Alberta's Local Governments
Politics and Democracy

Alberta's Local Governments

Politics and Democracy

Jack Masson with Edward C. LeSage Jr.

 The University of Alberta Press

First published by
The University of Alberta Press
Athabasca Hall
Edmonton, Alberta
Canada T6G 2E8

Copyright © The University of Alberta Press 1994

ISBN 0–88864–251–2 paper

Canadian Cataloguing in Publication Data

Masson, Jack K.
   Alberta's local governments

   Includes bibliographical references and index.
   ISBN 0–88864–251–2

   1. Local government—Alberta. 2. Alberta—Politics and
government. 3. Provincial-local relations—Alberta. 4.
Democracy—Alberta. I. LeSage, Edward C., 1948– II. Title.
JS1721.A5M37 1994   320.8'09712   C94–910676–3

The University of Alberta Press would like to acknowledge, with grati-
tude, the financial support provided by the Alberta Foundation for the
Arts, a beneficiary of the Lottery Fund of the Government of Alberta.

COMMITTED TO THE DEVELOPMENT OF CULTURE AND THE ARTS

Printed on acid-free paper. ∞

Printed and bound in Canada by
Quality Color Press, Inc., Edmonton, Alberta, Canada.

Contents

Acknowledgements

Without the many people who provided countless hours of their time, this project would never have been possible. Over the years, ideas were discussed with innumerable University of Alberta students taking courses on local government and with administrators enrolled in the local government certificate program offered through the University's Faculty of Extension. With their questions and comments, these students kept me intellectually honest. Particularly appreciated were the many administrators who explained carefully why this theory or that example was, or was not, relevant. This work would have been impossible without their insightful comments.

A number of bright and energetic research assistants not only collected materials for me, but also offered helpful suggestions for interpreting data and placing it within its rightful context. In particular, I want to thank Stuart Munro, Jim Rochlin, Ruth Rochlin, Caryn Duncan, Greg Poelzer, and Yi-chong Xu for their help.

I want to give special thanks to the Honourable Roy Farran, who was most helpful in providing information about the Lougheed era in Alberta government.

I offer thanks to the faculty and staff of the Department of Political Science at the University of Alberta, who have been most helpful and supportive. Special thanks to Alice Lau, a dedicated professional and department librarian, who counselled me on source materials and then spent innumerable hours locating them. There is no better reference librarian to be found in the province!

Edward LeSage, Director of Government Studies in the Faculty of Extension, provided the kind of support that makes writing and research a pleasure. Although Edd came into the actual research and writing stage late, he tightened up the manuscript's organization, focused unfocused chapters, and made me reconsider concepts which were not well thought out in the manuscript's earlier stages.

Judith Johnson, in her role as editor, is another person who deserves thanks for all of her helpful comments. Judith is responsible for the readability of this work.

The support and encouragement of Mary Mahoney-Robson, at the University of Alberta Press, was particularly appreciated.

Last, but certainly not least, are the anonymous outside readers who examined an earlier version of this publication for the University of Alberta Press. The book was substantially improved as a consequence of their suggestions.

1

Democracy and
Theories of Local Government

Introduction

Local government in Alberta, a hybrid of British, American, and Canadian political institutions, has been shaped into its present forms through innovation. A student of Alberta local government must be familiar with numerous different types of municipal governments and their intricate and varied relationships with governments at the provincial and federal levels. Unlike senior governments, local government is characterized by experimentation; the adoption of features of both presidential and parliamentary systems has created a hodgepodge of government structures and municipal-provincial relationships.

Apart from its complexity, local government often is misunderstood because there is little consensus on its goals. For example, the early "public choice" school of government conceived of local government primarily in economic terms. No *a priori* assumptions were made about the organization of government, although there was an emphasis on the advantages of municipal competition in revenue raising and the production and delivery of services. Citizens voted with their feet; that is, they chose to live in a municipality most compatible with their own economic ends.[1] Warren Magnusson criticized the public choice model's underlying assumption that "the municipality lacks any purpose beyond the purposes of the individual within it."[2] Today few if any public choice theorists believe local government consists solely of providing goods and services. The main stream of contemporary public choice theory embraces community self-determination and the empowerment of ordinary citizens so they are able to play a major role in municipal government decision making.[3]

Another popular view of local government is that democratically elected councillors should be furthering democratic ideals.[4] Yet others believe that the goals of local government should be similar to those of the Greek city-state—to strengthen direct democracy by allowing the citizen to be involved in policy making and administration.[5] It is these points of view that animate this work on Alberta's local governments.

Democracy

Canadians are fortunate in having inherited a tradition of stable and good government whose power and authority are derived from the people. Unfortunately, far too many people take democratic government for granted, which is a mistake since democracy is easily eroded. In order to counter tyrants and anti-democrats it is essential to understand the basic precepts of democracy.

Although most Canadians subscribe to the concept of democratic government, many are not familiar with its intellectual origins or the mechanisms involved in making it work. The term *democracy* has its roots in the Greek words *demos*, "the people," and *kratein*, "to rule." In its broadest sense, then, democracy is found wherever the people somehow rule. In a democracy citizens implicitly give their consent to be governed, even though particular policies may be repugnant to them. In other words, the people give government its legitimacy by consenting to a process of governance. But democracy is more than rule by a majority, for it also encompasses the concepts of political equality and basic rights such as freedom of speech and assembly. According to a modern political theorist, Tom Pocklington, political equality means that each and every citizen has an equal opportunity to influence governmental policy making. The caveat is that the nature of the social system gives some people more resources and opportunities to influence policy making than others.[6] In a discussion of basic political rights, Pocklington explains that every citizen has a vote which has the same weight as the vote of every other citizen.[7]

The concept of democracy is seldom challenged. But critics do question whether or not the democratic process can safeguard the rights of minorities. If a majority continues to pass legislation oppressing a particular minority, what is its protection from "majority tyranny"? Many argue that a minority is protected only to the extent that the majority does not erect barriers to prevent it from winning elections and, by definition, becoming the majority. It follows that a persecuted minority with no hope or expectation of becoming the majority may withdraw its support from the political system and attempt to overthrow the government by force. Although democracy's proponents admit that it is impossible to guarantee that a minority will not be tyrannized under a democratic system, they ask whether there is a better way to make governmental decisions than by majority rule and whether minorities are better protected under authoritarian and minority governments than under a democratic system. They emphasize that democracy is not a mystical concept but a process of governing in accordance with the wishes of the majority while at the same time respecting a minority's right to become the majority. The democratic process is difficult, time-consuming, and often frustrating, yet in almost every instance, given the opportunity, a country's populace will opt for democratic over nondemocratic government. It is no accident that many countries have nondemocratic forms of government, since it is easier to maintain power and to rule without having to consult or be concerned with the demands of the citizenry.

Direct Democracy and Its Use in Alberta

Just as in ancient Greece, from the standpoint of today's citizen the ideal way to make governmental decisions would be to hold a community meeting in which each citizen casts a single vote. The problem is that in modern Western society direct democracy is unwieldy and impractical for day-to-day policy making except in the smallest communities. However, there is a feasible alternative which enables the citizens of larger municipalities to engage in direct democracy. The plebiscite is a mechanism which enables the public to decide crucial public-policy issues.

David Butler and Austin Ranney, in an exhaustive study of referendums, identify two basic propositions of popular government: "(1) all political decisions should be as legitimate as possible, and (2) the highest degree of legitimacy is achieved by decisions made by the direct, unmediated vote of the people."[8] Discussing why the referendum leads to legitimacy in government, they write:

> People may or may not trust legislators ... but they certainly trust themselves most of all. Hence a decision in which all have participated (or at least had a full opportunity to participate) is more legitimate in their eye than one in which they have not participated. Moreover, decisions in which popular participation is direct and unmediated by others, as in referendums, produce more accurate expressions of their will than do decisions in which they participate only by electing others who make the decisions for them.[9]

Alberta's use of the plebiscite is a legacy from the first quarter of the century, when American municipal reformers, who called themselves Progressives, attempted to root political parties and special interests out of the political process and turn policy making over to the people.[10] The Progressives' fervent rhetoric extolling the virtues of direct democracy was well received, appearing just when special interest groups and party machines almost completely controlled the policy-making process in many American states and municipalities. Canadian reformers were intrigued by the Progressives' attempt to re-democratize government by employing three types of plebiscites: the initiative, the referendum, and the recall. The initiative enables anyone to draft a proposed law. When a number of people (usually 3 to 5 percent of the registered voters[11]) sign a petition, the proposed legislation is placed on a ballot for the electorate's approval or rejection. If approved, it becomes law. The referendum allows a legislative body that has passed a measure to refer it to the electorate for approval before it becomes law. The recall, a device allowing the electorate to remove a public official from office, is similar to the initiative in that it begins with a petition normally signed by a percentage of the voters in the preceding election. A special election is held shortly after the petition requirement has been satisfied, at which time the electorate determines whether or not the official is to be removed.

In 1913 Alberta's Liberal government, with the tacit support of its Conservative opposition, brought forward plebiscite legislation, an Act to Provide for the Initiation or Approval of Legislation by the Electors, which introduced a restricted use of the initiative and referendum. That same year Lethbridge's new city charter (Chapter 22, Section 10) provided for the recall of either the mayor or the elected city commissioner. In order to initiate a recall election a petition was needed with the signatures of at least 15 percent of those who voted in the previous city election. Although there is no record of any Lethbridge elected official being recalled, the recall provisions were in effect until 1955, when a new City Act invalidated the charter.

When the newly formed United Farmers of Alberta (UFA) came to power in 1921, one of its wings was composed of adherents to the American Non-Partisan League and supporters of the American Progressive movement, both of which advocated direct democracy. The UFA soon developed its own unique ideology, one tenet of which was the rejection of the political party as a means of governing. This stance provided a fertile environment for direct legislation that bypassed the party system. In 1921 the UFA's provincial platform endorsed "the principle of the initiative, referendum and recall."[12] However, a motion to legalize the recall was defeated at the UFA's 1924 convention. The recall was not revived as a political issue until 1935, when it was embodied in the theory of the new Social Credit Party, which also had a strong anti-party bias. C.B. Macpherson, discussing Social Credit's concept of representation and responsibility, writes:

> The only proclaimed line of responsibility was that by which elected members of the legislature were to be made recallable by their constituents. . . . This was quite in keeping with, though not required by, the social credit notion of a conglomerate electorate in each constituency. It was also quite in keeping with the fact that it was not by the constituency association that the elected member had originally been chosen as the social credit candidate.[13]

In March of 1936 the Alberta legislature passed a recall act which enabled a super-majority (two-thirds) of a riding's electors to recall their representative. Shortly thereafter, a bizarre attempt was made to recall three members of the Calgary council. Five councillors elected in December 1935 had run as official Social Credit candidates. Before they were allowed to run under the Social Credit banner, the Calgary Social Credit Association required them to sign a document stating that they would vote as a cohesive Social Credit bloc and espouse Social Credit principles in the administration of the city. After they were elected, Premier William Aberhart gave them both written and verbal instructions. They were to vote against any increase in municipal unemployment relief, against a request to the provincial government for a reduction in municipal debenture interest, and against a council proposal to tax provincial businesses. In November 1936 three of the five bolted, saying they would no longer take instructions from Aberhart or the Calgary Social Credit Association; henceforth, they would represent not only Social Creditors but "all classes of citizens in council matters."[14] Within days the three were told that the constituency association would trigger a recall election unless they recanted. Unrepentant, they were expelled from the party and again threatened with recall, although the provincial act did not provide for the recall of municipal officials.

Unsuccessful in ousting recalcitrant Social Creditors in Calgary, the party shifted its focus to Taber, where the mayor was also a sitting Social Credit Member of the Legislative Assembly (MLA). Charging him with not adhering to Social Credit principles at the municipal level, the constituency association tried to recall him as mayor, but discovered that the recall legislation applied only to MLAs in the provincial assembly. Moreover, a close reading of the 1936 Recall Act revealed that the number of signatures on a provincial recall petition must be at least two-thirds "of the total number of voters who were upon the voters' list" in the constituency. Since it was almost impossible to collect that many signatures, the association presented a resolution to the legislature to substantially reduce the number of signatures required by the act "to make the recall effective by a petition of 51% of the electors. . . ."[15] Taber's mayor also eluded attempts by "true" Social Creditors to remove him through a recall election.

Efforts to use the recall to punish dissident Social Creditors quickly ceased in the summer of 1937, when a coalition of Liberals and Conservatives in Aberhart's district of Okotoks-High River tried to recall the premier.[16] In October 1937 the Recall Act was quietly repealed retroactive to April 3, 1936, to ensure that this attempt would be unsuccessful.

In the last 30 years direct democracy provisions have slowly been eroded by politicians fearful that plebiscites would dramatically alter political power relationships and self-proclaimed public spokespeople with an interest in the maintenance of the economic and political status quo. Both groups profess to be committed to democratic precepts, but not to direct democracy, which they maintain undermines representative democracy.

Plebiscites are sometimes employed by municipal councils to avoid having to make "no-win political decisions," but most councils use them as seldom as possible. The threat of an easily initiated plebiscite makes it more difficult for councils to embark on policies which openly benefit traditionally well organized and well financed groups in the community, such as property developers and the owners of commercial buildings.

Another democratic mechanism with the potential to bring citizens directly into the policy-making process is the annual town meeting. A provision in the Municipal Government Act, Section 123(1), allows a council to hold "an annual meeting of the electors for the discussion of municipal affairs."[17] Although the act does not specify the powers of citizens at these meetings, at the very least penetrating questions on taxing, spending, and general policy making could hardly be ignored by council. And at the most, council could place major policy issues before a well-attended meeting for discussion and votes and bind itself to follow the dictates of the public.

Although many councils follow the letter of the legislation and call an annual town meeting, they carefully side-step the spirit of the law, which was intended to include the citizenry in the policy-making process. Some councils publicize an annual meeting as "council's annual report to the people." Any suggestion of a "give and take" discussion on major policy issues is carefully avoided. Other councils bury the annual meeting announcement in the section of the newspaper devoted to legal announcements, and still others hold the annual meeting during daytime working hours. When these tactics are employed, annual meetings are poorly attended. If few people turn out to question them about their performance, council members may assume that there are no complaints and congratulate themselves on a job well done. As an example, when only one person attended Beaumont's 1989 annual meeting the mayor remarked that the town was "in very good shape."[18] With only two citizens present, the Coaldale town council cancelled the 1988 annual meeting. The town manager explained the poor attendance by saying, "I'm just guessing but I presume there are no major issues to discuss at this time."[19] Other councils seldom or never call annual meetings, since so few people attend them.

If a council refuses to hold an annual meeting, Section 124(1) of the Municipal Government Act provides a mechanism by which citizens can call a meeting of the electors by petition.[20] This is seldom done because when a meeting is not held the councillors generally have already taken the electorate's pulse and are sure their action will not result in a political outburst. However, a council occasionally misreads the citizenry, as in the small town of Vauxhall in the spring of 1987. After the council decided to forego its annual meeting a fiery editorial in the local weekly newspaper sparked the formation of the Concerned Citizens Committee. In a town with a population of only slightly more than 1,000, the committee quickly collected more than 200 signatures on a petition. The council announced an annual meeting even before receiving the committee's submission.[21]

In contrast to the secretive or inaccessible councils described are councils committed to open government and proud of their well attended and spirited annual meetings. Almost 100 people attended a recent annual meeting in the Town of Fort Macleod. In the Village of Glenwood, with a population of less than 300, more than 30 people turned out to quiz their councillors and the administration. A number of rural municipalities also value a tradition of good attendance at their annual meetings.

Representative Democracy

The proper relationship between representatives and their constituents has been debated for almost 300 years. There are two theories of representation, mandate and independence. Mandate theorists begin with the premise that the ideal is to assemble all of a community's members in order to make governmental decisions, that is, the process of direct democracy. Since this is impractical in all but the smallest communities, the next best alternative is to elect representatives who are committed to doing their constituents' bidding. These representatives may exercise discretion on minor and unimportant issues, but must consult their constituents before voting on controversial ones. A representative who cannot in good conscience give unqualified support to the views of the constituency must resign. Independence theorists start from the premise that the business of government is too complex for the ordinary person. Therefore, constituents elect a representative to exercise good judgement in making legislative decisions, whether or not these choices reflect the views of the constituency. They argue that if representatives were bound by their constituents to rigid positions, compromise politics in any legislative body would be impossible.

Another modern political theorist, Hanna Pitkin, captures the essence of the debate between the mandate and independence schools with a question: "Should (must) a representative do what his constituents want, and be bound by mandates or instructions from them; or should (must) he be free to act as seems best to him in pursuit of their welfare?" After examining the arguments of the mandate and independence theorists, she concludes that what is striking about the debate "is how long it has continued without coming any nearer to a solution, despite the participation of many astute thinkers. Each in turn takes a position—pro mandate or pro independence—but the dispute is never settled."[22]

Pitkin notes that no representative subscribes completely to one theory or the other. When first elected, most representatives are determined to represent the positions and demands of their constituents. They soon find that it is extremely difficult to ascertain these positions; some issues evolve so quickly that it is impossible to poll constituents, and other issues actually are too complex for most constituents to understand. At the municipal level, representatives tend to vote according to their conscience rather than following the dictates of their constituents. Yet, when large numbers of constituents petition a representative to vote for a particular position, the representative takes their views seriously and usually votes accordingly.[23] In short, although representatives may favour independent representation, they generally adopt a position incorporating features of both independence and mandate theories.

Political parties are the usual mechanism for translating the views of the citizens to their representatives. But since municipal elections are nonpartisan, how do councillors learn what their constituents want? In very small towns or villages, council members consult their constituents on a one-to-one basis, but such a process is impossible in larger communities. A dated 1967 study of the Edmonton city council found that councillors identified business and welfare groups as those providing the information required for formulating policy.[24] A later study of council behaviour in five Alberta communities came to a similar conclusion: the councillors belonged to and were recruited into politics by community organizations, service clubs, churches, and civic and business groups.[25] It found that these organizations were both consulted and listened to by members of council.

An often overlooked precept of democracy is that the policy-making process be open to scrutiny. When decisions are made behind closed doors even the most conscientious representative may be tempted to place the interests of legislators and special interests above those of the public.

Representative Democracy in Alberta

The major problem with representative democracy is that representation means different things to different people; it is difficult to define. Since a basic campaign theme almost invariably focuses on the issue of representation, individual citizens may expect to be consulted on policy matters. On the other hand, "virtually all" elected representatives, according to Donald Higgins, "probably think of themselves as representing the 'public' for the sake of the 'public good.'"[26] This may enable some politicians to rationalize the representation of their own class interests or the interests of major campaign contributors by wrapping these interests in a pristine robe with a public interest label. To compound the problem, many representatives perceive that their responsibility in furthering the public good is to oversee the administration. As a consequence, their constituents may often be ignored as the representatives become mired in insignificant administrative decisions.

When people feel they are being unrepresented or misrepresented, they become cynical about the democratic process. More often than not, the press takes up the public's cause and begins to criticize the council. If council members, feeling they have been unfairly maligned, adopt a "siege mentality," what began as a small rift can become a wide gulf between the citizens and their representatives. On the other hand, Bettie Hewes, who was a popular and long-time member of Edmonton's city council, has a different view: "I have found in 15 years in public life that electors are seldom wrong and they have seldom sold me short as a result. And I have learned to trust them—I consult them often, I try to have that measure of humility and to listen carefully, and I trust them."[27]

Challenges to Representative Democracy

A number of legislative practices can undermine representative democracy. It is common for councils to hold secret informal meetings in which issues are discussed and policy formulated. The regularly scheduled council meeting then becomes nothing more than a formality, with council members unanimously implementing the policies hammered out at the informal meetings. As an example, The *Wainwright Star Chronicle,* in discussing a Tuesday council meeting, notes: "Several motions dealing with committee proposals were read and passed. Again, the motions were made up Monday and the majority of discussion took place the day previously."[28] In another case, a Department of Municipal Affairs review of Bruderheim's council was critical of its practice of holding "ad-hoc" informal meetings just prior to the regularly scheduled meeting or on alternate Wednesdays when the council did not meet. The review report read in part:

> The name ad-hoc may be a misnomer if, in fact, council is conducting committee business at these meetings. Council is reminded it cannot pass any resolutions at these meetings; it can only discuss issues. Any decisions made by council must be ratified by council at a regular council meeting. Council is encouraged to avoid excessive use of these private meetings if at all possible and, in so doing, remove the air of suspicion which frequently develops when the public does not know what has taken place.[29]

In 1987 the mayor of Drayton Valley defended the council's practice of assembling the evening before its regular session to hold a "government services meeting" because "our chances of talking back and forth only comes [*sic*] at these meetings." He added that these private discussions enabled the council to avoid in-camera sessions at its publicly scheduled meetings.[30]

Holding meetings in camera, that is, behind closed doors, is a more common method of fending off an inquiring public. Council members rationalize their actions by arguing that on certain issues the public does not have the same level of understanding as the council members and therefore if debate and decisions were made public the council would be subjected to unfair criticism. The mayor of Canmore was incensed after a *Calgary Herald* reporter charged the council with holding in-camera discussions on the 1987 budget. However, after one of the councillors agreed that "We haven't had a full budget debate by council for the last nine years or so," the mayor revealed a disjointed budgeting process so characterized by secrecy that even councillors were not privy to many aspects of the debate.[31] In an in-camera session the same year, the Hinton council awarded an Edmonton firm an accounting contract that was more than $5,000 a year higher than the bid by an equally qualified local firm.[32] When a controversial lease on Edmonton city land held by a private golf club came up for renewal, the council was split between one faction favouring renewal of the 40-year lease and another faction proposing that the city take over the course and make it public. With the discussions and votes cloaked in secrecy, the council renewed the lease.[33] Controversial decisions related to Edmonton's many tax concessions to developers also have been made in camera.

In 1988 open government was temporarily suspended when councillors for the Municipal District of Fairview and representatives of the Fairview School Division held meetings in camera to discuss renovations to a local school in general and "the fate of the [school's] community-use auditorium" in particular. A biting editorial in the local newspaper said, "It's hard to visualize subject matter more appropriate for public dissemination, but for reasons unknown or unstated, the school board felt the time was not right for Joe Public to learn of its plans."[34] A similar secrecy policy in some municipalities prevents the public from listening to a council's tape-recorded minutes. In the fall of 1986 several Calgary aldermen were upset when the council's legislative committee recommended continuing a policy which restricted access to tapes of council meetings. The committee's report explained that public access would make council members more liable to law suits.[35] Only months later, when a county council implemented a similar policy, the local newspaper's editorial writer responded: ". . . it seems that elected officials are afraid that someone listening to the tapes may misinterpret what is said. Balderdash."[36] In another case, the Vauxhall council adopted a policy requiring the town manager to supervise anyone who wanted to peruse its minutes.[37]

Rather than resorting to subterfuge, some municipal councils are straightforward in limiting participation. In 1988 the Fort McMurray council agreed, for the first time, to allow the public to attend the annual budget meeting. However, neither individuals nor the representatives of groups would be allowed to participate directly in the hearings. Mayor Knight explained that "if people have any concerns they can talk to myself or an alderman and it will be dealt with. We don't need a free-for-all kind of meeting."[38] In 1987 Red Deer's newly elected council members proposed establishing shopping mall political forums at which councillors would be able to meet informally with their constituents to discuss local issues. One of the five veteran councillors who voted against the motion apparently did not understand its objectives, for he justified his vote as follows: "I can see no advantage to it [the motion] whatsoever and I'm confident we will not increase the turnout at the polls."[39]

Of the many subtle means councils use to discourage segments of the public from becoming actively involved in the political process, the most common is to hold council meetings and public hearings during the day. Council's politically astute members realize the only people likely to be present will be those with flexible schedules, such as professionals, business owners, retirees, and farmers. Hourly and salaried workers not only would be unable to attend meetings held during normal working hours, but also would be under-represented on council itself. As an example, in the summer of 1988, with the citizenry deeply divided over the location of a brewery in Improvement District No. 17, the district's advisory council was asked to hold public hearings on the issue. The council scheduled a hearing in conjunction with its regular daytime council meeting in the Smith area. As a consequence, a large number of concerned people who wanted to speak to the issue in the Widewater and Wagner area some 80 kilometres away were effectively barred from participation.[40] The same year an *Edmonton Sunday Sun* political columnist, Allan Bolstad, took his city's council to task for holding one of its public hearings on a controversial city hall design at 1:30 P.M. on a Tuesday afternoon. "Council first decides whether it wants to hear from anyone. If it does, a time is arbitrarily set, inevitably during normal working hours. And 19 times out of 20, the public is forced to come to city hall."[41] Little had changed two years later, when an *Edmonton Journal* story, "Getting Heard by City Council Futile Exercise," cited numerous examples of citizens who were scheduled to speak before council but were delayed and inconvenienced until they gave up in despair. The most determined, who eventually were allowed to speak for five minutes, were equally dissatisfied. A business consultant summed up the latters' frustration when he said, "You had the distinct impression that everything was rigged."[42]

The Lethbridge council reserves an hour, commencing at 4:30 P.M., for citizens to speak on any issue without having to give previous notice. However, with such an inconvenient schedule it is not surprising that in 1988 "at least half the time not one citizen showed up with either a complaint or a thank you or a comment."[43] A similar situation occurred when the Innisfail council decided in 1987 to hold informal discussions so that citizens could voice their concerns. The first meeting was scheduled from

10:00 A.M. to 2:00 P.M. Another common ploy to discourage people from attending meetings and hearings is to follow a "flexible agenda" so members of the public will have no idea when a particular item will be discussed. Bolstad, in his discussion of the Edmonton council, writes: "It's not uncommon to see people wait two, three and four hours to be heard on any given item. As such, it's not surprising so few people try."[44]

Of course, there are many councillors committed to open government who oppose limiting citizen participation and using in-camera meetings for other than discussions of land acquisition and individual personnel decisions. As an alderman, Mayor Jan Reimer of Edmonton was critical of many council decisions which were closed to the public. In the fall of 1987 an advisory councillor for the Improvement District of Bighorn infuriated her colleagues when she disclosed the results of discussions held in camera which she thought should be open to the public. Council members requested an attorney to examine the possibility of bringing legal action against her for breach of confidentiality. In 1989 the mayor of Turner Valley informed the town manager that at an in-camera meeting the council had discussed changing her title and position from town manager to town administrator. Charging that he had violated confidentiality, the council forced the mayor to resign.[45] In the recent past the mayors of Edmonton and Calgary have questioned the use of in-camera meetings for very pragmatic reasons. Their administrations have been embarrassed by leaks to the press after these closed sessions.

Most citizens are incensed when they discover that their municipal council is attempting to escape public scrutiny by scheduling meetings at inopportune times or holding in-camera and informal sessions. Secrecy in government is not a phenomena found in only a few isolated municipalities with unenlightened councils; at the annual convention of the Alberta Association of Municipal Districts and Counties in 1978 an attorney counselled the delegates on the finer legal points of restricting citizen access to information. At one point "Mr. Sjolie suggested that a lawyer's advice can be presented to council members in informal briefings which are held before the start of their formal meetings where minutes are taken or during in-camera meetings where no minutes are kept."[46] Unfortunately, the Canadian public has no right to be privy to discussions held in camera unless it is mandated by provincial statute,[47] and no provincial legislation in Canada opens these meetings to the public. Since provincial legislatures also are guilty of operating in the shadows, their reluctance to enact municipal legislation may reflect a fear of establishing a precedent which could be used to open provincial legislatures to public scrutiny.

The Uneasy Relationship between Politics and Administration

In most communities the political and managerial functions of government coexist in an uneasy accommodation, although it may seem to many people they are diametrically opposed. Local politicians are not ideologues; they make use of professional expertise in adopting programs and formulating policies that will not generate undue controversy. At the same time, professional administrators realize that they have as much responsibility to the citizenry as they have to a professional management ethic.

Nevertheless, there are people who argue that the structure of government can be just as invidious and deleterious to representative democracy as council secrecy and deviousness. They are particularly critical of structures which emphasize professional management rather than representation, compromise, and politics.

The professional management approach to local government in Canada has its roots in both the civil service reform tradition of Great Britain and in a late-nineteenth-century business-oriented movement to reform American city government. While the British civil service reforms which were adopted in Canada recognized the interplay between parties and administration, the American proponents of professional management were less prone to do so. In an attempt to curb the power of strong local party organizations supported by new immigrants, middle-class business groups in the United States proposed reforms that would "take politics out of local government." In the interests of promoting efficiency and economy, local government would be run like a private business by a professional bureaucracy. Many local government administrators and elected officials in Canada were quick to espouse this approach. For example, in a paper presented to the Union of Alberta Municipalities Convention in 1909, a former mayor of Red Deer, H.H. Gaetz, argued:

It is contended by some that . . . the municipal and the business, have little or nothing in common, that the latter is conducted for the purpose of procuring a profit on the investment and operation, while the former is not conducted with this end in view. I contend however that there is no difference; that whether dividends to shareholders or the greatest material advantage to the ratepayers is the object . . . the principle is the same and that the methods which have proved successful in accomplishing the one aim will prove as effective in accomplishing the other.[48]

Almost as a logical extension of viewing municipal government as a business enterprise was an attempt in the 1930s to develop a set of principles for its efficient and scientific management.[49] Although later discredited, many of these principles were uncritically adopted by governmental reformers in both Canada and the United States.

Underlying one of the more extreme views of professional management is the attempt to depoliticize local government decision making. One justification for holding nonpartisan elections and electing councillors-at-large is the belief that this system will ensure the election of "reasonable people" with community-wide interests rather than narrow ideological or geographical ones. This tenet is best exemplified by the statement that "There is not a New Democratic, Liberal, or Progressive Conservative way to pave a street or catch a dog, there is only a right way." Those who subscribe to this approach tend to view politics as distasteful and divisive to the community; they perceive city government merely as a series of technical and management problems that can be solved by employing highly qualified engineers and administrators.

The major failing of this approach is that when partisanship is eliminated and council members are elected at large, the basic tenets of democracy suffer as council policy choices are narrowed and the process of political accountability becomes blurred. Even in small, relatively homogeneous communities there are social and economic cleavages. Nonpartisan and at-large elections weaken neighbourhood and minority claims in the "public interest," which is seldom, if ever, defined.[50]

In contrast are the proponents of political responsibility who argue that elected officials' accountability to the electorate is enhanced by a politically active citizenry. Political scientists have shown that partisan elections and ward representation lead to a higher voting turnout than do nonpartisan and at-large elections.[51] Furthermore, in nonpartisan electoral systems the middle class tends to vote and the working class tends to abstain from voting.[52] While the working class is represented on council in a ward system, it generally is not with at-large elections.[53]

A major tenet of management in the private sector is that the lines of authority and accountability should be crystal clear. Ironically, professional management in the public sector often obscures these lines, since the bureaucrat administering a public service may be insulated from both citizens and elected officials. In contrast, political accountability means that the elected official is directly responsible for governmental administration.

The difference between these two approaches also can be seen in the budgeting process. Proponents of professional management maintain that the experts, the professionals, should set the budget; proponents of political accountability claim that elected representatives should develop the budget in response to the demands of the citizenry, recognizing that establishing budget priorities is a highly political process.

Grass-Roots Democracy [54]

The ancient Greeks practised a form of direct democracy in which all citizens attended community meetings and made decisions by simple majority vote. As communities became larger, direct democracy gradually disappeared and has made only a limited appearance in modern times with the village assembly, or *Landsgemeinde*, in Switzerland, and the town meeting in New England.

In modern democracies public policy is made by elected representatives. But as population increased and many North American cities became as large as, if not larger than, many provinces and states, people became uneasy about the practice of democracy and the formulation of public policy at the local level. One response was a movement to bring the citizenry back into the policy-making process. Dubbed *grass-roots democracy*, it caught the attention of political theorists and people of all political persuasions across North America.

In the late 1960s and early 1970s people disenchanted with the impersonality of big-city government and the low rate of working- and underclass participation began to discuss ways of implementing grass-roots democracy at the city level. Writing in 1969, Milton Kotler advocated the decentralization of big-city government through the creation of semi-autonomous neighbourhood corporations that would have the power to tax and to distribute services. These corporations would be governed by the citizens in an open democratic system.[55] While others were advocating "participatory democracy," Carole Pateman argued that modern democratic theorists had lost sight of the values of widespread citizen participation in governmental decisions—values found in the writings of the classical democratic theorists.[56] Although Pateman was making a case for participatory democracy in the workplace, her ideas were soon adopted by militant urban reformers wanting to bring democracy to working-class neighbourhoods. The call for participatory democracy at the neighbourhood level was taken up by community and academic activists in a collection of readings entitled *Participatory Democracy for Canada*, published in 1971.[57] In the same year, Manitoba embarked on a bold experiment in efficiency and democracy in greater Winnipeg. Unicity, as it was called, amalgamated the region's municipalities into a single entity with a council comprising one member from each of 50 wards. In a token commitment to participatory democracy, Resident Advisory Groups (RAGs) were formed, each of which was "to advise and assist" one of the thirteen community councils composed of from three to six councillors. Neither the mandate of the community councils nor that of the RAGs was ever clear and as a consequence the Unicity experiment with participatory democracy failed.[58]

Many city politicians have rejected proposals for grass-roots democracy and neighbourhood government on the grounds that they were not practical. Other politicians redefined grass-roots democracy in such a way that they could claim it was being practised in their community and then carried on as usual. A continuing problem with grass-roots democracy is that it has been so loosely defined that it means different things to different people. At one time or another, door-to-door electioneering, marching on city hall, packing council chambers, and even stopping traffic at a busy intersection all have been labelled as the exercise of grass-roots democracy.

Political theorists define grass-roots democracy in two very different ways. For some, the term implies that small governing units are better than larger ones, since small units allow direct and personal contact between elected officials and individual citizens, making the citizen an integral part of the community decision-making process. They assume that elected officials in smaller communities consult their constituents on a one-to-one basis, and that the wishes of these constituents determine public policy. Other political theorists, disillusioned by small middle-class communities unwilling to enact policies which benefit working- and under-class people, advocate a two-pronged public participation approach. First, they believe in political centralization, the amalgamation of suburban and city municipalities in order to provide the larger government unit with adequate fiscal resources to carry out social programs. As a counter-balance to the larger body, the administration would be decentralized into small units over which the citizenry has some control.

Despite the imprecision of the term, it can be said that grass-roots democracy is an attempt to make democracy work in a complex society with an ever-increasing population, a society in which representative democracy is often unworkable. The sheer size of cities' populations makes it an impossibility for even the most conscientious councillors to meet and talk with more than a minute fraction of their constituents. Many elected officials, frustrated by the enormity of the task, have given up determining who their constituents are, let alone what they expect from government. Anonymous telephone polls are often used to replace the more personalized relationships between the citizenry and the elected representative which are so necessary to catch the nuances of the public's concerns.

Grass-roots democracy is a pragmatic process that borrows some concepts directly from representative and direct democracy and fuses and adapts other aspects of the two systems. Quite simply, grass-roots democracy can be viewed as a bridge between representative and direct democracy. The bridging process includes elected representatives in larger cities who are guided by their constituents in formulating policy, and the "barbershop politics" of smaller communities in which councillors seek advice from the man and woman on the street. It involves powerful citizen groups and the representatives who listen to and respect their opinions, and administrative systems that are responsible to the public as well as to the policy makers.

Participatory democracy includes mechanisms which ensure representation. As a check on elected officials who might refuse to listen to their constituents, or leave segments of them unrepresented, participatory democracy espouses features of direct democracy, such as the plebiscite and open town hall meetings. The plebiscite gives citizens the power to legislate policy directly and to override council legislation. In smaller communities, town hall meetings give citizens an opportunity to present policy proposals and question council about any of its actions.

Local Government Concepts and Alberta Local Government Policy

In the study of local government, as in any area of social science, theorists are continuously formulating, evaluating, and discarding concepts. Despite the amount of work which has been done in recent years, many definitions are still confusing and imprecise. The concepts of *decentralization* and the *optimum size for local government* continue to generate controversy and confusion, yet these are the concepts which the Alberta government uses to provide direction for its municipal policy.

In 1965 James Fesler wrote that decentralization was misunderstood because of its complexity in both theory and practice. As a consequence, people tended to classify political systems as either centralized or decentralized.[59] A quarter of a century later, the concepts of decentralization, direct democracy, and optimum government size have become interlinked, and while direct democracy itself is relatively easy to understand, it is nevertheless controversial.

Large numbers of North Americans, feeling alienated from seemingly gargantuan administrative structures and councils with inaccessible elected representatives seen only on television, are strong supporters of decentralization, which they believe will facilitate a more responsive type of government. Beset by the problems of living in a complex urban environment, they idealize the rural life style. Commenting on this phenomenon, Fesler writes, "The picture offered of a harmony among men in their little communities with a generous sharing of dignity, economic satisfaction, and happiness is often so inaccurate historically that one suspects it is borrowed from philosophers' portrayal of an idyllic state of nature before men organized politically or is a time-revered vision of the withering away of the state."[60] These disenchanted urban dwellers assume that small close-knit communities operate either as direct democracies incorporating the New England town meeting system or representative democracies with close consultation between the representatives and their constituents. As noted earlier, however, a number of political activists are skeptical about the supposed advantages of small units of government, which traditionally have been quite conservative. They point to David Rayside's recent study of an Ontario municipality with a population of less than 3,500 which found that "the agenda of local politics excludes anything that might be construed as interfering in the business of business."[61] As a consequence, many activists favour large, economically viable governments which are controlled politically by the working class but include small decentralized administrative units which provide for close citizen consultation and in some cases limited citizen control.[62]

The question of the ideal size for local government is related to the debate on decentralization and direct democracy. Recent studies employing public choice frameworks to examine municipal government in greater St. Louis, Missouri, and Allegheny County, Pennsylvania, maintain that one of the reasons the citizenry chose to maintain relatively small units of government was so that elected officials would be more accountable and accessible to the public.[63]

As will be seen in the next chapter, the Alberta government pays homage to local democracy while at the same time carefully maintaining authority by controlling access to fiscal resources and establishing municipal policy guidelines through provincial legislation. The provincial government determines the mechanisms municipalities use to select their representatives and to make policies and the Department of Municipal Affairs ensures that democracy is practised at the local level. The government is concerned that local government be democratic but that it not be too far-reaching. Quite simply, the provincial government takes most of its cues from municipalities with overwhelmingly middle-class councils that are disinclined to make major changes and nervous about the prospect of any increase in working- and under-class political participation which might change council power relationships.

When the Progressive Conservative government came to power in 1971 it was strongly committed to decentralization and the revitalization of small towns across the province. Decentralization was supported not as an abstract democratic concept, however, but as a policy proposed to gain the political support of rural Alberta.[64] In a 1965 speech before the Social Credit Party faithful, Premier Manning said "that within 10 years, 85 per cent of the population of this province is going to be in Edmonton and Calgary and that nothing could be done about it."[65] During the late 1960s, as Social Credit began to distance itself from its traditional rural base and court the electorate in Edmonton and Calgary, Peter Lougheed, then leader of the opposition, reached out for rural support. At the 1970 annual meeting of the Alberta Association of Municipal Districts and Counties, he promised that if the Progressive Conservatives formed the next government, growth would be balanced across the province and Edmonton and Calgary would not be allowed to expand at the expense of rural Alberta.[66] After Social Credit was toppled in 1971, Premier Lougheed put a policy into place to decentralize provincial departments and services whenever possible. Although this decentralization was not without political considerations, a conscious attempt was made to locate government offices in economically depressed communities. The party caucus established a decentralization committee which played a leading role in prodding departments to decentralize activities and in determining which communities were to benefit from the policy.

By 1973 the Agricultural Development Corporation had been located in Camrose and the Alberta Opportunity Company in Ponoka, and the Alberta Hail and Crop Insurance Corporation and Alberta Dairy Control Board were moved from Edmonton to rural Alberta. In the latter 1970s a research centre was established at Vegreville, a vocational centre at Fort McMurray, and a large provincial tree nursery at Smoky Lake. Undoubtedly the government was encouraged by the resolution supporting the government's policy which was passed at the 1973 annual meeting of the Alberta Urban Municipalities Association (AUMA). Jointly introduced by the towns of Bassano and Trochu and the villages of Acme, Beiseker, Carbon, Hussar, Rockyford, and Standard, the resolution urged that "the Provincial Government move further towards that stated goal of decentralization of agencies."[67]

In 1974 the establishment of Restricted Development Areas gave the province another means to control the growth of larger municipalities. Restricted Development Areas legislation was used in Edmonton and Calgary to reserve outer rings of land for utility and pipeline right-of-ways, easements for other municipal services, and transportation routes. The government expected that this legislation would also be used to freeze land for park use in urban areas.

In a speech entitled "Alberta's Industrial Strategy," presented before the Calgary Chamber of Commerce in 1974, Premier Lougheed stated that one of the government's goals was "to spread the growth on a balanced basis across the province and capitalize upon the potential of the smaller centres—to assure a better quality of life for citizens living within the metropolitan areas and also the smaller centres as a combined result."[68] Soon afterwards the Minister of Municipal Affairs said that the government "does not favor continued rapid growth for Calgary and Edmonton at the expense of the smaller centers of the province."[69] In November of the same year, in an address to the Edmonton Chamber of Commerce, Lougheed said, "Edmonton and Calgary . . . are large enough now."[70] To make sure there could be no question about the nature of the government's policy on decentralization and size, Lougheed reiterated it in September 1977 at a "Think West" conference:

> . . . part of our economic strategy is balanced growth. We do not want to see Calgary and Edmonton grow at the expense of the smaller centers. Primarily, our view as a government is to create the essential services and develop them in the smaller communities—the basic essentials of water and sewer, communication and transportation.[71]

In discussing another facet of his decentralization policy in 1980, Lougheed said, "In terms of regional expansion . . . we want a new thrust to expand our apprenticeship and technological courses to our college[s]. . . . to follow through in our program of decentralization of government services.[72] The decision was then made to locate Athabasca University in the Town of Athabasca and a new technology and trade school in Stony Plain.

Decentralization proceeded with little controversy throughout the 1970s, though neither Edmonton nor Calgary were very happy about it. In 1973 Premier Lougheed singled out Calgary as not being fully supportive of his decentralization policies.[73] Shortly thereafter, at the AUMA's 1974 annual convention, Edmonton sponsored a resolution, which was carried, asking the government to "indicate in greater detail its policies relating to the decentralization of growth in Alberta."[74] Dissatisfied with the government's response, Calgary sponsored a resolution at the 1975 AUMA annual meeting, which also was carried, that the government "clearly state the philosophy, scope and nature of its population decentralization policy and to provide specific details of the parameters of this policy."[75] In a terse response the government said that "it is difficult to couch in precise terms the several policies which constitute the Government's decentralization program," but added that "the Government's policy is to direct some of the new growth that Alberta surely will experience toward smaller communities." In 1976 the province, with no consultation, placed a five-mile-wide Restricted Development Area around Calgary which, among other things, stymied an annexation proposal favoured by the city administration.[76]

In 1979 decentralization became an underlying issue in Edmonton's massive annexation bid for the City of St. Albert, the entire County of Strathcona (including the unincorporated community of Sherwood Park), and significant portions of the County of Parkland and the Municipal District of Sturgeon. For the first time since the party came to power, the Tories split publicly, with Edmonton MLAs supporting the city's expansion and MLAs in outlying suburban ridings favouring the status quo. After the division in the party, little was heard of decentralizing and maintaining the viability of smaller communities until 1981, and then the policy was mentioned only in passing by a small number of government members praising its success.

With the onset of the recession, the government's attention shifted from policies for managing economic expansion to strategies for coping with high unemployment and reducing the public service; further decentralization of governmental activities was set aside. Then in 1985 the government's decentralization policy was attacked for the first time since it had been implemented. The Leader of the Opposition, Ray Speaker, maintained that while some government facilities had been decentralized, administration was still highly centralized, with "top-heavy control." To rectify this situation, he recommended that regional administrators be given substantially more responsibility and a system of "regionalized budgets" be put into place. Speaker also contended that the provincial government needed to work much more closely with municipalities in the provision and delivery of services.[77] The government did not respond.

Lougheed's decentralization policy remained intact but was apparently given a low priority by his successor, Don Getty, although in 1988 Getty responded to a question about Alberta's declining farm population by saying that "our whole program of decentralization" was a manifestation of the government's "desire to strengthen the entire agricultural community."[78] Little more was heard about decentralization until early January 1991, when Getty announced that the head office of the Western Canada Lottery Corporation was to be relocated from Winnipeg to Stettler, which was his constituency. To counter the criticism that the decision was motivated by crass political considerations, Getty argued that the relocation was in line with the government's policy on rural revitalization and decentralization. In the legislative assembly some months later, Getty clearly laid out his government's policy on decentralization. He explained:

> I want to make it very clear . . . that the government is determined to provide broad opportunities across this province and that we are going to work to maintain the strength and vitality of our smaller centres. We know the cities can take care of themselves. They grow and they grow, and they have strong industrial development and economic development initiatives. We are going to make sure the growth in this province is broadly distributed so there are opportunities all across Alberta.[79]

An Overview of Democracy in Alberta

In the course of nearly a century, the concept of local level democracy has become institutionalized in Alberta municipalities. In his historical study of Edmonton politics John Day notes that even before Edmonton was organized as a village, "open 'town meetings' of everyone were held when it was thought necessary."[80] Today the remnants of direct democracy are to be found in the plebiscite and annual town meeting. However, it is the institution of representative democracy to which the provincial government is committed and it is representative democracy which many sections in the Municipal Government Act address. But there are problems with local level representative democracy in Alberta, just as in other provinces across the country. In a great many communities where one would expect to find a functioning system of representative democracy, a number of factors preclude anything more than its facade. Edmonton and Calgary have become so large that the traditional mechanisms linking the representatives and the citizenry work only sporadically. In some communities councillors believe that there is no need for citizens to be involved in the decision-making process, since local government should be run as a private business, without politics. These councillors discourage citizen involvement, presuming it would lead to the creation of political divisions on issues for which they believe there is only one correct solution or policy. In other communities true representative democracy has diminished as councils, fearful of the electorate, embrace secrecy as an end unto itself. And in yet other communities there are councillors who, after years of public service, have lost sight of the functions of an elected representative. Some have become political prima donnas, suspicious and distrustful of their constituents, the administration, and even their council colleagues.

Municipal governments have two options. They can continue their present course with elected officials hoping they can maintain the support of a public which is beginning to question just how democratic they are. If this process continues, public support is likely to weaken, which will enable the provincial government, if it seems to be politically advantageous, to expand its powers and responsibilities at the municipal level. On the other hand, municipal governments can make substantial structural and procedural changes to allow the citizenry to become an integral part of the policy-making process. In short, municipalities can commit themselves to the precepts of grass-roots democracy.

Obstacles and substantial costs are involved in adopting a governmental system which focuses on citizen involvement and participation. The composition of many municipal councils would change substantially. Councillors elected only because an apathetic and cynical public had become disinterested in municipal politics would be replaced by councillors pledged to bring the people back into the political process. Councils would no longer consist primarily of businesspeople, farmers, professionals, and managers, all with an undifferentiated view of municipal government's role *vis-à-vis* the individual, governments, and society. Homogeneous councils with their camaraderie would be a thing of the past, as formerly unrepresented communities clamoured for representation and power. Meetings would become much longer, as council's diverse segments fought and compromised on virtually every policy issue. In short, decision-making would be less efficient but far more democratic than it is today.

2

Intergovernmental Relations

Introduction

Conventional explanations of the power relationships between federal, provincial, and local governments in Canada invariably begin with a discussion of their legal status. Although there are three major governmental sectors, constitutional status is given only to the federal and provincial governments; local governments are designated a responsibility of the latter in Section 92(8) of the Constitution.[1] Local governments' powers and very existence are conferred by statutory laws passed by provincial legislatures. In theory, this means provinces can create and abolish municipalities and increase and diminish their powers at will.

The terms used to describe the three governmental sectors—tier, layer, level, and stratum—all connote relatively rigid sectors of activity and superior and subordinate relationships. One student of intergovernmental relationships writes that "Canada is studied from the layer cake point of view, an approach that emphasizes the rigid division of power."[2] Statements such as "property taxes are the main source of *local level* revenue" and "local government is subordinate to the two *upper tiers*" are common. Even knowledgeable politicians occasionally depict local government as a less competent stratum. As late as 1976, Alberta's deputy premier characterized the municipalities as "children of the province."[3]

Possibly as a result of its subordinate status, there is considerable pessimism about local government's viability and its role in the future. In a discussion of the decrease in the legal responsibilities of municipal government, Charles R. Tindal and S. Nobes Tindal suggest that provincial control increases when a function appears to have "outgrown local government" and there is "concern on the part of the province about minimum standards in such areas as health and education."[4] Both politicians and scholars cite the changing fiscal relationships between the three governmental sectors as evidence that the two "senior levels" are increasing their powers at the expense of municipal governments. A report prepared by the Canadian Federation of Mayors and Municipalities in 1976 maintained that local governments' loss of power had reached crisis proportions.

> The outward signs are the steady loss of municipal power and increasing financial constraints. Grants from provincial and federal Governments come with so many strings attached and represent such a large part of municipal budgets that municipalities are becoming puppets in a show run mainly by Provincial Governments.[5]

Examining local government from a different perspective, the Tindals imply that municipalities themselves may be at least partially responsible for their subordinate status. "Our assessment of the present system of local government in Canada must conclude on a somewhat negative note.... Canadian local governments are not effectively fulfilling either of their basic representative or administrative roles. They remain weak even after two decades of reform initiatives."[6]

One of the reasons local government may appear to have lost power in the last several decades is that its place in the intergovernmental system is not well understood. With a few exceptions, the responsibilities of governmental sectors are not strictly delimited, and their relationships cannot be categorized precisely as vertical and hierarchical. In a federal system the functions and activities of governmental sectors often overlap, and power and fiscal relationships which reflect changing social and economic conditions are perpetually in a state of flux.

In 1960 Morton Grodzins suggested that rather than viewing the American federal system as a three-layer cake of federal, state, and local governments, the system should be seen as "characterized by an inseparable mingling of differently colored ingredients, the colors appearing in vertical and horizontal strands and unexpected whirls. As colors are mixed in the marble cake, so functions are mixed in...."[7] Grodzins shows that the federal government in the United States has always assisted municipalities with agriculture, forestry, employment, and highway grant programs which benefited local communities and were administered locally. Daniel Elazar agrees: "Contrary to the general impression, the federal government has been supplying direct aid to local communities since the early nineteenth century ... primarily in the field of internal improvements and secondarily in the field of education."[8]

The same phenomenon is to be found in Canada. Building on the theoretical constructs of Grodzins and Elazar, in 1979 Lorna Pawluk prepared materials for three Alberta case studies of federal-provincial-municipal negotiations which illustrate "the intermingledness of Canada's federal system, thus enhancing the credibility of the marble cake view."[9] After examining a number of policy areas, Pawluk wrote:

> All three Canadian governments are interdependent and intermingled. Federal agricultural, industrial development and housing policies influence migration to and settlement patterns in Canadian municipalities. Policing and housing bring the federal government into direct contact with municipalities, while health, welfare and education, once preserves of private and municipal institutions, now concern all three governments.[10]

Grodzins, Elazar, and Pawluk make what appears to be a simple but is actually an extraordinarily complex argument about intergovernmental relations: that the activities of the three governmental sectors (commonly thought of as levels) constantly overlap and intermingle. In short, the complexity and multidimensionality of intergovernmental relationships are illustrated by the many facets of their formal and informal ties and spheres of influence.

Governmental powers seem to be neatly categorized in the Canadian Constitution: federal powers in Section 91, provincial powers in Section 92, and municipal powers subsumed under Section 92(8). But while the distribution of powers and responsibilities seems to be straightforward in theory, in practice it is much less so. To illustrate the overlapping of formal powers, a Federation of Canadian Municipalities (FCM) report cites the Supreme Court of Canada decision upholding a Montreal bylaw prohibiting public assemblies in city streets and other public places. The court differentiated "the *preventive* nature of the bylaw . . . from the *punitive* measure relating to riots and other unlawful assemblies in the federal *Criminal Code.*" The report explained that "although 'criminal law' is a very important source of federal authority . . . the Supreme Court of Canada has recently seemed more favourably disposed to tolerate extensive jurisdictional duality."[11] Pawluk has found that police officers enforce provincial laws, municipal bylaws, federal statutes, and the Criminal Code without distinguishing between them.[12]

Education, housing, health, and social welfare are areas in which the three government sectors actively formulate policy and deliver programs. Responsibility for housing, for example, is shared by the federal Canada

Mortgage and Housing Corporation (CMHC), the provincial Alberta Housing Corporation (AHC), and similar agencies found in larger municipalities. The CMHC, among other things, provides funds for building low-income housing and loans money for housing rehabilitation, the construction and expansion of sewage treatment plants, and the purchase of land under land assembly programs. The AHC also assists municipalities with land assembly programs and the financing of low-income rental housing. Given such shared activities, one may want to question the conventional dictum that local government is the one closest to the people, since in some instances the government closest to the people is provincial or federal.[13] While policy-makers and bureaucrats are constantly meeting formally and informally to discuss jurisdictional issues, the public is concerned mainly about the adequacy of housing programs, rather than the identity of the agencies involved.

Provincial-Municipal Cooperation and Conflict

During the constitutional debate, when it was suggested that municipal powers should be constitutionally entrenched, a number of municipal politicians began to examine theoretical discussions of intergovernmental relations.[14] Generally, however, politicians have taken a practical approach to the distribution of governmental powers and responsibilities, which they consider to be important in "real situations" but not particularly relevant in the abstract. For example, local politicians tend to become involved in debates about sectoral responsibilities when a municipality is charged with a program requiring expenditures but is not given any additional revenue capability, or when a provincial government "caps" municipal government revenues.

Provincial officials and bureaucrats are equally pragmatic about power relationships. Although every province has an act delineating the responsibilities of municipalities, most of these are discretionary. Through overseer departments and agents, the province exercises power to ensure that municipalities carry out a small number of mandated tasks, but even these may be neglected or performed haphazardly unless a citizen makes a specific complaint to provincial authorities.

Municipalities and provinces occasionally operate at cross-purposes. In 1988 Premier Don Getty created a Provincial-Municipal Premier's Council "to deal with broad principles between the provincial government and municipal governments . . . to make sure that we are working in a coordinated way."[15] The premier's programs are carried out through the Department of Municipal Affairs, which gives advice and makes recommendations to municipalities and encourages them to amend and revise their policies so they will not be in conflict with those of the province.

The province also shapes local government policy by controlling municipal finance. With few exceptions, in its early years the provincial government was concerned not with municipal overspending but with parsimonious policies which prevented municipalities from meeting the service demands of an ever-increasing number of new residents. It was only after naive and over-optimistic city politicians, encouraged by business boosters and land speculators in the early part of the century, formulated policies which caused a land boom and bust of unprecedented proportions that the province finally exercised fiscal control over the municipalities. And even then the exigencies of the First World War mitigated the effects of the imposition of very severe financial constraints.

Until 1918 a land tax provided almost all of the revenue for cities. As a consequence, when "land boomers" subdivided thousands of lots in Edmonton and Calgary and sold them to small speculators in 1912 and 1913, each city's revenue base appeared to double and redouble in a very short time. Edmonton commissioners had so much confidence in the strength of the economy that they authorized between $4 and $5 million of expenditures over budget in 1912,[16] and the city councils of both Edmonton and Calgary sold large amounts of debentures to fund an enormous public works expansion. When thousands of speculators walked away from their unpaid lots in 1913, the cities had to retrench drastically to avoid bankruptcy.[17] Adding to their woes was an almost total cessation of building and railroad construction which dramatically increased the numbers of unemployed who needed public aid to avoid starvation.

As their income began to decline, some cities doubled their property assessments, which theoretically doubled their revenue and enabled them to double the amount of debentures they were allowed to sell. As an example, unimproved land in Calgary was taxed for as much as $5,000 an acre. However, as taxes increased, many landowners simply relinquished their property to the city; when the land was off the tax rolls, the city's financial situation worsened.

Although the provincial treasurer was forecasting a budget surplus in the fall of 1914, municipal pleas for financial help were ignored. In fact, the province passed an unearned increment tax on land that gave three-quarters of the tax revenue to the municipalities and one-quarter to the provincial government. The municipalities argued that they, "through their energy, their industry, their faith and their capital and credit, have made these lands increase in value," and were therefore entitled to all of the taxes collected on the unearned increment.[18] The government was unmoved. Municipalities also complained bitterly when the province gradually reduced its hospital and school grants, forcing them to make up the shortfall.

In order to curb city boosters' practice of offering "give-away" business incentives and tax exemptions, provincial legislation enacted in 1913 prohibited land sales and leases below cost, public stock subsidies, bond and debenture guarantees, and an assortment of tax exemptions.[19] This made little difference in Edmonton and Calgary, for the cities already were burdened with debt. Moreover, municipalities were still able to find loopholes in the acts, and legislative intent was circumvented again and again. Therefore, when a public utilities commission was established in 1915, it was given extensive powers to inquire:

> into the merits of any application of a local authority for permission to raise money by way of debenture, and to grant or refuse such permission: to manage sinking funds, supervise the expenditure of monies borrowed under the act, and to obtain from any local authority at any time a statement in detail of its assets and liabilities.[20]

Over the years, the commission's powers were increased on an ad hoc basis.

As the "Great War" progressed and Canada was asked to help finance Britain's military effort, the Dominion called upon the provinces to share the financial burden. In turn, to recoup its $800,000 contribution to the Patriotic Fund the Alberta Government enacted the Supplementary Revenue Tax, a two-mill surcharge on the land tax. Up to this time the government had successfully neutralized much of the criticism of its municipal policies by playing on the suspicions and antagonisms between city and rural politicians. But after having made numerous unsuccessful pleas to the provincial government for financial assistance and then being told their revenue base was to be further eroded by a war tax, the two groups formed a common front and demanded action. The government responded with a municipal tax policy which would splinter the new alliance. But then its spokesperson, Member of the Legislative Assembly (MLA) J.R. Boyle, announced that "we [the government] are not interfering in any shape or form in connection with any scheme of taxation of any kind a city may propose."[21]

The cities quickly proposed a variety of new measures, from the taxation of tenants to churches. But, as one might have expected, the focus was on the poll and income taxes, which would raise the most revenue. Although Minister of Municipal Affairs Wilfred Gariepy proclaimed the poll tax an excellent way to raise revenue, when the City of Wetaskiwin requested an amendment to its charter that would enable it to enact a poll tax the proposal was turned down by the province's municipal law committee.

A new tax policy announced in March 1918 included an income tax for municipalities. Although the Dominion Government's income tax was a lucrative generator of revenue, Premier Charles Stewart explained that the income tax was being left to the cities for the years 1918 and 1919 because the government did not have a collection structure in place.[22] After much bickering over whether income earned outside the city was taxable, Edmonton's charter was amended to allow for the tax.[23] Calgary's charter was similarly amended shortly thereafter.[24]

The province extended until 1921 the cities' right to collect an income tax, but their finances were still in disarray. Construction was down, the rate of unemployment was up, and the business boomers and hucksters had lost confidence in the future. Even before Calgary's income tax was terminated, the city was allowed to impose a poll tax. To encourage the real estate market, the tax was reduced for homeowners.

When the United Farmers of Alberta (UFA) came to power in 1921 little changed for the province's municipalities, which continued to totter on the brink of bankruptcy throughout the 1920s. At the onset of the Great Depression rural and urban municipalities were at odds over their shares of provincial financial aid. As economic conditions worsened for the province as well, few financial concessions were made to municipalities, whose financial needs had become critical. In 1925 the provincial government allowed cities to reinstate an income tax (renamed the service tax), but it was terminated in 1932 when the province imposed its own tax on income.[25] The 1919 Supplementary Revenue Tax, which the municipalities had been promised was just a temporary measure, was still in force in the 1930s despite continuing protests.[26] Municipalities were particularly incensed when told they would continue to bear 10 percent of the cost of maintaining the Old Age Pension program even though the Dominion Government increased its share of the cost from 50 to 75 percent. Earlier, the premier had explained: "The real reason for having the municipalities pay 10 percent of pension cost is that through their having a financial interest careful management may be assured."[27] An examination of the annual reports of the Union of Alberta Municipalities and Alberta Association of Municipal Districts during the depression era shows that their "key concern was taxation."[28]

When Aberhart's Social Credit government came to power in September 1935 Alberta's per capita debt was out of control and the province had no funds to pay its employees. When Aberhart set out to repair the fiscal damage, he did not forget the desperate plight of the municipalities. In *Urban Affairs in Alberta*, David G. Bettison, John K. Kenward, and Larrie Taylor note that Aberhart's appointment of "Mr. Charles Cochcraft both as Provincial Treasurer and as Minister of Municipal Affairs was not entirely coincidental."[29] The government moved quickly to aid bankrupt communities in southern Alberta, and when the federal government enacted the Municipal Improvements Assistance Act the province guaranteed federal loans to municipal authorities. In a discussion of Social Credit's early stance on provincial-municipal relations the three authors maintain that in general "the Social Credit government from 1935 to 1939 was not disposed to interfere with the autonomy and decisions of local governments." They explain that municipalities were not given absolute freedom of action, however, as municipal policy decisions were limited by "ad-hoc boards separated formally from the daily routine of governmental, departmental administration."[30] In particular, the Board of Public Utilities Commissioners was a powerful overseer of municipal finance.

During the Second World War the province's economic condition changed for the better, and by 1945 the government was able to reorganize its public debt and redeem all of its defaulted bonds. In the immediate post-war period the provincial government's financial health continued to improve, while the province's municipalities were forced to borrow to pay for badly needed capital projects which they had delayed for years. Just when many communities thought they had resolved their financial crisis, the discovery of oil at Leduc in 1947 brought tens of thousands of people into the province. An economist writes of this period:

> The contrast between provincial and local finance in Alberta suggests that there has arisen an imbalance in provincial-local responsibilities in relation to revenue levels. Local governments have found themselves faced with a rising demand for services unmatched by equivalent increases in revenue, and the municipalities have little choice but to raise tax rates on property. . . . The province, on the other hand, because of the breadth of its revenue system and the rapid development of natural resources, has seen its revenue grow more rapidly than the urgent needs for expenditure.[31]

The government responded to the municipalities' plight in 1950 with the Self-Liquidating Project Act which allowed municipalities to borrow provincial monies at low interest in order to build and expand utilities. In 1953 the province established the Municipal Loans Revolving Fund with $25 million capital for funding municipal capital projects at low interest rates. The central program to help municipalities, however, was a revenue-sharing scheme implemented in 1951 which gave them 40 percent of the province's gasoline tax. The Municipal Assistance Act was designed to provide the ratepayer with tax relief and municipalities with the funds necessary to meet their responsibilities. Both objectives were accomplished by tying the amount of the grant to the amount a municipality reduced its mill rate. In 1952, 50 percent of the gasoline tax was allocated for municipal assistance grants and the grant formula was altered after municipalities complained that it was too restrictive. The tax relief provision was relaxed, which enabled municipalities to increase their mill rate and still receive the grant, and the unconditional portion of the grant was reduced and an equalization formula used to distribute one-fifth of it.

By 1955 the provincial government had loaned municipalities $90 million through the Self-Liquidating Project and the Municipal Loans Revolving Fund. In 1956 the mechanism for lending funds to municipalities was completely reorganized and, perhaps inadvertently, the government relinquished its direct control over their capital spending. The two capital loan programs were terminated and the Municipal Financing Corporation (MFC) was created to be the vehicle for financing capital projects. The MFC was an independent nonprofit corporation funded by the province. Four of its seven board members were nominated by the government and the remainder were elected. In theory, the governmental majority dominated the board, but in fact it was never able to control the loans made to municipalities.

Under the MFC program municipalities borrowed low-interest loans worth hundreds of millions of dollars, yet many of them demanded even more funds. Bettison, Kenward, and Taylor point out that the municipalities were particularly interested in "how much were Calgary and Edmonton getting relative to all other local authorities."[32] In fact, the government was spending virtually all of its oil royalties on "assistance to taxpayers" and Edmonton and Calgary were receiving less provincial assistance than their percentages of the population warranted.[33]

When the Tories came to power in 1971 after more than 35 years of Social Credit rule, municipal politicians were somewhat apprehensive. Although rural-based Social Credit had initially been unsympathetic to the financial plight of cities, by the late 1960s it was actively courting an urban electorate. Peter Lougheed was cognizant of the importance of building and maintaining good municipal relationships, for Social Credit's neglect of rural municipalities had contributed to its defeat. Chapter 1 described Lougheed's commitment to economic decentralization and a revitalization of the hinterlands to counter-balance the growing economic strength of Edmonton and Calgary. A caucus committee on decentralization was established and, whenever possible, government enterprises were shifted from the large cities to outlying small towns in order to bolster rural employment and stimulate a faltering retail sector.

Lougheed had very firm ideas about provincial-municipal power relationships, which he transformed into policy. Shortly after taking office, when asked whether he would consider transferring any powers from the province to the municipalities, he replied that it is "not sound policy to transfer jurisdiction or responsibilities to local government if they do not have the fiscal capacity to meet them."[34] Knowing that the key to keeping municipal policy aligned with provincial policy was the control of municipal finances, he was careful to prevent the municipalities from becoming fiscally independent. Lougheed had spoken against revenue-sharing when Social Credit shared oil profits with the municipalities, and his opposition became government policy in 1971.[35]

As might be expected, Lougheed's stance on municipal autonomy was attacked by the opposition in the legislative assembly. Ho Lem, a former Calgary alderman and Social Credit MLA for Calgary McCall, accused the government of acting like a "high-handed dictatorial patriarch." He then called for a formula for distributing funds to municipalities which would "give them a measure of freedom and autonomy."[36]

Although his municipal policy was criticized, Lougheed was not insensitive to community financial needs. Shortly after assuming office he made MLA Roy Farran chair of a five-member committee with a wide-ranging mandate to examine provincial and municipal fiscal responsibilities.[37] The Farran report noted the rapid urbanization in the province, from 37 percent in 1951 to 76 percent in 1972, and pointed out that the municipalities, with their narrow property tax base, faced a financial crisis in providing the services the public expected. A manifestation of this was a municipal per capita debt of $580.40 in 1970, when the province was "to all intents and purposes debt free." On the basis of the committee's recommendations the province assumed total financial responsibility for hospitalization and public health services and a substantial portion of education costs. A Property Tax Reduction Act was followed in 1974 by a program to subsidize interest on municipal loans.

Despite this largesse, many municipalities believed that, given its ever-increasing oil revenue in the Heritage Trust Fund, the government should be doing far more. At the Alberta Urban Municipalities Association (AUMA) convention in 1977 a resolution was passed requesting the government to use the Trust Fund to reduce municipal debt. The government's response was decidedly cool: "It must be considered whether it is prudent to write-down or reduce the debt of municipalities which have higher relative levels of indebtedness, again primarily due to local choice, while in certain cases, municipalities through conscious pay-as-you-go policies, may have little or no debt."[38] The problem was resolved just before the 1979 provincial election, when Lougheed announced a $1 billion Municipal Debt Reduction Act which gave each of the province's municipalities and Metis settlements a $500 per capita grant to be used either to pay down the community's debenture debt or as an unconditional grant. With $648 million applied to debenture debt and $383 million distributed unconditionally, almost every municipality eliminated its long-term debt and many, particularly in rural areas, were able to deposit and earn bank interest on a substantial portion of their grants.

The municipalities were still dissatisfied, however, since government policies tended to increase the scope of conditional grants at the expense of unconditional ones. Table 2.1 shows that when the Conservatives came to power in 1971, 48.7 percent of municipal grant money was in the form of unconditional grants. This figure jumped to 61 percent in 1972 and then declined until it reached a low of 16.7 percent in 1981. For the next six years, the provincial government limited unconditional grants to no more than 20 percent of total grant funding for municipalities.

In 1978 AUMA commissioned two University of Alberta economics professors, Dr. Melville McMillan and Dr. Richard Plain, to examine provincial-municipal relations with a view as to how they could be improved. The following year *The Reform of Municipal-Provincial Fiscal Relationships in the Province of Alberta* attracted the attention of politicians and the news media with its municipal taxation recommendation: "... because it provides greater local autonomy but demands more municipal responsibility, the tax base sharing (i.e., a local personal income tax) alternative in conjunction with the selective reduction of conditional grants programs offers the most balanced approach towards correcting the municipal fiscal problem."[39]

The economists credited the government with providing adequate funding for municipalities but were critical of the imposition of fiscal restraints which affected their policy making and planning. Their recommendations on revenue sharing almost guaranteed that the government would ignore their proposals. In April 1979 a report by the Provincial-

Table 2.1   Provincial Fiscal Transfer to Municipalities by Year

| | Municipal Grants | |
Year	Unconditional Grants (%)	Conditional Grants (%)
1971	48.7	51.3
1972	61.0	39.0
1973	58.2	41.8
1974	34.3	65.7
1975	34.9	65.1
1976	33.8	66.2
1977	31.3	68.7
1978	28.3	71.7
1979	36.0	64.0
1980	26.4	73.6
1981	16.7	83.3
1982	19.2	80.8
1983	17.0	83.0
1984	17.9	82.1
1985	16.1	83.9
1986	16.9	83.1
1987	19.1	80.9
1988	33.9	66.1

Municipal Finance Council responded obliquely to the issues raised by McMillan and Plain. It argued that revenue sharing would seriously impair the provincial government's fiscal flexibility and "could introduce unnecessary problems and instability in municipal financing." The report defended the government's increasing reliance on conditional grants on the grounds that, unlike unconditional grants, they recognized "the variation in needs of individual municipalities."[40]

When the Advisory Committee on Provincial-Municipal Fiscal Relations was established in 1981 its members were told by the Minister of Municipal Affairs, Marvin Moore, "that it would not be useful for them to pursue any proposals for the sharing of either income tax revenue or natural resource revenue."[41] Instead the committee, working very closely with the government, recommended a 2.8 cent per litre gas tax that it estimated would generate $185 million a year, all of which would be targeted for municipalities. Even though the proposal was endorsed by the AUMA executive, at its October annual meeting the membership rejected it by a two to one margin and instead proposed that the government assign to municipalities 8 percent of its oil and gas royalties during the next five years. AUMA members were elected officials astute enough to realize that with the gas tax their constituents would curse each and every one of them and the municipality every time they filled their tanks.[42]

During the economic downturn beginning in the early 1980s, municipal concerns shifted from provincial restrictions on spending policies and control of grants and tax policies to reductions in provincial funding. Municipal grants were frozen or only marginally increased, a cap was placed on municipal borrowing, and the popular municipal interest subsidization program was terminated.

The formula for determining the amount of unconditional grants was changed in 1984 to reflect the "relative fiscal capacity" of each municipality. Although the Minister of Municipal Affairs said the new formula "will take from the rich and give to the poor,"[43] not a single municipality had its grant money reduced under the new formula.

Premier Don Getty's first address outside of the legislature was to the convention of the Alberta Association of Municipal Districts and Counties (AAMD&C), at which he announced that he was committed to funding municipalities with as few conditions as possible. He said that one level of government should not impose its views on another and went on to explain:

> It's the very argument that we have had with the federal government, in which the federal government . . . should not, in flowing funds into Alberta, then impose conditions out of Ottawa on the province. Now the argument stands up in the next step: that the province should not impose conditions on municipalities. They are elected. They are representatives of their constituents. If they are doing things that are wrong, their constituents will change it.[44]

Thus Getty committed himself to local autonomy and "no string" grants, but his immediate problem was the weakening provincial economy. Since operating grants to municipalities, schools, and hospital boards accounted for more than 40 percent of the provincial budget, Getty targeted them for trimming. However, after the Grants Structures Review Committee, struck by the Minister of Municipal Affairs in 1985, recommended that municipal unconditional grants should, at a minimum, reflect the annual increase in the consumer price index, unconditional grants were budgeted for a 4 percent increase for 1986/87.[45] To honour his commitment to the AAMD&C and to make his budget program more politically palatable, Getty initiated two new grant programs. In 1986 the Alberta Municipal Partnership in Local Employment (AMPLE) program was initiated to create jobs and rebuild infrastructures at the municipal level.[46] Although it was trumpeted as a $500 million grant over an eight-year period, only $22 million was budgeted for its first year, 1987.[47] In January 1988 the government announced the Alberta Partnership Transfer (APT) program, which would amalgamate the Municipal Assistance Grant (the principal unconditional grant for municipalities), the Municipal Police Assistance Grant, and the Public Transit Operating Grant[48] into a single cheque that could be used at the discretion of the recipient municipality.[49] However, Minister of Municipal Affairs Dennis Anderson was quick to point out that "we will continue to identify on the cheque and on the cheque stub the various components which will make up that one grant—in doing so, underlining the priorities of this government for the people of Alberta."[50]

Municipal councils were devastated when it was announced in January 1988 that in order to eliminate the provincial government's deficit by 1990, basic operating grants for municipalities, hospitals, and educational institutions were to be reduced by 3 percent.

Municipal disappointment about the size of provincial grants was tempered by increased autonomy in spending. Table 2.1 shows that the percentage of funds allocated by the Getty government for unconditional grants in 1988 nearly doubled the 1987 amount.

Local Authorities Board (LAB)

It does not take a close examination of provincial-municipal relations in Alberta to conclude that the province's imprint, sometimes barely discernable and at other times quite distinct, is found in almost every aspect of municipal planning and policy making. The province can use a number of mechanisms to shape the parameters of municipal policy, of which the most powerful is the Local Authorities Board (LAB).

The board's extensive powers are grounded in section 27(1) of the Local Authorities Board Act, which reads:

The Board has all the necessary jurisdiction and power
(a) to inquire into the merit of any application of a local authority for permission to raise money by way of debenture or on the security of stock . . .

(b) to supervise the expenditure of money borrowed by a local authority . . .

(c) to deal with the financial affairs of local authorities . . .

(d) to grant permission for the extension of the time for repaying the indebtedness incurred by a local authority for the cost of its public works . . .

(e) to separate land from an urban municipality . . .

(f) to order compromises of tax arrears . . . .

The board has additional powers. Although the majority of these are found in the Municipal Government Act, a number of other acts give the board power. As an example, under the New Towns Act the board's authorization is needed in order for a new town to proceed with its financial program. The Municipal Tax Exemption Act authorizes the board to determine which nonprofit organizations are to receive a property tax exemption and the Irrigation Act gives the board power to oversee the formation, amalgamation, and dissolution of Irrigation Districts.

The provincial government never formulated a long-range plan to give the LAB the immense amount of power that it wields today; rather, the board acquired power from its predecessors. As was noted earlier, the Board of Public Utilities Commissioners was created in 1915 to oversee and supervise the issuing of municipal debentures and the repayment of municipal debt after a number of municipalities had fallen upon hard times as a result of incurring excessive debts. In 1929, determined to further better relations with the municipalities, the United Farmers of Alberta government turned over ministerial approval for municipal annexations to the Board of Public Utilities Commissioners. Power kept accruing to the board and by 1934 it held almost sole authority over the creation of municipal debentures and annexation. In 1960 the Board of Public Utilities Commissioners was disbanded and subsequently a Public Utilities Board was created and given all of the powers which had previously been held by the Board of Public Utilities Commissioners. In 1961 the responsibilities for overseeing municipal debt and annexation were hived off the Public Utilities Board and given to a newly created Local Authorities Board. As will be seen in the chapter on governmental reorganization, during the 1970s the provincial Progressive Conservative government began to take back some of the strong powers of annexation that had accrued to the board over the years. Today, not only does the cabinet have the power to approve or disapprove of LAB decisions, it can also prescribe conditions for the adoption of annexation proposals.

Despite an erosion of its authority to make annexation decisions, the

LAB is still a powerful body. One reason for this is that it is an independent board with quasi-judicial powers and thus, apart from annexation issues, its decisions are final except on questions of jurisdiction or law, which can be appealed to the Court of Appeal.

Municipal Associations: Conduits in Provincial-Municipal Relations

Local government associations represent their members' interests before the legislative assembly and a number of departments, boards, and commissions concerned with policy making, administration, and budgeting at the local level. Although the provincial government is not required to work with local associations, Donald Higgins writes that, "it tends to serve the provincial government's political interests to accept the existence of such associations, to consult them, and to use them as a mechanism for furthering the province's own viewpoint."[51]

Skilful politicians and administrators may be able to change the fundamental direction of a municipal association so that it becomes a vehicle for the dissemination of the government's viewpoint rather than the articulator of a municipal position. In general, however, these associations serve as a conduit between their members and the provincial government. Particularly in a nonpartisan system, it is necessary that both the municipalities and the provincial government have mechanisms through which to communicate political information to each other.

Needless to say, municipalities are not homogeneous; they are rural or urban, large or small, wealthy or poor, and as a result are often in disagreement about goals and policies. Two critics of municipal association politics argue that associations "generally represent the lowest common denominator of opinion among the membership," with the consequence that the interests of individual municipalities become blurred.[52] The associations' professional staffs are aware of this problem and therefore support both legislation which benefits all members and legislation of interest to more specialized segments of the membership. An association also mediates differences between its members and, in some cases, functions as a cooperative buying agency that provides goods and services at substantially reduced costs. David Siegel, in a comparative study of Canadian provincial-municipal relations, describes an association's annual conference as the focal point for intergovernmental consultation, featuring an address by a minister and a host of resolutions: ". . . these resolutions form the main agenda for discussions between municipal association executives and the provincial government for the next year."[53]

The associations which are politically effective and have the support of their members are those that are just as knowledgeable and astute as their counterparts in the provincial government. They are staffed by full-time professionals who follow proposed changes in provincial legislation, develop and update position papers on intergovernmental relations, and present these papers to the government. Municipal associations are careful to remain on good terms with the news media, and almost all of them publish newsletters for their members. They may occasionally form alliances to present a common front.

While the departments of Municipal Affairs and Education often ask an association to comment informally on administrative and legislative proposals, municipal associations may also play a formal role in the legislative process. When the Municipal Statutes Review Committee was established in 1987, the Alberta Urban Municipalities Association (AUMA), the Alberta Association of Municipal Districts and Counties (AAMD&C), and the Alberta Association of Improvement Districts were asked to make nominations to the committee. A close working relationship generally develops between provincial departments and municipal associations to the benefit of both, since it reduces acrimony and conflict. However, two astute observers of associational politics, Lionel D. Feldman and Katherine A. Graham, question whether an association is able to maintain its independence when working so closely with the province. They write that "there is some evidence to suggest that . . . municipal associations in Canada have fallen under the influence of their respective senior government."[54]

Almost all urban municipalities in the province belong to the AUMA. In 1990 the association's membership of 292 municipalities represented 82 percent of the province's population.[55] Originally organized as the Union of Alberta Municipalities in 1905, its objectives were then to: (1) achieve uniform assessment in the various municipalities; (2) protect municipalities from unscrupulous corporations and promoters; (3) lobby for legislation benefiting municipalities; and (4) provide better ways of looking after indigent persons.[56] Although these were worthwhile goals, the Union functioned primarily to obtain additional funds for municipalities and to fend off the province's attempts to appropriate municipal revenues for its own use. Whether intentionally or not, the province weakened the association when cities were chartered individually.[57] Subsequently, rather than make legislative demands through the Union, a city's administration and its Board of Trade would lobby MLAs and departments for charter changes. Particularly corrosive of municipal cooperation was the animosity which developed between cities and other types of municipalities when only the cities were allowed to impose an income tax.

The Union was an informal organization until 1966, when it was incorporated as the AUMA. In 1969, at the request of its members, the AUMA established a Labour Relations Service to assist individual municipalities in their labour negotiations. In the 1970s and 1980s it became increasingly powerful as the provincial government came to rely on it for policy recommendations. The public has become aware of AUMA policy positions as a result of the media attention given its annual convention's "Bear Pit" session, a no-holds-barred question and answer period with government ministers whose departments have extensive dealings with municipalities. To keep the session honest, an outside person is brought in to moderate it.

Although the AUMA plays a prominent role in shaping municipal legislation, this role is not as large as might be expected. There are several reasons for this. The first is a function of the organization's own internal tensions, which are caused primarily by the division between large and small municipalities. Although all municipalities want to see an increase in "no-strings" unconditional grants, in other policy areas the concerns of small towns and villages are different from those of large cities. It is therefore difficult for the association to take firm positions on many issues; some proposals are compromises stated only in the most general terms.[58] Therefore, despite strength in numbers, the AUMA is always at risk of splintering.

The second reason why the organization has been less powerful than one would expect is a corollary of the first. Until the mid-1980s the AUMA's resolutions and political positions were not given the consideration the size of the organization would seem to command. As an example, the AUMA repeatedly requested that a yearly meeting be reinstituted at which its executive would meet with Premier Lougheed and the cabinet in order to discuss pertinent municipal policy and problems. At the AUMA's annual meeting in 1984, Minister of Municipal Affairs Julian Koziak defended the government's refusal to engage in such a meeting on the grounds that "the decision-making body of our government is the caucus, not cabinet" and that "we have 75 members of caucus, each of whom are equally important in terms of the political scheme of things in this province." Therefore, the type of high-level meeting requested by the AUMA should be held between its executive and government MLAs who at some time had held municipal office.[59] Many AUMA delegates found the explanation to be less than satisfactory.[60] But, in fact, since the AUMA traditionally has been controlled by politicians from smaller urban centres, Lougheed attempted to neutralize the political power of large cities by ensuring that all municipal policy issues were fed into the government through the organization.[61] The government did not see the AUMA as a major political threat since it was aware of the uneasy alliance between its large and small member municipalities and the compromises that had to be made on difficult issues.[62]

In 1991, when the AUMA responded to provincial cuts in city transportation grants, the organization acknowledged policy differences between urban and rural municipalities. The AUMA's president said that it was clear to cities that their transportation grants were being reduced while grants to rural municipalities were hardly affected. Very bluntly, he added that "if their [the provincial Tories'] political motivation was to encourage more MLAs to be elected in larger urban centres, you'd think they would be spending more money there."[63]

A smaller and more specialized municipal organization is the Alberta Association of Summer Villages. Founded in 1958, its membership in 1991 comprised 52 of the 54 summer villages. Almost all of its members also belong to the AUMA in order to obtain municipal insurance at attractive rates, but they rely on their specialized organization to present briefs and lobby the government for their primary concerns: adequate roads and bridges.

For many years rural municipalities have been represented by the AAMD&C. Its forerunner, the Alberta Association of Local Improvement Districts, was incorporated in 1910 to (1) forward the interests of all local improvement districts in the province, (2) endeavour to secure legislation relating to local improvements, (3) guard the interests of local improvement districts in any proposed legislation, and (4) work closely with the Department of Public Works. Since its inception it has strongly resisted provincial encroachment on local autonomy and has cautioned the provincial government against excessive centralization. Within a short time after its formation, the Alberta Association of Local Improvement Districts persuaded the province to create the Department of Municipal Affairs. The association probably wielded its greatest influence in the early 1920s, when its past president, Herbert Greenfield, was elected as head of a United Farmers of Alberta government. Greenfield resigned as premier and was replaced by J.E. Brownlee, who said in a speech before the association's 1925 meeting, ". . . I come in place of your old friend Mr. Greenfield. . . . I believe it was in the Municipal Convention that he was first initiated into the discussion of public subjects, and it became the training ground for his subsequent success."[64]

In earlier years there was often tension or even hostility between the

Alberta Association of Local Improvement Districts and the Union of Alberta Municipalities as a result of conflict over debt and how it was to be repaid. Urban municipalities perennially ran up large debts, while rural municipalities were frugal.[65]

Today, despite the province's urbanization, the AAMD&C successfully lobbies to ensure the government acknowledges rural concerns.[66] In addition to its lobbying activities, the association provides members with comprehensive insurance through its Jubilee Insurance Agency and acts as a cooperative for heavy equipment and supplies used by its members' engineering departments.[67]

One of the most powerful associations in the province is the Alberta School Trustees' Association (ASTA), which was founded in 1907 when Premier and Minister of Education A.C. Rutherford decided it would be a "good idea" to call all the school trustees in the province to a convention.[68] The province "paid for the notices and the publishing of proceedings of the first convention and also assisted in this matter with subsequent conventions."[69] ASTA's close relationship with the Department of Education began in 1909, when the Acting Deputy Minister of Education told its president that the department intended "to incorporate the suggestions of the trustees, as far as possible, into the Amendments of the School Ordinance and Regulations." Although active in its early years, "no evidence has been found to show that the organization was a functioning body in the 1914 to 1918 period so one must assume that it succumbed to the apathy of the individual trustees and to the demands of World War I."[70] When teachers united under the banner of the Alberta Teachers' Alliance after the war, the ASTA revived and joined forces with the Department of Education to oppose them.

During the 1930s the organization again foundered as trustees of some cash-starved school districts withdrew and other districts were consolidated, with the consequence that trustees lost their positions. In 1939 the provincial government passed the Alberta School Trustees' Association Act, which directed that "the board of trustees of each non-divisional school district and of each school division" be members of the association. This legislation resolved the membership problem, but its financial difficulties continued until 1941 when, in a remarkable tribute to the association's political power, an order in council empowered the Department of Education to deduct any unpaid ASTA fees from a district's education grant.[71]

This relationship between the ASTA and the Department of Education has continued to the present. In 1970, for example, the Department of Education asked ASTA to help rewrite the School Act; more than half of its suggestions were incorporated into the new legislation.[72] The provincial government may have provided such strong support and funding for ASTA because their goals are largely the same. First, ASTA has had a long-standing battle with its natural antagonist, the Alberta Teachers' Association (ATA), opposing teacher collective bargaining, minimum salaries, and continuous contracts. Undoubtedly, many politicians have sympathized with ASTA's efforts to limit the powers of the ATA. Second, most school trustees believe that it is their duty to protect ratepayers from "inordinate tax increases" and "irresponsible educational empire building," an attitude shared by both Social Credit and the Progressive Conservatives.

Although the Alberta Catholic School Trustees' Association (ACSTA), which was formed in 1958, is a part of ASTA, the organization holds its own convention at which members discuss the legislation, regulation, and financing of Catholic education. Since ACSTA represents 50 Catholic and separate school districts, with approximately 20 percent of Alberta's student population, the organization's lobbying activities are taken very seriously by the government.

Two more recently organized associations are the Alberta Federation of Metis Settlements Association, founded in 1975, and the Rural and Improvement Districts Association of Alberta, founded in 1976. The former represents the province's eight Metis settlements through a board consisting of the chairperson of each settlement council and four other members elected at large. The latter acts on behalf of improvement district advisory councils through a seven-person board representing the various areas of the province. Both organizations formulate briefs and pass resolutions that are presented to the appropriate provincial departments. Since the Association of Rural and Improvement Districts and the AAMD&C share many concerns common to rural areas, they work together in making presentations to the government.

The government has never established a formal cabinet-level committee to meet with the municipal associations and to coordinate the efforts of the various departments dealing with municipalities. Instead, ad-hoc committees composed of government ministers and municipal association representatives have been formed in response to specific problems. Walter Walchuk briefly discusses the formation in 1959 of the Provincial-Municipal Advisory Committee to "facilitate discussions between the UAM, AAMD&C and the Executive Council" and its dissolution in 1971. In 1962 Premier Manning established the Public Revenue and Expenditure Committee, which had among its responsibilities the examination of a diverse set of municipal concerns. Several years later it too was dissolved. After Lougheed came to power the Alberta Provincial Municipal Finance Council was created, with a wide-reaching mandate to examine issues such as municipal finances, delivery of services, and capital work projects.[73] When federal-provincial conferences were being held on the constitution, the Alberta government invited the AUMA and the AAMD&C to attend the meetings as observers. Although representatives from the two associations participated in the discussions, they were never made formal delegates.

At the 1984 AUMA annual convention, delegates passed a resolution asking the provincial government to formalize its relationship with AUMA through a "mechanism" to ensure the government consulted with the association on major municipal issues. After dismissing the resolution, the Minister of Municipal Affairs announced the formation of another ad-hoc committee with municipal association representation in order to establish a formula for borrowing and debt guidelines.

Shortly after Getty assumed office, Edmonton's Mayor Laurence Decore, an up-and-coming provincial Liberal, called for the establishment of a new ministry with a leader committed to being an "advocate of the cities" and a department able to deal with urban problems and accessible to its clientele. Implicit in his proposal was the formation of an urban municipal association with a formal role to play in the formulation of urban policy. Pledged to an administration with a smaller cabinet and unwilling to credit Decore with any political acumen, Getty dismissed his proposal out of hand. However, Getty began to meet informally with the AUMA's board of directors in order to discuss municipal policy. In January 1988 the Provincial-Municipal Premier's Council was founded with a membership comprising the premier, four cabinet members, and representatives from the AUMA, the AAMD&C, and the Improvement Districts Association of Alberta. Dedicated to bringing together "the ideas, concepts, and directions . . . [which] will underline that spirit of co-operation and of partnership which exemplifies our relationship with municipalities," the committee met twice between January 1988 and January 1990.

Politics as a Factor in Provincial-Municipal Relations

Astute politicians realize that as often as not a government's success in policy implementation depends on the policy stance and determination of other governments. In other words, from a strict legal perspective it may seem that provincial politicians always have the upper hand; but in fact they are often as dependent upon the goodwill and support of municipal politicians as the municipal politicians are on that of their provincial counterparts.

Political folklore is replete with tales of elected officials who have neglected their constituents and subsequently been defeated. MLAs attend a multitude of meetings, luncheons, and dinners in their ridings in order to demonstrate their accessibility and concern. Since it is necessary to be as time-efficient as possible, MLAs on the "rubber chicken circuit" tend to meet mainly with community business and political groups. Particularly in the larger municipalities, the mayor and council members are seen as key people who should not be ignored.

Municipal politicians consider it important to have access to and be on good terms with the MLA who is their principal spokesperson and advocate in the provincial government. As a consequence, much of the lobbying carried out by communities is with their MLAs who, in theory, act as conduits for information moving back and forth between the province and the municipalities. In 1988 the *Pincher Creek Echo* reported that MLA Fred Bradley held one of his regularly scheduled meetings with the Pincher Creek town council, which apprised him of its problems and financial needs. Bradley promised to speak to the Department of Municipal Affairs to determine the town's eligibility for provincial fiscal programs.[74]

When Ernie Isley was Minister of Public Works, he not only counselled municipal politicians to lobby both their local MLAs and his office for their public works projects, but also said that the more a community lobbied the more likely it was that its proposals would be reviewed. In 1986 High Prairie's mayor, Don Lorencz, took Isley's advice to heart and aggressively petitioned the government when a freeze was put on a planned provincial building in the town. In his own constituency, the *Grand Centre-Cold Lake Sun* accused Isley of not being aggressive enough in seeking funding for a new Grand Centre provincial building. Isley, in turn, criticized the council and the Chamber of Commerce for their lacklustre efforts on behalf of a tourist interpretive centre and concluded that as a result, Medicine Hat and Turner Valley would most likely get their centres first.[75] In contrast, the long-time mayor of Lethbridge, Andrew Anderson, had extensive contacts with politicians in the provincial government as well as with the city's MLA. During his term in office, a university was established in the city, the downtown core was redeveloped, and the city's rail lines were relocated.

An example of political naivete occurred in Carstairs in 1986. Rather than working through its MLA, who lived and practised law in the town, the Chamber of Commerce, backed by the town council, wrote the premier complaining that Carstairs had been ignored by the provincial government. In contrast, cognizant of the importance of MLAs in municipal-provincial relations, the Strathmore council spent some time in 1988 developing a lobbying strategy to enlist its MLA's support.

The relationships of MLAs with big city councils are much different from their relationships with small municipal councils. For each of the province's two largest cities there are nearly as many MLAs as there are members of council. MLAs in the same political party often work out common provincial-municipal strategies and meet with council members to discuss city problems. When caucuses are held haphazardly, or not at all, problems can occur.[76]

Party Politics in Provincial-Municipal Relations

Advocates of nonpartisan government have long held that provincial-municipal cooperation suffers if a province and a municipality are governed by different political parties. Although in Alberta provincial government is partisan and local government nonpartisan, innumerable candidates for municipal office have publicized their provincial party affiliation. In some instances candidates were elected who were well known and active members of an opposition provincial party; such was the case with Edmonton's New Democratic mayors Ivor Dent, who won one Edmonton election after another during the 1960s and 1970s, and Jan Reimer, who was elected in 1989 and re-elected in 1992.

In Social Credit's early period, when Alberta was predominantly rural, the provincial government worked closely with towns, villages, and municipal and improvement districts. Given this cooperation and an electorate which subscribed to one-party politics, it is easy to understand why the relationships between provincial and municipal politicians were so amiable. Contributing to Social Credit's 1971 demise was its desertion of its rural support base in order to court a growing urban electorate.

The Progressive Conservatives filled the political vacuum in the rural areas and also gained the support of the cities, with their new class of technicians and bureaucrats. Once again the electorate rallied behind one party, although a political chasm was widening between rural Alberta and the cities. Premier Lougheed seduced large and small municipalities and local level politicians of all political stripes with more than ample municipal grants almost every year. During Lougheed's administration, mayors and councillors who were members of opposition provincial parties openly criticized the premier and Tory policies without being penalized by the government. The party identification of municipal elected officials was apparently unimportant. After Laurence Decore was elected Edmonton's mayor in 1983, Julian Koziak, the Minister of Municipal Affairs, said, "I do not think the question of what his federal political leanings might be has any bearing on his ability to manage the affairs of city hall."[77] Progressive Conservative cabinet members with Edmonton and Calgary constituencies worked with city politicians and represented the cities' interests in cabinet meetings. An example of this was the role played in a conflict between Alberta Government Telephones and Edmonton Telephones Corporation by one of Lougheed's key lieutenants, Neil Crawford. It was rumoured at the time that Crawford, sympathetic to Edmonton Telephones, always took the city's position.

During the Lougheed years the public apparently was unaware of provincial and municipal politicians' differences of opinion on policy issues. One can only surmise that Lougheed was a masterful negotiator who resolved differences between municipalities and the provincial government behind closed doors.

The premier's successor, Don Getty, simply did not have Lougheed's political acumen. Shortly before the Tory leadership convention the party's three principal contenders, Don Getty, Ron Ghitter, and Julian Koziak, were invited to participate in the AUMA's Bear Pit, with its aggressive question and answer session. Evidently fearing he would be bested by Koziak, the Minister of Municipal Affairs, Getty first equivocated and then declined the invitation. Many of the AUMA's 1,100 delegates were disappointed and angry.

With the deterioration of the provincial economy, the financial resources Lougheed had used to mollify the province's municipalities simply were not available when Getty came to power. Moreover, Getty did not seem to know how to deal with Edmonton, where the Tories had lost ten seats in the 1986 election and the popular mayor was Laurence Decore, an unabashed provincial Liberal, who continued to draw political blood with deft jabs at the premier and his programs. Within a short time after Getty took office Edmonton Telephones had won the "telephone toll war" with Alberta Government Telephones, which gave the city utility a share of long distance phone revenue. And despite the province's objections, the city's other utility, Edmonton Power, continued its massive expansion of the Genesee Power Project.

In 1987, with the mayor exploring the possibilities of running for the leadership of the provincial Liberal Party, relationships between Getty and Decore became increasingly acrimonious. In a criticism of the provincial budget Decore blamed the Tories for doing little to alleviate the city's high unemployment rate and charged that the province was not cooperating with Edmonton. Getty responded with a list of job creation programs and accused Decore of not showing any political "class."[78] Months later Decore accused Edmonton's four Tory MLAs, including Getty, of failing to represent their constituents. Getty lashed back: "We're doing a lot for Edmonton—we're doing a hell of a lot more than city council . . . with the mayor running about the province, the Edmonton caucus really has to represent the city and we are."[79] In 1988 Decore again attacked Tory job creation schemes, and an angry Getty responded that the provincial budget included 20 projects which would pump $425 million into Edmonton.[80] Getty's Employment Minister Rick Orman said Edmonton's unemployment rate was substantially higher than Calgary's because Calgary's Mayor Ralph Klein "outhustled" Decore.[81]

Edmonton Sun columnist Allan Bolstad describes other provincial retaliations in response to criticism from Decore.

> On September 12, [1988,] the provincial government held a major press conference to announce a $6 million grant for an Edmonton concert hall. The hall foundation people were there . . . but no mayor. . . . "We wanted someone who had a depth of knowledge in municipal affairs," Anderson [Minister of Municipal Affairs] said yesterday, explaining why Cavanagh was selected. "Cavanagh is a former mayor."[82]

Also in September, when a press conference was called to announce the relocation of Edmonton's downtown rail yards and an expansion of Grant MacEwan Community College on the vacated lands, only representatives from Canadian National Rail and the college were present; Decore learned of the impending announcement only hours before it was made in a phone call from a friendly Tory MP. Less than a month later when Decore resigned to become the leader of the provincial Liberal Party, the council appointed one of its own members, a Tory, to serve out the mayor's term. One of Mayor Cavanagh's first pronouncements criticized Decore's poor relations with Getty, which he said had cost the city jobs, and promised "to have excellent relations with the provincial government."[83] Perhaps unintentionally, Cavanagh, a staunch Tory, revealed that Getty's quarrel with Decore had been detrimental to the city's interests.[84]

When Lougheed was in power and Edmonton was solidly Tory, the city benefited from informal meetings between the council and the Edmonton Tory caucus. The consultative process has deteriorated, however, with recent Tory losses. After the March 1989 provincial election, which left Edmonton with only two Tory MLAs, the city's council passed a resolution asking the premier to establish a tri-party Edmonton urban committee to look after the city's needs in the legislature and regularly meet with council. The major proponent of the resolution, alderman Ron Hayter, argued that the committee would ensure that the "city's concerns are addressed on the basis of urgency and merit" rather than partisan political considerations. Getty was unreceptive to the proposal.[85]

Getty's vendetta was costly for both himself and his party. In March 1989 only two Edmonton Tories were elected and Getty was defeated in Edmonton Whitemud by a Liberal candidate who had been Mayor Decore's administrative assistant. Another reaction to the Getty policy was the overwhelming defeat of Edmonton's Mayor Cavanagh, an outspoken Tory, by high-profile New Democrat Jan Reimer in the fall municipal election. Reimer made a determined effort to improve relations with the province by initiating the first of what was to become a series of meetings between the council and a truncated Tory caucus comprising the two Tories from Edmonton and two from the city's greater metropolitan area.

The loss of Edmonton seems to have had little effect on the way in which Premier Getty and his party treated other municipalities with an electorate sympathetic to one of the opposition parties. Early in 1989 the cabinet decided to hold the Western Premiers' Conference in Edson on May 25 and 26. However, it was necessary to postpone the conference after Getty lost in Edmonton and chose to run in a Stettler by-election. After Edson's New Democrat MLA, Jerry Doyle, attempted to embarrass the premier during the by-election by making the postponement an issue, the conference was moved to Camrose and rescheduled for the end of June. People in Edson were confused and disappointed. When the Federal and Intergovernmental Affairs Minister, Jim Horsman, was queried about the move, he said Doyle "brought it on himself." When asked if the decision was politically motivated, Horsman responded, "that's apparent, isn't it?"[86]

After Getty set a precedent for punishing municipal politicians who disagreed with him, Calgary's Tory mayor followed suit. Donald Hartman, appointed by council to fill out the term of Ralph Klein, who had become a MLA (and would later become premier) was positioning himself to run for mayor in the fall of 1989. In the spring the city administration decided to honour the Calgary Flames after they won the Stanley Cup. Invitations to the celebration were sent to community leaders and politicians; only the city's three Liberal and two New Democratic MLAs were not invited. After being harshly criticized in the news media, Hartman grudgingly apologized to them.[87]

It would seem that a factor in the Tories' declining fortune was the inability of Getty and the government to work with municipal politicians from different parties. In the short run, Getty was able to penalize municipalities and elected officials. In the long run, however, a provincial government is as dependent upon the municipalities as they are upon the province. Getty seems to have had little understanding of this symbiotic process.

Intermunicipal Cooperation and Conflict

Many students of local government limit their investigation of intergovernmental relations to the vertical connections between municipalities and the federal and provincial governments. They neglect the extensive network of formal and informal intermunicipal agreements used to solve problems that cut across municipal boundaries. This is a mistake on two counts. First, horizontal relationships are as important as vertical ones in making the governmental system operate responsibly. Second, since effective relationships between communities do not "just happen," but require competent and thoughtful political negotiations, it is worthwhile to examine them in detail in order to learn what works and what does not.

There is a major difference between vertical and horizontal relationships. In horizontal relationships municipalities deal with each other as equals; no municipality is able to impose its will on another, as sometimes happens in provincial-municipal relations. Although municipalities spend what may appear to be an inordinate amount of time bargaining and negotiating, the outcomes are usually equitable and are seen as being more legitimate than in a superior-subordinate relationship in which negotiations are often short-circuited in the interest of expediency by directives from above. Matthew Holden characterizes the intermunicipal negotiation process as being analogous to that which takes place among autonomous countries in the international system.[88] Some local governments, like some countries, are proud of their skilful negotiations, longstanding agreements, and good relations with their neighbours, while others take an almost perverse delight in fostering conflict and confrontation.

Unlike Calgary, which attempts to maintain harmonious relations with its neighbours, Edmonton has a history of confrontation with adjoining municipalities.[89] In 1985 Fort Saskatchewan's mayor Muriel Abdurahman took Edmonton to task. Noting that Fort Saskatchewan had been attempting to work with Edmonton since 1907 to prevent the city from dumping raw sewage into the North Saskatchewan River, Abdurahman said her city's environmental concerns were still being ignored as Edmonton's sewage flowed into the river during heavy rains.[90] Instead of viewing outlying municipalities as "parasites" taking advantage of city employment and services, she urged Edmonton to work with all of the area's municipalities to resolve their common problems.[91]

While Edmonton was dismissing Abdurahman's criticism, the city's sanitary landfill site was almost filled and it was seeking a new location. In 1984 Edmonton, Fort Saskatchewan, and the County of Strathcona had agreed to participate in a study to determine the best location for a regional landfill, but in 1986 both Fort Saskatchewan and the County of Strathcona stated that there were no plans to allow Edmonton to dump its garbage in their municipalities. Two years later the Municipal District of Sturgeon likewise refused to assist the city. Moreover, the County of Strathcona was a key opponent to Edmonton's unsuccessful proposal to establish the Aurum site near the county's border. It did not escape the public and the press that Edmonton's abrasive manner was bearing bitter fruit, for no neighbouring municipality could be found to alleviate the city's garbage crisis.[92] Shortly thereafter, the County of Strathcona requested the Edmonton Regional Planning Commission to amend the regional plan so the county could rezone for residential use a parcel of industrial land located near the Edmonton border. Nine members of the Edmonton city council attended the planning commission meeting on October 17, 1990, and all were adamantly opposed to the rezoning, arguing that allowing residences in the area would "significantly limit" the development of nearby industrial land in Edmonton.[93]

Edmonton is not the only municipality unable to get along with its neighbours. In 1987 and 1988 relations between the adjoining towns of Grand Centre and Cold Lake chilled when they were unable to agree on the location of a regional swimming pool. This occurred despite a history of jointly operated water, sewage, and dog pound facilities. In 1988 the *Westlock Hub*'s Michael Moss said, "Westlock's town council and the council of the Municipal District of Westlock love to despise each other. They live for the one opportunity to criticize the other's move...."[94] Another series of unresolved conflicts began in 1988, when the Municipal District of Bonnyville approved a piggery within two miles of the boundaries of the Town of Bonnyville.[95] Shortly thereafter the district council approved a subdivision with no sanitary or storm drainage which was to be located only a short distance from the town's water treatment plant. The district council was no more accommodating with adjoining Improvement District No. 18 than it had been with the Town of Bonnyville. Irritated by slow-moving discussions on a new contract to provide fire protection to improvement district residents, the district council decided to withdraw these services, leaving many small communities unprotected. The improvement district's administrator was shocked by the council's action, since the two municipalities had been within 30 days of signing a new contract.[96] A similar situation occurred in southern Alberta when the Coaldale town council adopted a strict policy of having its fire department respond only to fires within the contracted boundaries. The town's mayor was conspicuously silent about negotiating for fire protection with residents of the nearby County of Lethbridge.[97]

Some of the most acrimonious relations have occurred between Edmonton and Calgary, which from the early part of the century have competed with one another for provincial funds and for the honour of being Alberta's largest and most prestigious city. In 1931 both cities had come to a virtual halt and badly needed financial help from the province. Nevertheless, they were unwilling to make a joint presentation to the province for additional funds.[98] In recent years civic boosters and politicians have made jokes about the difficulties of living in "that other city," but in financial dealings they compete aggressively for business and governmental projects. Politicians have made careers out of belittling the intelligence and integrity of their counterparts in the other city. In 1985 after Calgary's Mayor Klein criticized Edmonton's administration for poor planning in allowing the development of a mega-mall, Edmonton councillors responded with a frenzied attack on Klein and the dowdy state of downtown Calgary. Two years later the Edmonton political establishment was again incensed when Klein made Edmonton the butt of a joke at a Calgary Rotary Club luncheon.[99]

Although confrontation occasionally is good politics, in other cases intermunicipal cooperation serves the political interests of individuals as much as it serves those of the municipality. Generally, it is considered beneficial to have open and established lines of communication with the elected officials and senior administrators of other municipalities in a region. Carefully weighing the advantages and disadvantages of intermunicipal agreements, astute and ambitious politicians quickly realize that the advocation and negotiation of well-publicized and popular intermunicipal agreements gives them invaluable visibility.

Even more important are the advantages which accrue to a region's municipalities when there is a widespread network of cooperation. Bargaining in good faith is a "win-win" strategy for each municipality. In many instances regional cooperation not only solves difficult problems but also results in substantial financial savings. In 1986 this point was made to a number of municipal councillors by an Assistant Deputy Minister for Municipal Affairs, who said that given the province's deteriorating financial situation, communities should "abandon their traditional confrontational stance and begin to work together. . . ."[100]

An abrasive council which deals with other municipalities only through legal counsel and legal proceedings may gain a temporary advantage. However, such short-term gains are far outweighed by the long-term costs. First, neighbouring municipalities soon become wary of legal action, with the consequence that even the simplest problem often is deliberately left unresolved. Second, the price in terms of both time and money is staggering for a municipality which always resorts to litigation. This point was made by Felix Michna, Planning Director for the City of Lethbridge, in explaining how his city benefited by maintaining ongoing and cordial relations with the county. In 1983, when the city was negotiating with the county over an annexation, the two governments worked together to reach an agreement and kept ratepayers informed of their every step. When the annexation proposal went before the Local Authorities Board (LAB), it had only token opposition.[101]

The amicable negotiations between the city and county of Lethbridge did not take place by chance. The two governments have carefully nurtured a nonadversarial relationship. A tradition of yearly meetings of elected city and county officials to discuss common concerns has undoubtedly helped to defuse what might become explosive confrontations. Particularly important has been what Lethbridge's city manager called "a political will to see this thing negotiated." Finally, areas of disagreement have been narrowed so that officials from the two governments are not engaged in endless wrangling.

When political and economic life was much simpler, area-wide concerns were resolved primarily through bilateral agreements. However, in the last few years municipalities have come to realize that their problems often affect a number of communities and thus it is necessary to have a synchronized and well organized response. An Alberta planner who examined a number of intermunicipal recreation agreements found that planners have assumed a leading role in the promotion of intermunicipal cooperation. Thomas Baldwin notes that the Red Deer Planning Commission fosters intermunicipal recreational planning among its members and that elected officials in the Municipal District of Fairview and the Town of Fairview work together to plan recreation policy. He examines the area-wide recreational facilities provided by the Town of Grimshaw, Improvement District No. 22, and the Village of Berwyn and concludes that intermunicipal cooperation in recreational planning "will become more popular as the benefits of such an approach are realized. It may not be on the basis of a formal agreement but will probably be on the basis of informal cooperation through a set of guidelines in a recreation master plan."[102] Perhaps Baldwin should have added that local authorities will turn to intermunicipal agreements to deal with increasingly stressful financial problems.

A different form of coordinated community action occurred in 1986 in southern Alberta when 70 community leaders representing ten municipalities, the Municipal District of Foothills, and the Foothills School Division met to work out a joint response to cuts in provincial funding and to explore more efficient ways of delivering services. This eventually led the towns of High River and Okotoks and the Municipal District of Foothills to cooperate to promote economic development. The chair of the High River economic·development commission explained that, "if High River is close to getting an industry, we should tell them at Okotoks so they could lobby and do whatever they can for us. It's better for both of us if the industry is here, rather than in Quebec. . . ."[103] Another example of intermunicipal cooperation occurred in 1989 when seven southern Alberta municipalities (the City of Lethbridge; the towns of Coaldale and Picture Butte; the villages of Coalhurst, Nobleford, and Barons; and the County of Lethbridge) signed a Peacetime Disaster Mutual Aid Agreement which entitled each municipality to call on any of the others in the event of a catastrophe.[104] The same year the provincial government encouraged six municipalities to form a unique regional task force in order to lease or purchase four major airports in the Edmonton region.[105]

It was only after the 1989 election placed mayors in Edmonton and Calgary who were determined to foster better relationships that the traditional rivalry, hostility, and acrimony between these cities began to abate. Despite very different political philosophies, Edmonton's Jan Reimer and Calgary's Al Duerr met regularly and collaborated on a number of issues. They discussed the feasibility of a connecting high-speed rail link and ways to increase municipal grants, as well as the apportionment of finance and industry between the two cities. After the provincial legislature's Special Select Committee on Electoral Boundaries released its report in November 1990 recommending that Edmonton and Calgary be under-represented in the legislature the two mayors met to coordinate their opposition to the proposal. Reimer summed up the new spirit of cooperation when she said that there would always be competition, "but it should be healthy and based on the two cities' strengths instead of . . . running down the other city."[106]

Federal-Municipal Relations

Despite the constitutional stricture on federal involvement in municipal affairs, the federal government controls airports and their location in the nation's cities, plays a major role in the placement and planning of rail lines, has post offices and routes in even the smallest communities, and supervises a nation-wide network of defense, penal, and park facilities. This is the reason provincial governments become suspicious whenever the federal government brings forward a program to help municipalities; they fear the national government is trying to increase an area of influence which is already quite large. Municipal politicians, on the other hand, seem much less concerned about an expansion of federal powers.

The Federation of Canadian Municipalities (FCM) is a national organization founded in 1976 whose purpose is to further the goals of municipalities and to facilitate cooperation between municipalities and the two senior levels of government. Its organizational structure is complex, since it includes both individual municipalities and associations of municipalities across Canada.

The FCM's predecessor was the Canadian Federation of Mayors and Municipalities (CFMM), which was formed by the merger of municipal and mayoral associations in 1937. Donald Higgins notes that the CFMM was created to lobby the federal government for financial aid for the unemployed, and improved economic conditions just prior to the Second World War made "the survival of the organization problematic because the problem of unemployment relief no longer applied."[107] While the CFMM continued to decline until 1976, when it had only slightly more than 200 member municipalities, the organization was revitalized and its membership began to increase after it resolved some of the inequities in its fee structure and made itself more relevant to the concerns of municipalities of all sizes.

Although the FCM has considerable influence on the formulation of federal policies that affect municipalities, the association has some inherent weaknesses. Feldman and Graham point out that many municipalities do not see any advantage in belonging to the FCM since, with municipal matters falling under the purview of the provinces, the federal government is not perceived as a major participant in municipal policy making. In addition, FCM membership represents only a minority of the nation's larger cities; the two social scientists note that "Canadian urban municipalities have ... exhibited a tendency to act alone when dealing with the federal government."[108]

From the viewpoint of many politicians and bureaucrats, the federal government's interest and influence in municipal affairs have been short-lived; the position of Minister of State for Urban Affairs, created in 1971, was abolished in 1979. But this view is much too narrow. In addition to its control of the transportation, postal, law enforcement, and defence networks listed at the beginning of this section, the federal government has had a lengthy history of involvement in local affairs.

For three-quarters of a century the federal government has participated with municipalities and provinces in various housing programs. The government's initial involvement in housing occurred after the devastating explosion which rocked Halifax in 1917 destroyed or damaged a substantial portion of the city's housing stock. To help survivors the government established the Halifax Explosion Relief Commission with trust funding of over $30 million.[109] In order to protect the capital, the trustees decided to invest most of this money in housing. They persuaded contractors and unions to build the housing at cost and convinced all three levels of government that it should be exempt from taxes. The housing project was a success, but since the trustees were determined to increase the size of the trust, its rent structure was based on the market. As a consequence, by 1923 more than half of the units were vacant. Although the federal government was involved with the Commission and the Hydrostone Project until it was sold in 1948, the President of the Central Mortgage and Housing Corporation recently said that the Halifax project "was not an auspicious beginning to the federal government's involvement in housing."[110]

A national program introduced in 1919 to provide housing for returning veterans funded more than 6,200 low-cost units in 179 municipalities. It was terminated in 1923 when the government decided that although housing for veterans was a worthwhile policy, housing should be a private sector responsibility.

In the depths of the depression the Dominion Housing Act was enacted to increase employment by lending funds to stimulate the construction of low- and moderately-priced homes.[111] Every province but Alberta participated in the program. When the Social Credit Party was elected in 1935 Aberhart was determined to put into policy the party's doctrine on credit and banking. What he did not realize was that in doing this he inadvertently challenged the power of the federal government. Party moderates prevailed in 1936 and no radical legislation was passed. But after the moderates were rooted out, two acts aimed directly at the financial community were passed by the legislature in 1937, only to be disallowed by the federal government.[112] Aberhart then brought forward two new pieces of legislation directed at undermining the banking system; in March 1938 the Supreme Court of Canada declared these to be *ultra vires.* Although hardly bruised by these thwarted attempts to apply Social Credit fiscal policies, financial institutions were understandably reluctant to do business in the province and quietly boycotted participation in the 1935 housing act and the 1936 Dominion Housing and Mortgages Act. Finkel writes that "fear of Social Credit's debt legislation had, allegedly, produced something of a capital strike in the province, causing investors to hold back planned building projects and financiers to withhold loan money from provincial businessmen."[113] Another federal initiative, the Municipal Improvements Assistance Act, enabled municipalities to modernize their utilities; however, Alberta's municipalities received only a token sum under the program. The 1938 National Housing Act was enacted to update the Dominion Housing Act,[114] but despite a lessening of hostilities between the province and the financial community, no loans were made under the National Housing Act or its 1944 successor until the year after Aberhart's death.[115]

After Ernest Manning assumed power, there was a subtle shift in the province's relationship with the federal government and the banking and finance community. In the 1944 election Manning had skilfully manoeuvred the Cooperative Commonwealth Federation (CCF) into the far left and garnered support from the business and banking communities which enabled him to remain in power. Both business and the federal government must have been relieved when in 1947 Manning abolished the militantly anti-business Social Credit Board.

The 1944 National Housing Act was enacted to consolidate the federal government's existing housing programs and to plan for a post-war program of reconstruction.[116] The act made it particularly clear that the federal government, and not local municipalities, was to make policy for the housing it financed.[117] Recognizing how important housing was to become, in October 1945 Parliament established the Central Mortgage and Housing Corporation (CMHC) to administer existing housing programs and to plan and coordinate financial arrangements with the provinces and the municipalities. As a result of Premier Manning's pragmatic interpretation of Social Credit ideology and the federal government's determination to involve all of the provinces in increasing the supply of housing, Alberta was an active participant in the NHA and CMHC programs. From January to June of 1945, 116 loans totalling $510,000 were approved in the province; between January and June 1946, 425 loans worth $1,925,000 were approved.[118]

Although many CMHC policies were determined in Ottawa, for four years a decentralized administrative structure and decision-making process resulted in many crucial housing decisions being made jointly by regional administrators and local authorities.[119] Then in 1949 CMHC announced that it would no longer initiate housing projects and in an internal memo laid out three principles: (l) the federal government's role in housing was to be primarily financial; (2) subsidized rental housing was to be a joint federal-provincial matter; and (3) there was to be no direct federal housing construction or operation. This "effectively cut the federal government off from direct negotiations with cities and substituted instead negotiations with the provinces."[120] Shortly after the discovery of oil in Alberta the economy boomed and there were housing shortages in Edmonton and Calgary. In 1950 the province asked CMHC to work directly with the two cities to resolve their housing problems. In line with its 1949 policy, the federal government responded that it "would deal with a city only if the province appointed it as its agent with complete authority to finalize any deal." A CMHC internal memorandum noted that since this condition would be completely unacceptable to a province, any pressure to deal directly with municipalities would be withdrawn.[121]

With the passage of the 1954 National Housing Act, the CMHC shifted from making direct housing loans in participation with private lending institutions to becoming an insurer of housing loans. Particularly important for municipalities was the stipulation that housing underwritten by the CMHC was to be approved by one of its inspectors. Bettison argues that this provision "led increasingly to the subservice of municipal and provincial planners to those who were in specialized positions backed by the source of funds, in Ottawa."[122]

The federal strategy of decreasing the importance of local authorities in the planning and administration of housing was not without its critics. In 1958 a memo of the Advisory Group of CMHC suggested that public housing should be the direct responsibility of municipalities, with the federal government providing the necessary financing. In 1961 an internal CMHC memo made the same suggestion and the following year the Advisory Group reiterated its 1958 proposal.[123] In Alberta the Department of Municipal Affairs established a Housing and Urban Renewal Committee comprising six members from the federal, provincial, and municipal governments. The committee was to resolve housing issues involving the three levels of government, but its suggestions fared no better than those made by the CMHC Advisory Group.

As it became clear to the municipalities that they were being systematically excluded from the planning and administration of housing programs, they proposed the creation of a federal Department of Municipal Affairs to change the rules on their participation. When the establishment of such a department was first proposed in 1962 by the Canadian Federation of Mayors and Municipalities (CFMM), which believed the provincial governments were gaining power at the expense of municipalities, it was discussed in Parliament and quietly dismissed. But when the federal Liberals were elected in 1963 there was renewed interest in urban housing and social problems. The following year the government committed itself to providing low-income housing and extending an urban renewal program initiated in 1955 which had been poorly funded.[124] The government also decided to work with municipalities (with provincial approval) after concluding they were best able to plan and administer public housing projects. Shortly thereafter, the Alberta Housing and Urban Renewal Corporation was established in order to coordinate the federal program with the province's municipalities.

For the next several years there was little change in housing policy or the patterns of federal-municipal relations until the government unintentionally precipitated a crisis by raising the interest rates on CMHC loans to slow construction and curb a rapid increase in inflation. As the housing industry declined, Prime Minister Pearson responded to requests from provincial and municipal leaders for a comprehensive policy on housing and municipal development by convening a conference on housing and urban affairs in 1967. The provinces, the CFMM, and the municipalities argued about representation at the conference. Allan O'Brien writes:

> The CFMM sought the right to be represented in view of the relevance of the subject for local government. Mr. Pearson advised that he had no objection provided all ten provinces agreed. Since such agreement was not forthcoming, no invitation was extended. Some provinces did invite municipal persons to join their respective provincial delegations either as advisors or observers.[125]

Perhaps it was this slight which galvanized the municipalities to demand entrenched powers in a new constitution. In 1969 Prime Minister Trudeau appeared unexpectedly at the CFMM's annual convention and in his speech asked the delegates to answer the question: "Do the enormously increased responsibilities and financial requirements of municipalities call for any change in the Constitution?"[126] Sparked by Trudeau's interest, the CFMM created the Joint Municipal Committee on Intergovernmental Relations (JMCIR), comprising representatives from municipal associations across Canada. Before preparing a brief for

Trudeau, the JMCIR sought to consult the provincial governments, who initially were reluctant to discuss sharing power with municipalities. The JMCIR eventually met with ten provincial municipal affairs ministers in Winnipeg in the late summer of 1970. The municipal delegation's brief asked that in the future municipalities be brought into the discussions on constitutional change and that tri-level talks be scheduled on the responsibilities of the three levels of government under the existing constitutional arrangements. An excerpt on the relationship between the province and the municipality illustrates the aggressiveness of the JMCIR:

> An examination of almost any of the provincial acts governing municipalities will indicate that the provinces apparently believe in their own infallibility where municipalities are concerned, regardless of the size or competence of the local government. The attitude, more often than not, is that of prohibition rather than of guidance and support, of domination rather than partnership.[127]

The ministers were amenable to holding tri-level talks to discuss governmental responsibilities but were not willing to discuss changing the constitution to benefit municipalities. In particular, British Columbia, Quebec, Ontario, and Alberta were wary of becoming involved in consultations which would legitimize a municipal role in constitutional discussions and negotiations.[128] In September Alberta's Premier Strom explained the province's position: "The municipalities tend to see the proper solution to their problems lying in a re-drafted Constitution, which, presumably, would on the one hand, guarantee their existence and responsibilities, and on the other, guarantee them adequate sources of income . . . we have concluded that municipal participation in re-drafting the Constitution is not the best means to solve municipal problems."[129]

The CFMM was furious that the municipalities were being shut out of the constitutional process by the provinces. In a brief to the federal government the following spring Ivor Dent, mayor of Edmonton and president of CFMM, wrote, "We reject the view that the Federal Government does not have the right to seek the views of Local Government and we deplore the result of this view which is the reluctance of ministers to hear those views even when invited by the mayors, and the refusal of federal officials to respect the integrity, authority and Boundaries of Local Government."[130] The federal government was unmoved by CFMM's attack, for it wanted to do nothing that would jeopardize the establishment of the Ministry of State for Urban Affairs (MSUA) which was to be proclaimed in June 1971.

Shortly after the provincial Tories came to power, New Democrat Grant Notley asked Don Getty, then Minister of Federal and Intergovernmental Affairs, whether municipalities would be represented at the next federal-provincial conference. Getty replied that the government had no objection to a municipal representative attending the conference as long as the federal government respected the legal relationship which existed between the province and its municipalities. Specifically, "we will not allow direct discussion or negotiations between the municipalities and the federal government to intrude into an area of our responsibility."[131]

Although the federal government was unwilling to enter the intergovernmental fray publicly, plans were being made for a national tri-level conference to be held in November 1972. Little was done at the first conference other than to agree on a second one, which was held in Edmonton in October 1973. At the second conference the CFMM presented three position papers on housing, land use, and transportation which all argued for the establishment of "locally defined regional boundaries" for the provision of services and finance, revenue sharing, and a greater use of unconditional grants.[132] There was little response from the federal and provincial governments. However, after an extensive discussion, a tri-level task force on municipal finance was established to examine the implications of revenue sharing. Even though Alberta's Premier Lougheed had made it very clear that he opposed revenue sharing, Alberta supported the task force. Dr. John Deutsch of Queen's University carried out the study, completed early in 1976, which documented the difficulty municipalities were having in raising enough money to meet their responsibilities.

The comprehensive three-volume report of the Tri-Level Task Force on Public Finance enabled Alberta's local politicians to compare their relationships with the province with those of other municipalities and their provincial governments. The figures indicated that Alberta municipalities were treated neither substantially better nor worse than municipalities in other provinces.[133] As one example, in 1974/75 Alberta municipalities received 14.4 percent of their total revenue from grants, with unconditional funding of $124.05 per capita and conditional funding of $191.96 per capita. In Ontario municipalities received almost exactly the same percentage of their funding from grants (14.2) but only $8.62 per capita was in unconditional grants and $189.74 was in conditional grants. In contrast, Quebec municipalities received slightly less of their total revenue from grants, 13.2 percent, but on a per capita basis they received $206.72 in unconditional and $119.69 in conditional funds. But it was the funding arrangements in Prince Edward Island which Alberta's municipal politicians must have looked upon with envy. The island's municipalities received 52.6 percent of their total revenue from grants, with the amount of conditional and unconditional grants being almost the same; $382.05 per capita from unconditional grants and $377.78 per capita from conditional ones. Despite the report's extensive data it was seldom used by individual municipalities, although the AUMA did cite it in pressing the government for greater fiscal autonomy.

The federal government dismantled the MSUA in 1979. Higgins notes that "the new ministry became something of an orphan child almost from its birth in 1971, undergoing a constant process of reorganization and experiencing frequent changes in ministers responsible for it. . . ."[134] The abolition of the ministry was a blow to municipalities across Canada, but it did not deter their quest for more powers and greater autonomy.

In 1976 the delegates at the AUMA's annual convention passed a resolution urging the province in its discussions of the patriation of the Canadian Constitution "to initiate and actively support amendments to recognize the importance of local government and the need for a new and permanent relationship between Federal, Provincial and Local Governments." The government's response to the AUMA's resolution was that "there are at present enough difficulties in Canada in clarifying responsibilities of the Federal Government and the provinces without entrenching in the Constitution, a third level of government."[135] Three years later in 1979 the delegates at the AUMA's annual convention passed another resolution calling on the provincial government "to advocate the statutory recognition of Municipal Governments in the revised Canadian Constitution." The province's response was almost identical to that in 1976.[136]

The same year, the FCM appointed a "blue ribbon" task force to examine a role for municipalities in a new constitution. On the basis of the committee's May 1979 preliminary report,[137] a resolution was passed at the organization's annual meeting in June. It was resolved that:

a. any specific discussions concerning the constitutional framework of Canada that are convened by the federal government should have representation from municipalities;

b. municipal jurisdictions should be clearly defined and written in new constitutional form so that the place of municipalities will be firmly established and entrenched in the structure of Canadian government; and

c. a new national financial arrangement must be formulated and must include income tax room for Canadian municipalities.[138]

In 1980 the committee's final report, entitled *Municipal Government in a New Canadian Federal System*, presented a carefully reasoned argument that municipalities, as a third level of government, should be entrenched in the Canadian constitution. A portion of the report discussed Alberta's position *vis-à-vis* the constitutional issue: "Alberta is opposed to any formal recognition of municipal government and entrenchment of rights and responsibilities in either a Federal or an Alberta constitution."[139] Provincial leaders believed that only the large municipalities would benefit from having municipal powers entrenched in a constitution, and that such an entrenchment would reduce not only the province's flexibility but also that of its municipalities.

In spite of the government's continuing hostility, in 1983 the AUMA passed a resolution "that the Government of Alberta be requested to negotiate with the Federal Government for the inclusion of the rights of Municipal Government within the Constitution." Predictably, the provincial government rejected the AUMA's position, but with a rationale different from that which had been used in the past. It argued that entrenching municipal powers in the constitution would "impose undue rigidities in the operation of the federal system and would hinder the effective development and implementation of Alberta's economic and social programs."[140] The issue remained dormant until 1991, when Edmonton alderman Ron Hayter, an FCM spokesperson, announced that Constitutional Affairs Minister Joe Clark had been receptive to a proposal giving municipalities constitutional recognition. He explained that rather than seeking specific powers, the FCM would ask "provincial governments to recognize municipalities as legitimate orders of government under provincial constitutions." Once this had been accomplished the federal government, in the preamble to the federal constitution, would give recognition to the municipalities.[141] The Alberta government did not reply publicly. Despite the concerns of governments in metropolitan areas across Canada, and the FCM's lobbying activity, municipalities were almost totally ignored when the new constitution was written. Following their failure to achieve legislated rights, Alberta's municipalities and those in the rest of Canada seemed to become dispirited.

Throughout the 1970s and well into the 1980s provincial governments were accused by the municipalities of undermining the MSUA and preventing the entrenchment of independent municipal powers in the constitution. On the other hand, the federal government fostered an image of itself as a caring and benevolent uncle of the country's municipalities whose hands were tied by unreasonable constitutional restrictions. All of this began to change in the 1980s when, as the result of federal economies, friction developed between municipalities and the national government.

In the wake of a spate of studies in the United States on the deterioration of the urban infrastructure (roads, bridges, docks, sewer and water lines, and such things as pumping plants), the FCM embarked on a similar study in 1984. Its subsequent report, *Municipal Infrastructure in Canada: Physical Condition and Funding Adequacy,* concluded that the infrastructure in Canadian municipalities had deteriorated. The cost of necessary corrective action was calculated to be $15 billion.[142] The First Canadian Conference on Urban Infrastructure, sponsored by the FCM in Toronto in 1987, called upon the federal government to assume one-third of the cost of renovation. The FCM's proposal received a decidedly cold reception from federal Environment Minister Tom McMillan, who stunned the conference's delegates when he told them the government was unable to help them financially and suggested that municipalities raise water rates to finance infrastructure repairs.[143] Mayor Laurence Decore of Edmonton responded by saying that the $8.5 million a year the city received from surtaxing water users was "only peanuts" compared to the $2 billion the city needed to restore and upgrade its basic structures.[144] In 1989 the FCM organized another conference entitled "The Big Fix," which again called upon the federal government to share the costs of infrastructure upgrading. The federal response was the same as it had been two years earlier: "given the current state of our own finances, the need to tackle the severe debt load, we do not see any way we can come up with funding for that program."[145] Less than three months later the federal government announced that the Canadian Forces Base at Penhold was one of the 14 military bases across the country either being closed or having its operations substantially reduced in the interest of federal economizing. Over a two-year period the jobs of 121 of the 264 military personnel and 123 of the 155 civilian employees, with an aggregate yearly payroll of $6 million, would be eliminated. The only hope held out for the Town of Penhold (population, 1,495) by its Member of Parliament was the possibility that the municipality might be eligible for a federal $90,000 economic adjustment cost-shared grant.[146]

In 1990 the FCM released a "future document" which depicted the municipalities' inability to expand their powers through constitutional representation. The report read that "the provinces have guarded . . . their turf jealously. . . . Thus the situation has somewhat left the Canadian municipal sector in the position of the 'bastard' child of government."[147]

An Overview of Democracy and Intergovernmental Relations

Although most municipal government officials are committed to local level democracy, it is either enhanced or inhibited depending upon how power is distributed and shared among governments. On the one hand, if local government is given wide-ranging powers and responsibilities, the citizenry will be actively involved in its operation, for government policies will be seen as having an effect on each and every person. Under these circumstances, local political leaders will be under the close scrutiny of the citizens and even the most ambitious will not be inclined to thwart the democratic process. On the other hand, if the powers of local government are so limited and constrained that the citizenry perceives its activities as being trivial, even the most determined effort to involve citizens in any aspect of decision making or government operation will come to naught. Quite simply, local government will be seen as a form of irrelevant "sand box politics."

During the early years of the Social Credit era, weak school governments were strengthened and the province's municipalities were invigorated by being provided with an independent source of revenue. Later chapters will show that Social Credit experimented with allowing the citizenry a much greater degree of direct democracy at the municipal level than that which is allowed today.

Over time, local governments have become pawns in the power struggle between the federal and provincial governments. Moreover, local self-determination and democracy are not values which either federal or provincial political leaders have targeted as political causes. During the debates on the 1981 Constitution the federal government did consider giving municipalities greater independence by entrenching municipal powers in the Constitution. However, the federal government was unwilling to confront the provinces on the issue. In 1985 Don Getty promised that mechanisms would be put into place to increase municipal self-determination and that there would be an expansion of "no string" unconditional grants for municipalities. Unfortunately, faced with a deteriorating provincial economy, the government reduced municipal grants instead. With their revenue base reduced, and prevented by statute from enacting a deficit budget, municipalities sought relief from many of their duties and responsibilities. During the latter 1980s newspaper accounts portrayed many citizens as disenchanted with local governments that were unable to meet their responsibilities.

In the last decade Alberta's local governments have shown themselves to be amazingly resilient in the face of adversity. Nevertheless, if the provincial government does not grant municipalities greater fiscal and legal autonomy, the durability of Alberta local government will be irreparably harmed.

3

Urban Governmental Structures

Introduction

Alberta municipalities are classified as either urban or rural, depending on their population and density. Cities, towns, villages, and summer villages are considered urban municipalities, and municipal districts, counties, improvement districts, and special areas are designated as rural. To be incorporated as a city, a municipality must have a population of at least 10,000; to be incorporated as a town, it must have at least 1,000 residents. A municipality must have at least 75 separate buildings occupied continuously as dwellings for at least six months of the year in order to be incorporated as a village, and it must have a minimum of 50 separate buildings occupied as dwellings at any time during a six-month period in order to qualify as a summer village.[1]

There are advantages and disadvantages in moving from one municipal category to another. In recent years one of the advantages of becoming a city has been acquiring eligibility for urban transportation funding. The mayors of Airdrie, Spruce Grove, and Fort Saskatchewan have admitted that the prospect of this funding was a major factor in the decision to apply for city status. On the other hand, municipalities which became cities during the 1980s had their Family Community Support Services grants reduced from $12 to $10 per capita. People in Sherwood Park, Canada's largest hamlet, have over the years debated the pros and cons of incorporation as a city. Sherwood Park residents not only are ambivalent about the financial benefits of becoming a city, but also are concerned about the issues of local autonomy and grass-roots democracy.[2]

One of the problems with Alberta's municipal classification system is that it does not recognize the unique status of Edmonton and Calgary, the two major metropolitan centres in the province, which are much larger than all the other cities. A number of years ago, one of the rising stars in Peter Lougheed's cabinet, David King, proposed that Edmonton and Calgary be governed under a separate municipal government act. He argued that "it is a result of their size, that they are so complex in terms of their responsibilities to their citizens and their relationship with the province, that we might consider the nature of that relationship to be different from the nature of our relationship with any other municipal government in the province."[3] King's idea was not new, for in earlier years both Edmonton and Calgary were governed under their own acts. However, his proposal received scarcely any attention in the news media and little support from other government members.

One of the factors that determines the degree to which our political institutions are democratic is their structure. A government can be organized in such a way that citizens are encouraged to vote and to contact their representatives on important business, or the public can be discouraged from active participation in the legislative process. Power can be concentrated so people are able to determine who is responsible for a particular course of action, or power can be fragmented to such an extent that it is impossible to assign responsibility and the process of representative democracy begins to break down.

Although there are major differences in Alberta's various forms of local government, certain characteristics are common to all. The most important is that power and control tend to be fragmented and distributed among a council, an executive, an administration, and a plethora of special boards and commissions. The executive's powers are limited. The mayor presides at council meetings and sits *ex officio* as a member of boards, associations, commissions, and committees but has little formal power to implement policy and plan effectively for the future. The mayor does not have the power to veto measures passed by council or sanctions which can be employed against its recalcitrant members. The mayor has little control over the municipal administration, since that power is vested in council; the council, not the mayor, has the power to hire and fire administrative heads.[4]

In general, the real work of council takes place in its committees, where bylaws are drafted and special research projects are carried out, usually under council's direction. Of the two kinds of committees, special and standing, the latter are by far the most important since they deal on an ongoing basis with such things as finance, engineering, and public works. Special committees are created in response to specific problems, and when they complete their task and report to council, they are abolished.

Councils are given wide discretion in the mechanisms they employ to arrive at decisions. Each council makes its own rules for calling meetings, governing its proceedings, and regulating the conduct of its members. A council determines how many meetings are necessary, although the mayor has the discretion to call additional special meetings. Even if a municipal council adopts an ill-conceived bylaw, the provincial government has adopted a policy of self restraint; Section 108 of the Municipal Government Act states that a bylaw passed by council "in good faith, is not open to question nor shall it be quashed, set aside or declared invalid, either wholly or partly on account of the unreasonableness or supposed unreasonableness of its provisions. . . ."[5]

Government by Council and Committee

Council-committee government is something of a misnomer, since all municipal governments have councils and committees. What differentiates the council-committee system from others is its weak executive, the mayor, who has only slightly more power than the other council members and the standing committees which oversee the administration. As a consequence, decision-making powers are decentralized.

The Canadian council-committee form of government is an amalgam of features borrowed from Great Britain and the United States. The practice of placing administrators under the purview of standing committees was borrowed from Great Britain; unfortunately, the integrative mechanism, the political party, which provided political accountability, was dropped in Canada. British local government is quasi-parliamentary in form, since the mayor is either elected or appointed by a highly politicized council operating under a strong party system. The party system acts to centralize responsibility and pull together the diverse centres of power located in the standing committees. While the direct election of the chief executive is borrowed from the United States, where in many communities the administration is directly accountable to the mayor, in Canada the chief executive has little control over the administration.

One student of local government, succinctly summing up the role of standing committees under the council-committee system, writes: "The committees exercise a general supervision over the work of the staff under their jurisdiction, consult with and advise the officials responsible for such work and make reports and recommendations to council on matters within their sphere."[6] Since this system of standing-committee supervision of administration tends to fragment the administrative structure, the mayor, by virtue of his or her power to sit *ex officio* on all committees, attempts to coordinate the activities of the municipal departments to ensure that they are not working at cross purposes.

An Alberta municipality employing a variation of council-committee government is the Town of Provost. It has an omnibus "Finance and General Government Services Committee" composed of two councillors and the municipal administrator. Membership on this powerful committee rotates every four months, with three sets of two councillors each serving one term a year. Protective services are overseen by two committees. The committee responsible for dog and pest control, emergency services, and fire and police services comprises two councillors, the fire chief, and the officer in charge of the town's RCMP. The disaster services committee includes a director and assistant director and two councillors. The transportation committee and the community service committee which oversees Hillcrest Lodge are composed of a councillor and the mayor.[7] Several other committees of only two councillors are the family and community services committee, the library committee, the utilities committee, the development committee, the standing policy committee, and the regional solid waste management committee. With 21 committees and only six council members, councillors by necessity sit on a number of committees. As an example, in October 1990 Councillor Stempfle was assigned to eight committees and the Court of Revision, which he chaired.

A prime requisite of democracy is that the citizenry be able to hold elected officials and administrators accountable. It is extremely difficult to locate administrative and political responsibility under council-committee government. The mayor has no formal sanctions to use on a recalcitrant council, and power is diffused. Under these circumstances it is not easy to determine the identity of the parties responsible for a particular policy. Since the mayor has little control over the administration, she or he often refuses to accept responsibility. The council as a whole is ultimately responsible, but often argues that administration is the duty of the standing committees. Standing committees tend to proliferate, further diminishing responsibility. Clearly, this form of government has a strong potential for political "buck-passing." Not only does council-committee government lack firm political and administrative accountability, it also runs counter to the professional management orientation to which most governmental officials subscribe.

Council-Manager Government

Like many other Canadian municipal institutions, the council-manager form of government was borrowed from the United States and then modified. The manager form of government, which originated in Staunton, Virginia, in 1908, was rapidly adopted by communities in North America and in Europe. It is found primarily in medium-sized middle-class municipalities committed to professionalism in government.[8] A number of Alberta cities and towns operate under council-manager government.

The manager's power is derived from Section 91 of the Municipal Government Act, which allows a council to delegate "any or all of its executive and administrative duties and powers to . . . a municipal manager." The underlying philosophy of manager government is that policy making is kept completely separate from administration; a hired professional administers policies formulated by council. Spruce Grove's bylaw C–10–86 states that the city manager shall:

(a) (i) suspend department heads subject to the advice of the Mayor;
    (ii) in the event there is no agreement between the Mayor and the City Manager, either party may appeal to the City Council;
(b) Direct, supervise, and review the performance of the administration of all departments, office and agencies of the City. . . .
(c) Implement all policies and programs approved by City Council;
(d) Prepare and submit to City Council estimates of revenue and expenditures and capital programs annually, or as required;
(e) Inspect and report to City Council or Committees of City Council on all municipal works and on the operation of all departments and offices. . . .
(f) Advise City Council on the financial condition and future needs of the City and make recommendations where desirable;
(g) Monitor and control civic expenditures including intra-departmental budget adjustments, within the budget prepared in consultation with City Council;
(h) Subject to the prior approval of City Council, consolidate or create any civic departments;
(i) Develop and recommend to City Council on policy matters relating to working conditions and compensation for all officials and employees and on the provisions of contracts negotiated with civic employee unions and associations;
(j) Develop and recommend policies to City Council from time to time as may be necessary or expedient for the health, safety or wel-

fare of the community or of its civic employees or for the improvement of the delivery of services;

(k) Provide an interface between the Administration and City Council for the flow of information and directives;

(l) Attend all meetings of City Council and Committees of Council unless excused therefrom and attend meetings of such Boards, Committees and Authorities, as required by City Council;

(m) Prepare and submit such reports and recommendations as may be required by City Council or its committees;

(n) Perform such other duties and exercise such other powers as may be required by City Council from time to time.

Although the bylaw specifies the responsibilities of the manager, it fails to deal with the dynamic nature of the office. The manager is expected to provide the administration with initiative and leadership. In giving the council policy advice, he or she must be highly sensitive to the local political consequences of any recommendation.

The council-manager plan is the purest example of the professional management ethic in government, since the manager is seen as being comparable to the private corporate manager who oversees day-to-day business operations. The manager is responsible to the council, an arrangement which, it is argued, is equivalent to the corporate manager being responsible to the corporate board. In almost all Alberta municipalities employing council-manager government the manager has three primary responsibilities: to make policy recommendations to council, to prepare a budget and submit it to council, and to oversee and coordinate municipal departments. In Edmonton all department heads report directly to the city manager, with the exception of the city clerk and the auditor general, who are responsible to council, and the chief of police, who reports to the police commission.

In the United States a manager can hire and fire department heads; in Canada, however, the manager can only make recommendations to council on hiring and firing. Council-manager government in Alberta, like council-committee government, is characterized by a weak executive. The manager is responsible to council, and the mayor has little power over administration.

Three major advantages are attributed to council-manager government. First, it frees the council from continually having to scrutinize the administration and enables it to devote its full attention to the formulation and evaluation of policy. The Town of High Level operated under council-committee government until it adopted council-manager government in 1988. When the change was made the two standing committees, planning and public works, were consolidated into a committee of the whole which met only once a month. The secretary-treasurer writes: ". . . the municipality is satisfied with recommendations coming forward from Management, then debated and decided upon by Council." Perhaps even more important: "The members attempt to minimize issues at the Committee of the Whole meetings in order to present an open government concept at the regular public meetings."[9] The second major advantage of council-manager government is that it brings into the municipality a professionally trained administrator who is given the power to coordinate departmental activities and evaluate staff performance. Nevertheless, it can be disquieting for councillors to see a manager actively exercising administrative powers. In 1988 the council in Lacombe disagreed about authorizing the manager to make land option agreements and purchases without consulting council. The opponents argued that it was not necessary to increase the manager's powers since "council can be brought together on an hour's notice to make a decision." The proponents said they had complete confidence in the integrity of the manager and that land speculation could be held in check if he were given this additional authority.[10] A third advantage of manager government is that while many council members have a relatively short-term policy perspective and evaluate and formulate proposals on the basis of their effects on the upcoming electoral campaign, the manager is not as constrained by politics and tends to take a long-term view of the policy process.[11]

Although the council-manager form of government was originally based on the belief that politics could be minimized in policy making, managers are now expected to work very closely with the council and the mayor. However, as Plunkett writes, since political power on council continually shifts, the manager should not be seen as playing favourites because if he or she finds him- or herself on the wrong side of an issue the only alternative may be to resign. Therefore, an optimal strategy is to present "the merits of a proposal and avoid any actions that seem an obvious ploy for support."[12] Plunkett also cautions that while the manager is accountable to the council, it is essential that the "ambiguous role of the mayor" be taken into account. He suggests that a mayor with a strong personality could bypass the manager and deal directly with department heads, justifying the action "on the basis of the obligation imposed on the mayor 'to oversee the conduct of all subordinate officers.'"[13] In short, a city manager needs to be politically sensitive and astute in dealing with the political arm of municipal government.

Council-Chief Administrative Officer Government

Since government by council and chief administrative officer evolved from the council-manager system, they have many characteristics in common. Like other forms of local government, this type originated in the United States. Council-manager government was widely adopted in California, where the municipal reform movement was extremely strong during the first half of the century. In the 1940s a number of communities were attracted by the idea of hiring a professional administrator, but were reluctant to relinquish direct control. They made the manager an agent of council. The consequence was a variant of the council-manager system.

The major difference between the manager and chief administrator forms of government is that while council delegates all administrative responsibilities to a city manager, it assigns specific duties to a chief administrative officer. The chief administrative officer directs and supervises other administrative officials only to the extent that he or she is specifically authorized to do so by council.[14] Unlike a city manager, the chief administrative officer does not have a general grant of power. But, like a city manager, the administrative officer acts as an advisor to council, making recommendations and preparing technical reports.

One study argues that:

> In practice . . . because of the wide difference in the attitudes and the needs of councillors, the abilities of CAOs and the needs of the municipal corporations, the informal role of a CAO may be very similar to the formal role of a manager; and the powers and duties that are assigned, informally, to a CAO may be very similar to the powers and duties that are assigned, formally, to a manager.[15]

Since the same study maintains that from the council's point of view, there is no real distinction between a manager and a CAO, it seems to miss the essential difference between the two forms of government. When a council decides to bring a professional into its administration, it has the choice of either delegating its powers to a manager or retaining them by appointing an administrative officer. Admittedly, the chief administrative officer may be allowed to function in much the same way as a city manager, but, at any time and on the shortest notice, the council is able to halt the administrative officer's activities. This important distinction does not escape council members who are constantly on guard against any erosion of their powers.

Although the Municipal Government Act makes no mention of a chief administrative officer, Section 60 of the act refers to a municipal administrator: "A council, by by-law may provide that the duties and responsibilities of the office of the municipal secretary and the treasurer be combined into one office to be designated as the municipal administrator [who may] . . . do anything that by this or any other Act is to be done by the municipal secretary or the treasurer." Sections 58 and 59 of the act specify the duties of the secretary and the treasurer, in contrast to Section 91 which, in a discussion of a manager's powers, allows a council to delegate "any or all of its executive and administrative duties" to a manager. Therefore, it is clear that in Alberta the terms "chief administrative officer" and "municipal administrator" are synonymous. A council may choose to create the position of municipal administrator for fiscal reasons. Under the Municipal Government Act every municipal council is required to appoint a secretary and treasurer. Since very small municipalities cannot afford to hire two administrators, they may combine the positions into that of a municipal administrator and save themselves a substantial amount of money.

Council-Commission Board Government

In recent years council-commission government has been the most controversial form in Alberta. Like the council-manager system, it attempts to apply professional management practices to local government. However, it differs from council-manager government in that the council delegates administrative and executive powers to a board comprising senior administrators and the mayor rather than to a single administrator.[16] The mayor therefore has a much stronger administrative role than in the other forms of government discussed so far. Although council-commission government brings considerable professional expertise to bear on municipal problems, it has the disadvantage of being overly complex, with almost infinite lines of political and administrative authority and responsibility.

In order to describe this form of government, Calgary's council-commission system is examined in detail. City council formulates policy, which is carried out by four professional commissioners who are appointed and dismissed by council. A chief commissioner, commissioner of finance and transportation, commissioner of planning and community services, and commissioner of operations and utilities are each directly responsible for the supervision of a number of city departments. The mayor and the four commissioners constitute the commission board, which determines how council's general policy directions are to be carried out. Under the direction of the chief commissioner, the activities of the commissioners are coordinated to ensure that they will not be working at cross purposes. The commission board also makes policy recommendations directly to council, and in many cases these recommendations carry more weight than those coming from council's standing committees.

Although not formal standing committee members with voting privileges, commissioners are resource personnel for standing committees, and actively participate in their discussions. As an example, in Medicine Hat the commissioner of finance sits on the finance committee, the commissioner of public works sits on the public works committee, and the commissioner of community services sits on the community services committee. Normally, a standing committee meeting is not held unless at least one commissioner is present. The chief commissioner has the authority to attend any standing committee meeting. In addition to coordinating the commission board and sitting on a number of standing committees, the chief commissioner has other important responsibilities, which include keeping the lines of communication open between the administration and the mayor and council and advising them on policy and administration. The chief commissioner must also consult with the committee that prepares the council's agenda. This is an extremely important responsibility, for, by acting as the "gate-keepers" for policy proposals, the chief commissioner and the agenda committee can structure council's policy direction. In his description of the commission government that prevailed in Edmonton from 1904 until 1984, Lightbody concludes, "Not surprisingly, most council business originates from commission board reports, which have a considerable impact in the structuring of political choice."[17] It should be noted that the mayor is also a member of council's agenda committee and, moreover, is the only committee member allowed to place additional items on the agenda without majority committee approval.

In 1968 Calgary's bylaw was amended to make the chief commissioner, rather than the mayor, the chair of the commission board. The mayor now sits *ex officio* on the commission board, but plays only a limited role in its activities. This restriction is unfortunate, since the mayor is the linchpin in the whole system, the bridge between the formulation of policy on council and its administration through the board.[18]

Council-commission government in two other Alberta cities differs significantly in structure and operation from that in Calgary. In Medicine Hat the mayor has an inordinate amount of power on the commission board. This came about in 1982 when a consulting firm commissioned to evaluate the city's government by council and chief administrative officer recommended that it be replaced by a council and commission board.

Although it was argued that the Municipal Government Act could be construed to indicate that the mayor could be "designated as the Chief Commissioner and thus be expected to play a very active role on the Board," the consultants did not make such a recommendation.[19] Instead, they proposed a board consisting of a commissioner of finance and administration, a commissioner of utilities, a commissioner of community services, a commissioner of operations, and the mayor, serving as chair of the board. Conspicuously absent was a chief commissioner. As a consequence, after the city adopted the consulting firm's recommendations the mayor not only chaired the commission board but also began to function much like a chief commissioner. When another consulting firm was employed to review the council-commission structure in 1985, it said diplomatically that the mayor "has a very strong and pervasive influence on the Board" and then recommended that council appoint a chief commissioner.[20] Although there was council support for a chief commissioner, the mayor rejected the proposal out of hand, arguing that "although the mayor's double role as the administrative and legislative leader is often difficult, it is manageable and what the people want."[21] Yet another review of the city's governmental structure occurred in 1988, and although it was generally agreed that the mayor was too powerful in his role as the chief administrative officer and the city's major elected official, the mayor again prevented any changes from being made. Today the commission board is composed of the mayor, who is its chair; the commissioner of finance, who is vice-chair; the commissioner of public works; the commissioner of utilities; and the commissioner of community services.

Red Deer, the other city with council-commission government, has only one commissioner who coordinates and has broad supervisory powers over municipal departments and works closely with council's standing committees. Though a commissioner *ex officio*, as in Medicine Hat, the mayor does not have an active role on the commission. In reality, the functions of Red Deer's single commissioner differ little from those of a city manager.

The major advantage of council-commission government is that, like council-manager government, it allows the council to devote its time to consulting constituents and to making policy without being distracted by everyday administrative matters. Its major failing is its complexity; its structure and processes are confusing to most citizens, and even members of the administration are often baffled by poorly defined lines of authority. Even when the mayor is chair of the commission board, power remains diffused and administrative responsibility is distributed among a number of commissioners.[22] An equally serious problem is the secrecy surrounding commission board deliberations and decisions. In an examination of the era of council-commission government in Edmonton, James Lightbody writes, ". . . in much the same way as the environment of the newsroom rewards consistency with the general editorial orientation of a newspaper, upwardly mobile civic managers do not upset applecarts in Edmonton. Rarely do internal struggles over policy alternatives reach the public ear, even though some have been fierce."[23]

Edmonton and Fort McMurray discarded council-commission government during the 1980s. Although citizen activism flourished in Edmonton in the 1970s, there was a general feeling that the administrative structure which had been created in 1904 was impregnable. Lightbody explains that citizens ". . . became increasingly cynical about their participation in a process so dominated by bureaucratic continuity, cohesion and apparent secrecy."[24] Moreover, in Edmonton it was charged that the commission board, rather than council, was making policy. When a popular mayoralty candidate, Laurence Decore, pledged in 1983 to dismantle the city's commission board, he garnered 61.2 percent of the popular vote.

In contrast to Edmonton, from the time it was implemented in 1982 until its demise in 1987, controversy over Fort McMurray's council-commission system involved its cost and not its operation. Opponents argued that the small community was over-administered by four highly-paid commissioners, each with a retinue of secretaries, clerks, and department heads. In 1984 Mayor Chuck Knight explained, "I have no problem with the commissioner system but if I had my druthers there would be two less commissioners. . . . Originally the four commissioners were recommended contingent on the go-ahead of the Alsands development and the fact Alsands didn't take place substantiates my opinion."[25] Two years after council-commission government was implemented, a private consultant's opinion that it needed only some "fine tuning" did not silence its critics. Shortly thereafter, the number of commissioners was reduced to three. Two positions became vacant in 1986, at the bottom of the economic downturn, and in response to public pressure the commission was replaced early in 1987 by a system in which six managers reported directly to a chief administrative officer.[26]

Generally, the disadvantages of council-commission government outweigh its advantages. Although it employs highly trained professionals, power is diffused and administrative infighting often occurs.[27] The complex structure of council-commission government is not only difficult to understand, but it also limits public participation in policy making and the administrative process. With council-commission government, as with other forms, if democracy is to prevail at the local level each citizen must be able to identify the person responsible for political and administrative decisions. Unless power is concentrated so that deliberate long-range policies can be planned and coordinated, council wallows in a sea of indecision and the public is confused.

Government by Council and Executive Committee

A council-executive government was proposed for an Alberta municipality as early as 1923, when Mayor D.M. Duggan suggested that Edmonton's governmental structure be completely revamped, with its executive to be chosen by council.[28] According to Donald Higgins, the principal advantage of this quasi-parliamentary form of government is that it "most closely parallels the Cabinet form at the federal and provincial levels of government," with its fusion of the administrative and legislative functions.[29] An executive committee is composed of the mayor, who usually sits as its chair, and three to five councillors selected by the mayor, appointed on the basis of the number of electoral votes received, or serving in rotation. A major disadvantage of council-executive government is that power is fragmented, since the major and members of council are popularly elected and have independent bases of political support.

Although it has been used by the City of Montreal since 1921, the council and executive committee system has only recently been adopted widely across Canada.[30] In Quebec City, Hull, and Laval in the late 1960s government was restructured to create a strong executive committee which enabled the mayor to exercise leadership and to streamline policy making by council. The committee's members were chosen by the mayor. The executive committee was adopted by Toronto in 1969, Winnipeg in 1971, and Ottawa in 1980.

In Alberta, Section 47 of the Municipal Government Act gives council the authority to establish an executive committee with the power "to make decisions or orders, enter into contracts, [and] execute agreements or documents. . . ." Subsection 2 of the act makes it absolutely clear that "all decisions, orders, contracts, agreements and documents made or executed by the executive committee are as valid and enforceable as if made directly by the council that delegates the powers." Despite this legislation, only Edmonton has established an executive committee and its mayor does not have nearly as much power as the mayors in Quebec cities that employ this form of government.[31]

Lightbody argues that the groundwork for executive committee government was laid during the 1970s, when there was "the erosion of public confidence" in the managerial style of government by council and commission.[32] In 1981 Edmonton hired a private consultant to determine how the policy-making process could be improved. The consultant recommended an executive committee system, with the committee to comprise the mayor and three councillors chosen by the mayor. In June 1982 the council supported the general concept of an executive committee, but set aside the proposal during the 1982/83 budget crisis in order to focus on the city's financial problems. In the fall of 1983 Laurence Decore swept into the mayor's chair, with one of his platform promises having been to dismantle the city's commission board and replace it with an executive committee and city manager. Despite the opposition and delaying tactics of council members who supported the status quo, government by executive committee was adopted in January 1984.

Like its counterparts in other Canadian cities, Edmonton's executive committee is the nerve centre of city government, responsible for finance, policy planning and administration, and providing direction for council. In the area of finance it is directed to: (1) prepare the annual budget, determine tax rebates, and monitor the administration's financial performance; (2) call for tenders and award contracts; (3) recommend to council which civic organizations are to receive grants and their amounts; (4) recommend to council the rates and charges for services such as transit fares, utility rates, and license fees; and (5) settle claims on behalf of the city. In the area of policy planning and administration the committee is directed to: (1) develop long-range policies; (2) act as the policy coordinator between the manager and the council's standing committees; (3) monitor the level of service provided to the public; (4) control and give direction to the city manager; and (5) enter into collective bargaining agreements with city employees. The executive committee provides direction to council in a variety of ways. It structures the activities of council by making recommendations and drafting bylaws. It sets the council's agenda and directs and coordinates the flow of information and business between council, its committees, and the administration.

It was more than two months after the executive committee and manager system was adopted before some members of council became aware of its ramifications. After the executive committee approved a controversial land swap, a council member not on the executive committee argued that the power to approve land sales, swaps, and purchases should be returned to the full council. A member of the standing committee on utilities and finance wondered whether his committee had any function now that almost all fiscal and utility matters were being handled by the executive committee. Yet another councillor was concerned about the number of letters from the public being routed past the standing committees directly to the executive committee.

Political pundits were not surprised when attacks on the executive committee came to a virtual halt after the method of selecting the persons who were to sit on the committee was changed. Initially, Mayor Decore proposed that the executive committee be composed of the mayor and the city's "six senior councillors." The member receiving the most votes in each of the city's six two-member wards would become the "senior councillor." After several councillors pointed out that an executive committee comprising half the council members would be unwieldy, Decore decreased the size of the committee to four members who would be chosen in rotation from among the six senior councillors. This solved the size problem but left unresolved the bitterness and frustration felt by councillors who were not eligible to sit on the executive committee. In October 1985 the bylaw was amended to allow every councillor to sit on the executive committee.[33]

Following the 1986 municipal election, the mayor was directed to poll council members as to whether or not they wished to serve on the executive committee. This established a list of members who would serve an equal amount of time on the committee in rotation. Once the membership debate was resolved, the question of executive committee power was not raised again until the fall of 1990, when a politically ambitious councillor and opponent of the mayor, Patricia Mackenzie, made it an issue. Mackenzie attempted to limit the executive committee, which Mayor Reimer used as an instrument to further her popular policy proposals.

Although Edmonton is the only Alberta municipality to have adopted the executive committee form of government, at the 1982 annual meeting of the Alberta Urban Municipalities Association (AUMA), Calgary Alderman Brian Lee argued that an executive committee would "counter-balance the strength and influence of city commissioners."[34] The underlying assumptions of executive committee government were examined by Medicine Hat three years later in 1985. A consultant reviewing the legislative and administrative structure created for the city in 1982 advised "that each alderman be accorded authority equal to that of all other aldermen on council." Although the report observed that "Council has not chosen to establish an Executive Committee of Council similar to the Edmonton example,"[35] it recommended that a new standing committee with powers "to review, monitor and recommend changes" in the organizational structure as well as oversee "management audits" be established.[36] The responsibilities of that committee were similar to those of Edmonton's executive committee.

Government by executive committee and city manager results in increased accountability and administrative efficiency and facilitates long-range planning. A close-knit executive committee coordinates and orchestrates both council and administration. The executive committee system works most successfully when the committee is composed of like-minded individuals who are able to work together. In short, the mayor must have the power to appoint people who share her or his views on policy and administration.

When partisan politics are entrenched at the local level, the mayor appoints party members and appeals to their party loyalties in formulating and carrying out policies. In the absence of a party system, the mayor must be able to appoint council members whose loyalty and votes can be depended upon. In Edmonton, however, political considerations prevented the adoption of a system in which the executive committee would be chaired by a mayor who had the power to appoint councillors to it. When Decore had proposed the executive committee system, his political advisors suggested that the Toronto model be followed and that the committee be composed of the persons who topped the polls in each ward.[37] What eventually evolved was a system in which Edmonton voters selected two candidates for council but were unable to specify which was to serve on the executive committee. Nevertheless, as has already been noted, either method would have been criticized by those not eligible to sit on the executive committee and for this reason the system was changed to allow every councillor to become a member. However, this still did not eliminate the potential for problems if an executive committee were composed of members opposed to the mayor's program or determined to undermine it in order to compete for the mayor's chair in an upcoming election. In short, the mayor may be forced to work with executive committee members who are openly hostile to him or her or to each other.

One can speculate that a popular mayor with a majority of council members sharing his or her values might amend the executive committee bylaw to give the mayor the power to appoint members to the executive committee unconditionally. Or one might posit that with the adoption of party politics at the local level the executive committee would be changed to bring a municipal form of parliamentary government to Edmonton. The former scenario is possible only if the public accepts the idea of a strong executive, while the latter is nothing more than a flight of political fantasy.

Special Purpose Boards, Commissions, and Committees

Although all municipalities employ boards, commissions, and committees created by council, Alberta's cities are characterized by a large number of these semi-autonomous bodies. Each has a narrow focus and often only a tangential relationship with the mayor and council, yet their predominantly nonelected members make and administer a sizeable portion of municipal policy. An example of the scope of special purpose bodies is shown below.

Edmonton Special Purpose Boards, Commissions, and Committees in 1991
1. Boxing and Wrestling Commission
2. Charitable Appeals Committee
3. Community and Family Services Advisory Committee
4. Court of Revision
5. Custom Transportation Services Advisory Board
6. Development Appeal Board
7. Downtown Business Association
8. Downtown Development Corporation
9. Downtown Parking Advisory Board
10. Edmonton Advisory Committee for Services for Disabled Persons
11. Edmonton Air Service Authority
12. Edmonton Ambulance Authority
13. Edmonton Area Hospital Planning Council
14. Edmonton Convention Centre Authority
15. Edmonton Convention and Tourism Authority
16. Edmonton Economic Development Authority
17. Edmonton Historical Board
18. Edmonton Housing Authority—Nominating Committee
19. Edmonton Northlands
20. Edmonton Police Commission
21. Edmonton Public Library Board
22. Edmonton Research and Development Park Authority
23. Edmonton and Rural Auxiliary Hospital and Nursing Home District no. 24
24. Edmonton Space Sciences Foundation
25. Edmonton Taxi Cab Commission
26. Fort Edmonton Park Management Committee
27. Greater Edmonton Foundation
28. Kingsway Business Revitalization Zone Association
29. Kinsmen Park Management Committee

30. Landlord and Tenant Advisory Board
31. Memorial Hall Trustee
32. Municipal Non-Profit Housing Association
33. Names Advisory Committee
34. Old Strathcona Foundation
35. Parks, Recreation and Cultural Advisory Board
36. River Valley Steering Committee
37. Royal Alexandra Hospital Board
38. Snow Valley Ski Club Board

More often than not all special purpose bodies are classified together, but it is important to keep in mind that each is created in response to the demands of a very specific clientele. For example, professionals argue that libraries are too important to be subject to the scrutiny of a municipal council interested in cutting departmental budgets to the bone in order to be re-elected. As a consequence, the Libraries Act specifies that libraries will be administered by boards.

Municipal councils are directed to appoint community members to most boards; almost invariably a council appoints one or two of its own members. Since it is unlikely that all board appointees will have relevant backgrounds, professionals lobby to ensure that board policy will reflect their views. "It is not uncommon in agencies which have boards as policy making bodies for most of the policies ultimately adopted to be generated within the bureaucracy of the agency and to be 'sold' to the commission by the administrative head."[38]

A variety of groups and associations attempt to remove narrow interests from council control in order to influence the formulation of policy. As examples, for a number of years a representative of the Calgary Associated Dog Fanciers sat on the city's Advisory Committee on Animal Control, and both the Urban Development Institute (an association of property developers) and the Alberta Mortgage Loan Association were represented on the Calgary Housing Commission.

A board occasionally asserts its authority and directly opposes council on a particular policy issue. This occurred in the Town of Bonnyville in 1989 when the council decided that a new library building project should go to public tender after having agreed with the Library Board that it would be built under the authority of a project manager. After five of the six board members resigned in protest, the council changed the composition of the board in order to exert more control over its actions. First, the board's size was reduced from six to five members. Then the number of public members on the board was reduced from five to three and the number of councillors increased from one to two.[39] In 1986 the Medicine Hat council advertised for people to apply for positions on the Family and Community Support Services Board, but after receiving letters from interested citizens, the council decided to fill all of the board positions with its own members.[40]

Although their opponents argue that semi-independent boards, committees, and commissions tend to fragment policy making and over-represent special interests, supporters such as an Alberta management consultant contend that:

> ... these groups can and do serve a useful purpose through handling particular areas which might otherwise be seen as an administrative function or a Council member responsibility. These bodies serve to enlarge the "ear" of Council to its residents and act as a screening device, sifting through presentations and distilling action recommendations for Council. . . .[41]

Councils often create special-purpose bodies in order to remove politically explosive "no win" issues from council chambers. An example of an attempt to do this occurred in Edmonton, where considerable controversy has surrounded the question of whether the city's river valley should be maintained as parkland or developed as a mix of park and residential areas. In the spring of 1983 a council member suggested that the issue be resolved by establishing a special-purpose body to formulate policy on river valley development. Rather than absolve itself of its responsibility, however, council rejected the suggestion.

Some conscientious councils create advisory boards, commissions, and committees in order to further grass-roots democracy by bringing into the political process a number of citizens who would otherwise be excluded. These councils make advisory appointments in order to represent the views of segments of the community which have inadvertently been socially and politically marginalized. However, there are many other councils that create advisory bodies and appoint large numbers of citizens to them in order to co-opt their political opponents. That is, once they are brought into the administration, they will feel they have a stake in its success and will support a broad range of council policies in addition to their own private interests on a board or committee. Other councils use board appointments to develop linkages with powerful political and economic interests in the community which have otherwise resisted becoming involved in local affairs.

Equally important is the fact that board appointments are often political rewards in a system that offers few opportunities for patronage, since virtually all civil service positions are filled on the basis of merit and examination. After the 1986 Calgary municipal election, Mayor Klein and several aldermen rewarded their supporters with a variety of appointments to special purpose boards. One of Klein's political supporters and a long-time friend was appointed to the Boxing and Wrestling Commission, while another was appointed to the Economic Development Authority. One of the three citizens appointed to the Calgary Planning Commission was a developer who had provided Klein with his campaign headquarters at no cost. A principal fund-raiser was appointed chair of the Calgary General Hospital Board and the legal advisor for the mayor's campaign became chair of the Police Commission. Alderman Ann Blough had a campaign worker appointed to the Development Appeal Board, and one of Jon Havelock's workers was appointed to the board of the Calgary District Hospital Group. But politicization of the board appointment process creates losers as well as winners. In order to make his appointment to the Boxing and Wrestling Commission, Mayor Klein first created a vacancy by opposing the renomination of one of its members.[42] That same year in Fort McMurray, two members of the Community Services Advisory Board were unceremoniously removed from office; one had run unsuccessfully for alderman twice and the other was a vocal critic of council.

Even when members of boards and commissions receive no remuneration, there may be costs in efficiency and performance when appointments are made as political awards. As an example, in 1987 an Edmonton alderman complained that the effectiveness of the Edmonton Convention and Tourism Authority was being damaged by council-appointed cronies who were "not particularly interested in tourism."[43] The same year the city council in Calgary terminated the representation of four animal welfare groups on the Advisory Committee on Animal Control after the committee criticized a new dog control bylaw which included a mandatory leashing provision. Alderman Theresa Baxter, in explaining the change, said, "The committee had become like a lobby group for one segment of the population."[44]

More important than the reasons why special purpose bodies are created and why people seek positions on them is their effect on policy making. Many of the municipal structures employed in Alberta diffuse responsibility. Special purpose bodies further fragment power and make it virtually impossible for an administration to develop and carry out a comprehensive body of policy.

Another failing of special purpose bodies is that, although many formulate and implement important policy, they are one step removed from control by the citizenry because board members are appointed, not elected. At the AUMA's 1989 annual convention, Edmonton introduced Resolution B15, which would have changed the Municipal Government Act to prevent citizens from appealing rulings by taxi commissions to the council. The Minister of Municipal Affairs responded that the government would not abolish a person's right to appeal a taxi commission decision. However, despite the government's concern for the rights of the ordinary citizen, democratic control of policy making continues to be eroded by a plethora of special purpose boards.

Finally, the argument most often used to justify a special-purpose body, that it removes a subject from the political arena, is patently false. These boards, commissions, and committees do not depoliticize areas of policy making, operation, and administration; rather, they remove these functions from the control and scrutiny of the citizenry. If ever the tired proverb about the fox guarding the chicken house applied to politics and government, it applies to special interests which control their own activities through membership on special-purpose bodies.

Governments of Villages and Summer Villages

The term "village" conjures up an image of a small community with close-knit social and political relationships. Although the Village of Coalhurst has a population of almost 1,300, most of the province's 122 villages have between 200 and 400 residents and provide a fertile ground for grass-roots democracy. The recent spate of village incorporations, however, has been driven almost solely by financial, rather than political, considerations. As an example, when residents on the south shore of Lac La Nonne met in 1987 to discuss the incorporation of the Summer Village of Birch Cove, they were motivated primarily by the prospect of lowering their property taxes an estimated 50 percent. The new municipality would be eligible for free RCMP protection, while road maintenance, fire fighting, and garbage collection would be contracted for with the private sector and other municipalities. As one might expect, opposition by the County of Lac Ste. Anne was generated by the prospect of a loss of $80,000 in capital assessment and $64,000 in tax revenue.[45] For almost a decade the residents of the Village of Fort Assiniboine have been trying to decide whether or not the community should revert to hamlet status.

Although local autonomy enters into the discussions, the debate has focused on the cost of running the village, its $250,000 capital debt, and taxation issues.

The Municipal Government Act makes allowance for the small scale of village society and allows villages to be governed by as few as three councillors who democratically select one of themselves as mayor.[46] Although it is unlikely the provincial government considered the implications of this practice, the effect is to centralize power and allow the chief executive effectively to formulate policy.[47] In the absence of partisan politics at the local level, particularly in small communities, the choice of a chief executive is based upon friendship, shared values, or an egalitarian belief that the position should be rotated. Whatever the reason, there is a much closer relationship between the mayor and the other councillors in the village council than in a municipality in which the mayor has an independent basis of electoral support.

Although village government has had its share of failures, it is more innovative than town and city government in the provision of services. There are instances of villages contracting virtually all of their services from other units of government such as municipal districts, counties, or improvement districts. It is also common for village councils to use their initiative to contract with the private sector for the provision of community services.

The governmental structures for villages and summer villages are similar. Aside from small differences specified by the Municipal Government Act and Local Authorities Election Act, substantial differences occur in only three areas. Since a summer village is the most populous during the summer, it is not required to hold an election on the third day in October, as is a village, but is given the option to hold the election when it is most convenient for the villagers.[48] Another difference is that although the Local Authorities Election Act specifies that one must be a Canadian citizen to vote in a village election, in a summer village a proprietary elector (a person who is liable for property assessment and taxation) or the spouse of a proprietary elector is eligible to vote in the municipal election. In short, if one is a proprietary elector it is not necessary to be a Canadian citizen in order to vote in a summer village. Finally, while a village must have an office within its corporate limits, the office of a summer village is to be located "at a place selected by the council," which often is outside the municipality.[49]

A particularly contentious issue is that many summer villagers pay substantially less taxes than ratepayers in other municipalities. In 1977 a special concession allowed summer village property to be assessed at a lower rate because most residents of summer villages occupy their homes only during the vacation season and their children make no demands on local educational facilities. However, it was argued that the tax concession was not equitable and a mechanism was put into place to phase it out. In yet another turn-about, the phase-out policy was halted in 1984.

Urban Governmental Units in Transition

New Towns

Following the discovery of oil at Leduc, oil companies embarked on a massive exploration across the province. Whenever a strike was made, hundreds of people moved into the area. Hanson describes these instant settlements as consisting "mainly of a main street with hastily constructed business buildings and hundreds of trailers."[50] populated by transients who had little or no interest in the affairs of the community.

Even after families began to settle in the new towns, their demands for services were often blocked by workers who had no interest in taxing themselves for educational facilities, parks, and water and sewage systems. In 1956 the provincial government responded by passing the New Town Act to provide financing and assistance for the development of new communities.[51] The intent of the legislation was two-pronged: to develop institutions to further local-level democracy and to provide interim financial support. The province administers and makes decisions for a new municipality through a town board of provincially appointed and locally elected members. The board's chairperson is always provincially appointed. Grande Cache is a typical example of the democratic evolution of a board of administration. When it was designated a new town in 1966, its board consisted of three provincial public servants from Edmonton.

Shortly after the New Town Act was implemented, a number of towns were incorporated: Drayton Valley, Cynthia, Hinton, and Lodgepole in 1956; St. Albert in 1957; Swan Hills in 1959; Whitecourt in 1961; Fort McMurray in 1964; High Level in 1965; Grande Cache and Rainbow Lake in 1966; and Fox Creek in 1967. A majority of these communities eventually became fully self-governing municipalities. Cynthia and Lodgepole reverted to hamlet status in 1959 and 1970, respectively. Rainbow Lake is the only community that remains a new town.

Other communities applying for new-town status were turned down after the provincial government decided that they were unlikely to become financially sound and to be able to repay provincial loans. For example, the Hamlet of Smith applied to the Alberta Provincial Planning

Board for new-town status in 1968. After an economic feasibility study the board concluded that, as there was little prospect that Smith would attract new industries or expand existing ones, the request should be denied. The most curious instance of a community being denied new-town status occurred in Slave Lake, the population of which increased from 500 to 3,500 in a ten-year period. The provincial government, as much as the town's administration, was responsible for putting the community in a precarious financial position. In 1970 the Alberta government and the federal Department of Regional Expansion signed a federal-provincial agreement to promote long-term economic expansion in this area. Incentive grants of slightly more than $5 million encouraged $14 million of investment in wood and wood product plants just outside the community's boundaries. A Department of Municipal Affairs publication describes the financial chaos that resulted:

> The municipal government . . . was required to spend approximately $3 million ($1300 per capita) from its general budget to upgrade roads, the water system and the sewer system. The rapid growth of the town and Mitsue Lake Industrial Park [where the new wood and wood product plants were located], which is outside the town's taxation area, committed the town's tax base and borrowing power to providing only the most basic public works infrastructure. The development of recreational and community facilities suffered as a consequence.[52]

Faced with an ever-increasing financial burden and encouraged by the Planning Division of the Department of Municipal Affairs, the Slave Lake council applied for new-town status in order to obtain provincial funds, even though it knew that, with a change in status, the community would no longer be self-governing. The application went to the cabinet, where it was turned down.

In 1969 the New Town Act was completely rewritten, although the basic philosophy of the 1956 act remained unchanged. As under the 1956 act, the board of administration required the approval of property owners for any money bylaw, issuance of debentures, "or for any other matter or thing that shall take place." The Alberta Planning Board approves all matters relating to the planning and development of the town and the Local Authorities Board all matters relating to the town's development and operation. The provincial government provides a new town with grants and loans and purchases its debentures.

Since 1967 the province has not designated any more fast-growing communities as new towns. Moreover, the new towns created between

1956 and 1967 have had their status changed as soon as they were fiscally viable. In 1982 the new towns of Grande Cache, Fox Creek, High Level, and Rainbow Lake were scolded by the Department of Municipal Affairs for denying residents their democratic rights and were encouraged to become self-governing municipalities. Shortly thereafter all made the change except Rainbow Lake.

Lloydminster

When Lloydminster was founded in 1903 the main street was located on the fourth meridian that was to become the boundary between Saskatchewan and Alberta. In 1905 Sir Wilfrid Laurier brought forward legislation to divide the North-West Territories along the fourth meridian into two provinces almost equal in size. Lloydminster residents wrote letters to the Prime Minister pointing out the difficulties of being separated into two provinces and requesting the divisional line be moved slightly one way or another so the village would be in one province. Their plea was to no avail; Laurier responded that only the provincial legislatures had the authority to shift provincial boundaries.

In February 1906 the municipality's residents held a plebiscite to determine in which province they wished to live. Although the vote was 79 to 35 in favour of Saskatchewan, neither province was willing to acknowledge that a straw vote had even been held. In July 1906 the Alberta portion of the community was designated the Village of Lloydminster, Alberta, and in April 1907 the Saskatchewan sector became the Town of Lloydminster, Saskatchewan.

As a result of the vagaries of urban settlement, the Saskatchewan portion of the community grew much faster than the Alberta side and by the time amalgamation was considered, the Saskatchewan portion was twice as large. Although the two communities were a single economic and social unit, sharing a common main street, churches, and social institutions, outbreaks of political rivalry occasionally occurred. More important, neither community was large enough to develop badly needed water and sewage systems.[53] Finally, in the early spring of 1930, elections were held in the town and village to ascertain whether or not the respective electorates favoured giving their representatives the authority to approach the provincial governments for the necessary legislation to amalgamate. The electorate in both communities voted overwhelmingly for amalgamation. On March 21, 1930, An Act Respecting the Amalgamation of Lloydminster was passed in Alberta and on March 27 an almost identical act (the Lloydminster Municipal Amalgamation Act) gained assent in Saskatchewan. The two provincial acts established what came to be known as the Lloydminster Charter, which united the two municipalities and their school systems and transferred their assets and liabilities to the newly amalgamated municipality and school system. In effect, this meant the municipality functioned under neither the Town Act of Alberta nor the Town Act of Saskatchewan but under its own unique charter. In 1958 both provinces approved a new charter for Lloydminster which gave it city status.

Today, Lloydminster is completely integrated politically, with the electorate ignoring whether council candidates reside in the Alberta or Saskatchewan portion of the community. The 1958 charter made the city's financial affairs and powers somewhat more complicated than those of other Alberta municipalities, since it operates under both provinces' municipal government acts and must receive approval from both when borrowing money and dealing with annexation and amalgamation. The charter specifies which of the provincial acts apply to the whole city and which apply only to one portion.[54] Since 1982 the city has operated under a council-commission form of government, with a single commissioner. However, since the commissioner reports to council, it is council-manager government in all but name.

The arrangement by which the two provinces have joint custody of Lloydminster has produced some financial benefits for the city. The city borrows money from the province that gives it the best terms. But for the most part the dual arrangement has been worrisome for the community's business people and residents. Since Saskatchewan levies a sales tax and Alberta does not, businesses in the Saskatchewan portion of the community are at a disadvantage, for if they collect the tax their customers shop in Alberta. When the Cooperative Commonwealth Federation was in power, sales taxes were not collected in the city,[55] but after the Liberals were elected in 1964 tax laws were stringently enforced by the Saskatchewan Treasury Department. The *Edmonton Journal* reported:

> Six plainclothes policemen are reported cruising the streets of this border town conducting spot checks of shoppers suspected of tax evasion. The policemen are carrying out government instruction to enforce the Saskatchewan sales and tobacco tax regulations, which Lloydminster residents are said to have been avoiding by crossing the street and shopping on the Alberta side of town.[56]

The sales tax issue was eventually resolved by making the public responsible for either paying the tax at the time of purchase or mailing it to the provincial treasurer; fines were to be imposed for failure to comply.

In a similar case, before Alberta taxed tobacco products, merchants in the Saskatchewan portion of the municipality were disadvantaged since they had to collect a 10 percent tax on tobacco.

Taxation has not been the only irritant. Commercial truckers operating in the municipality are almost forced to purchase dual licenses for their vehicles and professionals and tradespeople must be licensed in both provinces if they want to practise throughout the municipality.

Fortunately, the location of Lloydminster is such that there have been few annexation and amalgamation cases. The one involving the most territory was a 1965 bid to annex some 13,000 acres in both provinces. In order to hold hearings on the city's application an ad hoc joint committee was established by both provincial governments. The committee's decision had to be ratified by the two provincial cabinets before the annexation process could be completed.[57]

Although the Lloydminster Charter approved by an order in council in 1971 provided a mechanism for resolving tax, utility, and education problems in the divided city, citizens have been disadvantaged by being governed under two different sets of provincial laws. Despite Lloydminster's size, it does not have a permanent court and as a consequence there are only sporadic court sittings for civil and criminal offenses. Residents in the Saskatchewan portion of the municipality travel to Battleford for court appearances; those in the Alberta portion are somewhat more fortunate, since the court sits in the municipality four weeks out of the year.

National Park Townsites: Banff, Jasper, and Waterton

Since Jasper, Banff, and Waterton are located in national parks where the federal government has had exclusive jurisdiction, their residents have been denied the rights of self-government enjoyed in other Alberta municipalities. The Rocky Mountain Park Act of 1887 established the communities of Banff and Jasper as train and park service towns entirely under federal jurisdiction. From the beginning these communities were operated as miniature fiefdoms, with the citizens passive observers of town policy made by the federal government. The policy that land in the townsites could only be leased allowed the federal government to control municipal planning and development.

Citizen dissatisfaction with the federal government's autocratic municipal policy making led to the establishment of citizen advisory committees in Banff in 1921, and in Jasper in 1927. Members of these locally elected committees sat on various park committees administering the two communities. Over time, the committees gained a modicum of power.

The Natural Resource Transfer Agreement of 1930 was particularly important, since it gave Alberta limited jurisdiction in the townsites. It allowed "Alberta laws to operate . . . to the extent they are not 'repugnant' to Federal laws and . . . taxing Acts to apply . . . unless expressly excluded by Federal laws."[58] As a consequence, education, police protection, hospital and health services, recreation and library services, building and fire inspection, and social services came under provincial jurisdiction. Although the federal government relinquished a great many of its responsibilities and powers, in each townsite the park superintendent continued to formulate policies which were carried out by the townsite manager.

The townsite advisory committees were especially important in providing representation on the school boards, which became embryonic municipal administrations. In recognition of the townsites' special status, provincial acts were amended to allow the school boards to levy taxes and provide library, recreational, and social, as well as educational, services. The province designated the two school boards as having the same status as incorporated municipalities so that they would be eligible for grants and transfer payments.[59]

After the federal government began to change its policies on leasing townsite lands in 1958 a number of studies examined the feasibility of self-government.[60] Less than three years later a federal government proposal to discuss self rule for Banff was rejected by residents who believed self rule would lead to an expansion of the town's boundaries to the detriment of the park. Nevertheless, over the years local autonomy became a part of the local political agenda and when in 1970 the Banff school board held a self-rule plebiscite, 86 percent voted in favour.

In 1972 Alberta's Department of Municipal Affairs released *The Banff-Jasper Autonomy Report,* which suggested that the federal government and the province collaborate on making the two townsites autonomous and independent municipalities. The report recommended that the transition from a federal townsite to a municipality be undertaken under the New Town Act which provides for a council composed of both elective and appointive members. The report went on to suggest that this council be made up of both federal and provincial appointees as well as locally elected members. It also advised the town to work closely with the provincial and federal governments to devise strict planning and development controls. The most controversial recommendation was that "only persons essential to the basic functions of each town, will be permitted to own or lease property within the townsites."[61]

Opponents of local autonomy in Banff argued over lease rents and when another plebiscite was held in 1977, residents voted overwhelmingly against self rule. In 1980 the federal government, after reassessing the townsite's land, doubled lease rents for most residents. However, it was merchants, who had been paying very low lease rents, who bore the brunt of the increases when their rents were raised as much as 1,500 percent. The federal government added insult to injury by letting the roadways deteriorate and then in 1985 increasing the cost of water and garbage collection by 35 percent and tripling the business license fee. The Banff Municipal Committee was created in 1986 to assist the federal park administration in administering the townsite and to act as an interim transitional body in the event the citizens decided upon self rule. But it was the federal government's neglect of the townsite's sewer system, resulting in its failure and the spewing of human waste into the Bow River in the fall of 1987, which galvanized the self-rule forces. The movement gained momentum after the federal government announced it wanted to turn Banff over to the residents and promised that if the townsite became self governing lease rents would be substantially reduced. In February 1988 federal Environment Minister Tom McMillan encouraged Banff residents to seek self rule and warned that the maintenance of the status quo was no longer a viable option for them, since the federal government would begin recovering as much of the cost of providing services in the townsite as was feasible. Despite the efforts of local environmentalists who maintained that the federal government could best control town development, in June 1988 the residents voted almost two to one in favour of home rule.[62] The Banff Municipal Committee governed the town until January 1, 1990, when it was incorporated and its governance turned over to its first elected council.

From the early 1960s there were close parallels between the self-rule movements in Banff and Jasper. In both communities there were strong proponents of local autonomy as well as opponents who valued low lease rents from the federal government far more than self rule. Finally, in the late summer of 1986 when the community seemed to lean toward autonomy, tri-level discussions commenced among federal park officials, officials from Alberta Municipal Affairs, and the Jasper townsite committee. But all of the participants misjudged the public's mood and a hurriedly scheduled October plebiscite on self rule was narrowly defeated by a vote of 631 to 528. A townsite committee member explained that many park employees feared they would lose their jobs if self rule were approved and as a consequence rallied their supporters to the polls.[63] The federal government's policies of increasing lease rents and recovering the cost of providing services in park sites were applied in Jasper just as they had been in Banff. In 1987, after residents' annual taxes were raised an average of $71.06 to pay for services, self rule was again discussed. Only days after the citizens of Banff opted for self rule, federal Environment Minister Tom McMillan said that "there's an even stronger case in Jasper than in Banff for self-government" and that people in Jasper should not be governed by absentee landlords residing in Ottawa.[64] Nevertheless, Jasper residents seemed to be waiting to evaluate the effects of local autonomy in Banff before committing the townsite to self rule.

The number of people living in Waterton townsite in Waterton Lakes National Park is minute compared to the thousands of permanent residents of Jasper and Banff. About 100 people live in the townsite year-round, with several hundred college students employed in the Prince of Wales Hotel and motels and restaurants to serve tourists during the summer months. Although business people are unhappy with the Park Service's escalating land lease rents, a residents' committee has not been formed to explore self rule. In 1988 the president of the local chamber of commerce said, "I think we would like to be based on a municipal taxation basis, but I don't think we could ever get to the point where we could be doing all of our garbage system, [and] street system."[65]

An Overview of Urban Governmental Structures

Two factors stand out in an examination of the various forms of urban government. First, unlike the provincial government system, in which the legislative function is carried out by the legislative assembly and the executive function by the cabinet, the legislative and executive functions tend to be combined in municipal councils. The councils initiate policy proposals, formulate the proposals by passing bylaws, and oversee the municipal bureaucracy. In addition, bureaucrats often work hand-in-hand with council in formulating policies. In short, the legislative and executive functions of municipal councils are indistinct and tend to overlap, a feature that often leads to confusion and frustration among council members as well as the public. Furthermore, in Alberta's local governments formal power is dispersed rather than concentrated. Neither the mayor nor, for that matter, anyone else is given enough formal powers to control the administration or to implement major policy decisions. As a consequence, the only way leadership can be exercised and a distinct policy direction can be established is through the use of informal power.

Until the late 1960s people accepted the foibles of local government. Its supporters argued that the experimentation found at the local level more than made up for its deficiencies. But in the last three decades people increasingly have been demanding a say in the way revenue is raised and in the mix of the services which are provided. People today are not nearly as complacent as in the past, when they tended to leave the business of government almost solely to their elected representatives. They want a say in the raising of revenue and the provision of services. Although the mechanisms described in Chapter 1 enable citizens to bypass the political establishment with direct legislation and to channel their demands to the elected decision makers, these processes are awkward and time-consuming. Nevertheless, change occurs, though in most cases it is incremental rather than dramatic and cataclysmic.

4

Rural and Evolving Forms
of Local Government

Introduction

During Alberta's earliest period of settlement, when crops were often destroyed by stray livestock and prairie fires, the territorial council provided mechanisms for establishing herd and fire districts.[1] In 1887 the Statute Labour Ordinance, which recognized both the need for roads in rural areas and the cash-poor position of many settlers, was passed to enable local units of government to build and maintain roads. A road district's poorer residents could work on road crews to fulfill their obligation, while more affluent settlers could pay cash. A day's labour was valued at $1.50, and the amount of land a person owned determined the amount of the obligation.

In 1890 the functions of labour and fire districts were combined in the Statute Labour and Fire Ordinance. The ordinance was amended in 1893 so that any township with a population of eight or more residents could be designated a labour and fire district. Upon passage of the amended ordinance, Lieutenant-Governor MacIntosh said:

> ... sixteen new districts have been created with eminently successful results. Thus, without unduly creating machinery for excessive taxation, an element likely to encourage organized local improvement has been introduced, and will no doubt result in educating these communities in methods so necessary for the promotion of self-reliance.[2]

By 1896 the province's 36 fire and labour districts were indicative of the success of this unique form of local government.

Although Alberta had a population of only 170,000 in 1905, news of its rich agricultural land brought waves of immigrants and the population grew to over 400,000 in slightly less than ten years. Since the province could not afford to develop rural areas, it promoted new local government units that would be capable of raising revenues and providing a variety of services for rural residents.

In 1897 the statute labour and fire districts were enlarged and renamed local improvement districts. But already many people were critical of the roads being built by farmers ill-equipped with engineering skills. As a consequence, most of the local improvement districts were abolished in 1903 and replaced with larger districts governed by three to six elected councillors. The size of the districts was expanded to 216 square miles in 1907 and to 324 square miles in 1912, when the Rural Municipality Act was passed. Eric Hanson, in his seminal work on Alberta's local governments, describes the act's provisions:

> ... the province was divided into nine-township squares. ... Once these new nine-township units were laid out their residents could apply for incorporation of the unit as a rural municipality provided there was at least one person per square mile in the area. If the areas concerned had been organized as small local improvement districts before 1912 and if their residents did not petition for municipal organization, the minister of municipal affairs could *direct* reorganization of the areas as nine-township local improvement districts operating under The Local Improvement Act of 1907. ... units which did not request incorporation or organized local improvement district status became unorganized local improvement districts *at the discretion* of the minister of municipal affairs.[3] [Emphasis added.]

Thus the act created two new forms of local government for rural areas: the rural municipality and the organized local improvement district. In 1912 there were 55 rural municipalities and 90 local improvement districts, the main difference between them being that the rural municipality had a much stronger financial base than the organized local improvement district. Rural municipalities had the power to issue debentures and levy taxes on land, while organized improvement districts could assess taxes only on an acreage basis at a rate not to exceed seven and one-half cents an acre.[4] There were slight differences in the political structures of these two forms of government. Improvement districts had ward representation while councils in rural municipalities were elected either from wards or at-large. In almost all rural municipalities, the electorate opted for ward representation.

By the winter of 1917 Alberta had 80 local improvement districts and

88 rural municipalities, most of which had been organized in newly settled areas. A few rural municipalities were created and then dissolved as
people became fearful of excessive taxes and municipal debt. An authority
on the historical development of Alberta's improvement districts writes,
"Although the provincial government attempted to reduce this fear of
increased taxes (for example, by requiring an increased accountability of
councils to ratepayers on financial matters), the reluctance to organize
rural municipalities persisted; most organizing only occurred in newly
settled areas of the province."[5]

In 1918 the province changed the name "rural municipality" to
"municipal district" and compelled all organized improvement districts
to become municipal districts. By the end of the year there were 167
municipal districts. In very sparsely settled areas with limited financial
resources the provincial government established and administered an
even larger number of improvement districts.

Alberta farmers had suffered financially throughout the 1920s and
during the Great Depression farm income virtually disappeared. As a
consequence, a number of municipal districts collapsed because they were
unable to collect taxes. Three reverted to improvement district status in
the late 1920s, and some municipal districts in southeastern Alberta were
dismantled and designated as special areas administered solely by the
provincial government. Despite these reverses, 143 municipal districts
were operating in 1940.

After the success of school consolidation in 1936 the government
thought that, in the interests of economy and efficiency, the 143 municipal districts also should be consolidated. The Municipal Districts Act was
amended in 1941 to allow consolidations and despite some opposition the
number of districts was reduced to 60 by 1944 and to 28 by 1962.

The Improvement Districts Act was amended in 1942 to promote similar consolidations. The 216 improvement districts had been reduced to
50 by 1962 and to 24 as the result of another effort in 1979. Neil Gibson, a
senior administrator with the Department of Municipal Affairs, provides
the rationale for the government's 1979 consolidations:

... the purpose behind the enlargement [was] to combine weak and
strong economic areas in order to provide a wider and more diversified
tax base, thus permitting the expenditure of tax revenues over a wider
area. The Improvement Districts Act specifies that the tax revenues
must be spent in the district in which they are collected; quite often,
prior to the enlargement, the Improvement District with the more
buoyant tax revenue had a far sparser population and fewer areas that

required services such as roads, street lights, waste disposal grounds, etc. In the enlarged administrative units, the revenue from the more affluent areas could be spent in areas less fortunate, but still be within the boundaries of a single improvement district.[6]

In all cases, the principles upon which the Department of Municipal Affairs effected consolidations were that the new units were to reflect common social and economic interests, their boundaries were to follow township and range lines, and their administrative centres were to be accessible to all their residents. On balance, the consolidations seem to have been successful since, although the elected policy makers became slightly more remote from their constituents, consolidation resulted in a more equitable tax burden and more uniform service standards.

Municipal Districts

Only 18 municipal districts existed in 1982, but their numbers increased when the provincial government began encouraging improvement districts to become municipal districts. The municipal districts of Clearwater and Cypress were formed in 1985 and Brazeau in 1988. An examination of Table 4.1 shows that in 1988 there were 22 municipal districts in Alberta, ranging in population size from 138 residents in Bighorn to 17,484 in Rocky View.

A close examination of Table 4.1 shows that municipal districts differ substantially in the amount of their revenue base and in the percentage of total revenue which they derive from property taxes and special levies. Bighorn has the smallest total revenue and Acadia derives the least revenue from property taxes and special levies, while Rocky View has the highest total revenue. Bighorn obtains a greater percentage of revenue from property taxes and levies than any of the other municipal districts. Some municipal districts are highly dependent on the property tax, while others are not. In short, the diversity in the table figures illustrates the diversity in the economic bases of municipal districts.

The authority for municipal districts is embedded in the Municipal Government Act, which gives them full taxing and spending powers and allows them to borrow money. The act also gives the municipal district additional powers appropriate for the governance of a rural area. For example, it can make grants to encourage veterinarians to practise in the district and give cash advances to district farmers for spring feeding and "for any other good and sufficient reason."[7]

Table 4.1   Municipal District Population, 1988 Total Revenue and 1988 Property Tax

Municipal District	Population[8]	1988 Total Revenue	1988 Property Tax and Special Levies
Acadia No. 34	618	1,071,064	192,346
Bighorn No. 81	138	1,005,719	720,783
Bonnyville No. 87	10,384	5,613,514	2,368,087
Brazeau No. 77	5,448	6,155,392	4,149,213
Cardston No. 6	4,419	3,185,229	898,438
Clearwater No. 99	9,848	9,302,801	4,966,954
Cypress No. 1	4,795	8,921,274	4,707,477
Fairview No. 136	1,903	1,883,362	782,513
Foothills No. 31	9,432	5,809,370	2,852,274
Kneehill No. 48	4,996	6,860,231	4,216,443
Peace No. 135	1,527	1,956,183	615,320
Pincher Creek No. 9	3,093	3,617,887	1,892,448
Provost No. 52	2,725	3,294,505	1,577,710
Rocky View No. 44	17,484	18,039,084	7,903,143
Smoky River No. 130	2,853	3,722,269	1,066,952
Spirit River No. 133	848	1,330,982	414,591
Starland No. 47	2,120	3,912,505	1,844,415
Sturgeon No. 90	14,019	8,457,584	4,289,721
Taber No. 14	5,284	5,688,669	1,811,951
Wainwright No. 61	3,937	5,622,209	2,861,674
Westlock No. 92	6,992	5,406,791	1,884,510
Willow Creek No. 26	4,733	3,545,443	1,216,981
Totals	117,596	114,402,067	53,233,944

Although municipal districts have almost the same powers as urban municipalities, in the past their primary goal was to develop a dependable network of roads for their widely dispersed rural residents. A history of the province's municipal districts and counties highlights the emphasis on transportation. In the Municipal District of Provost, "as the number of Model T Fords increased, road building became the first concern of the councils."[9] Roadways were equally important in the Municipal District of Spirit River, where "road building became a major concern" during the 1920s.[10] However, records show that during the depression, one after another of the municipal districts suspended the construction and maintenance of roads in the interest of providing as much help as possible to farmers. Following the Second World War funds again were spent on road-building equipment. Equally important, as the standard of living in rural areas rose, municipal district councils were urged to add and upgrade services. In the last 20 years a number of municipal districts have installed sewage and water systems in some of their more populous hamlets. Cardston purchased a golf course in 1970 and Westlock operates its own ski hill and golf course.

Municipal districts have little to do with formulating educational policy, since school divisions with elected trustees are responsible for the operation of schools. However, as is the case with most municipalities, the municipal district provides financial support for the school division. After the school board has prepared its budget, it requisitions the municipal district for any funds needed in addition to those obtained from the province under its School Foundation Program.[11] According to Section 136(4) of the School Act, "If the municipality fails to pay to a board the amount required from time to time as hereinbefore provided, the amount becomes a debt due, owing and payable by the municipality to the board." Municipal districts often have problems with the requisition system, since regardless of the effect on expenditures in other fields, this requisition must be paid.

The municipal district governing structure is straightforward, as the act specifies that the council "shall consist of the same number of councillors as there are electoral divisions." Councils normally have from four to nine members. Rocky View had seven electoral divisions until 1983, when the Minister of Municipal Affairs ordered the number of divisions to be raised to eleven since the population of municipal districts had substantially increased. The seven electoral divisions ranged in population size from 1,200 to 4,600; after four new divisions were added, the range was from 1,300 to 1,900. The minister was not swayed by a council majority which argued that if the council's size were increased it would be more costly; the new councillors and their support staff would have to be paid and council meetings would take longer if more members were debating issues.[12]

Once elected, councillors choose a chief executive, called a reeve, from their own ranks. Since the 1920s this method of choosing a chief executive has been controversial, with opponents arguing that the chief executive should be elected at-large from the entire municipal district. Although the Department of Municipal Affairs considered the election of chief executives in the 1970s, the idea was dropped. When a Pincher Creek councillor brought the proposal forward at a meeting of the Foothills-

Little Bow Association of Municipal Districts and Counties in 1984, it was overwhelmingly defeated.

Particularly striking in the AAMD&C's *Story of Rural Municipal Government in Alberta* is the number of municipal district councillors re-elected term after term. Three councillors from the municipal districts that were organized as Foothills had a total of over 100 years of council service. After reorganization, Jack Sutherland continued as a Foothills councillor until he died after 47 years of service.[13] An Acadia councillor had 38 years of service, a Wainwright councillor 37, and a Kneehill councillor 35. In virtually every municipal district, one or two people have been councillors for 20 to 30 years.

The municipal district's administrative structure is straightforward. The secretary-treasurer and other administrative personnel are selected by, and responsible to, the council. To bring a higher level of expertise to administration, some municipal district councils have hired professional administrators and managers.

Municipal districts adjacent to large cities, such as Taber (east of Lethbridge), Rocky View (adjoining Calgary), and Sturgeon (north of Edmonton), must reconcile the demands of commuting "hobby farmers" for suburban amenities with farmers' desire for fewer services and lower taxes.[14] On the other hand, acreage owners revolted when the school board requisition in the Municipal District of Foothills increased 93 percent between 1981 and 1982 and the council was forced to increase its tax assessments by 50 percent. The acreage owners, with almost no support from district farmers, formed the Foothills Ratepayers Association, which encouraged ratepayers to withhold the increase when they paid their 1982 taxes. Rocky View, the municipal district in which the minister increased the number of electoral divisions, has been deeply split between farming and nonfarming residents and much of the hostility to the minister's proposal occurred because it would divide nonfarming electoral divisions and increase their political power. As the examples illustrate, municipal districts are becoming more heterogeneous and, consequently, their councils must deal more with conflicting demands and controversial political issues and less with purely administrative responsibilities.

Another politically charged campaign occurred in the Drayton Valley area in the late 1980s when it was proposed that the western portions of five rural municipalities be consolidated into a new governmental unit. In 1970 and 1979 residents petitioned Municipal Affairs to create a separate county, arguing that they were not being served by representatives who responded only to constituents in more populous areas. Again in 1984 rural residents complained that they were being ill-served by their elected representatives. This time Municipal Affairs responded with *The Drayton Valley Area Municipality Feasibility Study*. Although the study concluded that a new government was financially feasible, many people living in the area were more concerned with the effect a new government would have on educational policy and boundaries. When an election was held in September 1986 to determine whether some 2,100 residents of three counties, an improvement district, and a municipal district favoured establishing a new municipal district, 60 percent voted yes. But the issue was far from resolved, for people in two of the six voting regions opposed the resolution because of the continuing uncertainties over school closures and education boundaries. Just as opposition to the plan began to mount, the Minister of Municipal Affairs announced in December 1987 that effective January 1, 1988, Improvement District. No. 222 would come into existence with interim boundaries until the citizenry expressed its point of view on the matter in a March 1 plebiscite. On the basis of the March vote the boundaries were readjusted and on May 12 it was announced that Improvement District No. 222 was to be converted to the Municipal District of Brazeau on July 1.[15]

Improvement District No. 7 became the Municipal District of Badlands on January 1, 1991, after more than a decade of controversy. During the 1980s many urban municipalities made plans to annex nearby hamlets with the tacit encouragement of the Department of Municipal Affairs. Angry over what they saw as the improvement district's gradual dismemberment, residents agreed to a substantial property tax increase, staged over a three-year period, in order to prove they could manage their own affairs. Next, to forestall any further territorial adventurism by urban municipalities, the advisory council requested the Minister of Municipal Affairs to convert the improvement district to a municipal district. In September 1989 Ray Speaker agreed that the improvement district should become a self-governing municipal district.

Evolution of County Government and County Politics

The economic prosperity generated by a wartime economy in the early 1940s and an oil boom in 1947 revived municipal district finances. However, citizens were confused by the overlap of school divisions and municipal and hospital districts. Eric Hanson explains that "tax rates differed within municipal districts because those districts embraced parts of several school divisions and hospital districts, and each of the latter units requisitioned amounts that necessitated the levying of different rates in different parts of a municipal district."[16] In short, a farmer living in a school district and a hospital district on one side of the road often paid substantially higher or lower taxes than the neighbour across the road in a different district. Such disparities inevitably caused hard feelings and charges of tax inequities.

Until 1931 school boards and local councils each levied their own taxes and collected them independently. Although this system enabled citizens to pinpoint responsibility for fiscal policies, it tended to promote unnecessary competition and animosity between the two bodies. As a consequence, municipal councils were charged with levying and collecting taxes for both the local government authority and the school board, which obtained its funds by requisitioning the governmental unit. However, municipalities were unhappy with their new responsibilities and in 1931 at the annual convention of the Alberta Association of Municipal Districts a resolution was passed calling for the establishment of a county system in Alberta.

Over time, many municipal districts were frustrated by school and hospital requisitions. They saw school boards building large cash reserves at a time when municipalities were not merely short of cash but facing taxpayer rebellions. However, municipal councils' major criticism was that the school boards' system of requisitioning gave them an unofficial veto over the whole range of municipal fiscal policies. On the other hand, after being denied a portion of municipal reserves, many school officials criticized councillors for failing to recognize the importance of education. Many officials felt that municipal councils were concerned only with keeping mill rates and taxes at an absolute minimum, a practice that undermined educational goals. More often than not, school officials, hospital officials, and municipal district councillors planned and made policy without consulting each other.

The provincial government became increasingly concerned about uncoordinated policy making that confused and alienated residents of municipal districts. In 1941 a Department of Municipal Affairs report stated: "No reasonable person will dispute the fact that the outlook for the future is not a bright one . . . and it will be especially difficult for local self-government to continue functioning efficiently under the present set-up."[17] The government made several attempts to solve the problem, first by providing in 1946 that the school board and municipal council would each send a member to the other's meetings to facilitate communication and then, in 1948, by establishing an appeal procedure for a municipal district whose school board(s) requisitioned an amount exceeding the previous year's requisition by more than 20 percent.[18] Unfortunately, these measures did little to alleviate the conflict between school and municipal districts.

In 1950 the government passed the County Act, which provided for the creation of an omnibus authority by combining a municipal district and a school district into a single body to make policy and plan and administer all local governmental services within its geographical boundaries.[19] Such a radical restructuring of local government was bound to upset vested interests. A Department of Municipal Affairs paper entitled "After Twenty Years" discusses the "violent criticism" of the County Act. It reads in part:

> It was opposed as "an attempt by the Department of Municipal Affairs to take over the running of school districts," as a plan "to centralize and regiment the entire Province in Counties" or more tersely as "dictatorial centralization."
> . . . Opposition to the system was unaccountably strong in the teaching profession and among school trustees (who saw in it "the deterioration of school affairs in favor of roads, sidewalks and other public services"). Individuals were certain that counties would mean increased taxes, the loss of personal contact with their local councils, decreasing importance of elected officials, reduced services and even their own disfranchisement.[20]

The province was more circumspect in its policy on the establishment of counties than it had been in its earlier policies on school reorganization and municipal district consolidation. It agreed initially that no more than four counties would be formed and that after four years each must hold a plebiscite on its continuance. Moreover, under the act the provincial government could not form a county unless it first received a resolution to do so from a municipal council or a school division. When the electorate in the first four counties overwhelmingly supported the county concept, the government changed the act to allow more counties to be established and to make the vote on the retention of the county system optional.

At about the same time, the provincial government established the Co-terminous Boundaries Commission to straighten out the tangled and overlapping boundaries of municipal districts and school divisions. After devising seven criteria (physical features, nature of production, ability to pay, size in relation to administration, inclusion of nondivisional schools, existing pattern of school centralization, and the location of railroads, highways and market centres), the commission negotiated with municipal councils, school boards, teacher associations, and other interested groups to develop boundaries which would be satisfactory to all parties. There is little doubt that the Co-terminous Boundaries Commission played an important role in Alberta's county movement; its resolution of political and administrative conflict made county government acceptable to rural residents.

The County Act came into effect on July 1, 1950, and less than two weeks later the Grande Prairie council passed a resolution asking that the municipal district be converted to a county system. When Vulcan's council met on August 8 its members were equally enthusiastic and sent a petition to the Minister of Municipal Affairs to "erect a County in this area as soon as it can be arranged."[21] As adamant in their opposition as the councils were in their support, the municipal districts' educational establishments opposed the formation of the new counties at every step, but to no avail, for on January 1, 1951, the counties of Grande Prairie and Vulcan commenced operation. One year later Ponoka became the third municipal district to be converted into a county. Only in Sturgeon, which was incorporated as a county in 1960, did the electorate reject the county form of government after the four-year trial period. The electorate decided in a plebiscite to terminate county government in the spring of 1965 and on July 12 an Order in Council discontinued county government and Sturgeon reverted to a municipal district with school divisions.

By 1988 there were 30 counties with annual revenues ranging from those of Thorhild, with $7,720,000 ($2,044,000 from taxes and grants in lieu of taxes), to Strathcona, with $115,619,000 ($55,685,000 from taxes and grants in lieu of taxes). Table 4.2 shows that the population of counties ranges between under 2,500 and over 50,000, with the median being approximately 6,000. Economic and social diversities are equally wide, as are variations in levels of service. Various spending patterns are found, with roadways, protective services, education, and recreation accounting for different proportions of the budget.

Other than having an educational committee, counties have essentially the same political structure as municipal districts. The county council is composed of five to eleven councillors, each of whom is elected from an electoral division. Although most county councils have seven members, the number of councillors is determined by the size of the county. Paintearth and Lamont, for example, have five members, while Athabasca has nine and Grande Prairie has eleven.

Despite the provincial government's early attempt to bring all local government policy making and administration under the aegis of a single authority,[22] hospital districts remained independent of the county. The County Act originally provided for the amalgamation of municipal,

Table 4.2   Counties and Their 1989 Populations[23]

Athabasca No. 12	5,979	Paintearth No. 18	2,439
Barrhead No. 11	5,728	Parkland No. 31	20,926
Beaver No. 9	5,400	Ponoka No. 3	7,739
Camrose No. 22	7,475	Red Deer No. 23	13,911
Flagstaff No. 29	4,406	Smoky Lake No. 13	2,789
Forty Mile No. 8	3,335	St. Paul No. 19	6,595
Grande Prairie No. 1	12,042	Stettler No. 6	5,179
Lac Ste. Anne No. 28	7,765	Strathcona No. 20	51,744
Lacombe No. 14	8,911	Thorhild No. 7	3,094
Lamont No. 30	4,287	Two Hills No. 21	3,086
Leduc No. 25	11,278	Vermilion River No. 24	8,112
Lethbridge No. 26	8,266	Vulcan No. 2	3,656
Minburn No. 27	3,894	Warner No. 5	3,579
Mountain View No. 17	8,886	Wetaskiwin No. 10	9,521
Newell No. 4	2,439	Wheatland No. 16	5,409
Total Population		247,870	

school, and hospital districts under a single unit. However, when many rural residents strongly opposed the abolition of hospital districts, the provincial government decided not to jeopardize its policy on counties and left the hospital districts intact. Reformers and proponents of county government see the existence of independent hospital districts as forestalling completely rational and efficient policy making and administration at the county level.[24] Nevertheless, it is unlikely that the provincial government would be willing to precipitate a political showdown by abolishing hospital districts and transferring their functions to the county.

Since it was not necessary to provide for the representation of hospitals, the provincial government was able to keep the county's political structure simple and straightforward. Its policy-making body was to be composed of no more than eleven councillors who would select the county's chief executive officer, the reeve, from their own ranks.[25] At its first meeting of the year, the county council was to appoint three members to a school committee which was to be augmented by representatives appointed from towns and villages within the country. It is particularly important to note that the school committee cannot levy taxes, purchase property, or enter into any legal agreements.

In 1977 the County Act was amended to clarify the nature of educational representation on county councils. The council's education committee, which is the county's board of education, would consist of at least three county council members[26] and additional school representatives appointed from the county's educational units (i.e., the towns and villages in the county). An educational unit with a population of 2,000 or less was allowed one representative; one with a population of 2,000 to 4,000, two; and one with a population greater than 4,000, three. The act reads: "The number of school representatives appointed to the board of education shall not exceed the number of electoral divisions that exist within the county." In short, this means that town and village education representatives cannot exceed the number of county councillors. This provision caused a problem since, in many cases, the number of authorized representatives exceeded the number allocated to form the school board. When such a situation occurs, "the county council shall meet with those school representatives . . . and determine a system of rotation which will permit those positions on the board of education to be filled."

The counties which employ the rotation system allow all of the authorized educational representatives to sit on the school committee or board, but permit only some of them to vote. Since the rotation system is often based on a population formula, representatives of some smaller communities are almost always relegated to nonvoting status. This has been contentious, as smaller towns and villages feel they are being squeezed out of the educational policy-making process. But larger communities also complain about county educational representation. In 1989 the Raymond town council was concerned because Raymond's schools constituted 60 percent of the county's student population and yet the town school board only had two members on the nine-member County of Warner school committee. Being somewhat unfamiliar with the County Act, the town council asked the Raymond school board to examine the possibility of the school becoming independent of the county.

An almost unsolvable representation problem is that if a county councillor or reeve is a sworn elector of a *separate* school district he or she is ineligible to sit on the education committee, since it is the county's *public* board of education. If only one or two councillors are separate-school supporters, it is difficult although not impossible for the council to carry out its educational responsibilities. However, if most of the council members are separate-school supporters, the council is unable to act on educational matters.[27]

Self-determination and local control became major issues in 1981 when the government attempted to amend the County Act. Bill 25 would have abolished the power of the county council's education committee or school board to formulate and administer its education budget. The effect would have been to reduce the committee or board to little more than an advisory body to the county council. Small towns and villages fought the proposal, feeling that it would end local control over educational policy. Their opposition, in concert with strong lobbying against the bill by the Alberta School Trustees Association and the Alberta Teachers Association, resulted in it being dropped after second reading. In 1981 Shirley Cripps, MLA for Drayton Valley, introduced an amendment to the County Act which would abolish the rotation system on the county school committee. Minister of Municipal Affairs Marvin Moore was unwilling to support the amendment and it died on the order paper.

At one time a municipality with city status could not be represented in the county school system.[28] With the passage of Bill 72 of the County Act in 1983, a city was given the option to either remain with the county school system or establish its own educational system. When Fort Saskatchewan and Spruce Grove became cities they held referendums on the future status of their school systems; in both cases the public decided that the responsibility for education should remain with the county.

In 1983 a committee drawn from the departments of Municipal Affairs and Education began a review of the County Act.[29] Its "County Act Review Report," submitted in 1987, proposed several major changes to the act, including the elimination of the education committee rotation system and, if necessary, the implementation of "a modified system of representation."[30] It also recommended that the county school committee be given substantially more power:

> . . . council [would] have the authority to appoint corporate officials (secretary, treasurer, auditor) and the power to borrow money and pass bylaws. The board of education would have all the other powers of a board of trustees. The reeve would have all the powers of a chairman of a board of trustees under the School Act with respect to those matters reserved to the council. The chairman of the board of education would have the chairman's powers and responsibilities with respect to all other matters.[31]

The committee also wanted to rectify the disenfranchisement of the permanent residents of summer villages with populations of less than 150, since a quirk of the County Act made them ineligible to vote in any school election. Since school supplementary requisitions accounted for more than half of the total tax bill in many summer villages, residents wanted a say in the selection of school representatives. The committee recommended: ". . . that these electors be eligible to vote at the election of the county councillor for the electoral division in which the summer village is located."[32] Although the County Act Review Committee's report encouraged the critics of county government who felt that county education was being "short-changed," the legislature has not acted on the committee's recommendations.

Since the inception of county government, the Alberta Teachers' Association (ATA) has been its unrelenting foe. The association's 1987 report on the County Act, which was submitted to the Minister of Municipal Affairs, stated its basic premise: "education is sufficiently important to warrant its own independent local government."[33] If over the years county councillors had been generous with educational funding, the ATA might have been more tolerant of county government, but for the most part this has not happened. The ATA explained why labour unease, teacher frustration, and strikes occurred in a number of northern Alberta counties: "There are . . . frustrations over money for roads, culverts and grading but not for schools and frustrations over county councillors who don't care one bit about the education system other than to make sure that teachers are kept in their place."[34] In reply, county councillors insist that education is well funded but that tax dollars are occasionally squandered by the educational establishment.

In recent years many citizens have allied themselves with teachers in opposing county government. Some critics manoeuvred county councils into conducting referendums on the continuance of county government but, to their chagrin, the electorate overwhelmingly supported the county form.[35]

The focus of controversy in Strathcona was the representational imbalance between rural and urban councillors. Four rural councillors represented 38 percent of the county's population while another four members represented the hamlet of Sherwood Park, with 62 percent of the county's population. Following the 1986 municipal election the council chose as reeve a person who lived adjacent to Sherwood Park, but representation continued to be an issue. Encouraged by the Department of Municipal Affairs, which had directed the county to adjust its electoral boundaries to reflect population numbers more accurately, several councillors proposed the immediate realignment of electoral boundaries. In early 1987 the council considered implementing a comprehensive study of the county's future, but realized such a study might not satisfy the electorate. A plebiscite was called for April 6 to decide whether or not to preserve the existing county system or adopt another form of government.[36] After a raucous political campaign, 35 percent of the electorate turned out and 9,331 of 10,615 voters (88 percent) favoured continuing the existing system. However, less than a year later the Strathcona Board of Education struck a committee to examine the feasibility of separating the school board from the county. Perhaps to avert another campaign to dismantle the county, in the spring of 1989 the size of council was increased, making the ratio five to four in favour of the urban councillors.

In 1956, four years after the County of Ponoka was created, residents voted to retain the county system. In 1989 the educational establishment and Citizens for County Change led a campaign to convert the county into a municipal district with an independent educational government. Arguing that county councillors could not be expected to understand complex educational questions in addition to municipal matters, they presented a 477-signature petition to council calling for a referendum on the issue. On March 6 the electorate voted 1,552 to 537 to retain the county system.

Shortly after being elected to the Grande Prairie council in 1986, B. Desrosiers argued that councillors were too busy to manage both educational and municipal affairs. A seven-day strike by teachers in the fall of 1987 sparked a campaign by a portion of the educational establishment and many parents for an elective school board. Parents for Change collected enough signatures to force a plebiscite on changing the county into a municipal district,[37] but the council ruled not only that a number of signatures were illegal, making the remainder insufficient, but also that the County Act itself invalidated such plebiscites. Members of the educational establishment in the County of Camrose also argued it should revert to municipal district status, with an independently elected school board. In 1983 an elected school trustee for the Village of Hay Lakes initiated an unsuccessful petition for a referendum on the form of the county's government.

The provincial government is concerned about inequities in educational representation on county councils, and it is likely that in the near future county government will again be examined with a view to making major changes in its structure. The County Act Review Committee report proposed a "provision for the establishment of modified counties" which would closely follow the structure of the traditional municipal district. Moreover, even the Department of Municipal Affairs does not seem entirely satisfied with the county system. In 1989 one of its senior bureaucrats said that the advantages of centralized administration in a county system may be offset by the "fuzzy focus" of divided county administration and the time commitment county councillors must make in order to attend both school board and municipal meetings.[38] Perhaps even more important is that in asking to have its own "independent local government," the educational establishment implicitly favours accountability in financing, with education units setting rates and collecting taxes.[39]

Hospital Districts

The government's role in medical and public health care has changed dramatically in the past hundred years. At the turn of the century, the government assumed responsibility only for controlling epidemics and maintaining minimal health standards. Medical care and hospital service were regarded as purely private matters and, for the most part, hospitals were administered and supported by churches and charitable societies. When the public finally accepted a governmental role in the provision of health facilities, the responsibility was felt to be a local one. Hospitals were initially established only in the large cities; rural areas did not have an adequate financial base.

The Public Health Act enacted in Alberta in 1906 provided for the establishment of a Provincial Board of Health, health districts, and local health boards. The Rural Municipalities Act enacted in 1912 made municipalities responsible for health and the prevention of infectious and contagious diseases. Shortly thereafter, the newly formed United Farmers of Alberta (UFA) began to criticize the Liberal government for its short-sighted hospital and health policies. After delegates to a 1917 UFA convention passed a resolution calling for the division of the province into hospital districts of approximately equal size, the Liberal government enacted the Municipal Hospital Act.[40] However, the act was defective and had to be re-enacted a year later. In 1919 a cabinet-level department of health was established.

The provincial government had attempted to induce local governments to build and operate hospitals by providing a grant of 70 cents a day for each hospital patient. This grant was far too small to enable rural municipalities to operate hospitals. Consequently, rural residents were particularly supportive of the Municipal Hospital Act, which provided for the development of a hospitalization plan to serve hospital district residents.

Hospital districts were designed to be strong local institutions with policy-making and financial powers. After one or more municipalities petitioned to have their geographic area designated as a hospital district, a provisional hospital board was appointed which drafted provisions for the new district. To ensure political support, a plebiscite had to be held before the district could be created. If the vote was positive, the provisional board was replaced by one comprising a designated number of representatives directly elected by the ratepayers in each ward in the hospital district. As the district's policy-making body, the board had wide-reaching powers to purchase land, construct facilities, operate an ambulance service, and generally oversee hospital operations. The district obtained its revenue from three sources: patient fees, the provincial grant of 70 cents a day per patient, and requisitions from local units of government within its boundaries.

The first three districts were formed in 1918 and 1919 were operational by 1929. Constrained by the scarcity of local fiscal resources during the Depression, few new districts were established during the 1930s, but when more local funds became available after the Second World War their number grew rapidly, reaching 80 by 1960.

A hospital policy enacted in 1959 divided the province into 32 potential auxiliary hospital districts. In 1964 eighteen auxiliary hospital districts were incorporated with their own boards to provide long-term treatment and care for patients with chronic illnesses. The same year the Nursing Homes Act made it possible to amalgamate some 30 private nursing homes in the province with auxiliary hospital districts, which were then designated as auxiliary hospital and nursing home districts. By the end of 1964, 18 auxiliary hospital and nursing home districts had been formed. In areas not served by auxiliary hospital districts, nursing home districts were established.

In 1961 a new Hospitals Act provided for the establishment of general hospital districts to provide "acute" or "active" care. In order to straighten out the tangle of different types of districts, the Hospitals Act was changed in 1970 to allow the establishment of multi-purpose health care districts. Municipal and general hospital districts were permitted to amalgamate with auxiliary hospital and/or nursing home districts and to operate under a single district board.[41] Following are the number of different kinds of health care districts in Alberta in 1991.

Municipal and General Hospital Districts	29
General/Auxiliary Hospital Districts	1
General/Auxiliary Hospital/Nursing Home Districts	71
General Hospital/Nursing Home Districts	3
Auxiliary Hospital/Nursing Home Districts	7
Auxiliary Hospital Districts	1
Nursing Home Districts	2
Districts without hospitals, with active governing boards	4
Districts without hospitals, without active governing boards	4

Today the majority of health care districts are governed by five- and six-member boards of trustees which can be elected, appointed, or have a combination of elected and appointed members.[42] Section 27 of the Hospital Act states that "the board has full control of that hospital and has absolute and final authority in respect of all matters pertaining to the operation of the hospital." In her 1984 address as President of the Alberta Hospitals Association, Lois A. Radcliffe explained that the role of the hospital board "can be divided into three interrelated roles: a management role; a political role; and a community relations role." She added that "in order to formulate policies, the members of the board must be kept well informed . . . be familiar with statutes and regulations, hospital and medical staff bylaws, contracts and agreements . . . as well as the quality of medical care, financing, technologies, and the administration of the institution."[43]

Hospital trustees are unique in that they represent two constituencies. The traditional one comprises district residents, who elect hospital representatives directly or elect a municipal council that appoints members to the board. Their other constituency is composed of hospital district patients. The board monitors expenses and user charges to ensure that hospitals are operating efficiently and providing services at the minimum cost. Trustees work very closely with the board-appointed hospital administrator to ensure that patients' interests are protected.

As the provincial government assumed more responsibility for health care, the grass-roots principles under which hospital districts were governed began to erode. One change made in the Hospital Act in 1955 allowed municipal councils to decide whether hospital board members were to be appointed or elected. If they were to be appointed, the trustees could be from either the council or the public. So many hospital trustees were being appointed rather than elected that a resolution was passed at the 1983 AUMA convention which read in part:

WHEREAS the most effective, efficient, and responsive hospital operation requires direct accountability of the trustees of the Hospital District to the citizens thereof; and
WHEREAS the result of such a mixture of appointed and elected trustees is that the Board in total is still not accountable to the electorate, particularly if the elected trustees are in the minority compared with appointed trustees. . . .
BE IT RESOLVED that the Government of Alberta be requested to make it mandatory that all Hospital Board trustees be elected in accordance with the Local Authorities Act.[44]

Table 4.3   Elected and Appointed Hospital and Nursing District Boards
in Alberta (1984)

Hospital Board Type	Municipal and General Hospital Distr.		General Hospital and Nursing Home Dist.		General, Auxiliary Hospital, and Nursing Home Dist.		Auxiliary and Nursing Home Dist.		Nursing Home Dist.	
	No.	%	No.	%	No.	%	No.	%	No.	%
Appointed	9	22	5	56	5	12	6	60	1	50
Elected	9	22	0	0	8	20	0	0	1	50
Part Elected & Part Appointed	23	56	4	44	28	68	4	40	0	0
Total	41	100	9	100	41	100	10	100	2	100

In 1984 a Hospital Election Act requiring that all trustees be elected was introduced in the legislature by Dr. D.J. Carter (Progressive Conservative from Calgary Egmont). The statistics he used in his presentation are shown in Table 4.3.[45]

Particularly striking is the large number of hospital boards in 1984 whose membership was composed solely of appointed members and the small number with wholly elected boards. Moreover, the number of elected trustees in the "elected" and "part elected and part appointed" categories is overstated, since it includes elected members of a municipal council appointed by that council to a hospital board. A 1984 report commissioned by the Alberta Hospital Association (AHA) entitled "Alberta Trusteeship: Strength In Caring" found that out of 629 board members, 354 were appointed and only 275 were elected (this latter figure included the municipal appointed members). The AHA, which has a history of opposing all-elective boards, argued that there was little if any difference between a directly elected trustee and a municipal councillor appointed as a trustee. "Both types of trustees are popularly elected . . . the municipal councillor cannot be seen as less responsive. . . ."[46] Unfortunately, the AHA provided no data to indicate that directly and indirectly elected hospital trustees were equally responsive.[47]

When another bill requiring the direct election of hospital trustees was introduced in 1987, proponents of the status quo included Dianne Mirosh, a Tory member from Calgary, who said she supported "a balanced blend of democratic process" with a hospital board composed of both elected and appointed members. She explained that elections were costly and time-consuming and would prevent many devoted people from serving on hospital boards.[48] The bill quickly died after the New Democrats' health critic charged that many of the trustee appointments were governed by political patronage and Tory cronyism.[49] When the direct election of trustees was again proposed a year later, the Minister of Hospitals and Medical Care said the Alberta Hospital Association had convinced him that such legislation would not be in the best interests of either hospitals or the public.[50]

Hospital boards are currently elected in Drumheller, Ponoka, Lacombe, and Red Deer. In 1987 the Stettler town council passed a resolution to "support in principle the concept of an elected hospital board,"[51] but the following year the town learned that the county favoured a board composed of both appointed and elective members.[52] In early 1989 residents of the City of Wetaskiwin requested an elective board for the Wetaskiwin Hospital District after hospital employees and the public complained that board meetings were closed and trustees were unresponsive to their needs. Closely related was a request that the board, with an almost wholly appointive membership, be expanded from nine to eleven members and that Wetaskiwin's representation be increased from three to four. The rationale for the request was that the city was growing faster than the county.[53] That same year a Grande Prairie county councillor advocated elective health boards that "would allow through direct democracy the discussion and input of the general public concerning health questions."[54] Although most municipalities were attempting to democratize hospital boards in 1989, the Town of High River decided to appoint members to the High River Hospital Board rather than electing them, as had been the practice for some years.[55]

Irrigation Districts[56]

Southern Alberta, with its sparse vegetation, long winters, and hot, dry summers, was not attractive to settlers during the province's early period. Several large irrigation projects developed with private financing never became economically viable, although legacies of this early entrepreneurship, the Alberta Railway and Irrigation Company and the Canadian Pacific Railway irrigation works in southern Alberta, have been incorporated in the present irrigation districts. Recognizing that private ventures would be inadequate, Alberta enacted the 1915 Irrigation District Act that allowed farmers to organize for the purpose of floating bond issues for the construction of irrigation projects. Six additional irrigation district acts were enacted between 1919 and 1968, when a single Irrigation Act replaced all previous irrigation legislation.

Today almost one million acres in southern Alberta are served by 13 irrigation districts ranging in size from the Ross Creek District, with 527.6 hectares (1,319 acres), to the St. Mary River District, with 109,720.4 hectares (274,301 acres). In addition to water for irrigation, district reservoirs provide drinking water for approximately 125,000 people in 50 municipalities.

The Irrigation Act explicitly describes two very different kinds of districts. An "outer boundary district" encompasses all of the land parcels within its boundaries although only parcels which receive water are on the assessment roll, while a "parcel system" recognizes only parcels on the assessment roll as being within the district.

The farmers holding land in an irrigation district elect a board of directors charged with policy making and administration. The Irrigation Act gives the board wide-ranging powers that may have a major effect on every farmer in its jurisdiction. Each year the board establishes an annual water rate to cover the cost of operating and maintaining the district. Since irrigation rates are a charge against land, if an irrigation district bill is not paid the district can place a lien against the crops grown on the land. The district even has the power to take title to the land in question and sell it to recover the money that it is owed. The board also can contract with parties outside of the district for irrigation waters and negotiate government-guaranteed loans for operating costs and capital replacement. Section 44 of the act allows the board to enter into cost-sharing agreements with the governments of Canada and Alberta as well as other local authorities for the construction, extension, and rehabilitation of a district's irrigation works.

The size of an irrigation district's board of directors is determined by the size of the district. Under the Irrigation Act, the board consists of three directors where the assessment roll of a district shows that 36,000 hectares (90,000 acres) or less are classified as irrigation land; five directors in districts with 36,000 to 80,000 hectares (200,000 acres) of irrigation land; and seven directors in districts with more than 80,000 hectares of irrigation land. The directors have a three-year term of office. A district may elect a new board every three years or stagger the elections and hold them annually. Although board members are often elected by acclamation, when elections are contested the turnout is in the range of 25 to 40 percent. In explaining an electoral turnout of 25 percent, an irrigation district administrator said that it indicated people generally were satisfied with irrigation policy and felt they could easily discuss any problems with irrigation officials, who were always accessible.[57]

An irrigation district is administered by a manager appointed by the board of directors. The manager is responsible for hiring and overseeing an administrative and operating staff and for keeping the district's records.

An irrigation district would seem to exemplify local self-government and grass-roots democracy. Its formation depends on a petition from landowners within the proposed district boundaries and its elected board of directors is given wide-ranging policy-making and administrative powers. In addition, the Irrigation Act outlines in detail the procedure a board uses to poll the district's electorate on questions of policy. But it is here that democracy begins to break down, for the act (Section 105) states explicitly that "the board is not bound by the results" of any poll. This is just one manifestation of the provincial government's reluctance, from the first Irrigation Act in 1915 to the present, to give farmers the power and responsibility to manage their own affairs.

The main instrument the province has at its disposal to control the activities of irrigation district boards is the Irrigation Council, a provincial agency with at least seven government appointees. Council members must be water-users but not members of the civil service. Appointments to the council are made by the Minister of Agriculture, the Assistant Deputy Minister of Environmental Engineering Support Services, and the Department of Agriculture's Director of the Irrigation Division; the chairperson is selected from the appointees by the Minister of Agriculture.

Although the ostensible purpose of the Irrigation Council is to develop and coordinate a province-wide irrigation policy, it has the power to shape the membership of irrigation boards and to influence and overturn their decisions. When an irrigation district is formed, the council appoints its first board of trustees and designates one of the appointees as chairperson. Subsequent boards are elected; however, the council has the power to dismiss any or all members of a board and appoint new ones if: (1) the board has defaulted on the payment of any of its liabilities; (2) the board is not complying with the Irrigation Act and as a consequence the interests of the district's water users have been harmed; and (3) "there exists with respect to the board or the district any state of affairs of a serious nature that is or may be prejudicial to the interests of the water users or the board's creditors." This last provision gives the council almost unlimited power to control the composition of a board of trustees. Equally important, the annual water rate set by the district board must be approved by the Irrigation Council. The board also needs permission from the council before it is allowed to borrow money for capital projects.

Most irrigation district boards work amazingly well, with disagreements about rates, water flows, and delinquent accounts being settled informally by the district manager. In the event that a question related to assessment rates cannot be resolved informally, the complainant has recourse to a Court of Revision made up of all the board's members. Complainants who remain dissatisfied can appeal to the Alberta Assessment Appeal Board. In 1990 the government established an "Irrigation Appeal Tribunal" to resolve disputes between water users and irrigation district boards without costly legal action.

In recent years irrigation districts have faced many complex and controversial issues. For example, in order to expand an irrigation reservoir's storage facility, it is often necessary to flood adjoining farmland. As a result, a large acreage is taken out of production, with the consequent loss of tax revenue, and an angry farmer may bear a life-long grudge against the district.

Although irrigation districts are seldom in the news, the government is well aware of their importance. In 1980 the province announced that it was providing $123 million from the Heritage Trust Fund to fund a new Irrigation Headworks and Main Irrigation Systems Improvement program. The largest project funded was the rehabilitation and expansion of the Lethbridge Northern Irrigation District's main canal, which provided irrigation to an additional 70,000 hectares of land.

In the future, the control of water resources will become increasingly important. If drought conditions continue in the American West and Midwest there will be increasing pressure on western Canada to channel its water to the United States, and irrigation districts in southern Alberta will be caught in the middle between American and Canadian agricultural interests. The provincial government is currently considering the possibility of transporting water from the Mackenzie Valley to drought-prone areas of southern Alberta. If such a project is ever approved, new irrigation districts will be created and the responsibilities of existing districts will be greatly increased. As new canals are constructed decisions will have to be made as to which agricultural interests will receive water and at what price.

Drainage Districts

Very few Albertans are aware of the drainage districts in the central and western parts of the province, all of which practise a form of grass-roots democracy. Nine drainage districts, ranging in size from 2,600 to 74,720 acres, have been established for flood control, lake-level stabilization, and the improvement of soil drainage. The first, the Holden Drainage District established in 1918, was followed by the Dickson and Daysland Districts in 1919 and the Hay Lakes District in 1922. The other five districts (Bearshill Lake, Manawan, Cameron, Big Hay Lake, and Cygnet) were not formed until the late 1940s and 1950s.

For the most part, the day-to-day operations of drainage districts are financed by drainage service charges and a drainage ditch improvement grant from the Alberta Water Management and Erosion Control Program. Although drainage districts received $234,000 in provincial grants for 1989/90, the amount was decreased to $207,000 for 1990/91.

The 1990 statement of revenue and expenditure for the Holden Drainage District illustrates the importance of provincial grants. The district raised 34 percent of its revenue ($26,411) from drainage service charges and penalties and 56 percent ($43,000) from a 1990 government grant.[58] Administrative costs accounted for only 4.8 percent of total district expenditures. With the exception of a minuscule amount for banking, the rest of the funds were spent on brushing, bank leveling, ditch maintenance and cleaning, and culvert and bridge maintenance. The 1990 statement for Hay Lakes shows that it also maintained a lean administration, expending its funds almost solely for ditching.

The policy-making and administrative structure of drainage districts is similar to that of irrigation districts. A board composed of three elected trustees is the policy-making body which establishes drainage rates and decides which drainage projects are necessary and determines the amount of debentures needed for them. In order to vote for the trustees a person must be a Canadian citizen at least 18 years old who owns land in the irrigation district. Since there are fewer than 200 eligible voters in each district,[59] it seems that drainage districts effectively meld direct and representative democracy. An annual meeting is held at which the eligible voters elect trustees and express their concerns and policy preferences to the board. In most cases, however, the nominees are unopposed and the election is by acclamation. As an example, over a 20-year period it was necessary to hold only one election in the Holden Drainage District.[60]

If an election is held, an interesting procedure is required by the Drainage Districts Act. The district's secretary lists the trustees in order of the number of votes they received, with the trustee having received the fewest votes at the top of the list. "Each year the trustee whose name appears first on the list shall retire to make room for the trustee elected at the annual meeting." At their first meeting, the trustees elect a chairperson from their own ranks. They then appoint the secretary-treasurer and any other administrative and engineering personnel required, although the secretary-treasurer is often the only administrator.

When a debenture is needed the board of trustees drafts a bylaw which is submitted to those eligible to vote on drainage district matters. A super-majority of two-thirds of those voting is required to pass a debenture bylaw. Monies raised through the sale of debentures are used for the construction of drainage works as well as for a district's operation, although the use of debenture money for the latter is unusual.

Despite what seems to be almost an ideal model for democratic government in a small polity, the provincial government carefully controls the activities of a drainage district's trustees. Section 64 of the Drainage Districts Act gives the Lieutenant-Governor in Council power to order an election of new trustees or at any time appoint an official trustee, who is given the same powers as the board, to conduct the affairs of a district. A provincial Drainage Council, consisting of no more than three members appointed by the Lieutenant-Governor in Council, has almost total control over the activities of drainage district trustees. The rates established by a board of trustees must be approved by the Drainage Council, as must any debenture issues. In addition, the council can require a board to furnish information on anything it has done or is proposing to do, and has the power to "forbid an act or course of conduct proposed to be done or entered upon by a board." In short, when drainage district government is realistically examined, it becomes clear that the province allows the districts very little autonomy.

Regional Service Commissions

In the 1970s many municipalities were concerned that their service infrastructures were not capable of meeting the needs of the ever-increasing numbers of people entering the province. In both large and small municipalities, sewage, water treatment, and waste disposal systems were in danger of being overwhelmed in a few years. Moreover, it would be necessary for municipalities to purchase sophisticated equipment to meet the province's new environmental standards. Although some municipalities cooperated to produce and deliver these services in order to realize economies of scale, many small municipalities feared that if a larger municipality provided them with services their autonomy would be jeopardized. The larger municipality might apply to amalgamate them, arguing that as long as it was providing services to outlying municipalities, it also should be governing their areas of jurisdiction.

In 1975 the Alberta Department of the Environment carried out a study to determine "the most appropriate way to develop the water supply and sewage disposal facilities . . . to the year 2001" for the Edmonton metropolitan region.[61] Later a number of provincial departments, the Edmonton Regional Planning Commission, and several private consultants carried out another study which was released in July 1978, just before Edmonton's expansion bid for St. Albert and the County of Strathcona. The report, which recommended that several regional authorities be established to develop and provide water and sewer facilities, was criticized by the City of Edmonton because the recommendations undercut its expansionist arguments.[62] The region's outlying municipalities gave guarded approval to the proposals, for they could see regional authorities as a feasible alternative to amalgamation with Edmonton. In December 1981 the provincial legislature passed the Regional Municipal Services Act which created multi-purpose regional service commissions (RSCs).

Section 3 of the Regional Municipal Services Act states that the objectives of the commissions are "to provide water, sanitary and storm sewerage and waste management services . . . with respect to more than one municipality." The act gives a newly created commission substantial powers, including the right to expropriate a municipal utility within the district's boundaries and the ability to float bonds and debentures to finance the building and operation of water and sewer plants and lines and waste disposal sites. A RSC project does not adversely affect the municipal debt capacity of the commission's individual municipal members.[63]

The size of the commission board and the number of representatives from each member municipality are determined by the Minister of Municipal Affairs. Since the boundaries of a service commission encompass several municipalities, each municipality designates one or more councillors to serve on the board. In other words, representation is indirect. Each RSC is given the authority to enact its own bylaws and board decisions are made by majority rule. However, under Section 13, if there is a dispute between one RSC and another one or between an RSC and a municipality over rates or compensation, "the dispute may be submitted to the Public Utilities Board for an order on any terms and conditions that the Public Utilities Board may impose."

Initially, multi-functional RSCs were envisioned that would carry out a variety of services related to water, sewage, storm sewers, and waste management. However, since the early RSCs evolved to give water boards greater financial and organizational flexibility, they were uni-functional. As an example, the Parkland Water Board became the Capital Region Parkland Water Services Commission, the Northeast Water Board became the Northeast Water Services Commission, and the Strathcona Leduc Water Board became Capital Region Southwest Water Services Commission.

Of the current 15 regional service commissions, six are suppliers of water (Henry Kruger Regional Water Services, Capital Region Northeast Water Services, Capital Region Parkland Water Services, Capital Region Southwest Water Services, Capital Region Vegreville Corridor Water Services, and Highway 14 Regional Water Services).[64] Three regional service commissions are organized for the collection of sewage (Tri-village Regional Sewage Services, Northeast Pigeon Lake Regional Services, and Capital Region Sewage) and four are concerned with waste management (Big Country Waste Management, Lethbridge Regional Waste Management, North Forty Mile Regional Waste, and Long Lake Regional Waste Commission). Two regional service commissions have dual responsibilities. The Foothills Regional Service Commission is responsible for sewage collection and waste management, while the Cold Lake/Grand Centre Regional Utility Service Commission supplies water and collects sewage.

Although the structures of regional planning commissions and regional service commissions are similar, in that their membership comprises municipalities in the commission's service area, there is far more conflict on planning commissions. Of seven regional service commissions which responded to a mail survey in late 1991, only two mentioned any conflict on the commission board and in both cases it was negligible. As of 1991, only small urban and rural municipalities have been members of regional service commissions. There is little doubt that if a service commission is created that includes both large and small municipalities, it will encounter the same type of conflict over representation and rural versus urban rights that occurs on regional planning commissions.

Alberta Metis Settlements, Democracy and Self-Determination

Alberta has only recently taken steps to rectify the neglect of its Metis population by providing it with land and some degree of self-determination. Tom Pocklington documents the government's policy for the Metis, which was much worse than that for the country's Indians who, by treaty, secured legal title to large blocks of land and were given agricultural implements, ammunition, free education, and medical care. In contrast, "At the end of the nineteenth century and in the early decades of the twentieth century, most of the Metis were living in scattered bands, landless, disease ridden, and without hope of pursuing their traditional manner of life."[65] After a well-meaning Roman Catholic priest convinced the federal government to establish a farming community for Metis to be run by the church, the colony of St. Paul des Metis was founded in 1896 in the east-central part of the province. The church was apparently more concerned with propagating the faith than teaching farming methods, and the colony failed and was dissolved twelve years later.[66]

Little was heard of the Metis in the early part of the century, for they were not visible in the cities and were not represented in government. At the onset of the depression, fearful that they would lose what little the government had given them, the Metis established the Metis Association of Alberta (MAA) in 1932 to represent their interests. Through some shrewd political manoeuvres that included playing off one political party against the other, the MAA persuaded the government to create a royal commission to examine "the problems of health, education and general welfare of the half-breed population of the Province."[67] In 1936 the Ewing Commission, as it was called, submitted a shoddy 15-page document calling for the establishment of two isolated colonies where Metis could learn how to farm but at the same time follow their traditional ways.

The government responded to the Ewing Commission recommendations in 1938 by enacting the Metis Population Betterment Act specifying how an association which would control and administer a colony should be established, the form it should take, the procedures to be followed for elections, and the relationship between the association and the government. Pocklington notes that when the act was amended in 1940 the sections calling for "conferences and negotiations between the Government of the Province and representatives of the Metis population of the Province" were expunged and sections were added "which grant legal powers to the cabinet, to the minister with the approval of cabinet, or to the minister alone."[68] The government was able to control the Metis associations at every turn.

Shortly after the passage of the act, a committee of Metis leaders and government officials began meeting to discuss the establishment of colonies. Seven were founded in 1938 and 1939. Over time the colonies amalgamated and split; in 1960 the government closed an uninhabited settlement, as well as an ongoing one. Eight settlements existed when the Metis finally achieved a modicum of self-government in 1990.

The government's paternalistic stance in its relationship with the settlements seems to have been of little concern to the Metis until 1960, when the Metis Population Trust Account was established by an order in council. Revenue for the trust was to come from timber and grazing leases, hay permits, surface right compensation from oil companies, and "all moneys received from the sale or lease of any other of the natural resources of the areas."[69] The Metis interpreted this clause to mean that sub-surface oil revenue was to be a source of trust revenue, although the government asserted that this was neither the intention nor the meaning of the order. Anti-government feelings simmered until 1975, when the Federation of Metis Settlements of Alberta (FMSA) was incorporated to press legal action for oil royalty revenue which had accrued to the provincial government from Metis settlement lands since the late 1930s. Relationships between the government and the FMSA hit a low point in 1979 when government agents raided the eight settlement offices and seized materials relevant to Metis litigation. Shortly thereafter responsibility for the Metis was transferred from the Department of Social Services to the Department of Municipal Affairs, which established the Metis Development Branch. In a parallel move there was an investigation by the provincial ombudsman and a joint Metis and government committee was established to review the Metis Population Betterment Act. Perhaps stung by criticism of his government's treatment of the Metis, in 1985 Peter Lougheed worked out an agreement in principle to guarantee them settlement lands and political rights.

After lengthy negotiations the government and the FMSA reached a series of compromises which culminated in 1990 in the passage of four relevant acts. The FMSA agreed to terminate its lawsuit to obtain oil royalties and to relinquish its stand on the ownership of subsurface mineral rights. In return, the Metis were guaranteed the ownership of their settlement lands (480,000 hectares, or 1,875 square miles) and provided $30 million a year ($15 million for capital projects, $10 million for operations and maintenance, and $5 million for future development) for seven years for the development of education and recreational complexes. After that the settlements would receive $10 million annually for ten years. The most controversial legislation was the Metis Settlement Act.

The Settlement Act established eight settlement corporations governed by elected councils with extensive powers to control their own destinies and finances.[70] Each council is composed of five members with a chairperson selected by the councillors from among themselves. Elections are held annually; since councillors have a three-year term of office, one or two are elected each year. Although the councils' powers and responsibilities are identical in some respects to those granted to municipalities by the Municipal Government Act, there are substantial differences. One of these is that it is extremely difficult for Metis councils to change settlement policy through legislation, since Section 222 stipulates that the 24 major policy areas designated as "General Council Policies" cannot be altered without the unanimous approval of all eight councils. Even if all of the settlement councils agree on a particular policy change, it is still subject to a ministerial veto under Section 224.[71] Additional sections of the Settlement Act give the Minister of Municipal Affairs extraordinary powers. Under Section 176, "if the Minister considers that the affairs of a settlement are managed in an irregular, improper or improvident manner," he or she has the power to dismiss one or more councillors as well as any of the settlement administrators or to "direct the settlement council or an employee or official of the settlement to take any action that the Minister considers proper in the circumstances." Sections concerning conflict of interest are also much stronger than those found in the Municipal Government Act.[72] Under Section 16, a candidate for council who fails to file a financial disclosure statement with the returning officer is disqualified. Section 25(e) disqualifies a councillor if "the councillor uses information gained through his or her position as a councillor that would not have been available to the councillor as a member of the public to gain a financial benefit either directly or indirectly."

When the Metis Settlement bill was before the legislative assembly, members of the opposition took the government to task for giving the Minister of Municipal Affairs authority to disqualify councillors and almost unlimited veto power over the actions of the settlement councils. The government responded that the bill was drafted jointly with the Metis and ratified by Metis settlement members by a margin of 77.6 percent in favour, with a 67 percent turnout rate.[73] A 1985 article in *Municipal Counsellor* explains the government's position. Both the Director of the Metis Development Branch and the Assistant Deputy Minister of the Improvement Districts Operations Division, in discussing new legislation governing the rights and responsibilities of Metis, carefully avoided the term "self-government" and instead used "self-administration."[74] When the Metis government acts received their second reading in the legislature in 1990, Robert Hawkesworth, New Democrat from Calgary Mountain View, noted that they were "not establishing self-government for Metis people on Metis settlements" but rather, "it's clear that what's being followed by the government with this legislation is to establish a form of local government." The Attorney General, Ken Rostad, was quick to respond that self-determination, not self-government, was being promoted. Moreover, "this is unique, made-in-Alberta, not imposed by the Government of Alberta on the Metis, but developed together to something that we think they can work with, that they think they can work with. . . . The government structure that's proposed in these Bills is the structure that the Metis want, not the structure that we are trying to impose on them."[75]

An Experiment in Nondemocratic Government

A single case of the province wielding almost dictatorial control at the local level occurred in the Fort McMurray region in 1973 and 1974. During the development of the Syncrude oil sands plant, workers and materials were brought into the area so quickly that a public service catastrophe seemed imminent. The provincial government responded by creating the Northeast Alberta Regional Commission on June 6, 1974. Its mandate was to ensure that the public services, facilities, and accommodations needed for the development of the oil sands were "provided in an orderly and efficient manner." More specifically, the commission was to coordinate provincial government policies and interests with those of municipalities and the private sector in order to provide housing, educational facilities, and urban planning in the Fort McMurray area. The commission also was to ensure that, if the area's unprecedented growth continued, there would be minimum friction between government and the private sector. From the time it was created the commission was controversial, for it gave almost unlimited powers to a single commissioner appointed by the Lieutenant-Governor in Council.

The commissioner had the power to override provincial legislation and to formulate and carry out policy. The act creating the commission allowed the commissioner to: (1) exercise power binding the local authority; (2) do anything that a local authority is required to do by bylaw or resolution; and (3) execute any agreement on behalf of the local authority. The act further stated that "a local authority *may not exercise* [emphasis added] the power, duty or right assigned, or any other power, duty or right so as to effectively interfere with the exercise by the Commissioner of any power, duty or right assigned to him." Finally, the act stated:

> to enable the Commissioner to carry out his functions with the diligence and dispatch that the circumstances may require, the Lieutenant-Governor in Council may make regulations, with respect to the Region, varying, substituting, adding to or making inapplicable any of

the provisions of the following Acts and the regulations thereunder: (a) The Improvement District Act; (b) The New Towns Act; (c) The Municipal Government Act; (d) The Municipal Election Act; (e) The Municipal Taxation Act; (f) The Planning Act; (g) The Local Authorities Act; (h) The School Act; (i) The School Election Act; (j) The Northlands School Division Act; (k) The Alberta Hospitals Act; (l) The Health Unit Act.

The only power denied the commissioner was the authority to levy a tax or impose a licence fee.

Fortunately, Fort McMurray's first and only commissioner, R.V. Henning, had no interest in exercising many of his all-encompassing powers. Henning had just retired as a commodore from the Canadian Navy and settled into a position at the Banff School of Advanced Management when he was asked to become the first commissioner. As the Fort McMurray boom gained momentum, he ensured that the necessary public service infrastructure was put in place. In 1975 he took one of his first major actions when he overruled provincial legislation preventing the construction of new schools until existing schools were 80 percent filled. Without additional space, some of the new families would have been unable to place their children in the school system.

When Fort McMurray was granted city status and began to manage its own affairs in 1980, the commission became less important. With the collapse of the Alsands Project and a delay in heavy oil development at Cold Lake, the boom ended, and with it the need for the commission. Its operations were discontinued in September 1982, and it was finally phased out the following spring. Few people realized what immense power the government had delegated to a single person for almost a decade.

Improvement and Rural Districts

Improvement districts, which are administered by the Department of Municipal Affairs, are located primarily in sparsely populated rural areas that cannot finance their own local government services. Although the 18 improvement districts account for 67 percent of the province's land area, they have a population of only about 62,800. Table 4.4 reveals striking disparities in population among improvement districts.

Until quite recently the Department of Municipal Affairs held the position that it was not feasible for an improvement district with a small population and a limited tax base to become self-governing. As a conse-

Table 4.4 Improvement Districts and Their 1991 Populations[76]

I.D. No. 4 Waterton	150	I.D. No. 16	5,332
I.D. No. 5	409	I.D. No. 17	11,539
I.D. No. 6	128	I.D. No. 18	9,193
I.D. No. 8	7	I.D. No. 19	1,620
I.D. No. 9 Banff	1,461	I.D. No. 20	2,922
I.D. No. 12 Jasper	4,475	I.D. No. 21	2,992
I.D. No. 13 Elk Island	29	I.D. No. 22	3,991
I.D. No. 14	8,536	I.D. No. 23	6,942
I.D. No. 15	2,801	I.D. No. 24 Wood Buffalo	282
I.D. Total Population		62,809	

quence, the department provided public services to improvement district residents. Alberta Transportation assisted in the construction and maintenance of roadways and the Forestry branch supplied fire protection in wooded areas. School districts and divisions requisitioned the Department of Municipal Affairs for funds.

Despite the pervasive influence of the provincial government in the affairs of improvement districts, they resemble municipal districts so much that they are often referred to as "rural municipalities" in legislation. They have municipal planning commissions, development appeal boards, and courts of revision that function in the same way as in incorporated municipalities, and they also receive municipal assistance grants. However, improvement districts differ from regular municipalities in two important areas, policy making and administration.

As a result of a movement in 1942 to convert some of the more economically viable improvement districts into municipal districts and to consolidate others into larger and more efficient units, their number decreased from 216 in 1941 to 61 in 1944. There were 50 improvement districts in 1961, 24 in 1969, and only 18 today, five of them coterminous with park boundaries.

No mechanism existed that allowed improvement district residents to express their policy or administrative preferences until 1957, when the first appointed resident advisory committee was organized in what was to become Improvement District No. 10. Although most districts eventually had resident advisory committees, a member of the first one, without elaborating, characterized its first two years as a "very rough start."[77]

The government did not take the advice of the committees very seriously. In 1974 Marvin Moore, who was later to become Minister of Municipal Affairs, said, "at least their views are taken into consideration much more than they were during the early years."[78] Surprisingly few residents expressed dissatisfaction with this arrangement, even though autonomy would mean that the districts would receive less revenue from the provincial government, with a corresponding increase in property taxes.[79]

In the mid-1970s the government began to change its improvement district policies. The Improvement Districts Amendment Act allowed them to have the same services as municipal districts, and the Minister of Municipal Affairs intended to give advisory committees much more responsibility in the determination of district policy. However, the government's new policy languished until 1979, when the minister indicated that improvement districts would be undergoing major changes during the 1980s. He announced three goals for the districts: (1) to increase the number of advisory councils and councillors, particularly in the northern and remote areas of the province; (2) to encourage self-government; and (3) to decentralize decision-making and administration to the local level in order to provide a higher level of service.

As elected "advisory councils" replaced the appointed "advisory committees," the Department of Municipal Affairs hoped that improvement district residents, having experienced a measure of democracy, would be encouraged to opt for the self-governing status of a municipal district. In 1980 the Minister of Municipal Affairs stated in a speech to advisory council members that the advisory councils would have to become much more knowledgeable about the revenue-raising function of local government and should begin to consider "a lot of new things that we can call services to people."

The first test of the Municipal Affairs policy of encouraging improvement districts to become self-governing came in July 1979. The advisory council for Improvement District No. 1, located in the southeastern corner of the province, asked the Minister of Municipal Affairs to undertake a study to assess the feasibility of becoming a municipal district. Not surprisingly, a Municipal Affairs Special Projects Branch report concluded that the area could operate as a viable municipal district. Minister of Municipal Affairs Marvin Moore almost immediately began to mount a campaign to convince residents of the virtues of self-government, and funds were budgeted for pamphlets, newspaper ads, and radio announcements.

In late 1980 and early 1981, Municipal Affairs held a series of meetings throughout the district to discuss the department's report. The meetings made it clear that many residents were opposed to the change, fearing they would lose grants and subsidies which they believed would be offset by at least a six mill increase in the property tax. Minister Moore countered that taxes would increase whether the improvement district became a municipal district or not. After the 1980 election, the advisory committee's membership was almost evenly split over the issue. In April 1981, with a 40 percent turnout, 295 residents voted in favour of becoming a municipal district and 518 against.

After Municipal Affairs lost this skirmish, the department's tactics changed under the direction of a new minister, Julian Koziak. Provincial subsidies for improvement districts were cut and discussions were held on the feasibility of calculating their transportation grants as if they were municipal districts. Moreover, Koziak decided unilaterally to convert several improvement districts into municipal districts, a policy hardly likely to endear him to supporters of democracy and local self-determination. After Assistant Deputy Minister Robin Ford explained in an information meeting that improvement district government "actually gives the minister of municipal affairs the powers of a kind of dictator," a member of the audience retorted, "so we have democracy imposed by dictatorship."[80]

Koziak maintained a low public profile while the Department of Municipal Affairs conducted studies on the financial and administrative feasibility of the conversions. In the early spring of 1984 he announced that improvement districts No. 1 and No. 10 would become, respectively, the Municipal District of Cypress and the Municipal District of Clearwater on January 1, 1985.[81] Next, he announced that the agricultural and rural areas of Improvement District No. 7 would be absorbed by the County of Wheatland and the municipal districts of Starland and Kneehill. Although Koziak planned that the small remaining sliver of Improvement District No. 7 would be absorbed by its neighbours or become a municipal district, neither happened.

Improvement District No. 8, located west of Calgary in the foothills around Canmore, was a special case. It was one of the districts Koziak had examined to determine whether it could be converted to a municipal district. In fact, a majority of the residents favored the conversion, since they feared portions of the improvement district would be annexed by adjoining urban municipalities. In 1982 the advisory council commissioned its own study on the feasibility of becoming a self-governing municipal district, followed by three additional studies in 1984 and 1985. Since the provincial government had already taken a portion of the improvement district in 1983 for the Kananaskis Country recreational area, and the studies concluded it would be in the improvement district's best interest to become a municipal district, the advisory council was anxious to act as quickly as possible. But now it was Municipal Affairs which stalled until it had a chance to evaluate the success of improvement districts No. 1 and No. 10. Finally, Minister of Municipal Affairs Dennis Anderson announced that effective January 1, 1988, Improvement District No. 8 would become the Municipal District of Bighorn. But residents were shocked to discover that the government had splintered off the improvement district's sour gas field, making the new municipal district half the size they had expected it to be. Many felt that a heavy price had been exacted for the right to self-government.

In order to provide direction for the provincial government's attempts to convince improvement districts that they should be self-governing and pay for their own services, the Improvement Districts Association of Alberta (IDAA) in 1989 drafted "A Framework Proposal for Increased Local Government Autonomy for Improvement District Residents." The paper explained: "The process of transition from improvement district status to Municipal District (M.D.) status has not been a predictable, well planned process and has resulted in some rather painful municipal government experiences for some I.D.s as they achieve incorporation."[82] The thrust of the IDAA's proposal was that a transitional form of government, a rural district, should be created to facilitate an improvement district's evolution into a self-governing municipal district. The report candidly discussed the transition of power and responsibility from the provincial government to a rural district as well as the importance of providing a new government with an adequate financial base. Eighteen months after the Department of Municipal Affairs received the IDAA report, it responded in a paper entitled "The Rural District: A Concept of Transitional Municipal Government." The report, which had been prepared in cooperation with the IDAA, endorsed the idea of rural districts and discussed the transition process, all the time emphasizing the development of a corporate strategy "that would outline the process and requirements leading to a long-term goal of local government autonomy."[83] The report also focused on developing an adequate financial base, identifying relevant service responsibilities, and employing an administrative staff. The importance of nurturing democratic institutions and making provisions for grass-roots democracy was ignored. Unfortunately, the Rural District Act passed in 1991 closely followed the Department of Municipal Affairs report and emphasized corporate strategy rather than the development of democratic institutions.[84]

Special Areas

In the early part of the century the federal government's policy of giving a quarter section of western land to anyone who would improve it, coupled with well-advertised low rail fares, lured hundreds of thousands of home-steaders to western Canada. The population of east-central Alberta grew rapidly after track was laid into the area in 1909, rising from only 283 residents in 1906 to 13,170 in 1911. Prospects of large crops coupled with high war-time grain prices boosted the population to 24,500 by 1916.[85]

With little knowledge of the semi-arid region's climate and no under-standing of dry-land farming practices, farmers allowed stock to over-graze the land and broke sod in areas where wheat should never have been planted. A drought which began in 1916 seemed to become progres-sively worse each succeeding year. The Tilley East bloc, more than one and one-half million acres in the southern section of the area, was partic-ularly hard hit. According to a local historian, "At the height of the settle-ment there were 2,386 resident farmers in the area but by 1924, this num-ber had declined to 645. Even in 1924 it was more puzzling to determine why anyone remained than to understand why the vast majority left."[86] After the departing settlers defaulted on their loans, financial institutions gained control of abandoned farms and acreages. It was fortunate that these institutions paid property taxes, for tax money provided the only funding for many of the bloc's small municipalities and school districts.

In 1926 the United Farmers government established a commission to investigate conditions in the Tilley East bloc. The commission's recom-mendations were incorporated into the Tilley East Area Act of 1927. Some municipalities not considered to be economically self-sufficient were dismantled, while others were consolidated with larger municipal units. School districts were reorganized in the interest of economy and efficiency, and lands the settlers had abandoned were seized by the provincial government. An important provision of the act was the cre-ation of a powerful government-appointed Special Areas Board which was directly responsible to the government's executive committee.

In the early 1930s the government commissioned two more studies on the economic and human conditions in east-central Alberta.[87] On the basis of the studies the Berry Creek Area Act was passed in 1932 to reor-ganize the schools and stabilize government finances, and in 1934 the boards of Berry Creek and Tilley East were amalgamated.

Conditions continued to worsen throughout east-central Alberta and during the 1930s the whole region was ravaged by drought and depres-sion-level commodity prices. Most of the farmers had no crops and those who did were unable to sell them. The combination of drought, the depression, and an inability to pay property taxes drove thousands of Albertans from their farms. Tax sales were held, but there were no buyers; the farm families remaining had virtually no income.

In 1938 the province passed the Special Areas Act, which reorganized 37 improvement and municipal districts in east-central Alberta and established six special areas comprising 3.2 million hectares (7.8 million acres) to be administered by the Department of Land and Mines. Being large and sparsely populated, special areas have many of the same characteristics as improvement districts. In fact, they are so much alike that Section 6 of the Special Areas Act states that "all of the provisions of the Improvement District Act . . . apply to every special area as if it were an improvement district."

Eric Hanson, discussing government policy for special areas, writes: "One of the first objectives . . . was to assist people to move out so that the remaining farmers could get enough land to make their operation economical. The province provided grants to farmers who wished to move to other farming districts."[88] Since the special areas were first established, 810,000 hectares (2 million acres) have been amalgamated into adjoining municipal districts and the remaining acreage has been reorganized into three special areas. The government tidied up the fiscal loose ends in 1939 by writing off all tax arrears up to 1935.

In order to exert direct control over farming practices and to return the land to grass, the province froze sales of the 607,500 hectares (1.5 million acres) of Crown lease land in the area and the 810,000 hectares (2 million acres) the province seized under the Tax Recovery Act. Then the province leased the land to individual farmers under strict land-use regulations. When land was seized for nonpayment of taxes it was generally understood that titles would remain in trust until back taxes had been paid and the land rehabilitated. However, long after these conditions were met, the province still held the land. The government owned 70 percent of special area lands by 1944.

Although the provincial government's policies were well intended, they were not without their critics. In 1935 the municipal districts of Sounding Creek and Collholme moved to maintain their political autonomy by proposing the consolidation of three municipal districts into a much larger one which would have the right to lease land and be eligible for provincial loan assistance. They concluded their proposal to the Minister of Municipal Affairs with a strong plea for self-government. In December 1937 the Sounding Creek administrator received a letter which said that for some time the government had been investigating "whether or not your Municipal District would be able to carry on its affairs under a council or, whether it would be better to make other arrangements for the administration of the district . . . it would be in the best interest of all concerned for an official administrator to be appointed to administer the affairs of your own and other neighboring municipalities."[89] Needless to say, the municipal districts' politicians and administrators, as well as many residents, must have been extremely disappointed by the government's stance on local autonomy.

Modeled after the Tilley East Area Act, the Special Areas Act provided for a three-member Special Areas Board appointed by the Minister of Land and Mines. Under Section 28(2) "the Minister may delegate to the Board or the chairman of the Board any power, duty or function relating to special areas conferred . . . on the Minister by this or any other Act." Since the minister is given almost unlimited political and administrative powers for the governance of the special areas, the board has the potential to be extremely powerful. In 1948 the special areas were transferred back to the Department of Municipal Affairs, which has administered them ever since.

Until 1982, appointments to the Special Areas Board were made by the Deputy Minister of Municipal Affairs, who appointed long-term residents well acquainted with the problems peculiar to the special areas. The only apparent criticism of this process is contained in a 1977 legislative interim report that stated: "They have tended to sit for very lengthy periods . . . the negative aspect of such lengthy tenure has been a certain lack of innovation in approaching continuing problems—for example, water development."[90] The board is responsible for all public land administration, including the issuance of cultivation and grazing permits and leases; it is also responsible for tax assessment and road construction and maintenance. In short, in addition to its public land control duties, it performs many of the functions of any municipal council. To maintain contact with area residents, the board has decentralized its administrative structure; the main office is located in Hanna and field offices in Consort, Youngstown, and Oyen. Since a number of agents are involved in service delivery to special areas, the Department of Municipal Affairs has created a special areas branch to coordinate administration and policy making by the Special Areas Board, the Deputy Minister, and other government departments.

The Special Areas Act provides for resident participation in the policy-making process through an elective advisory council whose members have a three-year term of office. Although the advisory council is extremely important today, this was not always the case, for the Special

Areas Board was established in 1938 but did not meet with the advisory council until January 1940.[91] The council originally comprised 18 members each representing a subdivision of the special areas, but was reduced to 13 members as the geographic area of the special areas diminished. In each of the 13 current subdivisions four or five residents are elected to assist in the preparation of a road program which is reviewed by the board.

Although the advisory council has no binding powers, its recommendations to the board are always given serious consideration. In 1977, after interviewing members of the Special Areas Board, a legislative intern wrote that board members "regard committee recommendations seriously and try to avoid rejecting any proposals brought forward."[92] A small step to democratize the policy-making process was taken in January 1982 when the government appointed two advisory council members to the board. The third member, its chairperson, is still appointed by the Deputy Minister of Municipal Affairs.

During the 1980s the government sold much of the land it had been leasing to farm families, and 40 percent of special area land is now privately owned. The Alberta government provides the residents with municipal assistance grants, road grants, and culture, youth, and recreation grants, while the board strikes mill rates and collects royalties, taxes, crop shares, fees, and a variety of other revenues, all of which are retained in the region. Most of the 6,010 people who lived in the three special areas in 1986 were involved in agriculture. The farms in special areas are generally prosperous. Despite minimal road, police, and fire services, the residents seem satisfied, for their taxes are relatively low. Many older farmers have not forgotten that they once lost their land because they were unable to pay their taxes.

It was because the special areas were governed undemocratically by fiat for decades that it was possible to prevent an excess of people from settling there and repeating a vicious cycle of land depletion. Moreover, with policy being made by decree it was possible to enforce the use of scientific agricultural practices to restore the land. The provincial government attempts to justify its half-century-old policy of closely controlling the administration of special area government by avoiding the issue of democracy and focusing on the financial benefits. Special Area Board chairperson Abner Grover says that people support special area administration because it provides reasonable service without forcing them into debt.[93] The *Municipal Counsellor,* published by the Department of Municipal Affairs, refers to a survey of 840 special area residents in 1987 that shows that 90 percent of the respondents "are satisfied with the administration of the Special Areas and are in favor of maintaining the areas as they are today."[94] In a book commissioned by Municipal Affairs, Walter Walchuk extolls the virtues of special area administration: "there is a sense of success amongst the board members that should be shared. This would facilitate the replication of some of these positive features elsewhere and ensure that the present strengths are carried forward in the administration of the area." He praises the board for the way it meets with its advisory council and deals with the council's resolutions twice yearly in two- and three-day sessions and comments favourably on the restraint shown by special area residents and their advisory committee representatives who "seldom demanded more than they could afford." Walchuk only briefly ponders issues of democracy, when he asks the rhetorical question: "Is the existence of some form of local municipal government in all areas of the province of paramount importance, superseding concerns with financial viability?"[95]

Hamlets

Since 1905, provincial acts have referred to hamlets, even though they have never been strictly defined and their numbers as a result are difficult to determine.[96] The Municipal Government Act, R.S.A. 1980, states in Section 1 that a hamlet is land which has been registered as having been subdivided into lots and blocks, but a hamlet can also be any area that the Minister of Municipal Affairs designates as such. Little is said of governance and administration, although Section 277 of the same act states that in response to a petition from a majority of a hamlet's landowners, 50 percent of the taxes collected from the hamlet for municipal purposes must be used for public works in the community. Section 266 allows a municipal district council to levy a special tax on hamlet property to pay the cost of bringing water into the community and the Improvement Districts Act, R.S.A. 1980, states that if a hamlet is located in an improvement district, the minister can supply it with water and fire-fighting equipment.[97]

Whether an agglomeration of lots and buildings makes a hamlet or not is more than an academic question to a community's residents. The Alberta Hamlets Street Assistance Program provides grants for street improvements, and other assistance programs are available for policing and the construction of water and sewer systems in communities identified as hamlets.[98]

At the request of confused local-level politicians and administrators, the Municipal Government Act was amended and expanded with a view to clarifying the definition of a hamlet. In the fall of 1980 a hamlet was defined in terms of its geographic area: "an unincorporated community consisting of a group of 5 or more occupied dwellings, a majority of which are on parcels of less than 1850 square metres, with a defined boundary, a distinct name and the existence of or provision for nonresidential uses, that is designated as a hamlet by the council for the municipal district in which the community is located or by the Minister." However, the act still did not adequately describe the political and administrative dimensions of hamlets. In 1983 the delegates at the Alberta Association of Municipal Districts and Counties convention passed a resolution requesting the provincial government to clarify its definition of a hamlet.

With attention focused almost wholly on the problems of definition, one can understand why self-government, grass-roots democracy, and bureaucratic control have been non-issues. Undoubtedly, many hamlet residents have willingly relinquished local control to a municipal district or country in return for low taxes and "hassle-free administration." Pleas for self-government, such as were made by ratepayers in Bragg Creek in the late 1980s, have been the exception rather than the rule. Residents of the hamlet, which is located in the Municipal District of Rocky View, were debating the virtues of becoming a village. In the fall of 1987 a group favouring village government sent out a newsletter calling for a meeting on the issue. The newsletter read in part:

> The M.D. of Rocky View, with its large administrative area, is not set up to represent concerns of our small community. If you do have concerns, wouldn't these best be served by you or your neighbors, rather than a municipal council who possibly doesn't understand what you really want? When was the last time anyone asked you what you would like.[99]

When the meeting was held, the major issue was not representation and self-government, but rather that ratepayers in the hamlet were paying substantially more in property taxes than they were receiving back in services. The proponents of village government argued that 425 landowners in the hamlet paid more than $100,000 in yearly taxes, excluding school levies, and received services costing $65,000. In addition to establishing equity, they argued that incorporation as a village would make the community eligible for a number of provincial grant programs for such things as libraries and family and community services and "this money would tend to stay in the community instead of being spread around the municipality."[100] Opponents feared that with incorporation the community would lose its unique life-style. In September 1989 more than 83 percent of the residents cast ballots on the issue: "Are you in favour of incorporating the Hamlet of Bragg Creek into a Village?" The electorate overwhelmingly favoured the status quo, with only 16.3 percent voting in favour and 83.7 percent voting against.[101]

Municipal district and county politicians are quick to point out that hamlet residents are not disenfranchised, since they can vote for municipal district and county council candidates who represent their interests. However, one can debate whether a hamlet in the far corner of a rural county or municipal district can be adequately represented. Equally important, one can ask the same questions about hamlet residents that are asked about the residents of improvement districts. In short, do the residents of hamlets know their own interests or not? If they do not, then do the province and the county or municipal district have a responsibility to tutor hamlet residents on the virtues of democratic rule and self-government?

An Overview of Rural and Evolving Forms of Government

Overall, Alberta's policy on local autonomy and self-determination has differed little from that of other provinces. Policies generally have been paternalistic but not overbearing, and the government has recently attempted to provide more democratic institutions for residents of isolated and sparsely settled areas.

With the exception of special areas, recent government policy has been that municipalities should become self-governing if they can manage their own financial affairs. Thus several improvement districts became municipal districts during the 1980s and there was a major policy shift on the governance of Metis settlements. However, many rural residents are still "second-class citizens," unable to exercise the same democratic rights as those living in urban municipalities.

Residents of special area lands have not enjoyed self-government for more than half a century. Given the provincial government's belief that an area must have the economic resources to become financially viable before it can become self-governing, there seems little likelihood that special areas will enjoy local autonomy in the near future.

During the latter 1980s, when the Department of Municipal Affairs was commissioning one study after another to determine whether or not an improvement district was ready to become a municipal district, the ideals of democracy and local autonomy were generally cited, but unless a unit had a solid financial base the department did not approve the conversion. Little thought was given as to whether a community had a political infrastructure able to govern and exert leadership or whether or not the citizens were committed to local-level democracy.

Improvement district advisory councils have long been aware that the Department of Municipal Affairs is interested primarily in their financial viability. Moreover, until quite recently individual councils and the Improvement Districts Association of Alberta (IDAA) hesitated to criticize the department. The IDAA has now begun to reject the government's paternalistic stance and to demand control over government policies which affect improvement districts. In 1989 President Bill Mahon of the IDAA said, ". . . do residents of Improvement Districts want to be masters of their own ship or do they want the bureaucracy in Edmonton to do it for them?"[102] Six months later Minister of Municipal Affairs Ray Speaker announced that an agreement-in-principle had been worked out with the IDAA to create a new category, that of rural municipality, which would allow residents to play a much more active role in local government.

The Department of Municipal Affairs has the expertise which can be brought to bear to create other forms of government as unique as the rural municipality. If Klein's Tory government or its successor gives Municipal Affairs a freer hand, then innovative plans may be brought forth to further democratize rural government and to bring democracy to the special areas.

5

Governmental Reorganization

Appropriate Government for Metropolitan Areas

The appropriate number of local governments for a given geographical area, and their optimal size, are issues which have generated dissension and conflict between government professionals and the citizenry for more than half a century. On one side of the issue have been administrators and municipal experts aghast at what seems to them to be an ever-increasing number of governments with overlapping responsibilities in metropolitan areas. They seek to increase efficiency and decrease the cost of services by expanding the size of government in order to gain the advantage of economies of scale. They claim that consolidating governmental units and administration within one government reduces wasteful duplication of services and allows for comprehensive regional planning. Outside consultants sympathetic with this viewpoint are often employed to determine whether or not a municipality should be restructured to make it more efficient. Their recommendations almost invariably support the traditional reformers.

On the other side of the issue are citizens who interpret proposals to increase the geographical area and population covered by the government of a metropolitan area as a device to dilute the political power of neighbourhoods and ethnic and socio-economic groups and make a mockery of local self-determination. They maintain that having a number of governments in a metropolitan area gives citizens more effective political representation and offers them a greater opportunity to control public policies. In short, they argue that although the presence of a number of governments in a metropolitan area might seem to be untidy, it gives ordinary citizens a greater degree of political control over elected officials and administrators.

More often than not, economic arguments have dominated the debate over the pros and cons of the proposals to reform municipal government. Often overlooked has been that people are just as concerned with democratic values as they are with economic ones. Fortunately, in the last decade the conflict between the two sides has begun to abate. Moreover, a number of studies have shown that there is not one best organizational arrangement for government which is appropriate for all metropolitan areas. Rather, the preferences of an area's citizens and their elected officials for democratic institutions and the provision and production of services can lead to a variety of governmental arrangements.

Difficulties of Evaluating Governmental Performance

Since budgets and spending guidelines are central to the enterprise of government, it is not surprising that governmental performance is measured in dollars and cents. Whether or not it is appropriate or even possible to assign monetary values to the full range of government services is a moot point; administrators do so because the public expects it.

"Hard" services such as the provision of water, sewage treatment, and roadways are the easiest to measure in monetary terms, but difficult measurement problems must still be addressed. For example, while it is relatively easy to determine the cost per kilometre of asphalt paving, it is more difficult to determine the total cost per kilometre of asphalt versus gravel. Gravel is cheaper, but the cost resulting from broken windshields and vehicle damage is much higher. Are roadway costs to be measured solely in terms of the per-kilometre cost of roads or should the cost of wear and tear on private and public vehicles be included in the calculations?

As one might expect, performance measurement is the most difficult for "soft" service areas such as education and welfare. One reason is that, more often than not, neither the public nor the politicians agree upon the goals in these areas. For example, in evaluating the performance of a welfare agency one segment of the public will focus on how quickly clients are removed from public support and into the labour force, while another segment will focus on the adequacy of support for housing, food, and medical care. Even when there is agreement on what is to be measured, it is often difficult, if not impossible, to calculate the success or failure of social services in monetary terms. As a consequence, it is necessary to employ other forms of measurement.

Sometimes there is a general agreement about what is to be measured, but the use of two entirely different measures leads to very different conclusions. For example, there has been a long-standing controversy over whether it is more efficient in monetary terms to employ one or two officers in police cars. The advocates of one-officer cars claim tremendous savings in labour costs. The advocates of two-officer cars maintain that when one-officer cars patrol high-crime areas the officer is inclined to be extremely cautious and patrol the fringe rather than the core. They cite statistics which show a much higher fatality rate for one-officer patrols and argue that a price cannot be placed on human life. Thus the question of whether it is more efficient to patrol with one-officer or two-officer police cars remains unanswered.

These examples are simple, but they show that the issues are extremely complex and the bases of evaluation are controversial. In weighing the pros and cons of governmental reorganization proposals, it is important to ascertain whether everyone is using the same scales; more often than not, one group is citing direct dollar costs while another is employing nonfiscal measures or very indirect measures of monetary costs.

Intellectual Roots of Municipal Reorganization

During the 1930s and 1940s, hundreds of small school districts were consolidated to make them more efficient and to improve the level of education for Alberta's youth. Premier William Aberhart, who had been a teacher, made educational reorganization a priority when he was elected in 1935. The impetus for his program came from his own classroom experience, rather than from the educational establishment. Today reorganization efforts are focused on the municipality as well as the school district. The proponents of municipal reorganization maintain that in the interests of efficiency and better planning small rural municipalities should be consolidated and those adjacent to a large city should be absorbed into it.

The movement to reorganize municipalities has its intellectual roots in the American Progressive Movement, which flourished in the midwestern and western United States in the early twentieth century. Although the Progressives initially focused on removing corruption from municipal politics, it was but a short step to proposing programs to increase municipal efficiency. The first systematic exposition of the disadvantages of having a number of independent municipalities within a metropolitan area was made in 1922 by Chester Maxey, an American reformer and academic, who wrote:

> ... one handicap under which practically every city of magnitude is laboring is political disintegration ... the metropolitan district finds

itself obliged to struggle for civic achievement amid conflicts, dissension and divergencies of its several component political jurisdictions.[1]

Maxey's assumption that a metropolitan region is a single social and economic entity is shared by a leading authority on Canadian local government, who said in 1958:

> In the metropolis, where the government is politically fragmented, the problem becomes even more acute, for its inhabitants are economically and socially interdependent irrespective of the sector in which they live, and, as a result, many requirements and needs of the metropolis are area-wide in character.[2]

Although Maxey presented a number of arguments for the reorganization of municipal government, he outlined only sketchily solutions of large-scale annexation and consolidation. Following his seminal work a number of articles and textbooks incorporated his ideas, but his arguments were not systematically synthesized until Paul Studenski published *The Government of Metropolitan Areas in the United States* in 1930. Studenski carefully examined the reformers' proposals in terms of their benefits and political feasibility, then suggested a solution for the "metropolitan problem" of too many governments in an urban area. Studenski erred, however, in assuming that a metropolitan area with many governments was always inefficient and that consolidation always increased administrative efficiency.

The followers of Maxey and Studenski still maintain that the ideal is a single governmental unit.[3] They see no alternative to eliminating the expensive duplication of administrative personnel and facilities such as city halls and police and fire stations. They also believe the planning process is orderly and rational only when region-wide government is adopted, and bolster their arguments by citing case after case of fragmented planning which has caused unfavourable "spillover effects" in adjoining communities.[4]

In the early 1950s the government of Ontario and the municipalities in the greater Toronto region examined the feasibility of governmental reorganization and in 1953 the Ontario government imposed a two-tier form of metropolitan government on the region's 13 municipalities. Services deemed to be local in nature (such as fire protection) were to remain the responsibility of the municipalities, while area-wide services (such as health and planning) were to be the responsibility of the new first-tier metropolitan government. Representation on the metropolitan council was indirect, with each of the 12 smaller municipalities having one representative chosen from its council and Toronto's city council having 12 representatives. Many of the proponents of two-tier metropolitan government maintain that it has all of the advantages of regional government while maintaining the identity and viability of smaller municipalities.

In 1961 an article in the *American Political Science Review* challenged the traditional reformers' perspective on metropolitan reorganization and triggered a debate which still continues today.[5] Rather than making *a priori* assumptions about overlapping governmental responsibilities and ideal forms of city government, the authors utilized a theory of public goods to examine governance and the delivery of services in metropolitan areas. Focusing upon political representation, political control, local self-determination, and economies of scale in the production of public goods in order to determine an optimal scale of government, they argued that there could be wide variations in the number and kinds of public and private organizations in a metropolitan area. They emphasized the importance of distinguishing between decisions about the *provision* of public goods and decisions about the *production* of public goods. The following distinction between provision and production is from a recent monograph by the Advisory Commission on Intergovernmental Relations (ACIR).

... provision refers to decisions that determine what public goods and services will be made available to a community. ... Provision covers taxing and spending decisions about public goods and services, determinations of service standards, the monitoring of service delivery, and the securing of accountability to standards. ... Production refers to how goods and services will be made available ... [and] the process of combining resource inputs to make a product or render a service.[6]

It is emphasized that provision and production functions are activities which can be, and often are, separated, since "the appropriate scale of organization for provision is frequently quite different from the appropriate scale for production."[7] As an example, a municipality may decide to provide a high level of policing services by contracting with other municipalities, the province, or the RCMP for policing rather than producing the service itself. In this case, the size and structure of the municipality consuming the police service are much different from those of the municipality producing the service. Moreover, the provision function has to be separated from production in order to explain municipal contracting with the private sector for such services as garbage collection. Since 1961 the provision/production distinction has provided the major rationale for those who maintain that under certain circumstances governmental diversity can enhance local level democracy and lead to a more efficient production of public goods.

Metropolitan Reorganization Today

Modern reformers believe that the adoption of a single unit of government for a metropolitan area brings order to the often chaotic delivery of services by a multiplicity of municipalities. They maintain that the changing nature of the metropolis has led to tax and service inequities and a patchwork of local governments that frustrates attempts at regional planning. The decentralization of manufacturing, retailing, and housing has been devastating for many large cities. Manufacturing plants in search of cheaper land have moved their facilities from the city core to outlying industrial parks, eroding the core's industrial tax base. Middle-class single-family housing is developed on cheaper land in suburban communities rather than expensive high-density land near the city centre. The unintended consequence is that the core is left with a disproportionate number of lower-income and welfare families. These pockets of urban poor are afflicted with social disorganization, high levels of crime, and a myriad of housing, health, and educational problems. The costly programs required to respond to these problems place ever-increasing pressure on the city's declining industrial and residential tax base. A 1981 report commissioned to support the City of Edmonton's proposal to annex St. Albert and Sherwood Park discusses this phenomenon:

> There is a whole range of facilities and services which outlying communities cannot afford or do not wish to provide, and public housing is one example. There is none in St. Albert or Sherwood Park. . . . Edmonton currently pays for public housing not only for its own residents, but also for those from surrounding communities who for one reason or another, find it necessary to live in less expensive accommodation. In this, as in other areas, Edmonton once again carries the financial burden of a service used by all metro residents.[8]

Moreover, the critics of decentralization argue that the middle-class residents of outlying communities who are employed in the central city use its cultural and recreational facilities but fail to pay their share of service costs which are funded primarily with property tax revenue.[9] They point to the service and fiscal disparities in a metropolitan region in which some municipalities provide low levels of service and have low property taxes while others provide high levels of service and have high taxes. In particular, they note anomalies such as the working-class residential community with small older homes and no commercial tax base which, despite high property taxes, can afford only low levels of service and an incorporated area with an industrial park and few residences which has high levels of service and very low residential property taxes. In short, the proponents of amalgamation believe it would eliminate tax and service inequities and force all businesses and residents to accept their fiscal responsibilities.

Amalgamation is also justified on the grounds that larger municipalities have more influence with senior levels of government and are in a better position to promote economic development. In 1987 Member of the Legislative Assembly (MLA) Ernie Isley said, "One larger community would have more lobbying clout with the province than would two smaller communities. It could do a better job of lobbying and promoting itself for economic development."[10] When the villages of Entwistle and Evansburg considered amalgamation in 1986, an Evansburg councillor argued that the two "should amalgamate to have a political position to decide their own futures."[11]

An additional argument is that the increased use of the automobile coupled with changes in communication technology have made the metropolitan region an integrated and interwoven unit. Autonomous communities thus fragment government activities that are regional by nature. As an example, the discussion of transportation in Edmonton's annexation proposal said:

> An integrated service should offer more attractive and convenient transit routing, scheduling and service. More major destinations could be serviced between the two communities [Sherwood Park and St. Albert] in the core area, saving travel time and transfer inconvenience.[12]

In a consolidated metropolitan area, land use can be planned on a regional basis. Autonomous municipalities, each developing its own land-use plan, are likely to work at cross purposes. An industrial park in one municipality may border a suburban neighbourhood in another and large tracts of potential park and farm land are eroded in the absence of regional planning. The planning mechanism is discussed in detail in Chapter 12.

The arguments made by the proponents of major urban governmental reorganization and amalgamation are persuasive, but nevertheless they raise questions. For example, how realistic are the reformers' assumptions about the urban social and economic system? When governmental units are consolidated, what is the ultimate effect on the public? The argument that a number of government activities are inherently regional has a doubtful basis. Although many students of local government attempt to distinguish local from regional services, the distinction is arbitrary since, with the exception of planning, persuasive arguments can be made for any municipal function being either local or regional. Furthermore, those who attempt to make the local/regional distinction seldom base their arguments on what would seem to be the most important factors, a governmental unit's population size and its decision-making capabilities.

One can question whether it is necessary to embark on a policy of consolidation to solve problems created by changing economic and social conditions. It is possible to plan regionally with a number of governments. Furthermore, rather than viewing the existence of municipalities with disparate service levels and tax rates as a problem, one could argue that this diversity gives citizens a variety of options related to location, taxation, and lifestyle. A recent report on metropolitan reorganization states:

> Among the issues that can be addressed by nesting smaller units into larger ones is distributional equity. One popular view is that fiscal equity is best obtained by enlarging the size of jurisdictions to encompass economically diverse communities, creating a broader tax base and, in theory, allowing more resources to be distributed to poorer areas.[13]

Communities experiencing a decline in their tax base and facing costly social problems could be assisted either by direct government grants or by a provincially administered redistribution of commercial and residential tax revenues based on a needs formula. Finally, in theory, municipalities working closely on an ongoing basis with their local government associations should be able to lobby senior levels of government and promote economic development without resorting to amalgamation. In short, regional urban problems may be resolved without destroying an area's smaller municipalities, with their potential for grass-roots democratic government.

Economics of Governmental Reorganization

In spite of the difficulties of evaluating governmental activity, many people do so using a variety of fiscal and nonfiscal criteria. This initial examination of governmental reorganization focuses on its economics.

There is no question that under certain conditions smaller municipalities benefit by consolidating some services with those of other communities. Many of them cannot justify the expense of buying and maintaining firefighting and road-maintenance equipment used only a few times a year; others cannot afford to employ full-time administrators even though they may wish to upgrade and professionalize their operations; and some cannot afford to install needed water and sewage systems. However, communities are advised to be cautious about consolidation. Cost increases (diseconomies of scale) often are encountered in units serving larger populations, for the following reasons:

> . . . most government services require relatively close geographic proximity of service units to service recipients; this prevents the establishment of huge primary schools, fire houses, police stations, or libraries. Urban government services are also labor intensive, with wages and salaries often accounting for more than two-thirds of current costs. The resulting concentration of manpower can increase the bargaining power of labor and this, in turn, increases costs. While there are economies resulting from bulk purchases of supplies and equipment, such savings can be outweighed by inefficiencies resulting from top-heavy administration and the ills of political patronage in very large scale governments.[14]

In Alberta's small and mid-sized communities economy and efficiency have been major considerations in promoting consolidation yet, ironically, these factors are also primary impediments to governmental amalgamation. This seeming anomaly can be explained by examining two proposed amalgamations. In 1980, at the height of Alberta's economic boom, Stony Plain borrowed $5 million to develop an industrial park. The town's timing could not have been worse, for shortly thereafter the provincial economy went into a tailspin. By 1984 Stony Plain had one of the highest municipal debts in the province; slightly more than $2,200 per capita. Amid rumours of impending bankruptcy, with investors and entrepreneurs avoiding the town, its mayor believed amalgamation with nearby Spruce Grove, which had a $5 million reserve and a small debt, was the answer to Stony Plain's financial woes. A study commissioned by the Department of Municipal Affairs recommended amalgamation. However, Spruce Grove residents lost their enthusiasm for the project when the report predicted that after amalgamation they would pay substantially more in property taxes and Stony Plain residents would pay substantially less.[15] The two communities did not amalgamate. A similar scenario was played out in the adjoining towns of Turner Valley and Black Diamond in southern Alberta. After having worked together successfully to provide their residents with recreational facilities and fire protection, they requested Municipal Affairs to conduct an amalgamation feasibility study in 1986. The study showed that after amalgamation Black Diamond, with more residents but a smaller industrial and residential tax base, would have an 8 percent decrease in taxes while Turner Valley's taxes would increase by at least 17 percent. Shortly thereafter, the Turner Valley council terminated the discussions because, as the mayor explained, "we don't see any advantage."[16]

Evaluating Public Sector Monopoly Behaviour

In the private sector the cost of consumer goods is lowest in openly competitive industries and highest in uncompetitive industries. For example, international airline executives met regularly in the past to set fares. When the cartel was broken and the airlines began to compete with one another, fares plummeted. Similarly, the existence of natural monopolies in the private sector, such as telephone and power companies, often results in organizational complacency and inefficiency which in turn lead to higher prices for the consumer. In spite of being tightly regulated, these monopolies turn handsome profits. Economists deplore monopolies' production costs, their bureaucratic inefficiencies, and the inordinately high prices that are charged the consumer.

In the public sector one normally finds a single producer of governmental services within a municipality. Although a municipality is seldom thought of as such, the organization and processes it employs to deliver public services resemble those of a classic monopoly. However, it is argued while the municipality may have a monopoly on the provision of public services at the local level, in theory at least, an imperfect form of competition exists regionally. As knowledgeable residents become aware of neighbouring municipalities' taxes and service levels they can determine which communities seem to be the most and least efficient. The same information is often used by candidates in municipal electoral campaigns and as a consequence incumbents encourage the administration to be as efficient as possible. Residents who are dissatisfied with taxation and services have the option of moving to another municipality with a more efficient administration and more desirable taxes and services. When governmental units are consolidated into a single regional unit, this incentive for efficiency and cost-consciousness is lost, since the public has no measuring stick against which to evaluate a regional unit.

This argument makes a series of critical assumptions, the validity of which will vary from one metropolitan region to another. The first is that taxation levels accurately reflect the degree of municipal efficiency. In fact, in most metropolitan regions the level of taxation is as much a function of the presence or absence of an industrial tax base as it is of the level of governmental efficiency. Second, it assumes the electorate has access to accurate information on levels of taxation and costs of services for all the municipalities in a region. While some municipal officials may point with pride to an efficient administration, others successfully distort and hide service costs, particularly if they reveal inefficiencies. The third assumption is that the electorate is well-educated, interested in politics and economics, and motivated to seek out tax and service information. While this may describe a portion of the electorate in an upper-income community, it is much less likely to be true in a poorer community. Finally, it is assumed that if citizens have done their homework on taxes and services, they are able to act on the information. However, many people are unable to "vote with their feet" by moving, regardless of their dissatisfaction with their municipality. A low-income family in an older low-rent community is unlikely to be able to afford to live in a middle-class community of high-rent single family dwellings, even if it does have a more efficient governmental structure.

Noneconomic Factors and Governmental Reorganization

Today, the opponents of governmental reorganization and the proponents of municipal autonomy make noneconomic arguments far more often than economic ones. An important noneconomic factor is the strong emotional attachment and loyalty that people develop towards their communities. They identify themselves as being residents of Jasper, Medicine Hat, or Rocky Mountain House as often as they identify themselves as being Albertans. "Business boosters" appeal to citizens' loyalty and exhort them to shop in their own town rather than an adjoining one. The community may be too small to produce municipal services efficiently and property taxes may be high, but most residents are strongly attached to it and believe governmental reorganization would destroy their heritage and identity.[17]

Another significant noneconomic factor involves accessibility to administrators and elected officials. The public's perception of government is that the greater its size, the more distant and remote it becomes from the citizenry. In particular, people in large cities feel it is difficult for them to reach their elected representatives to discuss services and taxation or municipal policy. In short, the grass-roots democracy and policy making that are often found in smaller municipalities are absent in larger municipalities. Another factor not often discussed is that office holders and administrative personnel in the communities that would be absorbed by city expansion oppose consolidation because they are afraid of losing their jobs. Administrators in small municipalities are aware that they are not as well trained as their big-city associates and that they could be demoted or left unemployed as a consequence of amalgamation.[18]

Municipal government is time-consuming; city policy makers working as many as 70 hours a week often insulate themselves from their constituents with receptionists, secretaries, and administrative assistants. As a consequence, citizens are intimidated and feel it is fruitless to try to penetrate the city hall maze. In smaller communities elected officials and the bureaucracy are perceived as being more accessible. Although studies of small-town politics in the United States indicate the electorate participates in community affairs at about the same rate as it does in large cities, they also show that residents of small towns feel that if they wanted to participate, their elected representatives would be accessible and responsive. When the issue of amalgamation or annexation arises, opponents invariably argue that the proposed municipality's policy makers and administrators would be distant from, and inaccessible to, the citizenry. In the mid-1980s when the Town of Redcliff considered amalgamating with the City of Medicine Hat, more than ten times its size, Redcliff's police chief said that if the two communities were amalgamated, people in the Redcliff area would no longer have personal contact with their police officers. One of the town's more vocal opponents of amalgamation argued that the citizenry would lose control over school and municipal policy making. "The city could end up with 12 councillors—11 from Medicine Hat and one from Redcliff."[19]

On the other hand, community loyalty and accessibility to local decision makers must be kept in perspective. The province has experienced explosive growth in the last two decades and many mobile Albertans have little emotional attachment to the municipality in which they live. Since it takes time to develop community identity, newcomers are not likely to have the same sense of involvement as second- and third-generation residents. For some people, service levels and tax rates are far more important than community identification when they choose a place in which to live.

Governmental Reorganization in Alberta

From the province's very beginning, population trends and economic factors have resulted in some communities annexing land for expansion and other communities amalgamating with their neighbours. This pattern continues today, with few of the province's municipalities maintaining static boundaries. Although most of the changes are relatively small, a controversial annexation or amalgamation request can have political repercussions at the highest levels of the provincial government.

Unlike many provinces, Alberta does not have an explicit policy on urbanization; however, it has had an unofficial policy on community growth and economic expansion dating back to the 1930s. Although school government was reorganized when much larger school districts were created in the 1930s and 1940s, the Social Credit government was committed to maintaining the autonomy of local municipalities during its 1935–1971 reign.[20] In 1950 the County Act creating an all-purpose unit of local government was passed; by an order-in-council, the provincial government was given the power to incorporate all or a part of a municipality, school division, or hospital district into a county. Some counties were created, but since Social Credit had a largely rural support base, it was not in its interest to promote the expansion of politically antagonistic urban centres.

The discovery of oil in 1947 was followed by rapid economic expansion and urban growth that caused financial problems for the province's towns and cities. The government responded by providing loan assistance programs to municipalities, developing district planning commissions, and, in 1954, establishing the McNally Commission to examine and make recommendations for the cities of Edmonton and Calgary on the "financing of school and municipal matters," as well as "the boundaries and the form of local government which will most adequately and equitably provide for the orderly development of school and municipal services."[21] In January 1956 the commission submitted its final report recommending "that each metropolitan area would be best governed by enlarging each of the present cities to include its whole metropolitan area."[22] The premises upon which the recommendations rested were similar to those espoused by Maxey and Studenski a quarter century earlier:

1. It is unjust and inequitable that wide variations in the tax base should exist among the local governing bodies that comprise a metropolitan area where that area is in fact one economic and social unit.

2. A metropolitan area which is in fact one economic and social unit can ordinarily be more efficiently and effectively governed by one central municipal authority than by a multiplicity of local governing bodies.[23]

The commission recommended that Edmonton be enlarged from 107.5 to 290.1 square kilometres (41.5 to 112.02 square miles) and that Calgary be increased from 128.2 to 271.4 square kilometres (49.5 to 104.77 square miles).

According to Peter Smith, "... the McNally Commission completely misjudged the will of the Provincial Government and the strength of its attachment to the ideals of local autonomy and self-government."[24] Taking the position that "the metropolitan problem" was caused by a lack of fiscal resources, the province ignored the commission's recommendations. In 1956 it established the Municipal Financing Corporation and greatly increased its grants to Edmonton and Calgary.[25]

Although the Provincial Conservatives promised that an urbanization policy would be forthcoming when they took office in 1971, an official policy was never adopted. However, as was noted in the introductory chapter, Premier Peter Lougheed was committed to an unofficial policy of slowing the growth of Edmonton and Calgary, revitalizing smaller municipalities, and encouraging province-wide economic diversification in order to stabilize the rural-to-urban migration which had accelerated in the 1960s. The government was not hostile to local government amalgamation and expansion as long as its purpose was to strengthen smaller communities. As a sign of its commitment to the revitalization of rural areas, a special act was passed by the legislature in 1979 amalgamating a number of financially troubled Crowsnest Pass municipalities. The towns of Blairmore and Coleman, the villages of Bellevue and Frank, and eleven small hamlets in Improvement District No. 5, almost all of which were contiguous, were amalgamated into the Town of Crowsnest Pass.[26]

Although the Progressive Conservatives have been in power for more than two decades, the party's policy on urban and rural development still has not been translated into legislation. There is little doubt that Lougheed's policy of diversifying and slowing the growth of the province's two major urban centres caused dissension within the government caucus and the cabinet. The Klein government is no likelier than the Getty government to be willing to risk further eroding the Tories' already diminished urban political support by advocating a "no growth" policy for Calgary and Edmonton.

Before examining the machinations of the province's largest cities to increase their size, one should understand the annexation process specified by the provincial government, which paradoxically has the potential to undermine local autonomy. In Alberta both the Local Authorities Board (LAB) and the cabinet are vested with powers to evaluate and rule on amalgamation proposals.[27] The LAB is a quasi-judicial body which derives its power from the Local Authorities Board Act, Section 30 of which states:

> the Board has, in regard to the amendment of proceedings, the attendance and examination of witnesses, the production and inspection of documents, the enforcement of its orders, the payment of costs and all other matters necessary or proper for the due exercise of its jurisdiction or otherwise for carrying any of its powers into effect, all the powers, rights, privileges and immunities that are vested in the Court of Queen's Bench.[28]

Until 1975 the LAB was the final authority on annexation and amalgamation petitions, which could be initiated only by a municipal council, by a majority of the land owners in the affected area, or by the Minister of Municipal Affairs with regard to land in an improvement district. That year the Municipal Government Act was amended to require that LAB decisions be referred to the provincial cabinet for approval. However, aggrieved parties had no recourse to cabinet if the LAB turned down their annexation or amalgamation petitions. Two years later another amendment was added to the act which further diluted the LAB's power. It reads in part that when Crown land "has a common boundary with a municipality, improvement district or special area ... the Lieutenant-Governor in Council may, by order, annex all or part of that land." In 1978 the act was again amended to give the cabinet more power over annexation proceedings. In addition to the power to approve or disapprove LAB decisions, the cabinet was authorized to "prescribe conditions" for the adoption of an annexation proposal. In 1981 the LAB's powers were further weakened when the act was amended to give the Lieutenant-Governor in Council the authority to bring about an annexation or amalgamation and completely bypass the LAB and its procedures. The cabinet is now the ultimate authority in matters of municipal expansion and development and the LAB's decision is only an interim step in the process. Today an annexation proposal is initiated in one of three ways: (1) by a municipal council petitioning the LAB with respect to land in or adjoining a municipality, (2) by the Minister of Municipal Affairs with respect to improvement district or special areas land in or adjoining a municipality, and (3) by the Lieutenant-Governor in Council, who can effect an annexation at any time without consulting the LAB. The annexation and amalgamation process has become politicized and democratic practices for reorganization have not been institutionalized at the local level.

Amalgamation and Annexation in the Edmonton, Calgary, Leduc, and Medicine Hat Regions

Facing a massive influx of new residents during the 1960s and 1970s, neither Edmonton nor Calgary had any intention of waiting until the province developed a policy on urbanization. The two cities expanded their boundaries as quickly as possible. Calgary, which had almost no neighbouring communities, applied in 1978 to annex 11,200 hectares (28,000 acres) and was granted approval for the annexation of 6,400 with virtually no controversy. Edmonton was less fortunate, since there were municipalities on its borders which jealously guarded their local autonomy.

Edmonton was particularly unhappy with the provincial government's cool response to the McNally report recommendation that it be allowed to increase its size almost threefold. Nevertheless, the city managed to expand from 107.5 to 177.7 square kilometres (41.5 to 68.6 square miles) through piecemeal annexation over five years. In 1967, in an effort to pressure the provincial government, the city commissioned an economist to conduct "a study . . . in regard to extending the City's boundaries in all directions."[29] The economist's report recommended that the city's size be increased from 222.7 to 756.3 square kilometres (86 to 292 square miles). Since the report was commissioned by the city, the recommendation that a single unit should govern the metropolitan area was not unexpected, nor was it surprising that the arguments were based almost entirely on economic considerations. Although the report had its shortcomings, it was well received by almost everyone except the provincial government, which appeared to ignore its recommendations.

Between 1968 and 1979, Edmonton continued its policy of gradual annexation while at the same time issuing reports and news releases to justify regional government. In March 1979 the city made a bid to the LAB to annex more than 186,800 hectares (467,000 acres) which would increase its size from 318.6 to 1,813 square kilometres (123 to 700 square miles). This proposal included the City of St. Albert, the unincorporated community of Sherwood Park, the entire County of Strathcona, and significant portions of the County of Parkland and the Municipal District of Sturgeon. In December of 1980 the LAB awarded Edmonton much of the area it asked for, with the exception of the City of St. Albert and the unincorporated community of Sherwood Park and lands to the east of it. The LAB's order went to cabinet, where it was disallowed rather than revised. Subsequently, a new order was issued which awarded Edmonton 34,400 hectares (86,000 acres).[30] In this bitter political fight Edmonton, St. Albert, and the County of Strathcona spent over $7 million for consultants to justify their respective positions.[31] Predictably, Edmonton's mayor said the city would continue its attempt to increase its size and less than a year later the city bid for an additional 3,320 hectares (8,300 acres). At about that time the economy turned downward and residential construction came to a virtual halt. For the rest of the 1980s further annexation was not an issue as the city attempted, with some difficulty, to digest the areas it had already acquired.

In the late 1970s the City of Leduc, to the south of Edmonton, and the County of Leduc clashed over planning and the county's failure to recognize the extensive use being made of city recreational facilities by county residents. In the spring of 1985 Leduc's Mayor Oscar Klak, in a comparison of Leduc and Edmonton, said; "It [Edmonton] doesn't concern itself with a joint agreement [for recreation facilities] with surrounding territories," and, "If we had a more industrial base we wouldn't have this problem." He then hinted that Leduc was considering the annexation of the Edmonton International Airport and the Nisku business park, both on the county's eastern boundaries.[32] The county offered to increase the city's annual recreational grant from $19,000 to $120,000 for three years in order to deflect the annexation bid, which would have cost the county 25 percent of its revenue if it were successful. The city was not to be so easily mollified and in October submitted an annexation application to the LAB for 8,000 hectares (19,700 acres) of county land including the airport and the industrial park. The city based its need for additional land on a 40-year projection.[33]

If the annexation were successful, residential and commercial taxes in Leduc could decrease by as much as 25 percent and taxes in the county could increase as much as 19 percent. However, Klak argued that everyone would win, since when the Genesee power plant in the western part of the county came on stream the county's taxes would be even lower than they had been before annexation.[34] The county reeve, Norman Bittner, accused the city of simply making a tax grab, asking, "Would it be prudent, self-reliant or responsible for the county to give up a stable taxation base which has been carefully integrated over four decades, in exchange for the promise of grants and tax revenues from an unfinished power plant?"[35] In early 1987 the reeve and deputy reeve set about organizing anti-annexation grass-root groups across the county. They counselled people to contact their MLA and members of the Leduc council. When the reeve was asked whether there should be a business boycott of Leduc he answered, "that would be your decision."[36] The annexation campaign became so divisive that community leaders were alarmed. In early 1988 the incoming president of the Leduc Chamber of Commerce was cheered when he said, "Although the subject is a sensitive one . . . let us all believe that no matter what the decision of the cabinet, our elected officials will take it with a good measure of grace and mend the rifts that have torn us asunder."[37]

The LAB's ruling surprised everyone. It decided the city could not annex the airport but recommended that the two municipalities share the airport's revenue.[38] Since the LAB had no authority to order a binding agreement, it suggested that the city and county jointly plan how the airport would be developed and marketed.

The Leduc decision was important, for it introduced a new approach to resolving municipal conflict. In 1990 the City of Fort Saskatchewan and the County of Strathcona were unable to resolve their differences over Fort Saskatchewan's bid for 1,144 hectares of land for a proposed $800 million petrochemical complex. In February 1991 a LAB ruling which was endorsed by the cabinet ordered that the city and county either work out an agreement by June to share an estimated $4 million industrial tax revenue or the issue would be sent to binding arbitration. The LAB's decision was lauded by both parties. Strathcona's Reeve Iris Evans said that "the traditional method of annexations has not dealt adequately with . . . financial matters and we're looking forward to doing that now between ourselves."[39] Unfortunately, the two parties were unable to come to an agreement and subsequently began lobbying cabinet ministers and their MLAs. Moreover, Fort Saskatchewan maintained that the government exceeded its power by making tax sharing a part of the annexation order and the city filed a lawsuit to nullify it. In November, after the Minister of Municipal Affairs made one last unsuccessful attempt to reconcile the differences between the two municipalities, he rescinded the LAB ruling and had a senior judge on the Court of Queen's Bench appointed to arbitrate the dispute.

Calgary's annexation scenario differed substantially from that of Edmonton. After the province turned down the McNally Commission's recommendation to increase the size of Calgary, the city acquired 67.4

square kilometres (26 square miles) in 1956 and then quietly waited until 1961 to bid for an additional 195.5 square kilometres (75.5 square miles). Although the proposal included the amalgamation of Forest Lawn, there was only slight opposition and the LAB gave the city everything it asked for. In 1963 the city acquired the small community of Montgomery and in 1964 the community of Bowness; in both cases there was some opposition from local citizens' groups and politicians, but the LAB ruled in favour of Calgary. In 1971 a group of property speculators and a large real estate company filed a request for the annexation of 170 hectares (419 acres) of farm land on the city's northern border to develop modestly priced housing. Despite protests from the Calgary School Board, which was concerned about the area's isolation from existing schools, the LAB once again ruled favourably.

In 1974 Calgary administrators proposed to annex 514 square kilometres (198.5 square miles) north and south of the city, a takeover which would have almost doubled Calgary's size. In reaction to the city's explosive growth, increasing capital debt, and the secrecy surrounding the proposal, an anti-annexation citizens' group soon formed. As a consequence, the controversial proposal was submitted to the electorate and soundly rejected by almost two-thirds of the voters. Despite this setback the city administration was determined to expand its boundaries, as the population of Calgary was increasing at the rate of 30,000 people a year and was projected to double by the year 2000. In 1978 the city submitted a proposal to the LAB to annex 130 square kilometres (50 square miles) of land north and southeast of the city for residential development. The proposal was approved by the LAB but the annexation order was substantially revised in cabinet; consequently, slightly less than 65 square kilometres (25 square miles) were annexed in 1979.

In January 1983 the LAB approved the annexation of three land parcels totalling 1,800 hectares (4,500 acres) which it was estimated would give Calgary a twelve-year supply of land for development. Shortly thereafter the city planning department made two massive annexation proposals despite the fact that population growth had ground to a halt during the 1982/83 economic downturn. One proposal, based on older population and market predictions, called for the annexation of 329 square kilometres (127 square miles), the other for 241 square kilometres (93 square miles). The latter proposal soon became the centre of political controversy, dividing city planners and Mayor Ralph Klein from the other members of council, who were preparing for a fall election and very much aware of the increasingly vocal anti-annexation citizens' group and the heavy anti-annexation vote in 1974. Although the planning department adamantly maintained that it was necessary to annex at least 241 square kilometres (93 square miles) to meet the needs of residential and industrial expansion until the year 2014, some members of council and a new anti-annexation group, 20th Century Calgary, suggested the city examine other options. With increasing numbers of people settling in the outlying communities of Airdrie, Okotoks, Cochrane, Strathmore, and High River, one option was to encourage the growth of satellite communities. This would relieve Calgary of the extraordinarily high costs it would incur in developing a massive service infrastructure for the newly annexed areas. However, many people feared that Calgary's growth would be restricted in the future as the rapidly expanding satellite communities gained political power.[40] Another option was to increase the density in the city's core by committing financial resources to upgrade deteriorating areas in order to encourage people to remain in the city rather than fleeing to suburbia. Unfortunately, it was not known whether a policy committed to core city high-density apartment and townhouse living would reverse the exodus of the middle class.

Calgary was not willing to gamble with the implementation of innovative but untried policies. It modified its 1983 proposal and continued to pursue a policy of territorial expansion which had the uncritical support of the city's businesspeople and real estate developers.[41] In 1986 Calgary announced that it would begin negotiations with the municipal districts of Foothills and Rocky View to annex 256 square kilometres (98.5 square miles) of land so that the city would have an adequate supply for residential and commercial development until the year 2020. Unlike Edmonton, Calgary adopted a conciliatory stance towards its neighbours and spent almost two years bargaining and negotiating agreements with them.[42] Finally on February 27, 1989, the three municipalities signed an annexation agreement which would give the city 245 square kilometres (95 square miles). With this intermunicipal agreement in hand, the city expected the LAB to approve the annexation as a matter of course and was shocked when the amount of land was reduced to 158 square kilometres (61.3 square miles).[43] The board approved the annexation of approximately 128 square kilometres (49.6 square miles) of land from the Municipal District of Rocky View and 30.2 kilometres (11.7 square miles) from the Municipal District of Foothills.

The Town of Redcliff, a tenth the size of neighbouring Medicine Hat, has been embroiled in a controversy over amalgamation for several decades. But unlike expansion-minded Edmonton, Calgary, and Leduc, Redcliff has attempted to interest Medicine Hat in absorbing the town along with its financial liabilities. In 1962 the two communities considered amalgamation but the problems related to Redcliff's debt could not be resolved. In 1968 and again in 1972 the merits of amalgamation were discussed in Redcliff. In 1979, 760 citizens signed a petition calling for annexation which was rejected by council, but when the electorate was given the opportunity to vote on an amalgamation feasibility study in the 1980 election, it was defeated 730 to 421. Amalgamation again became an issue in 1985 when people in Redcliff compared their property taxes and natural gas rates with those in Medicine Hat, which were extremely low. The leader of the group proposing amalgamation said that "it's becoming too expensive, running a small town."[44] After Redcliff held a spring special election in which 753 people voted in favour of amalgamation and 608 were opposed, the two municipal councils struck a committee to discuss its feasibility. As in the past, the problems centred on whether or not Medicine Hat was willing to assume Redcliff's liabilities and on the $4.59 million cost of bringing Redcliff's services up to the same standards as those in Medicine Hat. If amalgamation occurred, Medicine Hat ratepayers could incur a tax increase of approximately 8 percent. Since this was unacceptable to Medicine Hat, the provincial government was approached for an $11 million grant to cover the costs of the amalgamation.[45] After the province turned down the request because an amalgamation grant "would not be perceived as equitable in other communities," Medicine Hat terminated the amalgamation discussions.[46]

Evaluating the Reorganization of Local Government in Alberta

In moving from policy to process it is important to remember that a major problem with reorganizing local government in Alberta is that the process itself is flawed. Although many communities are able to adjust their boundaries through a series of mutual accommodations and compromises before approaching the LAB, irreconcilable differences may exist between the proponents and opponents of annexation. Such conflict is exacerbated by the nature of the LAB hearings. Two political scientists who were participant observers in Edmonton's major annexation proposal, T.J. Plunkett and James Lightbody, emphasize that the LAB hearings are a judicial type of process and adversarial in nature.[47]

> ... the LAB process works reasonably well in dealing with the conventional or typical annexation requests. But the Edmonton application did not fit into this category for it raised other substantial issues not generally dealt with in the conventional annexation hearing, for exam-

ple, the amalgamation of two existing and viable municipalities. . . . Because the City was, by the nature of the process, the initiator of the annexation application it also became quickly designated as the aggressor by the interveners who emerged as the defenders of the status quo. It was in the interests of the latter, by virtue of the adversarial process which quickly emerged, to smother any attempt to maintain a focus on the wider issues involved. . . .[48]

Plunkett and Lightbody argue that the quasi-judicial nature of LAB hearings inhibits the intervention of individual citizens and groups. In conclusion, they suggest that if the province had employed an investigative team from the metropolitan area's municipalities it "would have eliminated the adversarial process, might have initiated research independent of municipal bias and could have provided a means of hearing all parties concerned without resort to tedious cross-examination."[49] Implicit in their conclusions is that such an approach would facilitate intermunicipal cooperation rather than the conflict generated by the current LAB process.[50]

It is important to remember that almost from the province's beginning, population trends and economic considerations have been the major factors in community annexation and amalgamation. This pattern continues today—few municipalities have static boundaries—although most of the territorial changes have been relatively small and uncontroversial. Only in Alberta's two largest metropolitan areas has a combination of population pressure and business "boosterism" resulted in expansions of thousands of acres at a time. While the sheer size of Calgary's annexations has been controversial, it has been in Edmonton, surrounded by municipalities jealously guarding their autonomy, that the controversy has been most intense. Efficiency and economy-of-scale arguments have been made frequently to justify expansion in both cities, but there is no evidence that either Calgary or Edmonton evaluated the effects of an increase in size on its administrative structure, fiscal capacity, or service delivery capacity. This may not be negligence but rather an indication that for the cities' administrations and the provincial government, the arguments made for territorial expansion are merely ammunition in very highly charged political conflicts. This is the point made by Lightbody in his examination of the dispute between Edmonton and the province over the ownership of the long-distance telephone revenue generated in the city. He argues persuasively that local autonomy was a "red herring" the government used to mask the real issue, which was the maintenance of the viability of a provincial telephone system whose policies benefitted rural Alberta.

What was never revealed in public were deep, and genuine, caucus concerns for the viability of the rural telephone system maintained by AGT. Alberta's legislature, not atypically, is significantly imbalanced to the advantage of rural districts; the subsidization by urban centers of the costly rural lines was a most tangible political issue for members who, at the best of times, were suspicious of the motives of the cities. Indeed, it was these latent bogies, far more than the pious platitudes about local autonomy, which had frustrated Edmonton's initiatives to bring institutional order to the metropolitan region by means of an extensive annexation in 1979.[51]

A facet of governmental reorganization which is seldom addressed and about which the public seems to be little concerned is the farm land which is taken out of production and lost with urban expansion. One of the most detrimental effects of annexation has been the loss of huge tracts of prime farm land to residential and industrial development. Although both Edmonton and Calgary have given lip service to the preservation of agricultural land, they have allowed expansion to erode prime land at an alarming rate. A study by the Environment Council of Alberta found that between 1977 and 1979, Calgary and Edmonton each annexed 8,400 hectares (21,000 acres) of farm land for residential and industrial use. During the same period, Alberta's smaller communities were just as guilty of neglecting to safeguard the province's agricultural future. Red Deer annexed 640 hectares (1,600 acres) and other central Alberta communities annexed 2,200 hectares (5,500 acres), of which 93 percent was prime farm land.[52]

The calculations in the preceding paragraph do not include 34,400 hectares (86,000 acres) annexed by Edmonton in 1979, 85 percent of which comprised some of the province's finest prime number one and number two farm land.[53] Edmonton's council eventually made a commitment to preserve less than 10 percent of it for agricultural purposes. When Calgary made its 246 square kilometer (94.7 square mile) annexation in 1989, farmers were promised the use of their land until the area was ready for development, but there was no commitment to preserve it as agricultural land in perpetuity. Municipal policy on the preservation of farm land is summed up best by the area manager of one of the province's large land developers. He maintained that although municipalities pay lip service to preserving farm land, they actually give it low priority, and, "if the municipal officials aren't concerned about it we won't be. If all the municipal councils passed resolutions saying we won't develop class one land, we'd get the message."[54]

Edmonton is not atypical in failing to calculate the costs and benefits of annexation. In 1979, in an attempt to convince metropolitan area residents of the virtues of annexation, the city distributed a fact sheet entitled "About the Edmonton Boundaries" in which Mayor Purves promised, "Regional service levels would remain at current standards or higher in present Edmonton, and will improve in the outlying areas. This is particularly so for protection services such as fire and police."[55] The exuberance felt by Edmonton's administration after the city was awarded 34,400 hectares (93,224 acres) began to wane with the downturn of the Alberta economy in the early 1980s. As Edmonton's residential, business, and industrial growth declined, it was unable to maintain the level of services the areas had enjoyed before they became part of the city and taxes in the annexed areas skyrocketed.

Although businesses located in annexed rural areas were receiving far lower levels of service than their counterparts in the city, it was decided by city hall that their tax structure would be the same as that of core city businesses. The tax increase was 100 percent. A report prepared by the city's assessor demonstrated how rural land owners would substantially increase the city's coffers. For example, the taxes levied on one Strathcona County farm would increase from $439 under the county's tax structure to $1,498 under the city's structure; taxes on a Parkland County farm would be raised 366 percent, from $279 to $1,300.[56]

As taxes increased in the annexed areas and levels of service began to decline, residents were particularly concerned about fire protection.[57] The council and the administration slowly phased some city services into the annexed areas, but no special provisions were made for the new residents to exercise political power. They were submerged into a political system composed of six wards and twelve councillors who viewed their constituents, first and foremost, as "core city" Edmonton residents.[58]

With the city in the midst of a recession in 1983, no funds were budgeted to service the newly annexed industrial and commercial lands. As a consequence, in the spring of 1984 a former Edmonton alderman and a number of disgruntled property owners living in the area organized the Edmonton Rural Fair Tax Association. The unhappy citizens, who were paying high taxes but who still had to truck in their water and truck out their garbage, believed their tax rates should be lowered. Some 5,000 of them presented a petition to Edmonton's council requesting that taxes be rolled back to pre-annexation levels, but the petition was summarily dismissed.

Belatedly, in December 1984 and the spring of 1985, the Minister of Municipal Affairs made a number of ad hoc policy announcements promising substantial rebates to ratepayers in the annexed areas for the taxes they had paid from 1981 through 1985 and an assessment of farm buildings at rural rates in the annexed areas until 1991.[59]

Several Edmonton council members became increasingly critical of the shabby treatment meted out to the city's newest residents and the effect of annexation on city finances. In January 1983 Jan Reimer complained, "Annexation hasn't benefitted Edmonton at all, we'll be paying years down the road for road maintenance and snow clearance in the new areas."[60] Ed Ewasiuk proposed the city "de-annex" a sizeable portion of the land it had annexed in 1981 by turning it over to the province or back to its original owners.[61] In 1985 Mayor Laurence Decore said, "We spent hundreds of thousands of dollars on a great big annexation that now appears to be pretty clear we didn't need." Then he qualified his statement by saying, "But we're just wasting money if we say 'take it back.'"[62]

In 1986 the debate continued as to whether the city's newly annexed areas had been fairly treated. Residents argued that they were paying $3.6 million a year for services they did not receive, such as water, transit, and sewage services and garbage collection, and for greatly reduced police, fire, and ambulance services. Facing yet another budget crisis, and unwilling to forego a single dollar of revenue, the city manager responded, "The philosophy of measuring taxes against services received could be carried to a ridiculous extent where, for example, certain families who no longer have children attending school could request a rebate or a reduction in mill rate to account for school taxes."[63] One of the city's aldermen dismissed the residents' plea for relief with the comment that "it's a tired argument but at that time our annexation team made some very strong and optimistic promises . . . no one could forecast a recession at that time."[64] After having broken faith with people living in the annexed areas, neither the city's administration nor its aldermen seemed to realize that their actions were seen by many as undermining representative democracy in the city.

Edmonton has not been alone in the mistreatment of residents of newly annexed areas. During the 1988 Calgary annexation hearings opponents discussed the problems they had encountered. One person related that he had owned farm land very close to the northwest sector of Calgary which was taxed at the rate of $2,500 a year. Several years after his land was annexed he received a tax bill from the city for $43,000 and an explanation that the land would no longer be taxed as agricultural land but would be taxed as "city land." After a two-year battle and legal fees of $15,000 he won his fight, but only because he was tenacious.[65] In another case the property taxes on a newly annexed farm increased from $347 to $6,100 a year.[66]

Ironically, the debates which took place in Edmonton and Calgary over the servicing and taxing of annexed lands were almost identical to those that occurred in the provincial assembly in 1918. During Edmonton's great boom in 1912, millions of dollars were borrowed to finance capital projects and thousands of square hectares, both subdivided and undivided, were added to the city. After the speculative bubble burst in 1913, the city's finances deteriorated and the mill rate was substantially increased. An MLA from Edmonton argued "that much of this land had been forcibly brought within city limits by the legislature itself against the protests of property owners. A great deal was taken in that never should have come in and it had resulted in taxes piling up which amounted to confiscation of the land." Premier Charles Stewart was sympathetic with the property owners but maintained that the fiscal interests of the cities also had to be considered. He suggested that the differences between the city and the land owners be resolved by the Board of Public Utilities Commissioners, which had been established as a nonpartisan body several years earlier.[67] Then, as now, the issue was never settled but left to subside of its own accord.

In Crowsnest Pass many people disenchanted with governmental reorganization felt they had been misled by its proponents. They had supported amalgamation after being told it would result in much higher levels of service at little additional cost. Once amalgamation was carried out, the province provided "one-time" grants to help offset servicing imbalances among the amalgamated communities. However, the funds were quickly spent and the new administration embarked on an ambitious program of road paving and curbing and gutter installation. In 1982 the cost of this program in addition to the $200,000 needed for facilities in the Crowsnest Pass for the 1984 Alberta Winter Games resulted in property tax increases of 17 percent for homeowners and 10 percent for businesses.[68] This triggered the formation of the 600-member Crowsnest Pass Ratepayers Association, which sought a referendum on abolishing the amalgamated municipality. After learning that the municipality could not be abolished by referendum, the association focused its attention on downgrading service levels and freezing spending. In 1985, still dissatisfied over the level of taxes and services, the owners of nearly 2,000 hectares (5,000 acres) of land near the municipality's eastern boundaries petitioned the LAB to join the Municipal District of Pincher Creek. They argued that since their land was agricultural they would be more comfortable in a rural and agricultural municipality. In a Pyrrhic victory the LAB ruled that 160.4 hectares (400 acres) were to be transferred to the municipal district and the rest to remain within Crowsnest Pass.

Crowsnest Pass is a classic case of bringing together a number of communities whose residents have different expectations of service and taxes, and imposing a single tax and service standard. In addition to being criticized for upgrading roads and installing curbing and gutters, the new professional administration was admonished for spending funds on meetings, conventions, and travel. In all likelihood, the disagreement between those favouring higher service levels and those committed to limited services and what they define as accountable administration will continue for several years before an accommodation is reached.

In an evaluation of governmental reorganization in Alberta it should be emphasized that many more annexations and amalgamations have been implemented with minimal controversy than have resulted in continuing conflict. Two factors seem to determine whether or not a reorganization will be successful: first, whether the proposal involves people and communities or only vacant land; and second, whether there is an attempt to reach an accommodation with the governmental unit losing territory or uncompromising "power politics" are employed.

Some municipalities are simply more politically aware of the necessity of viable and ongoing relationships with their neighbours. In the 1980s Medicine Hat, Lloydminster, and Lethbridge recognized the importance of negotiation and compromise and accomplished annexations with little conflict or animosity. In 1981 Medicine Hat entered into protracted negotiations with Improvement District No. 1 over a proposed 3,600 hectare (9,000 acre) annexation. The city was persuaded by the district to annex a road allowance that would require substantial improvement with the expansion of the city boundaries. As a result of the improvement district's concern about the annexation of prime farm land, the size of the area to be annexed was reduced by 256 hectares (640 acres).[69] In a 9,600 hectare (24,000 acre) annexation bid in 1981, the City of Lethbridge established a joint planning committee with the County of Lethbridge. A series of compromises included a reduction of the annexed area to 5,504 hectares (13,760 acres), an agreement that the city pay $75,000 for each of five years to reimburse the county for lost tax revenues, and a property tax reduction of almost $400 a year for each of the 36 county residents in the annexation area.[70] In 1982 Lloydminster negotiated an agreement with the County of Vermilion River and the rural municipality of Wilton to annex 1,400 hectares (3,500 acres).[71]

Until Edmonton's recent affliction with "annexation indigestion" the city was reluctant to restrict its growth to the relatively unpopulated southern sector of the region. Unlike those in Calgary, Edmonton politicians seemed to have taken a perverse pride in being publicly abrasive rather than negotiating with neighbouring municipalities on territorial issues.[72] Edmonton's uncompromising stance during its 1980/81 annexation battle has not been forgotten by municipalities on the city's borders. A decade later, "Edmonton baiting" in the St. Albert and Fort Saskatchewan council chambers is a "win/win" strategy and good political theater, for a deep-seated resentment still exists.[73]

An Overview of Local Government Reorganization in Alberta

During the 1980s the population pressure on Alberta's larger municipalities eased as net migration into the province declined to zero. Growth-related problems were placed on the back burner as municipalities dealt with a province-wide fiscal crisis. With a recovering economy in the 1990s, people are again moving into the province and municipalities once again face problems associated with increasing size. It can be expected that governmental reorganization will be resurrected as a solution for population-related problems and that the opponents of reorganization will bring back their traditional arguments against it. However, after years of debate on the issue, many people are beginning to realize there is not a "single best solution" for size-related problems. A combination of physical, fiscal, and political circumstances will determine an optimal public/private and government configuration for the production of services, which may or may not be the same configuration that will be used for their delivery.

The realization that, in resolving size-related problems, what works for one community may not work for another does not mean an end to political manoeuvring in this area. But it does mean that political discussions will be less dogmatic and have less of the fervour of the expert, which in the past often characterized the governmental reorganization debate. The emergence of a new political mood may lead to a conscious attempt to bring the public into the debate and further enhance democracy at the grass roots.

6

Policy Makers and Democracy

Rational and Incremental Policy Models for Decision Makers

For as long as social scientists have studied politics there have been heated arguments about policy making at the community level. Although scholars and practitioners developed myriad theories, only a few have captured the public's imagination. One of these is the rational model of decision making as a step-by-step process, described by David Braybrooke and Charles Lindblom: "The ideal way to make policy is to choose among alternatives after careful and complete study of all possible courses of action, all their possible consequences and after an evaluation of those consequences in the light of one's values."[1]

The steps employed in this model are as follows:

1. Identify the problem.
2. Identify and clarify the goals that would solve the problem and then rank them according to their relative importance.
3. Identify all alternative policies that would achieve each identified goal.
4. Assess the costs and benefits of each alternative policy.
5. Select the goal and the policy to achieve it that would provide the maximum benefits at the least cost with the fewest unwanted side effects.

Policy makers who employ this strategy are assumed to be above bureaucratic politics, internal council dissension, personality politics, and the influence of neighbourhood and interest groups. The rational model makes a number of other questionable assumptions, the first being that a problem can be clearly identified and that policy goals can be delineated and then ranked. In the real world, the definition of problems and policy goals often turns out to be subjective, and all too frequently policy is for-

175

mulated without "the problem" ever being clearly defined. The second assumption is that governments have large numbers of administrative personnel assigned to gathering and processing the information required to make rational decisions. This is seldom the case in large cities and in smaller communities, where the secretary-treasurer has little or no time to collect and consider information on policy issues, most decision making tends to be a "seat of the pants" exercise. Third, the assumption that decision makers have unlimited time to identify problems and rank goals is implicit in the model. In the real world, however, some issues require an immediate decision and a problem can seldom be put aside for six months or a year while a council explores all of its ramifications. Finally, the rational approach assumes that once a particular goal and policy are selected, council will adopt them in spite of politics, which are always integral to the policy process. In short, while the rational model of decision making has some appeal for practitioners and students of local government, it neither recognizes the complexity of issues facing municipal councils nor accounts for political considerations.

A general principle underlying almost all policy making is that decision makers tend to eliminate policies that are unpredictable. While innovative policies may be discussed, they are usually discarded in favour of familiar precedents. Since council members tend to be no more disposed to gamble with the municipality's resources than they are with their own, most policy decisions perpetuate the status quo.

Another general principle of municipal policy making is that councils attempt to avoid controversy by relying on routine methods in making decisions. Incremental budgeting is an example. Rather than evaluating the merits of each policy area, a council often increases all departmental budgets by a fixed percentage, usually approximating the inflation rate. The "spend-service" practice is also common; if a service appears to be inadequate, a council increases its budget rather than examining any underlying problems.

Policy making takes place in the context of goals which almost all municipalities adopt, such as to make the community a good place in which to raise a family and to prevent a decline in population. These goals are often couched in terms so general that very often two diametrically opposing policies can be interpreted as leading to the same goal.

Moreover, although policies are often rationalized in terms of furthering a general community goal, a specific policy decision is normally a response to an immediate problem. One year the major problem may be deteriorating roads and the next year it may be the destruction of property by young hooligans. Each time the council tackles the problem at hand and then at some later date "fine tunes" its policies to ensure that the same or similar problems will not reoccur. This "real-world" process of decision making was first identified by Charles Lindblom, who called it *incrementalism*.[2] Lindblom also coined the term *"muddling through"* to describe the activities of decision makers who are continually making incremental changes in policy rather than employing a comprehensive rational approach. Thomas Dye, building on Herbert Simon's concept of "satisficing," adds a further dimension to incrementalism:

> Rarely do human beings act to maximize all of their values; more often they act to satisfy particular demands. Men are pragmatic: they seldom search for the "one best way" but instead end their search when they find "a way that will work." This search usually begins with the familiar—that is, with policy alternatives close to current policies. Only if these alternatives appear to be unsatisfactory will the policy maker venture out toward more radical innovation. In most cases modification of existing programs will satisfy particular needs, and the major policy shifts required to maximize values are overlooked.[3]

Lindblom was criticized for advocating a conservative stance in policy making, despite the fact that he was only attempting to explain how the process actually operates. A more telling criticism was that the theory failed to explain why many policy makers were deeply concerned with long-range goals, since incrementalism, by its very nature, precludes setting and meeting general goals.[4] This criticism was met when Amitai Etzioni developed a hybrid model of rationalism and incrementalism, dubbed *mixed scanning*. He suggested that policy makers pursue generalized long-range goals by occasionally "scanning," while making a series of incremental policies. If they are moving too far from their general goals, policy makers change the direction of their line of incremental decisions.[5] Since Etzioni explained the role of mixed scanning in policy making almost a quarter of a century ago, the concept has gone through several metamorphoses although its basic idea is little changed.

Changing Policy Directions

A dramatic change in the socio-economic composition of a community invariably results in a fundamental change in its policy direction. An example is found in the case of Spruce Grove, which became a bedroom community for Edmonton when many young families were attracted by its cheaper housing. Spruce Grove had a population of 465 in 1961, 1,110 in 1970, and 11,918 in 1988. In 1966 the community spent $2.47 per capita for recreation and community services; by 1970 this amount had increased to $13.34 and by 1988 it was $176.60 (for a total expenditure of $2,104,700). A major shift in spending priorities occurred over the years as a younger population, including many professionals working in Edmonton, demanded more recreational and park facilities, cultural activities, and libraries.

The fundamental direction of municipal policy making is often changed by the provincial government, either directly through legislation or indirectly through manipulation of the grant structure. Legislation is enacted to "encourage" municipalities to make major policy shifts, such as giving greater consideration to the environment. Other provincial policies may have unintended but dramatic spin-off effects on municipalities. Provincial agricultural policies may encourage young farmers to live in a particular rural area or farmers' children to remain on the farm, or they may discourage rural residents from pursuing farming as a career and encourage them to move into the city. In either case, the municipalities affected are forced to re-evaluate their overall policies and spending priorities.

The grant structure, which is examined in Chapter 10, is often used to induce municipalities to make major policy shifts. *Conditional matching grants* (grants designated for a specific project that require the recipient to allocate funds for the project equivalent to a percentage of the provincial grant) often require a municipality to change its spending priorities.

Well organized community groups also are able to bring about fundamental changes in policy direction. If a group has politically astute leaders and committed members, the council generally will meet its demands, even if they result in a radical departure from existing policy.

Although candidates campaigning for council often pledge to redirect municipal policy, they rarely carry out their promises. Due in part to the absence of party systems on the local level, municipal government structures tend to fragment political power. Individual council members with innovative proposals seldom have the power or influence to bring about major policy changes.

In some communities, bureaucracies with thoughtful and farsighted administrators are the principal agents of change and initiative. However, a great many bureaucracies resist attempts to change the fundamental direction of policy making since their members have settled into a routine that has been established with much effort, time, and money. Any major policy change will force them to learn a new routine. Moreover, the greater the change in policy, the less predictable are its effects on the organization. Thus they see a major policy change threatening their job security, personal power, bureaucratic status, and income. The irony in all of this is that in every highly professionalized bureaucracy there are individuals with the education and expertise to develop innovative policy alternatives for the elected decision makers.

From Policy Directive to Bylaw

After council formulates policy, or legislative intent as it is sometimes called, it must be translated into a bylaw in order to have legal standing. In other words, bylaws are the vehicles which convert policy into legislation and legislation is the basis upon which a municipality is governed and regulated. The caveat to this conversion process is that a bylaw must always be based on a provincial legislative act which explicitly delegates authority and power to the municipalities.[6] Section 99 of the Municipal Government Act (MGA) reads:

(1) The powers and duties imposed or conferred on a municipality by this or any other Act are vested in and are exercisable by the council of the municipality.

(2) Except as provided in this or any other Act, a council may exercise and perform the powers and duties imposed or conferred on it either by resolution or by by-law.

(3) A council may exercise or perform by by-law any power or duty that is stated in this or any other Act to be exercisable by resolution.

Although legislative authority is conferred by a number of provincial acts, municipal powers for the most part are derived from the MGA. Occasionally a council enacts a bylaw with only a tenuous link to a provincial act. When this happens the bylaw is part of the municipality's legislation until someone challenges the basis of its authority. If the court determines that the bylaw is without authority it rules it to be *ultra vires*, or outside the municipality's jurisdiction. A bylaw is also in question if it conflicts with another provincial act or with federal legislation. In either case, the court decides whether or not the municipal legislation is in conflict.

Since bylaws must be general in scope but specific in meaning, they have to be carefully drafted. Various municipal associations and the Department of Municipal Affairs have prepared model bylaws which municipalities can copy with minor modifications for their own use.

However, appropriate models are not always available and the municipality may be forced to draft its own bylaws. Although elected officials are advised to write concise bylaws in simple and straightforward language, many municipal bylaws are wordy, obscure, and unintelligible. One of the dimensions upon which legislation is evaluated is its clarity and comprehensibility. If it fails to meet these criteria, regardless of how commendable the council's intent, the legislation fails.

A bylaw always begins with a preamble stating the reason(s) why it should be brought forth and citing the legislative authority which gives a municipality the right to enact such a bylaw. Some people humourlessly refer to this as the "whereas" section, for it often includes a number of statements beginning "whereas," followed by "and whereas" and culminating in a "therefore."

A piece of legislation is often unclear because many of its key terms are vague. Important terms should be succinctly defined in the section just prior to the substantive portion of the bylaw. The substantive section may contain any number of subsections depending upon the nature and complexity of the bylaw. Every sentence in this section should be absolutely clear. Complex and incomprehensible sentences, which easily can be interpreted in a number of ways, provide the basis for legal action.

After the bylaw has been drafted it has to pass three council readings before it becomes law. Section 105 of the MGA reads:

(1) Every by-law shall have 3 separate readings before it is finally passed, but not more than 2 readings of a by-law shall be had at any one meeting unless the members present unanimously agree to give the by-law 3rd reading.

(2) If a by-law does not receive 3rd reading within 2 years from the date of the first reading, the readings are deemed to have been rescinded.

(3) If the by-law is defeated on 3rd reading, the previous readings are deemed to have been rescinded.

A bylaw passed by council must be signed by either the mayor or the person who presided at the time the bylaw was passed and the municipal secretary or the acting municipal secretary at the meeting.[7]

As circumstances change, it often becomes necessary to amend or repeal a bylaw. In either case, it is necessary to go through the same procedure used to implement it, that is, three readings.[8] There are no fixed rules that determine whether a bylaw should be amended or whether it should be repealed and another bylaw drafted and implemented in its place. However, an amendment cannot be used to reverse the general intent of a bylaw; the purpose of an amendment is to make changes that do not affect its general intent. Rather than worrying about whether an amendment might change the intent of a bylaw, councils often repeal the pertinent bylaw and replace it with another.

Following is an Edmonton bylaw enacted in 1992 which illustrates many of the above points about the process of making bylaws.

BYLAW NO. 10287
Being a Bylaw to Deal with the Provision of Ambulance Service Within the City of Edmonton
WHEREAS City Council provides an ambulance service to the whole of the City of Edmonton.
NOW THEREFORE the Municipal Council of the City of Edmonton duly assembled enacts as follows:
1. The Council hereby prohibits any person other than the City from providing a public ambulance service within the City of Edmonton.
2. Any person who contravenes Section 1 of this Bylaw is guilty of an offense and upon the issuance of an offense ticket, shall pay a fine of $2,500.00.
3. Every day during which such contravention continues shall be deemed to be a separate offense.
4. Bylaw No. 6535, and all amendments thereto, is hereby repealed.
5. Bylaw No. 2573, and all amendments thereto, is hereby repealed.
FIRST READING 24th day of November, 1992.
SECOND READING 24th day of November, 1992.
THIRD READING AND PASSED 24th day of November, 1992.

Under sections 106 and 414(9) of the MGA, a bylaw is binding two months after it is enacted, even though there might be a lack of compliance with the MGA: (a) in either substance or form, (b) in the proceedings prior to the passing of the bylaw, or (c) in the manner of passing the bylaw. However, within one month of the final reading of a bylaw dealing with pensions, an application can be made to nullify it. In all other cases an application can be made to nullify a bylaw within two months of a final reading. The caveat to all of this is in Section 108, which states that a bylaw passed in good faith "is not open to question, nor shall it be quashed, set aside or declared invalid, either wholly or partly, on account of the unreasonableness or supposed unreasonableness of its provisions. . . ."

Cat Bylaws: A Case Study

Beginning with the 1971 Alberta Urban Municipalities Association (AUMA) convention a resolution was routinely passed almost every year calling for a change in the MGA to enable municipalities to license cats. However, the public seemed to have little interest in cat control until the summer of 1986, when city hall telephone lines in Edmonton and Calgary were overwhelmed by callers complaining that roaming felines were urinating and defecating in their yards and caterwauling into the small hours of the morning. A Red Deer couple claimed a vicious cat attacked their six-year-old daughter and in Fort McMurray "one person phoned us [city hall] saying a cat had done several hundred dollars of damage to his motorcycle by scratching up his customized paint job and tearing the bike's seat."[9] In Medicine Hat a petition was presented to council signed by 1,300 people who wanted cats controlled. Across the province, city councillors directed their administrators to prepare cat control bylaws. As just one example, the bylaw drafted in Calgary restricted the number of cats living in a household to two and made an animal's owner responsible for its behaviour and subject to a $2,500 fine if a cat disturbed the owner's neighbours.

Outraged cat owners responded by threatening political retribution if a cat control bylaw were passed. To add fuel to the controversy, newspapers reported on the activities of vigilante cat haters. The *Edmonton Sun* gave prominent coverage to the "Cat Killer of Lamont" who lived in a small town 56 kilometres east of Edmonton; he had become notorious over the years by shooting cats who trespassed on his property. Lethbridge's council passed a cat control bylaw in late summer but other councils were beginning to see that cat control was a "no-win" issue and simply waited for the controversy to subside in the fall.

The issue of cat control emerged again in the summer of 1988. After weeks of public hearings, wrangling, and compromises, the Calgary and Edmonton councils rejected controversial cat bylaws. Predictably, this did not settle the issue, which re-emerged in 1990 when Red Deer enacted a bylaw fining cat owners who allowed their pets to roam and permitting disgruntled neighbours to trap cats on their property. Shortly thereafter a similar bylaw was passed in Calgary.

When an issue has emotional overtones as strong as those generated in the cat control controversy, careful politicians step aside until the public participants have clarified the issues and revealed their political strengths. The adroit bureaucrat advocates neither the status quo nor a change in policy, but is painstakingly careful to appear unbiased.

The Chief Executive as Policy Maker

Chapter 2 of this book pointed out that Alberta mayors do not have the powers normally given to a chief executive in government, since they have no right to hire or fire members of their administration. In 1983 a Tory Member of the Legislative Assembly (MLA), Janet Koper, questioned the Minister of Municipal Affairs about "a growing municipal concern that the strength of the mayoralty in our province is not commensurate with their responsibility." The minister responded that he did not believe a serious problem existed and that he would hesitate to increase the power of the mayor without a recommendation from the municipalities.[10] With few formal powers, the politically astute mayor in Alberta builds a power base for the exercise of leadership in policy making by garnering widespread public support. Council members tend to defer to such a mayor because they know they may not be re-elected if the public sees them as attempting to sabotage the mayor's program.

With a city-wide constituency, the mayor has a much broader mandate than councillors elected from wards. As the community's political leader, the mayor has a distinct advantage over other council members. The mayor of a large city is often working within an international context. Mayors also are invited to perform ceremonial functions, from inaugurating new municipal projects to entertaining visiting dignitaries. They attend endless business and testimonial breakfasts, lunches, dinners, and evening events, in addition to an occasional wedding reception, christening, or funeral. Such functions give a mayor the opportunity not only to build political support but also subtly to reward supporters and punish detractors by attending some events and politely refusing to attend others.

In large municipalities, where personalized politics are less feasible than in smaller communities, the mayor often uses the news media, giving reporters "inside stories" on city hall in a tacit exchange for favourable publicity. Radio stations in Calgary and Edmonton have donated public service time to mayors whose "nonpolitical reports" occasionally include mild recriminations directed towards a balky council. Moreover, when council is discussing an important issue, it is the mayor's opinion reporters seek. Other elected officials and administrators are rarely invited to make their views known on radio and television and receive much less coverage in community newspapers. Perhaps the only advantage they have is that their activities are scrutinized less closely by the news media.

Both Calgary and Edmonton have had mayors who were masters at marshalling public support. William Hawrelak, who served as mayor of

Edmonton from 1951 through 1959, had such strong support that although he was convicted of "gross misconduct" in a land transaction and forced to resign, he was re-elected in 1963. After being removed from office in 1965 for conflict of interest, Hawrelak assiduously cultivated his own Ukrainian community as well as other ethnic groups and bided his time until 1974, when he was again elected mayor. Bolstered by the overwhelming support of the electorate and by the sheer force of his personality, his policies were supported by council after council.[11] In the same city, in the fall of 1983, a coalition of ethnics and young professionals placed Laurence Decore in the mayor's chair.[12] His disarming manner with the public and feisty stance towards the provincial government endeared him to the voters, who re-elected him in 1986 with a 62 percent majority. When Premier Ralph Klein was Mayor of Calgary, he was immensely popular. He was re-elected in 1983 with 85 percent of the vote and increased his percentage of the popular vote to 90 for the 1986 election. A former television reporter, Klein knew how to communicate with the public. Although both Decore and Klein had critics in council, for the most part they were reluctant to challenge a mayor with immense public support.[13]

Mayors who rely only on their status as community leaders are in a tenuous position; an astute council member attuned to the electorate and unwilling to defer to a mayor's leadership may undermine his or her authority. When Donald Blake studied the Edmonton council in 1967, five of the aldermen he interviewed stated that they were the equal of the mayor in policy making. One told him, "As I see it, in Edmonton there was a tendency on the part of councils to accept that their mayor and commissioners run the city. Council has equal responsibility with the mayor in the development of policy."[14] For more than two decades Edmonton councillor Ed Leger, who considered himself "council's watchdog," derailed many a mayor's programs. After relations between Decore and Leger deteriorated, he threatened the mayor with "trench warfare right to the end of the term,"[15] but his strategy backfired and he lost his seat in the 1986 election.

The most effective way to build and maintain power on council is to control a strong and cohesive local political party. For some time sporadic attempts have been made to build party organizations in Edmonton and Calgary, but they have encountered a number of obstacles, not least of which is public opposition to party politics at the local level. (See Chapter 9.) Consequently, the mayor is forced to rely on other methods, two of which are described by Donald Higgins:

It is . . . not unusual for certain traditions to develop around the office of mayor, traditions that in effect endow it with extra power. For example, the decisions on which members of council or which non-elected citizens should sit on which committees, boards, commissions, and authorities is sometimes delegated to the mayor. Similarly, it is common for mayors to initiate much of the action in council, and to represent the city in negotiations with other governments and other outside interests. . . .[16]

Although the mayor has little more formal power than any single councillor, it is the mayor who is looked to for direction in policy making at a newly elected council's first meeting. Unless the mayor loses momentum as leader, council members and the administration will bring forward suggestions, expecting them to be synthesized into concrete legislative proposals that the mayor can present to council. Normally, it is the mayor, working in conjunction with the clerk, who sets the council's agenda, although any councillor has the right to place an item on the agenda. A shrewd mayor can manipulate council's behaviour by placing contentious issues at the end of the agenda, where they are likely to be dispensed with quickly by tired members. However, council can vote to change the order of items on the agenda. Given the power under the MGA to preside at all council meetings, the mayor can appear to be fair and objective and still steer the council subtly in a particular direction. The perception of the mayor as honest and impartial is becoming even more important politically as communities allow their council meetings to be televised.

Mayors have found that hard-earned support from the public and council members can quickly fade if there is a loss of credibility. In December 1988, after Terry Cavanagh was appointed mayor in Edmonton, an equipment failure occurred at the city's water treatment centre. Perhaps in an attempt to show that he was "on top" of the situation, Cavanagh told the press that he knew about the problem early in the evening rather than the following morning, when he actually heard about it. He admitted to the press that he had lied, and most aldermen gave him the benefit of the doubt. But just one month later he told council that there had been no communication with anyone in the County of Strathcona over the location of a sanitary landfill site when, in fact, he had discussed the issue with the county reeve. When confronted with a statement by the reeve that they had talked about the issue, Cavanagh said that he did not consider the conversation to be communication, since that he believed it meant "they send me a letter . . . with somebody's signature on it."[17] Council members were much less charitable this time. The distortion of the truth became an issue in the fall election, in which Cavanagh was overwhelmingly defeated.

Exercising leadership is far more than having the aura of authority, setting the council agenda, presiding at its meetings, and appearing unflappable on television. Bettison, Kenward, and Taylor discuss the national prominence and influence that Mayor Ivor Dent of Edmonton wielded as President of the Canadian Federation of Mayors and Municipalities (CFMM) during the early 1970s. They write that he was "proven politically effective" by the brief he presented to the federal government on behalf of CFMM which appealed for a partnership between the two levels of government and called for constitutional change.[18] Shortly after he took office, Mayor Al Duerr made a concerted effort to "sell" Calgary throughout North America and the Far East. He achieved national prominence as his efforts paid off and companies began to move their operations into the city.

To exercise leadership while one has few formal powers is truly an art. A successful mayor knows when to compromise and how much can be conceded without destroying his or her legislative program. The discerning mayor knows which council members serve from a sense of duty, which serve to further business connections, and which are politically ambitious; the mayor's appeals, promises, and compromises are different for each group.

During his reign as mayor in the 1950s Bill Hawrelak controlled Edmonton's city council in much the same way a champion chess master manipulates the board pieces. After his overwhelming electoral victory in 1985, Laurence Decore used a two-pronged approach to engender council support. By assigning them to task forces which had high political visibility, he appeased aldermen who at one time had been decidedly cool towards him. Decore also held regular pre-council "tea parties" to resolve political problems informally behind closed doors. Shortly after taking office, he had gained the support of almost all of the councillors for his new programs. Even ever-irascible Ed Leger was a Decore admirer for a short period of time.[19] Rod Sykes, mayor of Calgary from 1968 to 1977, found that he could maintain a high level of public support by being abrasive towards councillors who threatened his programs. This tactic, combined with his "boosterism" in a city with a strong business ethic (Sykes had been vice-president of Marathon Realty, the real estate arm of Canadian Pacific), intimidated council members. Unlike Sykes, Ralph Klein, who was mayor of Calgary from 1980 to 1988, cultivated an image of himself as informal, folksy, and able to get along with almost anyone.

The former co-chair of the Calgary Economic Development Authority, in explaining how Klein was able to exercise executive leadership, said that in addition to having a natural ability to communicate, Klein "has a unique quality that all politicians would like to have and that is an appeal that cuts across every economic sector."[20]

A much different approach was taken by Strathcona County's reeve, Jim Common, an active member of the Baptist Church. Common explained that he could provide the electorate with the "moral leadership" to which it was entitled and make difficult and unpopular political decisions because "My own Christianity plays a major role in my decision-making. It helps when it comes to facing tough decisions."[21]

If a mayor falters in setting the direction of policy making, the vacuum may be filled by an ambitious councillor. The wielder of the gavel has power only if council members heed the dictates of the chair; mayors have been known to pound their gavels to no avail while bedlam prevailed in the council chamber. During one session of the Calgary council Ralph Klein repeatedly hammered for order as two councillors screamed at one another for over eight minutes. Afterwards an angry and frustrated Klein said, "I guess the only way to have control of the situation is to throw the bloody gavel at them."[22]

Some of the most acrimonious politics occur when a mayor fails to exercise leadership and the council is left with a power vacuum. This occurred in Calgary when Mayor Klein resigned to enter provincial politics and the council chose alderman Donald Hartman to serve the remainder of Klein's term of office. The new mayor lurched from one political crisis to another, alienating council members along the way. In a celebration honouring the Calgary Flames after they won the National Hockey League championship, Hartman presented the team's captain with a bronze statue which was the first of 500 that a local businessman planned to market for almost $900 each. Although the mayor denied knowing that the presentation of the statue was a marketing gimmick, the businessman insisted that Hartman had been aware of the commercial venture. Shortly thereafter the mayor endorsed a "Respect for Life Week" sponsored and inspired by the Calgary Pro-Life Association. After five aldermen questioned Hartman's ability to function as mayor, he lost his temper in council and harangued them for more than 20 minutes. Three days later he invited council to a private meeting to resolve their problems but the rift was so deep that a good working relationship never developed. Another leadership failure occurred in Hanna in 1981. After being elected to office on a platform of tax reduction, the mayor failed to gain council's support and resigned in frustration. In 1982 an Irvine council member accused the mayor of "dictatorial tactics" and of not allowing councillors "the opportunity to participate in decisions." Another councillor charged that "the decisions are all reached beforehand by the mayor."[23]

In some instances council members have made a conscious effort to undermine the mayor. In the fall of 1991 a coalition of conservative Edmonton aldermen amended a procedural bylaw so that the liberal mayor would no longer be able to select the chairpeople for council's standing committees. Rather, standing committee members would choose their own chairpeople.[24] A two-year resident and political novice won the Hinton mayoralty contest in 1983 on a reform platform. Charging that the previous council was a tool of private land developers and that many of its members were in conflict of interest, she alienated the members of council, all of whom had been re-elected. The mayor resigned when she in turn was charged with conflict of interest after four stormy months in office. Although he had been Calmar's mayor for more than four years, Bruce Tremblay resigned in 1985 because of "a strong personal conflict between myself and some of my fellow colleagues . . . which has created unnecessary and wasteful use of council's time and town funds."[25] In other cases where there have been irreconcilable differences the executive has prevailed. Four of Granum's six councillors resigned after accusing the mayor of being an autocrat. They maintained the mayor made important decisions without advising council and often arbitrarily reversed council's decisions without its knowledge. In High Prairie in 1987 the mayor sent letters to several councillors suggesting they resign. He explained: "The people who elected me mean a hell of a lot more to me than the people sitting around that chamber. I really hope I can get some resignations. Then we could get people to run for the right reasons."[26] After being asked by the councillors to investigate the council and the town's administrative structure, the Department of Municipal Affairs reported:

> It appears to the council that the mayor sees his position as having a great deal more power and authority than the position actually carries. Some individual councillors feel belittled by the mayor if they bring forward ideas or resolutions that the mayor does not agree with. Some councillors feel they have been attacked in public by the mayor.[27]

It is clear that a mayor's ability to function as a policy leader is dependent upon whether or not the council members will give him or her the freedom to do so. Another important factor which will be examined shortly is whether a council is cohesive or fragmented.

Council's Policy-Making Function

Since the mayor has few formal powers in Alberta, one might assume that council members would play a major role in formulating policy. In fact, many of them merely go through the motions of attending meetings and performing their duties. In effect, for a number of reasons, council members tend to practise incrementalism in policy making. There are no municipalities in which council membership is considered to be a full-time position. In smaller communities, where only a few hours a week are devoted to council business, policy issues are left to the mayor and the administrator by default. Except in Edmonton and Calgary, individual councillors have little if any staff assistance. Councillors are expected to do their own research and resolve constituents' problems themselves. When scores of decisions are made during a council session individual councillors are often unfamiliar with some issues. Important policy motions may be made and passed in a perfunctory fashion. At budget time the volume and complexity of information make it impossible for council to consider more than a few budget items in detail. Council members often focus on the merits or deficiencies of very minor items in order to show that they are "on top of the budget."

Although it is difficult to become well informed about the many motions and resolutions presented before municipal councils, members have not favoured proposals to enlarge councils to make their work load more manageable. When St. Albert's mayor suggested increasing council by two members in 1989, most aldermen said they were not overworked and one of them proclaimed that he spent much less time on council business in the 1980s than he had in the 1960s, when the work load was "more onerous."[28] When Lethbridge's mayor made a similar proposal the response was almost exactly the same; one member admitted that the aldermen were spread "too thinly" at times but did not think that adding to their numbers would solve the problem.[29] Aldermen in Fort Saskatchewan agreed that they were overworked, but were unenthusiastic about increasing council's size. One alderman suggested that the work load could be lightened if more members of the public were appointed to boards and commissions.[30]

Since municipal councils are small and in some communities meet only once a month it is important that councillors attend every meeting so that the responsibilities are shared equally. Less conscientious councillors are sanctioned under Section 29 of the MGA, which, with the exception of several reasonable exemptions, disqualifies a councillor who "is absent from the regular meetings of the council for an 8-week period. . . ."

This occurred in Mundare in 1988 when a rookie councillor elected in 1986 missed more than eight weeks of council meetings. Although he asked council to pardon his behaviour, after consulting with the Department of Municipal Affairs the Mundare council disqualified him.

Councils occasionally revolt against inept mayors. However, even when there is a complete leadership vacuum, most councillors hesitate to fill it, feeling that the time and energy required would be wasted. An individual councillor is in a much weaker position than the mayor. Unlike the mayor, the councillor cannot claim to speak for the whole community and there are inevitably other members who are unwilling to support a colleague's attempt to exercise leadership.

Although it is not usual, occasionally a council is so torn by dissension that its energy is dissipated in internal fighting rather than being directed to policy making. When this occurs, civic workers' morale is impaired and the municipal government functions only sporadically. In 1979 a rift occurred between councillors who had lived in Morinville for many years and recent arrivals who commuted to work in Edmonton. The newcomers wanted to preserve the charm of the community with a no-growth policy, while the old guard favoured policies that would attract industry and reduce the town's dependence on the residential property tax. With neither group willing to compromise, business ground to a halt and some councillors resigned in frustration. In the early 1980s a similar situation developed in Carstairs, a community with relatively low housing costs located only 37 miles north of Calgary. The commuters and long-time residents elected to council were unable to work together and four councillors resigned over a 21-month period.

In the spring of 1986 the Strathmore town council was irrevocably split four to three over the actions of two of its councillors. Council had decided upon a particular proposal to deal with storm drainage and sewage effluents to which three councillors with an alternative plan were opposed. When council representatives met in Edmonton with government ministers in order to obtain funding for the town's proposal, two of the dissident councillors put forward their own proposal, which had been defeated in council. At the next council meeting the two councillors were asked to resign. When they refused, the following motion of censure was passed: "be it resolved that the Council . . . do by this motion, censure the said Councillor[s] . . . for such actions, deliberately undertaken in disregard to advices given, so as to make their continued office of municipal councillor untenable to the citizenry of the said municipality."[31] The unrepentant councillors refused to resign.

An Edmonton alderman already considered by his colleagues to be slightly eccentric for advocating such policies as saving the city's magpies and reducing the gopher population with animal birth control, lost his credibility after it was revealed that he had been previously convicted of assaulting his wife. When he suggested the city consider using a landfill site which council and the board of health had already decided was unsound, one council member called him an "idiot" and the mayor commented that "it must be a full moon."[32]

Personal feuds can impair council's performance. In Calgary in 1986 Jim Bell alienated the mayor and 13 other councillors when he sent a letter to his constituents accusing six of his colleagues of illegally supporting a plan to help the Stampeder Football Club, in spite of the fact that the city solicitor had expressed an opinion that their actions were legal. Angry aldermen responded that in the future Bell would find it difficult to get even a pothole repaired in his ward. His action impaired not only his own performance as a councillor but also that of his colleagues, who were drawn into a time-consuming conflict which distracted their attention from more important policy issues. Two years later Alderman John Schmal demanded an apology from council colleague Dale Hodges after Hodges said that Schmal should be removed from the police commission for discussing police personnel matters with the press. In a confidential letter, Schmal wrote, "I think it's important that we respect each other as colleagues. . . . it seems reasonable for me to expect that you will withdraw the remarks you made with a public apology." Hodges did not believe an apology was necessary.[33]

In Edmonton a long and bitter feud between two veteran councillors, Ed Leger and Ron Hayter, affected the morale and performance of all members. The combatants had to be separated in the committee structure and council debate often degenerated into a discussion of personalities. After Leger was defeated, Hayter shifted his enmity to Lance White, a formidable opponent. Their infighting also had a deleterious effect. In the 1990s Alderman Patricia Mackenzie's close friendship with Mayor Jan Reimer unraveled. After establishing herself on the political right, she led a council move to cut funding for social services and child care. When the mayor attempted to restore the funding, Mackenzie lamented publicly that Reimer was not a leader who could develop a consensus.[34]

The high-profile cases of dissension between council members and the mayor may have influenced the Lougheed government's decision not to extend to elected municipal officials the kind of immunity to libel enjoyed by members of Parliament.[35] The government may have feared that immunity would lead to even greater divisiveness, irresponsibility, and "mud slinging."

It must be emphasized that despite the publicity they generate, conflict-ridden councils are the exception rather than the rule. Councils in most Alberta communities subscribe to the professional management premise, and council members working together over time tend to develop close personal ties.[36] Moreover, as we will see shortly, many councillors have similar socio-economic characteristics, a factor that diminishes conflict.

Scott McAlpine and Stan Drabek found that councils in Grande Prairie and Calgary between 1983 and 1986 were characterized by bloc voting. Grande Prairie's council had two identifiable voting blocs; membership in one was a function of councillors' terms in office and occupations, and membership in the other was primarily a function of age. Four voting blocs were identified in Calgary. One bloc was composed of younger members with lower educational levels; another comprised younger members on the political left; the third was made up of older members associated with business who had served for a number of terms on council; and the fourth included members who voted together but who were not "strongly associated with any particular background variable."[37]

Nothing can be more destructive to legislative programs than a council on which politics revolve around personalities. Astute mayors focus on issues and avoid personality discussions so as not to compromise their ability to gain support. However, this strategy does not require the mayor to avoid close personal relations. Fragmentary evidence indicates that friendships with key council members are extremely important in gaining support for a mayor's policy proposals. An examination of council voting behaviour in Edmonton found that friendship patterns provided the most reliable indications of how members would vote,[38] and one can assume this applies to other Alberta communities as well. On the other hand, there are isolated instances of personal relationships which have deteriorated so badly that council members have physically attacked one another. In the Village of Clyde in 1986 a councillor laid assault charges against the mayor, charging that in the midst of a council discussion the mayor grabbed him by the shoulder, shook him violently, and shouted, "I'm going to kill you."[39] Fortunately, such incidents are rare or there would be a complete breakdown of the decision-making process, which is based on discussion, compromise, and respect for others, whether one agrees with them or not.

Council Committee Policy Making

Although individual council members do not normally initiate comprehensive proposals, they play an important role in the policy-making process through their membership on standing committees. Policy is legitimated in the council meeting with the passage of bylaws, but most of the work and political bargaining take place in the council's committees. There are standing committees which are permanent and ad hoc committees which are temporary and created to deal with specific issues.

To understand council politics one must understand the dynamics of the committee system. Except in small villages with only three councillors, where work is carried out by a committee of the whole, committees structure council discussion and determine policy direction. They are able to do this because council usually accepts the recommendations of committees and enacts them as policy with little discussion or dissent. It is understood that committee members have developed special expertise in particular areas and that many hours have been spent discussing the pros and cons of a committee's proposal. Committee recommendations are subjected to close scrutiny and vigorous debate only when there is dissension on council or when other councillors have lost confidence in the abilities of committee members. The latter occurred in Fairview in 1988 when a councillor questioned why a proposal he brought forward in council was being referred to a standing committee. He maintained that "we, as councillors, are the truly elected representatives of the people and we should be able to bypass committees."[40]

One potential disadvantage of council policy is that, since most councils have several standing committees, proposals from any single committee tend to be narrowly focused. In the absence of a strong mayor who exercises leadership, policies developed by committees often work at cross purposes and overall municipal policy lacks direction. An astute mayor, knowing that one or two hostile committees can wreak havoc with the chief executive's policy program, attempts to exercise as much control as possible. However, although the mayor usually sits *ex officio* on all committees, it would not be feasible to attempt to control the standing committees by attending all of their meetings.

Members of standing committees develop expertise respected by other councillors. When they recommend one type of bylaw rather than another, they have structured the council's policy alternatives. Conversely, if a committee wants no action taken on a particular issue, it makes no report to council and the status quo is maintained. Both private and public interests in a community realize that the work of committees is a crucial step in the policy process and do their best to influence members.

Over time, most chairpersons gain the loyalty and support of committee members. In the full council it is not unusual for members to vote on the basis of loyalty to the chair of their committee, even for a bylaw they do not support wholeheartedly. Astute chairpersons often use this "loyalty support" to build a power base on council. On the other hand, a chairperson can quickly lose this support by speaking for the committee before council without having consulted the other members.

Socio-Economic Composition of Council

Council members bring to office the values that have been shaped by their social backgrounds. Many studies have shown that working- and middle-class people have different perceptions of the roles of business and labour in the community. They also differ in their views on education, community amenities, and thrift. Therefore, the socio-economic background of a council is an important factor in policy making.

Since the socio-economic characteristics of people elected to council do not mirror the socio-economic composition of their communities, it is likely that in any community some social classes will be overrepresented and others will be underrepresented on council. A number of studies of Canadian municipal councillors show they have predominantly professional and business backgrounds.[41] A dated 1971 study of political recruitment in Edmonton, Calgary, Red Deer, Lethbridge, and Medicine Hat found that:

> Whereas 49 per cent of the councillors have incomes over $20,000 just slightly more than 1 per cent of the populace from which they were selected have comparable incomes. Similarly, while less than 10 per cent of their constituents have gone beyond high school, over two-thirds of the councillors received some university or post-secondary education . . . 80 per-cent of the aldermen . . . fell into the traditional middle class white collar occupations of the managerial, professional and clerical nature.[42]

An Edmonton study corroborated these findings. "For the decade commencing in 1974, 87 per cent of successful candidacies have come from professional (including teachers) or business ranks."[43] Only one working-class person has been elected to the Edmonton council in the decade.[44] In smaller communities the only divergence from this trend is the large number of farmers elected to municipal positions.

A number of factors contribute to the predominance of middle-class managers and professionals on councils. First, studies have found a direct relationship between level of education and political involvement. Many people with a limited education find it difficult to comprehend complex issues and tend to avoid active political participation. On the other hand, a disproportionate number of better educated middle-class citizens are interested in politics and seek public office, many of them calling upon skills they have developed through membership in community organizations. Another important factor is that public service is more feasible for people in occupations with flexible hours, such as teachers, business owners and managers, lawyers, and farmers, than for people with rigid schedules, such as blue-collar workers and those in service occupations.

Professionals and business people also are attracted to local politics because of the high visibility it gives them in the community. Insurance agents, for example, often run for political office because it is good for business. Local government's strong policy focus on real estate and land use also attracts lawyers, architects, and engineers who are involved in property transactions. Given the predominance of these people, it is not surprising that the management ethic dominates the policy-making process. Even in municipalities with ward systems, which provide better representation for the working class, professionals and business people predominate on council. It is not uncommon that a business person elected in a working-class ward votes consistently with a business coalition on council. However, during the last two decades the public has begun to recognize the political nature of city hall and in communities with ward representation more working-class wards are being represented by working-class councillors.

Since it takes a number of years for a person to obtain the requisite amount of education to become a professional or enter the business world, it is not surprising that few municipal councillors are young. For this reason, younger citizens often believe that their interests are not represented in government. However, there are exceptions. In 1985 a hard-working and politically astute 18-year-old defeated six business candidates and two former aldermen to win a seat on city council in a Medicine Hat by-election. After he appealed to young people to work in his political campaign, more than 50 of them volunteered to distribute campaign literature door-to-door and put up lawn signs.

Unlike federal and provincial legislative bodies, where women have only token representation, municipal councils include a sizeable number of women. Although city councils are dominated by men, in some smaller municipalities the council consists largely of women. Social scientist Susannah Wilson explains why municipal politics provide a better environment for female politicians.[45] Since women generally have far less earning power than men and are not as well supported by the network of campaign funding sources, the lower cost of campaigning at the municipal level allows more of them to participate. Wilson also notes that at the provincial and federal levels the support structures necessary for many woman politicians simply do not exist. Female legislators with children must find adequate child care facilities and deal with the problems and costs of maintaining two residences suitable for children.

Although proportionately more women are members of municipal councils than members of Parliament and legislative assemblies, many have had to contend with male councillors who hold stereotypical views of the role of women. Margaret Crang, who was elected to Edmonton's council in 1933, rejected the notion that women politicians should passively follow the dictates of their male colleagues. An early feminist, Crang said that "a woman can decide questions of better food and housing that come up in connection with relief, better than a man."[46] More recently, Patricia DuBoise, mayor of the Town of Nanton from 1986 to 1989, said in a discussion of male chauvinism and sexual stereotyping, "Councillors and some of the townspeople themselves thought I would be a pushover for a sob story." She added that when she was first elected to council she was expected to make and serve coffee at council meetings, as well as to cut the cake. In order to dispel the idea that a female's role is to provide males with food and drink, DuBoise sat on council for four years before serving coffee.[47]

An irritating issue for some Alberta women is the practice in cities of calling the members of municipal councils "aldermen" rather than "councillors."[48] The term alderman is a venerable one, and women have only recently criticized the term as sexist and insulting. Nevertheless, many cities, including Toronto, Windsor, Winnipeg, Montreal, Fredericton, and Whitehorse, have adopted the term councillor, even though many of their officials did not believe the use of alderman was sexist. In 1983 the Red Deer council, with one female member, voted to continue to call themselves aldermen. Alderman Roy McGregor assured the council that the term had no sexist connotation.[49] When the issue was raised in Edmonton in 1986 the three female council members were divided. Jan Reimer, a woman of politically liberal sentiments, said that the term did not bother her but since it was offensive to some people, thought should be given to changing it. Politically conservative women on council thought the issue was trivial.[50] A year later Calgary's male commissioners argued in a report to council that "alderman stands out historically as the most appropriate term,"[51] but the issue is far from being settled.

Consultants

In the last 30 years municipal governments have made increasing use of private consultants who are often as important as elected officials in the policy-making process. Yet, for the most part, consultants tend to be invisible except to politicians and the bureaucracy. As the services they provide have become more technical and complex, municipalities of all sizes find they require skills which are unavailable among their own civil servants. Some service areas have become so technical or the circumstances so unique that the elected representatives do not even know what policy options are open to them. Municipalities find they need expert advice in areas that at one time were served adequately by municipal employees, such as the design and construction of swimming pools and ice arenas.

When the Alberta economy was booming during the 1970s the planning consulting industry expanded along with it. Oil and petro-chemical firms made increasing use of planning consultants, as did municipal governments and land developers. When land and resource development came to a halt and real estate and resource companies cut back on their use of consultants in the early 1980s, the Alberta planning industry was in disarray. Don Drackley, Gary Willson, and John Steil explain, "During the good years, the industry had forgotten how to promote . . . [planners] had little in the way of promotion programs and often lacked the necessary organizational skills to develop them."[52] The planners eventually rebounded, however, and established the Alberta Planning Consultants Association. In the early 1990s many planning consultants began to repackage their expertise as the provincial economy began to diversify with large pulp and paper projects.

One of the reasons that consulting is a growth industry is that the public has become increasingly critical of the size and cost of local bureaucratic structures. By employing private consultants rather than hiring additional personnel, a council is able to claim that it has put a cap on bureaucratic expansion and expenses, even though contracting with consultants is often as costly as hiring additional municipal personnel. However, the cost of consultants shows up in a different budget category; thus the use of consultants pacifies critics of big government.

Another reason for the increased use of consultants, particularly in smaller municipalities, is the realization that it is possible for the council to have access to the same level of administrative expertise that is available in the largest cities. Knowledgeable senior administrators in smaller municipalities can obtain expert advice and technical studies from consultants employed on a contractual basis at a fraction of what it would cost to hire a large full-time professional staff. However, caution must be exercised. A careful cost-benefit analysis is seldom done to determine whether it is cheaper to employ a private consultant or to hire additional municipal employees. According to Ron Duffy, "Firms have consultants ranging from the costly expert to the less expensive staff person. Hiring the right person or the right combination for the job increases cost-effectiveness."[53] In addition, unless the municipal council knows *why* it is employing an outside expert, the consulting firm will charge $200 or more an hour to identify the consultant's task before anything else is done. To carry out a well-defined assignment it may be possible to employ a competent technician, such as a computer programmer, rather than a highly paid systems analyst.

Municipalities have recently begun to hire employment consultants, commonly called headhunters, to locate suitable candidates for commissioner, manager, and administrative officer positions. In the past a special committee would be struck to advertise, interview, and select a suitable candidate who, more often than not, was already a public servant in the municipality. Today few council members are willing to spend the time necessary to select the best qualified candidate. Moreover, it was argued in Edmonton that the use of a consultant who charged $40,000 plus expenses "serve[s] to bring an objective and unbiased point of view" to the selection process.[54] However, there are exceptions. In 1985 the Airdrie council decided it was not necessary to pay a consultant between $15,000 and $20,000 to locate a suitable person for the city manager's position. Instead, a five-person committee composed of the mayor, an alderman, and three professionals was formed to evaluate the candidates.

A common strategy of many municipal councils has been to depoliticize a contentious issue by referring it to a private consultant. A student of politics explains this strategy:

The shifting of issues to private consultants by public officials has a great deal of middle class, business oriented responsibility. Further, since the private consultant is an unknown to the general public, and often from a distant city, the potential political retaliation or economic retaliation is removed.[55]

An Airdrie alderman, explaining why it was necessary to spend $4,500 to hire a consultant to conduct three public meetings and attend a two-day training session in order to develop a vision of the city in the year

2020, said, "My major concern is that it not be seen as a political document . . . to achieve this we thought it was necessary to have someone
from outside as a facilitator."[56] The fee is insignificant when compared
with the $300,000 the City of Edmonton spent in 1988 to hire a consulting firm to recommend whether or not Edmonton Telephones should be
sold. With the Chamber of Commerce on one side of the issue and the
Edmonton and District Labour Council on the other, council attempted
to defuse the controversy by basing its decision on the consultants' report.
The public was not convinced that the report, which focused on economic considerations, should be the determining factor in making policy
on the utility.

Many councils hire private consultants to legitimize a policy decision
that has already been made. The consultant gives a stamp of "scientific
approval" to a decision that is wholly political. As an example, the City of
Leduc paid approximately $200,000 to three firms to bolster the city's
plan to annex a substantial amount of prime industrial land in Leduc
County. The mayor argued that the reports of consultants were necessary
when the city made its case before the Local Authorities Board.[57] A horde
of private consultants approved diametrically opposing policies when
Edmonton attempted to expand its boundaries in the late 1970s. Edmonton, St. Albert, the counties of Strathcona and Parkland, and the Municipal District of Sturgeon each hired one or more consultants to legitimize
its position, and paid them substantial fees. None of the consultants in
the Leduc or Edmonton annexation cases made recommendations not in
accord with the views of their municipal employers.

The use of consultants is particularly controversial when they are
employed by councils to do work which could be accomplished competently by members of council or the municipality's public service employees. Gordon Hall, President of CUPE (Canadian Union of Public Employees), pointed out that city council justified paying Grande Prairie senior
civil servants some of the highest salaries in Canadian municipalities of
comparable size because of their administrative skills, but at the same
time spent thousands of dollars on consultants.[58] The public is also
becoming increasingly irate over what it sees as a wasteful use of public
funds to pay consultants for studies which are of questionable use.[59]

Civil servants are often demoralized when the council delegates to
highly paid outside consultants the work they are capable of doing. In
1985 the general manager and staff of Edmonton's Water and Sanitation
Department were upset when a local engineering firm which had been
awarded a $930,000 contract in 1984 to be the management consultant

for the south leg of the Light Rail Transit (LRT) line ignored the capabilities of the public sector. In a memo to council the manager wrote, "Municipal officials from other cities and engineering consultants and contractors from all over North America and overseas came at one time or another to see our deep sewer projects as well as Phases One and Two of the LRT, to discuss our methods and learn from our experienced staff." He added that although his department was not asked to continue work on the LRT, "last week, I was contacted by a local consulting firm which was awarded the design work contract . . . requesting consultations and advice on various aspects of tunneling practice."[60] Mayor Decore responded that he believed much of the LRT work should be contracted out to the private sector: ". . . it may cost a little more, but it has given Stanley and Associates an opportunity to get more work."[61]

Public Responsibilities and Private Interests[62]

Until the 1980s legislation governing municipal conflict of interest was confusing and ambiguous in Alberta. The section of the MGA under which most conflict of interest charges were made said that "A member of council shall not vote in the council on any question in which he has a direct or indirect pecuniary interest." Because the conflict of interest legislation was vague and the government had failed to provide municipal councils with adequate guidelines, overly cautious councillors often abstained from voting on issues that touched them even remotely for fear of being in conflict of interest. For several days in 1975 the Edmonton council was without a quorum in dealing with a rent control bill, since councillors abstained because they were either landlords or tenants. Shortly thereafter the MGA was amended so that a council member would not be in conflict of interest "if the member's interest . . . is one which is in common with all other, or a substantial number of other, persons in the municipality."

But the legislation was still unclear. For example, in a complex case in Cochrane in the early 1980s, the councillor affected thought pecuniary interest "meant receiving some gain, like money under the table."[63] In 1985 the AUMA and the Alberta Association of Municipal Districts and Counties (AAMD&C) worked closely with the Assistant Deputy Minister of Municipal Affairs, Tom Forgrave, on a report which made recommendations to clarify the legislation and to ensure that businesspeople and professionals elected to council would not be penalized. The legislation adopting the committee's recommendations required council members to disclose the nature of their pecuniary interest on matters being considered by council.

Another change allowed councils to sign contracts with companies in which council members or their families had an interest provided those members did not take part in council decisions affecting the companies. Municipalities were given the right to enact a bylaw requiring councillors to provide the council with a list of the companies in which they had an interest and to impose a substantial fine if they failed to comply. The legislation also allowed a councillor to appear before the council on matters about which any citizen has a statutory right to be heard, such as zoning and changes in land use, although any councillor who appeared as a private citizen was not allowed to participate in council's decision on the issue in question. Even before the legislation received its third reading, the City of Calgary prepared a "Declaration of Pecuniary Interest" form which aldermen were expected to fill out whenever an issue before council could affect or be affected by their private interests.

There are a number of reasons for the growth of conflict of interest cases. One is simply that some elected officials have been unwilling to forego business activities that place them at risk of betraying the public's trust. In other cases, rather than exercising caution, councillors vote on issues that they realize may place them in conflict of interest. This happened in the Village of Hillspring in 1989 when the mayor cautioned one of the councillors that he should leave chambers while a road allowance issue in which the councillor's father-in-law was one of the major claimants was being resolved. The councillor not only failed to heed the mayor's advice, he voted in favour of a motion which gave his father-in-law the use of the road allowance. The court later ruled that his actions constituted a conflict of interest.[64] In Medicine Hat the previous year a councillor who owned a plant nursery voted in favour of a strict Sunday shopping bylaw which exempted garden stores from closure. This occurred despite the fact that the mayor and municipal secretary had discussed with him any business interests which "might give him a problem in voting." After the court ruled that he had been in conflict of interest, the councillor still did not understand what he had done wrong. A councillor in the County of Beaver who was chair of the Grande Prairie school board signed a contract in the spring to teach in the fall, but failed to resign from the council. He explained that since he would not begin teaching for several months he did not believe he was in conflict of interest; more important, he did not want to leave his district unrepresented by resigning early.[65]

In local government, as elsewhere, a few people have questionable ethics. A number of years ago the mayor of the Village of Hairy Hill voted to extend a sewer line to serve one additional residence, his own.[66] In 1980 the mayor of Coutts voted to have water and sewer taxes imposed on properties in the village's northern sector but the bylaw was drafted so as to exclude the mayor's own property in that area.

Two Edmonton mayors have been involved in business dealings resulting in conflict of interest charges. Mayor William Hawrelak was ousted from office by the court in 1959 for "gross misconduct" in a land deal with his brother-in-law.[67] After he was re-elected, a corporation in which he had a 40 percent interest sold land to the city. Since the municipal act held that a councillor could not participate if he or she "held more than 25 per cent of the shares of a corporation undertaking a contract with the city, the judgment on March 10, 1965, was against him [Hawrelak] and he was removed from office."[68] In 1980 the city administration released a report showing that since the election of Cecil Purves in 1977, some $88,000 in contracts had been awarded to companies in which the mayor had an interest. The following month another report revealed that one of his companies received over $10,000 from the city for leased dump trucks. In September 1979 the mayor acquired a quarter interest in 40 acres just outside the city's boundaries. Three months later he apprised the city clerk of his interest but failed to make it known to the public. In December 1980 Purves voted in favour of a resolution approving a pre-annexation agreement for a large area of land which included his own holdings. When the case was brought to court, the judge in a controversial decision exonerated the mayor. Nevertheless, his business dealings with the city became a major issue in the 1983 municipal election, in which he was defeated by a margin of more than two to one.

Conflict of interest does not always involve politicians who are furthering their private economic interests at the expense of their public responsibilities. As an example, resolution no. 70 passed at the AUMA's 1977 annual convention pertained to conflict of interest by municipal and provincial politicians who owned and controlled newspapers. The resolution read in part: "the Government of Alberta should establish legislation requiring members of the Provincial and Municipal Governments owning and controlling various segments of the news media . . . to be subjected to the same 'conflict of interest' provisions as those applied to the members of the Provincial Cabinet during their tenure in political office." The government responded that it was irrelevant whether or not politicians promoted political preferences in newspapers they controlled. As will be seen in a later chapter, this point of view is controversial since the press has the potential to formulate policies and direct municipal policy making.

The ramifications of conflict of interest issues extend much further than the immediate consequences of a biased vote on council. If democracy is to work, citizens must be able to trust elected officials and believe they are committed to the public interest and not to private profit. As an example, in December 1990 a number of Calgary aldermen were concerned about what the voters would think if they accepted large and expensive Christmas floral arrangements from a major property developer, Oxford Development. Several of them sent their bouquets to senior citizens' homes and the Salvation Army so there would be absolutely no question in the public's mind about any improprieties.[69] It is essential that elected officials be beyond reproach in both their public and private dealings.[70]

Although it may seem that conflict of interest is rampant, in most Alberta municipalities elected officials are honest and hard-working. If they do overstep the bounds of conflict of interest, it is generally inadvertently and unintentionally.

Politics as Vocation or Avocation

One issue that always provokes the public and generates countless news stories is an increase in council salaries. Albertans are committed to efficient administration and professional management in local government. High-powered and high-salaried commissioners and managers oversee municipal departments in a number of cities, and professionally trained city managers and administrators are employed by towns. In many smaller towns and villages, clerks and treasurers are encouraged to upgrade their skills. In contrast, most mayors and councillors have no formal training or professional qualifications for their positions. As a consequence, the public tends to think that politicians do not deserve salaries as high as those of the professionals. This argument was made as early as 1913 by an editorial which said: "It is well to remember that Calgary prides itself upon a very good system of commission government. The commissioners are well paid to do the actual work. Why spend another $12,000 a year for aldermen when such good material as is this year available is ready to serve for the honor of serving?"[71] One reason for this attitude is a belief that making public policy is simple enough that any ordinary citizen with an interest in politics and administration should be able to do it well. A second reason is that council duties are seen as being part-time. Finally, while the community applauds individuals who, in the interest of the public good, serve a term on council, it often takes a dim

Table 6.1   1990 Remuneration of City Mayors and Councillors

	$
High remuneration for mayor	78,596
High remuneration for councillor	39,298
Low remuneration for mayor	8,000
Low remuneration for councillor	5,000
Mean remuneration for mayor	35,758
Mean remuneration for councillor	14,458

view of those who want to make a career of municipal politics. In 1917, when the City of Calgary decided to hold an advisory referendum on whether or not council members should receive a salary, an editorial in the *Calgary Herald* said: ". . . to pay the aldermen The Herald sees a direct waste of public money. It should be an honor sought after by the best citizens to be chosen aldermen of a city such as Calgary, and we do not believe public spirit is so moribund among our people to offer them a few paltry dollars in order to induce them to serve their fellow citizens."[72]

Councillors in Edmonton and Calgary who spend many hours sitting in council and committee meetings feel betrayed when their constituents question a salary increase. The electorate in turn becomes angry when councillors set their own salaries and then berate their critics.

Mayors in Edmonton and Calgary often hold office for a number of terms, work full-time for the city, and are paid accordingly. Although aldermen's salaries are lower, they are still appropriate for a full-time position. An Edmonton alderman's salary was $39,298 until May 1, 1991, when it was scheduled to increase 17 percent to $45,978. Calgary aldermen receive a base salary of $30,582 plus a $15,291 tax-exempt stipend for expenses.[73] While Lethbridge, Medicine Hat, St. Albert, Grande Prairie, and Red Deer pay their mayors full-time salaries, they pay their aldermen a part-time equivalent, a practice that has at times been controversial. Council salaries in smaller Alberta cities are much lower because the councillors have fewer responsibilities. Moreover, in most municipalities a conscious attempt has been made to discourage people from viewing municipal politics as a full-time career by paying councillors part-time wages. The evidence in Table 6.1 would be even more striking if high salaries in Edmonton and Calgary did not distort the mean remunerations for both mayor and councillor. Camrose pays its mayor $22,700 and its aldermen $10,000 per annum. Leduc and Airdrie pay their mayors $15,000 per annum and their aldermen much less. The lowest salaries for cities are in Drumheller, where the mayor receives $8,000 and the aldermen $5,000 a year.

With few exceptions, mayors' salaries have not been an issue. The president of the Edmonton Chamber of Commerce said in 1986, "I've always viewed the mayor's position and the salary he takes for it as almost a community service."[74] One reason for this kind of support may be that politicians who become mayors generally are more politically attuned to the electorate than councillors are. Another explanation may be that the community views the position of mayor as full-time, while that of councillors is considered part-time. Whatever the explanation, voters in Calgary and Edmonton have vehemently opposed attempts by aldermen to increase their salaries.

In 1978 Calgary's council approved a salary increase of 48 percent for councillors and 24 percent for the mayor. Only the threat of a plebiscite forced the council to revoke its decision. In 1981 the council's Committee on Role and Remuneration developed a simple formula to increase aldermen's salaries by adjusting them annually on the basis of the Calgary Consumer Price Index; salaries increased 13.3 percent for 1982. In 1983, however, when the council limited city commissioners and department heads to no more than a 3 percent increase, it also limited its own raise to the same amount. The cost of living formula was disregarded for 1984 when council froze its salary but was used to increase the salary 2.4 percent for 1985. That year council members, unhappy because their salaries were not keeping up with the cost of living, established an independent three-member salary committee headed by retired Chief Justice W.J.B. Kirby. The Kirby Report recommended that aldermanic salaries be adjusted upward so that by January 1, 1990, they would be equivalent to the salaries of MLAs and from that time onward would be tied to them. The report also recommended that the mayor's salary never be less than double that of an alderman and that none of the recommendations be implemented until after the 1986 election. In March 1987 another council study re-affirmed the Kirby Report recommendations. Finally, in November, council approved the recommendation to tie council salaries to those of MLAs, with the consequence that council salaries were to increase 41 percent over a three-year period. When it seemed the issue was finally settled, in the spring of 1988 the MLAs raised their annual salary by $8,700, which meant council salaries would also increase. The council ratified the new salaries in September but deferred the increase until after the 1989 election. The *Calgary Herald* and many citizens claimed that the increase was unjustified.

The 60 percent salary increase which Edmonton's council approved in

1978 was rescinded after a group of angry citizens circulated a petition calling for a plebiscite on the issue. Subsequently council almost doubled the yearly salary so that by 1982 it was $23,500, where it remained until 1986. With frozen city hall budgets and downsized departments, the council was unable to raise salaries again until 1985, when it established an independent remuneration committee chaired by Judge C.A. Kosowan and composed of labour, business, and senior citizen representatives. The committee recommended in June 1986 that the mayor's salary increase $7,000 to $60,000 and council members' salaries increase 5 percent to $24,675; the increases were not to go into effect until after the October 1986 election.

Just after the election, criticizing the remuneration committee for suggesting that they worked part-time and should be paid accordingly, the aldermen gave themselves a 15.6 percent salary increase plus an additional $6,000 a year for council members serving on the executive committee.[75] An editorial in the *Edmonton Journal* claimed that "the way in which it [the salary increase] was carried out is unconscionable. . . . Decore, who introduced the proposed increases in a surprise addition to the regular council agenda, later denied the handling of the matter had been orchestrated to avoid public opposition."[76] Still not satisfied with his salary, less than eleven months later Alderman Hayter proposed that Edmonton follow in Calgary's footsteps and tie council salaries to those of MLAs.[77] A "wage parity with MLA plan" adopted in March 1989 would raise council salaries by 51 percent over three years. City hall's phone lines were jammed by angry callers and council salaries became an issue in the 1989 election. After MLAs raised their salaries to $57,505, in the late summer council members agreed to hold their salaries to no more than $44,322 by 1991. This limit was subsequently increased. In September 1989, after deciding not to run for another council term, Alderman Julian Kinisky said, "I'm not proud to be an alderman. I'm almost ashamed now," and then explained that one of the reasons was that half of his council colleagues did not work hard enough to justify their 51 percent increase.[78] Just when the controversy over salaries was beginning to diminish it was revealed that the city's aldermen had been meeting in closed sessions in order to formulate a pension plan for themselves. Needless to say, the debate over the remuneration of aldermen has excited the political passions of the people living in Edmonton.

One of the most forceful arguments that city councillors have made to justify full-time salaries is that their duties and responsibilities are not only comparable to those of MLAs, but they also work longer than MLAs.

Table 6.2 1990 Remuneration of Mayors and Councillors in Towns and Villages[79]

	Towns ($)	Villages ($)
High remuneration for mayor	30,000	5,200
High remuneration for councillor	18,000	4,000
Low remuneration for mayor	1,200	600
Low remuneration for councillor	750	360
Mean remuneration for mayor	8,147	2,253
Mean remuneration for councillor	4,547	1,488

The Kirby Report states:

> The duties of a Member of the Legislative Assembly are largely concentrated over a period of several months when the Legislature is in session. The duties of Aldermen extend over the full twelve months. The problems to be dealt with by a Member of the Legislative Assembly are general in nature and contact with individual constituents is less frequent than that of Aldermen. Aldermen must respond daily to problems and complaints which are of immediate and pressing concern to their constituents. Their social and community commitments are more extensive.[80]

In smaller municipalities, where council meets less frequently, few if any local politicians maintain they should be paid as full-time professionals. Members of the community who "do their civic duty" and stand for election often receive little or no financial compensation for their service. In 1986 in the Town of Crowsnest Pass there was a heated council discussion about whether or not council salaries and honorariums should be cut. After one councillor proposed that the remuneration for attendance at special council meetings, committees, and board meetings be reduced to $50 per meeting another councillor argued that members who had to forego an income in the private sector should be compensated. A third councillor responded that a seat on council should not be thought of as a "money-making position."[81]

Table 6.2 shows that while some town and village councillors and mayors are adequately compensated, others receive so little that service on council is a financial hardship for them. In one of the larger towns in the province, with a population of more than 5,500, the mayor received a

Table 6.3   1990 Remuneration of Reeves and Councillors in Counties
and Municipal Districts (does not include expense allowance)

	Counties ($)	Municipal Districts ($)
High remuneration for reeve	48,000	25,161
High remuneration for councillor	30,000	22,247
Low remuneration for reeve	1,200	1,299
Low remuneration for councillor	1,200	2,160
Mean remuneration for reeve	8,843	10,547
Mean remuneration for councillor	9,200	10,455

base salary of $600 a month and a council member $300 a month in 1990. Considering the size of the community and the time it takes council members to carry out their responsibilities, they must be serving either out of a sense of responsibility or for the status involved in being a community politician. In the Town of Vulcan the mayor and councillors are paid $65 and $48, respectively, for each meeting they attend, and have no-voucher expense accounts of $65 a month. Table 6.2 shows that although in one village the mayor receives $5,200 and councillors $4,000, in 1990 the mean remuneration for council service was less than $200 a month. In the Village of Clive the mayor and councillors each receive $25 for every council and committee meeting they attend, while in Lavoy they receive only $20 for each council meeting and nothing for committee meetings. Chauvin's councillors are paid $6 an hour for attending council and committee meetings plus reimbursement for any expenses incurred. Summer village councils must labour because of a sense of civic duty, for they receive little or no remuneration and certainly no social status or civic glory. Among others, the summer villages of Silver Beach, Sundance Beach, Point Alison, and Castle Island pay their councillors no salary.

It should be pointed out that the data in Table 6.3 are based on a 35 percent response rate to a 1991 mail survey of Alberta municipalities. Nevertheless, they do reveal wide variations in reeves' and councillors' salaries in counties and municipal districts. Several of the more heavily populated rural municipalities pay their elected representatives full-time salaries. In the County of Parkland the average salary for councillors is $30,000 per annum and in the County of Strathcona the reeve receives $4,000 a month and a councillor $2,000 a month, a third of the Strathcona salaries being nontaxable. In the Municipal District of Sturgeon the reeve's salary was $30,171 and a councillor's $23,582 in 1991. However, the mean remunerations in Table 6.3 show that these figures are the exception.

Lutz Perschon, Manager for the Municipal District of Cypress, responded to the salary survey by writing that "the MD's philosophy is to keep things lean."[82] Annual salaries of $7,000 for the reeve and $6,000 for each councillor reflect this philosophy.[83] In the Municipal District of Cardston the average salary for councillors is $6,123 per annum and the Municipal District of Badlands pays the reeve $450 a month plus expenses and the other councillors $350 a month plus expenses. Surprisingly, in several municipalities the reeve's remuneration is less than that of the councillors. In 1990 in the County of Forty Mile the reeve received a salary of $7,715 and a subsistence stipend of $4,845. Five of the eight remaining councillors had a higher total remuneration than the reeve. The reeve of the Municipal District of Smoky River received $15,694 and one of the five other councillors received $15,949.

Breaches in Understanding

Many politicians do not understand why the citizenry is concerned about the increasing professionalization of municipal councils and opposed to council salary increases. All too often politicians decide that their salaries should be raised and then designate a council committee or salary task force to explain to the community why higher salaries would be in its best interests. When council members' motives and strategy are questionable, the public becomes angry and disillusioned. Edmonton Alderman Hayter said in 1987 that the public seemed to think alderman should be under-paid.[84] In the County of Beaver one councillor said that he felt "we are working too cheap." Another Beaver councillor, Fred Meyer, said, ". . . [I] won't sit here for that kind of money."[85] Such comments made publicly do not endear council members to their constituents.

In larger cities the justification for increasing council salaries is that councillors work a minimum of 40 and sometimes as many as 70 hours a week. But since many aldermen also hold part- and full-time jobs, the public is skeptical of the number of hours they claim to work. In 1988 Calgary Alderman Don Hartman defended the time spent on his consult-ing business by arguing that council benefitted from having members with business experience, while Alderman Ron Leigh maintained that the 50 to 60 hours a week he devoted to council still allowed him to sell insur-ance and Alderman Tim Bardsley denied that his law practice conflicted with his responsibilities as a full-time alderman.[86] In Edmonton, two of the most vocal advocates for paying aldermen on a full-time basis have been Lance White and Ron Hayter, both of whom have done extensive consulting work while sitting on council. However, the activities of many aldermen have undercut their claims that one can be a responsible and conscientious full-time council member and still engage in other business or professional activities. As an example, the *Edmonton Journal*'s city hall reporter, John Geiger, found that on the day people tried to complain to their aldermen about the salary increase they had given to themselves, only three members were in their offices. Earlier, Alderman Julian Kinisky had explained that some council members "just visit here occasionally."[87] Two months later a Calgary alderman objected to adjourning council at 10:30 P.M. because this would institutionalize two-day meetings and limit the ability of aldermen to hold part-time employment.[88]

Even when the public recognizes the many hours aldermen spend on council and its committees, salary increases are often opposed because of a perception that councillors are greedy and concerned only with their own interests and those of family and friends. In 1986 several Calgary aldermen employed family members as aldermanic assistants. After public criticism when this was discovered, council adopted a policy which prevented a councillor's dependants from being employed by the city but allowed the employment of a relative who lived independently and not in an alderman's home. In an in camera meeting in 1988, architect Eugene Dub, who had been a member of Edmonton's council from 1977 through 1988, was awarded an untendered $1.38 million contract to design the new city hall. The justification for not putting the contract to bid was that since Dub had won a 1980 design competition for a city hall that was not built, he deserved the 1988 contract. Moreover, a Dub supporter, Alderman Lance White, argued that the city was saving $750,000 by not having to stage another architectural competition.[89] What was left unsaid was that Dub already had received $250,000 for his 1980 design. After he produced a controversial design which the public did not like, council gave him the opportunity to prepare another plan. Since the second design was for a city hall that would cost 57 percent more than the first, it was necessary for council to increase Dub's fee, which was based on a percentage of the building cost. In 1989 council raised Dub's payment from $1.46 million to $2.26 million in an in camera agreement that was kept secret for more than a week. An *Edmonton Journal* editorial concluded, "City council has given us a classic example of how not to do things: it has chosen to spend public money in a series of private arrangements."[90] The same year, not long after Edmonton's council gave itself a substantial salary increase, four aldermen flew to Toronto to attend the Grey Cup Game between the Hamilton Tiger-Cats and Saskatchewan Roughriders. It was well publicized that the city was paying all of their expenses and that they were staying in $135-a-night rooms at Toronto's Western Harbor Castle and had $75 game tickets.[91] In contrast, Regina councillors who were representing their city at the game paid part of their own expenses. A year later Alderman Patricia Mackenzie made a 27-day junket to the Far East in order to promote the city's interests. The trip cost Edmonton over $14,000, including hotel expenses of $5,400.

Council salary increases are frequently justified on the grounds that as the community becomes larger council members are representing greater numbers of people and doing more work and should be paid accordingly. This rationale was used by Lethbridge's council in 1988 to raise its salaries substantially after comparing them with those of other councils.[92] The difficulty with this argument is that it does not take into consideration the city's governmental structure or whether or not the duties and responsibilities of council members are in fact greatly affected by any increase or decrease in a municipality's size.

Edmonton's Jan Reimer argues that aldermen work even harder than MLAs. She points out that nonpartisan aldermen have to be much more familiar with issues than MLAs, who are able to fall back on "party policy" rather than developing carefully formulated positions. The only possible fault with arguments equating the responsibilities of aldermen and MLAs is the assumption that being an MLA is a full-time job. If that assumption is questionable, then the argument fails.

Whether councillors are underpaid or overpaid is of little importance in itself. Rather, the controversy over council's compensation is a manifestation of several much larger issues: whether recognition should be given to the work of professional politicians at the community level, whether paying council members a substantial salary would enable people to sit on council who would otherwise be unable to do so, and what the implications of having full-time council members are for the governmental system. There is no doubt that council members in large cities spend 25 to 50 hours a week on council business: sitting on council and its committees, serving on independent boards and commissions, consulting with managers or commissioners, and meeting with constituents. Over time, councillors learn how the city operates and who are the key participants in the administration. In addition, advocates of the professionalization of local politics reason that councillors are making decisions for multi-million- or even billion-dollar enterprises and should, like their counterparts in the private sector, be well paid for doing so. Finally, proponents argue that paying councillors a living wage ensures that no one is barred from council solely for financial reasons.

For each of the arguments made for full-time council members and the professionalization of local politics, critics have well reasoned counter-arguments. They begin by questioning the underlying premise that local politics should be professionalized, suggesting that professional local politicians could become as distant and unresponsive to the public as those in the provincial and federal governments. Some critics argue that participation in local politics should always be viewed as an avocation rather than a full-time career, therefore local politicians should never be paid more than a part-time salary. Other critics are willing to pay politicians full-time wages for full-time work, but they fear that if councillors are paid salaries that are often more than double those of their constituents, money, rather than a commitment to public service, will become the primary motivation for becoming a councillor. Finally, critics fear that as salaries become higher, people will spend even more on electioneering in order to win a well-paying job. They note that the high cost of campaigning is already the principal financial barrier to public service in a large city.

Surprisingly, neither the proponents nor the opponents of full-time council members have considered the issues in addition to questions of compensation and the councillors' relationship with the public. Two scholars of local government who recently examined these issues maintain that "the potential cost to the organizational effectiveness of municipalities with full-time politicians is that a growing amount of its administrative leaders' energy and time will be focused internally on managing an increasingly complex and demanding political relationship, and turned away from an external focus on the quality of services provided to the public."[93] They argue that with a full-time council the relationship between administrators and council members begins to change, as many of the council members take it upon themselves to spend a good deal of their time overseeing the municipal bureaucracy.

There is no definitive answer as to whether or not the local political system should be further professionalized. The only thing apparent is that communication and understanding between many local politicians and the citizenry have broken down. If the issues of salaries and professionalization are to be settled to the satisfaction of both parties, the breach must first be repaired. One of the ways this might be done would be through the creation of a commission, completely independent of council, that would use carefully constructed guidelines to determine whether or not salary increases are justified and if so, by how much. Needless to say, how the commission is chosen, its composition, and the formula it employs to determine salaries must be accepted by both the public and council. Ironically, in 1979 the province was considering such a commission until the

AUMA convention passed a resolution "that the AUMA approach the Provincial Government stating that it is not in favour of the establishment of a commission to govern rates of remuneration for elected officials."[94] Shortly thereafter the government quietly shelved its plan to establish a remuneration commission and defuse council salaries as a political issue at the municipal level.

An Overview of Policy Makers and Democracy

The engine of government is the policy-making process, for it is here that elected representatives determine the scope of governmental activity, who pays for government, and who benefits from it. Very often electoral candidates promise new directions in council policy making and a reallocation of the municipality's services and resources. But newly elected councilors soon find there is a paucity of time, staff, and resources to plan for new policies. Innumerable regulations, human variables, and other factors may affect a policy proposal, but the specific effect of any one of them is unknown. As a consequence, many municipal councilors, whether newly elected or veterans, find the policy process chaotic and confusing.

Despite the difficulty of unraveling the complexities of policy making, there are tenacious, astute, and politically perceptive elected officials who are able to change a council's direction. They understand that since the structure of municipal systems is divisive and fragments power, it is necessary to create political power informally. However, this is particularly difficult since, for the most part, at the municipal level political parties do not exist to coalesce and consolidate power in governmental systems that are fragmented. As a consequence, elected officials seeking political power are forced to rely on the prestige of their positions and the friendships they have nourished.

Many municipal officials see the public as compounding their difficulties in formulating public policy. While most politicians accommodate themselves to the normal push and pull of democratic local government, many feel unfairly stigmatized by an unduly suspicious citizenry. The suspicion does not attenuate with a politician's length of tenure. In fact, long-serving politicians may be under greater suspicion than neophytes, as the public may view these officials as making a living off politics; that is, the public may view them as professional politicians. In Alberta most evidence suggests that amateur politicians are widely favoured. Amateurism presumably keeps government closer to the people by discouraging the development of a political class and by making it more likely that elected officials act in the public interest instead of their own limited interests. It should be added that despite the amount of discussion on this issue, there are not clear-cut answers as to whether policy making and democracy are enhanced or impaired by either professional or amateur politicians.

7

Bureaucratic Behaviour
and Democratic Institutions

The Municipality and Its Civil Servants

Section 57(1) of the Municipal Government Act (MGA) prescribes that soon after a municipality is formed the council will enact a
bylaw appointing a municipal secretary and defining the person's duties;
section 59(1) requires a similar bylaw for the appointment of a treasurer.
However, recognizing that very small municipalities may be unable to
afford both a secretary and a treasurer, the act allows the two positions to
be combined, with the person holding them being designated the municipal administrator. The MGA also directs every municipality to appoint at
least one senior civil servant as an assessor and one as an auditor, and
gives the council wide discretion in making other senior and junior
appointments. For example, the act allows a council to appoint a comp-
troller to maintain books and records and to employ a municipal engineer and municipal solicitor, on either a full-time or a fee basis. Section
82 allows a council to employ anyone it considers necessary in order to
meet the municipal responsibilities specified in the act. The employees
required to make local government work could range from sanitary and
building inspectors to playground attendants and community nurses.
Section 82 also authorizes the appointment of one or more commissioners or a municipal manager who may be given wide-ranging powers
defined under Section 91, which states that "council may, by by-law, provide for the delegation of any or all of its executive and administrative
duties and powers to one or more municipal commissioners or to a
municipal manager."

The powers of commissioners and the manager are acknowledged by
the procedures a council has to follow in order to dismiss them. While
other civic employees serve at the pleasure of council or under the terms

of the bylaw governing their appointment, commissioners and managers can be dismissed only by a two-thirds majority vote of all council members.[1] Although the mayor has the power to suspend any other municipal employee, a commissioner or manager can be suspended only by a council resolution and a written statement must be provided with the reasons for suspension clearly stated. The act attempts to insulate commissioners and municipal managers from a council which might act erratically or be politically unstable.

Commissioners and managers normally have an employment contract with their municipality which includes provisions that must be followed if the employee is dismissed. In the unlikely event there is not an employment contract, the council is required by Section 95 of the MGA to give three months' notice prior to termination. A senior bureaucrat being dismissed for no justifiable cause is normally granted one to two months of salary for each year of service up to a maximum of one year. If an administrator is fired for incompetence or improprieties it is not necessary to give him or her notice.[2]

While the MGA protects senior administrators from the whims of elected officials, it also lays out their responsibilities to the municipality. Section 94(1), which is explicit as to what constitutes a conflict of interest, reads: "No person having an interest in a contract with the municipality shall be appointed a municipal commissioner or municipal manager, and neither . . . shall, during his term of office, have an interest, direct or indirect, in a contract with the municipality." A commissioner or manager who acquires an interest in a business which has a contract with the municipality is subject to immediate dismissal without compensation. However, the legislation makes allowances for reasonable financial dealings with the municipality. As an example, an administrator who contracts with a public utility for power is not in a conflict of interest, nor is one who purchases property from the municipality if it has been advertised for sale by public tender in the community newspaper.

In specifying administrative powers and procedures for termination, the MGA differentiates substantially between municipal administrators and managers. An uninformed council occasionally reclassifies a clerk/treasurer or municipal administrator to manager with unforeseen consequences. The small town of Millet reclassified its senior administrator to manager in 1986 and made a six-month probationary appointment. At the end of the probationary period the council found it necessary to abolish the manager's position in order to rid itself of a manager who was protected because of the position. In 1987 the council of the County of Thorhild directed one of its members to investigate whether or not the secretary-treasurer's position should be upgraded to that of county manager. The councillor reported back to council that since most rural administrators preferred being called county managers, he had prepared bylaws to convert the position and appoint the person who was then secretary-treasurer to manager. The meeting became raucous. One councillor, charging that his colleagues were not aware of the difference between the two categories, asked the mayor, "Is your manager going to take over your duties?" He then stated, "We're not big enough for a manager." Another councillor was concerned that if the senior administrative position were converted into that of manager, that person would be able to hire a secretary-treasurer.[3] The change was eventually made, but not without acrimony.

Senior municipal administrators, whether they are clerks, treasurers, municipal administrators, commissioners, or municipal managers, have joint responsibilities, that is, responsibilities assigned to them by their council and statutory responsibilities specified in the MGA. The latter provisions relieve councils from having continually to specify the duties and responsibilities of their administrators. Although the two sets of responsibilities are almost always complementary, a senior administrator will occasionally be given a council directive that conflicts with the MGA's statutory requirements. Needless to say, the act takes precedence. However, since a council's actions also are governed by the statutory provisions, an administrator is rarely put in the uncomfortable position of having to choose between serving council or following the dictates of the act. The act's provisions on the duties of administrators are not overly restrictive, since they are meant to further, not hinder, the interests of municipalities.

Municipal Administrators' Responsibilities

In smaller Alberta municipalities, secretaries, treasurers, and municipal administrators are at the apex of the administrative structure. With statutory responsibilities under the Municipal Government Act, the Local Authorities Act, the Municipal Taxation Act, and the Tax Recovery Act, they are expected to be administrative jacks-of-all trades.

Section 58 of the MGA delineates the responsibilities of the secretary, who is directed to: (1) attend all regular and special council meetings and record the minutes and the names of council members present; (2) ensure the safety of council's bylaws in their original form; (3) keep a record of all other materials as charged by council; (4) prepare and deliver all of the reports and materials that the Department of Municipal Affairs requires of the municipality; and (5) call special council meetings when required to do so by a council majority, the mayor, or, in a municipal district, the reeve.[4] The secretary has a number of additional responsibilities that may include consolidating the municipality's bylaws and keeping them current.

The Local Authorities Election Act also assigns a number of responsibilities to the secretary, who is particularly busy during elections. While large municipalities appoint a returning officer to carry out election procedures, in smaller ones the secretary often serves as returning officer. Even in a municipality with a returning officer, the act stipulates that the secretary: (1) provide the returning officer with information and assistance and a sufficient number of ballot boxes; (2) safeguard the nomination papers and safely keep the ballot boxes for six weeks after the election; (3) destroy electoral materials after the returning officer examines the voting results; (4) be present with the sealed ballot boxes if a recount is necessary; (5) record the name of any person guilty of election bribery; (6) have all election materials available for examination by a judge in the event of an election irregularity; and (7) order a new election if a judge decrees the election invalid or the elected members disqualify themselves. In addition, if a bylaw requires a list of voters, the secretary may be directed to prepare it and to appoint enumerators.

The Municipal Taxation Act directs the secretary to: (1) prepare an assessment roll for the municipality and school districts with a description of all assessable and non-assessable parcels including their assessed value and owners' names and addresses; (2) prepare and maintain a supplementary assessment roll if directed to do so by council; (3) prepare a tax roll, send out the tax notices, issue receipts for payment, and issue a statement as to whether taxes have been paid or not; (4) mail assessment notices and keep a record of the mailing date; (5) keep a record of property owners with tax arrears; (6) notify the complainants and the assessor of the annual meeting of the Court of Revision and keep a record of its proceedings; (7) amend the assessment roll immediately after the court's decision; (8) notify a property owner if an assessor appeals the court's decision to the Alberta Assessment Appeal Board; (9) notify the Alberta Assessment Appeal Board of Court of Revision appeals along with the particulars of assessments under appeal and prominently post a list of the appellants and the time and place of the board's sitting; (10) appear at the appeal board hearing with the assessment roll and other materials pertinent to the appeal and, after the board's decision, amend the assessment roll accordingly; (11) notify the affected parties whenever a change is made in the assessment roll; and (12) post public notices of tax seizures. Many other minor duties also are prescribed by the MTA.

Section 59 of the MTA directs the treasurer to: (1) collect the municipality's monies and pay its bills; (2) maintain its fiscal records; (3) ensure that the books, records, and accounts are up to date and ready for the auditor; and (4) ensure that either a complete or an abbreviated financial statement and the auditor's report are published "in such manner as the council considers advisable in order to give such information to the ratepayers concerning the financial affairs of the municipality as the council considers reasonable and proper."

The Tax Recovery Act directs the treasurer to: (1) notify authorities collecting taxes if they have attempted to collect taxes on nontaxable property; (2) prepare a list of properties in tax arrears for more than a year and send it to the pertinent officers of a municipality; (3) post a list in the treasurer's office of properties in tax arrears; (4) send to every relevant authority a list of the parcels offered for sale because of tax arrears two months prior to the sale; and (5) send a registered letter to the property owners in tax arrears four weeks before the tax sale.

As was noted earlier, the MGA does not delineate explicitly the responsibilities of a municipal manager, but rather gives council the authority to assign the person wide-ranging "executive and administrative duties and powers." Section 91(2) of the act reads: "The municipal commissioners or the municipal manager . . . shall exercise the powers and duties set out in this Act, and any other powers and duties vested, confirmed or delegated by by-law or by resolution of the council."

Whether the senior administrator is a secretary, treasurer, municipal administrator, municipal manager, or commissioner, statutory duties and responsibilities constitute only a part of his or her job. Especially in smaller municipalities the secretary, treasurer, and municipal administrator are expected to be generalists well versed on any activity that remotely touches the council and the administration. As a village administrator for Nampa succinctly put it, an administrator's duties are "everything; tax rolls, water billings . . . you name it." The responsibility for almost innumerable duties and a high level of stress led to the resignation of Fort Assiniboine's municipal administrator in 1988. She was expected to attend meetings of the village council which often lasted past 1:30 A.M. and to be at work on time the following morning. Moreover, she was required to enforce the bylaws as well as help to formulate them, as the village did not have a bylaw enforcement officer. The letter of resignation shocked the council into addressing the administrator's concerns so that she might stay on and continue her duties.

Since the senior administrator is the key link between the municipality and the public, he or she must be sensitive to the feelings of disadvantaged and minority groups in the community. Only six months after he was appointed Edmonton's city manager, Richard Picherack offended two of the city's ethnic communities while making a report to council on the revitalization of the inner city. "Significant immigration has come from Asian and Caribbean nations," Picherack said, "these immigrants tend to locate in the same area . . . and gang activity has been noted." A spokesperson for the city's Caribbean Cultural Association said "he has pre-judged us when he says we're prone to criminal activity." A representative of the Edmonton Vietnam Association was more blunt: "I think he's prejudiced." Picherack's information had been presented to an eastern Canada meeting of the Canadian Association of Police Chiefs and then extrapolated to Edmonton, but he had not done his homework, for there was no history of ethnic gangs operating in the city. He then compounded his error when, rather than publicly apologizing, he denied "attributing the gang activity to any ethnic minority."[5]

Whether it is a question about the future direction of the municipality or about the building permit required to build a patio, it is the senior administrator who is contacted. A small municipality's administrator is often given a general mandate to encourage business expansion and tourism through a promotional campaign that may require him or her to collect data and prepare brochures on the community's amenities, labour force, markets, and transportation. The administrator is expected to be familiar with personnel management and contract negotiations, to be a competent office manager, and to be able to interpret and prepare simple contracts and understand basic legal documents. It is the administrator who deals with neighbouring municipalities and the Department of Municipal Affairs on a day-to-day basis. If its administrator is not aware of current provincial and federal grant programs and regulations, a municipality may miss out on substantial grant monies. Rural administrators are expected to have some knowledge of matters such as weed and forest fire prevention and control, and county administrators should be familiar with the School Act and school administration.

Finally, the administrator is obliged to advise council on its statutory duties. For example, the MGA requires council to appoint one or more auditors each year to examine the administration's financial statement. If this appointment is neglected, the administrator must remind council of its responsibility.

Bureaucrats and the Dimensions of Policy Making

In democratic governments the citizens elect representatives to formulate policies.[6] However, elected officials can hardly be expected to be familiar with all aspects of government operations, let alone their current status. Once council decides on a general policy, senior bureaucrats (municipal managers, department heads, section chiefs, and their assistants) are responsible for drafting the detailed rules and regulations necessary for its implementation. If a bylaw is ambiguous, senior bureaucrats interpret and "fine tune" it to make it workable. Over time, administrative rulings set precedents which establish the limits of a policy's parameters: if the policy is regulatory, the rulings determine to whom it applies; if the policy is social or fiscal, the rulings determine who is eligible for benefits. Of necessity, elected officials seek advice from career civil servants and delegate lower-level decision-making powers to them in the interest of rational policy formulation and efficient implementation. Democratic values are preserved if:

(1) Decisions made by administrators . . . fall within the limits of overall policy set by elected officials.
(2) Discretion is exercised so as to further or at least not conflict with the objectives that the appointed decision-makers know or can find out are held by their relevant elected superiors.
(3) The information, advice, and recommendations . . . are designed to facilitate the elective decision-makers' choices and are not seriously slanted toward some particular point of view in order to close their options.[7]

Career administrators who have long been involved in managing municipal affairs are viewed as resident experts by elected officials. Councils rely on these experts to identify issues of concern to the public and to provide alternative solutions to problems. Some bureaucrats argue that they should play the major role in the development of police, fire, planning, and other service policies.[8] However, some career bureaucrats are as subjective as the most biased elected officials. Two social scientists describe the process by which many administrators subtly change policy recommendations:

. . . the amount and kind of information, the method of presentation, the manner in which alternatives are identified and appraised, and the

making of, or abstention from, recommendations—all provide opportunities for the bureaucracies to impress their own discretion and preferences. . . . The object is constant: to guide the official's decision into
the channels which the bureaucrats regard as wise and prudent.[9]

Although elected officials are not oblivious to this problem, they seldom have the time or expertise to evaluate administration proposals. Perhaps this was the reason that Laurence Decore, Liberal Party leader and
former Edmonton mayor, said in a 1989 speech to candidates for municipal office, "go in with skepticism of administrators after getting elected."
He followed this by saying that "lots" and then changed it to "some"
administrators "don't do their homework."[10]

Administrators rarely make proposals affecting their own power, prestige, and salaries so blatant that a council would see them as motivated by
bias. However, in the Town of Nanton in 1988 a former administrator
breached the unwritten rule not to state publicly that a good deal of
municipal policy is made by the administration and not by elected politicians. After the town advertised for an administrator rather than hiring
the person the former administrator had groomed for the position, the
angry administrator said that while "mayors and councils come and go,"
it was really the administration which "runs the town."[11]

Astute politicians and students of administration have long been aware
that senior administrators can make or break a policy. Policy makers normally formulate new programs in general terms in order to give the
bureaucracy a certain amount of flexibility. Some administrators resolve
program ambiguities in their own favour, that is, to minimize their workload while increasing their power and prestige. Policy directives are necessarily broad, since it is impossible to anticipate all the day-to-day decisions required to make a policy work. Administrative flexibility, more
commonly called administrative discretion, permeates the bureaucracy,
but it is greatest at the top. For example, a municipal manager directed by
council to formulate a proposal to provide for greater citizen participation in municipal affairs might believe that council has been "sold a bill of
goods" by a totally self-interested group and stall in the hope that council
will forget the issue. A manager might refer council's proposal to a citizen
group or private consultant "for further study," calculating that it will be
forgotten or buried in political controversy. Similarly, a manager hoping
to reorient council's policy direction might advise it that a proposal did
not follow precedent or that council might not have the proper legislative
authority to proceed.

With a few important exceptions, lower-level civil servants such as mail clerks and stenographers cannot influence policy as individuals, but they can have a significant collective effect. If they choose to work slowly or inefficiently, a policy may become so expensive or so ineffective that it must be terminated. For example, if workers balk at office automation, the costs of doing business after implementation can be higher than when the old "tried and true" methods were employed.

Some lower-level civil servants, often called "street-level bureaucrats," have a fair amount of discretion in the performance of their duties and are able to change policy direction within their spheres of influence.[12] They are directly involved with the public and include building, fire, and public health bylaw enforcement officers, all of whom have the discretion to enforce regulations strictly or merely issue mild warnings. Police officers decide whether a minor traffic offence results in a warning or a ticket. Even school teachers can be street-level bureaucrats because what and how they teach can undermine a board's educational policy. An example occurred in the small community of Eckville where, unknown to the school board, a high school teacher preached anti-Semitism in his classes for years.

Policy makers face a dilemma: if they attempt to curtail bureaucratic discretion by creating very specific policy directives, the result is rigidity in policy implementation. Moreover, it is difficult and time-consuming to develop detailed long-range policies.

Normally, the bureaucracy balks only when a council adopts a particularly novel policy or radically changes an existing one. Most policies are a continuation of the status quo. A great many municipal administrators, probably even more so than council members, oppose change because it makes for an unpredictable future. However, it is a mistake for people to maintain unequivocally that the bureaucracy is a conservative force, since many innovative ideas about budgeting, personnel management, and administration have originated in administration.

Most bureaucrats are conscientious public servants who believe that it is the council that must ultimately formulate policy. Sensitive to the criticism that they often subvert the will of the public, they make a conscious effort to be impartial. When administrators appear to be expressing a policy preference, they may be merely anticipating the preferences of the council. Often their objections to policy are objections to technical aspects that would make implementation difficult. While most bureaucrats shape policy, they generally do so within parameters that are acceptable to council.

Administrator Salaries

Virtually every council recognizes the importance of employing qualified administrators. Experienced professionals demand salaries commensurate with their qualifications, but councils are reluctant to make administrators' salaries public for fear they will be charged with squandering the taxpayers' money. The Alberta Urban Municipalities Association (AUMA) conducts a yearly survey of its members' compensation and conditions of employment. The survey results are classified by the AUMA as "confidential comparative information" sent only to "Chief Administrative Officers, Personnel Managers of municipalities, Chairmen of Municipal Personnel Policy Committees, the Municipal Affairs Department and to other Public Sector Employer Organizations." If the survey results were made public, with a description of the administrators' responsibilities, citizens might understand why professional municipal administrators are required rather than suspecting a cover-up. Calgary had a similar restricted policy on the wage structure and proposed salary increases for its senior bureaucrats. While the administration was negotiating wages and benefits with the nine unions representing city employees in 1989, a consultant's report on wages for department heads and commissioners was judged to be confidential and not in the public domain.

The inflationary pressures of the late 1970s and early 1980s affected administrators' salaries in both the public and private sector. The yearly salaries of managers and commissioners in Alberta's larger municipalities are comparable to those of senior administrators in the private sector, ranging from $60,000 to more than $130,000. When Mayor Laurence Decore dismantled Edmonton's council-commission government and replaced it with an executive committee-city manager form, he wanted an outstanding person for the job. Although the council said the new manager's salary should fall in a range of $82,000 to $99,000 a year, Decore convinced it to hire Cy Armstrong for $120,000, making him the most highly paid city manager in Canada.[13] Armstrong, who had been chief executive for the regional municipality of Hamilton-Wentworth in Ontario, said he could not accept the job for any less. After serving one term of office Armstrong resigned and Richard Picherack, the Commissioner of Community Services for Metro Toronto, was selected to replace him at a salary of $133,000 a year.

Although small municipalities have traditionally paid their administrators low salaries, many councils have recently increased the salaries of senior administrators substantially in order to attract better-educated candidates. Particularly striking in Table 7.1 are the administrator salaries

Table 7.1   1990 Salaries of Senior Administrators in Urban Municipalities[14]

	Cities ($)	Towns ($)	Villages ($)	Summer Villages ($)
High	133,000	73,000	46,000	29,000
Low	57,500	22,000	930	1,800
Mean	72,018	48,062	22,765	8,700

Table 7.2   1990 Salaries of Senior Administrators in Rural Municipalities

	Counties ($)	Municipal Districts ($)
High	103,000	78,000
Low	47,000	37,000
Mean	67,000	53,000

at the high end in villages and summer villages. The salaries reflect both the emphasis which citizens in these smaller municipalities place on having a professional public service and the effect on administrator salaries of fierce competition for the services of outstanding administrators. On the other hand, in several villages the administrator is paid less than $100 a month. Nevertheless, in some of these villages the administrator has a strong sense of loyalty and obligation. In the 1990 survey of administrators' salaries, one wrote that "we just do not have big dollars, so all our salaries suffer. . . . My salary would be a lot higher in a larger town, the responsibilities are just as hard. Here I have to be lawyer, engineer etc. as we cannot afford to hire everything out. I do all the financial statement and budget work for the auditor . . . this saves us lots of money."[15] Another administrator with a relatively low salary wrote that she considered herself fortunate to work for a wise council whose decisions reflect the best interests of the community.

A 1983 survey of senior administrators found the highest salaries reported were for county and city administrators. More county administrators than city administrators reported salaries of over $45,000, 43 percent of those in counties versus 25 percent of city administrators. Although the 1990 data in Table 7.2 should be considered tentative, since they are based on a mail-out questionnaire with a response rate of less than 30 percent for salary information, it seems that there has been a reversal in the relationship between city and county administrators since 1983. Tables 7.1 and 7.2 show that the highest salary for a city administrator is $30,000 more than that for a county administrator and the lowest salary for a city administrator is $10,000 more than a county administrator's lowest salary. These differences are also reflected in the mean salaries of city and county administrators, the mean salary for city administrators being $5,000 higher. If the figures for all urban administrators are compared with those for all rural administrators, it is apparent that municipal district administrators have higher mean salaries than town, village, and summer village administrators, but that is to be expected since municipal district administrators generally have greater responsibilities related to the larger populations and geographical areas of municipal districts.

Profile of Senior Municipal Administrators

Although somewhat dated, province-wide surveys in 1976 and 1983 developed profiles of Alberta administrators which facilitated comparisons between the two time periods.[16] Perhaps the most remarkable finding was the increase in the educational level of local administrators in only seven years. The 1976 survey showed that 25 percent of administrators had neither obtained a high-school diploma nor taken other academic courses. In 1983 very few administrators fell into this category. While 23 percent of respondents had "some college" in 1976, the percentage had doubled to 46 percent in 1983. Only one administrator in 1976 reported having a college degree, as compared with 22 administrators (14 percent) in 1983. As might be expected, the educational level of senior administrators is highest in larger municipalities and lowest in villages and summer villages. Yet the 1983 survey found that among village and summer village administrators 30 percent had some college and 7 percent held college degrees. The impetus for increasing educational qualifications has come from the Department of Municipal Affairs, the Local Government Administrators Association of Alberta, and the University of Alberta's Faculty of Extension, which offers a comprehensive set of courses leading to a professional certificate in local government. Equally important, although there are no statutory requirements, municipal councils are recognizing the value of well-educated employees.

Despite the marked increase in administrators' educational levels between 1976 and 1983, the difference in age distribution was much less dramatic, and there was no appreciable change in the male/female ratio. The category with the largest percentage of local administrators in both surveys was the 36 to 45 year age group, 29 percent in 1976 and 40 percent in 1983. A major difference in the two surveys was the percentage of senior administrators over the age of 55, almost 18 percent in 1976 and only 8 percent in 1983. If retiring administrators were being replaced, one would expect to find a similar difference between the percentages of administrators in the younger age categories, but the contrast was not as great as expected, with 27 percent aged 35 and younger in 1976, and 32 percent aged 35 and younger in 1983. The surveys indicated that the one-to-two ratio of women to men among senior administrators did not change from one time period to the next. Few women held senior administrative positions in larger municipalities; they tended to be employed by small villages and summer villages and in half of these the position was part-time. In the 1983 survey women constituted 78 percent of village and summer village administrators, 25 percent of the senior administrators in cities and towns, and 15 percent in municipal districts. Not a single woman in the sample was a senior administrator in a county, special area, or improvement district. Without entering into a debate on covert sexual discrimination in the workplace, one can conclude that men enjoy a clear advantage as senior municipal administrators in Alberta.

The 1983 survey showed that while almost all administrators have a strong commitment to their career and their community, there is a wide disparity between the ideal and the actual job. Although most municipal councils give their senior administrators financial recognition, a number fail to give them professional recognition, treating senior administrators as little more than glorified clerical help. A key question asked of the administrators related to the importance of personal fulfillment and growth. Ninety-nine percent said it was very important but, when asked how much opportunity for growth and fulfillment they had on the job, only 30 percent replied that it was substantial and 15 percent responded that there was none. Municipal district administrators were the most satisfied, with 42 percent saying that their job gave them ample opportunity for personal growth; special area and improvement district administrators were the least satisfied, with not one person giving high marks for personal growth. Associated with personal growth is the opportunity to learn new job skills. Almost all respondents replied that it was very important to learn and develop new skills, but only 28 percent said their job gave them the chance to do so and 21 percent indicated their job offered no such opportunity. This disparity can be partially accounted for by the stance municipal councils have taken on educational upgrading. In another 1983 survey which asked 108 Alberta reeves, mayors, and councillors whether their municipality had established policies for the training and development of senior administrators, 50 percent responded affirmatively and the other 50 percent said their municipality had no policy on personnel development.[17] Responses to a follow-up question indicated that only one-third of the municipalities had an annual budget item for the educational upgrading of senior administrators.

A related survey question dealt with the importance administrators place on having highly marketable skills; 91 percent said that this was very important, but only 18 percent replied that their job provided them with such skills. Particularly surprising is that 25 percent felt that their job provided them with no marketable skills.

Another question concerned the importance of personal autonomy on the job. Well over 90 percent of the respondents said that it was very important, but only 47 percent said they had "a lot" of personal autonomy. Municipal district administrators were the most satisfied, with 73 percent reporting "a lot" of autonomy, while special area and improvement district administrators were the least satisfied, with only 25 percent replying that they had considerable autonomy.

Job security is important to municipal administrators, as it is to most salaried employes. However, while 88 percent of those surveyed indicated that job security was very important to them, only 41 percent felt their job to be completely secure and 15 percent replied that they had absolutely no job security.

Thirty-eight percent of the municipal administrators felt their job responsibilities were unclear, a factor which contributes to job dissatisfaction. But the most surprising finding was that, although a substantial number of administrators were dissatisfied with the nature or conditions of their work and distressed by the lack of professional recognition from council, almost all had a strong commitment to their profession, to their employer, and to doing a good job.

Municipal Administrators' Relationship with Elected Officials

None of the elected officials in the 1983 survey of Alberta municipal elected officials said they had an unsatisfactory relationship with their senior administrator. Some 66 percent stated the relationship was excellent, 30 percent that it was good, and 4 percent that it was only fair. When asked to identify "the most difficult problem" in their relationship with the chief administrator, 48 percent replied they did not have a problem. The problems elected officials had with their administrators did not fall into any single category, but rather covered a wide spectrum. The two

Table 7.3   Pressure on Administrators by Council

Government Unit	Hardly any Pressure (%)	Some Pressure (%)	A Lot of Pressure(%)
County	23	32	46
City	25	13	63
Municipal District	62	0	39
Town	36	25	39
Village/Summer Village	28	39	33
Special Area/Improvement District	25	50	25
Average	32	29	39

most frequently mentioned were administrators' lack of management skills and poor communication skills.[18]

Data from the 1983 administrators' survey show that administrators had a somewhat different perception of their relationship with elected officials. Fifty-nine percent said they had an excellent relationship with elected officials and only 4 percent said the relationship was poor, but when asked if they were subject to unreasonable demands by council, two-thirds of the administrators said they were working under duress. The percentage who reported "some" or "a lot" of pressure from council varies little by type of municipality, except for county administrators. For reasons not easily explained, almost two-thirds of the municipal district administrators said they were free from council pressure. On the other hand, almost half of the county administrators said they were under "a lot" of pressure from their councils.

Although almost 60 percent of the senior administrators reported being subjected to unreasonable council demands, 98 percent rated their relationship with council as good to excellent. Only one county and two village/summer village administrators said they had a poor relationship with council. Perhaps the reason for these seemingly contradictory findings is that administrators feel pressured to defer to council members on contentious issues in the interest of maintaining their jobs, but at the same time do not find that the issues are resolved to their satisfaction.

To ascertain how much a council relies on its senior administrator for policy and administrative direction the 1983 administrator survey asked, "When making policy recommendations to council, how often would you say your recommendations are adopted?" Table 7.4 shows that 72 percent of the administrators had 75 percent or more of their recommendations adopted by council. City administrators, although harried and pressured,

Table 7.4   How Often Council Adopts the Policy Recommendations of
             Senior Administrators

Government Unit	Percentage of Recommendations Adopted					
	0%	25%	50%	75%	100%	Don't make recommen- dations
County	0	10	10	33	43	5
City	0	0	0	38	38	25
Municipal District	0	0	23	46	8	23
Town	0	0	11	45	38	7
Village/Summer Village	4	4	20	24	38	9
Special Area/ Improvement District	0	0	13	63	13	13
Average	1	3	14	38	34	10

appear to be respected by their councils, since so many of their recommendations are adopted. In contrast are the village and summer village
administrators who work with councils that meet infrequently and are
often composed of part-time and inexperienced councillors. Since the
administrators provide continuity from one administration to the next,
one would expect that most of their recommendations would be adopted,
but the survey found that for 28 percent of them, 50 percent or less of
their recommendations were adopted. A puzzling finding is that 10 percent of all senior administrators said they did not make recommendations, including 25 percent in cities and 23 percent in municipal districts.
Either these administrators have abrogated some of their responsibilities
or their recommendations have been rejected so many times that they
have ceased to make them.

Serious discord between a council and its senior administrator is seldom publicized. The reason for this is that widely publicized charges of
mismanagement hang like an albatross around an administrator's neck,
making it impossible for the person to find another position. During the
mid-1980s two councillors in Fort McMurray charged the mayor with
constantly interfering in the city's administration. The mayor admitted
that he took an active role in managing the city, but the commissioners
were unwilling to comment on whether or not his actions constituted
administrative interference.[19] When relations break down between an
administrator and elected officials the administrator usually resigns qui-

etly. In the Town of Calmar, with a population of just over one thousand, 14 municipal administrators were hired during a ten-year period until one of them revealed the reasons for their resignations. In March 1987 the outgoing administrator explained that for the last two years the mayor had spent 40 hours a week in the town office looking over his shoulder. His successor tendered her resignation after being on the job less than five months. She explained that "unfortunately the Mayor has not allowed me to use any initiative and has constantly interfered in the operation of the office. And furthermore, I have received no cooperation from her or members of council in reaching an amicable solution."[20] In 1981 Drayton Valley's two senior administrators resigned after the council brought in an economic consultant to evaluate the town's finances. When asked about his resignation, one replied, "Let's just say we've [the administrator and the council] come to an agreement on an early retirement."[21]

In the few instances where dissension is publicized, the administrator is almost invariably dismissed, as in Coronation, where the senior administrator's competence became an issue in the 1980 election. One of the most highly publicized cases involving an administrator's competence occurred in Brooks in 1981 when council appointed one of its own members, Johannes Wannet, as town manager although he had no relevant experience. Before being elected to council he had owned and operated the local bakery. Controversy over his appointment and competence divided council for the next two years and became an important issue in the 1983 election. A major political realignment occurred when five new councillors were elected, and in a special session before the new council held its first regularly scheduled meeting the manager was dismissed. Wannet retaliated with a wrongful dismissal suit for $108,000 for three years' salary and $42,000 in overtime pay.[22] On January 11, 1985, the court held that his action was without merit and he was ordered to pay court costs. Wannet then filed a defamation suit against the *Brooks Bulletin* and Councillor Gerry Pelchat. On the basis of information provided by Pelchat the newspaper had run a story in 1984 entitled "Inexperience added to cost of 1983 town audit." In February 1988 the defamation suit was dismissed, with the justice explaining that Wannet had been called "inexperienced and he in fact was inexperienced."[23]

Although the Wannet case was highly publicized, innumerable councils have quietly agreed to financial settlements to avoid a wrongful dismissal action being brought against their municipality. Moreover, plaintiffs often are successful in court or in negotiated settlements when they contest their dismissal.[24] After the small community of Strathmore fired its municipal secretary in 1987, she began judicial proceedings against the town for unlawful dismissal. Rather than go to court the town negotiated a settlement which gave her three months' salary and paid her legal costs.

Negotiated settlements occur as often in large municipalities as in smaller ones. After Laurence Decore defeated Cec Purves for mayor in October 1983 he moved quickly to shape Edmonton's administration to suit his own policy purposes. Decore dismissed a number of people he felt had been too closely tied to the Purves administration and negotiated settlements with other senior administrators after he abolished the commission board and replaced it with an executive committee.[25] The day after Decore was sworn to office he told the woman who had been the community coordinator for Purves that she was being fired, since he wanted to place one of his own people in the position. She challenged the dismissal and won a $17,000 court judgement.[26] When Decore demoted a woman who had been secretary to four Edmonton mayors, she filed a suit for wrongful dismissal and settled with the city for $25,000. In December Decore negotiated a $192,000 settlement with the commissioner of finance for his resignation and a month later another commissioner resigned with a $152,000 settlement. The city's productivity management coordinator was dismissed in the fall of 1984; facing a wrongful dismissal suit, the city settled with him for $100,000 three years later. In March 1985 the former chief commissioner and city manager received $180,000 when he agreed to resign, and in 1987 the general manager of Edmonton Telephones resigned in exchange for $137,000. Just when it seemed the mayor had his own administrative personnel in place, allegations of sexual harassment in the law department led to the resignation of the city solicitor, who eventually negotiated a $160,000 settlement with the city.[27]

When administrators work very closely with strong-willed council executives, personality conflicts occasionally occur. Politically astute senior administrators often develop alliances with council members to counter the chief executive's dominant position. In the Town of High Prairie in the 1980s, for example, the appointment of John Jarvie as the town administrator was supported by councillor Don Lorencz, who later became mayor. As mayor, Lorencz suspended Jarvie after a disagreement, but the council converted the administrator's position to that of town manager (who can be hired and fired only by a council majority) and appointed Jarvie to the position. Protected by the mayor's antagonists on council, the town manager carried out council's directives and battled with the mayor for several years until he finally resigned. Only then did Jarvie explain that the basis of their disagreements was a difference in personalities: "just two different people with two different philosophies."[28]

High Prairie is particularly interesting since at one point a group of citizens suggested that if the council and the administration could not resolve their differences the mayor and council should resign and another election be held to elect a council able to get along with the administration.[29]

After an altercation in the Town of Brooks in 1988, councillor Heather Miyauchi pressed assault charges against the town manager, Neil Brodie, who countered with charges against the councillor. Although the events surrounding the actual incident are ambiguous,[30] in a six to one vote the council agreed Brodie should be reimbursed for any legal expenses arising from Miyauchi's charges against him. In addition, an ad hoc committee which council struck to examine the incident asked Miyauchi to make an apology and censured her for breaching the chain of command in town hall. The manager was exonerated of the charges but shortly thereafter resigned to take a position in Camrose.

There are other examples of senior administrators who feel they have such strong political support on council that they routinely battle with council members and openly "politic" to bring about a reversal of council policy. This occurred in Edmonton in 1990 when the general manager of city transportation, John Schnablegger, in attempting to protect other bureaucrats, jousted with alderman Brian Mason. In an intensive council session dealing with a mismanaged sewer planning and building program, Schnablegger attempted to "stonewall" Mason with bureaucratic jargon, but the senior bureaucrat finally admitted that a multi-million dollar sewer line was not only unnecessary but could exacerbate pollution in the North Saskatchewan River. The *Edmonton Journal's* city political columnist, John Geiger, wrote: "It was a brilliant performance from Mason, who has been trying for months to get answers to uncomfortable questions about the Highlands sewer. Not only was he able to expose serious concerns about the project, but he was able to do so in a public forum."[31] Less than three weeks later Schnablegger was again in the news after he convinced a number of aldermen to reverse themselves on protecting a neighbourhood from being bisected by a new transportation line. In the morning the council had agreed to delay clearing the route for a month, but after coming back from lunch it rescinded the motion and voted to proceed. An angry Mason said, "My understanding is that Mr. Schnablegger was displeased with the decision of council and exerted his effort and influence to reverse it. . . . I'm concerned that Mr. Schnablegger and the transportation department seem to have an inordinate amount of influence with a significant number of council members. I think the policy direction has to come from the politicians and not the administration."[32] With council's support on the issue, an unrepentant Schnablegger responded to Mason's criticism by saying that he was only doing his job. Schnablegger continued to joust with city hall's elected representatives until March 1992, when he was forced to resign.

After Calgary commissioner George Cornish called for a 4 percent tax increase in 1986, Mayor Klein said any increase should be limited to 2 percent and intimated that Cornish was unduly influencing two newly elected councillors. Speaking before the Calgary Personnel Association, he said he was concerned that a politically astute and experienced administrator could "lobby an inexperienced politician for the administration's point of view. That can be the danger of a permanent bureaucracy dealing with a small and transient elected body."[33]

There are probably as many incidents of senior administrators having the unqualified backing of council as there are of councils fighting with their administrators. A case in point is the twelve to one vote by the Calgary council in 1987 to give the city's retiring chief commissioner a lucrative "golden parachute." Chief Commissioner George Cornish and council's personnel committee worked out a retirement package which gave him one-third of his final salary as chief commissioner ($109,000) for each of two years in exchange for working 75 days each year as a consultant to the city.[34] The Town of Redwater's council gave its unqualified support to its manager in 1988 after receiving a 300-name petition calling for the person's dismissal. Summarily dismissing the petition, the mayor speaking on council's behalf explained, "According to us, the town manager is doing a good job; and to the auditors, he is doing an excellent job."[35] The council in Magrath supported its town administrator even after he pleaded guilty to falsifying unemployment insurance paperwork for a town employee and was sentenced to spend weekends in the Lethbridge Correctional Centre. The mayor explained: "I've said it to my own kids. If it's nothing serious I'd help them out the first time. The second time they're on their own. I feel the same way about Rod [the administrator]. Everyone is entitled to one mistake."[36]

Although there are councils which administrators know will be supportive if they run into trouble, there are others which they find unpredictable. As a consequence, an administrator often feels vulnerable to outside political pressures in the community. The 1983 survey of administrators asked how much pressure (defined as unreasonable demands) administrators had from the general public, developers, and community businesspeople. Eighty-eight percent of the respondents from cities, special areas, and improvement districts reported "some" or "a lot" of pressure. Administrators felt the least pressure in municipal districts, but even then 54 percent reported "some" or "a lot" of pressure.

The discussion to this point has provided examples of conflict between administrators and elected officials, but there are also instances of communities in which the boundaries of their respective roles have become indistinct. George Cuff, a municipal management consultant and long-time mayor of Spruce Grove, describes a category of senior bureaucrats as "political eunuchs." These "voteless politicians" are expected "to provide politically tinged advice on all matters to council, based on policies designed to win votes, not on those which make the most administrative sense."[37] A somewhat different situation occurred in the Town of Raymond. For some time the community's mayor was also its fire chief and questions arose as to whether his primary loyalty rested with the fire department or the council. One town councillor was highly critical after "the mayor took the fire department away from under the by-law and protection committee and placed it under administration." Another councillor said that "we've asked him to give serious consideration to stepping down [as fire chief] . . . it's hard to be objective when you're the mayor, fire chief and the fire department's representative to council."[38] However, nothing in the MGA prevents an elected official from simultaneously holding a municipal administrative office.[39]

Businesspeople often attempt to influence municipal administrators to further their own ends. In the 1983 administrators' survey, 54 percent of the respondents indicated that land developers had attempted to exert some or a lot of pressure on them; in special areas and improvement districts the figure was 88 percent and in cities 100 percent. Most village and summer village administrators are spared this type of pressure; 64 percent of them replied that developers seldom if ever made unreasonable demands. On the other hand, almost 50 percent of the village and summer village administrators replied that businesspeople often made unreasonable demands on them; for city and town administrators the percentages were 63 and 58 percent, respectively. The majority of county and municipal district administrators were fortunate; 69 percent of municipal district administrators and 64 percent of county administrators reported little or no pressure from business interests. Asked to name others who attempted to influence them, only a few administrators replied. Five town and two village and summer village administrators named local organizations. Only one respondent, a town administrator, reported undue influence from a labour union.

One of the more bizarre policies to prevent municipal civil servants from being influenced by the business community was implemented in Vegreville in 1987. Council passed a resolution which allowed it to bar municipal employees from socializing with people who conducted business with the town. The first time a municipal employee was caught socializing, the person would receive a warning letter from the mayor; after any subsequent socializing, the employee was subject to dismissal.[40] There are no reports as to whether or not the policy was strictly enforced.

Professionalism and Municipal Administration

Defining professionalism and determining which occupations are professions have challenged academics for some time.[41] William Goode identifies an abstract body of knowledge and an ideal of service as the two core qualities of professionalism.[42] Goode's criteria are useful but incomplete, as professionalism cannot be understood without also considering the relationships between society, the state, and the professional occupation. Since many occupations affect the welfare of persons and society, governments regulate them through licensing, fees, and inspections. However, governments may assign these powers to professional organizations. In some cases, professional bodies can apply legal sanctions against unauthorized persons who perform activities claimed by the profession, penalize members for improper practices and conduct, and bar from practice members judged to be unprofessional. Governments exact obligations from professions when ceding them powers, the principal one being the requirement that their members act as their colleagues' trustees. Professional organizations are also expected to take appropriate action to deal with members' misconduct or incompetence.

Although an application of the factors that define a profession seems to indicate that public administrators are professionals, Don K. Price maintains that no administrative or managerial position in the public sector can be regarded as professional since public administrators operate under the direction of politicians and thus do not have the autonomy associated with professionalism.[43] Price argues that in democratic societies public administrators should never presume to be professionals, since professionalism would conflict with their democratic responsibility to follow the dictates of nonprofessional politicians. The argument fails on two counts. First, it assumes that autonomy in work is an absolute when it is not, even in law and medicine. Second, despite what Price has to say, in an ideal bureaucratic-political relation there is a separation of function. In short, when the ideal is honoured there is autonomy for the administrator.

A second argument made against public administration being a profession is that its body of knowledge, that is, its theory, is not sufficiently complex and codified to qualify as professional knowledge.[44] The difficulty with evaluating this charge is that the same criticism is often made generally of social science theory, of which public administration is a part; little of it is predictive, much is speculative, and a great deal is normative. Just as social scientists make allowances for the deficiencies of their disciplines, the same is done for public administration.

Administrators in North America have aspired to be professionals for more than a century. A professionalized administration was part of the American Progressive agenda to remake government into a technically modern and businesslike organization. At the beginning of the modern age, a competent and well educated administration was needed to implement electrification and massive infrastructure projects. Moreover, Progressives believed that modern techniques of administration could be used to cleanse cities of municipal administrators beholden to political machines for their jobs. They also thought that a professionalized administration would attract into the public service better educated and less corruptible people with middle-class backgrounds. Not unexpectedly, the fervour for professionalizing administration soon spread from the United States to Canada.

One of the earliest attempts to advance professionalism in municipal public administration was mounted shortly after the turn of the century by the International City Management Association (ICMA).[45] In recent years the ICMA has promoted local government professionalism through a variety of continuing initiatives, including publishing texts that codify municipal practices, defining professional education requirements, and developing a code of professional ethics. The ICMA also sponsors ongoing administrative research.

The International Institute of Municipal Clerks (IIMC), like many other international organizations of administrators, is based in the United States but has a large contingent of Canadian members. Municipal finance officers are represented by the Governmental Finance Officers Association (until recently the Municipal Finance Officers Association). The Association of School Business Officials International (ASBO, formerly the Association of School Business Officials of the United States and Canada) has promoted school business administration professionalism since 1910.[46]

All of these associations have adopted agendas promoting professionalism that are similar to that of the ICMA. They encourage their members to invest time in professional development. The IIMC issues credentials for the completion of educational requirements and solicits universities to assist in the promulgation of its educational program, while ASBO sponsors training courses and issues letters of recognition to those who complete an organized program of study. All of the international associations have codes of ethics and publication programs. Through annual and regional conferences and special seminars, they also provide venues for the discussion of technical matters.

As one might expect, given the number of international associations, there are few purely Canadian ones. A notable exception is the Canadian Association of Municipal Administrators (CAMA), which is closely affiliated with the Federation of Canadian Municipalities (FCM) and tends to draw its members from the nation's larger municipalities.

Alberta has two long-established municipal administrators' associations, as well as an "umbrella society" promoting local government management professionalism. In 1921 the Alberta Association of Municipal Districts drafted a constitution for an association of rural municipal administrators entitled the Alberta Rural Administrators Association (later to become the Alberta Rural Municipal Administrators Association, ARMAA), which held its first convention in Calgary in June 1922. Urban municipal administrators were slower to organize. The Urban Secretary-Treasurers Association of Alberta was formed in 1959 and has since undergone two name changes. In 1973 it became the Urban Municipal Administrators Association and in 1980 its current title, the Local Government Administrators Association (LGAA), was adopted.

Both associations promote the exchange of information among administrators through regional zone and annual meetings which often feature speakers from Alberta Municipal Affairs. Government departments concerned with municipal affairs use these meetings to explain new and revised programs and policies as well as to give administrators advice. In addition, lawyers, accountants, and a variety of experts often appear on zone meeting agendas. In recent years the LGAA has worked closely with the University of Alberta's Government Studies Program to offer its members pre-conference training sessions.

The LGAA and ARMAA advise government departments and a variety of organizations on municipal administration matters. The top echelon in the Department of Municipal Affairs solicits their reactions to government proposals on policy and legislative change. ARMAA representatives are consulted on various issues by the Alberta Association of Municipal Districts and Counties (AAMD&C), and LGAA representatives sit on a number of Alberta Urban Municipal Association (AUMA) committees.

As early as 1924 rural and urban administrators asked the University of Alberta to develop a course on municipal administration. Although this initial effort was unsuccessful, the idea was resurrected 13 years later with the birth of the Municipal Refresher Course, which has run continuously since 1939. The university's extension department formulated a program of studies in close cooperation with the Department of Municipal Affairs and the municipal associations. The program is particularly important because it brings together urban, rural, and school officials to discuss problems which are common to all three groups.

The close ties and collaboration between the university, the associations, and the government over the years led to the development of a University of Alberta municipal administration certificate program in 1958. That program expanded so that by the 1990s two certificate programs, as well as a number of workshops and technical assistance courses, were being offered through the university's Faculty of Extension.

Despite having worked together on the development of an educational program, when it came to establishing standards for professional education and conduct, the associations acted independently. Finally, in 1980, both recognized the need for an advanced management program and they joined forces with the University of Alberta to create the Senior Executive Fellows Program in 1984. At about the same time, ARMAA and LGAA were hammering out the framework for a society to improve the professional educational opportunities available to municipal administrators. Although the Society of Local Government Managers of Alberta (SLGMA) was registered under the provincial Societies Act on February 23, 1988, this was a provisional measure since the organization was already working to gain recognition under Alberta's recently proclaimed Professional and Occupational Associations Registration Act (POARA), which was granted on February 27, 1991.

POARA registration is significant for three reasons. First, it is a recognition by the province that the SLGMA has met the test of being a professional organization.[47] Second, with POARA recognition are requirements specifying the internal organization of the professional association as well as governing the conduct of the association's members. POARA makes provisions for the professional association to deal with complaints against its members and specifies the procedure and penalties for complaint and discipline cases. Charges for contempt of court can be brought against witnesses who fail to attend a discipline tribunal or who refuse to be sworn. In every case, procedures for the professional organization's discipline tribunal conform to established principles of administrative law. Third, POARA provides for the formation of Registration and Practice Review Committees with extensive powers. The Registration Committee can approve, reject, or defer membership applications, while the Practice Review Committee defines the parameters of professional practice by establishing practice standards and investigating charges of malpractice.

The complaint-handling machinery in POARA provides the public with a recourse against any incompetent practices and unethical behaviours of senior municipal administrators. This is the principal difference between registration under the Societies Act and registration under POARA. The former concerns itself little with administrative practices, while a key role of the latter is to protect the public from incompetence and fraud.

The Society of Local Government Managers of Alberta recently created a committee to encourage post-secondary institutions to offer professional education in local government administration. SLGMA members sit on senior University of Alberta committees which are concerned with education for professionals. Although it is much too early to evaluate the long-term consequences of this relationship, it seems a synergy is evolving which is leading to the rapid professionalization of the upper echelon of municipal administration in the province. With three strong associations of local administration it is to be expected that there are stresses and strains between the executive bodies of the LGAA, the ARMAA, and the SLGMA, as well as jurisdictional conflicts. However, issues are being resolved, since there is strong commitment to professionalization on the part of the province, higher education, and the associations of municipal administrators.

Commitment to Professionalism

The surveys of Alberta administrators show that the majority are sometimes, if not often, pressured by council and community business interests. Resisting this pressure requires a strong commitment to public service and professionalism. In recent years Alberta's municipal administrators have become better educated, actively involved in professional associations, and increasingly sensitive to their role in policy making. Many municipal councils have recognized their senior administrators by awarding them salaries commensurate with those of other professionals. Still, there is a wide gap between the professional recognition administrators feel they deserve and the recognition they receive.

The 1983 survey of administrators asked how committed they were to professional values. Fifty-six percent replied that they had a strong commitment, 37 percent some commitment, and only 7 percent no commitment at all. Although most administrators consider themselves professionals, many do not have professional status. When asked how much status their job gave them in the community only 19 percent replied that it gave them a substantial amount, while 22 percent said it gave them no status at all.

Only well qualified and highly professional senior administrators can ensure that council policies are competently implemented and administered, yet many councils have not acted to professionalize their administrations. It has already been noted that as late as 1983 many municipalities still had no policy on educational upgrading. When administrators were asked in the 1983 survey whether they had an opportunity to learn new job skills, 21 percent of them replied negatively. The breadth of opportunities for advancement within an organization is an indication that it is committed to professionalism; 69 percent of the administrators who responded to the 1983 survey said that there were no provisions in place to allow them to advance.

One would expect council attitudes to be reflected in the public's perception of senior administrators. Commissioners and managers in larger municipalities are generally recognized as highly trained professional administrators and an astute council realizes that the success or failure of many major policies rests squarely on these administrators. It is in smaller municipalities and in those with less percipient councils that opportunities for educational upgrading are limited and administrators have little status in the community. Ironically, it is these same communities, with their part-time councils, that need highly trained and professional senior administrators.

The Department of Municipal Affairs is aware of some of these difficulties in smaller rural and urban municipalities and helps administrators to keep abreast of reporting deadlines, new regulations, and pertinent planning and legal decisions through its *Municipal Counsellor* publication and departmental directives. Despite the department's encouragement, skill upgrading is taking place much too slowly because many administrators receive mixed signals about the advantages of additional training. While the Department of Municipal Affairs urges administrators to become better qualified, many municipalities give no financial recognition to the administrator who does so. The implementation of enforceable education and salary guidelines tied to one of the municipal grant programs would eliminate this problem. In other cases Municipal Affairs encourages administrators to become more knowledgeable, but fails to provide funds to cover course fees and the wages of one- and two-day replacements so administrators would be able to attend pertinent seminars and workshops. All of this could easily be resolved if the provincial government would make an ongoing financial commitment to develop quality administration in all of its municipalities.

A Future for Alberta Municipal Administration

As the educational level of municipal administrators has risen, they have become almost as familiar with the basic principles of democratic theory as with the technicalities involved in keeping municipal books and following rezoning bylaws. Great strides have been made in the twentieth century to democratize governmental institutions. The challenge today is to eradicate the occupational inequities which have long affected women and the disabled, natives, and other visible minorities. As the result of persistent patterns of preferential employment, most senior municipal administrative positions are held by middle-class and middle-aged white males.

The federal government has recognized that the victims of inequities in the workplace often have narrow occupational choices and face formidable barriers to promotion to the upper echelons of an organization. Broad policy guidelines have been adopted, but the government has so far been unwilling to pursue the type of aggressive affirmative action programs, with quotas and substantial penalties for noncompliance, that are in place in the United States. Carol Agocs, in an examination of affirmative action in Canada, explains:

> In general, the federal approach to affirmative action in Canada has been to encourage voluntary initiatives, with government agencies offering support, persuasion and incentives rather than regulation and the threat of penalties. Employers are being invited and even implored, but so far not compelled, to take affirmative action. Affirmative action, American style, is not being transferred to Canadian soil, although Canadians can learn from observation of the U.S. experience. Canada has chosen to chart its own distinctive course toward affirmative action. But, so far, that path has not led to effective results in the form of significant change in patterns of occupational inequality.[48]

Strong affirmative action programs with quotas are an anathema to many Canadians who are convinced that they distort the employment market and are unfair to senior civil servants who are already in the system. The report of the Royal Commission on Equality in Employment dismisses a quota system in hiring as being "too rigid" and presents employment equity as being a flexible Canadian alternative.[49] In order to achieve employment equity an organization establishes a percentage of employment for which a group should strive.[50] Agocs explains how this is to take place: "Goals are achieved by dismantling organizational practices that adversely affected the hiring and career development of qualified target group members in the past, and establishing new policies and measures that facilitate their participation."[51]

The Alberta government has made efforts to promote women into management positions; however, it has been slow to encourage municipalities to rectify employment inequities. At the municipal level, when senior bureaucrats and councillors refuse to explain their employment decisions, the public becomes suspicious of their motives. As an example, just one month after Rimbey's Recreation Director went on maternity leave in 1989, the town council passed a motion in camera calling for her resignation. After a citizen leaked this to a critical *Rimbey Record*, council reversed its decision and the town manager wrote the director confirming council's action. The director returned to work a month later, but within ten minutes she was informed by the manager that her position had been terminated. Neither the mayor nor the manager was willing to provide an explanation for their actions.[52]

In 1978, just a decade after female city hall employees were asked to resign if they married, Calgary adopted its Equal Opportunity Program. Since then the city administration has made a conscious effort to fine-tune the program and eliminate employment barriers which discourage applications from women and minorities. Nevertheless, the Work Force Analysis Advisory Committee reported to council in 1989 that, despite the city's best intentions, white males were dominant in the city administration. Only 23 percent of city employees were female, 4 percent were members of visible minority groups, and 1 percent were native. Even more telling was the distribution of men, women, and minorities. Out of 32 upper-level managers only two were female, yet women held 80 percent of the clerical jobs in city hall. Only one of the upper-level managers was a member of a visible minority; the transportation director was a black man. The committee's chair, Dr. Maria Eriksen, concluded, "At this point it looks like the City of Calgary is one of the last havens in Canada for Anglo-Saxon men."[53] The city's equal opportunity coordinator, in defending the employment statistics, said that the city's policy on hiring was "one of neutrality as opposed to intervention."[54] Although council was not willing to embrace affirmative action, it did direct the administration to actively seek to hire women and minorities.

Edmonton's attempt to rectify employment inequities in a public service dominated by white males also has been hindered by its reluctance to enact aggressive policies to aid women and minorities. Although in 1990 three of the administration's eighteen general managers were female, as compared to only one in 1985, women primarily held clerical positions.[55]

In 1990 Mayor Reimer called upon the administration to develop a recruitment plan in order to increase the number of traditionally disadvantaged employees, but she was unwilling to call for employment equity or the enactment of hiring quotas. Given such a tepid policy, it is not surprising that a 1992 survey found that the number of women managers in the city had increased by less than 1 percent over a three-year period.[56] Although a city personnel department survey of civic workers found that 33.7 percent of women respondents agreed that their employment opportunities were limited by gender, Alderman Lillian Staroszik said that women did not need special treatment in employment. She explained that "if women are educated they can compete."[57]

Fire departments in Edmonton and Calgary have successfully maintained their fire halls as male-dominated enclaves. Although several hundred young and physically fit women have taken the cities' written and physical exams to become firefighters, by the spring of 1992 each city had hired only one female applicant. By establishing identical physical standards for males and females the departments have been able to disqualify virtually every woman. The president of the Edmonton Fire Fighters' Union defended the department's policy on the basis that "my life's on the line every . . . day I get on the truck."[58] However, the Edmonton Fire Department is filled with middle-aged men who have not taken a fitness test since they were hired 15 to 20 years ago and whose physical condition is unlikely to be as good as that of many of the young women who failed their physical exams.

A city concerned about fairness in employment, Lethbridge in 1988 adopted a two-pronged employment policy: a "pro-active native recruitment program" to interest natives in city civil service positions and help them with the application process and an "equal opportunity employment program" to ensure that only factors related to the nature of a job were being considered in making employment decisions.

Although few other municipalities have attempted to update their hiring practices, Alberta's local governments can hardly be faulted for their employment policies since the federal and provincial governments have not acted aggressively to rectify employment inequities. On the other hand, because many citizens deplore practices that create male bastions of employment and privilege, municipal administrations in Alberta have an opportunity to offer the leadership necessary to rectify employment inequities in the public and private sectors throughout the country.

An Overview of Bureaucratic Behaviour and Democratic Institutions

Municipal administrators and public employees often are caught up in a classic paradox: on the one hand the public applauds them for being "helpful civil servants" and on the other hand they are chastised for being "uncaring government bureaucrats." Municipal administrators face an equally difficult dilemma in their relations with members of council: they are expected to be experts capable of giving council advice on a variety of municipal matters, but they are also expected to leave the formulation of policy entirely up to council. Although the Municipal Government Act delineates the responsibilities of the municipal administrator, unfortunately, it is unable to establish the limits of administrative discretion. As a consequence, the distinction between administrative flexibility and policy making often is blurred and what is defined as flexibility in one municipality will be defined as policy making in another.

For the most part, Alberta's municipal administrators are well rewarded, but they are subject to much more scrutiny and criticism by many more people than their professional counterparts in the private sector. Undoubtedly, the reason so many senior municipal administrators report being under enormous mental pressure is that they face the demands described above, which they see as being irreconcilable.

Despite the pressure and scrutiny which Alberta municipal administrators have had to endure, in a relatively short time they have achieved professional status. Administrators' educational levels and knowledge have increased dramatically in the last two decades. Moreover, some municipalities are beginning to make a conscious attempt to break "the old boy network" in municipal administration by recruiting well qualified women and minorities. Perhaps when this recruiting practice becomes the norm the public will be less critical of the municipal bureaucracy.

8

Interest Groups and Democracy

Interest Groups and Policy Making

Interest groups have had "bad press" in recent years despite the important role they play in democratic policy making. Particularly in the print media and on American television, interest groups and lobbyists are portrayed as undermining democracy by subverting the legislative process with threats and bribes. The irony is that in today's complex society interest groups are essential to the democratic process, since they are often the only agents able to make legitimate demands on the political system over an extended period of time.[1]

In order to understand interest group politics it is important to keep in mind that few interest groups have lobbying and other political activities as their sole purpose. For most groups, lobbying is only a secondary activity to further their primary goals. For example, a religious organization may lobby city hall for a zoning variance to allow it to enlarge the church parking lot.

A charge often brought against interest groups is that the government is unduly influenced by their powerful and prestigious members, who know how the political system can be manipulated to further their own ends. It is generally acknowledged that some interest groups have far more power than others, but few people would argue that only these groups have an effective voice in a liberal democracy.[2]

The following sections discuss business groups, municipal employee associations, ratepayer associations, select-interest community groups, and broad-interest grass-roots community groups. Some of these groups are overtly political. A characteristic differentiating their members from members of other groups is that a large segment of them joined the organization specifically in order to make their views known to city hall.

Business Groups

A common saying heard in city halls across the province is that "the business of government is business." Donald Higgins explains why there is some truth in this cliché: "Because regulation of land is the single most important area over which local government in Canada has significant jurisdiction, it is particularly that part of the corporate sector involved in real estate that has interests which are most directly promoted or impeded by municipal government."[3] Since council is concerned with property development, from zoning and the issuance of development permits to the preservation of historical buildings, it is not surprising that real estate interests attend council meetings and sponsor candidates for political office. In 1984 a realtor contesting an Edmonton by-election sent letters to the real estate community soliciting campaign contributions, in which she explained how she would reward her supporters: "Those aiding me in the by-election will be remembered by me as long as I am in council."[4]

The real estate industry is particularly well organized and assiduous in developing working relationships with politicians. Very often the public is given the impression that one set of rules applies to the business community in its dealings with city hall and another set of rules applies to everyone else. In 1989 several business-oriented Edmonton aldermen were upset when council decided not to postpone a rezoning hearing after an attorney representing a developer sent a letter to city hall only days before the hearing requesting a postponement because he had prior commitments. One of the aldermen who voted against the request explained that a number of people who were opponents of the rezoning had already made arrangements to take time off from work to attend and it would be unfair to them if the request were granted. Alderman Ron Hayter responded that in the 18 years he had served on council it was the first time an attorney's request for a postponement had been denied.

In addition to real estate development firms, other businesses are interested in council policies. When councils consider enacting bylaws that set business hours and regulate certain types of business practices council chambers are packed with people clamouring to speak to the issue. Business representatives make concerted efforts to establish personal rapport with council members and senior bureaucrats by having dinner with them, sending small gifts at Christmas, and assisting them in minor business transactions. As a consequence, the business community usually has far better access to council than ordinary citizens. Mayor Terry Cavanagh identified so closely with the Edmonton business community that several times other members of council cautioned him that he was overstepping his authority. Shortly after his appointment to the mayor's chair, without conferring with council, he took it upon himself to advise Canadian Pacific Hotels that the city would consider offering $1.5 million in tax concessions in return for renovating its Hotel Macdonald.

Social scientist Norton Long explains why business is looked upon so favourably by almost every segment of the community:

> Public and reporters alike are relieved to believe both that there is a "they" to make civic life explicable and also to be held responsible for what occurs. . . . The community needs to believe that there are spiritual fathers, bad or good, who can deal with the dark: in the Middle Ages the peasants combatted a plague of locusts by a High Mass and a procession of the clergy who damned the grasshoppers with bell, book and candle. The Hopi Indians do a rain dance to overcome a drought. The harassed citizens of the . . . city mobilize their influentials at a civic luncheon to perform the equivalent and exorcise slums, smog, or unemployment. We smile at the medievals and the Hopi, but our own practices may be equally magical.[5]

In 1989 Lloydminster's Mayor Pat Gulak invited some 400 owners of downtown property to a private meeting at city hall to discuss how the central core could be revitalized. It was not revealed whether they exorcised any downtown demons.

Although businesses, independently and through their associations, lobby city council extensively, their inherent competitiveness prevents them from acting in concert except on a few issues that affect them equally, such as a business tax increase and the promotion of growth in the community. Chambers of Commerce, found in almost every urban municipality in the province, lobby council, present briefs, and develop a close relationship with councillors, yet they rarely take a strong stand on issues. Chamber membership encompasses large and small businesses throughout the community. Since almost any business issue before council benefits some people at the expense of others, a chamber's stance on most issues is either extremely moderate or nonexistent. For example, redevelopment of the city core is strongly supported by downtown businesspeople and strongly opposed by the owners of businesses in suburban shopping centres. A zoning variance allowing competing businesses to enter a neighbourhood will be opposed by the existing businesses. Then there are the "pariahs," such as escort services, massage parlours, "love shops," and pinball and video arcades, opposed by businesspeople who fear they will attract a clientele that will drive out their own customers.

Ironically, many citizens and elected officials believe the Chamber of Commerce is a unified organization and the major political force in the community. Municipal councils routinely make grants to assist the local chamber in promoting business. The president of the City of Leduc's Chamber of Commerce explained that it was a "sweet deal" for the city to give the chamber a $16,000 grant since it relieved the city of having to do anything related to business promotion. The president also noted that the chamber arranged business seminars, contests, political forums, parades, and the community clean-up, all of which are costly activities.[6] On a much smaller scale, in 1989 the Mannville council made a $1,000 grant to the Mannville and District Chamber of Commerce to pay some of the organization's operational expenses and to enable it to promote the village.

Despite the close bond between the chamber and council in most communities, a councillor occasionally questions funding for business interests. In 1985 St. Albert alderman George Kuschminder opposed a $20,000 municipal grant to the St. Albert chamber, asking, "Why is there this desperate need to promote St. Albert.... I don't believe bigger is beautiful...."[7]

Lobbying municipal council for a business promotion grant is only one of many political activities of the Chamber of Commerce. When the municipal budget is being prepared, the chamber is quick to point out how services can be maintained with no tax increase by increasing administrative efficiency. In some communities the chamber is directly involved in the budget process. In others, the chamber is routinely consulted on major policy proposals. As just one example, in 1985 the Fort Saskatchewan council adopted a "buy local" policy giving preference to local suppliers which copied almost exactly a motion passed by the Chamber of Commerce.

Given the chamber's aura of political power, it is not surprising that in some communities chamber leaders are involved in municipal politics. In December 1985 the president of the 4,000-member Edmonton Chamber of Commerce, Bruce Campbell, said business leaders were needed on council because a number of citizens wanted aldermen who were capable of making decisions. As it turned out, this was the opening of his own campaign for council, to which he was elected in October 1986. In a somewhat different case, several years ago a minor controversy erupted after a newly elected Didsbury councillor who was also president of the Chamber of Commerce released a parking study, which was prepared for the town by the Red Deer Planning Commission, to the chamber before it was presented to council.[8]

The Urban Development Institute (UDI) and the Canadian Home Builders' Association (CHBA), formerly the Housing and Urban Development Association of Canada (HUDAC), represent the real estate industry at the national level. Both have well organized Alberta affiliates with professional staff versed in the techniques of lobbying municipal councils and senior bureaucrats.

The UDI, incorporated in Alberta in November 1958, was the first Canadian organization to represent only land developers. Today the Alberta division of the UDA has over 100 members representing more than 35 development companies, as well as several hundred associates, in chapters in Calgary, Edmonton, and Red Deer.[9] The organization has an elected board of 15 directors whose political activities are carried out by its Provincial Liaison Committee. Both board members and professional staff maintain close working relationships with bureaucrats and elected officials in provincial and municipal governments.[10] A UDI newsletter discusses the activities of the Edmonton chapter: "Ongoing and open lines of communication with those municipalities which govern Edmonton and surrounding areas are carefully maintained in order that UDI is sought out and consulted prior to these municipalities taking any action which will involve our membership's livelihood."[11]

The UDI is prepared to bring legal action when municipal policies adversely affect developers. When the Cochrane town council passed a bylaw in the early 1980s prohibiting a development that would block the view of an existing development, the institute successfully challenged the bylaw in court. The UDI also is a member of the provincial government's Joint Liaison Committee, which includes several assistant deputy ministers from the Department of Municipal Affairs and representatives from the CHBA. In the past the committee has dealt with topics such as property assessment and taxation, the assessment of vacant land, land reserve requirements, and restricted development areas. The UDI is also a member of the City of Edmonton General Managers' Liaison Committee, whose membership consists of representatives from the UDI, the mayor's executive assistant, and the general managers of the departments of transportation, planning, recreation and parks, finance, and water and sanitation.

The UDI attempts to thwart policies requiring developers to build costly community facilities free of charge or to donate valuable land for transportation corridors as a trade-off for obtaining approval for subdivision developments. In addition to its political activities, the UDI carries out a public relations program, for it is well aware of the public's image of land developers. The program includes a speakers' bureau that provides experts to community groups at no cost, and promotes ties with colleges and universities.

The CHBA consists of more than 4,000 member companies in 80 local associations and ten provincial councils across Canada. In Alberta the CHBA is the parent organization of an integrated two-tier Alberta group with municipal chapters. The CHBA Alberta Council, with more than 1,000 members, constitutes the upper tier; the lower tier comprises CHBA chapters in the larger cities.[12] The association's political activities are delegated as follows: the national CHBA lobbies the federal government, the CHBA Alberta Council lobbies the provincial government, and the local chapters lobby their respective municipal councils. Since many housing programs and policies involve more than one level of government, the three levels of the CHBA often coordinate their activities.

In principle, the Alberta CHBA subscribes to a free market in housing. Realizing, however, that a free market is unrealistic and that government involvement in housing is increasing, the organization has followed a strategy of developing close relationships with the provincial and municipal governments, through membership, for example, in the Joint Liaison Committee. This tactic has been so successful that the CHBA is consulted at every stage in the formulation of government policy on housing.

A small number of influential businesspeople prefer to lobby council at the local level on an individual basis rather than have their views expressed through an umbrella organization. Unlike most property developers, Edmonton's Ghermezian brothers, who own and operate West Edmonton Mall, maintain a high level of public visibility. They have involved themselves in municipal elections, made presentations before council, and threatened the city administration with dire consequences unless their demands were met. At one raucous council meeting at which a rezoning bid on land adjacent to West Edmonton Mall was being discussed, Nader Ghermezian persisted in interrupting aldermen from his seat in the visitor's gallery until he eventually convinced council of the merits of his proposal.[13]

Unions and Municipal Employee Associations

Unions and associations of municipal employees influence the policy making of many urban and rural municipalities. A major problem faced by all municipal employees is the erratic stance councils take on personnel issues. A council's decisions on such policies reflect the community's economic viability. During periods of prosperity municipal councils grant generous wage and benefit settlements rather than face the possibility of a bitter strike, an irate and inconvenienced public, and unforeseen political consequences. In hard times, however, councils often claim that it is their duty to lay off municipal employees and keep wage increases to a minimum. Although such a policy divides councils and embitters municipal employees, it generally has substantial public support.

The first municipal employees' union founded in Alberta was a local of the militant Industrial Workers of the World that organized Edmonton outside labourers in 1912. Almost immediately, 250 of its members struck for higher wages but were forced to return to work on the city's terms.[14] The abortive strike broke the union. Less than a month later the Lethbridge police force participated in a strike which also was unsuccessful.[15] Four years later, Edmonton's outside workers organized again and were issued a charter by the Trades and Labour Congress. A labour historian chronicles the subsequent rapid expansion of unionization:

> Their lead was soon followed by city inside workers in Calgary and municipal employees in Lethbridge and Medicine Hat. By 1919 a municipal federation had been formed in Calgary to negotiate with city council. It included, in addition to city hall staff and labourers, police and fire fighters, teamsters, electricians and street-railway workers. In 1919, the first local of hospital workers in the province, Local 8, City Hospital Employees, was organized to represent workers at the Calgary municipal hospital.[16]

For the next three decades municipal unions used the strike threat as their principal strategy. With the formation of the national Canadian Union of Public Employees (CUPE) in Alberta in 1963, municipal unions have become much more politically sophisticated, recruiting widespread public support in order to influence councils. In addition to strong CUPE locals in Edmonton and Calgary, the union has organized municipal employees in almost all Alberta cities and in many smaller communities, for a total of 140 locals. Fire and police employees have also been organized in some communities, although not by CUPE. Fire department employees are unionized in nine municipalities, and nine municipalities have a unionized police force.

A newcomer to the municipal scene is the Alberta Union of Provincial Employees (AUPE), which has traditionally represented provincial employees such as those working in hospitals, community colleges, and universities. The union entered the municipal field in 1983 after a group of Bonnyville town employees requested AUPE representation. The town unsuccessfully contested the union's right to enter the municipal field before the Alberta Labour Relations Board and then appealed the board's decision to the Court of Queen's Bench, which also ruled in favour of the union. Although the town accepted the court's decision and began negotiations with the AUPE, the Alberta Urban Municipalities Association (AUMA) and Alberta Association of Municipal Districts and Counties (AAMD&C) feared that the union was so powerful it would be able to overwhelm any municipality it decided to organize. The organizations lobbied the Minister of Labour for changes in legislation preventing the AUPE from organizing at the municipal level and also attempted to enlist the support of CUPE. In both cases they were unsuccessful.

In the 1980s relations between councils and municipal unions became much more confrontational as municipalities attempted to pare their budgets and their staffs. CUPE intensified its organizational campaign. Although 2 and 3 percent yearly wage increases were being awarded, the negotiations were protracted and often bitter. Neither management nor labour was being greedy; municipal revenues, grants, and taxes were static while inflation was increasing, and workers' buying power was shrinking as municipalities frantically implemented policies to control spending.

In the winter of 1982 Calgary and Edmonton decided to minimize tax increases by laying off a large number of civic employees, including many police and firefighters. To garner public support, the administrations leaked information on the generous salaries and benefits received by police and firefighters during the prosperous 1970s. In addition, the public was led to believe that civic employees were primarily responsible for the financial crises. The unions responded by initiating legal action to prevent the layoffs and mounting a public relations campaign to win over the citizenry or frighten it into supporting their position.[17] The disputes were eventually settled, with only a small number of people losing their jobs and municipal staffs to be decreased by attrition. However, the civil service was demoralized and the public confused by the charges and counter-charges made by administrations and public employee associations. Mayor Cavanagh, for example, claimed during his election campaign that CUPE's endorsement of his opponent Jan Reimer was unethical and a "blatant attempt to muscle votes for an opponent."[18]

Although the Alberta Rural Municipal Administrators' Association is little known outside the ranks of professionals in the Department of Municipal Affairs, it plays a major role in the provincial government's formulation of municipal policy. The organization of municipal administrators was established early in the century when poorly paid rural administrators were being given increasing responsibilities.

...as early as 1914, the secretary-treasurers were holding informal meetings probably in small local groups with Department of Municipal Affairs officials who instructed them as to the interpretation and application of the various Acts. . . . by 1918, they were talking seriously of an association and some type of courses to better qualify themselves for their duties. . . . The municipalities in many cases preferred to keep the position [of secretary-treasurer] as a sort of political plum or sinecure for friends and relations.[19]

After the Alberta Association of Municipal District Secretary-Treasurers was formed in 1922, the Department of Municipal Affairs and the Alberta Association of Municipal Districts provided the organization with small grants. From its inception the association formulated positions on municipal issues which then were referred to the provincial government for consideration. The association has been concerned with upgrading the salaries and status of its members as well as defining the qualifications for a municipal secretary-treasurer. In 1939 the University of Alberta's Adult Education Division began to offer refresher courses for members of the association.

Over the years the association has continued to work closely with the Department of Municipal Affairs and with other groups in the development of municipal policy and legislation. "The most important association[s] over the years . . . [were] with the councillors group, [and] the Alberta Association of Municipal Districts and Counties."[20] In 1968 the organization's name was changed to the Alberta Association of Municipal District and County Secretary-Treasurers in order to recognize the increasing number and importance of county administrators. However, the length of the name was cumbersome and in 1972 it was changed to the Alberta Rural Municipal Administrators Association.

The Alberta Teachers' Association, with more than 30,000 members and 90 locals, is the most powerful political force at the municipal level today.[21] As teachers have attempted to gain professional recognition in salary and status, the organization has had a stormy history. In 1918 its predecessor, the Alberta Teachers' Alliance, splintered from the Alberta Educational Association (AEA), which it felt was not representing the interests of teachers, particularly the issues of salaries and tenure, and broader concerns about the inadequacies of the educational system. Membership in the AEA had been open to all laypeople and professionals who had an interest in Alberta education, which was discussed once a year at an annual meeting. Both the Department of Education and the Alberta School Trustees' Association were alarmed by the militancy of the

Teachers' Alliance, which, among other things, had employed a paid organizer; they fought the ATA throughout the 1920s and 1930s. When militant Edmonton high school teachers held a two-week strike in 1921, the Alliance won, but the organization suffered a severe setback five years later when teachers in Blairmore were locked out and the trustees hired an entire new staff. The teachers sued the district for unlawful termination and lost.

When a United Farmers of Alberta (UFA) government was elected in 1921, one of its first pieces of legislation lowered the entrance requirements for normal schools (the teacher colleges of the time) in order to flood the province with new teachers who could be hired at a very low wage. Both the provincial Department of Education and the school trustees rejected the Alliance's proposals for a pension plan, tenure, and dismissal procedures. In 1935 the Teaching Profession Act changed the name of the Alliance to the Alberta Teachers' Association (ATA), the only benefit the teachers received from the legislation.

It was not until Premier Aberhart swept into power under the Social Credit banner in 1935 that the ATA received government support. Teachers were given job protection and in 1939 the Teachers' Superannuation Act was approved, a first step towards the creation of an adequate pension scheme.

Today the ATA is a powerful association that is the collective bargaining agent for every Alberta teacher. It also has the authority to discipline its members for unprofessional and unethical conduct. Acutely aware that the economic welfare of its members is directly related to the province's basic education grant and to districts' supplemental requisitions, the ATA continually lobbies both sources. Teachers are encouraged to run for office and to become involved in local educational politics. The Alberta School Trustees' Association has attempted to counter the increasing influence of the ATA, with only limited success.

Ratepayer Associations

Ratepayer associations are generally political cohorts of business groups, since they also are concerned with running government efficiently and limiting taxes. Disagreements between ratepayers and business associations usually concern the relative weight of business and property taxes. Although Donald Higgins found that ratepayer associations had "developed at least as far back as the early part of this century in many municipalities, both large and small, in Canada,"[22] they are seldom mentioned in Alberta newspapers before the 1930s. In Calgary and Edmonton, ratepayer associations often formed spontaneously to vent the wrath of property owners, captured newspaper headlines, and then disappeared. These short-lived organizations have not been a political force in either city, possibly because ratepayers have always been able to attend a municipality's annual meeting and quiz the council about its fiscal policies and tax levels.

In recent years rural areas have spawned a number of ratepayer associations. In the 1960s and 1970s, "hobby farmers" on the fringes of Calgary and Edmonton found themselves locked in political battles with traditional farmers. Believing they were being inequitably taxed, that there was evidence of municipal fiscal mismanagement, and that they were being denied services, the disgruntled suburbanites formed ratepayer associations. By the early 1980s there were at least eight of these associations in Alberta, most of them on the outskirts of the two major cities, although several decidedly rural associations were also formed. A letter from the President of the Bearspaw, Glendale Ratepayer Association describes its membership as "upper-middle to upper levels . . . the acreage owners and large farmers are in the $70,000 plus per year level; some small farmers and older residents, $40,000 plus. Most acreage owners tend to be professional management or own their own companies."[23] According to its president, the Leduc Residents Association comprises "farmers and acreage owners of middle to upper middle level incomes."[24]

When the Wetaskiwin County Ratepayers' Association was founded in 1987, its first committees dealt solely with tax assessments and the cost of public works. Eventually, however, most rural ratepayer associations, like their urban counterparts, tend to focus on tax inequities. For example, the Homeowners Association of St. Albert was organized in 1986 after a general re-assessment substantially raised residential property taxes. The Fort McMurray Civic Taxpayers Association was formed in 1988 in order to force the mayor and council to resign because property taxes had been substantially increased after the first assessment in nine years. Although the association circulated a petition calling for a property tax reduction which several thousand people signed, the council ignored it and also refused to resign.[25] The association was re-energized in 1989 when the council called for a 3.8 percent tax increase.

In the Municipal District of Brazeau, the Twin Rivers MD 77 Ratepayers Association also has been a thorn in the side of the municipal council. In the spring of 1991 at a raucous annual meeting orchestrated by the

association, five separate motions were made calling for council resignations. People stood in lengthy lines in order to question the councillors
about the costs they incurred in attending conferences; their wages; and
per diem, mileage, and subsidence rates; as well as road allowances and
road construction in the district. An editorial in the *Western Review* said
in part: "Almost 400 angry residents believe they are not well represented
by council. . . . MD residents are standing firm against their council, only
this time, they believe the only way to get what they want is to oust those
in the highest power at the MD."[26]

The level of political activity for both urban and rural ratepayer associations varies widely, from functioning as a watchdog at municipal council
meetings to becoming deeply involved in electoral politics. At the organizational meeting of the Wetaskiwin County Ratepayers' Association in
1987 the president said, "It's very important that we get involved. . . . We
have to get some more communication going with county administration, and develop some solutions."[27] In contrast, the Balzac Ratepayers'
Association hired a former mayor of Calgary, Rod Sykes, to represent its
members, who lived in the 176 square kilometres of land that the City of
Calgary was attempting to annex in 1988 from the Municipal District of
Rocky View. The association wanted to freeze assessment values and taxes
on land and buildings until the area was developed. While the Strathcona
Acreage Owners' Association does not endorse county council candidates,
the Foothills Ratepayers' Association backed a full slate of candidates in
the 1983 municipal district elections and persuaded the Minister of
Municipal Affairs to change the district's electoral boundaries to guarantee equal representation. In a candid moment, the president of the
Bearspaw, Glendale Ratepayer Association wrote:

> We supported a candidate in the last councillor election to try and get
> acreage owners to vote for a non farmer; unfortunately the man was a
> hobby farmer and lost badly. This election we will try again but it
> might be the kiss of death to any serious contender to be supported by
> a ratepayer association with the large farmer vote.[28]

After the Claresholm council voted to build a new water storage reservoir in 1984, the Claresholm Ratepayer Association managed to force the
issue to a plebiscite by claiming that the project would necessitate substantially increasing the residential property tax.

While ratepayer associations have been able to exert some influence on
municipal councils, they have been less successful in encouraging their
members to attend meetings. The Brooks Renters' and Ratepayers' Association, 80 percent of whose members are ratepayers, had a membership

fluctuating between 50 and 60, 15 to 25 of whom regularly attended meetings. Less than a year after it was organized, the Wetaskiwin County Ratepayers' Association had a turnout of only eight out of a membership of 49. The president said that she could not understand why an association which was formed "to encourage citizen participation in county affairs and improve communication between council and ratepayers" was unable to attract more than 49 members out of a total of 9,521 ratepayers in the county.[29]

Select-Interest Community Groups

A select-interest group is often successful because it has achievable goals which are modest and narrow. Such an organization's leaders and members realize that their coalition is temporary and will be disbanded when it has accomplished its mission. For example, in April 1981, when the Brooks council appointed a town manager many people considered unqualified, the Brooks Concerned Citizens Committee was formed almost immediately. It circulated a petition protesting the appointment and held several well-attended meetings, eventually forcing the council to hire a management consulting firm to evaluate the town's administration. When the town manager was finally dismissed, the citizens' committee disbanded. After a severe storm in 1981 caused extensive basement flooding and sewer backups in the southeastern part of the city, a Southeast Edmonton Flood Action Committee formed to pressure city council to upgrade the area's sewer system. Over nine months, the group held a number of well-attended public forums, distributed 7,000 flyers throughout the community, and had several meetings with city aldermen. As a result of this incessant pressure, in April 1982 the council decided to start sewer improvement work in the area approximately 15 years ahead of schedule. Its work competed, the committee disbanded. In the summer of 1983 an ad hoc group of 30 middle-class residents on Medicine Hat's Fourth Street organized to halt a developer's plan to build a five-story apartment building in the neighbourhood. A petition accompanied by individual appeals to council members was successful; council quashed the development and the group was dissolved. In 1989 a small group of acreage owners and farmers who lived in the County of Strathcona organized the Stop Aurum Dump (SAD) association which played a major role in the defeat of Edmonton's proposal to establish a landfill in the area. SAD's membership grew from ten to several hundred in a short period of time, and the association raised thousands of dollars to hire consultants to evaluate Edmonton's dump site and to place informational ads in the media. After forcing the city to abandon its plans for Aurum, SAD was disbanded. A somewhat less effective single purpose organization was founded in Edmonton to oppose a proposed transportation corridor down 114 Street. The 114th Street Area Protection Coalition, composed primarily of middle-class professionals, challenged the bylaw giving the city the right to establish a transportation corridor. It was the city that eventually wore down the coalition; the street was widened, with substantial loss of housing.

A council often deals with a well organized interest group by striking a "blue-ribbon citizens' committee," ostensibly to obtain a different perspective on an issue but in fact to defuse a potentially explosive situation by co-opting its leadership with a committee appointment. These committees seldom represent more than a very narrow segment of the community's business and political leaders.

Not all select interest groups are well organized and their membership figures are often suspect. The Friends of the Athabasca (FOTA) environmental association was apparently formed only shortly before it approached the Athabasca County council to express its concerns about the building of a new pulp mill. According to an *Athabasca Advocate* reporter, "This delegation though was not as well prepared with their presentation as they should have been, as several times during the presentation they were at odds with one another."[30] A Lethbridge citizen, Norm Duce, established the Committee Opposed to Rampant Extravagance (CORE) to contest the construction of a new city hall in 1984. There was some question whether CORE's membership consisted solely of Norm Duce or whether it had the 200 members he claimed for it.

Broad-Interest Grass-Roots Community Groups

Although citizen groups were not accepted as a legitimate part of the municipal political process in Alberta until the late 1960s, Edmonton's extensive network of community leagues and Calgary's community associations have been powerful neighbourhood organizations for nearly three-quarters of a century. An Edmonton ratepayer association formed in 1912 became a community league in 1921, but the first organization established specifically as a community league was the 142nd Street District Community League, later known as the Crestwood Community League, which was organized in 1917. The league, with a constitution influenced by that of the American Neighborhood Club Movement, lobbied the city for better streetcar scheduling and such amenities as electricity and sidewalks for suburban neighbourhoods.[31] Other leagues soon formed and the Edmonton Federation of Community Leagues was established in 1921. The *Edmonton Journal* reported that in a public meeting before the 1924 municipal election the federation asked the mayoralty and aldermanic candidates whether they were in favour of the federation being represented on many of the city's boards and whether they approved of using public school facilities for children's recreational activities.[32] Community associations were created somewhat later in Calgary. The first was the Mount Royal Community Association, founded January 22, 1934, followed by the Scarboro Community Association on March 19 of the same year. The organizations proliferated in both cities and by 1988 there were 136 leagues in Edmonton and 120 community associations in Calgary.

In both cities the organizations have been, with few exceptions, only peripherally involved in politics.

> Although the Edmonton Federation of Community Leagues hovered on the fringe of issues such as the ward system, or the proposed downtown coliseum, it was not able to command the allegiance of its constituents who, in any case, were more concerned with the expansion of recreational services to their rapidly growing clientele.[33]

Nevertheless, in recent years several leagues and associations have become politically active. After lobbying by the Hillhurst-Sunnyside Community Association, the Calgary council made some minor changes to a proposed LRT route. In 1988 the Brentwood Community Association had enough political influence that the LRT's manager was directed by the Chief Commissioner not to attend any community meetings to discuss the extension of LRT into the community. In Edmonton the River Valley Community League played a major role in council's decision to reverse a long-standing policy of acquiring river valley land for parks and open space. In Calgary the Millican-Ogden Community Association took the opposite position when it convinced council not to decrease the community's open space by approving the construction of a large housing project.

Although political activists in both cities are optimistic that community organizations will evolve into effective political forces, a number of formidable obstacles exist. Perhaps the most serious is that with recent changes in demographics, many leagues and associations are in danger of collapsing for lack of volunteers to run and administer their programs. As the number of single-parent and two-income families continues to grow, fewer people in the community are donating their time and energies for community service. In addition, people have begun to wonder whether activating the associations might foster narrow and self-serving politics. After Edmonton's Federation of Community Leagues opposed a scheme which would have provided additional funding for multicultural groups in 1986, the federation was accused of opposing multiculturalism and community cultural centres for fear they would displace the leagues in meeting community recreational needs.[34] In addition, since community associations tend to be the strongest in communities comprising predominantly single-family dwellings, they sometimes act like ratepayer associations. In 1989 several Calgary community associations discussed sponsoring a mayoral candidate who would quickly pay down the city's outstanding debt.

As Alberta has become a multicultural society, ethnic communities in several larger municipalities have developed broadly based citizen groups that function as their political arm. When Calgary was considering scaling down the size of its Chinatown by one-third in 1982, the Chinese community quickly organized to convince the administration that the proposal was faulty. The United Calgary Chinese Association and the Chinatown Ratepayer Association, long active on the Calgary political scene, have been moderately successful in maintaining the viability of the Chinese community. Edmonton's small Italian community spent six years in a tenacious attempt to persuade city council to rename a small neighbourhood park to commemorate John Cabot. The Giovanni Caboto Society held a number of meetings, worked with the press, and met with various aldermen and senior city administrators. Its efforts were rewarded in 1981 when the playground was renamed Giovanni Caboto Park.[35] Astute politicians in communities with organized ethnic associations are careful to consult them and provide cultural grants. In 1986 the Lethbridge council made a $500 grant to the city's Japanese community in order to help it seek compensation from the federal government for its mistreatment of Japanese-Canadians during the Second World War. When Don Hartman was a Calgary alderman he assiduously cultivated the city's Polish and Italian communities and had their support at election time.

In the 1960s student activists learned organizational techniques and the tactics of direct confrontation. Once graduated, most changed their life-style but they did not forget the effectiveness of well-organized group action or lose the desire to participate directly in the democratic process. In his analysis of the changing atmosphere of Edmonton politics, James Lightbody describes another facet of the growth and legitimization of citizen participation in Alberta.

The source of this challenge was an unintended consequence of the rapid expansion of the University of Alberta's faculty (which tripled in size) and the research staff at other agencies such as the Research Council of Alberta. By far the greatest number of recruits for these institutions were either American by birth or Canadians who had received their post-graduate education in the United States. They were not only highly qualified but had also been subject to . . . the rhetoric of direct citizen participation. . . .[36]

Providing dedicated members and leadership skills, these academics and a number of recently graduated students were instrumental in forming neighbourhood citizen groups committed to political action.

City halls in Edmonton and Calgary recognized this new force and attempted to control it by plugging it into the political system. In 1971 Edmonton embarked on an ambitious three-year experimental pilot project combining the decentralization of social services with citizen participation for ten communities with a population of 40,000. The West Edmonton Social Task Force, or West 10 as it was popularly known, assembled in a central community office people from the provincial Department of Health and Social Development, city social services, city parks and recreation, the public school board, Canada Manpower, the federal Local Initiative Program, and a number of volunteer agencies. Two community development officers were employed to activate residents, who were to "oversee" the project through a 15-member area council. In reality, the council was advisory, as the various federal, provincial, and city employees were responsible to their respective departments. This anomaly eventually led to a drastic restructuring of the citizen participation component of the project. When the West 10 council took its mandate seriously and attempted to integrate and control all the services and agencies, the departments resisted and eventually the provincial government withdrew from the program. Although the chair of the first West 10 council said he was committed to "participatory democracy" with "most decision-making lying with the people and higher levels of government serving in a coordinating capacity," he later admitted that the citizens' area council had been a "sham."[37] To prevent the "radicals" from taking control, the organization was restructured with a board composed of representatives from established community groups, such as the Westmount Christian Council and the Westmount Ministerial Association. Although the West 10 project was renewed at the end of its three-year trial, its funding was cut and the citizen participation component was eventually discarded.

The low level of citizen involvement in the West 10 experiment was related to the council's lack of power. Some 900 residents were initially involved in the movement. However, the activists among them soon saw that the council was powerless and that citizen participation was merely "window dressing." At its first annual meeting in 1972 approximately 100 people turned out to elect council members; at its third, fewer than 45 people showed up, only eight of whom agreed to stand for election to the 15-member council.

In Calgary, Mayor Sykes attempted to mobilize community leaders as a nucleus for a broadly based citizen organization. The "Citizens' Open Government Study" (COGS) was composed of middle-class professionals from civic organizations and prominent individuals who were expected to recruit additional participants.

> First of all, participants would increase their own awareness of civic politics, their confidence to pursue it, and their commitment to its success. Secondly, the committee's recommendations would open the door to greater opportunities for participation in government by Calgarians.[38]

Either the organizational structure was faulty or the COGS members were unable to generate greater interest, for the study failed to develop a broadly based citizens' organization. After 15 months it submitted a number of recommendations to council, but little action was taken on them.

It is difficult to generate and maintain political involvement at the grass-roots level. The few middle-class groups that have become involved in community politics have been frustrated by unanswered letters and unreturned phone calls, given too little time to respond to proposals affecting their neighbourhoods, and refused the information they need to respond intelligently to council proposals. Working-class neighbourhood groups bear additional burdens. Since their members generally have less education, fewer of them are able to comprehend complex policy issues and possess the negotiating skills so crucial in dealing with council. They are less "connected" with the community's socio-economic elite, who tend to dominate the local political scene. Yet, despite these problems, an apparatus for grass-roots participation is in place. As a consequence there are numerous instances of working class neighbourhoods besting city hall. Leadership, organizational skills, and citizen attitudes towards local government are the key factors in determining whether or not community organizations will further democracy at the neighbourhood level.

The Media

Associations of broadcasters and newspapers lobby for legislation ranging from reduced newspaper mailing rates to zoning changes for proposed newspaper plants and radio and television towers. Although students of politics are more interested in the effects of the media on public opinion, this is a murky area. One problem is that "empirical studies . . . which have actually demonstrated influence relationships or tested formulations, seem to have lagged far behind the conceptual part of the enterprise."[39] Another difficulty is that newspapers, radio, and television serve diverse segments of the public in varying formats—there is not a single media influence but rather different media, each with wide-ranging influences. Moreover, since virtually all forms of media compete with one another for advertising dollars (which are directly related to the size of their reading, viewing, and listening audiences), they often follow public tastes and interests rather than lead them.

In shaping public opinion at the community level, newspapers are more important than radio and television. In a survey of city managers in American cities with populations of over 100,000, newspapers were seen "as much more interested in, associated with, and influential in municipal affairs than either television or radio."[40] There is evidence for a similar pattern in Canadian communities.[41] Radio and television stations carefully tailor their programming to the public's demand for entertainment. Radio focuses on providing music with occasional encapsulated accounts of national and international news. It is unusual for a radio station to devote time to council events and local political issues. Local television stations are even more reluctant to commit resources to reporting on municipal politics, and when they do, the coverage tends to be in the form of superficial 15-second segments. Perhaps this is why so few municipal candidates in Alberta use the broadcast media during their electoral campaigns.

Large city dailies have a somewhat different news focus than smaller community weeklies and urban "throw-away" advertising newspapers. A substantial portion of the political news in a large daily is national and international and is supplied by the wire services. Nevertheless, provincial political news is important and full-time reporters are assigned to cover the legislature and provincial departments in Edmonton. City hall and local political issues are covered, but must compete with international, national, and provincial events. In contrast, the smaller weekly newspapers, whose *raison d'être* is the community, focus on local events, politics, and personalities.

Regardless of the size of a newspaper, there are constraints on its content and tone. Since newspapers depend on the good will of advertisers, who are generally among the community's social and economic elite, an astute editor is careful not to offend them. Edwin Black, in a study of the news media in Canada, defines four factors that result in "the tendency for small newspapers to support community notables." They are:

1. The publisher's vulnerability to local social and business pressure.
2. Vocational training of traditional gatekeepers (city and news editors etc.) which leads them to omit or bury news items that might call into question the socio-cultural structure and people's faith in it.
3. Reporters' reliance on authority figures for news sources.
4. The journalistic concept of professionalism which emphasizes rationality, decisions rather than discussion, depersonalization of local legislative proceedings, legal language, and respectful treatment of local notables.[42]

By deferring to the established norms of the community's socio-economic elite and by selecting the material to be published, the newspaper helps to establish a community's political agenda. However, newspapers differ in their effect on different segments of the community. An American study found that members of lower-income groups tended to obtain their news from radio and television rather than from newspapers.[43] Yet a study of the media in the 1968 Edmonton election found that respondents with a low interest in the election and low levels of political competence "showed the closest association between voting and both editorial reading and information."[44] However, the same study found that the *Edmonton Journal*'s endorsement of the major civic party running for office in the city had almost no effect on the way the paper's readers voted in the municipal election.

Although editorial endorsements are largely ignored by the citizenry, every community has a small number of educated, informed people who follow the issues and express their opinions in the letters-to-the-editor column. These letters are taken into consideration by council, although it is difficult to determine whether they represent the community's general interests or individual opinions. Moreover, knowledgeable council members are aware that editors often select letters to be published which support their newspaper's political viewpoint.[45]

Little is known about the extent to which newspaper "agenda setting" influences council policy making. In a study of this phenomenon, Edwin

Black looked at three smaller Ontario communities, Belleville, Kingston, and Peterborough. With mixed findings, he concluded: "The ability to influence local decisions appears . . . to be a function of the prevailing structures of debate and decision making. The ability may not be generally inherent in local newspaper reporting as such."[46] One might expect to find a similar pattern of influence in Alberta; that is, in many communities a close relationship exists between issues raised by newspapers and those dealt with by council, while in others the newspaper is viewed as an irritant, provoking controversy and developing issues the council does not consider relevant. An example of the latter scenario occurred in July 1988 when the Edson council banned the press from its board and committee meetings because committee reports were being published before councillors had an opportunity to examine them. The council eventually allowed the press to attend board meetings, but it could not attend committee meetings without being invited. In 1987 Didsbury's mayor cautioned council members that if they were concerned about a matter it should be discussed in council rather than with the press. He added that the press had a responsibility not to portray council as "a bunch of blundering idiots."[47] That same year the Village of Holden adopted the following guidelines for both the council and the media: (1) at the beginning of each council meeting the agenda will be available for the media; (2) questions by the media about council items will not be answered during or after the meeting but only by telephone; (3) the media will emphasize the major points made during council meeting and not remarks made by the councillors during the discussion period; and (4) the media will respect council's wishes in reporting issues to the public. Council was particularly concerned that members not be quoted out of context. One councillor explained that since Holden was not a highly structured city council, "we make informal quips . . . [and] there is no reason to report those comments." He concluded by saying that councillors should not always have to be on guard with the press.[48]

Both provincial and municipal governments in Alberta have attempted to muzzle the press at one time or another. The most brazen attempt was made in 1937 by Premier Aberhart, who rushed the Accurate News and Information Act through the legislature to rectify what the government considered to be scurrilous attacks on Social Credit programs. The first section of the act gave the chair of the provincial Social Credit Board the power to require a newspaper to publish a corrected version of a story which distorted government policy, while the second section gave the chair power to require a newspaper to reveal its sources of information. In both cases, a newspaper that refused to comply was subject to closure and substantial fines. The act was ruled to be *ultra vires* by the Supreme Court of Canada before it ever came into effect and the government was roundly criticized for attempting to control the press.[49]

More recent relationships between community newspapers and councils have occasionally become as acrimonious as they were during the Social Credit era. In the late 1970s the *Edmonton Journal* persisted in attacking a council it considered inept. The council responded by encouraging a second daily, the *Edmonton Sun*, to begin publishing in the city. Shortly thereafter, alderman Ed Leger, the butt of numerous *Journal* editorials and editorial cartoons, proposed unsuccessfully that all city advertising be given to the *Sun*. When the *Journal* criticized other members of council, the city began to publish its own eight-page tabloid and distributed it free to Edmontonians. Its editor admitted the paper was "relatively bland" and that "elected and administrative officials obviously do have a vested interest in what goes out."[50] The tabloid was seldom read and the costly venture was terminated.

Edmonton is not the only municipality that has experimented with publishing its own paper. Since 1983 the County of Camrose has published a newsletter, co-edited by a civil servant and a councillor, which is sent to county residents. The Milk River town council began to publish a newsletter in 1987 to "let people know what we're doing."[51] In early 1989 the County of Parkland initiated a bimonthly newsletter containing information it thought would interest residents, as well as items from council meetings. In less than six months the newsletter was upgraded to a newspaper carrying the county's legal notices and reporting on all school board and county council meetings. The reeve claimed that there was nothing wrong with the county having its own newspaper, since it did not control or censor the stories.[52] In contrast, when a councillor for the Municipal District of Rocky View asked the council for financial assistance to publish a newsletter for her constituents, the reeve was opposed on the grounds that the newsletter could be used for political purposes during municipal electoral campaigns.[53]

Small town weeklies are particularly sensitive to their financial balance sheets and many rely on the publication of municipal legal notices and council minutes for their continued existence. In return for publishing minutes and notices the council contracts with a weekly newspaper for free distribution to all of its ratepayers. The legal authority for this is found in Section 150 of the Municipal Government Act, which reads in part: "A council by bylaw may provide for publication of the minutes of its meetings and of information concerning other municipal subjects and for that purpose may cause circulars to be prepared and distributed to all proprietary electors or to all proprietary electors and all other adult residents of the municipality." The County of Strathcona justified a $20,000 mail subsidy to the *Sherwood Park News* on the basis of a 1987 telephone survey which found that 88 percent of the respondents said the newspaper was their primary source of information on the county council and its policy making.[54] The same year Improvement District No. 17 contracted to have local newspapers delivered to inform all of its ratepayers about council activities.[55]

A council is occasionally charged with attempting to muzzle the press by withdrawing an offending newspaper's advertising revenue. In 1981 the editor of the *North Peace Pictorial* accused the Grimshaw council of trying to drive him out of business because he criticized the financial arrangements for a proposed curling complex and called for the mayor's resignation. He complained that the council gave all of its business, payment for 1,800 subscriptions, to his competitor without considering the electorate's preference in newspapers.[56] In 1982 the publisher of the *Sturgeon Gazette* charged the Bon Accord council with terminating a $36,000 contract to supply the community's 600 residents with a newspaper at half cost because the paper published a letter to the editor criticizing the municipal administrator.[57] In 1987, after a heated public hearing, the Town of Grand Centre decided not to renew a contract for legal advertising and resident subscriptions with the *Grand Centre-Cold Lake Sun*. Although the hearing was meant to deal with the financial aspects of the contract, the paper's reporting and editorial policies were also discussed. One councillor had heard criticism of the paper "on the street." Another responded, "the real issue here is that some people are upset about editorial content," and speculated that councillors wanted to punish the paper for the way it covered the news.[58]

In 1984 Edmonton's council was angered by a *Journal* writer who criticized the city's Genesee power plant and an editorial which described it as a white elephant. Mayor Decore said the editorial "lacked the proper research that people who write that kind of comment should do," and an alderman called the editorial "grossly misinformed."[59] In 1990 an Edmonton alderman accused the *Journal* of giving a peep-show operator too much news coverage, saying, "this guy couldn't have bought the publicity he's gotten in the past two weeks."[60] However, council did not attempt to sanction the *Journal* for its conduct in either incident. The Stettler council and administration were incensed when a front-page story in the *Stettler Independent* suggested that the town's property taxes were some of the highest in the province. They responded with a stinging letter to the editor, but there was not even a hint that the newspaper would or should be reprimanded.[61]

Electioneering provides another important source of revenue for small community weeklies. It is common for a candidate to drop off a biography and news release when making arrangements to place paid political advertising. Not unexpectedly, a struggling weekly is much more interested in writing a human interest story about a candidate who buys advertising than about one who does not.

Repression of the freedom of the news media can range from the actual use of physical force to subtler forms of censorship. The Calgary alderman who assaulted a television cameraman because he would not move his equipment from a spot the alderman considered to be inappropriate falls into the former category. When the alderman was charged and pleaded guilty to assault, the press was publicly vindicated. At the other end of the spectrum, when a licensing bylaw was being discussed in Cardston in 1984 the mayor said that "if the press and public show up, we'll go into camera and hash this thing out."[62] Controlling the press through secrecy or manipulation is much more serious than the use of force, for the issues involved are invariably more complex and media repression less apparent. The previously discussed situations in which advertising contracts have been withheld are examples of this type of censorship, as is the suppression of freedom of information on the grounds that it conflicts with other values such as personal privacy and public safety.

In 1987 the *Lethbridge Herald* surveyed daily and weekly newspapers throughout the province to determine whether any governmental jurisdictions were impairing the freedom of the press. The survey found that while municipal councils and school boards generally provided newspapers with relevant information and had good relations with them, hospital boards and police agencies tended to make policy in secret. As an example, the Sylvan Lake hospital board routinely held two board meetings, "one where the press and public are excluded and one the following night where they go through the motions publicly. Candid discussion is behind closed doors."[63] In a forum in November 1989 the Alberta Press Council said the relationship between the police and the press was improving but problems remained to be resolved, particularly in smaller communities. A weekly newspaper in Lloydminster, for example, was denied any police news after it published an editorial criticizing a Checkstop program. The publisher of the *Grand Centre-Cold Lake Sun* agreed that "the Mounties by and large don't trust the media."[64]

Despite their commercial focus and the vagaries of the public, the media play a vital role in determining whether democracy is to be a success or a failure. In community after community, the public relies on the media for open political discourse. In theory, the media strengthen grass-roots democracy by bringing the views of politicians to their constituents and the views of the citizens to their representatives. The public believes the media have a tremendous amount of influence in municipal politics. However, it fails to realize that the media are constrained because commercial enterprises cannot afford to diverge too far from prevailing political norms. In addition, since the media tend to be relatively conservative and, with a few rare exceptions, to support the status quo, investigative reporting and exposés of politicians and political events are the exception and not the rule.

An Overview of Interest Groups and Democracy

Alberta has a rich mosaic of groups which represent almost every segment of society. Most of these groups have been organized to serve some particular need of their members, a need seldom defined as lobbying legislators and bureaucrats or advancing a particular political agenda. Nevertheless, members of "nonpolitical groups" often call upon their organizations to take political stances. Given the number of organizations in the province and the fact that most of them are involved in governmental activity at some time or another, virtually every citizen is politically represented, although some are better represented than others.

A social scientist writing about interest groups in the United States maintains that they have become so powerful they have completely undermined the democratic process.[65] According to Theodore Lowi, the contract between the government and the citizens guaranteeing them protection in return for their obedience and loyalty originated in the Declaration of Independence. He argues that over time the contract has been subtly reshaped by interest groups so that it is the groups, rather than the citizenry, that give the government its legitimacy. Admittedly, many interest groups are politically powerful and play key roles in the formulation of policy in both Canada and the United States. Moreover, some groups occasionally engage in activities outside the sphere of legitimate politics. However, rather than undermining the democratic process, interest groups enhance it by providing a voice for individuals unheard among the many in an undifferentiated mass society. Without interest groups, only the rich and the powerful would be heard by government.

9

Parties, Representation, and Elections

Politics of Parties

A pervasive characteristic of the Alberta electorate is its commitment to nonpartisanship, rooted in the American municipal reform movement and the philosophy of the United Farmers of Alberta and Social Credit parties.

In the late nineteenth century large cities in the eastern United States were controlled by party machines whose power base was predominantly ethnic. These machines helped non-English-speaking immigrants to survive in a hostile urban environment by providing them with welfare not offered by federal or state governments. In return, the machines asked only for political loyalty and the immigrants' votes. The party machine was effective because it was a true grass-roots organization, originating at the block level. Councils were controlled by neighbourhood leaders, who used their friendships and contacts in the party hierarchy to help their constituents.

Municipal councils were composed of pragmatic grass-roots working- and lower-middle-class politicians, each of whom controlled a neighbourhood fiefdom. They were not concerned with efficiency, since inefficiencies, "sweetheart" municipal contracts, and the diversion of public funds to supporters kept them in power. During this period, the labour movement recruited millions of immigrant industrial workers. In many American cities the party machine and organized labour existed in a symbiotic relationship, each using the other to further its own ends.

Labour's attempts to seize power at the local level, political machines thriving on governmental inefficiency, skyrocketing municipal deficits, city bureaucracies bloated with political appointees, and elected ward councils comprising neighbourhood politicians unconcerned about broader public issues—all were anathema to the business community, the upper-middle class, and many academics. An astute observer of the American political scene writes that these critics and reformers held the view:

> . . . that urban problems were apolitical, requiring little more than the application of honesty and good business practices. This perspective manifested itself in an emphasis on efficiency and economy as the prime goals of city government [and the belief that] . . . professionals, experts, and the well educated . . . were more fit to govern than others.[1]

The reformers viewed the political machine with its attendant evils as the problem; the solution was to replace it with a businesslike system of government. Specifically, the reformers advocated that (1) party politics be replaced by nonpartisan elections; (2) neighbourhood or ward representatives on council be replaced by councillors elected from the city at large; (3) the political franchise be restricted solely to the middle and upper-middle classes, that is, to people who had a substantial stake in the community and paid property taxes; and (4) municipal government be run like a private corporation.[2]

Concurrent with the rise of nonpartisanship in the United States was a movement away from ward politics to the election of councillors at large. As the two movements reinforced each other, working- and lower-middle-class council members were replaced by business people, professionals, and members of the middle class. Although the reformers were unable to restrict the political franchise, they did maintain the status quo.

Although party machines never developed in Canadian cities, partisan politics and the occasional municipal scandal occurred in some communities late in the nineteenth century.[3] The reform movement in Canada, however, was initiated by the business community not primarily in response to patronage, corruption, or inefficiency, but in reaction to labour's quest for power and a perceived threat from the large numbers of impoverished Europeans settling in the country's major cities. Reformers believed they could protect their communities from the political activities of "less responsible" segments by limiting the franchise and abolishing the mechanisms that could enable the "underclass" to gain power—political parties and neighbourhood or ward representation.

While reformers were active in eastern Canada, their influence was greatest in the west, penetrating the region "through the medium of periodicals, newspaper reports, and books as well as more directly by virtue of trips by leading western reformers."[4] An urban historian found the Calgary newspapers preoccupied with reports of municipal corruption in American cities and proposals for reform.[5]

As was noted in earlier chapters, Alberta's civic and business leaders were determined to tighten their grip on municipal government and to bring a businesslike approach to its administration. A new Calgary charter in 1893 raised property qualifications for council positions from $600 to $1,000.[6] Edmonton's 1904 charter replaced council-committee government with a council-commission form which was to make the city's administration much more efficient. It also provided for representation at large and included "a cumulative voting clause allowing holders of property to cast up to four votes on referred money by-laws, and a property qualification for municipal voters."[7] Both Lethbridge and Calgary abandoned neighbourhood or ward representation in 1913 in favour of representation at large. The American commission form of government was adopted in Lethbridge, while Edmonton's council-commission system was copied by Calgary and Red Deer.

A paper on political parties presented by a former mayor of Red Deer before the 1909 convention of the Union of Alberta Municipalities summarizes the then prevailing feeling about parties among Alberta reformers.

> Our Municipal Councils know nothing of party politics and its baneful influence, dividing men on lines having no bearing upon the interests of the Municipality; neither bossism nor the vested rights of Public Service Corporations have yet thrown about us their demoralizing influences.[8]

A major reason the electorate was so receptive to the reformers' call for nonpartisanship was a basic anti-party tradition pre-dating the establishment of the province itself.[9] From 1888 through 1905 the territorial government operated along strict nonparty lines; Macpherson writes that even when partisanship was introduced with the formation of the province, "as long as the provincial administration elected by party methods devoted itself officially to the provision of the desired physical helps to the rapidly growing economy it served well enough. But it was supported less for its party principles than for its business efficiency."[10] The American Non-Partisan League, whose ideas captured the imagination of Albertans in 1916 and 1917, called for the replacement of the outmoded party system by a "business government."[11] The United Farmers of Alberta (UFA) had adopted much of the Non-Partisan League's philoso-

Table 9.1   **Alberta Attitude towards Party Politics by Size of
Community**

Favour Parties at the Local Level	Large City	Small City	Town	Village
Yes (%)	32	28	26	28
No (%)	68	72	74	72
No. of respondents	391	182	135	145

phy when it was elected in 1921.[12] Social Credit theorists depicted the
party system as nothing more than a mechanism "to direct public attention to a profitless wrangle in regards to methods."[13] Even after having
been in office for a number of years, William Aberhart remained adamant
in his opposition to political parties, describing the party system in 1942
as a "vicious and alarming negation of democracy in its true essence."[14]

An Edmonton survey in 1968 and a province-wide survey in 1971
found that most respondents rejected party politics at the local level.[15] In
the Edmonton study, almost 60 percent of the respondents were opposed
to partisan municipal elections. The results of the 1971 survey, presented
in Table 9.1, show that fewer than a third of the municipal residents in
Alberta were favourably disposed to party politics. A surprising finding
was the almost negligible variation between the responses of residents in
large cities and those in small villages. One would expect to find much
stronger support for parties in large cities with diverse and competing
socio-economic and ethnic groups than in smaller, relatively homogeneous communities.

A study of Calgary's Ward Seven in 1977 suggests that the city's electorate was growing somewhat less hostile to municipal parties. While only
38 percent of respondents agreed "with the idea of locally-based political
parties contesting local elections," another series of questions related to
the perceived advantages and disadvantages of local parties in Calgary
revealed much stronger support for them. Table 9.2 indicates that, in
every case, more respondents felt that the advantages of parties outweighed their disadvantages. Since one of the underlying assumptions of
the reform movement was that corruption was associated with municipal
parties, one would expect a substantial number of respondents to make
the same association, yet only 11.3 percent appeared to believe that local
parties would lead to more corruption in city government. Nevertheless,
the relatively high percentage of respondents who agreed that parties
"make no difference" probably opposed their introduction into Calgary

Table 9.2   Calgary Ward Seven: Advantages of Local Political Parties

Parties would:	Help (%)	Hinder (%)	Make No Difference (%)	No Opinion (%)
Keep the cost of city government low	25.7	13.4	39.7	21.2
Reduce bickering in city council	38.4	12.0	31.8	18.8
Keep corruption out of government	22.9	11.3	44.9	20.9
Provide long-term planning for the city	46.6	7.5	21.9	24.0
Provide better social services, e.g., welfare	33.6	6.5	36.3	23.6

politics, since there would have been no reason to disturb the status quo.[16]

The Calgary study suggests that the reformers' legacy of a strong municipal anti-party tradition may be being replaced by an indifference to political parties on the local level. In October 1983 Laurence Decore, a federal Liberal who was quite open about his party affiliation, won the Edmonton mayoralty election by a landslide.[17]

For the most part, Alberta elections are nonpartisan and municipal councils are not identified with political parties, except in the largest cities.[18] This is not unexpected, since large cities provide a more fertile environment for local party activity than do smaller municipalities. Since campaigning is expensive in large cities, it is advantageous for candidates to campaign collectively on a party ticket in order to make the most efficient use of their time and financial resources. Moreover, a political party provides candidates with the organizational and promotional expertise necessary to win elections in large cities. In smaller municipalities the financial clout and organizational skills of a political party are much less important, since campaigning is more personalized. People in smaller communities also associate party activity with what they consider to be the evils of the big city and all of its political machinations.

In recent years there has been a substantial decline in the fortunes of municipal parties in the larger cities. In the 1989 election no parties ran candidates in Calgary, and in Edmonton all but one of the parties had been disbanded. Walter Walchuk offers a provocative explanation for the decline of parties. He argues that with improved and cooperative human relationships, the nature of democracy will change. Among other things there will be "a shift from the competitive nature of the party system . . . to a cooperative system of citizens elected on the basis of individual merit."[19] The problem with his explanation is that although there has been a decline in the importance of municipal parties, people are no more cooperative today than they have been in the past.

The Partisan Bias of Nonpartisan Elections

Even though the overwhelming majority of local governments in Alberta hold nonpartisan municipal elections, it is impossible to rid local government of partisan considerations. As one politician said, "There is no such thing as nonpartisanship. If there were there would be no need for elections."[20] Quite simply, since different philosophical perspectives on raising and allocating fiscal resources are found at the local as well as the federal and provincial levels, local political decision making has a partisan component, even though it is covert rather than overt.[21]

The partisan bias of nonpartisan elections in Alberta has been studied by James Anderson and James Lightbody. Anderson maintains that in the province's early years, Liberals and Conservatives covertly running on civic slates were able to thwart the attempts of socialists and labour representatives to capture city halls. "On balance, the non-partisan camouflage appeared to have benefited Liberal and Conservative business-oriented interests in prairie cities during the reform era."[22] Making a similar point for Edmonton's more recent period, Lightbody writes, "Throughout the 1950s, the Citizens' Committee was extensively infiltrated by Liberals who employed their federal organization to advance municipal candidates, perhaps as a surrogate to realistic hopes elsewhere."[23] Shortly after Decore's 1983 victory in Edmonton, the provincial Liberal party claimed that 55 mayors and school board chairs elected across the province were, or had recently been, Liberal party supporters.[24]

A 1983 survey attempted to determine whether the Progressive Conservative, Liberal, New Democratic, and Social Credit parties were over-represented or under-represented on municipal, county, and municipal district councils and school boards. Senior municipal administrators were asked to identify the federal and provincial party affiliation of elected representatives. Despite a general reluctance to reveal political allegiances, the limited responses indicated that in Alberta cities the Liberals were over-represented relative to the percentages of votes received in federal and provincial elections. In towns, villages, counties, municipal districts, and school divisions, extremely fragmentary data indicated that almost all members were provincial and federal Progressive Conservatives. Since the NDP won 18.5 percent of the province's popular vote in the November 1983 provincial election, it would appear to be substantially under-represented on municipal councils throughout Alberta.

Given a high percentage of "don't know" responses, these results must be considered tentative, but it would appear that councils do have a partisan bias. Lightbody notes that in Edmonton, as in other Canadian cities, municipal elections "are essentially a middle class sport." Between 1974 and 1984, "87 per cent of successful candidacies have come from professional (including teachers) or business ranks."[25] Although Lightbody cautions the reader that such crude data tell nothing of the ideological orientation of the councillors, one could safely predict that this class of councillors is more likely to identify with the Liberals or the Progressive Conservatives than with the New Democrats. However, until there is a further examination of the federal and provincial party affiliations of municipal councillors, the extent and strength of the partisan bias in Alberta municipalities can only be a subject of speculation.

Party Politics in Local Government

The proponents of party politics maintain that at the local level, parties can perform functions that are just as important in making government responsive and accountable as the party functions carried out at the provincial and federal levels. At election time they provide comprehensive platforms so that voters can make considered decisions. If a party captures a majority of council seats, the electorate expects its members to transform platform planks into concrete municipal policies. It is argued that while a nonpartisan independent candidate might offer a comprehensive program, it is more difficult to predict the effect of his or her election, since other councillors will be motivated by their own, possibly incompatible, political philosophies and goals.

A majority party can be held accountable for its actions; if it does not perform as promised, the electorate can penalize the party by not voting for its candidates in the next election. A nonpartisan system, it is argued, lends itself to diffused responsibility; each incumbent can claim that a much better set of programs would have been produced if she or he had been supported by other council members.

Another argument is that parties democratize the political process by selecting candidates who appeal to diverse social and economic sectors of the electorate. In other words, a well-balanced party ticket includes representatives from business, labour, and various ethnic factions.

It is also argued that a party system generates a higher level of political participation. First, since parties use media more efficiently, their candidates' viewpoints are presented collectively at a much lower cost and citizens are exposed to more political messages, which raise their awareness and stimulate their desire to vote. Second, personalized campaigning is a major factor in eliciting the vote; parties have far greater resources, which enable them to canvass door-to-door, a strategy almost impossible for independent candidates in a nonpartisan system. Third, political parties present abbreviated programs to an electorate with a low level of interest in local politics and little knowledge of political issues. Party slogans such as "for business," "for fiscal responsibility," or "for the workers" simplify complex issues and enable politically unsophisticated citizens to participate in elections.

Finally, Lightbody notes that in a nonpartisan municipal system "a major part of the provincial government's distrust of local politicians has been based on the suspicion that they are neither very representative nor can they be held effectively responsible by electors for services under their administration."[26] He suggests that although a partisan system at the municipal level would not immediately change municipal-provincial power relationships, it would probably yield important benefits for the municipality.

> What is likely to occur in the larger metropolitan areas following the routinization of the municipal party system is the gradual return of functions to local council control as parties, finding themselves subjected to a rigorous competition for office, expand their programs in the form of pressure on the province to maximize their responsibilities for all local services.[27]

The proponents of nonpartisan politics argue that their position has been misrepresented by the advocates of partisan politics. David Siegel explains that one of the proponents' favourite arguments "is that those who oppose party politics are like the turn of the century reformers who see local government as pure administration and refuse to admit that it has a political element." He argues that modern proponents of nonpartisanship have never been so naive and that such an argument is "guilt by association" which must be rejected. He then presents a reasoned set of arguments for nonpartisanship. First, he maintains that unlike a party system with disciplined party voting, with nonpartisanship, individual councillors are directly responsible to their electors. In addition, in a nonpartisan system councillors are able to work together, since they are not forced into council combat because they openly wear party labels. Finally, he argues that intergovernmental relations may break down if the provincial government is controlled by one party and a municipal council by another.[28]

On balance, the rationale for nonpartisan local political systems does not seem to be as persuasive as that for partisan systems. First, few if any Canadian municipalities have been afflicted by "bossism" and political corruption. Second, in a nonpartisan system decision making tends to be more dispersed since power generally is more dispersed, while in a partisan system power tends to be concentrated, which enables the public to pinpoint political responsibility. Finally, in a nonpartisan system there is a tendency to maintain that political decisions are made in the public's interest, while in a partisan party system politicians are more likely to publicize who benefits and who pays.

Although there are examples of municipal nonpartisanship in other western industrialized democracies, concerted efforts to foster nonpartisanship have been made only in Canada and the United States. In both countries, its strongest advocates tend to be established political leaders and rural voters who fear that partisan government would erode their control over the political establishment.

Partisan Municipal Politics in Alberta

In a few Alberta communities the reformers' campaign for nonpartisan local elections has been opposed by a militant labour movement. Labour made a concerted effort to gain a foothold in Edmonton and Calgary, cities in which some candidates sponsored by provincial parties had been elected to municipal office. However, more common in Edmonton, Calgary, and Lethbridge were local parties with limited durability that were spawned by a business community fearful of labour's potential power and determined to instil and reinforce an ethos of civic and business boosterism in city hall.

During the first three decades of the century the labour movement in Alberta was deeply divided between radical unskilled and semi-skilled workers anxious to improve working conditions on the railroads and in the coal mines, and moderately skilled workers in the trades. Control of the movement seesawed between the two; however, both groups knew that success depended on electing labour members to municipal councils and the provincial legislature.

Particularly intriguing was the close relationship between William Irvine's Non-Partisan League and organized labour. Borrowing many of its ideas from the American Progressive Movement, which was active in the midwestern United States, the league aimed to transcend traditional politics and the evils of business exploitation through a coalition of farmers and labourers. Anderson documents the close relationship between the league and labour:

> ... Irvine and other League members were involved in setting up the Labour Representation League in Calgary in 1917 in cooperation with the Calgary Trades and Labour Council. By 1919 the Labour Representation League had evolved into the Independent Labour Party and later in the same year, it became the Calgary branch of the Dominion Labour Party. These parties . . . succeeded in electing a few candidates to municipal [office]. . . . At the urging of the Labour Representation League of Calgary, an organization with the same name was set up in Edmonton by . . . the Trade and Labour Council of the capital city. It, too, was transformed into the Independent Labour Party and then the Dominion Labour Party by 1919. It also achieved a measure of success in Edmonton civic elections in the post-war years.[29]

During the 1920s a short-lived alliance between democratic socialists and communists resulted in impressive gains for labour in Edmonton and Calgary that alarmed the business communities. Labour had six representatives on the Calgary council in 1923 and a majority of the seats on the Edmonton council in 1928.[30] Warren Caragata writes that "in both communities, candidates of the Canadian Labour Party contested and won seats on local school boards. . . . After the defeat of Joe Clarke (who was not a labour party member but depended on labour support) in Edmonton in 1920, business interests kept a firm grip on the mayoralty office."[31]

Most of Alberta's smaller communities took a nonpartisan, "businesslike" approach to civic administration, with the exception of Blairmore in the Crowsnest Pass. Some of the most bitter labour strife in Alberta's history had occurred in the Pass, where coal miners violently protested infrequent employment, dangerous and abysmal working conditions, and low pay. In 1932 water and electricity in company housing were cut off during a seven-month strike. In a municipal election immediately following the strike, Blairmore workers ran a labour slate and took control of the council with the purpose of retaliating against the management and owners of the coal mine. "A dog licensing tax was imposed, but only on purebreds, on the grounds that only the bosses could afford pure-bred dogs."[32] The town's solicitor said that council:

> worked out a taxation system whereby . . . the whole burden of taxa-
> tion fell on the company. . . . we put up these miners' homes and
> shacks for auction but nobody would bid when we told them not to
> and these miners lived there and drew rent relief. They'd give it to
> council; we applied it to their debts and in two or three years they got
> their houses back with taxes paid off.[33]

With newspapers throughout the province referring to "Red Blair-more," business became increasingly alarmed. In Edmonton, Calgary, and Lethbridge, professedly nonpartisan political parties with alphabet names, such as the CGA (Civic Government Association) and UCA (United Citizens Association), had already been organized to counter labour activity. In 1932 labour's threat was seen as particularly serious and business redoubled its efforts to provide financial support to attractive candidates for council. This move only intensified the activities of labour supporters. However, it was some time before labour realized that it would increase its electoral success by running candidates under nonpartisan political party labels rather than on a formal ticket.

Senior parties have not sponsored candidates at the municipal level in Alberta since the 1940s.[34] However, in 1971 there was a heated debate in the New Democratic Party as to whether or not Edmonton's sitting mayor, a party member, should run under the NDP label in the fall election. The mayor's labour supporters prevailed after arguing pragmatically that the mayor would lose the election if he ran openly as a New Demo-crat. In 1983 Laurence Decore, an extremely popular candidate and a well-known Liberal, was careful to respect the electorate's commitment to nonpartisanship and captured the mayor's chair in a nonpartisan cam-paign.[35]

Although senior political parties have not participated formally in municipal elections for almost half a century, they often offer advice to candidates for municipal office. As one example, in 1963 the president of the Alberta Liberal Association, Nick Taylor, was the finance chairperson for Grant MacEwan's mayoralty campaign in Calgary. Moreover, there is a close relationship between the local political arena and provincial and federal party organizations, which often recruit seasoned municipal politicians as credible candidates. Edmonton alderman Bettie Hewes entered provincial politics to become a Liberal MLA and alderman Ed

Ewasiuk left city government to join the inner circle of the New Democrats as an MLA. In Calgary, Art Smith became an alderman in 1953, a
provincial MLA in 1955, and two years later moved into federal politics to
represent Calgary South.

The practice of running candidates under the banner of "alphabet parties" has been adopted in recent years by a number of citizens' groups initially organized as broadly based lobbies. Although these quasi-party
organizations may win elections, their loose or nonexistent organizational
structure is not suited to transforming the demands of the electorate into
public policy.

> Three prerequisites need to be fulfilled in order to ensure both respon-
> sible and democratic policy-making at the local level. First, the politi-
> cal organization needs to possess temporal continuity. Continually to
> change an organization's name, while searching for the right combina-
> tion of name and platform to ensure electoral success, results only in
> thoroughly confusing the electorate. . . . Second, when local party can-
> didates are elected to council they must function as a political bloc to
> implement their campaign platform into policy. This simply has not
> been the case in Alberta cities, even though certain local political orga-
> nizations have been in power for years. Finally, in order to give the
> electorate a choice of potential policies it is necessary to have at least
> two viable political parties competing for power. In Alberta, seldom
> does one find competitive politics at the local level. Consequently, the
> electoral options are limited to one policy perspective, or the alterna-
> tive of voting for independent candidates. . . .[36]

Alphabet organizations generally fail to function as responsible parties
because they have been used mainly as campaign vehicles by candidates
who act as independents when elected. Faced with an overwhelming
majority of Albertans opposed to local party politics, members of electoral slates have been extremely reluctant to impose bloc voting on council. A candidate in the 1968 Lethbridge election stated that his party's
nominees "would work as a team although occasionally there would be
differences of opinion and they would be on opposing sides."[37] Alphabet
organizations' loose structure and lack of sanctions preclude the exercise
of party discipline. In 1975 an observer of Lethbridge politics wrote that
the Civic Government Association "is rather a loose organization which
simply gets 'good people' to run. . . . The CGA doesn't campaign beyond
putting up money for its candidates."[38]

Alphabet organizations usually languish after each election, only to revive just before the next, when they often either splinter, with dissidents initiating yet another electoral organization, or adopt another name, possibly that of a defunct party. Another factor weakening local parties is that they seldom run enough candidates to capture a majority of council seats, let alone a full slate. In Edmonton, Calgary, and Lethbridge there have been many instances of a party running a single candidate.

In the last decade support for local party politics has declined in the province's largest cities. A shift in the ideological position of a city's political opponents has taken place so that they no longer fit neatly along a classic left/right political continuum. Just emerging in Edmonton and Calgary is a new politics based on environmentalism. As environmental and related growth issues become increasingly important, one can predict that once again local political parties will appear to clarify these new issues of the 1990s for the electorate.

For an extensive discussion of local party politics in Edmonton, Calgary, and Lethbridge, the reader is directed to the Appendix.

Electoral and Representation Politics

In an ideal democratic voting system, each person has one vote and the candidate who receives a majority of the votes cast in the election wins. Simple as it may sound, few municipalities achieve this ideal.

The system of representation employed in a municipality can be structured to accomplish certain ends. A ward system is generally most advantageous to those at the margins of society; an at-large system of representation favours the middle and professional classes. However, the wards that eventually replaced at-large representation in Calgary and Edmonton were far too big to represent minorities adequately, and the middle and professional classes soon learned how to manipulate ward representation to their own advantage.

Although many communities have attempted electoral reform, most reform measures have been either diluted or totally eliminated. Calgary, as an example, used proportional representation longer than any other city in North America but eventually discarded it. Just as at-large and ward representation work to the advantage of some people and the disadvantage of others, election rules often are enacted to maintain the status quo or to favour a particular segment of society.

Plurality System

The municipal voting system in Alberta seems to be straightforward, simple, and unbiased; the candidate with the most votes wins. The "plurality formula" ratifies the election of the candidate who receives more votes than any other single candidate, but the successful candidate need not have a higher total than all other candidates combined. The plurality system falls short of being an ideal system since it allows candidates who do not have a majority of the vote to win and it does not necessarily produce a truly representative council.

In a nonpartisan election, candidates elected under a plurality system often receive less than a majority of the vote. An example of this occurred in Fort McMurray in 1986, when three candidates ran for mayor. Out of a total of 8,897 votes, the winning candidate, C. Knight, had 3,433 votes; the second-place finisher, E. Collicot, had 3,414 votes; and the third-place finisher, N. Costello, had 2,050 votes. Although Knight captured only 39 percent of the vote, he won the election.

In municipalities with a party system, such as Lethbridge, Calgary, and Edmonton during the 1930s, the plurality system rewards the strongest party out of proportion to the size of its electoral margins. For example, in the 1935 Lethbridge election a sizeable minority of the electorate voted for the Social Credit candidates, who lost. Under the plurality system the business-dominated Civic Government Association elected all the councillors and the quarter of the population expressing a preference for Social Credit candidates had no representation whatsoever. A student of electoral systems summarizes the effect of a plurality system as follows: "Like the Sheriff of Nottingham, electoral systems are apt to steal from the poor and give to the rich. . . ."[39]

The principal advantages of the plurality system are that it is simple and it seems to be very democratic. However, when people are elected to office who receive the most votes rather than a majority of votes, their legitimate right to hold office can be, and sometimes is, questioned.

Proportional Representation

In the early part of the century a number of cities in western Canada employed a system of proportional representation using the "single transferable vote mechanism" to rectify the inequities of the plurality system. The basic principle of proportional representation is that candidates of majority and minority parties and ethnic and community groups receive the percentage of seats on council equivalent to the percentage of votes they received in the election. In short, the system guarantees minority representation, and it has been opposed for just this reason. A 1922 *Edmonton Bulletin* editorial said that "proportional representation is only a scheme to enable minorities to keep the majority from governing."[40]

Proportional representation is used in multi-member constituencies that elect representatives who run municipality-wide. This system can be confusing, and requires further explanation. The proportional representation ballot lists all candidates and each voter ranks them in order of preference, marking a "1" for first choice, a "2" for second choice, and so forth, until every candidate is ranked. After all votes are counted, a quota is computed to set the number of votes a candidate needs to win. The formula is the total number of votes cast in the election divided by the number of seats to be filled plus one. After this figure is computed, 1 is added to complete the formula. For example, in a three-member constituency in which 600 votes are cast, the quota formula is [votes divided by (number of members + 1)] + 1, i.e., [600 divided by (3 + 1)] + 1. When the computations are made the quota figure is 151.

The first preference votes are then counted and any candidate whose vote reaches the quota is elected. Any surplus votes the winning candidate receives over the quota are redistributed proportionately to candidates who were second preferences on the winning candidate's ballot. Using the previous example of a three-member constituency and a quota to win of 151, candidate E in a five-person race receives 200 votes. Candidates listed second on ballots cast for candidate E would receive part of a vote for each ballot, that is, votes cast for E minus the quota divided by votes cast for E. The computation is (200 − 151), which is 49, divided by 200 or 49/200th of a vote or one-quarter of a vote for rounding purposes. If candidates B and C were each chosen second on 100 of candidate E's ballots, then 25 votes would be transferred to each one.

Following this step, the candidate with the least votes is declared defeated (dropped from the list) and the ballots on which the loser is listed as first preference are distributed to the other candidates on the basis of the second preferences on these ballots. An example would be a five-person race in a three-member constituency, in which candidate D, with the fewest first preference votes, and the person to be dropped from the list, has 35 first preference votes. On these 35 first preference ballots, candidate A is listed as second preference on 20 of the ballots and candidate B on 15. Twenty votes would be transferred to candidate A and 15 to candidate B. If this redistribution makes another candidate a winner, this winner's surplus votes are distributed as were those of the first candidate.

Again, the candidate with the lowest number of votes is declared defeated and the second preferences are redistributed. If any second preferences are designated for candidates already elected or defeated, the third preferences are distributed. This process continues until winning candidates are selected for all of the seats. It is worth noting that many voters will not express any more than a first preference. Therefore, it is impossible to distribute their votes after the first round of counting.[41]

Three problems plagued proportional representation in Alberta. First, many voters were confused about the ranking instructions on the ballot. In the 1923 Edmonton election a number of voters befuddled by the instructions dropped blank ballots in the box. Others marked either an "X" or a "1" by the names of all the candidates of their choice rather than ranking them. As a consequence, 2,448 ballots were spoiled, 1,100 for aldermen, 1,037 for school trustees, and 311 for mayor.[42] The Edmonton electorate did not seem to understand proportional representation any better the last year it was used than it had the first. In the 1927 election there were 3,842 spoiled ballots.[43] In Calgary's first proportional representation election in 1917 many voters continued to mark their ballots with "X" rather than numbers designating the order of their choices,[44] but six years later the city clerk said that although the number of spoiled ballots the first year was "greater than the year immediately preceding . . . a general improvement has been noted every year since, until at present the percentage of loss due to improperly marked ballots is less than 2 percent."[45] A letter from Calgary's city clerk to the clerk in Regina describes what was done to explain proportional representation to the voters.

> When the system was first introduced . . . we were fortunate in securing the assistance of the local press in an endeavor to educate the electorate in the proper marking of the ballot. Without this assistance, unquestionably, we should have experienced an unpleasant condition of affairs due to the rejection of the ballot as not being properly marked. The newspapers conducted a very active campaign with daily illustrations on how to properly mark the ballot, and by this means no end of confusion was averted.[46]

The second problem with proportional representation was that many people did not understand the mechanics of the system; even newspaper descriptions of how votes were transferred from one candidate to another were muddled. Especially confusing was the fact that, in a few instances, a candidate received only an average number of first preference votes but was elected after vote transfers were made. For example, in the 1927

Edmonton election, eleven candidates were running for five council seats, and a quota of 2,116 votes was required for election. Following are the first preferences:

Bellamy (CGA)	2,193	Dineen (Labour)	798
Sloane (CGA)	1,951	Pelton (Independent)	784
East (Labour)	1,922	Rehwinkel (CGA)	550
Bowen (CGA)	1,514	Herlihy (Labour)	485
Keillor (CGA)	1,227	Thompson (Labour)	375
Findlay (Labour)	914		

Bellamy won on the first count, but on the fifth count Sloane was elected when he received 190 votes upon Rehwinkel's elimination. On the sixth count East reached the quota when he received a substantial portion of Herlihy's votes. On the next count 110 votes were transferred from Findlay to Bowen, giving him his quota, and Dineen also received enough votes from Findlay to reach his quota.[47] Thus the candidate who placed seventh in first preference votes was elected to council. Adding to the confusion was a provision in the annexation agreement when Strathcona was brought into the city which guaranteed there would always be a certain number of south-side aldermen on council. During the 1920s the south side was guaranteed two aldermen irrespective of whether or not more votes were cast for south-side candidates than for north-side candidates. An *Edmonton Bulletin* editorial expressed the general frustration:

> For some five years the voters of Edmonton have been marking their ballots on the one, two, three, and on to fifteenthly, method; and leaving it to a group of election officials to decide who their votes were to be counted for, if for anybody, according to certain rules of procedure. . . . It would seem that when the people of a community cannot, at the end of five years understand in a fairly general way how their voting system works . . . the practical sense of the voters would probably lead them to abandon it.[48]

The third problem was the length of time it took to count the ballots and transfer the votes. The 1917 Calgary election was held on Monday but the results were not known until Tuesday morning. Flustered over how slowly the votes were being recorded, from 3:00 A.M. to 9:00 A.M. Commissioner A.J. Samis repeated over and over again to the waiting newspaper reporters that "the last count is now being made . . . and we certainly are going to elect a council this time."[49]

*Proportional Representation in Edmonton and Calgary
and a Note on Lethbridge*

In Edmonton and Calgary the proponents of proportional representation were government reformers and militant labour groups who felt disadvantaged by the plurality system. In both cities the system was implemented by plebiscite.

Calgary employed proportional representation longer than any other large city in North America, from 1917 to 1974.[50] The first time it was used, only ten votes separated the winner from the loser in the mayoralty race and 124 people, confused by the new system, had spoiled their ballots. However, the public soon came to understand and accept proportional representation and it was used for more than 40 years with little controversy. Although it is generally believed that labour benefited most from proportional representation, Foran argues that, for the most part, it operated as a neutral system. In fact, he writes, "it is probable that the election-at-large system worked against Labour's interests. Voting turnouts were higher in wealthier districts."[51]

It was 50 years before Calgary's business community challenged proportional representation, and even then it was done surreptitiously. As was explained earlier in the chapter, there was a tacit agreement between labour and business in the late 1950s that labour would accept reduced proportional representation in exchange for a ward system in which proportional representation would be used. After two plebiscites which favoured the ward system and the political machinations of council members fearful they would lose their seats if a change were made, a ward system employing proportional representation was adopted and first used in the 1961 election.[52]

Both a ward system and proportional representation are meant to represent minority interests in the community. The ward system assumes that minorities cluster geographically, while proportional representation assumes they are scattered throughout the community. Since the underlying premises of the two systems are quite different, when they are employed together, as in Calgary, they work at cross purposes. From the beginning, the citizens and politicians viewed the ward system as establishing the pertinent political ground rules. After the 1961 election an editorial writer for the *Calgary Herald* wrote that "with time now for citizens to become known in the smaller area of a ward there should be more people taking part in civic affairs and more direct connection with the citizens who know now who their actual City Council representative is."[53] With the focus on wards as the mechanism to ensure representation, people paid little attention to the proportional representation system. In 1971 a *Calgary Herald* news story attributed 6,256 spoiled votes on a fluoridation plebiscite to confusion over proportional representation.[54]

Despite support from the *Calgary Herald* for the abolition of proportional representation, city council was reluctant to refer the issue to the citizenry in a plebiscite, possibly fearing that a positive vote might entrench the system indefinitely. The issue was resolved in the spring of 1974 when the Municipal Government Act was amended to give council the power to change a municipality's electoral system without having to resort to a plebiscite. With little fanfare, on June 24 council instituted a plurality system. A *Herald* editorial applauded council's action: "It has taken many years, but Calgary is finally going to join the world of sane voting procedures and adopt the simple 'X' ballot abandoning the proportional representation ballot."[55] Paradoxically, one year later the delegates at the Alberta Urban Municipalities Association (AUMA) 1975 annual convention passed a resolution that the School Act be amended "so that urban municipalities may have proportional representation on County School Committees."[56]

The introduction of proportional representation in Edmonton was much more controversial than it had been in Calgary. When the question was submitted to the electorate in the 1922 municipal election, candidates for council campaigned for or against proportional representation and the city's two newspapers took opposing positions, with the *Edmonton Journal* being in favour and the *Edmonton Bulletin* opposed. Proponents brought Proportional Representation League spokespeople from Philadelphia and city clerks from Vancouver and Calgary to speak on its behalf. Vancouver's city clerk testified after having used proportional representation for two years that "it prevents a party from electing a full ticket, no matter how strong that party may be and most certainly provides for the fullest individual choice of candidates...."[57] Calgary's clerk testified that it was more democratic than the plurality system since it gave electors "a wider freedom in the choice of representatives."[58] But it was not the rhetoric of good government which swayed the electorate as much as the argument that proportional representation would enable labour to place more of its candidates on council. Despite a vigorous campaign by its opponents, the plebiscite passed by almost a two to one margin.

During the five years proportional representation was employed, from 1923 to 1927, Edmonton's *Journal* and *Bulletin* carried on a heated debate. Opponents who argued that proportional representation gave labour an unfair advantage felt they had been vindicated when labour aldermen fought a bitter but unsuccessful council battle in an attempt to forestall a plebiscite to review the proportional representation system.[59] The plebiscite was scheduled for the December 1927 municipal ballot. Some advocates of wards believed that if the electorate abolished proportional representation it would be replaced with ward-based representation, but the *Edmonton Journal* pointed out that even if proportional representation were abolished the city administration would have to lobby the government for enabling legislation to establish wards in the city.[60]

When it became clear in the fall of 1927 that the tide of public opinion was running against proportional representation its supporters again brought in speakers from the Proportional Representation League. The league's field secretary, Walter Millard, made a number of presentations to labour, women, and community groups. In meeting after meeting he was asked "if five aldermen are to be elected, why should I not have five votes instead of only the one the proportional representation system gives me?" His answer that each voter should be limited to electing only one representative since in a representative body an elector should have but one representative was not well received. Millard may not have been aware of Edmonton's strong eastern European ethnic makeup, for he noted that scores of English colleges and universities used proportional representation in governing themselves and that the Archbishop of Canterbury was one of the officers of the English Proportional Representation Society.[61]

Although many people had expressed opposition to proportional representation, it was defeated by a narrow margin of 1,222 votes out of 12,168 votes cast. A minor factor, but nevertheless an important one, was that the plebiscite was worded in such a way that a "Yes" vote on the ballot was a vote against proportional representation.[62] Shortly after the plebiscite the province amended the city's charter in order to abolish proportional representation and restore a plurality at-large electoral system.

Lethbridge's labour movement closely followed the machinations involved in the implementation of proportional representation in Calgary and Edmonton. After a labour candidate blamed the voting system for his loss in an extremely close race in 1923, the council directed the city clerk to examine proportional representation in western Canadian cities with a view to considering whether or not it would be appropriate for Lethbridge.[63] Despite a favourable report by the clerk, changes to the city's electoral system were shelved until 1928. Although labour promoted a council decision rather than a plebiscite, proportional representation was placed on the ballot. The *Lethbridge Herald* urged the electorate to vote against it, arguing that it would allow minorities to be elected and would create a divided council.[64] By a vote of 727 to 501, proportional representation was defeated.

At-Large and Ward Representation

Although the average citizen is not concerned about the mechanics of council representation, council members debate it extensively, for the form of representation will likely determine whether or not they will be re-elected. The issue is also important to business and labour interests, since each type of representation gives a different class of candidates an overwhelming electoral advantage.

In a ward system a councillor represents a geographical area, while in an at-large system a representative's constituency is the whole city. In the former, each elector is restricted to voting for candidates running in his or her ward, while in the latter each elector can vote for any of the council candidates. Depending on whether a ward system or an at-large system is adopted, there will be significant differences in the conduct of election campaigns, the formation of political alliances on council, and the development of public policy.

In the late nineteenth and early twentieth centuries in the United States, wards provided representation for great numbers of working-class ethnic immigrants in the large cities. (Although many European immigrants also settled in Canada, their political potential was limited by the business community's tactic of advocating a property qualification to exercise the franchise.) Wards were used to develop political machines in the United States. A machine's ward lieutenant would be the person constituents contacted to obtain city employment or have a teenager bailed out of jail. In return, the voter was expected to support the machine's ward candidate. Thus ward representation was closely linked with the party politics of the times. To eradicate the political machines and ensure that the "right kind" of people would be elected to council, reformers proposed that ward representation be replaced by at-large elections. As a consequence, at-large representation was linked with nonpartisan politics.

The connection persists today, though for different reasons. In American cities where nonpartisanship is linked with at-large representation electoral participation rates are low and the municipal council tends to be dominated by middle-class white businessmen. Today it is not the American reformer who fears wards and advocates at-large representation as much as it is middle-class white conservatives who are fearful of the power that could be exercised in a ward system if the increasing numbers of black, ethnic, and working-class citizens decided to exercise their franchise. Like political parties, ward representation tends to increase political participation. In an at-large election, even if an ethnic minority constituted 20 percent of the city's population, it would be outnumbered and outvoted by the predominantly white electorate. Ethnic and racial minorities often become cynical in such a situation and stay away from the polls, thus further decreasing the likelihood that they will be represented on council.

Proponents of at-large representation argue that it is not necessary for minorities to be represented on council in proportion to their numbers in the population, since they can be represented just as well by conscientious white middle-class councillors. However, a study by Susan Hansen indicates that participation rates are important for working- and under-class people. In a study of the degree of agreement on policy issues between the electorate and the elected officials, she found that three factors determine the extent of agreement: (1) whether there is a partisan or nonpartisan system (agreement being highest in a partisan system); (2) whether or not there is intense political conflict (agreement being highest in communities with a great deal of political conflict); and (3) whether participation rates are high (agreement being highest in communities with high participation rates). These findings lead to the conclusion that in a community with ward representation there will be higher levels of political participation and minorities will be elected to council. Since the voters and their representatives generally will agree on issues, the interests of minorities will be served and local democratic institutions strengthened.[65]

The advocates of at-large elections turn this argument on its head, contending that a council elected at-large expresses a community-wide view that diminishes conflict and promotes unanimity in policy making. After the first election in which wards were used in Calgary a veteran alderman, Clarence Mack, charged that they "divided and sectionalized" the city and fostered local interests instead of dealing with the city's major problems.[66] When the ward system was being debated in Fort McMurray in 1986, the mayor argued that a ward system would fragment government and the chief commissioner said, "for a municipality the size of Fort McMurray, it's established and proven to be one of the most divisive things that can occur."[67] The same year the point was made somewhat differently by Lethbridge Mayor David Carpenter, who said that the council candidates running at-large in the recent municipal election did not define issues on the basis of geography but viewed them as affecting the community "as a whole."

The proponents of at-large representation argue that in wards each representative takes a narrow view of the public interest in order to get re-elected. Moreover, the norm for policy making will be "council log-rolling," with each ward representative supporting the parochial interests of other ward representatives in return for their political support. Calgary

Alderman Sue Higgins complained that "Alderman Blough ended up with everything she wanted and I got nothing" after the council's operations and development committee failed to recommend the installation of stop signs in her ward but recommended they be installed in Blough's adjacent ward.[68] After charging his council colleagues with unfairly cutting back on his ward's recreational funding, Alderman Julian Kinisky said that if they wanted a ward war he would routinely oppose each and every recreational development in other areas of the city.[69]

Supporters of ward representation admit that policy making can be more time-consuming and less efficient in a ward system. James Lightbody describes the Edmonton council's difficulty in making a decision on the location of a new landfill site as an example of an issue so controversial that "they [the council members] could not work out a trade-off that was acceptable and so they are going to the ninth hour." He adds that despite the delay in making a decision, "no councillor is behaving irrationally . . . it's just that the common good tends to be more difficult to find in ward-based elections."[70] Rather than having the community interest defined by academics, professional bureaucrats, or conservative councillors on the basis of middle-class values (the norm with councils elected using at-large electoral systems), ward-elected councils work in such a way that policy is formulated by bargaining and compromise. The pertinent class and ethnic interests in each representative's ward become part of the community interest. In other words, since most communities are geographically segmented by race, ethnic origin, and class, only wards enable the diverse groups to be adequately represented. On the other hand, the opponents of ward representation argue that it solidifies racial, ethnic, and class identities that create even deeper cleavages in the community and corrode the council bargaining process.

The nature of the electoral campaign differs greatly in ward and at-large systems. A councillor elected from a ward represents a smaller number of people and therefore knows the constituents and their problems much better than someone elected at-large. In the election of a city council, even a person with limited financial resources can carry out a successful campaign in a ward, while election at-large requires an expensive media promotion.

Alberta's Local Governments and Political Representation

At-large representation was institutionalized in Edmonton when major reforms advocated by the American National Municipal League were incorporated into the city's 1904 charter. James Anderson writes that "in the absence of a ward system in Edmonton, labour and Eastern European immigrant groups concentrating in the eastern section of the city were largely unsuccessful in obtaining representation on city council despite organized attempts to do so."[71] Sporadically, for over half a century, labour unsuccessfully advocated the adoption of a ward system and the *Edmonton Journal*, with its middle-class orientation, opposed it, arguing that it would lead to divisions on council. Unstated was the fear that a ward system would break the middle-class business community's hold on council and possibly lead to a city party system. Not until the late 1960s, after the city had increaseed greatly in size, was serious consideration given to adopting a ward system. In October 1968, when the issue was finally referred to the electorate after council was shrewdly manoeuvred by one of its liberal members, 61.5 percent favoured the ward system. The council's response was to devise four strip wards running north to south (completely ignoring community, economic, and ethnic cleavages), with three councillors representing each one.[72] With 65 percent of the city's population living north of the North Saskatchewan River and seven of the twelve councillors living south of the river, strip wards were the only way incumbent councillors could ensure re-election in their home wards. The liberal community felt betrayed when Ivor Dent, a mayor who ran for election as a nonpartisan candidate but who was proud of his member-ship in the New Democratic Party, proclaimed that the north-south wards would "mean the best distribution of socio-economic areas" for represen-tational purposes.[73]

Even more important than the way incumbent councillors ensured themselves safe seats by adopting a strip-ward system is how the system affected Edmonton's working- and under-class areas.[74] Since middle-class communities almost always have a higher voter turnout than working- and under-class ones, in a strip ward with equal numbers of middle-class and working- and under-class residents, the middle class will elect its can-didate to council. Even with four wards completely heterogeneous in socio-economic composition and with no requirement that councillors live in the ward they represented, some council members were dissatis-fied.[75] Another plebiscite, held in conjunction with the 1974 civic elec-tion, asked voters, "Do you favour abolishing the Ward System and revi-sion to a system of nomination and election of aldermen for the entire city of Edmonton?" Slightly more than 53 percent opposed abolishing the ward system. For more than four years the council debated and held hear-ings on restructuring ward boundaries, but to no avail. In February 1979 a mayor's task force comprising a cross-section of middle-class citizens was created to review council's discussions and make recommendations on the ward system.[76] The task force concluded that there should be eight two-member wards, approximately equal in population and representative of neighbourhoods. In 1980 council increased the number of wards to six, each with two members representing approximately 81,900 people. Councillors generally agreed that the wards were much too large and cumbersome but decided not to increase the number of representatives because there was no office space for them in city hall. The ward issue languished until shortly after the 1986 election, when two council members, Ron Hayter and Jan Reimer, announced the ward system was totally inadequate and called for changes to be made.[77] After Reimer moved that the wards be increased from six to twelve, with one member elected from each, council referred the proposal to a committee chaired by Hayter. Although he made a concerted effort to obtain support for ward reform, public response was unenthusiastic, and reform efforts collapsed when Mayor Decore, who had just been re-elected with one of the largest majorities in the city's history, announced that he needed a lot of convincing that "we should shake up the system" and he had "difficulties" accepting the idea of single-member wards.[78] In September 1987 council narrowly defeated a proposal calling for twelve wards with a single member elected from each.[79] Alderman Lillian Staroszik explained that, in her opinion, Edmonton already had "probably the best possible representation."[80]

In February 1989 the council rearranged the ward boundaries to balance their populations.[81] The representation issue simmered until the fall, when aldermanic incumbent Patricia Mackenzie focused her campaign on city-wide rather than ward issues. After she explained that "I don't think there are a lot of ward issues," she was criticized for being insensitive to the needs of her constituents.[82] Shortly thereafter, Jan Reimer, a long-time proponent of ward change, was elected mayor. A newly elected councillor, Brian Mason, made ward reform his first priority. He proposed twelve single-member wards, arguing that a ward system with dual representation "creates some duplication, no one person is accountable, and it favors incumbents."[83] Champions of democratic representation were ecstatic until they realized that the opponents to ward change outnumbered its proponents.

Edmonton's wards have become so large that the smallest one is almost 50 percent larger than Alberta's third largest city. A census in April 1990 found that Ward 1 had a population of 101,708; Ward 2 a population of 101,973; Ward 3 a population of 109,571; Ward 4 a population of 84,561; Ward 5 a population of 96,999; and Ward 6 a population of 110,726. The province's third largest city, Lethbridge, had a population of 60,614 in 1989.

Calgary had four wards, each with three members, from 1893 until 1913, when the electorate voted 1,319 to 1,280 to abolish the ward system.[84] The at-large system was generally accepted until 1958, when a pro-business council promoted major changes to the proportional representation system. Labour countered with a proposal that wards be reintroduced if proportional representation were modified. An accommodation was reached and in a May 1959 plebiscite the electorate expressed its preference for a ward system by a margin of 12,497 to 6,975 (64 percent) even though there were no provisions in the City Act for ward representation. Despite the electorate's expressed preference for wards, ten council members maintained that the public did not understand the adverse effects ward government would have on the city and refused to vote in favour of a bylaw to implement the ward system. Provincial legislation in the spring of 1960 allowed a city to introduce ward representation provided that it was approved in a plebiscite with a super majority, that is, two-thirds of those voting. Only days before the fall election, in a raucous council meeting, third reading was given to legislation authorizing placing the issue of ward representation on the fall municipal ballot.[85] In the second plebiscite, with almost every area of the city favouring wards, the outcome was 20,263 to 9,262, or 68.6 percent, which met the two-thirds requirement.[86]

Just as in Edmonton, there was a controversy over the configuration of wards and, as a consequence, in the second plebiscite voters were asked to express a preference for block or pie-shaped wards. Although the *Calgary Herald* was a leading supporter of the ward system, the paper was uneasy about a system of representation which could give power to closely-knit neighbourhoods. The paper favored pie-shaped wards "because they take in all parts of the city, from outlying areas, to residential districts, to industrial sub-divisions, to the downtown business area."[87] Despite the *Herald*'s endorsement and the mayor's preference for pie-shaped wards the vote was 13,527 for block wards and 10,068 for pie-shaped ones.

Shortly after wards were introduced, council's composition began to change as several alderman decided to retire rather than campaign in a ward while others, having lost their support base, were defeated. As one example, George Ho Lem was elected to council in 1959 with the largest majority (24,182 first-choice votes) for an alderman in the city's history. In 1961 and 1963 he was re-elected in Ward 1, but with only small majorities. In 1965 he ran for re-election as an alderman from Ward 3, into which he had recently moved, but lost his seat to a political novice because the voters did not believe he would be able to represent the views of the ward adequately on council. Another example was alderman Ernie Star, who in 1960 received the second largest number of first-preference votes in the first count and maintained second place through the ninth ballot, when he was finally elected. When he ran for re-election in Ward 5 in 1962, it took three vote counts for him to be elected, while all of the other incumbents were elected on the first count. The basis of Star's electoral support had shifted when the ward system was introduced.

In the 1970s Mayor Rod Sykes established a Standing Policy Committee on Legislation and a Citizens' Open Government Study to determine how the electorate's viewpoint and demands could be incorporated in the policy-making process. Both bodies made similar recommendations which included expansion to 18 single-member wards. Stan Drabek, in a discussion of the council meeting that settled the controversy, writes:

> Figures were bandied about with abandon—sixteen, twelve, eight. . . . Council, ever mindful of past demands for more citizen participation indicated a dissatisfaction with the existent twelve member council but on the other hand it felt that a sixteen member council would be too large a representative body. . . . Ultimately, council on a close vote . . . decided on fourteen wards so that the new system would see one member elected per ward. . . .[88]

Unlike its Edmonton counterpart, the Calgary council has not been involved in determining ward boundaries. The task has been left to the administration, which has drawn boundaries to encompass historical neighbourhoods and to balance the wards north and south of the Bow River in order to defuse a north-south rivalry.

The major difference between the ward systems in Edmonton and Calgary is the number of constituents and the number of square miles each councillor represents. In Calgary, with 14 single-member wards, each councillor represents between 29,000 and 68,000 people (11,000 to 27,000 eligible voters). Although this hardly fosters a close working relationship between elected representatives and their constituents, it is far better than Edmonton's system.

The Progressive Conservative government has been little involved in the representation controversy. During the fracas over Edmonton's ward system the provincial government was unusually quiet; perhaps it was fearful that any proclamations or legislative debates on municipal representation could return to haunt it over its own representation in the provincial legislature.[89] In 1974 and 1975 Calgary Social Credit Member

Table 9.3   Calgary Eligible Voters and Population by Ward in 1990

Ward	Eligible Voters	Population
1	19,047	49,443
2	19,058	52,976
3	18,480	52,852
4	19,146	39,452
5	20,893	67,861
6	18,610	43,460
7	22,241	40,534
8	26,852	43,378
9	23,320	56,030
10	17,459	55,319
11	11,581	28,957
12	20,960	51,956
13	18,780	55,790
14	17,325	54,877
Total	273,752	692,885

of the Legislative Assembly (MLA) Roy Wilson introduced a bill allowing "municipalities to create any number of single or multiple aldermanic wards," but in both years the bill died after its first reading.[90] It was not until 1986 that the government became interested in political representation at the local level and then its concern was with school board elections. With more than 50 candidates running at-large for nine trustee positions on the Edmonton Public School Board, 20 percent (25,574) of the people who voted for municipal candidates failed to vote for school trustees. For almost three years the Department of Education recommended that the public and separate school boards in Edmonton and Calgary adopt a ward system. All of the boards eventually complied except the Edmonton Public School Board; most of the trustees resided in south Edmonton and would have found re-election difficult under a ward system.[91] In February 1989 the Minister of Education announced that if the Edmonton school trustees did not adopt a ward system by March 1 he would unilaterally impose one. Edmonton's trustees left it up to the Department of Education to devise a ward system. Even though the system which the Department of Education put together was complicated and confusing,[92] when the candidates were presented by wards in the 1989 election only 11.5 percent of those who voted for municipal candidates failed to vote for school trustees, a percentage far smaller than it had been when school trustees were elected at-large. The provincial government had finally recognized the highly political nature of school board elections and the importance of geographical representation in school budget and policy making.

Ironically, while the public in Edmonton and Calgary seems to favour a greater number of wards and elected representatives, in Crowsnest Pass there was a concerted effort in 1986 to reduce the number of councillors. Budget-cutting aldermen argued that a reduction in the size of council from ten to seven members would result in a substantial tax savings for each ratepayer, and proposed that two aldermen be elected in each of two wards and one alderman be elected in each of two wards for a total of six representatives plus the mayor. The proposal was defeated, but when citizens were later allowed to vote for candidates outside of their ward boundaries, Crowsnest Pass reverted to elections that were at-large in everything but name.

Plebiscites[93]

The first chapter notes that the plebiscite, one of the few direct democracy provisions which brings the citizenry into the policy-making process, was strongly endorsed by Albertans early in the twentieth century. Once it became accepted as a legitimate means for making public policy, provisions for plebiscites were incorporated into legislation pertaining to local units of government.[94]

Since a sizeable percentage of municipal income is spent on education, provisions in the School Act give citizens the right to intervene directly in the policy-making process. Section 111 grants the board of trustees extensive power to finance major capital projects, such as the construction and furnishing of new buildings, through the sale of long-term debentures. When the board decides upon such a policy it is required to give public notice in order to allow any objector to submit a petition within 15 days calling for a vote on the issue.[95] If 10 percent of the electors vote, and a majority are opposed, the board is bound by the electors' decision for one year. The same procedure applies if a board decides to build or purchase a school building for noneducational use. Section 58 allows the electors of a separate school district to dissolve the district. After the board submits the question to the electorate or 25 percent of the electors file a petition for an election, if a majority of the electorate favours dissolution the Minister of Education is bound to dissolve the board. Finally, the minister is given broad powers under Section 2 of the School Election Act to call for a plebiscite in a school district on "any matter or question."

Although citizens are given the right to petition council and call for a plebiscite, the procedure in Section 6 of the Municipal Government Act (MGA) is so complicated that the Department of Municipal Affairs recommends that the services of a solicitor be obtained during the development of a petition.

In 1988 a petition with 300 signatures was rejected by the council in Redwater for a variety of reasons. A witness had not attested that each signature was authentic and there was not a complete municipal address and printed name opposite each signature. The petition did not include a signed statement by the person representing the petitioners that any inquiries regarding the petition could be referred to this person. More important, the objective of the petition was not stated accurately and clearly on each page.[96]

Section 324 of the MGA gives the citizens broad powers of direct intervention. If a council passes a bylaw creating long-term debt (not payable within the current year) it must have a copy of the bylaw published in the municipality's newspaper at least once a week for two consecutive weeks.[97] If within 15 days of the bylaw's last publication a petition is filed with the municipal secretary for a plebiscite, the council must submit it to the electorate for approval.

Section 125 gives the electorate the right to petition council for "a by-law, or the repeal, amendment or suspension of any existing by-law or resolution dealing with any matter within its legislative jurisdiction." In order for the petition to be valid it must be signed by 10 percent of the people entitled to vote if it is in a summer village; 10 percent of the voters if the municipality has fewer than 1,000 residents; and 5 percent of the voters if the municipality has 1,000 or more residents. The council is required to give the proposed bylaw a first reading. It must be published within four weeks of the petition and a plebiscite has to be scheduled thereafter. If a majority of the electorate vote in favour of the bylaw, council is required to give it a third reading within four weeks.

Although Section 125 seems clear, plebiscites have foundered because its provisions were not strictly followed. In 1984 a divisive issue in Lethbridge was whether the city should proceed with the construction of a new city hall. According to Section 125, a plebiscite would have had to ask whether or not the electorate was in favour of a bylaw to rescind council's resolution approving the construction of a new city hall. Rather than placing such a convoluted question on the ballot, the council and the plebiscite's proponents agreed that the question would be simplified and city council would abide by the electorate's decision. The question was: "Are you in favour of commencing construction of a new city hall at this time?" The Department of Municipal Affairs pointed out that if the question were rephrased the plebiscite would not be legally binding. Nevertheless, since the council promised to be morally bound by the outcome, the simple question was put to the voters, who defeated it. In 1989 the Rose Ridge Citizen's Committee collected signatures for a plebiscite on whether or not a sour gas plant should be built just outside St. Albert's northern border. On the advice of their legal counsel, the Municipal District of Sturgeon's councillors decided that the plebiscite could not be held since the petition asked neither for a bylaw nor for the repeal of a bylaw.

Section 119 of the MGA allows a municipal council to submit to the electorate any question or plebiscite not specifically authorized by the act "but over which a council has jurisdiction." The council, not the electorate, is given wide-ranging power to trigger a plebiscite on any municipal issue over which council has authority. In Edmonton and Calgary the referendum has been used to block controversial or unpopular fiscal policies passed by council. In the late 1970s many blue-collar workers and retired people on fixed incomes had been affected by a decade of high inflation. They had been unable to muster support provincially or federally to curb government spending or increased taxation. Although property taxes in both cities were among the lowest in North America, plebiscite petitions were initiated in 1977 and 1978 to roll back substantial council wage increases in the two cities. In 1979 plebiscites also were forced on a $234 million downtown redevelopment project in Calgary and a $32 million convention centre in Edmonton. In each city the business community and civic boosters countered by spending well over $100,000 in highly professional campaigns.[98] Nevertheless, Calgary's electorate voted down the redevelopment project by a slim margin of 1,800 votes. In Edmonton 63 percent of the electorate, primarily from the city's middle-class polls, voted in favour of the convention centre. Supporters of the centre had mobilized broadly-based organizations to canvass door-to-door during both the petition and election campaigns. In contrast, the well-financed "Go Calgary" organization established to extoll the virtues of downtown redevelopment had almost no grass-roots support. Although it was able to produce thousands of buttons and posters there was no way to distribute them, for "Go Calgary" was a paper organization with few members and and almost no volunteers.[99]

During these campaigns a study was carried out to determine why people signed the plebiscite petitions.[100] Table 9.4 shows that, in both

Table 9.4   **Reasons for Signing Plebiscite Petitions in Calgary and Edmonton**

Reason for Signing	Edmonton (%)	Calgary (%)
Not opposed to project; wanted to show dissatisfaction with government	11	11
Not opposed to project; think it should be put to a vote (some respondents also wanted to show dissatisfaction with city hall)	44	55
Opposed to project for fiscal reasons	35	26
Don't know	11	8
Totals	101	100

cities, only a minority of those who signed the petitions were "tax cutters." More important, 44 percent of the respondents in Edmonton and 54 percent in Calgary were not opposed to the projects but thought the issue was so important that the electorate, rather than its representatives, should make the decision. This finding affirms the argument of democratic theorists who maintain that some political decisions are too important to be left to politicians. In both cities, although blue-collar workers and the retired initiated the plebiscite petitions and worked in the electoral campaigns, the socio-economic characteristics of those who signed plebiscite petitions differed little from those of the general population.

Within two years after the Calgary and Edmonton elections the provincial government made it more difficult to initiate plebiscites. At the 1979 annual meeting of the Alberta Urban Municipalities Association (AUMA), which followed the two plebiscites, a recommendation was proposed to the Minister of Municipal Affairs that would make it much more difficult to trigger a plebiscite election.[101] The government responded in 1981 by substantially increasing the number of signatures needed to initiate a plebiscite and stipulating that a petition for a plebiscite to amend or repeal a bylaw had to be received by council within 60 days after the passage of the bylaw. Taken together, these two provisions leave the structure of direct democracy intact, but strip it of much of its substance. Nevertheless, many people still believe the plebiscite process should be further restricted. In 1988 Lethbridge West MLA John Gogo introduced an amendment to the MGA making it much more difficult for citizens to use the plebiscite process to implement policy.[102] His private member's bill died after its first reading. A year later delegates at the AUMA annual convention passed a Calgary resolution to amend the Section 125 of the

MGA in order to restrict the time the proponents of a plebiscite had to gather a requisite number of signatures.[103]

Although the direct democracy provisions of the MGA are relatively clear, in the late 1970s the Edmonton council refused to comply with them twice. After the council voted itself a 60 percent salary increase in December 1977, a popular media personality, Fil Fraser, led a plebiscite petition campaign against the increase. Although more than enough names were secured to force the plebiscite, the council ignored the petition, maintaining that its actions were administrative rather than legislative and thus not subject to plebiscite. The *Edmonton Journal* took the issue to court, where the city lost.[104] The council also ignored the 1979 plebiscite petition on the convention centre, but was again required by the court to hold a plebiscite.[105] A similar situation occurred in Lethbridge in 1984 when a defeated mayoralty candidate forced a plebiscite on the building of a new town hall, which was Mayor Andrew Anderson's pet project and strongly endorsed by the Chamber of Commerce and the Lethbridge Construction Association. After 55.5 percent of the ballots rejected the proposal the mayor argued that because only 33 percent of the eligible electorate had voted, the decision was not truly representative of the people's feelings about the new city hall.[106] Two councillors who were fervent city hall boosters were instrumental in having the city hall question placed on the city's 1986 municipal election ballot. Once again the electorate turned down the proposal, with 53 percent voting against it. Less than one year after the second referendum the same councillors moved that the construction of a new city hall be initiated in 1988. Asked how they could reconcile such a request with the views expressed by the citizens in two referendums, councillor Ed Martin skirted the "public be damned" issue by saying that conditions had changed since the last referendum and it was council's responsibility to "do what we consider best for the long-term needs of the city."[107]

A major criticism of the plebiscite is that it short-circuits the established system of representative democracy. The argument is that the more the citizenry turns to plebiscites, the more reluctant elected representatives will be to make controversial decisions; as a result, people will lose respect for the legislative body and competent and respected members of the community will be less inclined to seek public office. In a recent study of the plebiscite process in the United States, however, Thomas Cronin found no evidence that legislators are constrained by the plebiscite, that it results in loss of respect for legislators, or that people are less inclined to seek public office when the plebiscite is in place.[108] In fact, local governments in Alberta were relieved when mandatory referral provisions in both the Alberta Lord's Day Act and the Public Health Act offered them a plebiscite "escape hatch," since Sunday openings and water fluoridation polarized municipal councils and created "no-win" situations for them.[109]

Opponents of plebiscites argue that they are expensive and that since voter turnout is often low, they enable a vocal and politically active minority to make public policy for an entire community. Because plebiscite elections often concern complex issues, they believe that the outcomes often reflect the decisions of a poorly-informed electorate.[110] But when these criticisms are weighed against the advantages of a mechanism that allows citizens to participate directly in the policy-making process, to practise grass-roots democracy in large as well as small municipalities, and to make elected representatives more responsive to their constituents, then clearly the use of the plebiscite should be expanded rather than contracted.

Election Rules and Practices

Election rules are seldom neutral; they operate to the advantage of some people and the disadvantage of others. As an example, until 1977 a British subject residing in Alberta could vote and run for municipal office even though he or she was not a Canadian citizen. This provision, which favoured British over non-British immigrants, was amended and today one must be a Canadian citizen to vote in an Alberta municipal election. Until 1983 an election rule which subtly discriminated against new candidates allowed a candidate's occupation to be shown on the ballot. Many incumbents listed their occupation as mayor or alderman in order to draw votes from apolitical electors who knew little about the candidates other than what they were able to learn from the ballot.

People who owned property in a municipality were favoured until 1977 by a rule that permitted them to vote for council members and money bylaws even if they did not reside in that municipality. An amendment to the election act now requires voters to be Alberta residents for six months before a municipal election and residents of the municipality on election day, thus eliminating for electoral purposes the distinction between those who own property and those who do not. For some time Section 324 of the MGA required that a bylaw creating long-term municipal debt be approved by a percentage of the proprietary electors in the community. However, Section 325 allowed a council to waive this provision. In 1986 Section 324 was amended so that it was not even necessary to waive the provision that a money bylaw be submitted to the proprietary electors; a money bylaw could now be enforced as long as it had been passed by council and approved by the Local Authorities Board.

Several sections of the MGA allow a council to favour proprietary electors, although it would be politically unwise for it to do so. Section 119(1) states: "A council may provide for the submission to the electors or proprietary electors of any municipal question or plebiscite not specifically authorized by this Act, but over which a council has jurisdiction." Section 150 gives a council the discretion to distribute a municipal newsletter to all residents or only to the proprietary electors. Under Section 433, which is seldom used, proprietary electors can request a provincial investigation of their municipality's financial affairs if a quarter of them sign a petition to the Lieutenant-Governor.

Although few people consider it discriminatory, even the choice of the age at which one is able to exercise the political franchise confers advantages on a particular segment of the population. When the minimum voting age was 21, 18-year-olds argued that if they were mature enough to marry and serve in the military, they were old enough to make intelligent political decisions. Shortly after the voting age was reduced to 18, some teenagers argued that it should be further reduced to 16 because the political system ignored their special needs and thus discriminated against them. Perhaps because the argument was not persuasive and the median age of the Canadian population has been increasing, the voting age has remained 18.

Until 1983 taverns had to be closed on election day so voters would be clear-headed when they cast their ballots. That year the new Local Authorities Election Act gave municipalities the option as to whether or not liquor could be sold on the day of an election. Although no drinkers have formally complained to the government that they were discriminated against on election day, a tavern owner in the Village of Fort Assiniboine made such a claim. After he declared his candidacy for council, the council passed legislation closing taverns on election day. Shortly thereafter, in a letter to the Minister of Municipal Affairs, the tavern owner wrote: "I am one of the three candidates in the by-election tomorrow and because of that my business punished by the two present councilmen . . . a small businessman . . . is subject to a $450 penalty (my loss of business today) because he dares to challenge the dictatorial policies of the two men village council." He added that the council had ignored a 23-signature petition requesting the bylaw be rescinded.[111] The minister was unable to act because the village had been given the right to exercise permissive legislation to control liquor during elections.

One of the most controversial restrictions on candidate eligibility is found in Section 22 of the Local Authorities Election Act, which states that a person is ineligible to be nominated as a candidate if "he is an appointed official or employee of the local jurisdiction for which the election is to be held." In 1989 an Edmonton Transit bus driver was forced to resign in order to run for a position on city council. Brian Mason, the driver, made the restriction an issue during the campaign and after he was elected to council. In the summer of 1991 Section 22 was amended so that, upon an employee's request, a council could grant him or her a leave of absence in order to run for municipal office.

Section 29 of the Local Authorities Election Act allows a municipality to discriminate against candidates with limited financial resources by requiring substantial deposits on the registration of nomination papers. A $500 deposit can be demanded by municipalities with populations of 100,000 or more and $100 by those with populations of less than 100,000. Most municipal politicians realize that it is a fundamental tenet of local democracy that everyone have an equal opportunity to participate in the political process, and no municipality except Edmonton has made money a criterion for political participation. This anti-democratic requirement was enacted primarily because of the efforts of a small group of self-styled reformers. In 1980 Cec Purves easily won his mayoralty race in the city because he had no well known or well financed opponents. But politics often attract strange people, and the election that year was no exception; none of the other mayoralty candidates were professional politicians and one boasted that he was "criminally insane" and sought to prove it by "blowing raspberries" during his free television commercials, interrupting the other candidates at election forums, and wearing a black pantsuit with a bell attached as his electoral garb. An *Edmonton Journal* political columnist asked how these "fringe" and "jokester" candidates might be eliminated so the "serious candidates" could be heard.[112] Professional politicians dominated the political scene in the 1983 and 1986 elections, but amateurs continued to file their election papers and campaign for office. With little organizational structure and campaign funding, they were invariably unsuccessful, but their political activities continued to annoy the columnist and Alderman Ron Hayter, who was determined to drive them from the political arena. In 1987 Hayter recruited enough council support to increase the candidate filing fee for mayor from $100 to $500. This did not deter the amateur politicians who filed as mayoralty candidates in the 1989 election despite the fact that it was very unlikely they would receive enough votes to have their deposit returned to them.[113]

Although a $500 deposit may discourage the frivolous, it also deters serious candidates from the under-class, who may be on welfare, and those on the ideological fringe who can ill afford to lose the money. At a time when property qualifications for holding office and voting have become almost an anachronism, the erection of financial barriers to prevent "undesirables" from running for public office is at the very least inappropriate.

One of the opponents of the $500 filing fee was Mayor Laurence Decore, who said he had attended many meetings with the other candidates and was strongly opposed to erecting financial barriers to prevent them from running for office. Instead, Decore suggested the city work through the Alberta Urban Municipalities Association (AUMA) to lobby the province to raise the number of nomination signatures to 250 for mayor and 100 for aldermen from the five specified under Section 27(1) of the Local Authorities Election Act.[114] The city prepared a resolution to that effect which was sent to the AUMA for presentation at its 1988 annual convention. Since smaller communities opposed the resolution, it died on the convention floor. Today the number of nomination signatures for council member or mayor remains at five.

Intermittently over the past two decades proposals have been made to limit campaign spending and contributions and to require the disclosure of the amount and the name of the donor of any contribution larger than a certain dollar figure. Such provisions are not unusual; legislation governs campaign finance in local elections in Quebec, Ontario, and Manitoba, as well as in all federal and provincial elections.

A resolution which was drafted in Edmonton and passed at the 1971 AUMA convention asked only that the province "consider legislation to place a ceiling on Civic Campaign expenditures." The provincial government dismissed it with the comment that limiting expenditures was "good in principle" but impractical. Undeterred, the Edmonton council passed a resolution requiring its members to disclose donations of money, goods, and services with a value of more than $100. Since the resolution had no legal basis in provincial legislation it was generally ignored by all but one or two aldermen.

At the AUMA's annual convention in 1977 a resolution was passed requesting the provincial government to enact legislation requiring municipal candidates to "disclose all donations of either money, goods or kind in excess of $100." The government responded that it would consider the request at the appropriate time but in the interim there was nothing to prevent a candidate from disclosing the source and amounts of campaign donations. The provincial government never did act on the resolution, despite the efforts of Ed Oman, a Tory representing Calgary North Hill, to bring forth legislation to curb the financial excesses of municipal campaigns.

Many smaller municipalities oppose any limits on campaign finance. They maintain that while such legislation might govern campaign activity in large municipalities, it would have little effect in smaller ones except perhaps to generate "red tape." In Saskatchewan the Advisory Committee on Local Election Financing addressed this issue in a 1990 report recommending that "Candidates whose expenditures do not exceed $1,000 be required only to submit a statutory declaration stating that their expenditures do not exceed this amount and disclosing total contributions received as well as contributions received, in the aggregate, in excess of $100.[115] This proposal simplifies campaign reporting but still provides enough information to indicate whether or not there has been any unusual campaign finance activity in a small community.

Despite the province's reluctance to enact municipal election expense legislation, some Edmonton aldermen were determined to control the escalating cost of running for municipal office and expose interest groups that attempted to purchase council influence with campaign donations.[116] After being elected to council in 1986 Pat Mackenzie voluntarily disclosed her campaign contributions in the hope that other council members would follow suit.[117] They did not. Little was heard of the issue again until January 1989 when Alderman Ron Hayter proposed a strong bylaw on campaign finance that would limit individual donations to $750 and require disclosure of the names of donors contributing more than $100. Each candidate's campaign expenditures would be limited to $5,500 plus 50 cents for each elector in a mayoralty race and to $3,500 plus 50 cents for each elector in a ward for aldermanic races. Other council members were quick to note there was no provincial legislation giving municipalities the authority to enact legislation to control election expenses and therefore such a bylaw would be unenforceable. Although the bylaw was not passed, Jan Reimer, a leading candidate for mayor, published the names of everyone who had donated $375 or more to her campaign and challenged the other mayoralty candidates to do the same.[118] Another leading candidate, Terrence Harding, promised to disclose any campaign contributions in excess of $325 but the other two major candidates refused to disclose the sources of their campaign funds.[119] At the AUMA's fall convention the cities of Edmonton and Lethbridge sponsored a joint resolution on campaign finance which was passed by the convention's delegates. The resolution asked the government to amend the Local Authorities Election Act so as to include either:

a) a provision allowing a local authority to enact a bylaw binding upon candidates for election to the local authority which may:
   - require the disclosure of all campaign contributions;
   - require the disclosure of all campaign expenditures;
   - limit the maximum amounts of campaign contributions and expenditures;
   - require audited statements of campaign contributions and expenses to be prepared and disclosed to the public; and
   - provide penalties for failure to comply with the bylaw

Or

b) provisions requiring the disclosure of campaign contributions and expenses, limiting the amount thereof, requiring audited statements thereof to be prepared and disclosed for the public, and providing penalties for failure to comply with such provisions, all of which may be brought into force for individual local authorities by bylaws of such local authorities.[120]

The resolution was sent to the Department of Municipal Affairs, which forwarded it to its Municipal Statutes Review Committee. Since that time little has been heard about campaign expenditures and legislation to curb their abuses.

Not all electoral rules are known by politicians, let alone the public. The political career of an Edmonton alderman was brought to a sudden halt after it became known that she had violated Section 22(1) of the Local Authorities Election Act which states that a person is ineligible to be nominated as a candidate "if on nomination day he is indebted to the municipality of which he is an elector for taxes in default exceeding $50." Catherine Chichak, who had been a member of the legislative assembly for eleven years and the Edmonton Separate School Board for six, was elected to council in October 1989. Shortly thereafter it was discovered that when she signed her nomination papers she was in arrears more than $8,400 in city business taxes. Despite Chichak's protests that she was innocent of deliberately violating the act and that the tax arrears were just an unfortunate oversight, several aldermen and more than 5,000 phone calls as well as letters to city hall called for her resignation.[121] When Chichak's case came before the Court of Queen's Bench, Justice Ronald Berger held that in overlooking the payment of her taxes she had been irresponsible and negligent but ruled that she could keep her council seat since she had not acted deliberately to avoid paying her taxes.[122] Even after the court exonerated her, Chichak was treated like a pariah by councillors who thought she should resign.

Campaigns and Elections

Political campaigns and elections are very different in large and small municipalities. Characteristic of city politics is the number of candidates seeking office and the many incumbents who win election after election. In large cities scores of people hoping to become full-time professional politicians view a position on council as a stepping-stone to a career in provincial and federal politics. In the 1989 municipal election there were 53 candidates for 14 council positions in Calgary, 43 candidates for 12 positions in Edmonton, and 20 candidates for 8 positions in Lethbridge. In contrast, few candidates are attracted to public office in most counties, municipal districts, towns, and villages. Prospective officials must be flattered and cajoled as appeals are made to their sense of civic duty.

In 1986 and 1989 the mayor and council were elected by acclamation in some Alberta towns and at the village level it was common for council candidates to run for office unopposed. As examples, in Redwater and Spirit River the council and mayor ran unopposed in both elections; in 1986 the mayor and council were elected by acclamation in both Bruder-heim and Blackfalds; in Black Diamond and Redcliff the council was elected by acclamation; and in Hanna, High Level, and Mundare the mayor was elected by acclamation. In 1989 the mayor and council were elected by acclamation in Cold Lake, Lamont, Lac la Biche, Killam, Vaux-hall, and Oyen; in Black Diamond, Morinville, Slave Lake, Provost, and Mundare the mayor was elected by acclamation and in High Level the council was elected by acclamation.[123] In the villages of Derwent, Stan-dard, and Ferintosh, and the summer villages of Cookson, Seba Beach, Bondiss, Pelican Narrows, Bittern Lake, Castle Island, Sundance Beach, and Bonnyville Beach, councils were elected by acclamation in both 1986 and 1989. According to the municipal administrator for Pelican Narrows, "We have never had to have a formal vote, councillors and mayor are always voted in by acclamation. We never have more candidates than offices."[124] The mail survey on political participation also found that election by acclamation was common in counties and municipal districts.[125] Table 9.5 shows the survey results for rural municipalities.

In the Municipal District of Fairview, where there were no contested elections for council in either 1986 or 1989, the secretary-treasurer indicated that "we recently had a councillor vacancy and had to extend nomination day to attract a candidate."[126] In the Municipal District of Smoky River, where four candidates ran unopposed in 1986 and there was only

Table 9.5   Survey Results of Rural Municipal Elections by Acclamation for 1986 and 1989

Municipality	Number of Councillors out of Total Number Elected by Acclamation 1986	Number of Councillors out of Total Number Elected by Acclamation 1989
Counties		
Flagstaff	2 of 7 by acclamation	6 of 7 by acclamation
Forty Mile	7 of 9 by acclamation	7 of 9 by acclamation
Lamont		3 of 5 by acclamation
Leduc	2 of 7 by acclamation	4 of 7 by acclamation
Mountainview	4 of 7 by acclamation	5 of 7 by acclamation
Paintearth	4 of 7 by acclamation	2 of 7 by acclamation
Parkland	2 of 7 by acclamation	
Red Deer	2 of 7 by acclamation	4 of 7 by acclamation
St. Paul	3 of 7 by acclamation	1 of 7 by acclamation
Stettler		7 of 9 by acclamation
Strathcona	2 of 9 by acclamation	1 of 8 by acclamation
Taber	2 of 7 by acclamation	3 of 7 by acclamation
Two Hills		1 of 7 by acclamation
Wetaskiwin	2 of 7 by acclamation	1 of 7 by acclamation
Municipal Districts		
Beaver	2 of 7 by acclamation	
Bonnyville	2 of 7 by acclamation	3 of 7 by acclamation
Cardston	council by acclamation	6 of 7 by acclamation
Fairview	council by acclamation	council by acclamation
Foothills	3 of 7 by acclamation	2 of 7 by acclamation
Peace	council by acclamation	3 of 5 by acclamation
Pincher Creek		1 of 5 by acclamation
Provost	4 of 7 by acclamation	6 of 7 by acclamation
Smoky River	4 of 6 by acclamation	5 of 6 by acclamation
Spirit River	3 of 4 by acclamation	3 of 4 by acclamation
Sturgeon		2 of 7 by acclamation
Westlock		5 of 7 by acclamation

one contested race in 1989, the Director of Corporate Services writes, "I don't believe that the results of the above noted elections show any definite pattern. As our area is basically agricultural with very limited numbers of acreages and or country residential parcels, everything stays pretty much at a status quo."[127] The administrator for the Municipal District of Peace, where the entire council was elected by acclamation in 1986 and three of the five councillors were elected by acclamation in 1989, believes that the reason so few people run for council is because the "demands of the residents appear to be increasing (paved roads, recreation, rural water lines) . . . and many people do not wish to undertake the responsibilities of being a Councillor."[128] The administrator for the Municipal District of Spirit River noted that in the 1986 election three of the four council members were incumbents who won by acclamation. In the 1989 election, three of four candidates again won by acclamation, but none of them were incumbents. The administrator writes: ". . . there appears to be a pattern whereby there is very little change in Council for spells of nine years. Then a totally new Council usually takes over."[129]

Elections in rural municipalities adjoining large cities are generally contested, since they have heterogeneous populations and candidates with divergent views. Nevertheless, there are still examples of candidates running unopposed. In the County of Strathcona two councillors were elected by acclamation in 1986 and one won by acclamation in 1989. Two councillors won by acclamation in the County of Parkland in 1986 and in the County of Red Deer two uncontested elections occurred in 1986 and four in 1989.

The Local Authorities Election Act prescribes measures that should be taken by municipalities when the number of candidates equals the number of council positions or when there are not enough candidates to fill all of the council positions. Section 34 states that if when nominations close the number of persons nominated for office is the same as the number of positions to be filled, all of the candidates are declared to be elected without the formality of an election. It is more complicated when there are not enough nominees to fill all council positions. Section 31 provides that the deadline for nominations will be adjourned to the following day, when nominations will be accepted between 10:00 A.M. and noon. This process continues each day for another five days until the requisite number of nominations is received. If at the end of this period sufficient nominations still have not been received, the Minister of Municipal Affairs is notified and may take any action he or she considers necessary, including recommending a change in the status of the jurisdiction.

Voter Turnout

If anything riles a newspaper editor, it is a low voter turnout. The day after Calgary's 1964 municipal election a *Calgary Herald* editorial chided the public:

> It is always a matter of puzzlement why so many people don't bother to vote. It can only be assumed that they don't take any interest in how their community affairs are being looked after by the government which is closest to them. They just don't seem to want to be informed and so, at election time, they say they don't know whom to vote for and let the whole thing slide.[130]

Although newspaper editors may not understand why the public votes in some elections and refrains in others, professional politicians and a sizeable number of citizens are aware that partisan elections increase turnout and nonpartisan ones decrease it. They know that when the incumbent mayor of a large city has virtually no opposition voter turnout is extremely light. Until the 1960s half of a municipality's councillors were elected every year for a two-year term. The turnout was almost always higher in mayoral election years than in the years when only councillors were being elected.[131]

In two Edmonton elections in the 1950s Mayor William Hawrelak was elected by acclamation and voter participation dropped below 20 percent in both. In 1980, when Mayor Cec Purves had virtually no opposition, the turnout rate was 21 percent. Three years later in a hotly contested race for the mayor's chair in which Purves was defeated the turnout rate increased to 34 percent. Table 9.6 shows that the voter turnout in Airdrie was 37 percent in 1986 but dropped to 29 percent in 1989, when the mayor was elected by acclamation. The table indicates that in most cities with contested mayoralty elections voter turnout is relatively high; however, other factors also affect participation rates. Contentious policy issues which divide the electorate almost invariably increase the percentage of people who vote.

One might expect that formal elections are not as important in small municipalities which are socio-economically homogeneous. Table 9.7 shows an opposite voting trend: the highest turnout occurs at the village level and the lowest in cities, which are characterized as being heterogeneous. The fact that the voting level for the three classes of urban municipalities remained virtually the same in 1986 and 1989 indicates that this relationship is relatively stable.

Table 9.6   City Voter Turnout Rates for 1986 and 1989

Municipality	Percentage of Voter Turnout 1986	Percentage of Voter Turnout 1989
Airdrie	37	29 (mayor by acclamation)
Calgary	37	49
Camrose	(not available)*	(not available)*
Drumheller	39	54
Edmonton	34	36
Fort McMurray	41	58
Grande Prairie	32	34
Leduc	35	41
Lethbridge	46	51
Medicine Hat	42	49
Red Deer	26	36
St. Albert	37	38
Spruce Grove	(council, mayor by acclamation)	35
Wetaskiwin	42	43

* The municipality does not keep a voter list.

Table 9.7   Average Voter Turnout in Villages, Towns, and Cities*
1986 and 1989

Municipality	Percentage of Voter Turnout 1986	Percentage of Voter Turnout 1989
Villages	61	59
Towns	48	51
Cities	42	41

* The data are based on responses from a spring 1991 mail survey.

For several reasons, the traditional interpretation of the relationships between communities that are socio-economically homogeneous or heterogeneous and voter turnout should be reconsidered. First, it was shown earlier that there is a correlation between the size of a community and the number of candidates elected by acclamation; a great many village and most summer village councils are elected by acclamation. Second, under

Section 49 of the Local Authorities Election Act it is entirely at the discretion of the municipality whether or not to enumerate the citizens and prepare a list of voters. Since many municipalities choose not to prepare voter lists, and therefore are unable to calculate voter turnout, the figures in Table 9.6 may be an anomaly. Third, the variation in voter turnout is especially wide in smaller municipalities. As an example, in the Village of Glenwood the turnout rate was 90 percent in 1986 and 78 percent in 1989, while in the Village of Boyle the rate was 20 percent in 1986 and 23 percent in 1989. Even in the same municipality there may be substantial differences in rates for different elections. In 1986 voter turnout in the Village of Sangudo was 38 percent but in 1989 it dropped to 15 percent. In the Town of Pincher Creek the rate was 30 percent in 1986 and 64 percent in 1989. Some cities have equally wide swings in participation rates. Almost invariably, a high rate is associated with a strong political personality or an issue that deeply divides the community. Finally, although Alberta political folklore holds that people in smaller municipalities are more civic-minded than people living in large cities,[132] until more electoral analysis occurs, this must remain an untested hypothesis.

Incumbents, Money, and Winning

For an election analyst, the single most important piece of information in predicting who will win a municipal election is whether or not the candidate is an incumbent. The power of incumbency is so great that in recent years in Edmonton and Calgary incumbents have been almost unbeatable. For this reason, in 1986 Edmonton alderman Lance White proposed council pass a resolution limiting its members to no more than three consecutive terms in order to allow new people to sit on council and revitalize the policy process. The resolution was defeated by long-serving council members who maintained that it would undermine the democratic process.[133] The issue emerged anew in the 1989 AUMA convention when Edmonton introduced a resolution (no. C2–8) to amend the MGA to limit an incumbent's term of office. The resolution read:

a) in a city or town, the length of service in any one elected office shall be limited to three consecutive terms;

b) in any other municipality . . . the length of service in any one elected office shall be limited to six consecutive terms;

c) in a city or town, an elected official may serve for an additional three consecutive terms in an elected office not held in the preceding three consecutive terms;

  d) in the event a by-election is held during the time a former elected
     official is sitting out (after serving three consecutive terms) the
     former elected official may seek re-election in that by-election;
  e) elected officials holding office when the legislation becomes effec-
     tive may run in two more elections, irrespective of how many pre-
     vious terms they have served.

The resolution was defeated and little has been heard since of limiting
municipal terms of office.

The key to winning in a municipal nonpartisan election is name familiarity, that is, the candidates who are best known usually win.[134] Although
some of the electorate closely follow the candidates and their stands on
issues, most people have only a marginal interest in municipal elections.
The candidates with whom they are the most familiar are incumbents
whose names they have seen in the newspapers and heard repeatedly in
the electronic media. In small municipalities with contested elections a
winning strategy is for a candidate to go door-to-door passing out campaign literature and introducing him- or herself to everyone in the community.

An issue of concern for both politicians and the public over the years
has been the escalating expense of carrying out an effective electoral campaign. It generally costs more than $200,000 to wage a feasible campaign
for mayor and a minimum of $15,000 to $20,000 to run for alderman in
Edmonton and Calgary. Many people who would be credible candidates
are unable or unwilling to make a major financial sacrifice to run for
office. Even Ross Algers, who received tens of thousands of dollars from
business for political campaigns when he was mayor of Calgary, said that
campaign spending had gotten out of control.

Failing being an incumbent, the next best thing for a candidate is to
have large amounts of money available to purchase door flyers and rent
billboards and television time. After winning the 1989 mayoralty race in
Edmonton, Jan Reimer opened up her campaign books, which recorded
payments of $51,235 for advertising, $44,517 for office and telephone
expenses, and $26,624 for signs. Her total campaign expenditure of just
over $131,000 was one of the lowest for a winning mayoralty candidate in
recent years.

Even without being an incumbent or having generous financial back-
ers, a candidate can win an election with determination and dedicated
political volunteers who are willing to make and erect lawn signs, work on
telephone banks, and distribute campaign literature. In 1986 a council
candidate in Calgary, John Schmal, began a door-to-door trek in July and

campaigned continuously until the October election. He won. The same year in the City of Airdrie the incumbent mayor was defeated by a hard-working candidate, Grant McLean, whose strategy was to knock on as many doors as possible and personally hand out campaign brochures and put up lawn signs. Edmonton's Jan Reimer was able to run a relatively inexpensive campaign in part because she received the endorsement of organized labour and many union members actively canvassed on her behalf.

Since few mayoralty candidates in recent years have been willing to identify the sources of campaign funding, Reimer's 1989 disclosure is particularly useful. Of the contributions to Reimer's campaign, individual donations accounted for 39 percent, donations from business and professional associations 30 percent, donations from unions 19 percent, and donations from developers 12 percent. The most Reimer would accept from any one source was $3,750. There were 18 donations of more than $1,000, of which the largest by an individual, her father, was $1,500. Eight of the donations of more than $1,000 came from labour unions.[135] The incumbent mayor's campaign finance chairperson announced a month before the election that contributions for Mayor Cavanagh had exceeded $100,000 and that 325 people had just attended a $100-a-plate fund-raising dinner for him. Like Reimer, the mayor placed a cap on the amount of money he would accept from any single source. Cavanagh's campaign manager said he would reject any single contribution in excess of $10,000 because he did not want to place himself in a position in which he might be compromised.[136]

Obtaining the endorsement of key members of the community is a time-honoured campaign practice. Conservative candidates seek the endorsement of the Chamber of Commerce executive, while liberal candidates look for support from union leaders. Candidates also attempt to take advantage of Alberta's multicultural tradition by obtaining the endorsement of ethnic groups. Although the conventional political wisdom is that when the leader of an organization endorses a candidate, the membership will also, it is based on two questionable assumptions. The first is that labour and ethnic groups are monolithic and have homogeneous political values; the second is that the rank and file will follow their leader in any political direction he or she chooses. Many members of ethnic groups feel patronized and are insulted when candidates seeking electoral support stumble through a few words of their language; others concur with their leader's endorsement and feel flattered by the attention they receive. James Lightbody, who was one of Mayor Decore's chief electoral strategists in his 1983 and 1986 campaigns, maintains that it is necessary to target the ethnic vote if a candidate is to win its support. To be successful, Lightbody argues that candidates have to work through an ethnic group's leadership structure.[137]

Although candidates in the larger cities know that the key to winning is name familiarity, some develop campaign issues they hope will differentiate them from the rest of the candidates.[138] From time immemorial municipal candidates have been pledging to hold the line on taxes, if not cut them, and to increase the level of services. Other favourite issues in virtually every election are almost diametrically opposed: bringing business into the community and controlling community growth. In the 1989 Edmonton election, as the incumbent mayor's support began to wane he tried unsuccessfully to pin a "red" label on front-running Reimer. At a campaign forum he discussed her "socialist hidden agenda" and suggested that if she were elected the city would be renamed "Redmonton."[139] His strategy backfired as he was soundly criticized by the newspapers and the public for "red-baiting."

After the ballots have been counted, losing candidates generally concede graciously and winning ones compliment their opponents for putting up a good fight. But this is not always the case; occasionally a losing candidate charges that the ballots have been miscounted or that an election fraud has been perpetrated. In either case, the Local Authorities Election Act provides a remedy.

Not only a losing candidate but any elector has the right to apply to the court for a recount as long as it is within 19 days from the time voting stations closed on election day.[140] After a recount application is made a judge determines whether or not it has merit. If it does, the court notifies the concerned candidates of the time and place of the recount so they can attend. At the recount the judge opens the packets of ballots and supervises the recount. According to Section 108 of the act any ballot is void that: (a) lacks the voting officer's initials; (b) lists votes for more candidates than are to be elected to the office; (c) has any marks that might identify the person who cast the ballot; or (d) has been torn or defaced in such a way that the person who cast the ballot might be identified. After the recount a statement with the results is posted at the judge's office.

As with the recount, any elector has the right to bring election issues before a judge as long as there are reasonable grounds for (a) supposing the election was not legal or not legally conducted; (b) supposing the person declared elected was not really elected; or (c) contesting the validity of the election of a member of the elected authority.[141] The judge, without formal pleadings, determines whether the affected person has a right to the office and if it is decided that irregularities occurred, the judge may declare the election invalid and order a new one be held.

Defeated candidates occasionally express anger about the outcome of an election campaign even though there was not a breach of rules. In 1989 this occurred in Leduc when Oscar Klak, who had served as mayor for nine years, was defeated by a one-vote margin after a recount. After the newly elected mayor said that he hoped he would be able to seek advice from his defeated opponent, Klak responded that no one could "expect a beaten mayor to come back and make this guy look good. He's on his own."[142]

An Overview of Parties, Representation, and Elections

Like most Canadians, people in Alberta tend to favour nonpartisan over partisan politics at the local level. Perhaps the difference between Albertans and others is that for years the nonpartisan tradition in Alberta was more pervasive, with provincial party leaders adamantly opposed to party government at any level. Nevertheless, municipal parties were formed in the large cities and they sponsored council candidates, although councils rarely came under party control. This was primarily because parties were in a constant state of flux, as they were created to function as electoral vehicles and then after an election were allowed to languish or expire.

In Alberta's small urban and rural municipalities municipal parties have had little appeal for the electorate. One of the reasons for this is that political activity tends to be more personalized in small towns than in large cities. Another reason is that small communities tend to be more homogeneous than larger ones, and as a consequence in many of these communities council decisions are made almost by consensus. Finally, the population size and geographical area of small communities allow much of their political recruitment, campaigning, and even governing itself to be carried out on a face-to-face basis. One can speculate that the personalized grass-roots politics often found in small municipalities make the activities of a municipal party redundant.

One of the most innovative municipal experiments was the adoption of proportional representation by Edmonton and Calgary during the 1920s, which drew a number of minorities into the political arena. Also during the 1920s and 1930s, the provincial government and many municipalities made an effort to use the plebiscite to decide major policy issues. However, over the years vigilant municipal politicians have successfully lobbied the provincial government to make it difficult for citizens to use this grass-roots political mechanism, with its potential to erode the professional politicians' power. Today the use of the plebiscite is much more restricted than in the past.

Some who are committed to increased democratization of local government are concerned about low rates of voter turnout and the paucity of electoral competition in small municipalities. They believe that an unopposed election or one with an extremely low turnout makes a mockery of democratic government. However, elections by acclamation and low turnout rates can also be interpreted as an indication that the citizens are so satisfied with council representation that they do not consider it necessary to vote, or that incumbents are so popular that opponents believe it is fruitless to challenge them. Regardless of their views on voter turnout and electoral competition, most citizens would agree that if local government is to be democratic, elected representatives must be accessible to the citizens and faithfully represent their constituents views.

10

Finance, Democracy, and Policy Making

Introduction

The allocation of the costs and benefits of government is not a purely technical exercise devoid of issues of democracy or representation. First, it must be determined which goods and services are in the public sector and therefore the responsibility of a municipal government. Unfortunately, there are no simple criteria that can be used in making this classification. Sometimes the constituents decide what is, and is not, in the public sector and at other times this determination depends on the values and goals of elected officials. Second, elected representatives have to make hard and often subjective decisions about which groups of individuals in the municipality are to bear the costs of government and which are to be the recipients of its largesse.

Complicating the issue is the fact that in Alberta, local government in urban areas with high service needs is growing much faster than local government in rural areas which traditionally have had lower levels of municipal services. Moreover, almost all of the 80 percent of the province's citizens who live in urban areas seem to be demanding more services and lower taxes.

The public trusts its elected representatives to make fiscal decisions as objectively and as equitably as possible. But the belief that equity and objectivity should prevail is often held only in theory; when fiscal decisions must be made, many people argue that "the rich should pay" or "the people using the services should pay." As groups compete for fiscal advantages and tempers become heated, democracy at the local level is strained to its limit.

In making public sector fiscal policy, it is dangerous to adopt schemes to enforce efficiency and rationality in municipal budgeting without citizen participation. Almost invariably these practices are borrowed from the private sector and as a consequence they focus on shaping future values for the community rather than providing mechanisms that enable the public to define its own goals. Politicians and administrators who espouse such schemes fail to realize that the implementation of fiscal policy at the municipal level is a "bottom-up" process, with the citizenry establishing and evaluating priorities. Moreover, the strategic planning process is often distorted in order to exclude the public. Ian Wight, in critically discussing "strategic planning," first used in the private sector, said that it is formulated in secret by corporate leaders seeking "to better position themselves in the marketplace." He cautions that using the same technique in the public sector "would likely lead to plans produced in a top-down technocratic rather than democratic manner."[1]

"Rational" methods of policy making have many labels and are packaged in a number of ways. Any scheme in which a policy expert identifies goals and values should be avoided because it is, quite simply, not democratic.

The Budget Process

Every council is concerned with making rational and equitable decisions about the rate and distribution of taxation, the amount and mix of public services, and the number and financing of capital projects. But few councils give much thought to the budgeting process which provides the framework for their decisions. Typically councils grapple with four interrelated issues: whether or not (1) the budget is balanced; (2) the budget is adequate to maintain existing service levels; (3) the budget provides for wage increases for municipal employees; and (4) the budget avoids excessive tax increases. If the answer to any of these is negative, the budget is reworked or the council must be prepared for sustained criticism and controversy. Budget makers perform a delicate balancing act as they attempt to minimize community conflict while satisfying both citizens and municipal employees.

Although much has been written about budgeting, almost all councils employ the same general rules. Taking into consideration an increase in property taxation equivalent to the rate of inflation, a council calculates revenue statistics for the coming year. Then expenditure decisions are made, with each department allocated an increase equivalent to the rate of inflation.[2] It is at this point that department heads make tightly rea-

Table 10.1 1988 Total Revenue Figures for Alberta Municipalities

Type of Municipality	Revenue in Dollars
Cities	$3,151,874,000
Towns	$319,461,000
Villages	$38,614,000
Summer Villages	$4,257,000
Counties	$662,550,000
Municipal Districts	$114,400,000
Improvement Districts	$43,929,000

soned arguments for additional funding. Their estimates are almost always only slightly larger than the current year's budget, for a request substantially larger is likely to be subjected to close scrutiny. Much municipal fiscal policy making is based upon the rule that past experience is the best guide—an incrementalist and conservative approach.

Local governments have four sources of revenue: locally collected taxes, user fees, borrowing, and provincial and federal grants. Every municipal council has worthwhile projects and programs, but many are chronically short of funds with which to implement them. Difficult revenue decisions must be made. What kind of taxes should be collected? What services should be fee-based? How much should the fees be? Should the municipality apply for any and every provincial cost-shared grant?

Table 10.1 illustrates the importance of municipalities in the province's fiscal planning and economic growth. In 1988 cities in Alberta had revenue in excess of $3 billion and counties, seldom thought of as major income generators, had a revenue of two-thirds of a billion dollars.

Just as there are legal and political constraints on the raising of revenue, there are constraints on municipal expenditures. The most limiting is that unlike the provincial and federal governments, Alberta municipalities are not allowed to budget for a deficit, although an allowance is made for miscalculations and fiscal emergencies. A municipality can incur a budget deficit in a given year, but under the terms of the Municipal Taxation Act enough revenue has to be raised the following year to recover the shortfall; municipalities cannot finance a deficit with long-term borrowing. Although these restrictions may seem onerous, the result is that municipalities maintain their fiscal integrity.

Property Taxes

Although the property tax is the major tax source for Alberta local governments, it is less than ideal. It has a low elasticity, which means that the generation of revenue each year does not keep up with the rate of inflation. Neil Ridler explains: "With positive growth, or merely inflation, municipal expenditures (through rising costs) will increase faster than tax revenues (with constant tax rates). Municipalities therefore will be forced either to raise tax rates or seek alternative income sources."[3]

Once a municipal council has determined how much revenue it needs to generate from property tax revenue, a simple formula is used to calculate the mill rate. The next step is to calculate the amount of tax for each ratepayer. To do this, each residential and commercial property in the municipality is assigned a value, that is, it is assessed.[4] Although the assessment process is simple in theory, it is complex in practice. A property's assessed valuation is based on the market value of its land and the depreciated replacement cost of buildings in the base year of the general assessment. A base land value is calculated by comparing a property with similar properties sold in the same and other areas.[5]

The property tax and mill rate formulas are relatively easy to understand. However, properties often are assessed at less than 100 percent of market value and the mill rates for properties differ according to their use. To further confuse the ratepayer, a number of properties are exempt from taxes.

In general, all land in Alberta is assessed at nearly 80 percent of its fair actual value except for farmland, which is assessed on the basis of its productivity. After depreciation has been determined, a building is assessed at 65 percent of its depreciated replacement cost and machinery and equipment are assessed at 50 percent of their fair actual value. In the 1980s two changes in assessment made property taxation more equitable. Since the Municipal Taxation Act had allowed land designated as urban to be converted to farmland for tax purposes, developers holding land were changing its classification and saving enormous amounts in taxes. A number of land parcels located in urban areas which had never been used for farming also were converted into farmland. By planting alfalfa on a large parcel of land in downtown Edmonton, a developer changed its status from urban to farmland and reduced his property taxes from $97,000 to $1,000. Some 1,500 parcels were converted to farmland in Edmonton alone.[6] In order to prevent municipalities from losing property tax revenue, the Municipal Taxation Act was amended in 1988 to enable the minister, by regulation, to alter the definition of farmland.[7] In addition, land parcels used for industrial or commercial purposes and designated as farmland were to be valued at urban tax rates.

A problem which developed in the 1960s was the proliferation of "hobby farms" owned by commuting urban workers who maintained their property should be assessed as farmland. Rural municipalities felt they were being cheated of property tax revenue and as a consequence the tax act was amended in 1988. While rural residences had previously been assessed at either rural or urban rates, the residence and the first three acres were now to be assessed as a residential site at 65 percent of market value and the remaining land assessed as farmland. Dennis Anderson, Minister of Municipal Affairs, explained that with the new system, "the hobby farmer with just a few acres would thus see only a small reduction in residential taxes; the farmer with a large tract of land will continue to qualify for the full basic exemption."[8] Nevertheless, when the change in taxation was implemented a number of full-time farmers in Strathcona County had sizeable tax increases. The taxes of a feedlot operator in Ardrossan who owned 10 acres and rented 400 increased from $28 to $675 a year and a chicken farmer's taxes jumped from $130 to $890.[9] It was argued that the tax system unfairly penalized the farmer who cultivated a small acreage intensively and helped the less efficient farmer with a large acreage but a lower gross income.

Between 50 and 60 Alberta municipalities employ a split mill rate. Section 96 of the Municipal Taxation Act states that a council can classify assessed property as residential, nonresidential, or farmland. If it does so, then under Subsection 2(a) the council can "establish a rate applicable to residential property that is less than the rate applicable to non-residential property and less than the rate applicable to farm land. . . ." In many Alberta communities the mill rate is split to benefit home owners. For example, for every $1,000 of assessment in Edmonton in 1988, home owners paid $25.52 in property taxes, owners of multi-unit rental housing paid $27.53, and owners of business and industrial property paid $39.18. Although owners of rental, business, and commercial property maintain they are unjustly discriminated against by a split mill rate, they seldom mention that they are able to deduct their property and business taxes from their income tax if the business venture is profitable, a deduction not available to owners of residential property. After making this deduction, property entrepreneurs and business people pay, in real terms, about half the property taxes they have been assessed.[10]

Another taxation issue is the number of nonprofit facilities in a municipality which are exempt from property taxes and yet receive full servicing. Under Section 24 of the Municipal Taxation Act, most church, school, and hospital land and buildings, as well as cemeteries, irrigation works, gas cooperative equipment, and land and buildings for senior citizen housing are exempt from property taxes. Section 25(1) exempts from municipal and school taxes lands and buildings used: (1) by an agricultural society, (2) by a nonprofit society for community purposes, (3) by Ducks Unlimited (Canada), (4) for a government-contracted nursing home, (5) by a nonprofit organization for a summer camp, (6) by the Canadian Youth Hostel Association, (7) by "a branch or local unit of the Royal Canadian Legion . . . and any other organizations of ex-servicemen," and (8) college buildings used for residential purposes. These exemptions tend to be somewhat more controversial than those listed in Section 24 and taken together can result in a substantial loss of revenue.[11] Under Section 25(2), councils are authorized to pass bylaws imposing municipal taxes on any or all of the properties listed in Section 25(1). However, councils are loath to enact such bylaws, since the proponents of tax exemption argue that if these organizations were forced to curtail their operations the municipality would have to assume many of their community service activities at great expense. In 1986 the Calgary council's finance and budget committee recommended that Royal Canadian Legion halls be taxed, since legion hall tax breaks that year had cost the city $177,585. The committee's recommendation angered an alderman who vowed to fight for a tax exemption on the grounds of the legion's eleemosynary activities; a single hall had contributed more than $150,000 to charitable causes in the previous year.

Tax exemptions became overtly political in 1988, when both Edmonton and Calgary adamantly opposed requests by some cultural societies for exemption from property taxation. After debate in the legislative assembly, Calgary's Jewish Center had been granted the same tax concessions as the city's YMCA and YWCA in 1982, but it was not until 1988 that other cultural groups became aware of the exemption (worth $118,504 in 1988) and sought similar privileges.[12] In Edmonton the Hungarian Cultural Society asked to be excused from paying property taxes after the provincial legislature exempted the Jewish Community Center in 1984, St. John's Institute (a Ukrainian organization) in 1986, and the German Canadian Cultural Society in 1987.[13]

Although taxpayers are often irritated by tax increases, they are incensed by apparently haphazard assessment practices. At a Fort McMurray public information program on tax assessment in 1988 a woman complained that her house was assessed as having three rooms and a bathroom in the basement when in fact the basement was undeveloped. The city assessor's explanation was that it was just assumed that if there were curtains on basement windows the area was developed. Another homeowner said that although the frost came through the walls of his small 50-year-old house in the winter, he paid $2,050 in property taxes. His response to the public information program was that he was through "fiddling around" and wanted some answers to his questions about assessment and taxes.[14]

The longer the time between assessments, the greater the likelihood of a change in the value of property and a corresponding change in assessment. Since a general assessment usually is conducted every eight years, ratepayers often find their taxes have doubled. It was for this reason that Spruce Grove in 1985 initiated a three-year pilot project to determine the efficacy of an annual general assessment. With tax increases only incrementally higher each year, the number of assessment appeals declined from 50 percent in 1982, when there was a seven-year assessment, to 17 percent after the annual assessment in 1985. An evaluation of the Spruce Grove experiment by the Department of Municipal Affairs concluded that "assessors and municipal staff developed an ongoing co-operative working relationship which facilitated the annual general assessment and assured a high degree of accuracy and consistency in the results."[15] Five other municipalities have since adopted an annual general assessment.

Another assessment pilot project was carried out in the Town of Okotoks in 1991 when the town's residential, commercial, and industrial properties were assessed at full value, that is, at 100 percent. After the town council notified ratepayers of their new assessment, some 400 people contacted the council and provincial assessors to discuss their assessment or the assessment process. An assessor who handled the majority of inquiries said that only three people expressed dissatisfaction with full-market assessment.[16]

Despite the complexity of assessment and property taxation, many ratepayers closely follow taxation policy and rates across the province. Each year newspapers publish Department of Municipal Affairs statistics on the average tax on homes in the municipalities. Table 10.2 shows the property tax homeowners paid in 1988 after receiving a homeowner grant or credit in five cities for a typical five-to-eight-year-old detached three-bedroom bungalow with a one-car garage.[17]

Figures such as these are read avidly by ratepayers who compare their taxes with those in other communities of the same size. Politicians and administrators in municipalities identified as being "high-tax" protest that comparing one municipality with another solely on the basis of tax rates is like comparing apples and oranges, while politicians and administrators in "low-tax" municipalities congratulate themselves on the good

Table 10.2 1988 Property Taxes for Typical Three-Bedroom Bungalow
in Alberta Cities

City	Tax	Mill Rate
Calgary	$1,286	11.7
Lethbridge	$1,141	13.6
Red Deer	$1,238	14.7
Medicine Hat	$831	10.5
Edmonton	$1,204	13.5

job they have been doing. The truth lies somewhere between the two positions; comparisons can be made, but cities often conduct general assessments in different years, and substantial changes in the figures can occur from year to year. Other factors seldom taken into consideration include the amount of industrial land in a community, and whether or not the municipality stabilizes the property tax with utility revenue.

Since ratepayers are interested in city government and have higher rates of political participation than the general population, councils are extremely sensitive to underlying dissatisfaction which might spark a taxpayer revolt. Ratepayers are told the administration is "lean and mean" and revenue from any additional increase in taxes will be used efficiently. The split mill rate and increases in user fees often are used to placate residential ratepayers. In 1987, in order to increase revenue and to make the property tax burden more equitable, properties in Edmonton which had not been assessed for several years were reassessed; as a consequence, many property taxes were doubled. In order to forestall ratepayers' complaints, council placed a cap on property tax increases; those whose taxes increased more than 13 percent were entitled to rebates. Of the approximately 200,000 property owners in Edmonton, an estimated 6,500 were eligible to apply for a rebate and received nearly $1.5 million in 1987 and $2 million in 1988. The major beneficiaries of the council's policy were the owners of high-value residences in the community. It did not come as a surprise to critics that many council members profited handsomely from the tax cap.[18]

Although the provincial government specifies both methods and standards for property assessment, the responsibility for conducting an assessment is delegated to the municipalities. When this power is coupled with their ability to exempt certain properties from taxation, split the mill rate between residential and nonresidential properties, and base assessment on valuations made as many as seven years earlier, the councils have considerable discretion in making property tax policy. But there are provincial restraints, since legislation requires a municipality to collect a certain number of mills for schools even though it has no control over how the funds are to be spent.

Only about 55 percent of all property taxation is used for municipal purposes, the remainder being collected for other activities. While education receives most of the property tax revenue which funds nonmunicipal activities, municipal governments are also responsible for collecting revenue for local hospital authorities and the Alberta Planning Fund, which supports regional planning commissions.

Contesting Assessment

Section 43 of the Municipal Taxation Act allows Alberta ratepayers who believe their properties have been assessed unfairly to appeal to a quasi-judicial body established by council, the Court of Revision.[19] An appeal can be based on the following allegations: (1) an error or omission has occurred in the assessment of a property; (2) the assessment on a piece of land or an improvement is too high or too low; (3) a property has been "in any way" wrongly assessed; (4) the name of a person is wrongfully entered on or omitted from the assessment roll; (5) a person assessed as a public school supporter is a separate school supporter or visa versa; or (6) the property has been classified incorrectly as residential, nonresidential, or farmland.

A council can establish a Court of Revision in one of two ways. When it is established through a bylaw, any councillor, commissioner, municipal employee, or municipal resident may be appointed to it. However, it cannot have more than five members. A court established by a resolution of council must include not less than three and no more than five councillors. In the past, courts have generally comprised only council members, but more recently they tend to include members of the public as well. For example, the Court of Revision of the Municipal District of Clearwater was composed entirely of council members until 1988, when one councillor and four citizens were appointed.[20]

The Municipal Taxation Act gives the court power to issue summonses and administer oaths to witnesses. In instances where a court has been established under bylaw, court procedures, such as whether sessions are to be open or closed, are spelled out in detail. In 1987 the chair of the Court of Revision for the Improvement District of Bighorn ejected an advisory councillor from a sitting of the Court of Revision on the grounds that people dislike making their complaints public. Another court member explained that a person appealing an assessment often had to present very personal information which is sometimes confidential. The councillor, who had been a member of the court in 1985 but was disqualified, said she had been attending the session as a ratepayer so she could report any "general trends" back to her constituents.[21]

A Court of Revision decision can be taken to the Alberta Assessment Appeal Board, which makes the final determination of the amount of an assessment. Its judgements can be appealed only on questions of law and jurisdiction. In recent years, as the number of appeals has increased, the board has expanded and now operates in three divisions. In 1988/89, 3,119 appellants filed on behalf of 17,195 items. Even though 8,258 of these were withdrawn before they reached the board, the remainder constituted an immense workload. The board's decisions are made orally and later confirmed briefly in writing. Detailed written decisions are available only when requested; 97 were issued in 1988/89.

Business Tax and Economic Concessions to Business

The business tax is assessed on the basis of the gross annual rental value of a property and cannot exceed 25 percent of its assessed valuation. The owners of businesses must pay the tax whether their premises are owned or rented. Since municipalities have the discretion to impose different tax rates for different classes of businesses, business tax issues often become political footballs, especially since many people do not fully understand why a business tax is imposed or for what purpose its revenue is to be used. They assume the tax is imposed to help business and its revenue used to support activities such as downtown revitalization and tourist promotion campaigns. In fact, most councils consider the tax a convenient way to raise monies for general revenue. As an example of the controversy over the tax, Edmonton until 1987 used five different classifications that tended to assign taxes by type and size of business. As a result, the rate for financial institutions was twice that for small businesses. After the owners of large businesses argued that discriminatory taxation would drive them out of the city, council adopted a uniform rate. A year later the Canadian Federation of Independent Business (CFIB) and the Edmonton Chamber of Commerce lobbied council to abolish the business tax on the grounds that it was retarding the city's economic recovery. There was not a general consensus in the business community that the business tax should be abolished. The Building Owners and Managers Association (BOMA) strongly opposed its abolition, since the owners of nonresidential properties would absorb any substantial tax increase. Possibly as a result of lobbying by the BOMA, the business tax was not abolished, although council froze it and then raised property taxes by almost 5 percent. Alderman Julian Kinisky explained that "it is important for us to try to give the business community as good a break as we possibly can."[22] Despite a newly elected liberal alderman's efforts to raise business taxes, they were again pegged at the current level in 1989, while property taxes were increased 5.5 percent.

Only Edmonton and Calgary derive substantial revenue from the business tax; in 1988 collections totalled $55 million for Edmonton and $75 million for Calgary. Most municipalities do not tax businesses and those that do receive insignificant amounts of revenue. Smaller communities are reluctant to enact a business tax for two reasons. First, if the tax is enacted the municipality is prohibited from taxing machinery and equipment. This is an important consideration since many smaller municipalities derive substantial revenue from taxes on equipment, stored oil and coal, and lumber company machinery. Second, many people believe business taxes drive businesses from the community.

While there has been considerable debate on the appropriateness and equity of the business tax, its proponents and critics agree that it is difficult to collect. Although the Tax Recovery Act allows a municipality to acquire land for nonpayment of property taxes, there is not a similar provision enabling a municipality to acquire the assets of a business for nonpayment of business taxes. As a consequence, during the economic downturn many businesses folded without making an attempt to pay their delinquent taxes. Edmonton alone wrote off $23 million in business taxes in the spring of 1989.

Although Alberta is one of four provinces allowing municipalities to offer tax incentives to business, this policy is extremely controversial, as the cost often is borne by the ratepayer. A business intending to expand often dangles the prospect of employment and economic diversification before city hall in making a bid for economic concessions. Astute firms try to spark a bidding war between cities so as to obtain the best bargain. They issue press releases extolling their firm's virtues and leak stories to reporters about politicians unsympathetic to concessions and insensitive to community unemployment. In short, they carefully orchestrate campaigns to place pressure on council members. In 1988 the executive director of the Calgary Economic Development Authority estimated that almost half of the 12,000 businesses that express an interest in locating or expanding in Calgary each year seek tax concessions and free utilities.[23]

Tax concessions almost always result in a fragmentation and realignment of traditional business and political alliances. Business is usually divided, with large firms favouring concessions and small ones opposing them. In 1989 a survey of 15,000 Canadian owners of small businesses found that 59 percent opposed, 34 percent favoured, and 7 percent were undecided about municipal tax concessions.[24] Organized labour also is divided; construction unions support concessions and other unions are either indifferent or opposed to them. These cleavages in the business and labour communities are often reflected in odd voting patterns and unusual liberal-conservative alliances on municipal councils.

In recent years Calgary has refused to grant business concessions, arguing that to do so creates inequities which ripple through the business community and ultimately hurt the ratepayer. In 1986 the Oxford Development Group asked for some $32 million in concessions for the construction of the downtown Eaton project, threatening to move to Edmonton if its requests were not granted. Calgary's council held fast and Oxford developed the project without concessions. On the other hand, major property development companies in Edmonton have been the beneficiaries of a number of financial concessions in exchange for promises to revitalize the downtown area and stimulate the economy. After council awarded one company a major grant, a long-time alderman explained: "There's nothing sinister about concessions and subsidies. They are common in farming, business and industry, especially in today's depressed economy. City council's decision was made in the same vein."[25]

Edmonton's council made substantial tax concessions to the CN Hotel Corporation in return for the restoration of the Hotel Macdonald, which was closed in 1983. Despite the concessions, the hotel corporation broke agreement after agreement with the city. In another case, the Triple Five Corporation received concessions worth more than $50 million for the development of the downtown Eaton Center.[26] The company was granted a tax holiday, economic incentives for constructing a parkade, and a special installment plan for the payment of current and delinquent taxes. The latter concession was particularly controversial, as council made it in camera.[27] Since the installment scheme enabled Triple Five to pay its taxes without having to borrow funds and pay interest, it came as no surprise when two development companies with shopping centre holdings requested similar benefits. Although other developers were not as successful as Triple Five, they still extracted sizeable concessions. Olympia and York obtained $5.4 million in tax concessions and Manulife $7.5 million, while Western Aerospace Technology negotiated a complicated lease agreement with the city which gave it more than $1 million in rental rebates over a seven-year period.

When Jan Reimer was an Edmonton alderman she occasionally ques-

Table 10.3 1988 Revenue from Public Utilities for Alberta Cities, Towns, and Villages

Revenue Source	Cities ($)	Towns ($)	Villages ($)
Electricity	821,854	7,751	0
Water	204,552	39,327	5,427
Gas	38,618	8,526	1,283
Telephone	234,712	0	0
Transit	90,134	0	0
Total	1,404,324	55,604	6,710
Percentage of Total Revenue	45%	17%	17%

tioned council's generosity to land development companies. Therefore it was not unexpected that when she became mayor requests for concessions would be scrutinized and existing concessions re-examined. As she worked on the 1990 budget, Reimer pointed out that the $6,410,000 in business concessions would cost the average residential ratepayer about $12 in additional property taxes. In particular, Reimer asked why the models and plans which property developers show to council as the basis for financial concessions are so frequently changed without council's knowledge or permission after the concessions have been granted.[28]

Utility Revenue

After the property tax, transportation revenues and proceeds from the sale of electricity, water, natural gas, and telephone service are the most important sources of internally generated revenue for Alberta's municipalities. Table 10.3 shows that in 1988 cities derived 45 percent of their revenue from public utilities. Since towns and villages are less likely to operate utilities, the percentage of their total revenue from these sources is substantially less.

The Municipal Government Act allows municipalities to own, operate, and establish the rate structure for a variety of public utilities and gives them the option of granting utility franchises to private firms for as long as 20 years. The firms are charged a franchise tax based either on their gross revenue or on a percentage of their machinery and equipment assessment. The provincial government closely monitors these rates through its Public Utilities Board, with which Edmonton in particular has had constant problems.[29]

Public transit systems generally lose money, while electric utilities and telephone systems provide revenue. Edmonton Telephones has been extremely profitable, particularly after Mayor Decore argued successfully that the utility should keep the long-distance revenue it generated. In 1987 Edmonton Telephones contributed $22 million to general revenue and over the years its income has grown steadily whether economic times were good or bad. Another successful Edmonton enterprise is the municipal airport, the only major municipally owned airport in Canada. Since 1968, when the airport was directed to become profitable, the city has had an average return on its equity of 17.1 percent a year.

Although public utilities are lucrative, the municipalities owning them are often embroiled in controversy. Some people argue that utility profits should be used to reduce property taxes, while others maintain that the consumers of public services should be the beneficiaries of "break-even" utility rates. Edmonton utility rates were manipulated for political purposes in 1983 when the council substantially increased water, sewage, and telephone rates in order to hold a property tax increase to no more than 8 percent. In effect, the consumers of public services subsidized property owners. Eight years later the policy of having the consumers of public services subsidize property owners was still in effect. A city planning department report showed that in 1991 the combined charges for power, water, sewer, and telephone services were higher than in any other comparable city in Canada. However, when utilities and property taxes were combined, the total rate was among the lowest in Canadian cities. Moreover, the city boasted that its 1992 property tax increase would be much lower than that of other cities.[30]

In contrast, Medicine Hat, which has its own electric utility and natural gas field, is committed both to keeping its residential utility rates as low as possible and to using utility profits to hold down property taxes. As a consequence, the city consistently has had some of the lowest property taxes and utility rates in Canada.[31]

Local Improvement Charges

In 1988 Alberta cities derived 1.7 percent ($53,867,174), towns 5.6 percent ($17,933,000), and villages 6.2 percent ($2,400,228) of their revenue from levies made on property owners for local improvements such as sidewalks, street lights, and paved lanes and roadways. Such levies are justified on the grounds that since local improvements directly benefit the neighbourhood and increase property values, property owners should pay for all or a portion of their cost.[32] Under Section 149 of the Municipal Taxation Act, the council, by a three-fourths vote, can decide what portion of the cost is borne by the property owner and what portion by the municipality. Normally a group of property owners will petition council for a local improvement project. The petition must be signed by at least two-thirds of the individuals or groups who collectively own property equal to at least half of the assessed value of the land to be affected by the improvement. A local improvement project can also be initiated by council, but it must notify affected property owners before levying charges. If a majority, who collectively own property equal to at least half of the assessed value of the land, oppose the project, council cannot proceed.

Opponents of local improvement taxes argue that many improvement projects are required in older areas housing lower income families who cannot afford to pay for them. Since upgrading a deteriorating area benefits the whole community, they argue that the costs should be covered by the property tax and shared by all property owners in the municipality.

In some communities amenities such as street lights and sidewalks are charged to developers, who recover their costs from purchasers. Although this practice and local improvement levies tend to hold down property taxes, developers maintain that when amenity and servicing costs are added to the price of a house and lot, lower-middle-class and working-class people cannot afford to purchase homes in new subdivisions.

User Fees, Sales of Goods and Services, and Fines

In the 1980s Canadian municipalities increasingly resorted to user fees to raise revenue and give themselves more fiscal autonomy. Neil Ridler, an economist, argues that the move to user fees was a reaction to the provincial and federal practice of attaching conditions to grants which distorted the priorities of local municipalities and limited their independence. He shows that the gross revenue raised by user fees increased from 5.4 percent in 1973 to 9.2 percent in 1982.[33]

Since user fees tend to generate political controversy, municipal decision-makers have had to justify their imposition. One criteria often used is that such a fee should not prevent low-income people from using a service so basic that it should be available equally to everyone regardless of economic circumstances. When Edmonton alderman Ken Kozak calculated the city could raise more than $900,000 a year by charging library patrons 25 cents for each book they borrowed, he was roundly criticized. Librarians, other aldermen, and members of the public said that such a policy would discriminate against the city's poor.

Another consideration in determining the advisability of imposing user fees is whether a service is primarily of benefit to individuals or to the entire community. Fees are charged for parking in municipal lots and metered spaces, for example, because these are used only by people who drive cars and not by the community as a whole.[34]

User fees may also be charged if people are likely to waste a resource if it is free. Whether the charge for water should be fixed or based on usage is debated in some Alberta communities. Only 20 percent of the residences in Calgary are metered. In plebiscite after plebiscite the electorate has voted against metering on the grounds that: (1) the city's flat fee based on land assessment is a form of user fee, with properties with higher assessments using more water than properties with lower assessments; (2) metering would reduce water consumption and delay the construction of a new water treatment plant; and (3) the installation of meters city-wide would be too expensive. Although Medicine Hat recently placed meters in all commercial and residential properties, many residents still view water as a commodity for which they should be charged only a token fee.

Another service affected by the user fee controversy is garbage collection. In recent years municipalities have spent substantial sums to upgrade older facilities and build new ones. Department of Environment programs provide funds to regional landfill authorities, and most urban and rural municipalities increase their budgets for garbage collection and disposal every year. Nevertheless, municipalities also levy a user fee for garbage collection and site maintenance which has been increasing more rapidly than the annual inflation rate. Many people object to paying user fees in addition to property taxes, and others, under the mistaken impression that service costs are covered by user fees, expect their taxes to decrease when such fees are imposed. However, taxes pay for only a portion of public services.

Few people object when municipalities sell outmoded and worn equipment and vehicles at public auction, or when a village office charges the public a nominal fee to use its photocopy and fax machines. But many people become concerned when municipalities buy and sell land and engage in land banking. The mechanics of land banking are relatively simple; municipalities purchase undeveloped land, hold it until it is needed, and then sell it on the open market at prices somewhat below those established by private developers. In theory, land banking breaks the monopoly of private developers, keeps down the price of serviced land, and allows municipalities to make a profit.

In the 1970s, with a buoyant economy and skyrocketing land and housing costs, the Alberta Mortgage and Housing Corporation (AMHC) provided municipalities with land banking assistance. The AMHC's program was to purchase a block of land and negotiate an agreement to sell that land to a municipality after a specified period of time, from five to fifteen years. The municipality was obligated to purchase the land for its original price plus interest, although in 1983 AMHC froze the interest charges. If a municipality was unable to sell the land for what it had paid for it, the AMHC would absorb 75 percent of the loss. The program worked well until economic growth faltered and many municipalities had agreements coming due on land that had declined to less than 50 percent of its initial value. In 1988 the Alberta Urban Municipalities Association (AUMA) surveyed its members to determine how many had a land banking agreement with the AMHC. Of the municipalities which responded to the survey, 3 percent of the cities, 62 percent of the towns, and 14 percent of the villages had such an agreement. Moreover, many of them were in financial trouble. In 1990 the AMHC phased out its land banking programs and allowed the municipalities with land purchase agreements to acquire the land at the current market price rather than the price at which the land had originally been purchased by the AMHC.

Red Deer pioneered residential land banking in the province and between 1956 and 1972 had purchased 750 acres for $1.3 million, serviced them for $3.7 million, and sold them for $9 million. By 1982 the city had a land inventory worth $50 million that had cost $19 million. Not surprisingly, private developers lambasted land banking as anti-business and a burden on the taxpayers. In 1978 the Red Deer branch of the Urban Development Institute (UDI, which is a provincial association of private land developers) complained that the city was selling lots at $5,000 to $6,000 below the price at which private developers could make a profit.[35] In the mid-1980s land sales declined and the UDI predicted that land banking would bankrupt the city. However, Red Deer limited its exposure to the vagaries of the housing market by servicing land only when development was certain to take place.

Edmonton's land bank operation has been very successful, accruing more than $185 million in profits up to 1991. Although the city placed these profits in a "Mill Woods Reserve Fund," the money was not used to purchase additional land for future development but rather was spent to construct a new city hall and reduce the city's debt. Medicine Hat also has a land banking policy to prevent the private sector from manipulating prices and to facilitate orderly residential development. After the city bought 491 hectares (1,197 acres) in 1981, the mayor said, "the city will use the land eventually. It doesn't matter if you're talking about 100 years, the city of Medicine Hat will get there one day."[36]

Municipal councils which have adopted land banking policies have almost invariably become factionalized and have been soundly criticized for competing with the private sector. After the province acquired 1,777 hectares (4,391 acres) of land adjacent to Edmonton in the early 1970s, some council members opposed its transferral to the city for development. When the land was marketed, council debated whether or not the city should be holding down land prices and competing with the private sector. During a Grande Prairie land banking debate one councillor summed up the opposition when he said, "I have always felt that land acquisition and development is better left to private enterprise."[37] In the 1980s, many councils which had engaged in speculation under the guise of land banking were left with large blocks of commercial and residential property which had been developed at substantial cost and for which there was no demand. With annual interest payments in the millions, the financial burden fell on the ratepayer.

Not of the same magnitude, but also controversial, is the practice of many rural municipalities of selling sand and gravel to their residents. Although many council members feel they are providing a worthwhile service, sand and gravel companies view the municipality as unfair competition. Even making the village office's photocopy and fax machines available to the public for a small fee may raise objections if a village store installs similar equipment.

Municipalities derive only a very small part of their revenue from fines. Under the provisions of the Highway Traffic Act and the Motor Vehicle Administration Act, the province allocates to municipalities the fines accruing from certain high-volume traffic offences. However, the 1989 AUMA convention passed a resolution which would "return to the municipality providing the police service, fines levied for offences committed in violation of the *Criminal Code* as well as provincial legislation for which enforcement is a responsibility of the municipal police service." The province dismissed the resolution on the grounds that the substantial amount of revenue generated from Criminal Code fines should remain with the province. Another issue is the Municipal Government Act provision which allows a council to impose a fine as large as $2,500 for a bylaw violation. With more aggressive enforcement substantially more revenue could be generated from fines, but it should first be determined whether the purpose of fines is to control people's behaviour and penalize them for bylaw violations or to raise revenue.

Privatization

David Osborne and Ted Gaebler write in *Reinventing Government* that although there are similarities between government and business, they are fundamentally different institutions. Yet, although government cannot be run like a private business, it can exhibit the entrepreneurial spirit often characteristic of the private sector. These authors argue that many politicians make the mistake of grappling with the wrong issue. Rather than debating whether or not there should be more or less government, they should be developing more innovative ways of governing. They explain:

> It makes sense to put the delivery of many public services in private hands . . . if by doing so a government can get more effectiveness, efficiency, equity, or accountability. . . . When governments contract with private businesses, both conservatives and liberals often talk as if they are shifting a fundamental public responsibility to the private sector. This is nonsense: they are shifting the delivery of services, not the responsibility for services. . . . When governments contract activities to the private sector, those governments still make the policy decisions and provide the financing. And to do that well, they must be quality governments.[38]

Although privatization has only a minimal effect on municipal revenue and expenditures, this issue can be politically explosive. Whenever council considers expanding or decreasing the extent of municipal governmental activities, the same questions are asked. What are, and what are not, government and private enterprises? Can government do something better or can it be done better in the private sector? When government produces services, is the playing field always level or is government competing unfairly with private business? Can a particular activity be done more economically by government or by private enterprise? There are no "definitive answers" to these questions.

Some people tout privatization as a panacea for every municipal financial problem. Others attack privatization as the death knell for municipal administrative harmony and public service unions. On balance, both sides greatly overestimate what privatization can and cannot do. Proponents of privatization argue that services can be produced more efficiently and at less cost by the private sector because, among other things, the private sector responds to competitive market forces. They also hold that competition in the private sector makes service providers more responsive to service consumers, that is, the public.[39] Supporters of privatization also argue, though more quietly, that it will curb the power of municipal unions. Opponents point out that union wage scales enable employees to pump economic benefits back into the community by purchasing homes, consumer goods, and personal services. Equally important, it gives them the income to enjoy a middle-class life-style. Those opposed to privatization also argue that it does not necessarily lead to competition, since private firms are generally given monopoly franchises.

Municipal unions oppose privatization. In particular, the Canadian Union of Public Employees (CUPE) contests it at every turn, since the issue is of uppermost concern for its rank-and-file membership. The privatization issue is crucial to CUPE's strategy for long-term growth; the union is determined to eliminate any roadblock to its continued expansion and any defeat of privatization will enhance its image in future organizational drives.

In the winter of 1988 when a contingent of council members and senior administrators in Calgary were considering contracting out services to the private sector, municipal unions orchestrated a campaign to mobilize and capture the public's support. The union's central argument was that people were willing to pay for the superior services it provided. The proponents of privatization pointed to the disparity between private sector and municipal salaries, which were in some cases as much as 50 percent higher. Mayor Klein supported the union's position, arguing that the city had a moral obligation to keep its employees working during periods of economic hardship.

The privatization debate had taken a bizarre turn in 1986 when the Edmonton Chamber of Commerce argued that the city's water and sanitation departments should be prevented from bidding on a Light Rail Transit tunneling contract. The Chamber's president explained: "It is an unnecessary intrusion into the private sector and a direct assault against the business community. If the city bids on this job, a number of qualified organizations will decide not to spend the time and money to bid the job. In short, competition will be discouraged and the city is less likely to get the best price."[40] Mayor Decore sided with the Chamber and the city manager eventually negotiated a compromise which allocated $6 million of the construction work to the city departments of water and sanitation and put $31 million out for private tender.[41]

Unfortunately, municipal debates on privatization often fail to deal with the real issues. As an example, when the privatization of garbage collection was being discussed in Calgary in 1989, Mayor Hartman justified his opposition as follows: "You hear some horror stories in New York and other cities where it gets into the Mafia . . . once they get control you have no control on pricing, it's as simple as that."[42] In Edmonton a study commissioned by CUPE documenting a number of privatization cases which had gone sour was dismissed out of hand by councillors Lance White and Bruce Campbell, a former president of the Edmonton Chamber of Commerce who called it "the product of a vested interest."[43] When a new council was elected, however, it included at least one opponent of privatization. In the spring of 1991 Alderman Brian Mason complained that the $14.4 million the city had paid to private consultants the previous year was "nothing but a massive subsidy to the private sector. It's using the private sector when you could do it more cheaply and with more accountability by doing it in-house."[44]

While recent debates about privatization have generally been restricted to service areas in which unskilled, semi-skilled, and skilled craft workers are employed, municipalities have for many years contracted out a sizeable portion of their accounting and legal work. Small municipalities employ local law firms on retainer and even some large municipalities with substantial legal departments employ firms thought to have specialized skills. As an example, in the spring of 1989 it came to light that a 16-year-old lawsuit against the City of Edmonton had been handled by the prestigious law firm of Milner and Steer at a cost to the city of $749,216. When the firm lost the suit, the city had to pay $2 million plus court costs.[45] So common is the contracting out of legal services that there was not even an editorial comment on the size of the fee.

Only recently have policy analysts and elected officials begun to grapple with the pertinent issues in the privatization debate.[46] In many communities, honest attempts are being made to work out compromises which protect the interests of both municipal workers and the public. In all likelihood, a two-tier wage system will eventually be implemented which will maintain the prevailing wage scale for long-term employees and provide another wage grid with lower starting salaries for new employees. Increasing numbers of municipal services may be contracted out, but with the proviso that the private sector must provide wages and benefits comparable to those in the public sector.

Grants to Municipalities

The amount of grants, or transfer payments, received from the provincial government is extremely important in the budget process. A general rule is that the smaller the municipality, the more important grants are in its budget. In any given year, as a percentage of total operating costs, grants to villages range between 25 and 30 percent, grants to towns between 17 and 23 percent, and grants to small cities between 10 and 15 percent. Edmonton and Calgary are much less dependent on provincial grants, which cover less than 10 percent of their total operating costs.

From the perspective of municipalities, grants are ideal; funds received from senior governments are viewed as being free. The more "free monies" municipalities obtain, the less dependent they are on politically sensitive property taxes, business taxes, and user fees. Equally important, grants cause little dissension in the community. There always is a certain amount of tension between municipalities seeking larger grants and the provincial and federal governments seeking to reduce them, but conflict with the government making the grant generally elicits community support for a local council.

Basically, there are two types of government grants, conditional and unconditional. Conditions are attached to more than 80 percent of provincial grant money. Municipal treasurers and most councillors prefer a system of unconditional grants. However, some councillors and heads of operating departments favour conditional grants. Since there is a decided difference of opinion over the merits of the two types of grants, friction develops within and between municipalities and municipal associations whenever there is any attempt to change the grant structure.

Each year the Department of Municipal Affairs provides an unconditional grant to every municipality in Alberta on the basis of relative need. The purpose of the grant is to enable municipalities to provide a range of services without burdening citizens unduly with taxes and user fees.

The provincial government has always used grants to encourage municipalities to adopt province-wide standards, and it was not until after the Second World War that municipalities began to request unconditional funding. In the 1950s members of a Provincial-Municipal Advisory Committee negotiated an unconditional Municipal Assistance Grant which gave municipalities half the proceeds of the province's gasoline sales tax, totalling $16.5 million by 1964. In 1965 the Social Credit government announced that the grant would be tied to the price of oil; under a new formula municipalities would receive one-third of the province's oil royalty revenue.

Although the municipalities were generally satisfied with the revenue-sharing agreement, the provincial government became increasingly concerned when an economic downturn affected its portion of oil revenue. When the economy was buoyant the government's 16.67 percent royalty agreement with the oil industry and the sale of drilling rights were extremely profitable, but by 1967 the province's natural gas industry was in decline and oil exploration had virtually ended. Premier Harry Strom, in an attempt to avert a provincial revenue shortfall, terminated the agreement with the municipalities.

When the Tories were elected in 1971 municipal councils hoped that the policy of coupling oil revenue to municipal grants would be re-implemented. Premier Peter Lougheed, however, stated unequivocally in 1974 that he was opposed to "a portion of any given item of revenue [being] allocated to another level of government."[47] Nevertheless, delegates at the annual convention of the Alberta Urban Municipalities Association (AUMA) adopted a resolution which called upon their association to "make the necessary representation to the Provincial Government to initiate a point system whereby municipalities can share, without increasing taxation, in that portion of income tax collected for the province based on the income of the citizens resident in a given municipality." Predictably, the government's response was that the resolution's revenue-sharing scheme was "not possible nor would it be equitable."[48] In 1975 St. Albert drafted a similar resolution to be presented to the AUMA's annual convention, but withdrew it at the last minute.

Beginning in the early 1980s and almost every year thereafter, municipalities again lobbied the government for a share of oil revenue. Each time, the Minister of Municipal Affairs responded emphatically that the province would not share its oil revenue with local governments.[49] In 1981 an AUMA advisory committee to the Minister of Municipal Affairs recommended an eight cent a gallon gasoline tax at the pump, with the revenue earmarked for municipalities as an unconditional per capita grant. With the minister's tacit support, the gasoline tax motion was presented at the AUMA's annual convention, where it was defeated by a vote of two to one.[50] Delegates feared that Alberta motorists would blame the municipalities for the additional cost every time they purchased a tank of gas.[51] The AUMA proposed instead that the province allocate to the municipalities 8 percent of the projected $64 billion it would receive from oil and gas royalties over the upcoming five years.[52] Irritated that AUMA delegates had voted down the motion supported by the minister, the government summarily rejected its counter-proposal.[53] The minister explained that "there just isn't a whole bunch of money lying around. The fund [Heritage Savings Trust Fund] is asset-rich and cash poor."[54] The government's Advisory Committee on Provincial-Municipal Fiscal Relations was specifically directed not to consider income tax revenue sharing or resource revenue sharing with municipalities in any of its deliberations.[55] At the AUMA's 1982 annual convention a resolution was carried "to ensure that a portion of revenue from depleting natural resources is invested in capital assets at the municipal level." The government responded that the issue was under study.[56] In 1984, when yet another revenue-sharing resolution was passed at the AUMA convention, the government claimed that "significant revenue is now being shared by the province to municipalities through a series of conditional and unconditional grants."[57]

Despite its reluctance to implement revenue sharing, the government was not ungenerous. Shortly before the provincial election in 1979 it overwhelmed the political opposition with the announcement that each of the province's 349 municipalities and eight Metis colonies was being given a $500 per capita grant in order to reduce its debt. The Municipal Debt Reduction Act allocated $648 million to municipalities to pay off their long-term debentures and $383 million as unconditional grants. Under a complex formula, every municipality received an unconditional grant whether or not the funds were sufficient to eliminate its municipal debt. The Minister of Municipal Affairs described the program as extraordinary: "it's never occurred before in any province in the history of Canada. I'm unaware that it has occurred anywhere in the world, when you consider a transfer of that amount of funds on a largely unconditional basis to another level of government, without some kind of standard agreement."[58]

When Don Getty came to power in 1985 it had become apparent that the four-year economic slump would become permanent unless some drastic changes were made in the government's taxing and spending policies. Moreover, the Getty government discovered that the previous Provincial Treasurer, Louis Hyndman, had overestimated revenue and underestimated spending and as a consequence the province faced a $2.5 billion deficit. One of the many measures used to stem the flow of red ink was to freeze some municipal grants and reduce others. Perhaps to soften the fiscal blow, in the fall of 1985 Getty promised that whenever possible he would implement unconditional grant programs, since municipal councillors "are the people who know the services they require and the best way to deliver them."[59] In 1984 the Minister of Municipal Affairs established a joint municipal-provincial Grant Structures Review Committee which recommended in December 1985 that the government implement a comprehensive system of unconditional grants.

In April 1986 the province announced an unconditional grant program that it "hoped" municipalities would use to stimulate employment and repair and upgrade roads, bridges, and water and sewage systems.[60]

Table 10.4 Per Capita AMPLE Grant to Municipalities by Year

Year	Per Capita Grant	Grant Millions
1987/88	$10.44	$24.8
1988/89	$25.72	$61.1
1989/90	$28.54	$67.8
1990/91	$25.70	$61.0
1991/92	$25.70	$61.0
1992/93	$25.70	$61.0
1993/94		$55.0 (estimate)*
1994/95		$55.0 (estimate)*
1995/96		$55.0 (estimate)*

* $167 million to be spent over three years

The Alberta Municipal Partnership in Local Employment (AMPLE) program, based on a per capita grant formula, was to give municipalities $500 million ($200 per capita) over an eight-year period, beginning with an initial $15 per capita grant in 1987.[61] Just when many municipal councils had decided how they would use their grants, Minister of Municipal Affairs Neil Crawford warned them at the AUMA convention in November that in the interest of fiscal responsibility the grant might be cut back to $12 per capita or even less. Eventually $24.8 million ($10.44 per capita) in AMPLE grants was distributed to municipalities for fiscal 1987/88. Although many local governments used their AMPLE grants to repair infrastructures and generate employment, some paid off debenture debt and still others placed the monies in a reserve fund for future projects.[62] In a few cases municipalities subsidized ratepayers by using AMPLE funds to reduce and stabilize the mill rate.[63] In January 1990 the government announced that the AMPLE program would be extended an additional year, but without additional funding. As a consequence, funding for the 1990/91 fiscal year was reduced 10 percent. Table 10.4 indicates that AMPLE funding will decrease again in the last three years of the program if the government makes no additional contributions.

Early in 1988 the conditional grant monies each municipality received for law enforcement, municipal assistance, and public transit were consolidated into a new unconditional grant, the Alberta Partnership Transfer (APT) program.[64] Although municipalities would receive a single unconditional payment, the program's overall funding would continue to reflect government priorities in the three program areas by specifying three separate allocations of money. In the first year of the program, 1988/89, municipalities received $147 million of APT funding. Since then there have been yearly incremental increases; for 1991/92 municipalities were scheduled to receive $163 million.

Throughout the Lougheed years unconditional grants for municipalities were based on relative need.[65] In 1984 all general purpose grants were consolidated into a Municipal Assistance Grant (MAG) with an equalization formula designed to narrow fiscal disparity among municipalities. The grant was to be phased in over a five-year period so that by 1989 every city, town, village, county, and municipal district would receive a municipal assistance grant of at least $25,000 and every summer village, improvement district, and national park school district at least $2,000. However, Municipal Affairs extended the phase-in period for an additional year.

In order to understand how the MAG program works it is necessary to keep in mind that the greater the proportion of property in a municipality which is assessed as nonresidential, the lighter the tax burden of residential property owners. If there is little nonresidential property in the community, almost all of the tax burden falls on the residential ratepayer. The MAG program is intended to enable poorer jurisdictions to provide the same level of services as those with a stronger tax base.[66] The Department of Municipal Affairs explains:

> This formula is designed to provide additional assistance to municipalities with lower-than-average financial wealth or "fiscal capacity." Under the formula, the fiscal capacity of a jurisdiction is measured by its equalized assessment per capita plus, in rural municipalities, equalized assessment per road kilometre. For summer villages, fiscal capacity is measured by equalized assessment per lot with a dwelling constructed on it.[67]

As an example of the MAG process, grants for the cities with the highest and lowest nonresidential assessments are compared for 1987 and 1988. Fort Saskatchewan had the highest nonresidential assessment for cities, 76 percent, and St. Albert had the lowest, 20 percent. When the grant for each municipality is converted to a mill rate equivalent, Fort Saskatchewan was awarded a grant equal to 1.3 mills and St. Albert was awarded a grant equal to 6.2 mills.

For many communities MAGs are essential if property taxes are to be held at an acceptable level and services maintained. The 1989 MAG provided the equivalent of 3.7 percent of the 1987 property tax revenue for cities and 15.7 percent for villages. For the Town of Raymond and the Village of Stirling, the 1989 MAGs equalled 29.4 and 33.8 percent, respectively, of their 1987 property tax revenue. Without the municipal assistance portion of their AMPLE grants, communities such as Raymond and Stirling would be forced to increase property taxes drastically in order to maintain current levels of services.

Conditional grants usually are given to a municipality on a cost-shared basis. That is, the provincial government provides a certain percentage of funds for a specified purpose and the municipality is required to provide the remaining funding. Until 1988, when police and public transit operating grants were rolled into the APT grant, the general trend had been a shift from unconditional to conditional grants. A 1979 study of municipal financing in the province found:

> In 1965 only 43.1% of grants were specific but by 1977 over 70% were conditional. . . . In 1959 transfers were made only for transportation and social welfare. By 1965 grants for recreational and cultural purposes made a modest beginning. By 1968 there were six separate conditional program areas and seven by 1975. While transportation still remains the most important conditional grant program area, grants for protection (policing) and for recreation and culture have become relatively large.[68]

From the provincial government's perspective, the shift to conditional funding had several advantages. Province-wide municipal policies could be established in areas such as recreation, highways, and sanitation. Cost-shared provincial programs could be implemented more economically. Above all, conditional grants enabled the province to control what it viewed as "irresponsible municipal councils."[69] On the other hand, the municipalities prefer unconditional grants, on the grounds that conditional grants with stringent guidelines alter their spending priorities and make their governments mere conduits for the administration of provincially designed programs, thus lessening local autonomy and weakening local democracy.[70] Although the provincial government argues that municipalities are free not to participate in grant programs, local governments are always under constituent pressure to obtain additional funding. To accommodate a new cost-shared conditional grant program, a municipality must either raise additional revenue or shift funds from an established program. Neither alternative is favoured by local administrators, who know that the process of changing budget priorities is often stormy.

In addition, conditional grant programs targeted for capital facilities often result in an *increase* in property taxes, for once a facility is in place the municipality is responsible for its ongoing operating expenses. Even when cost-shared conditional grants provide for operating expenses, such grants are normally tied to a high level of service. As a consequence, the municipality usually finds itself spending more on the service than it spent before receiving the grant.

Alberta's most recent grant program, initiated in 1987, allocates a portion of its annual proceeds from the Western Canada Lottery Corporation[71] to community groups and municipalities for "community facility enhancement." The program is contentious and has been called a Tory political slush fund, since the Minister of Career Development and Employment has complete discretion in the allocation of funds and is not accountable to the legislature.[72] In its first year $32.9 million was allocated for 907 projects, almost 80 percent of which involved renovating and upgrading recreational facilities. The largest grant, $600,000, was awarded to the Town of Manning and the smallest, $250, was made to the Summer Village of Seba Beach. Above and beyond the charge that the program's administration is too political, its purpose is also controversial. Critics claim that the public would be better served if lottery revenue were earmarked for health and education rather than recreation and cultural facilities. In 1989 the minister said that "the reality is that the lottery fund is an un-guaranteed fund" and for that reason education and health should not become dependent upon it.[73]

In any examination of the grant structure an important but often neglected tangential issue is the municipal census. With only a few exceptions the grants municipalities receive from the provincial government are based on a formula which includes a population component; in its simplest form a grant is determined by multiplying population by a predetermined dollar figure. Since a municipal census is costly, if the population is relatively static the figures from the federal census are used, a census which is carried out every five years. If a municipality's population is increasing rapidly it is important for it to provide recent census figures in order to receive all of the grant money to which it is entitled. Conversely, if its population is declining, a municipality is generally quite content to supply the provincial government with out-of-date figures!

Although Lethbridge's budget was lean in 1986, the administration decided to conduct a census, since each resident was worth $90 in government grants. Edmonton took a different tack in 1984 and 1985; rather than carry out an annual municipal census which it feared would show a decrease in population, the city continued to use its 1983 municipal census figures. When a census was carried out in 1986 for the civic election, it

Table 10.5 Grants in Lieu of Taxes Received by Alberta Municipalities in 1988

Type of Municipality	Total Dollars	Percentage of Total Revenue
Cities	$62,490,743	2.0
Towns	$12,565,288	3.9
Villages	$1,243,055	3.2
Counties	$4,289,681	0.6
Municipal Districts	$2,156,040	1.9

was found there were 11,421 more residents than in 1983. Since each was worth $520 in grant funds, the city had lost $1.18 million over a two-year period by deciding to use 1983 census figures.[74] In a somewhat different case, the Town of Rimbey was ordered to carry out a new census in 1987 when it was found that its municipal census figures for 1986 were substantially higher than the federal census figures for the same year, 2,106 as opposed to 1,786. After the new municipal census showed the town to have a population of 1,748 some of its grant monies were cut.[75]

Grants in Lieu of Taxes

Although federal and provincial governments and their agencies are generally exempt from taxation by municipalities, it is their practice to acknowledge their use of municipal services by making payments to local governments in lieu of school and general purpose taxes. These grants are based on an evaluation of Crown properties using the same municipal assessment formula that would be used if the properties were subject to taxation. They are an important source of revenue for Alberta communities containing federal and provincial government buildings and enterprises. Table 10.5 shows that grants in lieu of taxes are most important for towns and villages, where they constitute more than 3 percent of the total revenue, and least important for counties. Calgary, with a number of federal and provincial installations, is a major beneficiary of the program, and in 1988 received $20,204,000 from grants in lieu of taxes.

The federal government has generally been a good corporate citizen in Alberta communities and provided grants equivalent to the property taxes that would otherwise be assessed.[76] However, the federal Municipal Grants Act gives the minister the power to reduce the grant almost at will.[77] The parallel provincial act, the Crown Property Municipal Grants Act, makes it clear that a municipality does not have a right to the grant and that grants are made at the province's discretion. To emphasize this point, local governments must apply to the province for their grants every year. Nevertheless, municipalities assume they will receive equitable grants in lieu of taxes and were therefore shocked when the Alberta government announced in 1990 that the grants in lieu of taxes for 1990/91 would be 6 percent less than in 1989/90, that is, $37.36 million as opposed to $41.4 million.[78] The Minister of Public Works was unable to give the government's rationale for the decrease in funding.[79] Representations were made to the premier's office on behalf of the province's municipalities by the Alberta Urban Municipalities Association and the Alberta Association of Municipal Districts and Counties. In July Premier Getty announced the reinstatement of some $4 million in grants in lieu of taxes, claiming there had been a misunderstanding with the municipalities which had been resolved.

The Crown Property Act exempts a substantial number of properties in municipalities from payment of grants in lieu of taxes, including parks; museums; monuments; hospitals; mental institutions; trade, forestry, and agricultural schools; and colleges and universities.[80] While the provincial government, like the federal government, has generally paid for its share of municipal services, the AUMA passed a motion in both 1980 and 1981 requesting the province to reverse its policy of refusing to pay grants in lieu of taxes on nonprofit accommodation for senior citizens and the physically or mentally disabled.[81] In the spring of 1982, a study carried out by Edmonton's Real Estate and Housing Department on the impact of residential tax exemptions found that:

> In 1979, the Assessment Department estimated the total amount of municipal tax lost to be $980,000 for roughly 2700 apartment and bed-sitting units in 36 projects. By 1981, this figure had risen to an estimated $1.8 million for approximately 4300 units in 74 subsidized housing projects. . . .[82]

Municipal Affairs responded that the negligible amount of money at stake meant no community would incur a hardship. However, as criticism mounted and yet another resolution was passed at the AUMA's annual convention in 1984, the government decided that beginning in 1985 grants in lieu of taxes would be made for senior citizen housing. Speaking on behalf of the Alberta Mortgage and Housing Corporation in 1985, the Minister of Housing announced that the corporation would pay $3.6 million as a grant in lieu of taxes for self-contained apartments for senior citizens. At about the same time, Municipal Affairs announced it would be making an $800,000 grant in lieu of taxes to municipalities for private nonprofit apartment complexes for seniors.

Borrowing

Although Alberta's municipalities are prohibited from borrowing for operating expenses, they occasionally borrow in order to finance capital projects. Two urban economists describe borrowing as:

> the only practical way to finance local capital expenditures, since it would be very difficult to use current revenues such as property taxes to make such large outlays in any given year. One capital project might account for a very large proportion of the budget in some municipalities for the year. By spreading the costs of a project over a period of time there would be much less variation in tax rates on an annual basis.[83]

Municipalities originally were able to obtain funds for capital projects from the private sector, but during the Great Depression several municipalities defaulted on their municipal debt and others suspended borrowing for capital projects. After the Second World War and the 1947 oil boom, which indirectly provided municipalities with revenue, the stage was set for massive capital growth. However, private financial institutions had lingering suspicions about Social Credit fiscal policies and were reluctant to resume underwriting major municipal debentures. As a consequence, in 1950 the Social Credit Government passed the Self-Liquidating Projects Act which enabled municipalities to obtain 2 percent loans to extend or construct self-liquidating utility systems. Under the 1953 Municipal Capital Expenditure Loans Act, municipalities could borrow funds for capital projects at 3.5 percent interest. Three years later the government established the Alberta Municipal Financing Corporation (AMFC) to purchase municipal debentures at a very favourable interest rate, thus enabling small villages as well as large cities to develop worthwhile capital projects.[84] Local governments sold the AMFC debentures worth $844 million in 1981 and $1.12 billion in 1982, and the corporation maintained the interest rate at 11 percent despite surging rates in the private sector.

A number of villages had built up long-term debts of more than a million dollars when the provincial economy faltered and the government announced in April of 1982 that the Interest Stabilization Program that was keeping the cost of municipal debentures low would be discontinued in five years. By the end of 1984, municipal borrowing from the AMFC totalled $4.5 billion and the government was attempting to discourage further borrowing unless it was absolutely necessary.

When the AMFC was the major source of funds for Alberta municipalities it was relatively easy for them to obtain loans. A municipal council needed only to pass a bylaw authorizing the municipality to borrow money which was forwarded to the Local Authorities Board for approval. At the same time, a simple debenture form was sent to the AMFC and shortly thereafter the municipality received its funds. When provincial funds are not available, local governments must apply to the Canadian financial market, which is much more cautious than the AMFC. A municipality has to prepare a plan showing how borrowed funds are to be used and how the debenture is to be repaid. The plan then becomes the basis for a financial prospectus which underwriters and investors use to evaluate the municipality for investment purposes.

The two key factors that affect the interest rate a municipality must pay are its credit rating and the general level of interest. The credit rating is assigned to a municipality by one of four North American agencies.[85] Reference to a municipality's credit rating enables lenders to evaluate the risks in loaning funds and to charge an appropriate interest for the risk involved. All of the rating agencies use a similar scheme to denote the credit worthiness of government borrowers; ratings run from AAA, a bond of the highest quality, to C, a bond likely to default. Having a good rating is important, since the difference in interest between two adjoining categories is generally .25 percent. Over the life of a 20-year debenture in the tens of millions of dollars, a .25 percent difference in interest can be substantial. Although the likelihood of a municipality defaulting on its debenture payments is small, it occasionally happens and therefore a municipality's credit rating can vary throughout the life of a debenture, depending upon its financial health. As an example, if a municipality's primary industry moves to another jurisdiction, this could affect the municipality's credit rating.

The general level of interest is affected by myriad factors in and outside of Canada. Canadian interest rates once varied little over time, but since technological advances in communication during the 1980s linked the world's financial markets, interest rates are constantly changing. As international events can move interest rates up and down by as much as .25 percent in a very short time, a financial underwriter must work closely with a municipality to enable it to enter the market at the most opportune time in order to obtain the best rate and to diminish the underwriter's exposure to interest fluctuations by selling an issue as quickly as possible.

In 1983 Strathcona County's chief commissioner thought he had found a painless way for local governments to raise funds for capital projects while maintaining a modicum of independence from the provincial government. Taking his cue from municipal bond financing in the United States, he proposed that the federal government allow municipalities to sell municipal bonds with tax-free interest to private investors at interest rates substantially lower than the market rate. With the endorsement of the Minister of Municipal Affairs, the proposal was sent to Ottawa, where it now languishes.[86]

Although the Alberta economy has begun to revive, municipalities are more cautious about incurring debt than in the past and provincial funds are less accessible. Nevertheless, a short-sighted council unwilling to borrow for worthwhile capital projects may be jeopardizing its future by driving people into adjoining communities with more attractive services and amenities. When this happens, the municipality's tax base and services begin to decline, leading to further erosion of its population and economic vitality.

Budgeting During and After the Economic Downtown

In the halcyon years of the 1970s rapid economic growth provided municipalities with a safety net. As municipal property values and property tax revenue increased substantially each year, there was little likelihood a municipal administration would be embarrassed by a fiscal miscalculation. Moreover, the provincial government was much freer with funding for municipalities than it is today. During this golden era the size of many local bureaucracies increased substantially and wage increases well above the rate of inflation were routinely negotiated with civic employees. In the 1980s the safety net collapsed, and communities were divided by allegations of fiscal mismanagement and outcries against the size and cost of the municipal bureaucracy. As early as 1978, an independent auditor-general in Edmonton had criticized many of the decisions made by the city's commission board and recommended a number of improvements in the city's administration.

Alberta's municipalities became acutely aware that their ability to govern was directly related to their ability to raise sufficient revenue and to spend it efficiently. As the growth of population in urban centres began to slow down, budgetary processes were seriously disrupted. When Calgary showed a net decrease in population instead of a predicted 20,000 increase, its transportation operating grant, based on a $9.50 per capita formula, dropped to $5.9 million instead of rising to an anticipated $6.18 million. The city opted to take its 1982 and 1983 provincial Major Cultural Recreational (MCR) grant in 1981 and cut its funding for community association recreational programs. By 1983 Calgary also had incurred a long-term debt of over $1 billion, with debt servicing charges in excess of $100 million annually. Despite a succession of cutbacks, salary freezes, and wage increases substantially below the rate of inflation, the city's debt continued to climb until by 1989 it was $1.6 billion. Today approximately one-fifth of the city's operating budget goes to service its long-term debt, which is the second highest in Canada, surpassed only by that of Montreal.[87]

Calgary is not the only city which has had trouble with its revenue projections. The general manager of Edmonton's financial department said that in planning for the 1983 budget, the city estimated that it would collect $167 million in tax revenue. However, because of a "stagnant assessment base," only $164 million was collected. The Red Deer city treasurer announced that $2.3 million in commercial, industrial, and residential property taxes remained unpaid at the end of 1982. This figure represented 11 percent of the total property taxes for that year and was double the sum of unpaid taxes in 1981.

The Town of Stony Plain and the Village of Plamondon were in dire financial straits in 1983 as a result of municipal policies that had been based optimistically on uninterrupted population and economic growth. In 1980 Stony Plain embarked on an ambitious plan to develop two industrial parks; in the fall of 1983, the town found itself with a $12.4 million debt, including a $800,000 deficit for the year. The council made substantial cuts in services and enacted fiscal conservation measures: municipal salaries were frozen, the salaries of the mayor and councillors were reduced by 20 percent, and the positions of twelve of the town's 37 full-time employees were abolished.[88]

The Village of Plamondon (1982 population, 271) was encouraged in 1980 to upgrade its water and sewer system by a developer who proposed a 40-lot subdivision to house people who would be working in Fort McMurray. At the insistence of Alberta Environment, a $1.2 million water and sewage system was built that would be adequate for 1,000 people. The village's portion of the cost, $250,000, was to be shared by the developer. However, the council failed to obtain an agreement from the developer before constructing the system, and after the Fort McMurray project was cancelled, the developer vanished.[89] The developer's defection, combined with a substantial cost overrun, left the village with a $405,738 long-term debt and annual debenture payments of $60,220 for 21 years. In 1982 property taxes were increased 60 percent. Although roads in the municipality were unpaved and recreational facilities nonexistent, in 1983 the property tax on a basic five-year-old bungalow was $2,002, which was 75 percent higher than the tax on an equivalent property in Edmonton. Rather than raise taxes another 40 percent, in 1983 the mayor and council resigned and the administration of the village was assumed by the Department of Municipal Affairs. Only after the province made a $250,000 grant to the village was a Municipal Affairs administrator able to reduce Plamondon's mill rate from 202 to 148, which meant that the tax on the basic bungalow dropped to $1,480.

A series of unrelated economic events also pushed the Town of Grand Centre to the edge of financial ruin after it expropriated 119.5 hectares (295 acres) of land for a new sewage lagoon in 1981. Shortly thereafter the town was forced to cancel the project after the Department of Defense complained the lagoon would attract birds which would be hazardous for military aircraft at a nearby airport. The town council attempted to return the expropriated property and recoup the $375,000 which had been paid for it, but the offer was rejected by the six previous owners, who appealed the expropriation to the Land Compensation Board. The board agreed that they had been underpaid and awarded them $3.1 million in compensation plus another $.5 million in interest.[90] In early 1984 the town offered to give the land back to its previous owners, rezone it for industrial use, and pay them $1 million. The offer was refused and on June 4 the town's assets were frozen in a garnishee action, whereupon the Department of Municipal Affairs guaranteed a $250,000 loan which allowed it to continue operations. Shortly thereafter the expropriated land was classified as part of the town's water and sewage system, which entitled the town to provincial assistance. The province agreed to assume 75 percent of the town's debt .

The President of the AUMA has said that the reason for the financial plight of Alberta municipalities in the 1980s is not difficult to understand. His explanation was that some were lured into a "false sense of security" by the one-time $500 per capita grant to municipalities in 1979, while others expected the high funding levels of the 1970s to continue throughout the 1980s. Instead, the government abolished street assistance and housing incentive grants and made cuts in other grant programs. Many municipalities had been managed inefficiently during the buoyant 1970s, paid unnecessarily high prices for everything, managed their investments poorly, ignored employees' low productivity, and settled wage disputes quickly and expensively. He concluded by saying that some municipalities hired poorly trained people, while others provided little or no incentive for municipal employees to upgrade their qualifications, all of which led to poor morale and low productivity.[91]

Eventually some municipalities hired consulting firms to recommend more efficient and less costly procedures. Other communities, including Edmonton and Calgary, adopted a zero-based budgeting system, which requires each department to justify its total operation and total budget every year. In the City of St. Albert an overzealous alderman proposed eliminating the free coffee provided to staff and served at board and council meetings, "a luxury item we could do without."[92] Foolishness on council also occurred in neighbouring Edmonton. In December 1989 John Geiger wrote:

> At the start of three weeks of intensive budget hearings at city hall, budget chairman Judy Bethel vowed $1 million would be trimmed from the 1990 operating budget and property tax increases would be held to five percent. . . . Not only have these fake fiscal conservatives failed to trim $1 million from the budget, but they have actually added $1.4 million to the total. . . . Suddenly, instead of a five percent property tax increase, or even the 5.5 percent the city manager had recommended, Edmonton ratepayers were facing a 6.2 percent hike. . . . the politicians abruptly dumped the budget back into the lap of [the] Acting City Manager [who] was to go away over the lunch hour and return with $1.4 million in cuts. He was given two hours to come up with savings that these financial wizards had failed to find in three weeks.[93]

Council was no more rational in its deliberations the following year. Its budget meeting commenced at 9:00 A.M. on a Tuesday morning and ran continuously until 3:00 A.M. Wednesday morning. A motion to hold an additional meeting was defeated. An angry alderman, Brian Mason, suggested there was "a deliberate and bloody-minded exercise to ram through an unpopular budget when all sensible people were in bed."[94]

In 1987 a series of fiscal errors left the Calgary council's budget committee with a $4.4 million budget shortfall. After the first complete property tax assessment in twelve years, assessment officers overestimated by several million dollars the grants in lieu of taxes the city was to receive from the provincial and federal governments. They also overestimated by millions of dollars the amount of utility and business tax revenue.

Citizens might be more forgiving of such budgetary errors if elected officials were less cavalier. In 1988, Calgary's Mayor Ralph Klein attempted to minimize a 4.5 percent property tax increase by saying that it was "no big deal, no more than the price of a bloody caesar a month."[95] Two weeks later in Edmonton, Alderman Julian Kinisky, chair of council's budget committee, explained that the city's property tax increase was minimal since "it's going to total for the average household about $5 per month—less than a six-pack of beer."[96] In neither city was the analogy between an increase in property taxes and the cost of liquor appreciated by the public.[97]

An Overview of Finance, Democracy, and Policy Making

Although a few people believe government finance is a technical area best left to bureaucrats, most realize that it is their elected representatives who make the broad policy decisions as to who bears the cost of government and who receives its benefits. It is for this reason that many citizens carefully monitor whether their representatives' legislative action reflects the promises they made during their election campaigns and whether or not the provincial government is honouring its financial commitments to the municipalities. If the electorate finds there has been duplicity in the formulation of fiscal policy there often ensues a hue and cry to "throw the rascals out." The democratic process affects fiscal policies just as it does all of the others.

While the inner workings of a complex financial operation like property and business taxation are perhaps best left to the technicians, the economic principles upon which the tax policy rests can be understood by almost everyone if they are discussed in appropriate terms. Elected officials should consult with the public rather than obscure and confuse the issues, as is sometimes the case. More to the point, elected officials have a responsibility to develop grass-roots mechanisms in order to obtain citizens' opinions on fiscal issues. If elected representatives are unable to do this, then the public should be allowed to make policy directly by plebiscite. In short, in decisions affecting issues as important as fiscal policy, the public should be involved.

11

Municipal Activities

Classifying Goods and Services

The services performed by Alberta municipalities range from planning to garbage removal and disposal. Occasionally the public and its elected representatives ask why a municipality should be responsible for financing and administering certain activities. Whether or not the government should be regulating the production and distribution of goods and services in the private sector, and if so, to what extent, is also debated at all levels of government. Conflict and confusion may be reduced if goods and services are classified as those which are best provided by the private sector, those which are best provided by government, and those which are best provided jointly by the two.[1]

It also should be emphasized that entrepreneurial governments increasingly separate the making of policy decisions, which Osborne and Gaebler characterize as steering, from service delivery, which they characterize as rowing. They write that while steering organizations formulate policy, provide funding for operational organizations, and evaluate performance, they "seldom play an operational role themselves." As a consequence, they are able to cut across traditional bureaucratic boundaries in order to obtain the best that is offered in the public sector as well as make use of the most innovative and efficient operational organizations in both the private and public sectors.[2]

Goods and services best provided by the private sector are those that are available from several suppliers who control their distribution with a pricing mechanism. An economist would say they can be easily "excluded" or denied to people who do not meet the supplier's conditions. Examples are dry cleaning and automobile repair, services which are offered competitively to the public on an individual basis by several suppliers. Although such services are provided by the private sector, many people expect a modicum of government regulation to ensure adequate standards are met so the public will not be overcharged or harmed as a result of shoddy products or services.

Economists designate other goods and services as "collective," for their nature is such that it is extremely difficult to prevent people who are unwilling to pay for them from enjoying their use and benefits. For this reason, it is the government which produces and distributes collective goods and services. One example is the protection provided by the police officer who patrols a neighbourhood. Individuals who stroll and shop in the area benefit equally whether they pay for the patrol service or not. In other words, a service such as police protection is not divisible, so that individuals can be charged for it; it affects everyone in the community. Another example is the prevention of air and water pollution; businesses and industry are closely monitored by government agencies and violators of environmental laws are prosecuted. People who live or work in the region enjoy clean air and water whether or not they contribute directly to the costs of monitoring and enforcement. Since few people volunteer to pay for their fair share of collective goods and services, they are usually financed by governments from general revenue.

Few goods and services are purely collective, although there are a number, such as playgrounds, libraries, sidewalks, and roadways, that most citizens agree should be provided by the government. Although in theory it would be possible to prevent persons who fail to pay from using them, such a policy would be politically unwise. Another reason many of these activities are carried out by the public sector is by default; the private sector has not been able to devise a way to provide them at a profit.

Some goods and services which do not have collective characteristics, but were once generally considered public functions, have now been converted into private functions or sold by governments to individuals. Free public parking areas have been leased to private operators who charge motorists for their use. The conversion of free recreational and cultural programs to "user-pay" activities is particularly controversial. A seminal article by urban economist Wilbur Thompson puts the issue into perspective.

> . . . we must recall that it is the middle- and upper-income classes who typically visit museums, so that free admission becomes, in effect, redistribution toward greater inequality, to the extent that the lower-income nonusers pay local taxes (e.g., property taxes directly or indirectly through rent, local sales taxes). . . . No, I would not put turnstiles

in the playgrounds in poor neighborhoods, rather it is only because we do put turnstiles at the entrances to the playgrounds for the middle- and upper-income groups that we will be able to afford playgrounds for the poor.[3]

Echoing a similar sentiment, an Edmonton alderman recently said, "I'm all in favor of the concept of user-pay, but on the other hand you have to be careful you don't interfere with people's enjoyment of life because of their circumstances."[4]

Goods and services such as those provided by transit, power, water, and telephone systems are the most problematic, since they can be produced and distributed by the public or the private sector. By their very nature there is only one producer and distributor for them in a region, that is, they have monopoly characteristics. In each of these cases it would be wasteful and uneconomical to have more than one system serving a geographic area, therefore the goods and services are provided either by the public sector or by a single private-sector company which is given an exclusive franchise by government.

The service functions operated as municipal monopolies are often characterized as inefficient or dominated by politicized bureaucracies. In fact, as was noted in Chapter 5 on governmental reorganization, municipalities in a region often compete with one another in both the production and the sale of municipal services. Moreover, many of these services do have private sector competitors. Private schools compete for students with public institutions; private waste management companies compete with municipal sanitation departments; and private security companies compete with police departments to provide law enforcement services.

Fire Protection

From the turn of the century until the Second World War, fires were fought using the same techniques with basically the same type of equipment. During the war, the military devised new methods to extinguish aircraft fires quickly; shortly thereafter they were adopted by municipal fire departments, but few changes have occurred since then.[5]

Firefighting is only one of the many activities of a modern fire department. A vigorous inspection of buildings for fire code violations can reduce the incidence of fires as well as sensitize building owners and business managers to the importance of fire prevention. A well-planned school and workplace educational program can reduce considerably the annual cost of fires but, unfortunately, when budgets must be cut, the fire department's education program is often one of the first to be axed. Finally, fire departments must investigate the cause of every fire and file a report with the Provincial Fire Commissioner.[6] A well-trained investigation team is a deterrent to those who plan to profit from arson.

Despite the importance of fire protection, the Municipal Government Act does not require a municipality to have a fire department or even to adopt the National Fire Code of Canada. All of Alberta's large municipalities and most smaller ones have fire departments, and a number of other municipalities contract for fire services with an adjoining community, although this practice is considered to be less than ideal.[7] Edmonton and Calgary have modern state-of-the-art fire departments, as do several medium-sized and smaller communities in which councils give fire protection a priority. This tends to be the exception rather than the rule, however, since fire departments have generally been among those most affected by budget cuts, particularly in the 1980s.

In the early spring of 1983, in a political scenario reminiscent of the early 1930s, Edmonton laid off 87 firefighters as part of a program to limit property tax increases. Calgary's cost-cutting measures, while less dramatic, alarmed many people. Several smaller municipalities also adopted tight-fisted policies. In 1988 the Grimshaw town council gutted the fire department's proposed budget and cut the honorarium for fire chief from $2,000 to $1,200 and deputy chief from $1,000 to $750. Councillor Daryl Ferguson explained, "We don't want a full-time Fire Chief, we can't afford it."[8] The same year in the Village of Ryley the fire chief resigned after council frustrated his every attempt to upgrade the department. Council was unwilling to support the cost of cardio-pulmonary resuscitation training for firefighters, to purchase oxygen tanks for the department, or to install a fire alarm in the community hall.

It has been difficult to evaluate the effectiveness of fire protection programs because until recently there has been little work in this area, and that almost solely in an American context. This situation has changed. Current research in Canada includes that of James McDavid, who examined data from 104 fire departments across Canada in a comparative study of the costs and performance of departments staffed with full-time firefighters, those staffed with both full-time and part-time firefighters, and those employing only part-time workers. He shows that fire departments staffed with full-time employees are more effective but are considerably more expensive than ones staffed by part-time employees, since part-time departments have longer response times for residential fires and increased fire losses. He concludes that communities under 50,000 with a mix of full- and part-time employees "have reason to keep them. Having a core of full-time fire fighters ensures that response times are adequate, while allowing for the necessary additional manpower to come from the ranks of the part-time fire fighters."[9]

Water and Sewage

In small communities with dispersed populations, each family provides for its own water supply and sewage disposal with a well and a septic tank. As the population becomes more concentrated, however, the close proximity of wells and septic tanks begins to constitute a serious health hazard.[10] The provincial government therefore has established mandatory safety standards for municipalities. Water delivery and sewage disposal systems are exceedingly expensive; without provincial assistance the average municipality would be unable to operate them unless it placed an unbearable burden on its ratepayers. Alberta Environment, through its Water Supply and Sewage Treatment Grant Program and Regional Water and Sewage Grant Program, funds up to 90 percent of the costs of water and sewage plants on the basis of per capita grants ranging from $250 to $2,100. The municipal share is normally raised through long-term debentures repaid by the users through service and user fees, and the cost of the water and sewer hookup from the street to the house is borne by each homeowner.

Edmonton and Calgary have some of the highest charges for water and sewage in Canada. A 1988 study conducted by Edmonton's Strategic Planning Branch found that an average single-family dwelling in the city was charged $21.15 for water and $11.90 for sewer service each month. The costs for a Calgary residence were almost the same, $18.30 for water and $12.92 for sewer service, but they dropped sharply for the services in Red Deer, Medicine Hat, and Lethbridge. Medicine Hat charged its householders the least, with an average monthly water charge of $6.30 and an average sewer charge of $9.70.

Smaller municipalities often contract for water with larger ones; 17 communities near Edmonton purchase their water from the city. Although less common than in the past, many private companies also supply water to municipalities. As an example, in 1991 Canadian Utilities Ltd. announced that it had agreed in principle to a $10 million water distribution scheme to supply 6,000 people living east of Edmonton. If the venture is financially successful the company intends to develop similar systems throughout rural Alberta.[11]

Two particularly important water policy issues are pricing and usage, which theoretically should be inversely related. But in some Alberta communities the price of water is lowest per unit for the heaviest users and highest for the lightest users. As Bird and Slack point out, in such a situation the smaller user subsidizes the larger one.[12] In Calgary, 80 percent of the water users are unmetered; residents are charged what amounts to a flat rate for water regardless of how much they use.[13] In effect, low-income homeowners with postage-stamp lawns subsidize Mount Royal homeowners who keep their extensive properties lush and green throughout the summer. Plebiscites that offered voters an opportunity to abolish the flat-rate system were defeated in Calgary by five to one in 1959, four to one in 1966, and again in 1989, although the defeat was less lopsided than in the past. Similarly, in a 1966 plebiscite in Medicine Hat only 21 percent of the voters favoured water meters.

The amount of support for a policy of unmetered water is particularly surprising at a time when people are beginning to realize how wasteful and costly unmetered water can be.[14] For example, the per capita consumption of water declined by 22 percent when meters were installed in Redcliff in 1981 and in Medicine Hat in 1986 it was estimated that the 40 percent of the homes that were unmetered used 60 percent of the city's water.

Although many people are not concerned about pricing and usage, almost everyone worries about the purity of the water they drink. Since one community's cleansed waste water is another community's water supply, there is continuing controversy over the adequacy of water treatment and the taste and smell of waters in the province's large rivers. The Bow River southeast of Calgary, the South Saskatchewan River east and west of Medicine Hat, the Oldman River east of Lethbridge, the Red Deer River east of Red Deer, and the North Saskatchewan River east of Edmonton, all of which are used for recreation and provide drinking water for smaller communities, have been considered heavily polluted.[15]

Edmonton and Calgary are criticized not only by their downstream neighbours but also by their own residents. Citizens have been frustrated by mayors and councils that have been unwilling to make bold policy commitments and provide necessary funds to rectify poorly designed and deteriorating water systems.

Calgary has the dubious distinction of being the only city in Canada that allows the discharge of storm sewer water directly into a major drinking water reservoir; more than 20 storm sewers carrying street run-off flow directly into the Glenmore Reservoir. In 1988 Mayor Ralph Klein attempted to allay citizens' concerns by telling them that contaminants coming from upstream in the Bow and Elbow rivers were far more threatening to the water supply than contaminants flowing from the city into the reservoir. More to the point, he said the city did not have $60 million to construct a storm sewer diversion.[16] In Edmonton the intake for the city's water supply is downstream from 85 storm sewers that empty into the North Saskatchewan River. As the city grew, each spring thaw produced increasingly foul-smelling and vile-tasting drinking water. In 1986 a study commissioned by the city recommended that the intakes for the water system be moved upstream from the storm sewer outlets. The council repeatedly delayed the project, which was estimated to cost $96.7 million. By 1989 the furore over Edmonton's water quality had begun to diminish when it was rekindled by Klein in his new position as Minister of the Environment. He warned the city administration that it could no longer allow raw sewage to run into the river during heavy rainstorms, when the city's sewage plant was unable to process all of the effluents. Mayor Terry Cavanagh justified the city's policy by saying it had been in effect for 60 years and that it would be much too costly to reconstruct the sewer system. But the public was not placated; after a change in leadership in 1989 the council grappled in earnest with the city's water problem and decided to move the intake for its water supply upstream from the storm sewer outlets.

Edmonton and Calgary are not the only communities plagued by questionable water systems. As more pulp and paper mills are constructed in northern Alberta the rivers will become increasingly polluted. Pulp mills using large amounts of water discharge their effluents directly into rivers which are the source of municipal water supplies. Fort McMurray draws its water from the Athabasca River, with a number of pulp mills located upstream, and the Town of Peace River is dependent on the Peace for water which is shared with a large pulp mill.

Fluoridation

The most divisive issue faced by municipal councils in most Alberta communities has been the fluoridation of water, a measure instituted to protect children's teeth from decay. During the late 1950s and early 1960s fluoridation was the single most important political issue in many municipalities, with neither its proponents nor opponents willing to negotiate on the issue. Communities were deeply divided and neighbours become life-long enemies. Fortunately, municipal councils had an "escape hatch" in the provincial Public Health Act, which made it mandatory that a plebiscite be held after a council passed a fluoridation bylaw.[17] Unless a majority voting on the plebiscite supported the bylaw, it would be nullified. Almost invariably, however, whenever a plebiscite lost, the proponents of fluoridation called for another plebiscite which, under the Public Health Act, could be held in two years. According to Harlan Hahn, a political scientist who examined the voting behaviour of 168 Canadian communities that held referendums on fluoridation between 1955 and 1965:

> The question of fluoridation . . . seemed to offer a prime example of referendums that may provoke an outburst of immediate protest. In the first referendum, a relatively high rate of turnout usually was associated with a minority vote in support of the issue. By the time of the second referendum, however, voter concern and antagonism apparently had ebbed sufficiently to yield a smaller turnout that provided an average majority in favour of fluoridation. . . .[18]

Although it may have been true of other Canadian municipalities, Hahn's analysis does not accurately describe the situation in Alberta, where the fluoridation issue was so emotional that many communities remained deeply divided over a long period of time.

Edmonton plebiscites on fluoridation were defeated in 1957, 1959, 1961, and 1964. The issue finally passed in 1966 and fluoridation equipment was installed the following year. Although it took them 20 years longer, proponents of fluoridation in Calgary were equally tenacious. Votes held in 1957, 1961, 1966, and 1971 all were defeated, but after a group of high school students wrote to council calling for another plebiscite, the issue was put on the 1989 municipal election ballot and fluoridation was approved by the voters.

The reason this seemingly innocuous issue rocks communities is that it has ideological overtones. Antifluoridation forces in Alberta in the 1950s and 1960s brought in speakers from the United States, many of whom were ultraconservatives who maintained that fluoridation was a communist plot to subvert North America. Specifically, they argued that fluoridation is harmful to the nervous system and leads to memory loss, and that distributing it through the water supply would slowly diminish the citizens' will to resist the communist menace.[19] Both sides marshalled evidence to show that fluoridation was either a deadly poison, causing cancer and chromosome damage, or a completely safe chemical that, in minute amounts, did nothing more than prevent tooth decay. In the early campaigns the antifluoridationists won most of the battles, with only Fairview and Red Deer fluoridating their water in 1958 and Devon and Grande Prairie in 1959. But as ultraconservatives began to lose their credibility in the 1960s, an additional 26 municipalities opted for fluoridation.[20]

In the 1970s there was a decided change in the composition and tactics of the antifluoridation movement. Although the movement still had a conservative orientation, the communist conspiracy theory was quietly dropped and replaced by accusations that the North American medical and dental establishments were committed to dosing the populace with an unsafe chemical. Antifluoridation campaigns were led by proponents of holistic medicine and health food stores playing on people's fears and prejudices. Nevertheless, in the 1970s an additional 21 municipalities began to fluoridate,[21] and by 1989, 57 Alberta municipalities had fluoridated water.

In 1986 and 1987 a spirited battle in occurred in Camrose, where the electorate supported fluoridation by a margin of two to one in the October 1986 election. The opponents, angry that the Alberta East Central Health Unit had funded a full-page community newspaper ad supporting fluoridation and orchestrated a "get out the vote" campaign, refused to accept the electorate's decision and continued their fight. Particularly galling to them was the health unit's unrepentant director, who justified her unit's actions during the plebiscite campaign by saying they clearly fell within her authority. A letter-writing campaign to the *Camrose Canadian* and the packing of city hall chambers well into the summer of 1987 failed to persuade council to cancel the plebiscite's mandate. The opponents were apprised that another plebiscite could be held two years from the previous one.

The 1989 Calgary plebiscite ratifying fluoridation also was stormy. The opposition's principal organizer and strategist was Ross Brown, an activist in the four previous plebiscites, who remained aggressively on the offensive.[22] Brown and his Calgary Safe Water Association charged that aluminum companies orchestrated the fluoride campaign to create a market for their sodium fluoride byproducts and maintained that studies suggested fluorides might contribute to heart disease, cancer, osteoarthritis, and colitis. The city's health food outlets were recruited to distribute antifluoridation brochures and a long-time opponent of fluoridation, California holistic physician Dr. John Lee, was brought to the city to counter the testimony of innumerable medical authorities on the safety and benefits of fluoridation programs. When it became apparent that the electorate would support fluoridation, its opponents frantically began to write letters and appeal to city hall politicians, all to no avail.

Calgary's antifluoridation forces were unwilling to accept the electorate's 1989 decision and began to organize to force yet another plebiscite on the issue. The Health Action Network Society (HANS) composed of health food crusaders and political libertarians who do not believe the government should be involved in mass fluoridation of the water supply collected thousands of signatures on a petition calling for a plebiscite on the issue and on another petition calling for public meetings to discuss its pros and cons.

More than 70 percent of the province's population now drinks fluoridated water, but even after more than 30 years fluoridation still has the potential to become a highly charged ideological and emotional issue rather than simply being evaluated on the basis of its costs and benefits.

Garbage Collection and Disposal: Not in My Back Yard (NIMBY)

"Solid waste management," the euphemistic term for garbage collection and disposal, presents few difficulties in rural areas where farmers have traditionally dug their own refuse pits. It becomes a problem when population density increases to the point where private garbage dumps are not feasible. Before Edmonton implemented a recycling program and began to consider market forces in pricing garbage collection the amount of waste produced each year was staggering; at its peak, in 1980, the city disposed of 1.4 million tonnes of garbage.[23]

Some of the most contentious politics to be found in Alberta municipalities are generated by policies on garbage collection and disposal.[24] Virtually every municipal councillor and responsible citizen in the community supports recycling and environmentally safe and adequate garbage transfer stations and dumps, but nobody wants a recycling centre, a transfer station, or a garbage dump in his or her neighbourhood. As a consequence, many municipalities have begun to examine the "Vancouver solution." Vancouver has a contract with a private company which trucks the city's nonrecyclable garbage to a landfill in Cache Creek, located some 225 kilometres northeast. Although the Vancouver solution is expensive, it is politically feasible. Canadian Pacific Rail has announced that it is prepared to transport municipal solid waste by rail to distant landfill sites to resolve the NIMBY problem.[25] Although no Alberta municipality has availed itself of this service, Edmonton has investigated the possibility of moving the city's garbage by train to abandoned coal pits adjacent to the Genesee power plant 90 kilometres west of the city. The idea was abandoned when it was found the coal pits were not environmentally safe for garbage.

Perhaps more than any other Alberta municipality, Edmonton has been plagued by the NIMBY syndrome. When it was predicted in 1981 that the city's Clover Bar dump would be filled by 1986, a two-year study costing $400,000 was commissioned to locate another dump site. Twelve sites were recommended, two within the city's boundaries, five in the County of Strathcona, and five in other surrounding municipalities. Shortly thereafter the administration began holding public hearings both in and outside of the city. After acreage owners angrily protested at the meetings, rural politicians said that Edmonton would not be permitted to dump garbage in their municipalities. The administration was forced to choose a site in Edmonton. When the preferred site was rumoured to be adjacent to Mill Woods in southeast Edmonton, a Mill Woods Anti-Dump Action Committee was organized and threatened political reprisal in the upcoming municipal election. Council backed down and struck the Mill Woods site from its list. Almost in desperation, the council decided in 1983 to locate the new dump at Kelties Farms in Clover Bar (northeast Edmonton), even though the location was not recommended in the original consultants' report. After 10,000 residents of the adjoining community of Clareview signed a petition objecting to the location of the new site, council again backed down. Shortly after Laurence Decore was elected major in 1983 discussions were held with the area's mayors and reeves about the feasibility of a regional dump. In March 1984 Edmonton, the County of Strathcona, and the City of Fort Saskatchewan agreed to conduct a two-year study to find a suitable regional dump site.[26] Although their 1986 report identified five possible locations, it favoured a site in northeast Edmonton. But after the northeast residents again objected, Mayor Decore focused his attention on an alternative site located in a remote area of Lamont County northeast of Edmonton. Although it would be costly to truck garbage 90 kilometres it was politically ideal, since the administration would not have to deal with the NIMBY syndrome. In 1987 an agreement was reached in secret negotiations between the city and Lamont politicians, but when Lamont's citizens learned about it they angrily confronted their representatives, who backed out of the deal.

One of the side effects of the economic downturn was a substantial reduction in the amount of garbage generated by the City of Edmonton each year. As a consequence, the life of the Clover Bar dump was extended first to 1989 and later to 1992, which allowed the city more time to develop another facility. After the Lamont agreement collapsed, the city's Water and Sanitation Department was given until early spring to locate a dump site. Of the nine sites it recommended, one in Aurum was the most desirable politically, since council would not have to contend with a

NIMBY argument, but it had a price tag of $8.5 million. Moreover, the site was the least acceptable environmentally, since it had porous soil and abutted the North Saskatchewan River, and thus had the potential to contaminate both the area's groundwater and the river. The city administration assured council that the groundwater problem could be solved with a $1.6 million plastic liner and council elected to develop the Aurum site. However, it encountered a number of unanticipated obstacles. Strathcona residents, living just three kilometres from the dump site, organized to fight the decision. Mayors of three downstream Saskatchewan cities expressed concern that the dump would pollute the North Saskatchewan River, from which their communities drew drinking water, and several environmental experts said they were shocked by the city's choice. Minister of the Environment Ralph Klein expressed serious reservations to Mayor Jan Reimer in November 1989.[27] One month later the Edmonton Board of Health rejected the application to develop the dump, citing a number of environmental issues the city had not addressed. On the advice of the head of its waste management branch, the city decided to appeal the decision. At the same time, Mayor Reimer called on Edmontonians to cut down on their waste. Shortly thereafter the comprehensive Blue Box recycling program was put into operation, reducing the amount of garbage that was being generated in the city. To council's chagrin, in October 1990 the Board of Health again rejected its application.

After the Aurum dump was lost, Mayor Jan Reimer met with various elected officials to develop plans for a new dump, implement a fee structure to extend the Clover Bar dump, and arrange for the use of private dump sites. But Reimer was frustrated by the city administration's "preferred site" tunnel vision, which seemed to inhibit the development of an aggressive recycling campaign. She said, "There has been this love affair with Aurum. All the attention has been on trying to get Aurum approved and a great deal of resources spent on trying to prop it up."[28]

The Minister of Municipal Affairs and the Minister of the Environment next established a loosely organized committee comprising representatives from Edmonton, surrounding counties, and nine outlying municipalities in order to develop a regional dump site which would be used by everyone. After more than a year of closed-door meetings, the committee of regional politicians announced in November 1991 that it had identified three possible locations: two were in Edmonton and the other bordered Elk Island National Park. The cooperative approach unraveled a month later when outlying municipalities opted out of a regional solution. In early 1992 the city's administration began a preliminary evaluation of the two Edmonton sites. This caused a political furore and split the city council; representatives of both areas were adamant that a dump would not be located in their ward. Council attempted to resolve the garbage crisis before it became a major issue in the upcoming fall election. In late February the city's public works manager announced that the life of the Clover Bar site could be extended until 1998 by raising the level of the dump only one metre. The manager claimed that the city's recycling program was so successful that a much smaller landfill site would suffice. Thus a solution was found to the NIMBY problem by postponing it for at least two council terms.

The NIMBY factor is as important in small communities as it is in large ones. For example, in August 1988 Newalta Energy announced in the *Morinville Gazette* that it planned to establish in the town a transfer station, where refuse would be sorted and transferred from one type of carrier to another. Newalta scheduled a public meeting. After residents learned that the transfer station would handle highly toxic oil-field waste materials, they were livid, although several councillors initially supported the station because it would bring money into the community. In a town with a population of 5,000, more than 1,300 appeals against the proposal were filed with the Development Appeal Board (DAB). Equally important, several large demonstrations claimed that the transfer station was a public health risk that would result in decreased land values in the community. After three days of debate the DAB voted not to allow the transfer station in the town.

Other grass-roots political battles have occurred when politicians negotiate agreements for garbage collection and disposal without taking into consideration the views of the community in general or their constituents in particular. In 1982 the towns of High River and Okotoks and the Municipal District of Foothills, in conjunction with Alberta Environment, located a regional garbage dump in a sparsely populated area northwest of High River. Although the small number of rural residents affected were unable to change the dump's location, they succeeded in delaying its operation several times. In 1988 a similar controversy erupted in Water Valley, a hamlet 80 kilometres northwest of Calgary. When the Town of Olds negotiated with the County of Mountain View to ship its garbage to a dump site less than 300 metres from the Water Valley subdivision, residents took matters into their own hands. After they padlocked and strung barbed wire across the dump's gates and dug a trench in front of them, the Town of Olds decided not to use the dump; it had become too controversial.

As Alberta has become increasingly industrialized, the provincial government has become concerned about the disposal of both residential and industrial waste. The Reclamation Program for Derelict Land and the Alberta Solid Waste Management Assistance Programs provide 100 percent funding to assist municipalities with waste disposal. The derelict land program funds the reclamation of abandoned garbage dumps and sewage lagoons, while the waste management assistance program supports the purchase of sanitary landfill sites.

In order to resolve the problems of ever-increasing amounts of garbage and the NIMBY factor, municipalities, at the urging of the province, are beginning to explore the advantages of regional garbage dumps even though transportation expenses increase the cost of garbage disposal several hundred percent. One of the most innovative programs is funded jointly by the province, the towns of Innisfail, Bowden, and Penhold, and the County of Red Deer. Under the Central Alberta Waste Management Authority, solid wastes are compacted at five transfer stations and transported to the authority's dump site.

In Alberta's larger municipalities garbage collection and disposal are almost always classified as public activities. But a closer examination reveals that while residential garbage is collected by the municipality, commercial refuse tends to be collected by independent firms who dispose of it in private dumps. A study of 126 Canadian cities by University of Victoria researcher James McDavid found that in the early 1980s the yearly cost was $42.29 per household when garbage was collected exclusively by municipal employees, $32.31 when it was collected jointly by the municipality and private firms, and $28.02 when it was collected exclusively by private contractors.[29] After the study was publicized many people asked if there were any valid reasons why garbage collection should not be turned over to the private sector. A subsequent study by McDavid led to a surprising conclusion. When a municipality which employed a private firm to pick up residential waste was compared with an adjoining municipality which used public employees and had excellent union-management relations, the cost was lower for municipal collection. McDavid concludes that ". . . unionized employees can be responsive to changes in a municipality's environment and are willing to cooperate with management in mutually beneficial efforts to increase service efficiency."[30] Therefore, it cannot be said definitively that either privatisation or public collection of garbage costs the least; a number of factors must be examined on a case-by-case basis before one can determine which system is preferable for a given community.

Housing

Chapter 3 showed that since the end of the Second World War the federal and provincial governments have worked closely to formulate housing policy. According to Bettison, Kenward, and Taylor, "The Alberta Housing Act of 1952 . . . was as much related to the amendments of the NHA [National Housing Act] in Ottawa as it was to provincial need."[31] Initially, the act created the machinery for municipalities to acquire land and to construct low-cost housing for sale or rent. The act was amended in 1965 to allow municipalities to participate in a federally funded urban renewal program.[32]

In the late 1960s, with Alberta municipalities among the fastest grow-ing in Canada, serviced land and housing became increasingly scarce. Two factors were involved: housing could not be built fast enough to keep up with demand and, particularly in Edmonton and Calgary, a small number of companies held a virtual monopoly on outlying development lands and were able to manipulate prices.[33] Edmonton and Calgary housing costs escalated so quickly that many working- and middle-class families were priced out of the market. Housing crises had occurred before, but this one was particularly acute given the unabated population growth in almost all of Alberta's larger municipalities.

For a number of years Red Deer had a policy of purchasing undevel-oped land, holding it until there was a demand for it, and then selling it on the open market in direct competition with private developers. This policy of "public land banking," which was to break the monopoly of pri-vate developers, held down the price of serviced land and turned a tidy profit for the city. Between 1958 and 1972, the city purchased 303 hectares (750 acres) for $1.3 million, serviced this land for $3.7 million, and then sold it for $9 million. By 1982 Red Deer had a land inventory worth $50 million that had cost $19 million.

In 1967 the government created the Alberta Housing and Urban Renewal Corporation, renamed the Alberta Housing Corporation (AHC) in 1970. Perhaps encouraged by Red Deer's success, in 1968 the provincial government established a program administered by the AHC to assist municipal land banking. The AHC acquired land for residential develop-ment which a municipality could buy by paying the original cost plus holding costs. A municipality was eligible to participate in the program if: (1) a private sector monopoly was charging exorbitant prices for serviced land; (2) a private sector did not have the expertise or finances to pursue private land development; (3) the municipality was unable to acquire land because of inadequate finances or other technical inadequacies;

(4) additional growth in the municipality would further "the Province's balanced industrial growth program"; and (5) residential development was needed to relieve the "demands being placed on large urban centers."[34]

The AHC had the authority to acquire land without notifying the pertinent municipality. For example, in 1979 the province began to purchase 2,828 hectares (7,000 acres) of land northeast of Edmonton, between Namao and Fort Saskatchewan. Edmonton was unaware of the AHC's activities until June 1981, when the province notified the city. Meanwhile, unknown to Calgary, the province acquired 4,040 hectares (10,000 acres) between its northern border and the Town of Airdrie. In most cases, however, the AHC acted in concert with the municipalities. In 1969 the province, through the Alberta Housing and Urban Renewal Corporation, purchased and assembled 1,965 hectares (4,864 acres) southeast of Edmonton. This land became the core of Mill Woods, which eventually encompassed 2,626 hectares (6,486 acres). Shortly thereafter the city acquired the land from the province and began to develop it. The first lots in the new Mill Woods subdivision were sold to the public in 1973. Although the city could not bring its lots onto the market fast enough to thwart large developers, the Mill Woods project is considered a success. By 1989 Mill Woods housed more than 70,000 people and land sales had added more than $175 million to the city's coffers.

Despite its successes, land banking was controversial in Alberta. When Edmonton marketed Mill Woods lots at prices slightly below market prices, a sporadic debate occurred in council over whether the city should be competing with the private sector and attempting to beat down its prices. In 1981 Grande Prairie's council was almost evenly split over continuation of the city's land banking policy. One councillor summed up the opposition when he stated, "I have always felt that land acquisition and development is better left to private enterprise."[35]

Two interrelated events affected land banking programs. First, the federal government's 1981 National Energy Policy stalled the province's phenomenal economic growth and, consequently, the escalation in municipal land prices. Moreover, when it seemed that investment in real estate was the route to economic success, many municipalities embarked on a policy of commercial real estate development. The Alberta Mortgage and Housing Corporation (AMHC, the successor to the AHC) funded the land banking and the municipality agreed to purchase the land at some time in the distant future.[36] Shortly thereafter, the province's commercial real estate market collapsed and a number of municipalities were committed to purchasing expensive commercial land for which there was no market. Although in 1983 the provincial government froze the interest charges on lands purchased under the AMHC agreements, much of the property which had been land-banked had a market value far below its loan value and as a consequence municipalities were not honouring their purchase commitments. Finally, in March 1990 the provincial government announced a program which would cost as much as $50 million to terminate its role in land banking.[37] Municipalities would be allowed to buy land for which they were obligated at the market price rather than the much higher purchase price and would have three years to pay. In other words, the provincial government "let the municipalities off the hook" by subsidizing their purchases.

Although land banking has been terminated, the province still provides municipalities with grants for the Senior Citizen Lodge Program, a rent supplement for low-income parents and senior citizens, and a Community Housing Program which allows municipalities to provide rental housing for low-and moderate-income families. Under the Senior Citizen Lodge Program the AMHC provides capital financing for senior citizen housing as well a grant for up to 50 percent of an operating deficit to senior citizen foundations which oversee lodges. The Rent Supplement Program is designed to provide low-income people with adequate housing while at the same time limiting their rent to 25 percent of their income. The amount of the difference between the 25 percent of income and the market rent is subsidized by the federal and provincial governments, with the federal government paying 70 percent of the share and the provincial government 30 percent. The Community Housing Program provides the capital financing for rental housing. Canada Mortgage and Housing Corporation subsidizes up to 70 percent of a local housing authority's annual operating deficit and the remaining 30 percent is shared by the AMHC and Alberta municipalities.

Although the cost of housing is usually the most contentious, other housing issues may divide a municipality. In 1972 Calgary and Edmonton adopted a policy of dispersing subsidized housing projects throughout the community to avoid creating an inner-city ghetto. Since developers were required to dedicate 5 percent of the land in new subdivisions to public housing, many projects were located in new developments. In several instances, residents objected to the dispersal policy. A well-organized and articulate group from one of Edmonton's more exclusive subdivisions, Wolf Willow, persuaded the city and the Alberta Housing Authority (which was to finance the project) not to locate public housing in their neighbourhood.

Transportation

Contemporary Alberta is dependent on the automobile. Tens of millions of dollars are spent yearly by the provincial and municipal governments to build and maintain streets and highways. Simultaneously, municipal property tax bases are reduced as more and more "paved land" is taken off the tax rolls. Municipal councils and downtown businesspeople in larger cities curse the automobile for draining the middle class out to the suburbs. Smaller municipalities view the province's outstanding roadway system as a mixed blessing. On the one hand, it allows their residents the same access to cultural, medical, and educational facilities as the residents of larger communities; on the other, it gives people the mobility to spend their dollars in communities other than their own. In short, the automobile allows the large city to decentralize and expand but decentralization increases the number of people living in low-density suburbs in which the automobile is the most convenient mode of transportation.

For more than 20 years the province and municipal governments have been criticized for funding automobile transportation at the expense of other modes. In 1963, with its Metropolitan Transportation Study (METS), Edmonton embarked on a 25-year plan to develop a comprehensive freeway system. In the same year, the Calgary Transportation Study (CALTS) proposed an equally elaborate network of roadways. However, escalating gasoline prices, a concern that freeways would carve up neighbourhoods, and new policies to revitalize the core city and curb low-density suburban development led eventually to major changes in transportation policy in both cities. Hoping to avoid the automobile gridlock found in many American cities they planned the construction of Light Rail Transit (LRT) systems.[38]

In the early stages of the Edmonton LRT system council spent little time studying transportation needs, usage, or costs, since it felt it had to move quickly on public transportation in order to sidetrack any additional freeway plans.[39] Using an existing railroad right-of-way, the city constructed the first leg of the system, a 7.25 kilometre northeast line, for $64 million.[40] Although capital and operating costs began to increase, the system's usage remained relatively constant. A 1979 evaluation found that LRT "has not attracted a noticeable amount of new ridership [and] . . . patronage increases are due to residential growth rather than increased ridership from the established neighbourhoods."[41] In a 1991 study two University of Alberta Economists, John Kim and Douglas West, concluded that the city could operate a comprehensive public transportation system using buses at a fraction of the cost of an LRT system.[42] Despite

Kim and West's findings and the city's failure to carry out a comprehensive study of its transportation needs, the general manager of the city's transportation department is committed to expanding LRT rather than a comprehensive bus system, arguing that trains can carry four times as many passengers.[43]

During the 1980s council debated intermittently whether the LRT's southern leg should run along the Canadian Pacific right-of-way to Mill Woods or to the University of Alberta and then south. When it was finally decided to run the line to the university, another debate centred on whether the line from the university south should be above or below ground. People living along 114 Street convinced their MLA, Neil Crawford, that it should be below ground, and he promised to ask cabinet for $20 million to cover the additional costs. Crawford was not successful in his quest for the funds. In 1990 the city shifted its policy on the extension of the LRT system and began planning an extension to the more affluent west end rather than to the southeast and Mill Woods, which had been promised rail transit in the early 1970s. But when provincial grants began to diminish, the city decided early in 1992 that the LRT's southern terminus would be the University of Alberta. The "subway to nowhere," as even city hall has taken to calling it, is unlikely to be extended until the turn of the century.

Calgary embarked on a LRT system somewhat later than Edmonton after city planners convinced Mayor Rod Sykes of its merits. After a 20 kilometre southern leg was completed on schedule the city began construction of a northeast leg for which $218 million was budgeted. Because contractors made extremely low bids in order to hold their crews together during the recession and the project was carefully supervised, the final cost was $52 million below the estimate. The savings were used up quickly by council in its zeal to have the LRT in service to the Winter Olympics site. The construction on a 5.9 kilometre northwest leg began before the engineering work was completed and a number of cost overruns occurred.

Will the cities be able to absorb LRT operating deficits or will the province continue to provide grants for LRT operating costs? Is there any indication that population density in the two cities is increasing so that per capita transit operating expenses will stabilize? Until recently councils in Edmonton and Calgary had only educated "guesstimates" on transportation usage and fare elasticity. What is quite clear is that the overall transit usage in Edmonton and Calgary is quite low. Kim and West explain why the Edmonton LRT system will never generate the high ridership found on the Toronto and Montreal subway systems:

... the urban core of Toronto, which has a subway system, had a population density of 3671.02 per square km in 1986, almost twice that of Edmonton. Montreal, which also has a subway system, had a population density of 5643.57 per square km in its urban core, not quite three times that of Edmonton. There are also 158 census tracts in Montreal and 63 census tracts in Toronto that have population densities in excess of 10,000 people per square km, whereas there are no such census tracts in Edmonton and little likelihood of high density development in the near future.[44]

The LRT systems in both communities have not met the councils' ridership expectations, particularly in Edmonton. In 1991 approximately 120,000 people used the Calgary system daily, compared to 24,000 in Edmonton.[45] Edmonton bus ridership figures have been nearly as dismal: between 1980 and 1989 yearly usage had dropped from 51 million to 41.5 million riders, in contrast to between 46 and 47 million in Calgary.

Both Edmonton and Calgary depend on the provincial government to subsidize public transit operating costs heavily. Table 11.1 shows the aggregate amount cities in the province received in Public Transit Operating Grants between 1979 and 1989. Since the grant is set at $11.10 per capita, as the largest cities Edmonton and Calgary receive most of the funds.[46] Although early in the decade the government increased its grant each year approximately the same percentage as inflation, in 1984 this policy was abandoned. As a consequence, municipalities have had to place heavier demands on their ratepayers just to keep transportation spending even with increases in the cost of living.

Edmonton and Calgary also receive substantial grants from the Alberta Cities Transportation Partnership Program. At a cost of $500 million, the three-year program to "assist all Alberta cities in the development of safe, integrated transportation systems" was put into place April 1, 1989, replacing the Public Transit Capital Assistance grant. The program was initiated with much fanfare on April 11, 1989, when the Minister of Transportation announced a $18.8 million grant for extending Calgary's LRT line. Eight days later he announced a similar $16.5 million grant for the extension of the Edmonton LRT, but early in 1991 Edmonton was told that since the three-year program was being extended for another year the city would not receive $12 million of the $43 million due under the Transportation Partnership Program until 1992.

Alberta's medium-sized cities also are debating the amount of funds which should be expended on bus transit. As more of a city's population shifts outward to suburbia and quarter-acre estates, the cost of servicing

Table 11.1 Amount of Transportation Grants to Urban Municipalities
and to Counties and Municipal Districts, 1979–1989

Year	Urban Transportation Grant (000)	County and Municipal District Transportation Grant (000)
1979/80	$112,322	$20,422
1980/81	$133,161	$20,954
1981/82	$155,508	$33,970
1982/83	$210,054	$35,168
1983/84	$165,678	$30,407
1984/85	$149,455	$25,424
1985/86	$153,121	$29,696
1986/87	$144,524	$34,129
1987/88	$169,871	$28,899
1988/89	$122,807	$27,789

these low-density areas becomes excessive and often service is not provided in the evenings and on weekends. However, well educated and vocal
suburbanites are among the most politically astute in the city and are very
successful in maintaining transit service in their areas. Another perennial
debate relates to fare structure; how much of transit's operating expense
should be borne by the city and how much by the user? Calgary recovers
approximately 52 percent of its operating costs from the fare box, while
Edmonton recovers only about 41 percent. Which policy is more equitable? People in different cities have different levels of sensitivity to fare
increases. In 1988 Edmonton's council raised transit fares and ridership
decreased even though the new fares were in the bottom quartile among
Canadian cities. In the winter of 1990 the city again raised transit fares.

Various groups have proposed high-speed rail service between Calgary
and Edmonton with an intermediate stop in Red Deer. In the fall of 1986
the Red Deer council submitted to the Minister of Economic Development a Red Deer College study which concluded that 50 percent of the
city's residents would use high-speed rail service.[47] Shortly thereafter the
minister released the "Report of the High Speed Rail Review Committee"
which he had commissioned in January. The committee recommended
that a high-speed rail line not be developed, since it was unlikely it could
generate enough traffic to be economically feasible and because of its high
capital costs.[48] Four years later the mayors of Calgary and Edmonton discussed a high-speed rail link between the two cities as part of a gamut to
make a joint bid for Expo 2005. However, there was no public announce-

ment as to how the cities would distribute the financial responsibility for the initial project, estimated at $1.3 billion, and annual expenses of approximately $30 million.

Smaller communities and rural areas, in which automobiles are the primary mode of transportation, work closely with the provincial Department of Transportation, regional planning commissions, and municipal planners to design and build roadways. Although these communities do not have to allocate finances between roads and public transit, they are not without contentious issues. In some communities policies on street lighting and parking have been particularly controversial and divisive; in others residents argue about which streets should be paved.

Although municipalities criticize the provincial government for underfunding transportation, there is a close working relationship with the province on transportation issues. Cooperation is necessary because responsibilities are intermeshed; the maintenance of secondary highways and local roads and streets is the responsibility of the municipality, while the province is responsible for all primary highways except those within cities.

In a November 1985 pre-election announcement, Minister of Transportation Marvin Moore told the delegates at the annual meeting of the Alberta Association of Municipal Districts and Counties that the government intended to pave every secondary road in Alberta within ten years. Some rural road oiling grant restrictions were dropped and there were small increases in the transportation grants for smaller and rural municipalities but little else occurred. In February 1989 the government again announced its intention to pave every secondary road in the province within ten years. At the same time it introduced a six-year, $75 million transportation grant program. Two hundred and eighty towns, villages, and summer villages were eligible for a base grant of $80,000 plus a $100 per capita grant for the first 1,000 population and a $10 per capita allowance increase for every 1,000 increase in population. The government would pay out of this grant 75 percent of roadway construction costs and 50 percent of engineering costs. In addition, communities were eligible for a base grant of $2,000 plus a $10 per capita grant for safety equipment such as pedestrian signals and traffic barriers. Assured of provincial funding, municipalities made long-range plans to develop their transportation systems. Two years later, when the province failed to balance its budget, a number of programs were cut back, including the transportation grant. Municipalities were forced to make substantial changes in transportation projects which were being developed with the expectation that they would be financed primarily by the province. Mayor Jan

Reimer was particularly upset because Edmonton had to revise its schedule for extending the LRT and to cut back on a number of major roadway
projects.[49] After an intensive lobbying effort by the city supported by
Edmonton MLAs, the province approved a rescheduling of the construction and a $9 million advance against grants slated for the city in 1994
and 1996.

Table 11.1 shows that from 1979 to 1989 rural municipalities received
transportation grants ranging from $20 to $35 million yearly. However, as
with grants to urban areas, the funding provided failed to keep up with
inflation after the mid-1980s.

Despite provincial commitment and municipal studies and plans
devoted to transportation problems, neither level of government has progressed beyond a conventional view of transportation. As just one example, it seems no serious thought has been given as to how taxicabs might
complement bus and LRT systems. Edmonton and Calgary's taxi commissions are primarily responsible for setting the fare structure and controlling the number of cabs on the street; they have little to do with transit
systems and transit planning. In 1988 Calgary's commission seemed to be
far more concerned with increasing the price of cab licenses and various
and sundry fees than working out ways to reduce taxi fares for consumers
dependent entirely on cabs for transportation. The policies of Edmonton's taxi commission were equally bizarre, since in 1990 fares were raised
to 89 cents a kilometre with a $22.50 per hour charge for waiting time.

Viewing transportation policy as distinct and separate from policies on
housing, industrial development, and downtown revitalization is another
example of conventional thinking. Very often such policies are put into
place with no appreciation of the transportation problems they would
generate. In all communities a thoughtful integration of industry, housing, and retailing in a number of geographic sectors would eliminate
many transportation problems.

Keillor Road Policy Making: Community Pitted against Community

Southwest Edmonton is the fastest growing area of the city and its rapid
rate of growth is predicted to continue throughout the 1990s. A battle
between neighbourhoods over traffic is a by-product of the residential
expansion which has outpaced the provision of adequate roadways and
public transportation for this area. One of the quicker routes downtown
was along scenic two-lane Keillor Road, which wound through a portion
of the river valley for two kilometres and joined two-lane Saskatchewan
Drive, with parkland on one side and attractive homes on the other. The
route ran less than six blocks along Saskatchewan Drive before it con-

nected with a four-lane thoroughfare to the city's core. Although Keillor Road was never designed for more than 5,000 vehicles a day, more than 11,000 were using the substandard road and Saskatchewan Drive. The alternative route to Keillor Road took substantially longer, as a portion of it ran along 114 Street, which is a major commuter route to the city centre and the University of Alberta.

The communities of Belgravia and McKernan on either side of 114 Street had been fighting a losing battle with the city for several years. As noted earlier, their MLA had attempted to obtain money to construct an underground LRT through their neighbourhood, but the city's transportation department never seriously considered anything but an above-ground LRT for the area.

For several years the middle- and upper-middle-class homeowners in the Saskatchewan Drive area on the western edge of Belgravia petitioned council to close Keillor Road in order to prevent thousands of cars from driving past their homes daily. The closure was opposed not only by the southwest residents who used the Keillor Road short-cut, but also by many 114 Street residents living only six blocks from Saskatchewan Drive, for it would divert additional traffic onto their street. After many meetings of the three groups of residents and council's public affairs committee an agreement was reached: 114 Street would be maintained as a four-lane roadway with an above-ground LRT line on its west side and Keillor Road would be closed to through traffic on weekends and in the evenings until the LRT extension reached the Southgate Shopping Centre after 1997, at which time Keillor Road would be permanently closed. When the issue came before council the two Ward 5 aldermen who represented the 114 Street and Saskatchewan Drive residents as well as the thousands of commuters in the southwestern part of the city opposed the closure of Keillor Road. They proposed instead amendments calling for a partial closure of Keillor Road only after work had been completed on 114 Street and a reconsideration of permanent closure after the LRT reached the shopping centre. Saskatchewan Drive residents had an ally in Jan Reimer, who in her campaign for mayor had said in a number of southside election forums that Keillor Road should be closed and the roadway turned back into parkland.

After Reimer's election the battle escalated when Saskatchewan Drive residents began to park their cars on both sides of the street to narrow the roadway and delay traffic. Angry motorists vented their frustrations by breaking windshields, blaring their horns at all hours, and throwing eggs and rocks.[50] The city responded by prohibiting parking on one side of Saskatchewan Drive and promising that the issue would soon be resolved.

As her constituents fought among themselves, Ward 5 alderman Lillian Staroszik attempted to defuse the situation by calling for an outside consultant to study the southside transportation jumble, but her proposal did not have council's support. In December council stitched together a compromise: Keillor Road would be closed in 1992 when 114 Street was widened to four lanes with an LRT right of way on the west side. However, the compromise did not address the problem of ever-increasing traffic in the future.

There are clear winners and losers in the Keillor Road controversy. Belgravia residents in the Saskatchewan Drive area have managed to maintain the serenity of their portion of the neighbourhood and the value of their property, although there will be a long period of bitterness with nearby 114 Street residents. The southwest commuters will have a longer commute but may have a six-lane roadway to alleviate some of the traffic congestion. The overall losers are the McKernan and Belgravia residents on either side of 114 Street. With a major traffic artery and the LRT bisecting it, in all likelihood the area will be rezoned to higher density with walk-up and high-rise apartments in the 1990s.[51]

Recreation, Culture, and Libraries

Almost every community has at least one publicly-supported recreation facility. While a small village's facilities may consist only of a community hall and an outdoor baseball diamond, larger municipalities have, in addition to the traditional public park, public swimming pools, lighted tennis courts, and curling rinks which are costly to build and maintain. As a result of the increased emphasis which health professionals and the public now place on physical fitness, athletic facilities are considered to be a key component in any health program and funding for recreation receives far more support today than it has in the past. In addition to building and maintaining facilities, municipalities often provide grants to community groups which promote leisure-time activities. In Fort McMurray, Little League Baseball, the Fort McMurray Youth Soccer Association, the Noralta Figure Skating Club, Midget Girls Volleyball, and the Labatt Slowpitch League all received small municipal grants in 1988. In at least one instance, Calgary funded a local chess tournament.

The Department of Culture and the Department of Recreation and Parks have actively promoted recreational and cultural facilities at the local level. Particularly important for municipalities is their joint Community Recreation/Cultural Grant Program which is designed to provide direct assistance to municipalities and to encourage them to cooperate with volunteer community organizations in planning and developing cultural programs.[52] The initial five-year program provides an annual $20 per capita grant which must be divided so that at least 50 percent of the funding is designated for programs run by community organizations and no more than 50 percent is allocated to the municipality.[53] A minimum of 25 percent of the grant is to be used for cultural purposes. A number of other specialized grant programs administered through the Department of Culture have been beneficial for smaller communities. One of the more successful of these has been the Historical Publications Assistance Program, which provides funds to enable a community to document its past, thus promoting a sense of civic pride.

Many local politicians and administrators are surprised by the conflict generated by library issues. On one side are people willing to sacrifice other municipal services in order to have a superior library; on the other are people who never use community library facilities or services.

During the latter half of the 1980s, when Edmonton was under severe fiscal constraints, the percentage increase of the city's budget was always higher than that of the library's budget. The year 1988 was particularly striking, with the city's budget increasing almost 4 percent while the library's budget increased just .67 percent. An examination of the last item in Table 11.2, "Library Budget as % of Total City Budget," also shows that compared to the budget as a whole (and implicitly compared to other items in the budget) the library's share of city funds was decreasing each year. By the fall of 1989 the library system had fallen into such a state of disrepair that the council found it necessary to approve an 8.8 percent funding increase for 1990 which, however, failed to compensate for a decade of neglect. The following year, Alderman Ken Kozak proposed that council resolve to lobby the province for legislation allowing municipal libraries to assess a user fee.[54] He calculated that a charge of 25 cents for each book borrowed would raise $900,000 a year and put the library back on a solid financial footing. His proposal, which was dubbed "a tax on literacy," attracted widespread media attention and public support for the beleaguered library system. After almost 12,000 people signed a petition opposing Kozak's resolution, the President of the Friends of the Edmonton Public Library said, "You get a real show of support and then you can tap into it. . . . it's a very fortunate thing for the library."[55]

Although the Calgary council approved a 9 percent budget increase for the city library system in the fall of 1988, the Library Board cut evening service and decided to charge patrons $5 for a library card and $5 for a

Table 11.2 Comparison of Edmonton's Operating Budget and the Edmonton City Library Operating Budget, 1985–1989

	1985	1986	1987	1988	1989
Edmonton Operating Budget (000)	$476,885	$511,307	$525,462	$545,562	$571,678
% Increase of Operating Budget over Previous Year		7.22%	2.77%	3.83%	4.79%
Edmonton Library Operating Budget (000)	$13,657	$14,235	$14,397	$14,494	$15,115
% Increase of Library Operating Budget over Previous Year		4.23%	1.14%	0.67%	4.28%
Library Budget as % of Total City Budget	2.86%	2.78%	2.74%	2.66%	2.64%

renewal after three years. A year later aldermen charged the library with poor judgement and the misallocation of funds. After four years without a budget increase, in the fall of 1988 the Stettler library presented the town and county councils with a deficit budget for 1989. Both councils refused to approve additional funding. In 1989 a town councillor told the Cold Lake Library Board, "We are being faced with requests for a fire truck, police barracks, recreation department development and now a new library within the next four years. The taxpayers can't afford it. Somewhere, somebodies [*sic*] got to give up a project or two."[56]

A number of cities, towns, and villages castigated the provincial government for its low level of library support. In 1989 the per capita grant for municipal libraries was $3.96; for regional libraries, $2.73; and for community libraries, $3.18. Table 11.3 shows that provincial funding increased dramatically in the early 1980s, then levelled off and began to decrease as the government attempted to balance its budget, often at the expense of municipal services.

Table 11.3 Provincial Grant Funding for Libraries, 1979–1989

Year	Funding (000)	Year	Funding (000)
1979/80	$2,863	1984/85	$9,806
1980/81	$6,579	1985/86	$10,545
1981/82	$7,692	1986/87	$12,126
1982/83	$9,387	1987/88	$10,953
1983/84	$9,731	1988/89	$10,531

Public Health and Welfare

In Alberta's early years municipalities were solely responsible for public health. The Provincial Board of Health established by the Public Health Act delegated its responsibilities to local boards of health that did everything from enforcing sanitation in slaughter and ice houses to requiring that roller towels be installed in public washrooms. A number of Alberta municipalities received funds from the American Carnegie and Rockefeller foundations to improve local public health standards. After the Second World War, in response to public demand for better health services, the provincial government initiated a cost-sharing program under which it funded 80 percent of local health board costs and the municipality paid 20 percent. Since January 1973 local health districts have received all of their funding from the provincial government.[57]

Although welfare, like health, was initially the responsibility of the municipalities, cost-shared programs were implemented in 1919 when the province helped municipalities provide assistance to widows. The desperate plight of municipalities during the "Dirty Thirties" clearly indicated that their fiscal resources were inadequate for supporting welfare programs. As just one example, J.G. MacGregor notes that with a population of 79,197 (approximately 18,000 families) in 1931, Edmonton had 14,573 people (2,601 families) on direct relief.[58]

After the Second World War large numbers of people were demanding better welfare programs than the municipalities could afford. Others argued that social services largely funded by municipal property taxes were not a legitimate charge against real property.[59] Responding to the demand for more and better social services, senior levels of government began to accept the responsibility for social welfare. Local governments did not resist this erosion of their power and autonomy; they were happy to be rid of the increasing financial burden. In 1965 the Union of Alberta

Municipalities asked the provincial government to assume all community welfare services.

In 1966 the Social Credit government took over child welfare services from the municipalities and initiated a unique, locally administered, preventive social service (PSS) program. The major goals of the government were to:

1. *Prevent Welfare:* To prevent people from becoming dependent on government programs of financial assistance.
2. *Prevent Marriage Breakdown:* To prevent separation and divorce, which were perceived as leading to dependence on government and to child welfare problems.
3. *Reduce Child Welfare Intake:* Soaring illegitimacy rates and a structural flaw in the child welfare program were flooding the province's child welfare system. PSS and associated reforms were intended to slow this influx.
4. *Promote General Social and Physical Well-Being:* Although its meaning was not specified, a general statement of this kind was presented in most public justifications of the new PSS program.[60]

Funded 80 percent by the province and 20 percent by participating local governments, the program allowed a municipality wide latitude in developing and administering its own preventive social service programs, although each program had to be approved by the province. In order to gain support and provide the greatest benefits at the lowest cost, the program was to be offered through private social agencies which would be funded by the municipality. The Social Credit government placed no upper spending limits on PSS programs.

Both large and small municipalities responded by developing such diverse programs as drop-in centres and job placement services for transients, home care programs for the elderly, day care centres for working-class and handicapped children, alcohol and drug counselling centres, support programs for children of single parents, and family planning clinics. Edmonton and Calgary almost immediately incorporated many existing agencies into the new PSS program. Initially, this practice meant savings, since they were paying for the same services with 20-cent dollars. Very shortly, however, the two cities initiated a number of new programs in areas covered by PSS. Smaller communities had the option of establishing a regional PSS program, and after some initial hesitation many rural communities developed cooperative social welfare services.

Table 11.4 **Provincial Grant Funding for Family and Community Support Services**

Year	Funding (000)	Year	Funding (000)
1979/80	$19,735	1984/85	$26,000
1980/81	$29,045	1985/86	$26,200
1981/82	$18,341	1986/87	$33,300
1982/83	$23,800	1987/88	$32,300
1983/84	$25,200	1988/89	$33,700

In 1971 the newly-elected Progressive Conservative government placed a ceiling on provincial funding and changed the name of the program to Family and Community Support Services (FCSS). Only minor modifications have been made to the program since then.

One unintended consequence of the PSS/FCSS program has been that the communities, being free to devise their own programs, have engaged in substantial experimentation and innovation. The province has adopted several very successful programs that were initially developed by communities, including a coordinated home care program, a school readiness program, and a particularly innovative method of delivering day care services that was initiated in Edmonton. But, like any program which encourages experimentation, the FCSS program encountered criticism in some communities. During the 1980s many family planning clinics offering candid advice about abortion received FCSS funding. In 1988 a Calgary alderman estimated that the city had spent approximately $100,000 in legal fees over a three-year period defending the city's right to support the Calgary Birth Control Association (CBCA). Alderman Barbara Scott said that of the estimated $10 million in FCSS funding, about 98 percent went unnoticed because of the disproportionate amount of time and attention spent on the CBCA.[61] In a few communities councils controlled by anti-abortionists voted to withdraw from the entire FCSS program.

Undoubtedly, Family and Community Support Services is one of the provincial government's most successful cost-shared grant programs. It allows municipalities wide latitude in program development, has resulted in a number of innovations in preventive social services, and has given the province many inexpensive pilot projects to examine. All of this has been achieved without violating the principle of municipal autonomy. Since it is a social program, one might expect FCSS funding to reflect the increased demand for services during times of economic hardship. Table 11.4 is disconcerting because it shows not only that funding is not stable, but also that the FCSS program appears to be one of the first to be reduced when there is a provincial budget shortfall.

Another problem that the government has not addressed is that while FCSS funding is on a per capita basis, social problems are not distributed equally across the province. As an example, in 1989 Edmonton had 24 percent of the province's population and 40 percent of the provincial social allowance case load. Although the city funds approximately 40 FCSS programs, including boys' and girls' clubs, drop-in child care for single mothers, and home visits to senior citizens, some of its most important work involves helping the large number of destitute people in the city. In contrast, rural communities with lower percentages of impoverished residents have more latitude in the use of FCSS funds. When Edmonton's grants were cut in the early 1980s the city was not willing to cut its FCSS programs. As a consequence, the portion of FCSS funding paid for by the city increased from 20 percent in 1982 to 54 percent by 1989. When Mayor Decore pleaded with Neil Webber for an increase in FCSS funding in 1985, the Minister of Social Services denied there were any inequities in the grant system and concluded that "if there's any extra dollars they'll be going to rural municipalities rather than to the city."[62]

Although some members of the government have recognized that much more FCSS funding is needed in large cities, the program's formula continues to favour smaller communities. In 1990/91 FCSS programs in cities were funded at the rate of $12.60 for each resident and non-city programs received $13.60 per capita.

Public welfare policy has always been controversial, since some people are concerned mainly with the effectiveness of particular programs and others focus on their relevance and sensitivity to human needs. Since Alberta's FCSS program is one of the better plans, one might expect it would be less likely to be mired in political controversy. However, the furore over FCSS funding for birth control associations, the charges of inequities in urban funding, and the variations in overall FCSS funding over a ten-year period indicate that it is at least as political as any of the other provincial-municipal programs.

Economic Development

Every municipal council in Alberta is concerned with the community's economic vitality and its ability to weather a sustained economic downturn. Although a growing population and local economy place additional pressure on all municipal services, they also expand the community's business and property tax base. The "conservers," who prefer no growth in order to maintain a community's charm, tend to be in the minority. For the business sector, community growth is essential; a decline in population and commercial activity is a disaster. As an example, when the population of the Town of Brooks declined from 9,049 in 1981 to 8,060 in 1982 after the region's oil and gas industry collapsed, 60 businesses either went bankrupt or closed their doors.

It is not uncommon for businesses to be overextended in anticipation of rapid growth that will enable them to reap large profits and repay their loans. Therefore, when population and economic growth begin to slow down and then decline, the business community increases its efforts to persuade council to implement growth-oriented policies which generally focus on developing tourism or promoting new industries and expanding existing ones. This call for increased spending at a time when the local economy is stagnating almost invariably causes conflict between business-people and other members of the community who favour a reduction in municipal expenditures. In 1983 Alberta enacted legislation which provided a means to help stabilize local economies without dividing the community over costs. Under Sections 171.2 through 171.8 of the Municipal Government Act a community is allowed to develop a Business Revitalization Zone (BRZ) with its own self-governing board having wide-reaching powers. Under Section 171.4 the board in part may:

(a) improve, beautify and maintain municipally owned lands, buildings and structures in the area, in addition to any improvement, beautification or maintenance that is provided at the expense of the municipality at-large;

(b) acquire, by purchase, lease or otherwise, any real property necessary for its purposes and improve, beautify and maintain that property;

(c) promote the area as a business or shopping area;

(d) undertake interim improvement and maintenance of any property mentioned in clause (b) for use as parking and subsequently to dispose of that property, by sale, lease, exchange or otherwise, for public or private redevelopment for commercial purposes at a price not less than its fair market value.

The cost of revitalization is borne by the businesses in the area, which are assessed a tax each year to cover the BRZ's expenses. There are also provisions for a BRZ to develop capital projects to be financed with debentures which are repaid by "a levy on all business assessments in the area at a uniform rate that the council considers sufficient to raise the amount required for the payment of the annual instalments of principal and interest on the debentures."

The BRZ has been endorsed enthusiastically and implemented in a number of municipalities. Almost every community has a run-down area at its centre, and the BRZ offers a means to redevelop the downtown core.[63] In 1984 Calgary established the Uptown 17 BRZ to revitalize the area along 17th Ave. S.W. Shortly thereafter, BRZs were established in Lethbridge, Medicine Hat, Strathmore, Grande Prairie, and Lacombe.

In addition to BRZs other policies have been adopted to forestall the decline of city centres. After the West Edmonton Mall siphoned off a substantial amount from downtown retail sales, Edmonton's council made tax concessions worth tens of millions of dollars to downtown developers, eased downtown parking restrictions, rebuilt Jasper Avenue, developed a comprehensive underground pedway system, encouraged high-density residential development in the downtown area, and discouraged nonretail businesses such as banks and financial institutions from locating on "shopping streets." In the early 1980s the council in Red Deer reduced downtown business taxes by 38 percent and increased the taxes in outlying malls and strip shopping centres by 12 percent. Medicine Hat tried a somewhat different approach by locating a new city hall in the core and persuading the province to build a courthouse in the same area.

Edmonton and Calgary both have well staffed and professional business departments that aggressively promote their respective cities across North America, Europe, and the Far East.[64] Occasionally, a mayor will make a selling junket to extol the virtues of investment opportunities in the city to foreign entrepreneurs. In smaller cities and towns, economic development promotion is handled either by the administration or directly by the council. In a few cases it is delegated to the local Chamber of Commerce. Smaller municipalities can obtain grants from the Alberta Department of Tourism and Small Business to help defray the cost of bringing prospective investors to the community or sending a representative to visit businesses that might locate in it.

For many municipalities, a fully serviced industrial park is the key element in an economic development plan. During the buoyant 1970s many communities took advantage of an Alberta Housing Corporation (AHC) program under which industrial land was assembled and sold to municipalities over a 15-year period at cost (including the cost of holding the land). Although many industrial parks were successful, failures also occurred, particularly during the 1980s, when economic expansion ceased and the new facilities could not be leased. Rather than community assets, these industrial sites became a burden on the ratepayers who had to pay their yearly interest and operating costs.

There are other instances of economic development schemes which have turned into financial nightmares. The business communities in both Calgary and Edmonton enthusiastically supported the construction of large complexes which were to attract free-spending conventioneers. In both cities a special 1 percent business tax is assessed annually to operate the centres. Unfortunately, usage and revenues were substantially overestimated. The Calgary Convention Centre has incurred an operating deficit of between $1 and $2 million every year since it opened in 1974, a deficit for which the city is responsible. Despite having had the benefit of seeing how the Calgary Convention Centre fared, Edmonton began building its convention centre in 1979. Budgeted at $32 million, the cost of the centre ballooned to $100 million. Like its Calgary counterpart, Edmonton's centre has operated at a sizeable deficit each year. When Laurence Decore was mayor he became so frustrated by continually having to spend money on the convention centre that he suggested, "Why don't we just untie the thing and let it flow down the river?"[65]

Administration

While a variety of public services are eligible for provincial grants, Alberta municipalities bear almost the entire burden of financing expenditures for general administrative activities such as human resource and financial management and the department of the city clerk. The only function that receives provincial funding is property assessment. The cost of administration is affected by factors such as the number of administrative personnel, their salaries and fringe benefits, general expenses such as the costs of supplies, equipment, and postage, and the costs incurred in holding public meetings and elections. These expenditures often create stress between council and its civil servants, since council believes that if administrative expenses are minimized, more money can be spent on public services or taxes can be reduced.

The problem is that most council members wrestle with the wrong questions. Rather than asking how much or how little administration is needed, they should be asking what kind of administration is needed. A recent treatise on government in the United States succinctly states, "We do not need more government or less government, we need better government."[66]

It is perhaps because the wrong sets of questions are asked that the cost of administration at city hall occasionally becomes an election issue. Ironically, it is at the village level, where the public seems to be the most satisfied with administration, that its costs represent the largest portion of the

municipal budget. In 1989 expenditures on general government constituted 29.6 percent of total expenditures for Alberta summer villages, 18.2
percent for villages, 12.1 percent for towns, and 7.5 percent for cities. The
common-sense explanation of this inverse relationship is that it is a manifestation of economy of scale. That is, the specialized bureaucracies in
large cities are much more efficient than the generalist administrators
found at the village level. In addition, fixed administrative costs are larger
proportionately in villages than in larger cities. As one might expect, figures such as these often are used to justify the consolidation of smaller
urban governmental units. Opponents are quick to note that although
administrative costs in smaller communities may be proportionately
higher than in cities, problems are more easily resolved in smaller communities with accessible public servants than in municipalities where citizens often view the bureaucracy as inaccessible and unresponsive.

Pomp and Ceremony

By far the greatest number of governmental activities deal with fiscal matters, the delivery of services, and the internal functions of government.
Other activities that do not fall into any of these categories are symbolic
and ceremonial; their purpose is to further a sense of local identity and to
affirm patriotic, ethnic, and community values. "Symbolic policies" may
involve specifying a particular day to honour a prominent citizen or one
of the community's ethnic groups; naming new neighbourhoods, streets,
and playgrounds; and designating a variety of objects as being official representations of the municipality. Councils like making symbolic policies
since, in addition to being generally uncontroversial, they can be used to
pay off political debts and garner support for upcoming elections. But
even seemingly innocuous symbolic gestures can generate political controversy. For example, shortly after the death of Mayor William Hawrelak
in 1975, some Edmontonians wanted to honour his memory by changing
the name of Mayfair Park to Hawrelak Park. Although Hawrelak was
revered by many citizens, others felt he had been an irresponsible mayor.
Finally, after a year of controversy, on October 12, 1976, the council voted
six to five to rename the park.[67] Another seemingly innocuous symbolic
issue involves a beaver-pelt "chain of office" designed in 1986 to be worn
by Edmonton's mayor during official ceremonies.[68] When Laurence
Decore wore it he said, "I'm tingling, I feel so much pride," but shortly
after Jan Reimer took office in 1989 she caused a minor furore when she
refused to wear animal skins around her neck.

Ceremonial functions, like the designation of official days and naming of streets and neighbourhoods, are generally considered politically advantageous for council members. Medicine Hat celebrated its centennial by funding a day-long party of dancing and sports. When Leduc became a city the council voted to sponsor a celebration picnic. During the summer of 1983, after Edmonton's administration had laid off a number of firefighters, bus drivers, and police officers for fiscal reasons, the city honoured a short visit of Prince Charles and Princess Diana by spending $50,000 on a barbecue, accommodations, and a gift. As tens of thousands of people lined the streets to catch a glimpse of the royal couple, the very small number of citizens who objected to the expenditures were themselves criticized.

Municipalities have adopted flags, crests, coats of arms, official lapel pins, and their own letterhead stationary.[69] At conferences of administrators and councillors, lapel pins are exchanged and collected like baseball cards. Although lapel pins generally are uncontroversial, in 1987 an Edmonton alderman, Mel Binder, was upset that the pins given to his counterparts in the "sister city" of Harbin, China, had been manufactured in Taiwan and purchased from a Calgary supplier. He said, "this . . . is almost an embarrassment to the pride of Edmontonians, especially those who grew up and were educated in Edmonton."[70]

Since the Alberta Urban Municipalities Association (AUMA) began to display its members' flags at the annual convention, councils have been particularly concerned about their municipal banner—its size, shape, design, and the protocol for its use. In 1987, for example, the mayor of Camrose said, "Our flag is a non-flag. That was shown when city flags were flown at last fall's AUMA convention. You can't even see the city crest unless you are real close to the flag."[71] After a spirited flag design competition, Smoky Lake's council winnowed the entries down to five. One councillor favoured a design composed of fish, wheat, Ukrainians, tractors, and sunsets, while others favoured a blue flag with a tree in a triangle, a Ukrainian house in a square, and a flame in a circle. Edson's council withheld partial payment for flags it purchased when members complained the squirrels on the flag did not look like squirrels, what was supposed to be a coal cart looked like a garbage bin, and the fishermen seemed to be fishing in the middle of a highway instead of a stream.[72] In 1987 Fort McMurray's council developed flag protocols for its administrative staff and the public. Among other things, council stipulated the municipal flag was to be flown at half-mast whenever the provincial flag flies at half-mast and on the death of a city hall employee, a former mayor or alderman, or any prominent Fort McMurray resident. The council did not define "prominent." Fort McMurray has been similarly concerned about the use of its logo. After council refused to allow the city's Minor Hockey Association to use the logo the Operations Commissioner explained, "if you open your logo to one organization today other organizations might call."[73]

The province recognizes the value of symbolic functions through Alberta Culture's Heritage Day grants. The Heritage Day Act of 1974 proclaimed the first Monday of August a day for celebrating cultural heritage (the celebration can also be held on the preceding Saturday or Sunday). Heritage Day is one of the most important symbolic events in Alberta communities, largely because the Department of Culture funds up to 50 percent of the cost of municipal celebrations.

The province, elected officials, administrators, and the public all acknowledge the importance of municipal ceremonies, rituals, and symbols. However, councils are often criticized for focusing on these issues at the expense of what many consider more important ones. James Lightbody expresses concern that "these debates over municipal symbols reinforce the overall image of city politics as silly and irrelevant. . . . the rummaging about for a physical manifestation of civic identity does suggest a serious weakness, at least in the eyes of those in authority, in the fundamental legitimacy of North American municipal governance."[74]

Questionable Local Government Activities

Chapter 2 on intergovernmental relations emphasized that municipalities derive their power from provincial governments which circumscribe and control their activities. Stanley Makuch, an authority on municipal law, writes that "municipalities have very little authority from a legal point of view to initiate policies or to act independently of their provincial governments."[75] Nevertheless, a municipal council occasionally is involved in a questionable activity which is overlooked by the province if it is relatively inoffensive and there are no complaints. An example is a resolution passed in 1987 by the Cardston council which declared a coin minted by the town's Rotary Club to be legal tender until the end of the year. Although the town had no authority to pass such a resolution it was ignored by the Department of Municipal Affairs, which viewed it as a harmless tourist and business promotion.

Questions are raised when a council passes a motion on a controversial issue that is outside the municipality's authority. Such issues during the 1980s included disarmament, the deportation of an accused mass murderer, and abortion. Peace and disarmament groups attempted to obtain municipal support for their goals; in particular, Operation Dismantle, a national organization, made a concerted effort to build grass-roots support by mailing literature to municipal councils and asking them to support the disarmament movement with municipal resolutions. It also provided local groups with information and arguments which they made to councils under the aegis of their own organizations.

In the spring of 1983, at the request of local disarmament groups, several municipal councils decided to include a disarmament referendum on their October 1983 election ballets. However, the Alberta Urban Municipalities Association (AUMA) warned its members that in its judgement such a referendum was outside municipal jurisdiction and if it were included on the ballot, it could invalidate the election. In September Edmonton's Referendum Committee for Nuclear Disarmament applied to the Court of Queen's Bench for an opinion as to whether or not it was proper for council to place a disarmament referendum on the Edmonton ballet. After Chief Justice William Sinclair declared that it was legal and did not contravene the Municipal Government Act, several other councils voted to place the referendum on their October ballots.[76] The movement's sole success was a resolution by the Didsbury council declaring the municipality to be a nuclear-free zone. Apart from an anti-nuclear resolution by Strathcona County's school board in December 1984, disarmament receded as a municipal issue until the fall of 1986 when another national organization, Operation Ploughshare, called for municipalities across Canada to declare themselves nuclear-free. In the October election a nuclear-free zone referendum was passed in Cochrane and in the late fall councils passed similar resolutions in Lethbridge, Fort Assiniboine, and Hinton. Just as the movement was gaining momentum it received a set-back on December 16 when the Didsbury council voted unanimously to revoke the nuclear-free resolution it had passed three years earlier. The town's administrator explained that the action was taken to eliminate the "endless" letters and requests for donations from peace groups.[77] In the summer of 1988 Operation Dismantle sent letters to councils asking them to support resolutions calling for the federal government to cancel its nuclear submarine program. The letters were ignored by most councils, although Edson and Stony Plain debated the issue before deciding the resolution "falls completely outside the mission of town council."[78]

In January 1989 the Town of St. Paul orchestrated a campaign to rid Canada of Charles Ng, accused of mass murder. The town council first passed a resolution calling for the federal government to extradite him to the United States and then sent letters to other municipalities asking them to follow suit. Edson, Strathmore, High River, and Ponoka passed similar resolutions. As the St. Paul resolution was debated by council after council, two issues evolved. The first was whether or not municipalities had the power to make such a resolution; the second debate focused on capital punishment, since if Ng were convicted, he would likely receive a death sentence.

In late 1991 the council in Edmonton was deeply divided over issues which clearly were outside the authority of the city. The council's pro-business faction praised the acumen and foresight of a northern Alberta pulp and paper company, while the mayor and an alderman criticized the company's policy of logging on lands claimed by a small Indian band. A pro-business alderman, apparently unaware of his own shaky legal position, said to Mayor Reimer, "I would urge you in the future to refrain from expressing views on matters that do not fall within our mandate."[79]

In 1989 anti-abortion advocates vigorously lobbied councils to designate a particular week as pro-life, that is, anti-abortion. In Medicine Hat many people were upset when the mayor unilaterally signed such a proclamation without consulting with other council members. In Edson a "Respect for Life Week" sailed through the council with only one dissension, while in St. Paul a "Sanctity of Human Life Week" was proclaimed by a slim margin of four votes to three. Mayor Paul Langevin argued that such a declaration was not inappropriate for a municipal council: "I think every government can take a stand on any issue. There are issues that we can't legislate anything on but what we can do is send a message to the higher government."[80]

Especially in Edmonton, anti-abortion forces have made abortion a local issue, after having been largely unsuccessful at the provincial and federal levels. In the October 1989 municipal election the Alberta Campaign Life Coalition endorsed candidates in Edmonton for mayor, aldermen, and school trustees,[81] but almost all of these candidates were defeated. When Dr. Henry Morgentaler announced that he planned to open an abortion clinic in Edmonton, another pro-life group vowed that it would work through city hall in an attempt to stop him. It seems clear that in the future the emotion-laden issue of abortion will be used to test the limits of council powers and actions.

Policing

Policing certainly is not related in any way to questionable municipal activities, or is it? The public is aware that some type of relationship exists between the municipal police force or the Royal Canadian Mounted

Police (RCMP) and city hall, but is not quite sure what it is. Many politicians are no more knowledgeable about policing than the citizenry, and much of their confusion can be attributed to the Canadian Constitution. Since the responsibility for the administration of justice falls under the powers of the province, and policing is one of the components of the justice system, one would assume that municipal policing is a provincial function. On the other hand, our Canadian tradition of policing is based on the concept of the police officer as a professional public servant committed to working closely with the community. Implicit in this definition is some degree of citizen control over the police force. Police commissions have been established by many Canadian municipalities in an attempt to reconcile the province's constitutional policing powers with municipal expectations. However, most police commissions are structured in such a way that there is negligible public influence on law enforcement, personnel, fiscal, and disciplinary policies.

In 1988 the Alberta government substantially revised the Police Act to update it and clarify the relationships between the municipality and the police. In addition, using population as its primary criterion, it assigned financial responsibilities and defined municipal options for the provision of police services. Under the revised act every town, new town, village, and summer village with a population no greater than 2,500 receives "general policing services provided by the provincial police service at no direct cost" to the municipality.[82] Municipalities with populations in excess of 2,500 have five options. The one which is most commonly employed is to contract with the federal government for policing by the RCMP, an arrangement that must be approved by the provincial government. The contract specifies the level of police service for the community. Since salaries constitute the largest single expenditure item in a town's policing budget, it is critical to determine how many policing personnel are required. Office space, furniture, telephones, clerical support, janitorial services, and utilities are provided by the municipality, which must meet RCMP specifications. The major problem in contracting policing services from the RCMP is that citizens have almost no say about policing policies or procedures in their community. Although the officer of the RCMP unit in the municipality is designated as a liaison person between the unit and the municipality, the officer is directly responsible to the RCMP's K Division headquarters in Edmonton. The liaison function in the municipality is often delegated to the mayor, the municipal manager, or a council committee. In any case, even though the policing committee may have a "citizen member," it has virtually no power. Although the RCMP provides policing for over 60 Alberta municipalities, it is not responsible to either the municipality or the province; it is subject only to federal control.[83]

In a similar arrangement, municipalities can enter a contractual agreement with the provincial government for RCMP services. The cost of the arrangement is determined by the Solicitor General.

As of 1991, only nine municipalities had a police force: Calgary, Camrose, Coaldale, Edmonton, Lacombe, Lethbridge, Medicine Hat, Redcliff, and Taber. Even when a municipality maintains its own force, it has very little control over policing policy, which is the responsibility of the municipal police commission. The police commission, which may vary in size from three to twelve members, is appointed by council for a term of office not to exceed three years. If the police commission has fewer than five members, one of the appointees may be either a council member or a municipal employee. If a commission has more than four members, two of the appointees may be councillors or civil servants.[84] Councillors and municipal employees are ineligible to chair the commission.

The police commission is potentially a very powerful body, since it is responsible for: (1) establishing a municipality's police policy; (2) making all police force appointments except that of the Chief of Police, which is ratified by council; (3) conducting public inquiries relevant to policing policy; (4) monitoring complaints against the police and departmental discipline problems; and (5) allocating the policing funds it receives from the municipal council.

In the winter of 1982 a controversy erupted in Edmonton when city council decided during a fiscal crisis to terminate the employment of 94 police constables. The Edmonton Police Association took the city to court, which ruled that the city did not have the power to fire police officers; its role was to provide funds which the commission could allocate as it saw fit. Although the court was silent on whether the commission had the power to fire police officers, the implication of the decision was that it did.

The nature of the appointment process prevents councils from exercising any more than a modicum of control over police commissions. Controversy is to be expected as long as commissions attempt to assert their independence and councils persist in viewing police commissions as their agents. After the Medicine Hat council refused to reappoint two citizens to the police commission board after they expressed some strong views, a *Medicine Hat News* editorial proposed a solution:

One solution does exist, but it is one which only the provincial government can implement. Medicine Hat will have to make the police commission's politicization complete and more direct. Its members quite simply, will have to be elected and given the full powers and responsibilities of elected representatives. . . . Letting the people choose those who would oversee the operations of the police would make the system more responsive to the needs of the people and end, once and for all, the hypocrisy which hangs over police commissions like some shroud.[85]

The extent of citizen involvement in overseeing police officers and advising on law enforcement policy making is a divisive issue that is unlikely to be settled in the near future. A policy with the potential to defuse conflict between the public and the police is the adoption of community-based policing. When the police and the citizens work closely together at the community level, distrust and suspicion are gradually replaced by mutual respect and trust.

When the Police Act was revised in 1988 two of the most innovative provisions allowed municipalities to establish a regional policing agency under the tutelage of a regional commission and permitted intermunicipal contractual arrangements for the provision of police services. As of May 1992 neither practice had been adopted in Alberta, although one can predict that in the near future both will be commonly employed across the province.

Although police policy is often contentious, a prime source of discord is the effect of policing costs on municipal budgets. A provincial government report entitled "Police Commissions in Alberta, Structure and Functions" includes detailed sample police budgets for towns with populations of 6,000 and 13,000. The smaller town spent $548,592 on police services in 1987, with an estimate for 1988 of $595,151. The province recognizes the costs of policing by providing municipalities with a number of grants. The basic one is the Municipal Police Assistance Grant for municipalities with a population in excess of 2,500. Until the 1987/88 budget year the grant was on a strict per capita basis; a municipality contracting with the RCMP received $12 per capita and a municipality with its own police force received $18. For the 1987/88 budget year the province reduced a municipality's grant by 3 percent from the grant it had received for 1986/87. The province continued to distort what had been a straightforward per capita grant. For the 1988/89 year the grant was increased 1 percent over the 1987/88 grant; the 1989/90 grant was increased 5 percent over the amount received for 1988/89; and the 1990/91 grant was increased 3 percent over the 1989/90 grant. Following

Table 11.5 Medicine Hat Basic Police Grant

	1986/87	1987/88	1988/89	1989/90	1990/91
Amount	$750,906	$728,379	$735,663	$772,446	$795,619

is an example of how this shuffle affected Medicine Hat's basic police grant between 1986 and 1991.

A number of other grants, usually awarded on a one-time basis, supplement the basic Municipal Police Assistance Grant. The Police Phase-In Grant provides funds for five years to a municipality which decides to provide for its own policing. The Municipal Police Building Subsidy provides up to $50,000 to underwrite some of the costs of erecting a new police building or renovating an existing one. A police training grant pays up to 50 percent of the costs incurred by a police officer in employment-related studies. In addition, the province has devised several grants to strengthen the policing system in specific areas. The Summer Village Special Constable Grant provides $3,000 to enable a summer village to employ a constable. The Liquor Control Act Subsidy pays a municipality $7.00 per capita to hold in a jail cell intoxicated persons who have not been charged. In 1988/89 the province spent $98,749 for this program. The popular Crime Prevention Grant provides seed money for carefully planned crime prevention programs.

Although the government cut back on its police funding to municipalities in the late 1980s and substantially reduced the number of RCMP personnel policing rural areas, there are two reasons why there has not been a recognizable increase in crime in the province. First, the migration of young single men (especially those in the crime-prone age group between 16 and 25) decreased dramatically as oil-related enterprises declined. Second, the percentage of the population between 16 and 25 was already decreasing in the 1980s as the population as a whole grew older. If this trend were to continue there would be a smaller and smaller percentage of the population in the age group that commits the most crimes. However, during the 1990s there will be some changes in these trends, especially in northern Alberta, with the growth of the pulp and paper industry. One can predict that the crime rate will increase substantially and that northern municipalities in particular will be seeking additional funds from the government to cover increased policing costs.

An Overview of Government Activities, Responsibilities, and Democracy

A classification system has not been worked out which automatically determines which activities should be carried out by the public sector and which by the private one. However, since the nature of collective goods makes it virtually impossible for them to be profitably produced and distributed by the private sector, most people believe they should be provided by the public sector. With the exception of the few totally collective goods, such as defence, in recent years there has been a spirited debate over whether many of the services traditionally designated as public goods should continue to be produced and distributed by the public sector, or if some portion of them should be turned over to the private sector.

Although municipalities are responsible for many government activities, they are dependent on the provincial government for much of their funding. When the economy was in a downward spiral in the 1980s, the province responded by cutting back on its spending. With the government making conditional and unconditional municipal grants at less than the rate of inflation, municipalities had to spend more of their resources to make up the difference. The provincial government was willing to divest itself of program responsibilities and costs, but was unwilling to expand the municipalities' fiscal base. This situation is ironic, since until recently the municipalities had relinquished one major service function after another to the provincial government because they did not have the fiscal resources to provide the level of service that the public had come to expect.

Very little has been heard from the Department of Municipal Affairs about the dire consequences of the provincial policy of increasing municipal responsibilities without providing the necessary funding. If the trend continues, the public may become disillusioned with local-level policy making and administration and support for local government and local-level democracy will erode when service levels begin to decline. Yet many Municipal Affairs senior civil servants are committed to the precepts of local democracy and the active participation of the citizenry in policy making. Since senior administrators are responsible to the minister from whom they take their directions, one can understand their reluctance to speak out when the government implements a policy with long-term effects which may undermine local democracy.

12

Planning and Democratic Institutions

Introduction

Within the parameters laid out by elected officials and administrative personnel, municipal planners identify community goals and develop strategies to reach them through the efficient use of available resources. Equally important, planners are responsible for predicting the effects of any particular strategy or goal on the diverse and often conflicting group and class interests within a community.

While planning theoretically should integrate all of a municipality's service functions, in practice, planning at the municipal and regional levels is concerned almost exclusively with land use.[1] Moreover, even within this narrow focus, valuable community resources may be overlooked, elected decision makers are often presented with a narrow range of goals, and attempts to integrate land-use planning with a municipality's other functions are rare.[2]

Planners in an open democratic system are accountable to the public as well as to council. Several years ago Calgary's planning director, in explaining why the commission was meeting in camera, said the planning process was a "communication exercise" but that the communications should not be taking place in the news media.[3] In "The Seven Deadly Sins of Planning," Thomas Burton identifies one of these sins as "ignoring the community or giving it only token attention in the planning process." His point is that a planner is ineffective if the community is ignored. He also notes that "a myriad of different mechanisms exists whereby the planner can meet the letter of the law regarding public participation, without subjecting himself to the rigours of actually becoming involved with those who live in the community."[4]

Development of Planning in Canada

The city planning movement in Canada is rooted in two diverse intellectual movements, a belief in the value of beauty as an end in itself and the philosophy of utilitarianism. Shortly after the turn of the century, Canadian students who had traveled extensively in Europe lamented the image of the Canadian city; they saw it as ugly and unplanned in comparison to European cities. Other Canadians were excited by the architectural wonders displayed at the 1893 Chicago World Fair. In fact, "in later years, when leaders in the Canadian planning movement discussed its beginnings, they often traced the North American planning movement back to the Chicago World Fair."[5] The "City Beautiful Movement" emphasized broad thoroughfares, large parks, and graceful neoclassical public buildings and amphitheatres. However, its proponents were criticized for not dealing with important social problems in the city: housing for the poor and the working class and rampant suburbanization spurred by private greed and public boosterism.[6] During the latter nineteenth century, new immigrants and the poor were housed in crowded and unsanitary slums and shantytowns that were periodically ravaged by disease. In their headlong competition for profits, the captains of industry, often among a city's civic elite, showed little interest in creating acceptable environments for their employees.[7] By the late 1920s the City Beautiful Movement had collapsed, although its influences are still found in municipal and regional plans in Alberta.

The second and more lasting intellectual tradition was based on Jeremy Bentham's philosophy of utilitarianism, the basic tenet of which is that the greatest happiness should accrue to the greatest number. It linked a concern with social ills with the imposition of a code of moral behaviour on the poor and uneducated. An English planner, Thomas Adams, played a major role in giving the Canadian planning movement its utilitarian direction. He began his career as a secretary for the Garden City Association in London but soon became one of its principal lecturers, espousing well designed industrial communities with adequate housing for workers. Despite having no formal qualifications, and not being particularly innovative, Adams soon became a leader in the new town planning movement. He participated in drafting a town planning act and when it became law in 1910 he was appointed to the Local Government Board, which conducted public hearings on the planning process. Realizing that the act would necessitate a cadre of civil servants who would be involved in planning, Adams lobbied for the formation of a professional body that could offer training and sponsor research. In 1913 the Town

Planning Institute was established and Adams became its first president.[8]

Adams's move to Canada was precipitated by a change in the conception of planning. Canadian planning professionals disenchanted with the City Beautiful Movement had initiated a "City Scientific Movement" which, although not devoid of a concern with beautification, emphasized the importance of a healthy environment and fiscal and engineering considerations. In 1909 the federal government created the Commission of Conservation of Natural Resources, with a broad mandate to protect and best utilize the country's natural resources.[9] One of the commission's first staff appointments was an Advisor on Public Health, who was appalled at conditions in the nation's cities. He arranged a National Housing and Town Planning Congress in Ottawa to which Adams was invited from Great Britain. Adams was recruited to serve on the commission and within a few years his social philosophy and that of another staff member, Charles Hodgetts, were having a major impact on Canadian planning.

> The philosophical basis of the gospel which Adams expounded was the advanced utilitarianism of J.S. Mill. . . . In terms redolent of Mill, Adams asserted that a landowner had no "right to use his property to injure his fellows. Life is higher and more valuable under the law than real property . . . we have either to control the right of property so that it shall not endanger the right to live in wholesome surroundings or face inevitable decay." However, the negative restraint of private activity did not imply a positive collectivism for "we do not want to inaugurate socialistic extremes but to forestall them."[10]

While Adams was employed by the commission he drafted the planning legislation for a number of provinces. Although he incorporated some of his philosophical ideas, the legislation generally was modelled after the English act, which he had also helped to draft.

Despite a number of successes, by 1918 the Commission of Conservation of National Resources had begun to lose its political support and its chair, Minister of the Interior Clifford Sifton, retired. In 1920 Adams was working part-time on the commission and part-time as a private planning consultant. After budget cuts, the commission was dissolved the following year.[11]

Adams's concerns for housing reform, public health, and the professionalization of planning were adopted by the Town Planning Institute of Canada, established in 1918. Not surprisingly, the structure of the institute closely followed the British model. According to Michael Simpson, "The 'Grand Seigneur' of Canadian planning could boast that 'Probably in no country was there more activity than there was in Canada during the critical years 1914-19.' His opportune arrival at the outbreak of war may well have saved Canadian planning from nemesis."[12] Influenced by Adams, town planners with a social conscience were as concerned with economic and social problems as with the aesthetics of the city.

Although Adams's ideas on the mechanics of planning, which were rooted in an English tradition, were ultimately rejected as inappropriate for Canada, his basic philosophy is still accepted by a segment of the Canadian planning profession.[13] "He regarded the city as primarily an economic organism in which 'the first concern of a town plan should be to provide for the proper and efficient carrying out of business.' Mindful, however, of his reformist background, he added that 'complementary to the business side of a city is the provision of satisfactory and healthy living conditions for the people.'"[14]

Another set of ideas on government and planning was being introduced from the United States at about the same time that Adams and his disciples were providing a counterbalance to the City Beautiful Movement. To eliminate the evils of municipal party machines, American reformers advocated changing the structure of municipal government to "take politics out of government" and to "govern scientifically." Their program included, among other things, "value-free" comprehensive master planning based on a belief that planning was a rational technical exercise that could identify a single universal public interest. Master planning and the planner were seen as being above the give and take of municipal politics, which connoted divisiveness and controversy over community goals. One manifestation of this stance was an attempt to insulate planning from politics by placing it in the hands of a semi-independent planning commission. In a Canada influenced by the American reform movement, it was but a short step from a concern with alleviating social ills to a concern with reforming the local political system considered responsible for a great many of these ills. Paul Rutherford describes this movement in Canada:

> ... the bureaucratic method required the creation of an autonomous and trained administration dedicated to the twin ideals of economy and efficiency. To the reformers expert knowledge was a near panacea. ... The reformers hoped to minimize the influence of the amateur in all departments of civic government, to take administration out of politics.[15]

In short, an American package of political and administrative reforms was modified and adapted to the Canadian political environment in order to cure social ills.

This burst of energy in planning was followed by two decades of passivity as the "nation turned to priorities other than cities."[16] And yet it was during this lull that a set of radical planning ideas and goals was advanced. In 1935 the League for Social Reconstruction (LSR) published *Social Planning for Canada,* which discussed the problems caused by capitalism and advocated a system of socialist planning.[17] Tom Gunton discusses the socialist phenomenon:

> For the socialists, planning was a general technique of decision-making which would form the core of social organization instead of being a peripheral activity isolated to limited sectors of the economy. Private market forces would not be eliminated but they would be subordinated to a democratic planning process to ensure that they operated in the public interest. . . . all planning was subjective and political in the sense that it sought a particular set of ends, [and] was in stark contrast to previous theories which assumed planning was a scientific objective exercise above politics.[18]

Matthew Kiernan argues persuasively that the Canadian planning profession lacks direction because it has been driven by four intellectual orientations whose basic ideas are often in conflict with one another.[19] In his discussion of the first orientation he maintains that the "fundamentally ambivalent Canadian attitudes concerning the legitimacy of public sector intervention in the urban land market" reflect "the intellectual ancestry of Canadian planning." On the one hand, planners have been influenced by Americans with their view of private property as conferring on owners "virtually inviolable" rights, and on the other, they have been influenced by the British view that "land is a scarce public birthright, and that its use and development are matters over which the state has extensive and legitimate control."

The second intellectual orientation is "a powerful ethos of apolitical, anti-interventionist minimalism in municipal government," which limits local government to being nothing more than a prudent provider of hard services to community residents. As a consequence, social problems are not viewed as the responsibility of municipal government and even hard services "are normally interpreted as fundamentally technical exercises, devoid of political or distributional implications." Ron Clark, a virulent critic of the planning profession, argues that British-trained planners hired by Canadian planning departments and universities have misdirected the profession. "The British belief that planning is a value-free, apolitical science to be practiced with rigorous precision, employing a grab bag of pseudo tools . . . was the unfortunate legacy that British planners bequeathed to Canada."[20]

A third intellectual influence "is the persistent belief that, at best, planning remains a fundamentally rational and technical endeavour, undertaken by trained professionals in pursuit of incontrovertible and generally shared public goals." This ideological outlook minimizes the political dimension of planning and public policy. A 1976 cross-country survey of Canadian planners found that 42 percent believed there was a single public interest "that overrides narrower parochial interests."[21] According to Kiernan, a unitary public interest "bespeaks a distinct idiosyncratic sociopolitical outlook . . . the unitary public interest ideology implicitly adopts a fundamentally consensual rather than conflictive view of society."[22] The same study found that many Canadian planners were proponents of value-free comprehensive planning guided by scientific principles.[23]

Kiernan maintains that while the first three influences have remained relatively constant, the fourth did not emerge until the middle of the century. He points out that early planners were uncritically pro-development, but in the 1960s and throughout the 1970s many planners allied themselves with reform politicians and citizen activists who actively opposed development and urban growth. It was this activism and anti-business ethos which constituted the fourth intellectual orientation. Then another reversal took place: "In the current, post-recession era, planners in most Canadian cities find themselves not only more receptive to new development than was the case during the previous decade, but increasingly in the business of actually trying to catalyze it."[24]

Whether planners are for or against development is of little consequence. A more important question is whether planners' attitudes about their role in policy making will change in the foreseeable future. In their survey of Canadian planners, John Page and Reg Lang found ". . . a young, well paid, predominantly male professional group. . . . The past 10 years have been a period of rapid growth and change for the planning profession, accompanied by shifts in background from the dominancy of engineering/architecture to that of geography/social sciences."[25] As greater numbers of planners obtain an undergraduate education in the social sciences, which tend to focus on the problems of societal inequities, rather than in engineering, with its focus on technology, it is likely that planning will become increasingly liberalized and politicized.

Although radical planners with a socialist bent were in the spotlight during the 1930s, their numbers were small and their voices were over-whelmed by those of the traditional planners. More than a half century later the training and values of planners have become more humanistic and many of the radicals' ideas are being re-examined. Radical planners today espouse decentralized government and grass-roots democracy, especially where they benefit poorer citizens. More often than not, these planners are found at the neighbourhood level, acting as its advocates.

Development of Planning in Alberta

Alberta's second premier, Arthur Sifton, left an imprint of utilitarianism on the intellectual development of planning in the province that is still with us today. The premier's brother, Clifford Sifton, was the originator and chair of the Commission of Conservation that, according to P.J. Smith, "combined, in a single organization, the . . . mainstreams of pro-gressive social philosophy, environmental conservation and urban improvement. It also epitomized the adaptation of utilitarian doctrine to the Canadian setting."[26] Arthur Sifton was the province's representative on the commission during his 1910–1917 tenure of office.

Alberta's first Planning Act passed through all three readings on the last day of the 1913 spring session, receiving little press coverage and even less fanfare. The new act was based, with some slight changes, on New Brunswick's Town Planning Act of 1912, the first planning act in Canada. Since New Brunswick's planning legislation was closely modelled on the town planning section of the British Housing and Town Planning Act of 1909, Sifton indirectly brought English utilitarianism to planning in Alberta.

The year the new planning legislation was enacted, the province's cities were at the end of a major land boom. Working with developers, city administrators in Edmonton and Calgary had committed millions of dol-lars to streets, streetcars, and water and sewer lines to service newly planned areas which, as it turned out, would not be settled for many years. By mid-1913 Edmonton had incurred a debt of $22,313,968 and Calgary a debt of $20,633,605. Since the province's major cities needed a long and continuing land boom to justify their excessive capital spending, it was unlikely that the new planning legislation would be used as a deter-rent to speculation and growth.

While containing no definition of planning, the act focused on the "legal procedures by which town planning was to be implemented," and was very specific as to what area of the community was to be planned and regulated. Section 1(1) clearly stated that the act applied only to underdeveloped land on the community's periphery.[27] Despite this prohibition, the act contained a number of innovative provisions that have been incorporated into subsequent legislation. One provided a mechanism "for individual property owners to combine their land holdings for planning purposes," which made it possible "to prepare a single unified design for quite large tracts of land, commonly of a thousand acres or more." It went a step further: "the town planning scheme was also able to incorporate non-economic features in the public good, such as parks and open space. . . . In short, it offered the aesthetic order of unified design rather than the mechanistic order imposed by zoning and grid subdivision."[28] The only substantial addition to the act has been the requirement of a dedication of up to 5 percent of land for open and public spaces with no compensation in newly planned areas. Compulsory dedication of land was not to become part of planning legislation in other parts of Canada for 40 years.

The act gave the Minister of Municipal Affairs an extraordinary amount of power over municipal planning. To begin with, the minister's approval was necessary before any municipal planning scheme could be implemented. Even more important, the act gave the minister the power to require a municipality to prepare a planning scheme "in a case where a town planning scheme ought to be made." But, as P.J. Smith notes, "no Minister was ever put to the test."[29]

The onset of a recession in 1913 destroyed all interest developers or municipal administrators might have had in planning outlying developments. According to Bettison, Kenward, and Taylor, ". . . the 1913 Act was introduced at the very time when its authority was hardly needed. Rapid expansion of towns and cities had ceased and the next twenty years were to be largely consolidating, with slow but steady development in selected urban areas."[30] Although it would have little effect on the regulation of planning for a number of years, the importance of the 1913 Act is summarized by P.J. Smith:

> The only significance of the Town Planning Act . . . is its place in the history of the idea of planning and, particularly, its contribution to the Alberta view of planning that is in place today. The central point is simple: the principle of utility [utilitarianism] continued to be served. . . . the gospel of efficiency continues to be the only explicit ethic that supports the institution of planning.[31]

During the 1920s Edmonton and Calgary once again were beginning to expand into some of the partially developed areas created by the 1913 land bust. But conditions in the 1920s were far different from those prevailing when the first Planning Act was implemented in 1913. The municipalities responded pragmatically "by replacing or revising those parts of the planning system that were no longer thought to be effective; by filling critical gaps in the original system; and by adopting innovative responses to new concerns (or to renewed expressions of old concerns)."[32] By the late 1920s it became clear that the 1913 Act was outmoded. With the impetus provided by the government in power (the United Farmers of Alberta), the City of Edmonton, the United Farm Women of Alberta, and the Edmonton Local Council of Women, the 1913 Act was repealed in 1929. The UFA was committed to maximizing the quality of rural life and a "central planning agency designed to help the local communities to help themselves . . . was the obvious solution."[33] The City of Edmonton felt that the 1913 Act should be updated, and the United Farm Women of Alberta and the Edmonton Local Council of Women were concerned about the lack of legislation to prevent unsightly billboards along roads and highways. In 1928 "An Act to Facilitate Town Planning and the Preservation of the Natural Beauties of the Province" was passed, repealed, and then reintroduced in an amended form in the 1929 Town Planning Act.

The 1929 legislation was an amalgam of sections of the 1928 Act, the British Columbia Act, and some of the latest ideas in American planning theory and practice. P.J. Smith describes it as "the longest and most complex piece of planning legislation . . . in Canada . . . and, in its new provisions, the most complete expression of American planning techniques in Canadian law."[34] It provided for a Town and Rural Planning Board and a Provincial Director of Town Planning to establish provincial planning guidelines. It gave municipalities zoning powers by enabling them to prescribe permissible land uses in various areas of the community and to control densities, lot size requirements, and building heights and floor areas. The 1929 Act also gave cities, towns, villages, municipal districts, and improvement districts the right to establish a regional planning commission. As might be expected in a legislature dominated by rural members, small municipalities were favoured over very large ones; no governmental unit was allowed more than three members on a commission. However, under Section 18(4), the costs of a regional planning commission were borne "by the councils in the proportion which the total value of the assessable property in their respective municipalities as shown on the assessment rolls bear to one another." Thus proportionality was woven into the composition of a regional planning commission but only on its cost side!

Despite the onset of the depression in 1929 there was initially a considerable amount of interest in planning. Planning commissions were organized and professional staff hired in Edmonton and Calgary and some 50 municipalities adopted planning bylaws. But as the depression continued and money became increasingly scarce, interest in planning waned. No regional planning commissions were established and the province disbanded the newly created provincial planning branch to save money.

Fueled by a revival of agricultural prices shortly after the beginning of the Second World War, the province's economy began to revive. In 1942 the few amendments passed during the 1930s were consolidated into the 1942 Town Planning Act. Perhaps more important, when uncontrolled development began to take place beyond Edmonton's boundaries in 1945, city officials touted the advantages of a regional planning board. The following year the newly established Red Deer Regional Commission prepared a long-range plan for the development of the city and its outlying municipalities.

The 1947 Leduc oil discovery prevented a post-war slump in the province's economy and the cities of Edmonton and Calgary, again experiencing growing pains, did not want to repeat the mistakes of past expansions. Calgary and its neighbouring municipalities agreed to establish a regional planning commission. Two important planning events occurred in 1949 in Edmonton: the Edmonton Local Council of Women petitioned city council to establish a department of town planning and two McGill Planning Professors, Harold Spence-Sales and John Bland, were hired to examine the city's problems. Their report was submitted to the provincial government as a justification for changing the Planning Act to facilitate planning in Edmonton. The government responded with the Town and Rural Planning Act of 1950; its major contributions were provisions for the formation of district planning commissions, which were the direct forerunners of the province's regional planning commissions.[35] The district planning commissions, which were voluntary associations of municipalities, were given primarily advisory powers in a region; "no municipality was required to join, nor did they have to follow any advice the Commission offered."[36]

Shortly after the passage of the act, the Edmonton District Planning Commission (DPC) was established, followed by the Calgary DPC in 1951, the Red Deer DPC in 1952, the Medicine Hat DPC in 1954, the Oldman River DPC in 1955, the Peace River DPC in 1958, and the Battle River DPC in 1960. Wes Shannon writes that "it wasn't until 1953 when the District Planning Commissions ... were assigned subdivision approval authority, that agricultural land conservation became a more clearly defined regional policy."[37]

By the end of the decade seven district planning commissions had been established but with only advisory powers, they could not control land use effectively. This weakness was exemplified by the development of Edmonton's satellite community, Sherwood Park, in the County of Strathcona. Since a district planning commission could not make a decision unless a representative of the affected municipality was present at the hearing, the County of Strathcona simply did not send a representative to the meetings when the question of whether residential development should proceed in Sherwood Park was discussed. Development proceeded by default.

In 1957 the Planning Act was amended to require municipalities with populations in excess of 50,000 to prepare district general plans. This provision established the precedent that, under certain conditions, planning was mandatory. A second important amendment delegated final subdivision approval to regional and municipal authorities.

A review of planning legislation begun in 1961 by the Minister of Municipal Affairs culminated in a rewriting of the Planning Act. Partially influenced by the McNally Commission's recommendations on the need for providing orderly development in Edmonton and Calgary, the new act, which came into effect in 1963, changed the name of district planning commissions to regional planning commissions and required every commission to prepare a regional plan; no deadline was mentioned. It also reduced the number of bodies dealing with planning appeals and subdivision approvals. Particularly surprising was the elimination, with hardly a murmur from the planning profession, of citizen advisory commissions.

Two important changes to the planning act occurred in 1968. First, planning commissions were given subdivision approval authority for all of the municipalities within their jurisdiction. Second, an amendment directed each regional planning commission to complete a preliminary regional plan by 1972. Despite this edict, by the end of 1971 only the Edmonton and Calgary commissions were in compliance. It was not that the other commissions questioned the government's authority to issue such a proclamation, but rather that they could not afford to comply, since they had to rely on their member municipalities for funding. It was for this reason, among others, that the government set up the Alberta Planning Fund in 1971.

Prior to the establishment of the fund the province had contributed 60 percent of the funding for regional planning commissions and the member municipalities supplied 40 percent. Approximately two-thirds of the

Planning Fund came directly from the provincial government and the remainder from the municipalities, which were required to contribute an amount determined by a formula that took into account the inherent differences between small and large, and rural and urban, municipalities. While the Planning Fund was implemented to provide an orderly means to support the regional commissions, an unintended effect was to increase the overall percentage of operational costs for which the provincial government was responsible.[38] Michael Gordon and J. David Hulchanski argue that "this was a significant administrative change because it indicated an increased provincial commitment to the regional process and allowed the development of a broad framework to work with local municipalities in the preparation of land use bylaws and general plans."[39]

The Progressive Conservative government elected in 1971 recognized an increasing interest in environmental concerns by expanding the Department of the Environment. The government also realized that an effective planning mechanism was essential to control accelerating urbanization in the province, and throughout the early 1970s the Department of Municipal Affairs conducted a complete re-examination of planning in Alberta. As a consequence the act was rewritten a number of times, culminating in a new planning act in 1977.

P.J. Smith argues that all planning in Alberta, both municipal and regional, has been based on the utilitarian principles that there is "one best way" to plan and that the "public good" is easily determined by the citizenry. A Department of Municipal Affairs discussion paper discusses the utilitarian approach:

> . . . a philosophy characterized by planning as a technical activity "to be carried out by experts whose scientific knowledge equips them to judge that certain courses of action are 'best' because they maximize utility." . . . The old utilitarian approach proved less useful in the face of the increasing complexity of planning.[40]

Smith disagrees with the assertion that there has been a move away from "the old utilitarian approach" in the 1977 Planning Act. He argues that the "scientism" of the utilitarian approach is as pervasive in the 1977 Act as in earlier ones, and that its fundamental fault is that "it does not incorporate a principle of justice." He explains:

> Planning . . . is an allocative process in which scarce resources, notably land and public funds, have to be distributed among rival claimants.

Conflict . . . is inherent in the situations. . . . To resolve conflict, there has to be an ethic, and that ethic has to incorporate a principle of justice independent of utility [utility being loosely defined as the greatest good of the greatest number], since it will rarely be possible to prove, objectively, that the desire of one individual or interest group would contribute more to the general welfare than those of another.[41]

Although Smith is critical of the "scientism" of the utilitarian approach and is candid about the difficulty of determining the public good and public interest, he does not reject utilitarianism out of hand. Rather, he believes that if a principle of justice were incorporated into the utilitarian approach, many of its shortcomings would be rectified.

The 1977 Planning Act and the Planning Process

The 1977 Planning Act can be seen as an evolution of the utilitarian approach to planning. Section 2 states, "the purpose of the Act [is to] achieve the orderly, economical and beneficial development and use of land and patterns of human settlement . . . without infringing on the rights of individuals except to the extent that is necessary for *the greater public interest*." [Emphasis added.] An Edmonton legal authority maintained that the 1977 Act was largely a refinement of the 1970 Act it replaced. However, since the new act gave municipalities far more discretion, she believed that it would "offer planners greater opportunities for creative planning."[42]

At the apex of the planning authorities is the Alberta Planning Board; just below it are the province's ten regional planning commissions with authority over more than 90 percent of the province's population. Although the act directs a commission to act as a resource body on which its member municipalities can call for assistance in drawing up a municipal plan or a land-use bylaw, its most important function is to prepare a regional plan to which all its members must adhere. The regional plan first establishes goals, such as the preservation of agricultural land, and then develops broad but firm guidelines determining how the region's municipalities are to manage their land.

Since each commission board comprises representatives from its member municipalities, it would seem that regional planning directives are the collective goals of all of the region's municipalities and that regional policy making is a grass-roots process. While this is the case initially, the regional plans formulated by commission boards must be ratified by the Alberta Planning Board to ensure that they conform with provincial government policy. If a plan is not acceptable to the planning board, it is sent back to the regional planning commission for revision. The board has exercised this power a number of times. Many of the plans prepared by regional planning commissions are so detailed and technical that they are in effect regulatory instruments. The board returns these plans to the commissions to be rewritten as broad policies.[43]

After a plan has been approved, any amendments must also be submitted to the board. In addition, the board is the appeal body for subdivision decisions. Since the ratification of the Calgary Regional Planning Commission's regional plan in 1984 the board has overturned 11 out of 20 subdivision appeals made by the commission and in another case the commission's decisions were amended. Rulings of the planning board are subject only to an appeal to the Alberta Supreme Court and then only on questions of law, not on the planning substance of the decision.

Members of the Alberta Planning Board are appointed by the government and serve at its pleasure. Initially, the board was composed entirely of senior civil servants, deputy ministers, assistant deputy ministers, and department directors, all of whom represented departments with a direct interest in land-use planning. When Marvin Moore was the Minister of Municipal Affairs, a number of appointments were made on the basis of political considerations. The rationale for selecting these new members, designated "citizens at-large," was that regional planning commissions and municipal councillors "had for some years expressed dissatisfaction that Provincial servants could, on subdivision appeals, overturn decisions that had been made by municipally elected people."[44] After the composition of the board was changed, the civil service appointees and professional civil servants became increasingly reluctant to play an active role on it. Vicki Barnett, a writer for the *Calgary Herald*, explained that "because the citizens have more time to spend on matters than the bureaucrats, who have numerous other matters to attend to, they have heavily influenced decisions."[45] Perhaps even more telling was Barnett's comment that the board now had a rural slant. The long-term effect of politicizing the board was to give the province even greater control over regional and municipal planning decisions.

A regional planning commission acts as the subdivision approving authority for most of the region's municipalities.[46] After examining a developer's subdivision scheme to ensure that it does not conflict with the regional plan's guidelines for the area, the commission has three options: it can approve, approve conditionally, or disapprove the application. As the name implies, conditional approval stipulates conditions that must be met before the developer can subdivide.

While regional planning commissions establish broad provincial and regional guidelines, municipalities are allowed to do their own planning and some larger cities have established their own planning departments. Professional planners in the Planning Service Division of Municipal Affairs and the regional planning commissions work closely with municipal councils in preparing general municipal plans and writing land-use bylaws. A planner with the Battle River Regional Planning Commission describes his responsibilities:

> It's kind of a watchdog role . . . to ensure that planned changes are in the best interests of our region. It's a mentally tedious job. Planning. Paperwork. Meetings . . . and more meetings. There are the regularly scheduled meetings with four city and county councils—and two environmental commissions. There are numerous unscheduled, every day meetings with subdividers, special interest groups and farmers.[47]

Every municipality in Alberta with a population of 1,000 or more and every county and municipal district with a population of 10,000 or more is required to have a general municipal plan describing the municipality's land uses and proposals for future development. A council has the discretion to designate a portion of the municipality for an area and/or redevelopment plan. An area plan is not as detailed as a subdivision plan or as abstract and undifferentiated as a general plan and is often used in the redevelopment of older neighbourhoods.

Once it has developed a general plan, council must enact a very specific land-use bylaw based on its power to control zoning and development. A land-use bylaw divides a municipality into a number of districts with designated permitted and conditional uses of land and buildings. The bylaw can be very specific, limiting the floor areas and heights of buildings; specifying their character, appearance, lighting, and other details; and regulating the height of fences and placement of billboards. The other parts of the machinery necessary for carrying out a municipality's general and area plans are the subdivision control system and the direct control exercised by the municipality over public works programs.

Opportunities for public participation in the municipal and regional planning process are limited. Citizens can act only in an advisory capacity; there is no point at which they are directly involved in the formulation of planning policy. Section 62 of the Planning Act requires a council to "provide an opportunity to those persons affected by it of making suggestions and representation." Section 139 directs a council to hold a public hearing before giving second reading to a proposed general municipal plan bylaw, area structure plan bylaw, area redevelopment plan bylaw, or a bylaw that amends or abolishes any of the above.[48] Section 49 requires a regional planning commission to hold one or more public meetings before adopting a regional plan.

Since much planning concerns technical matters, members of the public often hesitate to make presentations for fear of appearing ignorant. In addition, since professional planners often feel threatened by attacks on their plans, any public meeting to discuss a proposed plan can become adversarial. In the late 1960s advocate planners began to use their expertise on behalf of citizen groups attempting to prevent the enactment of what they saw as ill-conceived plans. At public meetings advocate planners provide technical information and arguments to counter the proposals of municipal and regional planners.[49] Both Edmonton and Calgary espoused community-based advocate planning when they participated in the federal government's Neighborhood Improvement Program, which has since been terminated.[50]

Amendments to the 1977 Planning Act

Following the passage of the 1977 Planning Act there was a frenzy of planning activity as a dynamic economy attracted people to Alberta from across Canada. While population growth and economic activity in Edmonton and Calgary were among the highest in the country, the expansion of their surrounding bedroom communities was phenomenal, with populations doubling and redoubling. Encouraged by the province's policy on decentralization and by rural municipalities that wanted to strengthen their assessment base, industrial development began to take place in rural areas. In the early 1980s a combination of a decline in the price of oil, the federal government's National Energy Policy (NEP), and a shift in exploration activity to the Canadian frontier wreaked havoc on the provincial economy and adversely affected planning activity in the province. Gordon and Hulchanski note that the Alberta Planning Board pressured "regional planning commissions to alter the content of their regional plans and downsize their operation"[51] in the interests of fiscal responsibility.

There was a renewed concern with planning when the economy began to revive and larger urban municipalities again began to expand in the late 1980s. The government had made a number of important changes to the planning act after Premier Peter Lougheed's March 15, 1984, throne speech, in which he said that one of his major priorities was "a government-wide effort . . . to reduce or eliminate unnecessary or obsolete regulations which frustrate or complicate the lives of our citizens as well as the operations of business."[52] In 1988 Dennis Anderson, who was then Minister of Municipal Affairs, said, "the government was calling for all of its agencies to review their regulations with an eye to getting rid of red tape. It's a principle which will guide us in our policy-making."[53] In 1988 Anderson's views on red tape and the decentralization of decision-making were reflected by changes made in 16 sections of the Planning Act which granted municipal and regional planning bodies more discretion, including the authority to approve a subdivision plan even though it did not "meet every standard of the local land-use bylaw."[54]

In 1991 another series of amendments was made to enhance local autonomy. The government responded positively to 1987, 1988, and 1990 resolutions by the Alberta Association of Municipal Districts and Counties (AAMD&C) by amending Section 78 to give a municipality, rather than the Alberta Planning Board, the power to grant an exemption to allow a second dwelling on a residential parcel. An amendment to Section 117 gave municipalities wide latitude in determining how municipal environmental reserves would be used, subject to the approval of the Alberta Planning Board, while at the same time ensuring that the public's interest was being protected.[55]

Regional Planning Commission Politics and Dissension

Although membership on a planning commission is not automatically bestowed on every governmental unit within a commission's boundaries, in practice, the Minister of Municipal Affairs has given commission representation to virtually all affected municipalities.[56] Moreover, the Blood and Peigan Indian reserves each have one vote on the Oldman River Commission.

Political posturing and contention are to be found on all planning commissions, but most dissension occurs on those containing a major urban centre. Conflicts between urban and rural municipalities revolve around both money and issues reflecting traditional urban and rural values. Regional planning invariably specifies locations for industry, with its strong tax base. Although rural municipalities compete among themselves for resources, the cleavage is normally an urban-rural one. Rural municipalities often charge that a commission dominated by urban members approves outlying subdivisions with little concern for their effects on school population, roadway usage, and agricultural land. On the other hand, urban municipalities maintain that they should receive at least a portion of the property taxes from "bedroom communities," since commuting suburbanites use urban services without paying for them. Urban municipalities favour regional parks, while rural municipalities maintain that parks deplete the stock of agricultural land and attract undesirable urbanites to rural areas, where they engage in crime and vandalism.

The crux of the representation problem on regional planning commissions is that the larger urban centres favour representation based on population, while smaller municipalities maintain that representation should be on the basis of individual units of government. A report prepared in 1980 by the Alberta Association of Municipal Districts and Counties and the Alberta Urban Municipalities Association states that "Representation on the RPCs [Regional Planning Commissions] and the voting pattern of rural and urban members was a source of contention for both. There is a perceived urban domination in the eyes of the rural municipalities, and a small town-rural bias in the eyes of the larger urban municipalities."[57]

At an Alberta Planning Board seminar in 1983, the provincial government's quandary over representation on regional planning commissions was apparent. When the Minister of Municipal Affairs, Julian Koziak, was asked his position on planning commission representation, he could respond only by saying that the present system recognizes local responsibility and that a balance has to be struck between the interests of urban and rural municipalities.[58] While the Department of Municipal Affairs has attempted to resolve the problem by giving larger municipalities slightly more representation, this compromise has satisfied neither larger nor smaller units.

Section 51 of the Planning Act requires that a regional plan be approved by two-thirds of the membership of a regional planning commission. This provision was designed to prevent an urban-rural split; it was thought that, where there was a slight majority of rural or urban members, the requirement for a two-thirds majority would force the majority to negotiate compromises with the minority in order to obtain approval for the plan.

Considering that smaller urban and rural municipalities are overrepresented on regional planning commissions, one would expect the commissions' most outspoken critics to be the larger urban centres. With the exception of Edmonton, this has not been the case. A somewhat dated survey, "Municipal Attitudes Towards Regional Planning in Alberta," found rural municipalities to be much more critical of regional planning commissions.[59] The major reason for rural criticism is that as regional planning commissions have evolved from serving as purely advisory bodies to exercising real power, they have forced municipalities to conform to planning schemes that undermine local autonomy. Several rural municipalities used the term "dictatorial" to describe their planning commissions. Concern with local autonomy is also manifested by the number of respondents from rural municipalities who wanted subdivision approving authority delegated back to local governments from the planning commissions.[60]

Dissatisfaction with planning commission powers was expressed by a resolution passed at the 1979 annual convention of the Alberta Association of Municipal Districts and Counties.

> WHEREAS as it was the purpose and intent of the original Regional Planning Commission to act as an Advisory Board:
> and WHEREAS, the same Regional Planning Commissions have over the years obtained more and more authority in the subdivision and development of Municipalities;
> and WHEREAS, local autonomy of rural Municipalities is being eroded,
> NOW THEREFORE BE IT RESOLVED that the Government of the Province of Alberta be requested to implement legislation which would stipulate that the regional planning commissions are created for the sole purpose and intent of The Planning Act . . . without infringing on the rights of individuals.

A Municipal Affairs representative responded to the resolution by saying that "a certain amount of local autonomy must be sacrificed in the interest of securing the policy objectives which are of common concern to the municipalities within a given region." These objectives are to preserve agricultural land, curb "wasteful" urban sprawl, and prevent and control development in "environmentally sensitive areas." Somewhat later, however, the provincial government modified this policy to recognize the concerns of municipalities that felt they were losing their autonomy. At the Alberta Planning Board's 1983 seminar, the Department of Municipal Affairs presented a discussion paper that stated:

> When the Board speaks of regional planning commissions in the years ahead, it is referring to the utilization of non-regulatory and non-control-oriented methods of achieving regional goals and objectives. . . . Recognizing that the key decisions in a region are implemented by municipal governments, the development industry, private citizens as they go about the business of living, and the Provincial Government, the Board believes that the most effective long-term benefits for the community will be achieved if those with the responsibility for making decisions are allowed to do so, with as little interference from outside

as possible. The Government has constrained the extent to which Regional Planning Commissions can intervene in local decision-making, to those occasions when the regional concern dictates it, and then only in specific and defined ways.[61]

The irony of this exchange between the rural municipalities and Municipal Affairs is that a great deal of controversy was generated by Section 85 of the 1977 Act, which provided municipalities with far more control over planning than they had had since the early 1950s. With the minister's authorization, either a council or its municipal planning commission was given the power to act as its own subdivision approving authority.

Farmland preservation, urban sprawl, and environmental issues are the three areas in which regional planning commissions are expected to follow provincial guidelines. Unfortunately, government departments often make policies with little or no consultation with regional planning commissions; as a consequence planning commission goals are adversely affected. Even when the procedures established for the formation of a regional plan call for the participation of provincial departments at specific stages, these departments tend to provide "inputs" rather than consulting and negotiating with planning commissions as equals.

The regional offices of various departments do consult planning commissions, but generally only in order to determine how provincial policies are to be implemented at the regional level. Policy is formulated at the Edmonton headquarters of most provincial departments, which have no formal consultative links with regional planning commissions. Since upper-level decision makers have little information about the peculiarities of particular regions, their policies often conflict with the commissions' long-range planning goals. If the provincial government's policy on regional planning and the maintenance of local autonomy is to succeed, it will be necessary to establish a formal mechanism to coordinate the policies of provincial departments with those of regional planning commissions.

Democracy and Regional and Municipal Conflict

Regional planning commissions comprise municipalities with diverse interests that must be balanced against one another, especially since a two-thirds majority is needed for the ratification of a regional plan. The provincial government recognizes that many planning decisions benefit people in one geographical area at the expense of those in others, and has provided opportunities for interested parties to participate in the planning process. As a result, planning has become increasingly political. One of the reasons this politicization has taken place is that municipalities must compete for provincial funds. But it is also important to note that politicization is a result of the gradual democratization of the planning process and increased public participation.

A principal cause of the animosity between large cities and their outlying municipalities is the competition for revenues. With municipalities dependent upon inadequate provincial grants and locally derived property taxes for most of their funding, and with regional planning commissions trying to make binding decisions on the location of industry, it is not surprising that the politics of planning often become bitter. If municipalities had a broader revenue base there would be less competition for revenue-producing industries and, consequently, more emphasis on the development of regional plans that would mitigate social problems.

The argument that a lack of fiscal resources distorts planning decisions and causes an inordinate amount of hostility between governmental units is not new. It was made implicitly by Bettison, Kenward, and Taylor in *Urban Affairs in Alberta* in 1975.[62] In 1981 a Department of Municipal Affairs regional planning discussion paper argued that "the regional planning system becomes the battleground for what are essentially fiscal matters perhaps more appropriately handled through tax sharing, grants aimed at low or no-growth areas.[63] Perhaps the best case for fiscal policies such as sharing provincial income tax and oil and gas revenues with municipalities, allowing municipalities to enact their own sales taxes, and providing substantially larger conditional and unconditional municipal grants can be made on the basis of their effect on regional and municipal planning.

Despite intermunicipal competition for fiscal resources, planning is being democratized because astute planners and pragmatic elected officials believe that planners and politicians working together can move beyond traditional physical planning into the development of comprehensive physical and social plans not unlike the master plans envisioned by Thomas Adams shortly after the turn of the century. A contemporary term for this process is strategic planning. In 1989 the Deputy Minister of Municipal Affairs, Archie Grover, predicted:

> "Strategic planning" will become essential for survival. A strategic plan is the "roadmap" which guides an organization through turbulent times to its destiny. Community planners will be called upon to apply

their expertise beyond traditional land use planning issues to assist municipal governments to develop such broad strategic plans. These strategic plans will still involve land use and development issues, but will also likely involve all aspects of community life.[64]

Whether it is called comprehensive or strategic planning, planners and politicians know that if planning policy is to be successfully implemented the public has to be involved at all stages in the process, from the initial brainstorming phase through a final reading by council when policy is made. In 1988 Minister of Municipal Affairs Dennis Anderson, enamored with the writings of futurists, initiated Vision 2020, which was to be a long-range planning tool to cope with rapid change. The Department of Municipal Affairs provided municipalities with "future data" and resource personnel to interpret it and conduct public meetings and expected that elected officials, the bureaucracy, and the public would collectively forge a scenario for the future of their communities. Although "visioning" was soon put on the back burner after a change in ministers, Municipal Affairs continues to recognize the importance of public involvement in the planning process.

The "Green" Phenomenon in Planning

Planning in the Department of Municipal Affairs and in municipalities across the province has always been a conventional process. Nevertheless, radical planners operating at the margins of society have proposed democratic agendas for planning which ultimately captured the public's imagination. The concepts of advocate planning and public participation in planning were introduced by radical planners and only later accepted, albeit reluctantly, by the planning establishment.

Throughout the 1970s and into the 1980s radical planners railed against the many mega-developments being built in urban areas across the country. Suburban projects were charged with destroying the downtown core, and downtown projects with being disproportionate to the people who frequented them. In almost every case developers were accused of charging exorbitant rents to the detriment of small businesses and working-class people. In short, radical planners blamed the developers and financiers for making cities less liveable.

With the collapse of the development industry and an increasing public awareness of environmental issues, radical planners began to focus on the creation of a "green city." *City Magazine* devoted its summer/fall 1989 issue to the topic.

Today an environmental consciousness has put saving our planet as the number one concern. Green City is one aspect of this reawakening—a movement that sees the city as saveable and development of this green alternative as worthy of great effort. . . . The Green City idea embraces many threads, particularly environmentalism, bioregionalism, social ecology, and green. Green City is a rallying point. . . .[65]

In the same issue, "Green City: An Introduction" explains that in addition to such principles as energy self-sufficiency, clean air and water, parks, gardens, and open space, a commitment to grass-roots community involvement and cooperation is integral to the green city movement. According to John Young, a "preference for small-scale communities, participatory democracy, [and] belief in a 'natural relationship' between people and the earth . . . are elements of radical ideology which go back to the peasant revolts of medieval times . . . and which are echoed by Robert Owen and the Ricardian socialists of the 1820s and 1830s. . . ."[66] Thus radical planners, the majority of whom have socialist inclinations, find it appropriate to embrace a "green" perspective.

In the not too distant future, the country's planning establishment can expect radical planners to escalate their attacks unless it begins to demonstrate more concern for environmental issues. Now that the environmental movement has captured the attention of the public, radical planners may at last be able to begin to define planning's mainstream.

An Overview of Planning and Democratic Institutions

Historically, planning ideology in Alberta falls within the mainstream of the planning movement in Canada. In both cases an infatuation with the "City Beautiful Movement" soon cooled, to be replaced by a philosophy of utilitarianism. While the evolution of Alberta's planning legislation has been affected by the ever-changing social, economic, and technological factors at work in the province, a commitment to utilitarianism has remained intact.

The explosive population growth during the 1950s led to the creation of an expanding network of regional planning commissions to control and program growth. Although a commission has extensive powers, it works closely with its member municipalities, since the commission board is composed of the municipalities' elected officials. Most boards are divided by two philosophical and voting cleavages: an urban/rural split and a large/small community split. Both are a function of the communities' differing values and needs. However, increasing democratization and proportional representation on the boards seem to have mitigated some of this conflict.

Like other middle-level municipal servants, planners get caught up in bureaucratic paradoxes with no clear-cut answers. Municipal and regional planners are highly educated visionaries with a sense of municipal plans and mission. But often council members also see themselves as visionaries, with a decidedly different plan for the future than that offered by planning professionals. Therein lies the problem. In theory, the planner accepts the traditional bureaucrat's role of following the dictates of elected officials, but in fact the planner has been taught that certain land uses and plans are unacceptable no matter what the position of the elected representatives. Planners have to ask themselves whether one of their roles in a democratic system is to seek the support of the public when elected representatives refuse to heed their advice or whether they must follow the dictates of those who are elected, no matter how misguided their planning policies appear to be.

Planners are expected to work within a democratic framework, since it is the elected council that ultimately makes decisions on community planning. In a discussion of ethical problems planners often face, Nigel Richardson advises them to put aside "purely personal views . . . and unfocused notions like 'the public interest' . . . unless they can be translated into specific and defensible planning criteria." If a planner has a strong moral or religious conviction about an issue, "the proper course is to make his/her position known and suggest that he/she be relieved of the responsibility."[67]

Perhaps even more difficult for the planner is to define the appropriate relationship between the planning profession and the public. Legislation allows the public to be brought in at almost every stage in the planning process, but very often it is unclear whether the people are meant to have power or whether the consultation process is merely a facade. In short, for the planning profession, the parameters of grass-roots democracy are still unclear. Still, the proponents of democracy are encouraged by changes in education and values in the planning profession which are reflected in greater numbers of planners imbued with a sense of social responsibility and a commitment to grass-roots democracy.

13

Education Politics and Government

Introduction

In 1985 a prominent provincial Tory politician told a meeting of Alberta educators that education should be viewed as a rational enterprise rather than a "political game." Although the politician's remarks were well meant and mirror the view of a substantial portion of the public, it is no more possible to eradicate politics from education than it is to remove it from the provincial or federal levels of government. Harvey Tucker and Harmon Zeigler explain how the idea originated that educational policy making is beyond the pale of politics, noting that in the early part of the century schools of education adopted the reform ideology that government should be run as an efficient business enterprise.

> The key points of the ideology—efficiency, unity (for example, minimization of conflict), and professionalism—were welcomed by upper-class boards. Schools, like businesses, should be managed by experts. By 1920, the norm of school board nonparticipation in administration had become so pervasive that superintendents protested lay influence.[1]

Not everyone in the community subscribed to the view that education should be divorced from politics, but during Alberta's halcyon 1950s and 1960s education was rarely beset by serious political controversy. This period has been characterized as one in which "the authority or wisdom of the school was rarely questioned" and "education was held in high esteem by all."[2] For the most part, students were well-behaved and the educational system was supported by the community. Teachers thought of themselves as professionals who were above "haggling" over wages, which was just as well since many people believed teachers should make economic sacrifices in the interests of the community.

The permissive society of the 1970s made teaching more arduous.

Teachers facing classrooms of unruly and rebellious students responded by becoming militant and demanding higher salaries and better working conditions. At the same time a number of people disenchanted with the educational system argued there was an inverse relationship between the amount of money spent on education and "Johnny's ability to read." As property taxes mounted, education was often the scapegoat.[3] As just one example, while the average personal income in the province increased 293 percent between 1972 and 1982, the average property tax increased 415 percent in Calgary and 433 percent in Edmonton. People became aware of educational costs during the 1970s when funding from the provincial government did not increase as fast as educational spending. Although education grants increased in absolute terms each year, in relative terms, the provincial share of total educational revenue consistently decreased. As a consequence, school boards resorted to supplementary requisitions from municipalities and the municipalities were forced to raise property taxes.

In the 1980s a number of elected officials charged that the cost of education, rather than poor planning or land speculation, was responsible for municipal indebtedness. Politicians and community groups argued that a decrease in the quality of education was responsible for a decline in the reading of books and was even a factor in increasing drug use and teenage pregnancies. The pendulum is beginning to move in another direction in the 1990s as more sophisticated politicians and citizens realize that although education has its deficiencies, the focus should be on rectifying them rather than blaming the educational system for social ills. They understand that if society is to move ahead, education and educational spending must be given a higher priority than in the past.

Historical Development of Alberta Education

In Canada's early period the educational system was administered, operated, and financed by various churches, with limited government support. The Loyalists who fled to Canada during the American Revolution brought as part of their philosophical baggage the belief that the state had a moral responsibility to provide education for the masses. Although the Common School Act passed in Upper Canada in 1816 provided for the establishment of a school by the residents of any town, village, or township by local option, almost half a century passed before universal education financed by the public purse was fully accepted. Egerton Ryerson became Superintendent of Schools for Canada West in 1846 and his ideas shaped all aspects of Canadian education during the rest of the nineteenth century and influenced educational practices well into the twentieth. Ryerson was committed to uniform, free, universal, compulsory education that would further Canadian values. Fascinated by the highly centralized French and Prussian educational systems, he advocated a school system tightly controlled by a central authority with limited administrative duties to be carried out by locally elected school trustees. The system was to be financed at the local level. "The Ryerson tradition," as it came to be called, soon spread across the country and by the turn of the century it was firmly established in western Canada.[4] In 1867 the importance of public education was recognized in Section 93 of the British North America Act, which stated that "in and for each Province the Legislature may exclusively make Laws in relation to Education" provided that they did not affect "any Right or Privilege with respect to Denominational Schools. . . ." After Confederation, the federal government set aside one-eighteenth of all Dominion Lands as an educational endowment.

A series of bitter struggles led to the establishment of separate and "common" schools, both of which received provincial funds and were given the power to tax. One factor in the development of the educational system was Ryerson's belief that a specialized form of government was required for educational policy making and administration. A second factor was that since municipal government was out of favour at the time, bringing education under the fold of municipal government would doom it to failure. Frank Oliver, a North-West Territories legislator and principal proponent of the establishment of a school system in the territories, argued that education should be controlled and financed by an autonomous locally elected governmental body with its own powers of taxation, including the right to tax owners of nonresidential property.[5]

In 1884 the North-West Territorial Council passed an ordinance providing for public and separate schools, and school districts were established in Edmonton and Calgary. The 58 public schools and one separate school operating in the territories in 1885 had increased to 243 public and eleven separate schools by 1891. Eric Hanson describes the financial status of the early school districts:

> At first the school districts levied and collected their own taxes, but the territorial government often had to help in collecting arrears. . . . Dominion and territorial grants to schools were paid to the treasurers of the districts or directly to teachers as part salary.[6]

One of the first acts of the new Alberta provincial government in 1905 was the passage of a school act and the establishment of a department of education. The 1905 Alberta Act provided that the majority religious group, either Protestant or Roman Catholic, would form the public school district, while the minority religious group could form a separate district. In both cases district electors chose their own school board. Since in most communities Protestant electors predominated, public school districts generally provided an education for non-Catholic children and separate school districts provided an education for Catholic children.

Most districts requisitioned their funds from municipal and local improvement districts, while the others levied and collected their own taxes. Regardless of the method used, poorer districts often had difficultly obtaining sufficient funds to cover their debenture payments and pay teachers' salaries.

As waves of immigrants flowed into the province, new school districts were organized and educational facilities built. In 1906 there were 746 school districts (570 of which were operating schools) with 28,784 students and 760 classrooms. Three years later there were 1,250 districts (970 operational) with 46,048 students and 1,323 classrooms. By 1915 there were 2,478 districts (2,138 operational), 97,286 students, and 3,082 classrooms. The school systems were overwhelmed by the population booms in Edmonton and Calgary and classes were held in rented rooms while new schools were being built. Calgary School Superintendent Melville Scott noted in 1913 that "one-third of our present pupils are new to Calgary schools this year."[7]

Although legislation passed in 1913 allowed school consolidation, the number of districts continued to increase, since it provided little inducement for them to consolidate.[8] A few districts that merged voluntarily during the 1920s to provide high school facilities had financial problems, for they were still too small. The school divisions that were eventually created would include almost all of the consolidated school districts.

Alberta's school systems suffered when farm income plummeted during the 1920s and 1930s. The Department of Education's annual report for 1933 stated that some teacher salaries were months in arrears, and "school budgets have been scrutinized with so discriminating an eye that no provision has been made for purchase of physical equipment such as maps, supplies and books."[9] In 1935 a municipal inspector from St. Paul wrote that in some newly settled areas 75 percent of the people were on relief. Residents in at least three communities decided to delay organizing a school district "because they could not see their way clear to pay even a small contribution towards the support of the school."[10]

Although teachers suffered along with their students as the provincial government gave education short shrift, the public was less sympathetic towards teachers, who were "a living symbol of taxation in the community."[11] In 1906 the average salary of an Alberta teacher was $614.13 a year and a decade later it had increased only $200. Facing a severe teacher shortage, in 1918 the province finally amended the School Act to make the minimum salary for teachers $840. However, in rural areas it was common for a teacher to be employed no more than a year or two before being dismissed so a new teacher could be hired at the minimum salary level. The province's teachers had neither secure tenure nor a pension scheme, a state of affairs that suited the Department of Education and the Alberta School Trustees' Association (ASTA).

Given their poor salaries and working conditions, a parsimonious provincial government, and hostile local school trustees, it is not surprising that in 1918 teachers embraced the newly organized Alberta Teachers' Alliance (ATA), loosely modelled after the British National Union of Teachers.[12] Although reluctant to affiliate with organized labour, the Alliance was militant; in the spring of 1921, Edmonton, Lethbridge, and Calgary ATA locals threatened strike action in order to win recognition. Disputes were resolved in Calgary and Lethbridge, but in Edmonton 74 high school teachers participated in an unsuccessful two-week strike before returning to their classrooms. The strike confirmed ASTA's perception of the ATA as a radical labour organization which should not be recognized by the trustees. When the Liberal government was defeated in 1921, teachers expected to be treated more sympathetically by the United Farmers of Alberta (UFA).[13] Unfortunately, not only was education a low priority for the new government, but the Minister of Education, Perren Baker, was careful not to alienate the ASTA which, at that time, was rural-based and whose trustees had close ties with rural members of the provincial legislature. ASTA was unrelenting in its opposition to consolidated school districts, which would have reduced its membership, and to the demands of the ATA. Throughout the UFA period teachers' salaries remained virtually static, they had no pension plans, and there was little improvement in tenure conditions. With the exception of two school consolidations, no major changes were made in education policy until after William Aberhart's Social Credit victory in 1935.[14]

William Aberhart may be best remembered for his Calgary Prophetic Bible Institute radio preaching, but at the time he was known as a professional educator.[15] A teacher in Ontario before he came to Calgary in 1910, Aberhart moved up in the city's educational system and was appointed principal of a secondary school which became Crescent Heights High

School in 1927. Although education was not a major campaign issue in 1935, after Aberhart gained control of the government he decided to manage the education portfolio in addition to the premiership.[16] Despite the adamant objections of the ASTA, the new government soon passed major legislation that enabled the Department of Education to merge school districts by ministerial order and gave teachers rights for which they had fought for almost two decades.[17] Many parents did not take kindly to this loss of control over education.

The new administrative unit was the school division, which included up to 60 rural school districts. The responsibility for educational policy making and administration shifted from school districts to school divisions and, although the districts were left intact, they became primarily attendance units with limited advisory powers. Hanson describes the policy-making and administrative structure of the school division:

> A school division is administered by a board of trustees, three to five in number, each trustee representing a subdivision. A full-time secretary-treasurer is hired by the board to carry on the day-to-day administrative matters of the division. . . . A supervisor of schools, appointed by the department of education, is stationed in nearly every school division. His duties are to supervise school operations and to serve as an advisor of the board of trustees. . . . local school districts elect three trustees each; their duty is to advise the divisional board on local matters.[18]

From the perspective of school consolidation, the government's policy was a success: by 1941 there were 50 school divisions where there had previously been 3,450 districts.[19] The number of divisions had increased to 59 by 1954 but dropped to 30 by 1971 as a result of the creation in 1950 of counties with educational functions and the alignment of school division boundaries by the Co-terminous Boundaries Commission in 1953/54. Although the Social Credit government was determined to reduce the number of school districts, separate districts and those located in cities were not initially affected by the amalgamation process.

In 1935 the province's teachers were strong supporters of Aberhart's policy on school consolidation. Many of them had been left unpaid and destitute for months by districts whose excuse was that they were too small to collect enough taxes to pay their bills. Aberhart was as determined to modernize teaching and to improve the working conditions of teachers as he had been to consolidate school districts. When he taught in

Calgary he had a reputation for being a strict disciplinarian who required students to commit pages of facts to memory. Nevertheless, he implemented the major curriculum changes promised during his election campaign which brought progressive education to the province.[20] In the spring of 1936 the Teaching Profession Act was amended so that every teacher in Alberta automatically became a member of the Alberta Teachers' Association (ATA), the successor to the Alberta Teachers' Alliance.[21]

There is no question that many school districts were much too small to support an adequate educational system. Consolidation produced greater equalization of the tax burden and a higher degree of administrative specialization, but diminished community control over educational policy. Moreover, the consolidation of physical facilities meant that children had to be bussed to adjoining communities, and some residents argued that the loss of a school through consolidation led to a decline in community identity. On balance, however, few people advocated a return to the conditions extant in 1935 when the teaching profession was demoralized and there were almost 4,000 school districts, many of which had duplicate facilities and were fiscally unstable.

After losing battle after battle with the new Social Credit government, the ASTA passed a resolution at its 1938 convention calling for compulsory ASTA membership for all Alberta school trustees. William Roberts writes that the reason given for this was the newly strengthened position of the ATA, but "there was reason to suspect that trustees were concerned about their inability to influence the Government's decision to establish larger administrative units," among other issues.[22] Although the Alberta School Trustees' Association Act passed in the spring of 1939 gave the organization a public corporate identity, the government did not make membership compulsory until 1941.

Between 1933 and 1943 student enrollment fell each year. Despite an economic rebound in the late 1930s total school expenditures increased at an average annual rate of only 1.9 percent, with most of the growth occurring during the war years. Enrollment stabilized in 1944 before beginning a rapid increase in 1945 which continued for some 15 years; once again educational facilities were overwhelmed, as they had been in the province's early period. However, new oil revenues enabled the government to increase education spending. Record increases in enrollment each year peaked in 1960 and began a slow deceleration until there were actual declines in the early 1970s. Nevertheless, between 1961 and 1971 enrollment in Alberta elementary and secondary schools increased by 40 percent.

Table 13.1 County of Two Hills School Enrollment by Year

Year	Enrollment	Year	Enrollment	Year	Enrollment
1965	1,998	1974	1,427	1983	910
1966	1,960	1975	1,399	1984	868
1967	1,871	1976	1,384	1985	813
1968	1,748	1977	1,351	1986	779
1969	1,729	1978	1,258	1987	749
1970	1,712	1979	1,148	1988	724
1971	1,640	1980	1,069	1989	708
1972	1,558	1981	987		
1973	1,450	1982	940		

Although there was a general increase in school enrollment, the trends were very different in rural and urban areas due to Alberta's changing demographics. An ongoing migration was depleting the population of many rural areas while enrollments were surging in urban areas.[23] An example of rural decline is shown by Table 13.1.

Demographic trends also affect urban areas. As families with school-age children moved from the city centre to outlying suburban neighbourhoods in Edmonton and Calgary, inner-city schools were increasingly under-utilized while schools in new neighbourhoods were filled almost as soon as they opened. In Edmonton the Rutherford Elementary School, built more than 50 years ago, operated at capacity until the early 1970s, when enrollment started to decline; in 1986 the school was operating at only 21 percent of its capacity.[24] Although various plans were implemented to increase the attractiveness of inner-city schools, the Edmonton public district closed 11 schools between 1969 and 1985 and the Edmonton separate district closed 19 schools between 1973 and 1990.[25] There were even more closures in Calgary, 21 public schools and ten separate schools between 1975 and 1990.[26]

Although school closures may have the public's support, they cause havoc at the neighbourhood level, where they pit community against community and families with children against those without. The prospect of a school closure often brings out the worst in people involved in local politics. In order to counter education critics who maintain that deep financial cuts must be made in the interests of efficiency, many proponents of inner-city schools argue that their schools should be converted into multi-use educational and community facilities, but this idea has never captured the public's imagination in Alberta.

Education Funding

From the beginning, funding education has been difficult in Alberta, where an ever-increasing student population quickly overwhelmed the province's education grant structure. The per diem school grant, which was set at $1.20 in 1905, was gradually reduced to $1.00 by 1919. A policy implemented in 1901 of giving a school district a bonus for employing highly qualified teachers was discontinued in 1913. An incentive grant for districts which kept their schools open 160 days a year was repealed in 1913, as was another grant for districts in which a high percentage of students were attending school.[27] The post-war recession resulted in another round of cost-cutting.

> The per diem grant for rural schools was cut from $1.00 to $.90. For rooms that contained grades above the eighth the grant was lowered from $.50 to $.25 per diem. Newly organized districts obtained $.20 per diem for only two years. The library grant was limited to schools in the first six years after their organization. Special grants for schools with rooms used for community purposes, for technical education in one-room schools, for gardens and teachers' residences were all struck out. Town schools received a similar cut. Where there were two rooms the grant for the senior room was reduced from $3.00 to $2.00 per day. High School and consolidated school grants were reduced by fifty percent.[28]

This scaled-down provincial grant structure remained essentially the same until after the Second World War.

The government developed a crude equalization formula which provided poor districts and those with unique problems with more funds than wealthier districts with ordinary needs. As an example, in 1906 almost equal numbers of children attended rural and urban schools; 14,576 children in rural schools and 14,208 in urban ones. However, because the government recognized that the cost of educating a rural child was substantially higher than that of educating an urban child, rural schools received $93,000 and urban schools $50,000 in grants.[29]

The School Grant Act of 1913 continued to recognize the higher cost of rural education by giving rural schools special financial incentives. Moreover, since the government was encouraging district consolidation, it provided a special transportation grant to enable large districts to develop extensive bus systems. After the School Grant Act was amended in 1919, rural districts continued to receive more funds on a per capita basis than their urban neighbours. When the act was amended again in 1926, a tax equalization formula was devised so that all schools would have enough funds to operate for at least 160 days a year. Dent explains: "If the total assessment for any district was below $75,000 and more than $70,000, the district was given a special grant of twenty cents daily. For every subsequent drop of $5000 in the assessment, there was . . . a corresponding increase in the grant of twenty cents per day, until a daily maximum of $2.80 was reached."[30]

The 1926 equalization formula changed little until 1946, when it was completely revamped, making the number and type of classrooms the basis for formulating a district's grant. Although the grant formula differed considerably from what it had been in the past, the underlying philosophy of equalized assessment remained the same.

Major changes in the province's economy and demographics occurred after the Second World War. With a revival of agriculture, rural areas were no longer destitute. An oil boom attracted tens of thousands of people from outside the province who settled in the cities and overwhelmed the school systems. Beginning in 1948 changes were made in the equalization grant which narrowed differences in the amount of grants to urban and rural districts. In 1950 the School Borrowing Assistance Act provided funds for new schools which were being built primarily in urban areas and subsequent changes to the act provided more money for school construction.

Despite additional provincial funding, education costs continued to soar and school boards were forced to increase their requisition on municipalities for funds. This was one of the reasons why counties were created in 1950 which placed the power to tax and provide services for a given area under a single governmental authority. Under county government the county board of education submits its budget to the county council for approval. In an another attempt to cap requisitions on municipalities the government introduced a program in 1955 which provided a subsidy to any school district or division whose requisition did not exceed 25 mills. But costs continued to climb and by 1960 the grant program had become a conglomeration of basic and equalization grants. A district's basic grant paid for 100 percent of student transportation costs, 80 percent of teachers' salaries, 3.5 percent of costs for instructional materials, and $900 for every operational classroom. Depending upon a district's tax assessment, the pupil equalization grant provided between $2 and $9 per student and the classroom equalization grant provided between $14 and $23 per classroom. A $100 per student grant was available to districts with extraordinary increases in enrollment.

The School Foundation Program Fund (SFPF) introduced in 1961 to ensure that every school district had adequate funds to provide a minimal standard of education included an equalization grant which redistributed funds levied in high assessment districts to those with low assessments.[31] First, every municipality's total equalized assessment, including the assessment of residential properties and pipe and power lines, was determined by the Alberta Assessment Equalization Board and then a uniform tax of 32 mills was levied on the equalized assessment rate. Along with a provincial government contribution, the assessment money which was collected was distributed by the SFPF to the province's school districts following a complex and elaborate set of regulations.[32] The provincial government contributed additional special purpose grants.

In addition to the SFPF levy a district was allowed to obtain additional funds through a supplementary requisition to municipalities. This provision was made to enable districts with high assessments to provide new and innovative educational programs and to make the SFPF program more palatable. The government initially expected that the supplementary requisitions would be very moderate.

The SFPF relieved the financial pressure on local ratepayers. Table 13.2 shows that the province and the SFPF provided 92.3 percent of the total revenue for Alberta school districts in its first year of operation. However, in each succeeding year the province's share of educational funding decreased.

The "other local revenue" in Table 13.2 constitutes a small but important source of funds for school districts. Included in this category are various assessments made on parents for educational programs and supplies (for example, book rentals), cafeteria revenue, rental revenue for the use of school buildings by other school authorities and private organizations, revenue from sales of surplus assets, and charges collected by a number of small fee-based programs. This component of education funding, as a share of total spending, increased slightly after the School Foundation Program was implemented and then for a number of years moved in a narrow range. Nevertheless, it has occasionally been controversial, as in 1988 when the government brought in new education legislation and allowed schools to continue charging fees for instructional materials.

When the Progressive Conservatives were elected in 1971 one of their campaign promises had been to exempt residential property from the SFPF levy. Shortly thereafter, a blue ribbon Task Force on Provincial Municipal Fiscal Arrangements in Alberta was struck "to make an inquiry into the proper division of responsibilities" between the province and local authorities.[33] Following its recommendations, the government exempted residential property from the SFPF in 1974. After farm land was exempted in 1975, the SFPF component of education funding became a single digit.

Although owners of farm land and residential properties were no longer paying into the SFPF fund, the government was unwilling to make up all of the difference, and the provincial share of educational funding began a long and precipitous decline. As a consequence, education districts increasingly resorted to supplementary requisitions for their funds and once again rural and urban ratepayers were paying substantial property taxes to support local education. In 1982, 65.3 percent of the cost of local education was borne by the province. The Minister of Education's Task Force on School Financing recommended that the province assume 85 percent of local educational costs, with the other 15 percent to be covered by local property taxation, that is, by requisitioning municipalities.[34] The plan, which was not implemented, would have cost the government an additional $460 million for 1982 and an additional half billion dollars each year thereafter.

As the share of provincial funding decreased, the share of local funding increased. Table 13.2 shows that after a slow growth in the share of supplementary requisitions between 1961 and 1974 there was an increase from 15 to 26 percent in the next six years. The percentage size of local supplements slowed in the 1980s, however, after a protracted controversy with local authorities.

As might be expected, the continual decrease in the provincial government's share of educational spending generated controversy among municipalities, school districts, and the provincial government. Year after year at the meetings of the Alberta Urban Municipalities Association (AUMA) and the Alberta School Trustees' Association (ASTA), delegates passed resolutions requesting the provincial government to increase its share of school funding.[35] Each time the government responded that additional funds were not available from the province's general revenue. As school districts increasingly came to rely on local funding, municipalities had to increase property taxes to meet the larger requisitions. Not unexpectedly, many ratepayers blamed the increases on the extravagances of municipal councils rather than the needs of boards of education. In 1981 Edmonton sponsored a resolution at the AUMA convention calling upon the government to "amend such legislation as may be necessary to allow municipalities to collect taxes only for municipal purposes." The government responded that "the added cost and added bureaucracy outweighed the advantages of separate accountability."[36] Similar convention resolutions passed in subsequent years were given equally short shrift by

Table 13.2 Education Funding in Alberta by Source

Year	Prov. Gen. Rev. (%)	Prov. SFPF Levy (%)	Total Prov. Share (%)	Local Suppl. Req'n (%)	Other Local Rev. (%)	Total Local Share (%)
1950	27.0	0.0	27.0	68.3	4.7	73.0
1954	32.4	0.0	32.4	64.0	3.6	67.6
1956	45.2	0.0	45.2	51.4	3.4	54.8
1960	44.4	0.0	44.4	52.8	2.8	55.6
1961	47.4	44.9	92.3	5.4	2.3	7.7
1962	44.9	44.5	89.4	8.3	2.4	10.7
1964	46.4	43.3	89.7	8.1	2.2	10.3
1966	52.8	35.5	88.3	8.5	3.2	11.7
1968	51.4	30.1	81.5	15.2	3.4	18.6
1970	57.0	28.1	85.1	11.4	3.5	14.9
1972	56.3	27.1	83.4	12.6	4.1	16.7
1974	68.0	13.0	81.0	15.1	3.9	19.0
1976	68.4	8.4	76.8	19.0	4.2	23.2
1978	64.0	9.0	73.0	22.5	4.6	27.1
1980	59.1	9.6	68.7	26.1	5.1	31.2
1982	56.1	9.2	65.3	29.7	5.0	34.7
1984	55.5	8.4	63.9	30.4	5.7	36.1
1986	55.6	7.4	63.0	32.0	5.1	37.1
1988	53.0	7.5	60.5	33.9	5.7	39.6
1989	52.6	7.4	60.0	34.3	5.8	40.1
1990(E)	51.4	8.0	59.4	35.4	5.2	40.6
1991(E)	50.7	7.6	58.3	36.3	5.4	41.7

the government. A 1984 resolution calling for an amendment to the Municipal Taxation Act which would allow school divisions to become taxing authorities "and thereby account directly to the people who elect them" was dismissed by the provincial government with the comment that such a policy would merely duplicate the tax administration system without reducing taxes. The government concluded by saying that school board trustees were sensitive "to the effects of higher school taxes on local ratepayers to whom they are accountable."[37]

Although the government was unwilling to make any fundamental change in the education requisitioning process, it was not oblivious to the problems of education finance. In particular, the Department of Education was concerned about the extreme disparity between wealthy districts with a substantial business and industrial tax base and rural ones with property taxes based almost entirely on agricultural land. In 1984 an Equity Grant program was introduced which attempted to rectify fiscal inequities by basing the size of one of the major provincial grants on a combination of three components, a school division or district's fiscal capacity, the sparsity of its population, and its distance from major urban centres.[38] Three years later the Minister of Education, Nancy Betkowski, released a controversial report entitled "Equity in Education Financing" which proposed to equalize nonresidential assessment across the province. This was to be done by first pooling the nonresidential portion of all property taxes in a provincial Education Trust Fund. The money would then be re-allocated to school jurisdictions according to the criteria established for the equity grant—fiscal capacity, population sparsity, and distance from large centres. The Department of Education was surprised by the extent and depth of opposition to the proposal from school trustees, educators, and municipal councils. The ASTA's position was that corporate pooling was unwise unless the government could guarantee that the funds would be safe from raids by other departments and changes in political priorities. The ASTA's executive director admitted that small rural school boards supported corporate pooling, but said that the balance of the boards, representing two-thirds of the province's student population, opposed it.[39] Like the ASTA, the AUMA was concerned that the pooling scheme could be jeopardized if the government decided to make concessions on corporate taxes for political reasons. It also feared "the same rationale would eventually apply to pooling . . . corporate taxes collected for municipalities" which would result in a centralization of finance and a loss of municipal autonomy.[40] Faced with such intense opposition, the government put the policy proposal on hold.

In 1988, one year after the Department of Education floated its pooling proposal, Education Bill 27 was enacted. Although Betkowski adamantly maintained that equity was one of the principles upon which the legislation rested, provisions to enhance financial equity were modest at best. At the next sitting of the legislature, Premier Getty said in his throne speech that "enhanced equity funding will be implemented in 1989. Equal access to education . . . is a priority, and this grant will assist school boards with a small tax base or in sparsely populated areas."[41] Nevertheless, local school jurisdictions and municipal councils battled the government to a standstill over "enhanced equity funding," the euphemism for corporate pooling.

In January 1991 the Minister of Education, Jim Dinning, announced that the government was making a one-time $2 million allocation to remedy fiscal inequities. He warned that since the government was committed to balancing the budget, school districts should not expect such an allocation in the future and should seriously consider other alternatives. Only days later the Department of Education published a short position paper entitled "Education Trust Fund: A Proposal to Bring Equity to Educational Financing" in order to show how the implementation of the department's equity proposal would affect education. It said that in its first year of operation some $450 million would be collected and redistributed to school districts across the province. Funding for 106 of the 140 operating school boards, with 86 percent of the students in the province, would be increased, while the remaining 34 boards would be guaranteed the level of support they had received in the preceding year. The report also "estimated that non-residential mill rates would decrease in about 60% of operating school jurisdictions."[42]

Shortly after the minister warned that the time for putting an equitable school funding program into place was running out, the Education Tax Equity Council (ETEC), with representatives from 37 of the wealthier school governments, presented the government with an alternative proposal stating that any changes in educational funding must be minimized and that boards had an "historic right" to their nonresidential taxes which "must [and] will be protected."[43] Although the ETEC raised money for a campaign to convince the public of the merits of its position, the government did not act on its proposal.

At about the same time, the school board in Devon began to organize other tax-poor school systems and in October 1991 representatives from 43 district boards attended a meeting in Edmonton to urge the government to implement a plan that would provide school units across the province with equitable funding. Shortly thereafter they decided to initiate a lawsuit to force the government to ensure that all districts have equal financial resources so that equal educational opportunities would be available across the province.

Education Government

Education government has evolved in much the same way as its municipal government counterpart; it derives its authority from the provincial government which delegates to it certain areas of responsibility. Therefore, education government is not entirely autonomous. Proponents of school government autonomy express concern that provincial governments seem to be centralizing traditional education functions, an assertion that has been made for the past century.

Although there are many similarities between education and municipal governments, there are differences in their financing and elected official and administrator relationships. First, a sizeable portion of education government funding is obtained by requisitioning municipal government, which obtains much of its money from residential ratepayers. Second, educational administrators (such as school superintendents and principals) often influence or override the decisions of school boards that are elected to formulate policy. These two characteristics of education government generate a great deal of controversy.

The School Act outlines the policy areas reserved to the provincial government and delineates the responsibilities of local education government. Section 25 gives the Minister of Education the option to:

(a) prescribe courses of study or education programs including the amount of instruction;

(b) authorize courses of study, education programs or instructional materials for use in schools;

(c) prescribe the minimum total hours of instruction a board shall make available to a student in a school year;

(d) approve any course, education program or instructional material that may be submitted to the Minister by a board or another operator of a school for use in a school;

(e) subject to the right of a board to provide religious instruction, by order prohibit the use of a course, an education program or instructional material in schools;

(f) by order adopt or approve goals and standards applicable to the provision of education in Alberta.

Quite clearly the act gives the Minister of Education wide-ranging discretion to formulate educational policy and standards. But, in addition, the legislation gives educational units authority to make policies as well as share policy-making powers with the provincial government. As an example, Section 28 directs school boards to enroll students in a school and provide them with an educational program "consistent with the requirements of [the] Act." Section 38(1) states, "A board, in addition to its obligation to provide courses and education programs to its resident students . . . may develop or provide courses to any person on any subject." Section 40(1)(f) states that if the minister has not specified the number of hours of instruction a student should receive, the school board must do so. Section 33(1) gives local boards the discretion to prescribe religious instruction for their students and allows persons other than teachers to provide religious instruction. Subject to certain conditions, Section 79 grants local boards the authority to hire teachers and Section 88 the right to terminate their employment.

While school boards are given discretionary powers, they also are specifically mandated to carry out some activities and prohibited from carrying out others. According to Section 40 of the act, a board is responsible for designating the date schools open, the dates of summer and winter vacations, and the number and length of school recesses. Other mandated board activities include the provision of school health services for all students and transportation for those who live more than 4.8 kilometres from school. The act clearly specifies activities which are prohibited to a board: Section 32 prevents a board from imposing a tuition fee and Section 93 prevents it from employing a teacher who is not qualified under the Department of Education Act.

Although the School Act specifies which policy areas are solely the responsibility of the provincial government, which are shared, and which are, for all intents and purposes, the responsibility of the school board, there is confusion at the local level as to what constitutes board policy and what constitutes nonpolicy decisions which administrators must make to carry out board policy directives. A number of articles in the ASTA's official publication, *The Trustee*, have included policy schemas and definitions in an attempt to enable trustees to determine when policy ends and administration begins. Unfortunately, the distinction is never simple, since there are times when it is necessary for a board to spell out administrative details in order to ensure that a broad educational policy will be carried out as intended. And there are other times when, advertently or inadvertently, the tone of an administration is in itself an education policy. Tucker and Zeigler describe professionalized administrators who are able to "hive off" many of the policy-making functions of elected trustees.

> Because in most cases boards have no independent staff, the agenda for meetings is set by the administration. Setting the agenda is a highly significant political function, as it defines what is to be decided. It is therefore not surprising that school boards solicit and defer to policy recommendations from superintendents. School boards typically enact policies suggested by their professional staff in over 90 percent of the recorded votes.[44]

William Boyd explains that school boards often become conditioned to administrative policy making after being told repeatedly that they should defer to the expertise of their administrators in order to "produce the 'best,' most professional, scientifically sound educational decisions."[45] One study found that very few American school boards would oppose a superintendent's educational program. More than half of the boards surveyed indicated that in spite of board opposition their superintendent would manage to have his or her own way.[46]

There seem to be some differences between the behaviour and actions of boards in America and those in Alberta. In 1983 a study of Alberta school trustees reported that only 7.3 percent agreed and 91.5 percent disagreed with the statement "that the school district central office demonstrates little respect for trustee opinions." On the other hand, 40.2 percent of the trustees reported they were "expected to rely on other sources to guide [them] in decision-making" and 17.1 percent of them reported that they felt they had "limited influence over the decisions made in the name of the local school board."[47] Although American boards appear to be more deferential to their administrators than those in Alberta, the latter may be experiencing an erosion of their policy-making function.

If the increase in the powers of school administrators at the expense of those of the trustees were merely a manifestation of the struggle between two areas of government, few people would be concerned other than the losers in the conflict. Unfortunately, this is not the case. A number of years ago the assistant executive director of the Saskatchewan School Trustees' Association warned local school boards about the mechanisms the provincial government used to siphon power from them. He could just as well have been discussing how local administrators seize power from elected officials.

> Provincial consultants, directors and superintendents are available, on call, to offer advice and direction to school boards who have been told repeatedly that education is so complex that they should not act without the expert advice of these individuals. Certainly, the advice of professionals is both welcome and necessary. But, too much dependence on this expertise can reduce the position of the elected authorities to "rubber stamping" the recommendations. Too much reliance on expert advice is just another form of loss of local control of education because accountability for decisions is no longer clearly identifiable.[48]

To take this one step further, if the school trustees, who are the people's representatives, become little more than figureheads molded by administrators, then democracy becomes nothing more than a facade.

If school rule should ever evolve into a system of nondemocratic governance, it will not be for lack of directives in the School Act. Board members are elected except when there is a shortage of candidates or when positions must be filled quickly because of resignations. In such circumstances the Minister of Education has the authority to appoint school trustees. Although board members are elected to represent their constituents, there is a direct democracy check on their actions since the School Act enables the public to overrule certain classes of board decisions. When a board decides to borrow with debentures or proposes to construct or lease a building other than a school, it is required to give notice so the public has the opportunity to petition for an election on the issue. According to Section 186 of the School Act, "If the result of the vote is to defeat the proposal . . . the board is bound by the vote for a period of 12 months from the date of the vote." Moreover, depending on whether it is a debenture or building issue, during this period the board is prohibited from proposing debenture borrowing or constructing or purchasing a building for the project. The act also directs a district located wholly or partly within a city to call a public meeting on receipt of a petition.[49] The act does not define the types of issues which can be brought forward at such a meeting, although it would seem that there are no restrictions. In any case, the board is directed to send one or more representatives to the meeting.

The School Act structures boards to act democratically. Their meetings must be open to the public and in the event it is necessary to deliberate in camera, they cannot pass a bylaw or resolution at the closed meeting.[50] With the exception of the records of individual students and employees, an elector residing in a school district or division has the right to inspect virtually any board documents.[51] Like municipal councils, school boards must give a bylaw three readings, each of which requires a quorum constituting a majority of the board's trustees.

School Trustees

In theory, school trustees are the elected representatives on school matters for the voters in their district or division. But, in fact, this often is not the case. Tucker and Zeigler maintain that "most board members [in the United States] do not view their role as representing or speaking for, the public: rather they view their role as speaking for the administration to the public."[52] Trustee representation in Alberta probably lies somewhere between serving the ideals of representative democracy and acting as a voice for professional education bureaucrats.

The nature of education representation was debated in Edmonton and Calgary during almost every election, when hordes of candidates filed for trustee at-large positions, until legislation was passed in 1988 to establish a ward system for school trustees in cities with populations of over 300,000. Although there are many instances of community businesspeople and professionals being recruited to run for the school board, self-selection is the more common practice. Like municipal officials, many of those who seek to become school trustees are engaged in work which allows them a flexible time schedule. Others run for office for the sake of name familiarity or to further their own occupational goals. Many education professionals become candidates because they believe that the school system is failing the community or that too little or too much money is being spent on education. The nature of the selection process ensures that trustees do not mirror the socioeconomic and ethnic composition of the community.

Traditionally, school trustees have viewed themselves as public-spirited citizens willing to sacrifice time and money in order to further the interests of the community's children. Although few people could identify the school trustees who represented them, trustees were held in high regard. More recently, however, especially in the larger cities, many trustees have begun to view themselves as no different from other professionals. The role of the school trustee has become an issue in Edmonton, where citizens have begun to question recent increases in salaries and expenses. In October 1990 the city's Catholic community was outraged when expense account data released by the Edmonton Catholic School Board revealed that trustee Tony Catena received a total of $36,527 in salary, honoraria, and expenses between October 1989 and August 31, 1990. Catena maintained that since he put in 30 hours a week as a trustee he deserved the compensation he received.[53] Six weeks later Edmonton's public school trustees voted to increase their base salary to $15,874, the vice-chair's salary to $18,519, and the chair's salary to $21,165. In addition, the trustees increased the amount of their per diem and travel expenses and decided to pay themselves $75 for each special meeting they attended. Since most trustees will claim to have attended 30 to 60 special meetings a year, one-third of their salaries is tax-free, and they have generous expense accounts, the position of trustee has become, at least financially, the equivalent of a full-time occupation.[54] These examples indicate a decided change from the time when serving as a school trustee was considered an avocation rather than a vocation.

There have been substantial socioeconomic differences between those who represent urban and rural school districts or divisions. A 1978 survey of Alberta trustees reported that 29 percent of the respondents were farm owners or farm managers, and a much larger proportion of trustees in urban areas were professionals.[55] However, professionals and nonprofessionals differed little in their attitudes toward educational issues. The Alberta study also indicated that the larger the jurisdiction, the higher the trustees' educational level,[56] and in this case there were significant differences between trustees holding at least a university degree and those with a high school education or less. The latter tended to equate running a school with running a business; they believed a board should make policy which, among other things, establishes the parameters of administration. Trustees with more education were less inclined to favour a political and bureaucratic structure in which professional educators were subordinated to elected trustees.

Conflict of Interest

Like municipal councillors, school trustees may be accused of conflict of interest. The teaching profession tends to be close-knit, and it is not uncommon for several generations of a family to be educators and for people with shared professional interests to marry. Moreover, professional educators often seek positions on the school board in order to bring their expertise to bear on the formulation of education policy. Unfortunately, the interaction of all of these factors may inadvertently lead to what the public sees as a conflict of interest. Consider, for example, a trustee whose son or daughter has just begun to teach in a district. Is there a conflict of interest when in formulating education policy the trustee must consider cost factors in changing the district's student to teacher ratio that might result in the elimination of new teacher positions? Since trustees are responsible for negotiating and ratifying wage contracts with teachers, can a trustee whose spouse, child, or parent is a teacher be involved in the contract process without being in conflict of interest?

When the School Act was rewritten in 1988 one of the major objectives was to determine what constituted conflict of interest. Among other things, it was defined in terms of whether or not a trustee had a pecuniary interest in an issue before the board. Section 62(2) states that the pecuniary interest of a "spouse, children or parents of a person, or of the parents of the spouse of a person . . . shall be deemed to be the pecuniary interest" of that person. For example, a trustee is considered to have a contract with a school district if a family member has such a contract. On the other hand, a trustee does not have a pecuniary interest simply because he or she is a elector or taxpayer in the district or division or if an interest is "so remote or insignificant that it cannot reasonably be regarded as likely to influence the person." This means that a trustee who is a ratepayer is not in conflict of interest if he or she votes during a board meeting for an educational policy which would decrease the amount of tax paid by all ratepayers, including the trustee.

Section 64 of the School Act carefully delineates the activities which place a trustee in a conflict of interest. A person is disqualified from office if he or she uses information obtained while acting as a trustee to further his or her own pecuniary interests. A trustee is also disqualified if he or she owns 10 percent or more of a corporation which has a contract for the construction, maintenance, or repair of real property administered by the board.

The act makes allowances if a trustee discloses a pecuniary interest in a matter before the board or if a district education contract involves the employment of a trustee's spouse, child, parent, or spouse's parent. In either case, Section 65(1) of the act directs the trustee to:

(a) disclose the general nature of the pecuniary interest prior to any discussion of the matter; (b) abstain from voting on any question relating to the matter; (c) . . . abstain from voting the matter and; (d) . . . leave the room . . . until the discussion and voting on the matter are concluded.

Although provisions in the School Act enable trustees to conduct business with a school board without being in conflict of interest and legally disqualified from holding office, school policy making is still complicated. Conflict of interest, serious in urban educational districts, can be catastrophic in rural areas where the Department of Education estimates approximately 40 percent of school trustees are related to teachers. When a rural school board negotiates a salary contract with its teachers, trustees often have to abstain because a family member is a teacher. Since Section 55(2) of the School Act defines a quorum as a majority of the members elected to the board, it is unable to negotiate a contract with its teachers if more than half of the trustees must abstain from voting.[57] When the Alberta School Trustees' Association (ASTA) queried the Department of Education about the problem, the association was advised to "call another election."[58] Since another election would be both costly and no guarantee that a majority of the trustees elected would not be related to teachers, the department's advice is not helpful. At the 1990 ASTA convention two resolutions were passed to resolve the conflict of interest and quorum problem. One asked that the School Act be amended "so that a quorum for a board meeting will not be lost if individual trustees who have a conflict of interest on a specific issue must leave the room during discussion and voting on that item."[59] A change in the School Act to accommodate the resolution would mean that a quorum would comprise the number of trustees remaining after all who were in conflict of interest abstained. It is unlikely the Department of Education would approve such a policy, for in an extreme case a single trustee could negotiate and sign a contract with a district's teachers. Another resolution called for the School Act to be changed "to delegate power to a committee of trustees, or a committee of persons not members of a board of trustees or a combination thereof to reach contractual settlements with its employees."[60] Such a change, however, would probably create many more problems than it would solve.

An Overview of Education Politics and Government

School government in Alberta has changed far more than urban or rural government. Perhaps this is to be expected, since in earlier years property taxes for school support took precedence over taxes for other municipal activities. Over time, as attention has become focused on ways of reducing educational costs at the local level, numerous proposals have been made to reorganize school government and transfer more of the responsibility for financing education to the province. Current educational funding has its genesis in the School Foundation Program, which was introduced by the Social Credit government in 1961.

Although most trustees are totally committed to excellence in education and the precepts of democracy, there are a few who, by default, allow nonelected bureaucrats and interest groups to make education policy. The public is ill served by such people, whose motive for running for the school board seems to be to obtain a well paid position or a stepping stone to higher office. Unfortunately, it is this very small number of trustees who make newspaper headlines and give school boards an undeserved reputation for neglecting the concerns of the citizenry.

In the past inadequate finances and inefficient administrations have been remediated by school consolidations. Today it is apparent that districts need to be relatively large to be efficient and financially secure, but it is also recognized that many decisions about educational instruction should be made at the school rather than the district level. Schools should be given the responsibility for developing their own budgets and the authority to plan programs to meet the educational needs of their students.

One of the most important changes that has taken place in education is the province's emphasis on educational democracy. Numerous sections of the School Act specifically direct school districts to practise democratic decision making. In order to make educational democracy relevant, parents must be brought into the decision-making process in their children's schools. This is particularly important when schools are authorized to make important educational and budgeting decisions. Teachers and administrators should realize that when parents are made an integral part of policy making, they also become an active political force in the community, lobbying for better educational programs and teacher benefits.

14

Concluding One Era of Governance and Beginning Another

The introductory chapter argues that municipalities in Alberta are at a critical juncture in their democratic development. They can continue their current course, as the public becomes increasingly sceptical about the ability of local governments to remain viable and democratic, or the provincial government can make a concerted effort to revitalize municipal institutions. Since that introductory chapter was written, Don Getty announced his retirement in the early fall of 1992. The pundits predicted the defeat of a tired and dispirited Tory political machine in the next provincial election. Shortly thereafter, Ralph Klein won the Tory leadership race promising that he would enact a deficit reduction plan. When Klein became premier in December 1992, he remained true to his promise. In the spring of 1993 the Deficit Elimination Act was passed to balance the budget by 1996 and in the process reduce governmental expenditures up to $500 million for 1993/94. Klein called an election for June and campaigned on a promise that there would be spending cuts, no tax increases, and a balanced budget in the future. The Tories defied the pollsters and captured 51 of the 83 seats in the legislature.

With a number of dramatic political and economic changes, Alberta had declined from a "go-go province" in the 1970s, filled with optimistic people who believed anything was possible, to a province in the 1980s and 1990s with a stagnating economy, an ever-increasing debt, and a dispirited population. A dreary economic climate and several years of unbalanced provincial budgets took their toll. In the final years of the Getty government, the Department of Municipal Affairs tried to stem the flow of red ink by reducing expenditures to municipalities. As funding was reduced, municipalities were told to bear a greater share of the fiscal responsibility for local level activities, despite being shackled by myriad taxing and spending restrictions. When Klein came to power, he appointed as Minister of Municipal Affairs Steve West, who was ideologically committed to reducing the costs of government. After the Treasury Board instructed all departments to prepare scenarios on the implications of 20 percent and 40 percent spending cuts, West announced in the fall of 1993 that all municipal grants would be cut at least 20 percent. Four months later the government announced that over a three-year period it would eliminate the Municipal Assistance Grant program and phase out provincial funding for regional planning commissions.

As was noted much earlier, plans and programs to eliminate municipal inefficiencies have been proposed and adopted from time to time since Alberta became a province. Beginning in the late 1950s, a small group of American economists and political scientists examining municipal government proposed that many of its traditional services be turned over to the private sector. They argued that if contracts were let competitively, market forces would effect decreases in service costs and government would become more efficient. Although these ideas attracted little attention outside of the academic community, they provided an intellectual foundation for many of the fiscal arguments that would be made by Margaret Thatcher and Ronald Reagan. Although they were heads of foreign governments, both had a major impact on the thinking of many Albertans. During this period, the activities of conservative governments in Saskatchewan and British Columbia that espoused and experimented with free market concepts did not go unnoticed by Alberta provincial and municipal politicians and administrators. With all of these events forming a conservative backdrop, it is not surprising that Klein and his cabinet were strongly influenced in the 1990s by *Unfinished Business*, a book by New Zealand's former Finance Minister, Sir Roger Douglas, which purported to show that conservative fiscal policies had revitalized that country.

During the early 1990s provincial and municipal politicians and administrators also were influenced by two Americans, David Osborne and Ted Gaebler. In *Reinventing Government*, they argue that government must be entrepreneurial in the best sense of the term, and mission-driven rather than rule-driven. They explain that entrepreneurial governments "get rid of the old rule books. . . . They define their fundamental missions, then develop budget systems and rules that free their employees to pursue those missions."[1] Using example after example, they show that local governments can become highly creative and innovative.

Most elected officials and senior bureaucrats throughout the province are familiar with the ideas of Osborne and Gaebler. Nevertheless, while a great number of Alberta policy makers are aware of their focus on administrative and economic creativity, few seem to be cognizant of their emphasis on the importance of the citizen. Osborne and Gaebler write that people "hunger for . . . more control over matters that directly affect their lives."2 Moreover, they show that "participatory democracy" is an essential component of entrepreneurial government in the United States.

Ironically, while the provincial government maintains that it is concerned with matters of local democracy, democracy has often received short shrift. For example, Chapter 4 describes how the Metis settlements accord met many of the concerns of the Metis community but failed to provide for self-government. The same chapter discusses the rural district. Although this interim form of government was ostensibly created to prepare citizens to govern themselves, the provincial emphasis was on making the rural districts fiscally independent.

In the last decade the Alberta government has realized that local government must change dramatically in order to meet the challenges of the twenty-first century. One of its most ambitious endeavours has been to rewrite the Municipal Government Act and rationalize more than 100 provincial statutes dealing with local government. In 1986 the Minister of Municipal Affairs announced the formation of a Municipal Statutes Review Committee that would include representatives from the major municipal associations. A number of position papers were produced and subsequently discussed in public forums across the province.

Eventually an act was drafted to reflect the views of the public and the government. Instead of listing in detail every subject on which a bylaw can be enacted, it gives municipal councils a broad grant of power. It does this by first stating that a municipality "has the capacity of a natural person and the rights, powers and privileges of a natural person." The Minister of Municipal Affairs explains in a discussion guide that this allows a municipality to "do anything it needs to do to carry out the purposes of municipal government unless the ability to do it is limited by legislation."3 Next, the act identifies very general spheres of jurisdiction within which councils can pass legislation:

- Protection of persons and property
- Nuisances
- Gatherings of people and any public activity in a public place
- Transport and transportation systems
- Business and business activities
- Public utilities and services on which people and property depend
- Wild and domestic animals
- Any activity or thing that endangers or affects the safety, health, or convenience of others

- Any activity or thing that endangers or affects the environment
- Establishment and collection of fees and charges for services and activities provided or carried out by the municipality
- Bylaw enforcement
- Activities that affect good municipal government

According to its proponents, local government and administration would be reinvigorated by a new municipal government act. General grants of power would allow councils to formulate broader policies and give administrators more discretion in applying them. Local governments would be free to develop intermunicipal working agreements to solve regional problems. Finally, the champions of grass-roots democracy and local self-determination would have reason to be optimistic. Councils, responsible to the citizens, would have the legal right to address the problems and concerns of individual municipalities across Alberta.

Although the new municipal act has had a long gestation period, and many doubted that the provincial government would pass an act that gives municipalities more autonomy, the government is committed to the act. At the same time, however, the government decided in the spring of 1994 to decrease the number of school boards in the province from 142 to 60 in order to reduce administrative costs and increase efficiency. What was being proposed was greater centralization of decision making and a diminishment of community control over the educational establishment.[4] Sceptics wonder how the government can rationalize increasing the powers of municipalities while at the same time decreasing the number of school boards and many of their responsibilities.

There is another important factor to consider. As Municipal Affairs continues to reduce municipal grants, even conscientious and efficient councils and administrations will be unable to meet all of the public's demands for governance and services. Some administrators may be able to formulate programs that enable a municipality to be more efficient in all service areas, but in most cases municipalities will not be able to meet their commitments unless the province gives them greater fiscal autonomy. People in the community, not the provincial government, should determine whether or not municipal services and service costs should be increased or decreased.

Although it is possible that the new act emancipating municipalities will not be passed, this should not be a reason to predict gloom and doom at the local level. First, the citizenry seems much less complacent than it has been in the recent past; large numbers of people question the motives and actions of government at all levels. Second, within the news media are investigative reporters who are zealous in uncovering political and administrative wrongdoing. A diligent news organization, combined with a vigilant citizenry, forces government to remain responsive.

One can argue that although there may be fits, starts, and an occasional reverse, local governments in Alberta are moving toward grass-roots democracy and local self-determination. Some municipal politicians and administrators have begun to open the decision-making process to public scrutiny. With more information available, citizens soon replace cynicism with demands for greater accountability. Although people may be divided on a number of fundamental policy issues, there is almost unanimous agreement that politicians should be accountable to the public. When the democratic will also includes an expectation that each and every citizen has a role to play in decision making, then grass-roots democracy will be firmly planted in Alberta.

Appendix
Local Political Parties

Edmonton Party Politics

In Edmonton, quasi-parties, commonly referred to by their initials, arose to meet the demands of ethnic groups which felt they were not
being represented in city hall, a militant labour movement that seemed to
be gaining momentum, and a group of "straight-out reactionaries" who
wanted "a return to the simpler days of town government."[1] In the 1906
election, reformers who had adopted the ideas of the National Municipal
League and incorporated them into the city's new charter in 1904 were
defeated by populists. The 1907 electoral campaign was completely polarized. On one side, the Edmonton Labour Council endorsed candidates
pledged to fight for equal municipal expenditures in all areas of the city.[2]
On the other side, the winning one, was John McDougall, who created
the Commercial Party dedicated to running the city on business principles. But it was not simply a cleavage between labour and business which
had developed. John Day explains: "The East End put up slates of candidates in 1907 and 1908, which included ethic and labour union candidates."[3]

Labour campaigned unsuccessfully in election after election until 1914,
when the president of the Edmonton carpenters' union became the city's
first labour councillor. Joe Clarke, an avowed reformer, tied his political
fortunes to an emerging labour movement and was elected mayor in
1919, when three council candidates running under the banner of the
Dominion Labour Party won seats on council. On the heels of the Winnipeg General Strike in May of 1919, organized labour called for a general
strike in Edmonton. Mayor Clarke was sympathetic and a few months
later was re-elected with labour's support.[4] The election "forced a resur-
gence of the good burghers initially in the form of the Civic Government

459

Association (CGA), which campaigned on slogans of 'sound business government' and representation 'of all classes of our citizens.' . . . the resultant mobilization of conservative interests produced the Citizens' Progressive League (CPL) and Clarke's defeat."[5]

Labour continued to put forward candidates but it was not until proportional representation was introduced in 1923 that its fortunes again improved. The Edmonton central committee of the Canadian Labour Party developed a progressive seven-point platform and nominated four candidates for council and three for the school board.[6] Labour elected two councillors and two school trustees in 1923 and won an additional seat on the school board in 1924. In 1926 a former Member of Parliament who had lost in the preceding federal election defeated labour's candidate for mayor. However, labour gained control of council as well as half of the positions on the school board.

By 1927 the business community had concluded that proportional representation was responsible for its declining fortunes. Not only was proportional representation defeated, but labour lost control of council and seats on the school board.[7] As the twenties came to a close, business interests recaptured city hall, only to lose it again in the depression.

Throughout the 1930s and 1940s the pendulum swung back and forth between labour-endorsed candidates, labour-sponsored alphabet parties, and alphabet parties originating in the business community and the middle class. Deep-seated political cleavages within both labour and the moderates caused them to splinter into a number of short-lived political organizations.

Labour was especially prone to this phenomenon. For example, in 1934 the Communist Party, the Independent Labour Party (ILP), and the Canadian Labour Party (CLP) all ran candidates for council. In 1935 the ILP disappeared and the Communists adopted a united front strategy. In 1936, all labour candidates ran under the banner of the short-lived Edmonton United Peoples League (EUPL), which folded after the election. Its successor in 1937 was an umbrella organization, the Progressive Civic Association (PCA), whose candidates were supported by labour, liberals, and the new provincial Cooperative Commonwealth Federation (CCF). With the exception of 1939, the PCA nominated candidates yearly until 1944, when it folded, its supporters throwing their votes behind a full slate of CCF candidates. In both 1942 and 1943 CCF candidates split the labour-liberal vote. In 1942 Elmer Roper, CCF's President, was elected to council; another CCF candidate, Harry Ainlay, was elected to council for one term in 1943. After minimal success in three years of effort, the CCF abandoned municipal politics in order to put its energies into provincial and federal elections. The vacuum was filled by the newly created labour-backed Civic Democratic Alliance (CDA) which also folded after capturing only one seat in each of the 1945, 1946, and 1947 elections.

In terms of electoral success, the moderates fared somewhat better, although they created and dismantled organizations at will in order to devise a winning combination of issues and candidates. The business-oriented CGA run full slates until 1936, when it was replaced by the Citizens Committee (CC), which claimed support from "businessmen, working men and other responsible citizens."[8] It was Social Credit's entry into municipal politics that had led to the realignment. In his discussion of this period of Edmonton politics, George Betts writes:

> In October 1935, shortly after the civil election campaign opened, the Social Credit Advisory Board met to decide whether it should follow up its signal success at the provincial level by entering the municipal field. It was decided to run three aldermanic candidates . . . [who] were elected handsomely.[9]

In 1936 the three Social Credit candidates for council and two for the Public School Board all met ignominious defeat, despite strong support from the provincial party. Finkel discusses Social Credit's informal alliance with the Communist Party, with both parties nominating as their candidate a left-wing labour member who was not a member of either party. Labour wanted nothing to do with a candidate supported by Social Credit and threw its vote to another labour candidate, thus splitting the left and facilitating the election of a right-wing candidate.[10] Unity candidates sponsored by the Social Credit, Labour, and Communist parties in 1937 ran poorly.

Social Credit withdrew from the municipal scene in Edmonton, most of its numbers backing the newly created Progressive Civic Association, the rest supporting Citizens Committee candidates. From 1936 through the 1940s the CC fielded almost a full slate in every election and managed to elect more candidates to council than any other group. In addition, throughout the period it maintained a majority on the public school board.

With the demise of the CDA, labour was quiescent from 1948 until the Edmonton Labour Council ran two candidates in 1951; both lost, placing 11th and 13th in a field of 14. The leadership of the CC was attempting to co-opt labour, and labour was attempting to infiltrate the CC, thus it is not surprising that in 1952 one of the Edmonton Labour Council candidates defeated in 1951 was elected under the CC banner. In 1954 three of the five CC candidates identified themselves with labour.[11] The business community split; some of its members supported the CC slate and others founded the Committee for Sound Civic Administration (CSCA) that supported only non-labour CC candidates. While labour's conservative wing was invading the CC, its liberal wing formed the Civic Reform Committee (CRC) and nominated the secretary of the Alberta Labour Progressive Party and a previously defeated member of the federal Labour Progressive Party for council. When their candidates finished 17th and 18th in a field of 18, the CRC quietly dissolved.

The CC's power base was weakened in 1955 when a CC councillor deserted the party to form the Civic Voters Committee (CVC); he disbanded his one-man party after losing the election. In 1957, realizing that it had been co-opted by the CC, labour allied itself with splinter liberals to form yet another party, the Edmonton Voters Association (EVA), which ran a full slate of candidates, all of whom lost.[12] That same year, a long-time CC councillor left the party to run against the CC's Mayor William Hawrelak, and a large number of CC supporters formed the Edmonton Property Owners Association (EPOA) and nominated a full slate of candidates.[13] All of them lost, and the organization was disbanded. In 1959 the EVA again fielded a full set of candidates, all of whom were defeated; its disillusioned members sponsored only three candidates in 1960, and when they too lost, the organization folded.

CC's death knell sounded in 1959 when it splintered over the Porter Royal Commission's revelation that Mayor Hawrelak was involved in a land fraud. A fusion organization, the Civic Reform Association (CRA), was founded by dissident CC members and an NDP faction. The CRA split the EVA and the CC votes with a ticket headed by Elmer Roper and captured four of the six contested council seats and the mayor's chair.[14]

In 1960 the Civic Government Association (CGA) made another appearance, its first since 1936. The CRA had bifurcated; some of its members supported candidates running under the CGA label. The CGA won three council seats, the CRA two.[15] In 1961 the ranks of the CRA were further eroded when some of its members founded the League of Edmonton Electors (LEE); predictably, both LEE and CRA candidates lost and the organizations disbanded.[16] In 1962 the Civic Rights Protective Association (CRPA) was founded by members of the defunct EVA; its four candidates were defeated when the CGA captured all council seats, and the CRPA was dissolved. In 1963 two more alphabet parties were formed and Hawrelak returned to the electoral scene, running for mayor as an independent and defeating the CGA candidate. Supporters of the defunct CRPA established the United Voters Organization (UVO), which won two council seats. Former alderman and mayoralty candidate Ed Leger founded the Citizens Council (CC) and successfully ran for office as its only candidate.[17]

As the result of a 1962 plebiscite the electoral system in Edmonton was changed for the 1963 and subsequent elections; instead of six candidates being elected each year for a two-year term, all twelve members were to be elected every two years. With more positions to contest, there was a flurry of party activity. The CGA changed its name to the Better Civic Government Committee (BCGC), ran a full slate of candidates, and captured five council seats.[18] The UVO also nominated a full slate, including Leger, who switched from the CC. The resurrected CRA did surprisingly well, winning two council seats.[19] Almost immediately after the election, the UVO announced that it was disbanding, and the two members elected under its banner became independents. In 1966 seven BCGC candidates were victorious in a bitter campaign in which their party was repeatedly charged with being undemocratic and "the mouthpiece for the czars of downtown business."[20] Stung by these allegations, the BCGC broke up shortly after the election and its members proclaimed themselves independents. The CRA managed to elect one member, and three candidates running under a Labour banner were defeated by wide margins.

In 1968 the UVO, BCGC, and CRA (the more recent local parties) disappeared. However, several incumbents elected under the BCGC label in 1966, along with other members of the business community, established the United Civic Action Party (UCAP), which nominated a mayor and eight candidates for council. Although it failed to win the mayoralty contest, the new party captured five council seats. By this time the revolving doors of the alphabet parties had thoroughly confused the public.[21]

New legislation in 1968 changed the tenure of municipal office from two to three years and it was 1971 before another municipal election was held in Edmonton.[22] The unique characteristic of the issueless 1971 election was the total absence of municipal parties.[23] A new organization, the Concerned Citizens, endorsed candidates, as did the Edmonton and District Labour Council, but no candidate ran under a party label.

Lightbody offers an explanation of some of the permutations of Edmonton's municipal parties between the 1920s and 1974. He argues that the business-oriented Civic Government Association, which foundered early in the depression, was resurrected as the Citizens' Committee several years later. He maintains that municipal elections have "revolved around the slate-making activities of the Citizens' Committee, the name of the CGA from 1936 to 1959." When the CC splintered in 1959, the most prominent segment adopted the CGA label and other "new names and new groups were invented with increasing regularity . . . by 1971 fragmentation had become so great that local parties no longer existed. However, aldermen showing a business orientation retained total domination of the council." Particularly important in his analysis is that whether the Citizens' Committee or a splinter group was in power, its basic policy was to run the city "as a business and in the interests of the business community."[24]

Parties once again emerged in 1974. An environmentally sensitive segment of the city's "new class," comprising professionals and bureaucrats concerned about the development of a comprehensive freeway system which would invade parkland and open space, formed the Urban Reform Group Edmonton (URGE). Two of its candidates were elected to council. In addition, David Leadbeater, a University of Alberta student leader and avowed socialist, resurrected EVA, ran as its sole candidate, and captured a council seat. But, as Lightbody notes, "His election was 'accidental' insofar as none of the three incumbents stood for re-election in the ward and in a nonpartisan contest, where name recognition is important, many voters undoubtedly thought they were voting for his father, a very prominent Anglican clergyman."[25] Although the city's conservative business community was certain it was facing a socialist rebellion, in fact, the EVA candidate's victory may have been a mistake and URGE members were more committed to environmental issues and the quality of neighbourhood life than social policies which would benefit the underclass.[26]

In 1977 a group of conservative incumbents and new office-seekers adopted a variation of the CGA label and called themselves the Edmonton Civic Government Association (ECGA). After capturing a majority of council seats, the organization disappeared. Although David Leadbeater decided not to seek re-election, five candidates ran on the EVA label and lost. URGE again ran a strong campaign and increased its seats to three.

Four of URGE's eleven candidates and one EVA candidate were elected in 1980. A Fort Saskatchewan businessman created the People for Independent Aldermen (PIA) which, although endorsing candidates, spent most of its energies during the 1980, 1983, and 1986 elections railing against the "left-wing socialist" tendencies of URGE and EVA. In 1983 the business community founded the Responsible Citizens Committee (RCC), which ran almost a full slate of candidates and elected two of them. URGE began to decline; as the campaign progressed, some of its candidates were reluctant to mention their affiliation, and only two of them were successful. EVA's sole council member was re-elected.

Three URGE candidates ran for council in 1986 but only one, Jan Reimer, was elected and the political pundits generally agreed she would have won whether she had run on a party ticket or not. With EVA's council member having resigned to enter provincial politics, the party was dependent upon three novice candidates, all of whom lost. After the election little was heard of URGE until June of 1989, when it was dismantled. Only EVA ran candidates in the fall election. Of its three aldermanic candidates and one public school candidate, one councillor was elected.

Calgary Party Politics

Calgary's early civic councils were dominated by a business community concerned only with real estate and business expansion; the plight of the city's workers was ignored. Until 1915 labour was frozen out of the municipal political process by a requirement which restricted the franchise to owners of real property with an assessed value of at least $200 or personal property worth at least $400. Equally onerous was a qualification which until 1918 stipulated that a candidate for public office must own at least $1,000 of real property or personal property worth $2,000.[27] Only after the franchise was extended to all city residents did labour become politically active, and even then its involvement was limited. The Calgary Trade and Labour Congress encouraged its members to run for council but was hesitant to establish a labour party for fear of alienating the business community. Calgary's mayor from 1915 to 1918 had been a member of the Typographical Union but espoused nonpartisanship while in office. Two members of the Machinist Union were elected to council in 1916 and 1917 and served for two and three years, respectively. In 1918 a Calgary Trade and Labour Congress executive was elected to council and, with the exception of 1927, held his seat continuously for 17 years.

Facing increased labour militancy after an abortive general strike in 1918, the business community agreed with the Great War Veterans Association to create a "Citizens' Slate" of candidates for the fall municipal election.[28] Labour responded by running its own slate. Since the business slate enjoyed only limited success, the business community formed the Civic Government Association (CGA) in 1920 to ensure that city hall would not fall into labour's hands. "Election campaigns, especially between 1920 and 1923, were advertised in the press as struggles between business and labour, and as such were replete with class rhetoric."[29] Despite the business community's fear of "socialist gains" in city hall, the number of labour councillors remained constant at three or four in election after election, and the council was consistently controlled by the CGA.[30] Foran suggests a number of reasons for labour's failure: "1) the relative weakness of the union movement in Calgary, both in terms of its actual members and its success in securing the working man's vote; 2) the low level of voting turnout; and 3) the system of proportional representation which it is argued did not advantage labour."[31]

Throughout the 1920s and into the 1930s, labour continued to restrict its activity to endorsing candidates. Neither the Calgary Trade and Labour Congress nor the Dominion Labour Party was willing to confront the CGA directly with a formal slate. Not until the depths of the depression in 1933 did labour wrest control of council from the CGA, and then it was for only a very short period of time, until Social Credit entered the city's political scene. The Social Credit leadership may have believed the party would appeal to a municipal electorate because it defined itself as a movement rather than a traditional political party.

Social Credit entered the municipal arena in Edmonton, Lethbridge, and Calgary, but was most successful in the latter city. In 1935 three of its seven candidates for council and two school trustee candidates were elected. The party placed two additional members on council and on the school board in 1936, but the following year all of its candidates, including incumbents, were defeated, which left only two Social Credit members on council. Although there were two party members on council and two on the school board in 1938 and 1939, and one on council and one on the school board the following year, Social Credit's Advisory Board decided to stop running candidates in the city in 1940.

Neither the CGA nor the labour movement was deterred by the entry of the ruling provincial party into city politics. Labour captured three council seats and one school trustee position in 1935. At the height of Social Credit's popularity in 1936, when there were five Social Creditors on council, labour still held two positions. Labour's power ebbed in 1937, with only one council seat, but Finkel notes that a Communist, Patrick Lenihan, was elected alderman in 1938 with the help of Social Credit votes.[32] From 1938 through 1940 labour held two council seats; it elected two school trustees in 1938, one in 1939, and two in 1940. Buffeted first by the success of labour and then by that of Social Credit, most of CGA's candidates were defeated in 1935 and 1936; from 1937 through 1940 it placed two or three of its members on council in each election.

No elections were held in 1941 and 1942 as the federal and provincial governments, following the example of Great Britain, declared a "political truce" and suspended elections to avoid divisive political controversy during the war period. Alberta's CCF bitterly opposed this suspension of the democratic process and forced elections in many municipalities, including Calgary, in 1943. One of the three CCF candidates for the Calgary council was elected and labour also captured a seat. In 1944, with the city's labour movement throwing its support behind CCF candidates rather than running its own, the CCF captured two council and two school trustee seats. Shortly thereafter, the party withdrew from municipal politics and neither labour nor the CCF ran candidates in the 1945 election.

Almost immediately after the Second World War Calgary's labour movement split into the left-wing Labour Progressive Party (the Canadian Communist Party) and the moderate United Civic Labour Group (UCLG).[33] With labour splintered, the CGA won one election after another until the mid-1950s, when its hold on Calgary's council was finally broken. In each election from 1953 to 1955, a reunified labour movement ran a single slate, capturing two seats; CGA's candidates won three seats. The demise of the CGA occurred in the autumn of 1956 when, for the first time in a number of years, both CGA and labour members were beginning to vote as blocs. Alarmed by council's intense party politics, CGA supporters restructured their organization and changed its name to the United Citizens Association (UCA), which would encompass both labour and business positions and candidates. The UCA slate included several trade unionists in 1957, and five of its nominees won seats on council. Labour's left wing elected two members.

Until 1957, the Calgary Labour Council had occasionally endorsed labour candidates or nominated its own Labour Group slate. But just days before the election, the Labour Council decided that it would no longer endorse candidates, and the Labour Group soon vanished from the civic scene. Shortly thereafter, the Labour Council, in yet another policy shift, announced that it would run a Calgary Labour Council (CLC) slate in 1959. Although the CLC captured one seat, labour's influence in Calgary was waning. Under the proportional representation system, UCA's candidates received 37,023 first choice votes while labour received only 16,457 first choices, only slightly ahead of the 14,768 first choice votes for independents.

At about the same time, another event occurred which had a lasting effect on labour's civic political strategy. In 1958, anti-labour members persuaded the council to alter proportional representation, ostensibly because it confused the electorate and made it difficult for the administration to count votes. After much political manoeuvring and two plebiscites, changes in the City Act replaced city-wide proportional representation with a two-member, six-ward system, also using proportional representation. The anti-labour strategy paid off, for in 1961 the CLC captured only one council seat although it contested all of them.

Adding to labour's woes was the new major, Harry Hays, described in a *Calgary Herald* editorial as "young, vigorous and personable . . . the very prototype of the kind of mayor this Western city should have."[34] Despite having had no experience in municipal government, he insisted that a business approach be used to "clean up" and administer the city.

An unforeseen consequence of the ward system was the sporadic emergence of community-based political organizations contesting council elections. A group of dissatisfied citizens in north Calgary founded the North Hill Businessmen's Association (NHBA) and fielded two candidates in 1962, 1963, and 1964. One or both of them were elected each year.[35] Instead of nominating council members, the Bridgeland-Riverside-Renfrew Ratepayers Association endorsed selected candidates and provided some with financial assistance. Despite such community political organizations, the UCA held a majority of council seats throughout the 1960s. After the 1964 election, candidates backed by the UCA held six seats on council. In the 1965 election the UCA endorsed Jack Leslie, the winning mayoralty candidate, and five of its seven aldermanic candidates were elected. Once elected, however, UCA members did not operate as a disciplined voting bloc. The UCA executive announced in 1967 that the association existed only "to place good men in local government," not to give them policy direction. "Our sole function is to get responsible people and to get them to run for election. We assist in a financial way."[36] After the ward system was installed, the UCA no longer found it necessary to include labour members on its slate, which during the 1960s consisted typically of business people, oil executives, realtors, and a few housewives and teachers.

Labour decided that in order to exercise power it needed to expand its support base. The CLC was replaced in 1965 by the Civic Labour Association (CLA), which appealed as much to homeowners, tenants, and owners of small businesses as to labour. The CLA placed only one person on council in 1965 and 1966 and then folded. Its successor, the Civic Action League (CAL), called itself a "non-partisan civic political body," and announced it was going "to bring democracy back into civic elections."[37] After all of its five candidates lost in the 1967 election, CAL disbanded. Labour was so dispirited that it nominated no candidates after 1967.

With council's term of office changed to three years, 33 candidates ran for twelve seats in 1971. Labour's demise left the field clear for the UCA, which elected four members; the rest were independents. After UCA candidates won three council seats in 1974, the party disbanded. In 1977 the new Calgary Urban Party (CUP) attempted to capture the vote of the city's new professionals with a platform of social and planning policy reforms; all six of its candidates met ignominious defeat.[38] In the spring of 1980 the CUP executive decided that the city was not ready for party politics and, for all intents and purposes, disbanded. With no parties involved, the election contest revolved around disparate campaign promises made by 34 council and eight mayoralty candidates.

No political parties were represented in the 1983 aldermanic campaign, but two education parties sponsored candidates for the public school board and elected a total of five members. In 1986, as in 1983, no local parties contested council seats, but two education parties ran candidates for the public school board. Although the Better Education for Everyone (BEE) and the Save Public Education (SPE) campaign platforms were so vague that even the *Calgary Herald*'s election reporters could not understand them, party candidates captured 12 of the 14 positions. It was clear that with 38 candidates running independently, the electorate took its cue from the political parties. In 1989 wards were established for school board representation and all of the candidates ran as independents, as did the candidates for council.

Lethbridge Party Politics

Local party politics developed somewhat differently in Lethbridge than in Edmonton and Calgary. A party representing the city's business interests existed for almost half a century, changing its name only once although other alphabet parties periodically emerged and disappeared.

As Lethbridge's population tripled, from 2,313 to 8,060 between 1906 and 1911, organized labour kept pace, chartering a number of new unions. The Lethbridge Labour Council endorsed candidates for public office during this early period. During the 1913 recession the city's buoyant economy and growth began to decline. In an attempt to avert a fiscal crisis and to halt the growth of labour's influence, the city council adopted a system of government by nonpartisan commission in 1913.[39] Ironically, although labour had been rent by internal divisions and weakened by declining membership at that time, it was reinforced by the enmity of business interests and continued to endorse municipal candidates for more than a decade.

Although W.D.L. Hardie, first elected mayor in 1913, was an unabashed supporter of business, it was not until 1923 that he was seriously challenged in an electoral campaign. With the community's moral reformers, labour threw its support behind Dr. J.E. Lovering, who claimed that the unofficial policy of Mayor Hardie's administration was to tolerate gambling, prostitution, and drug dealing in the city. In an extremely close election, with Hardie counter-charging that Lovering treated "dope fiends and prostitutes" at Galt Hospital, Lovering was defeated.[40] In hard-fought campaigns in 1926 and 1928, Lovering again challenged Hardie unsuccessfully for the mayor's chair.

Facing another fiscal crisis, and with the business community determined to put a stop to labour's political activities, Lethbridge held a plebiscite in 1927 at which a city manager form of government was adopted.[41] An editorial in the *Lethbridge Herald* had argued: "It does away with civic politics and in this respect must tend to efficiency. . . ."[42]

Paradoxically, it was during the 1928 election, after the adoption of city manager government, that municipal parties first appeared in Lethbridge. The Dominion Labour Party (DLP), loosely affiliated with the federal party of the same name, ran a full slate and two of its candidates were elected to council.[43] The Citizen's Slate, committed to "business administration for conserving [city] capital assets," also elected two members. Independents took the rest of the seats. With three council seats to be filled in 1929, the DLP ran three candidates, all of whom lost. The Citizen's Slate had disbanded shortly after the 1928 election, but its members supported another new party, the Lethbridge Civic Government Association (LCGA). Endorsed by the business community and the *Lethbridge Herald*, the LCGA won all three seats. The newspaper had refused to print the DLP platform or any news of its activities.

In 1930 the defunct Citizen's Slate was resurrected and merged with the LCGA, which captured three seats; the fourth went to the DLP. The LCGA took all three seats in 1931. The following year the DLP and the LCGA entered into an agreement to ensure that neither would have to campaign. With four council seats vacant, the two civic parties agreed that the LCGA would run three candidates and the DLP only one, which would make an election unnecessary, as all of the candidates would win by acclamation. Although the plan failed at the last minute when an independent filed and forced the election, the two parties captured all four council seats. In 1933 the agreement broke down and both parties again offered full slates for three seats, all of which were won by the LCGA.

In 1934 taxes were in arrears, the welfare program was inadequate, and municipal services had been cut. The electorate turned on the LCGA, which had controlled council since its formation in 1929, and elected three labour candidates and only one from the LCGA. Although the

LCGA maintained a majority, with four seats to the DLP's three, labour was certain it would prevail after the 1935 election. The entry of a full slate of candidates running under the Social Credit banner upset labour's plans; despite having formulated a platform similar to that of the LCGA, Social Credit candidates received substantial labour support. A Communist Party candidate added to labour's problems, although he received only 185 votes. With labour splintered, the LCGA won all three council seats. Chastised by the *Lethbridge Herald* for bringing provincial party politics to municipal government, Social Credit withdrew from Lethbridge shortly after the election.

Both the DLP and the LCGA nominated a full slate of candidates to fill four council vacancies in 1936. The Communist and Social Credit candidates defeated in 1935 were adopted by the newly created Civic Progressive Association (CPA), which advocated a city industrial policy to reduce unemployment. Alienated by this odd partnership of right and left, large numbers of former municipal Social Creditors supported the LCGA, which won all four seats. A bizarre alliance was formed again in 1937, when Communists, Social Creditors, and a breakaway wing of the DLP all ran under the banner of the Lethbridge Citizen's Educational League–Non-Partisan (LCEL-NP). With the labour vote splintered between the DLP and the LCEL-NP, and with substantial numbers of Social Creditors voting for the LCGA, the latter won all three seats, with the result that every council seat was held by an LCGA member.

Its opposition dispirited by successive defeats, LCGA took all four seats by election in 1938 and acclamation in 1939. In 1938 a former LCEL-NP member running under an Independent Progressive Candidate (IPC) label was soundly defeated. In 1940 the DLP and LCGA negotiated an agreement similar to that in 1932: each would put forward only two candidates for the four vacant seats. They explained that this would allow the citizenry to devote its energies to the war effort rather than to an electoral campaign. The election was won by acclamation. In 1941 the DLP changed its name to the Labour Party (LP) and ran a full set of candidates, all of whom were defeated by the LCGA. In 1942 the LP and the LCGA again put forward only two candidates each for the four council vacancies and forestalled an election. In 1943 three LCGA candidates were elected by acclamation. The following year organized labour disbanded the LP and supported independent candidates, who won one council seat to the LCGA's three. In 1945 all of labour's candidates lost to the LCGA.

As Lethbridge emerged from the war years its political complexion began to change. The LCGA dropped "Lethbridge" from its name and became the CGA. More important, in the 1946 election labour resolved its internal dissension and united to support the Civic Labour Organization (CLO), which captured two of four seats, the others being won by a popular independent candidate and the CGA. Labour's momentum was stopped in 1947 when the CGA won all three positions. The *Lethbridge Herald* gave labour candidates only limited coverage and imposed a news blackout on the platform and campaign of a woman running as an independent.

In 1948 the independent councillor elected two years earlier created the Independent Civic Welfare Association (ICWA) and was re-elected under its banner. The CLO captured two seats and the CGA one. The CGA won all three council seats in an issueless lacklustre election in 1949. For the 1950 election, full slates were nominated by the CGA, the CLO, and the ICWA; nine candidates ran as independent labour.[44] The number of labour candidates, eight of whom had Ukrainian names, seemed particularly to offend the newspaper, which attacked them unmercifully. Each group elected a single candidate.

Both the CGA and CLO fielded a full slate of candidates for three council seats in 1951. Shortly before the election, the Lethbridge Citizen's Association (LCA) was founded by a coalition of women's groups determined to place a woman on council. The LCA candidate was elected with the overwhelming support of the city's women and the CGA captured the other two positions. There was less interest in the 1952 election; five candidates running under the CGA and CLO banners contested four seats and each group won two. In 1953 the LCA changed its name to the Lethbridge Women's Citizens Association (LWCA), under whose banner the female incumbent won. The CGA captured the other two seats. In 1954 one independent ran, the CGA and CLO fielded three candidates, and the LWCA one. For the first time in a number of years an independent was elected, as were one CLO and two CGA candidates.

The electorate was confused by several political metamorphoses in 1955. The LWCA changed its name to the Inter-Club Council for Women in Public Affairs, which decided to endorse candidates but not nominate them. The female incumbent who had successfully run in 1951 and 1953 was running as an independent and the *Lethbridge Herald* reported that the council's strong support guaranteed her re-election. In addition, the CGA and an independent each won a seat. The CLO became the Lethbridge Citizens' Organization (LCO) and attempted to broaden its support by making an appeal to the business and professional community.[45] The strategy backfired, as it alienated labour's left wing and failed to attract members outside the labour community. In 1956 the LCO's two candidates ran on a straight labour platform and one was elected, as were two CGA candidates and one independent.

The Lethbridge electorate must have been perplexed in 1957, when 13 individuals filed for four council positions. The Council for Women in Public Affairs supported four independent female candidates but refused to endorse the incumbent female councillor, who subsequently lost. After a quarrel with the LCO, the Lethbridge Labour Council founded the Civic Labour Committee (CLC) and ran two candidates. With labour split, neither party placed a member on council. The Lethbridge Taxpayers' Association (LTA) nominated three candidates, one of whom was a conservative labour member. Elected were one LTA councillor, two from the CGA, and a woman endorsed by the Council for Women in Public Affairs. Shortly after the election, the CLC disbanded and labour's factions were again reunited.

In 1958, with eight candidates running, the four council seats were filled by an independent and one candidate each from the CGA, LCO, and LTA. Labour did not participate in the 1959 and 1960 campaigns, and the LTA folded after failing to place candidates on council in either election. The CGA held a majority on council after each election. The 1961 political campaign was another lethargic one, with CGA candidates running for three seats and winning two; again, labour sat out the election.

In 1962 the mayor was to be directly elected for a three-year term for the first time since 1913. Three local parties and a host of independents contested the election. The CGA endorsed the incumbent mayor and two council candidates ran under its label. The Lethbridge Labour Council (LLC) nominated a candidate who subsequently lost. Yet another short-lived party was created when a number of people concerned about "the evils of planning" founded the Civic Improvement Association (CIA) and nominated a full slate of candidates. The CIA captured the mayor's chair, but the CGA won two of the three council seats. In 1963 the CIA died as suddenly as it had been born, with its advertising bills for the 1962 election still unpaid. Labour, wounded by its 1962 defeat, decided not to contest the election. The CGA filled the vacuum with party candidates, but only one of them was elected. In 1964 the CGA was the only party to nominate candidates, all of whom won handily. The 1965, 1966, and 1967 elections were almost repeat performances, with only CGA and independent candidates running. The party captured two of three council positions in 1965 and 1967 and one of three in 1966; an independent mayor was elected by acclamation in 1965.

For the 1968 election, the number of council members was increased from seven to nine, with five council seats and the mayor's position up for election. Charging fiscal wastefulness and involved in a heated controversy over the new location of the University of Lethbridge, the Independent Civic Association (ICA) offered a full slate of labour and disenchanted Social Credit candidates. The CGA, with a platform of civic responsibility, received the endorsement of the *Lethbridge Herald* and took every council seat; the ICA disappeared after the election. The next year, four CGA candidates were elected with little opposition.

In 1971, 15 candidates ran for council and two for mayor. Opposed only by independents, the CGA, with a full slate, captured the mayoralty position and four of the eight council seats. The 1974 election was almost a rerun: the CGA mayor won by acclamation and four CGA candidates were elected to council. In 1977 the *Lethbridge Herald*, reversing its longtime policy of giving tacit support to the CGA, advocated a return to nonpartisan campaigns on the grounds that the CGA had become too partisan.[46] The party quietly disbanded and its council incumbents ran as independents. Satisfied that partisanship had been eliminated from the local scene, the endorsed all the former members of the CGA. The Lethbridge Labour Council endorsed six candidates, two of whom were elected, for their "excellent work" in the community, whether they were pro-labour or not. In a quiet 1980 election, the mayor was elected by acclamation and 15 independents competed for eight council seats. Although three mayoralty candidates and a host of would-be councillors campaigned vigorously in 1983, no political parties were involved as all the candidates ran as independents. However, the Labour Council endorsed four candidates, of whom one won, and the Chamber of Commerce endorsed a single candidate who lost. Nonpartisan elections were also held in 1986. In 1989 a resuscitated CGA nominated five candidates, of whom only one, an incumbent, was elected to council. After the election the association was once again in disarray.[47]

Notes

1. See Tiebout, "A Pure Theory of Local Expenditure," 416–424, and Bish and Ostrom, *Understanding Urban Government.* For a discussion of the distinction between the provision and production of public services see U.S. Advisory Commission on Intergovernmental Relations (ACIR), *The Organization of Local Public Economies*, 5–34.

2. Magnusson, "The Local State in Canada," 591–592. Another critic, Robin Hambleton, maintains that it is faulty to apply the market model to municipal government because it is impossible for a person to switch from one municipal provider of public services to another without physically moving, since service providers always have a monopoly. Hambleton, "Consumerism, Decentralization and Local Democracy," 129.

3. One study states, "When citizens first petition and then vote to incorporate a new municipality, or vote to approve an annexation or consolidation in a referendum, or give their consent at the ballot-box to a tax-rate increase, they are participating directly in the governance of their local public economy." ACIR, *The Organization of Local Public Economies*, 35. However, a year later in a study of local government in Missouri's St. Louis County, the role of local democracy is qualified: "Although self-determination is important as a base rule for organizing local governments, it works only within limits. An important issue is how far self-determination should be carried. . . . In some circumstances, a strict reliance on self-determination exacerbates conflict." ACIR, *Metropolitan Organization: The St. Louis Case*, 156.

4. An important corollary is that local government is not controlled by any single person or group of persons but rather diverse groups have authority and influence and control multiple centres of political power in the community. The leading spokesperson for this approach is Robert Dahl, one of the major American political theorists, who maintains that at the city level there are a pluralist power structure and pragmatic policy-making; regard-

less of which group controls local government, its policies are legitimate as long as it has been democratically elected. It should be pointed out that Dahl emphasizes process rather than goals. See *Who Governs?* and Dahl and Lindblom, *Politics, Economics and Welfare.*

5. In a comprehensive analysis of this approach, Magnusson critically examines the work that has been done in the United States, England, and Canada. See "Community Organization and Local Self-Government."

6. Pocklington, "Democracy," 26.

7. *Ibid.,* 7–9.

8. Butler and Ranney, *Referendums,* 24.

9. *Ibid.,* 25.

10. However, it is important to note that the use of the plebiscite in Canada pre-dates the American reform movement. For example, the Canada Temperance Act of 1878 provided for the prohibition of retail liquor sales by local option. "This meant that the Act as passed in the regular way by Parliament was to go into force in a country or city if and when there was a favorable vote in that country or city under voting procedures provided for by the Act. In these circumstances, the electors of a country or city were confined to accepting or rejecting as a whole the statutory package of rules already fully determined by Parliament." Boyer, *Lawmaking by the People,* 26.

11. In the United States the onus is on the voter to register at the county court house in order to vote.

12. United Farmers of Alberta, *Annual Report,* 1920, quoted in Macpherson, *Democracy in Alberta,* 71.

13. Macpherson, 162.

14. *Calgary Herald,* November 30, 1936.

15. *Calgary Herald,* January 16, 1937.

16. Finkel writes that Aberhart blamed financiers and oil companies for the recall campaign. *The Social Credit Phenomenon in Alberta,* 70.

17. The act reads: "If so requested at any time by the written petition of the electors, the mayor, by public notice conspicuously posted in at least 10 widely separated places in the municipality, shall cause a public meeting of the electors of the municipality to be held on the date named in the notice, for the discussion of municipal affairs."

18. *Nouvelle,* April 17, 1989.

19. *Sunny South News,* May 25, 1989.

20. Section 124(2) specifies the number of signatures needed. In a municipality with a population between 1,000 and 10,000, 7 percent is needed. An additional stipulation for summer villages is that owners of at least 10 percent of the land parcels must sign the petition.

21. See *Advance,* April 23, May 28, and June 4, 1987.

22. Pitkin, *The Concept of Representation,* 145–147.

23. An example of elected representatives completely disregarding the views of their constituents occurred in the Municipal District of Rocky View in

1988. Throughout the spring, district councillors met in camera with Calgary officials to negotiate the annexation of 186.5 square kilometres of municipal district lands by Calgary. A survey carried out in the district by the *Rocky View/Five Village Weekly* found that 72 percent of the respondents were opposed to annexation. Slightly more than 71 percent indicated they were dissatisfied with the municipal district's performance during the negotiating sessions and 73.8 percent said that councillors did not keep them informed during the negotiating period. *Rocky View/Five Village Weekly*, June 21, 1988.

24. Blake, "Role Perceptions of Local Decision-Makers," 83–93.

25. Long and Slemko, "The Recruitment of Local Decision-Makers in Five Canadian Cities," 559.

26. Higgins, *Local and Urban Politics in Canada*, 371. Only limited research has been carried out in Canada on councillors' perceptions of their representational role. A study of Port Arthur and Fort William, Ontario, in 1970 indicated that the councillors in the two communities perceived themselves more as trustees than as delegates representing the views of their constituents. Alexander, "The Institutional and Role Perceptions of Local Aldermen." Journalistic accounts of council proceedings in Alberta seem to corroborate these findings.

27. Hewes, "Listen, Consult and Be Accountable," 4–5.

28. *Wainwright Star Chronicle*, March 9, 1988.

29. *Triangle*, January 27, 1988.

30. *Western Review*, November 24, 1987.

31. *Banff Crag and Canyon*, May 20, 1987. First the mayor asserted that "town Council has never told Parks and Recreation, for example, what their budget should be." She then explained that the council's Policy and Finance Committee reviewed and discussed each department's budget. However, the boards of many departments formulate their budgets in camera; the Parks and Recreation Board and Mount Rundle School Board No. 64 rarely allow the public to be privy to budget discussions.

32. *Hinton Parklander*, June 8, 1987.

33. *Edmonton Journal*, June 28, 1989. At one point even city staff members were ordered out of the hearing room while representatives from the private golf club held discussions with council.

34. *Post*, May 24, 1988.

35. *Calgary Herald*, November 4, 1986.

36. *Freelancer*, March 25, 1987.

37. *Advance*, May 28, 1987. Commenting on the council's policy, the municipal manager said, "It is a misuse of valuable time . . . to sit with the ratepayers while they read the minutes."

38. *Fort McMurray Today*, November 29, 1988.

39. *Advocate*, June 30, 1987. In the small village of Fort Assiniboine, with a population of just over 200, the mayor called for the assistance of an RCMP officer to maintain order when a citizen repeatedly challenged the council

on point after point. The mayor justified his actions on the grounds that the person "interrupted the meeting not respecting the position of council." *Westlock Hub*, May 1, 1989.

40. *Slave Lake Scope*, June 14, 1988.
41. *Edmonton Sunday Sun*, November 20, 1988.
42. *Edmonton Journal*, November 13, 1990.
43. *Lethbridge Herald*, May 5, 1989.
44. *Edmonton Sunday Sun*, November 20, 1988.
45. *Okotoks Western Wheel*, June 14, 1989.
46. "Access to Information," 7.
47. This point was established very early in *Journal Printing Co.* v. *McVeity* (1915), 33 O.R. 166. Stanley Makuch, an authority on municipal law, writes, "The common pattern of legislation in Canada is that no general right to information or to attend meetings is provided." *Canadian Municipal and Planning Law*, 269. More recently Southam, Inc., owner of the *Hamilton Spectator*, brought forward a case involving an in-camera meeting held in 1983 by a council committee of the Regional Municipality of Hamilton-Wentworth. Southam's attorney argued that the in-camera meeting contravened Charter of Rights legislation pertaining to "freedom of the press and other media of communication." The majority opinion in the Divisional Court did not address the Charter of Rights argument, but said, "the committee is not a decision-making body. It is confined to making recommendations to council and is not required by statute to hold its meetings in public." *Globe and Mail*, March 18, 1986.
48. Gaetz, "Municipal Legislation," 28–29.
49. Some of the more prominent principles were:
    1. Activities should be grouped by purpose, process, clientele, place, or time and made the responsibility of small units under the direct control of supervisors.
    2. Work units should be organized hierarchically, so that several are grouped under the control of a single supervising unit (or supervisor), which in turn is grouped with other supervising units under the control of a higher supervisor.
    3. There should be a narrow "span of control," with a limited number of subordinates under each supervisor, so that supervisory personnel can give sufficient attention to each subordinate unit or person.
    4. There should be a clear "chain of command" and "communication through channels," so that superiors will have full information about the activities of subordinates and be assured that their own directives will control their subordinates.
    5. Executives should have sufficient authority to appoint and remove their subordinates.
    6. Personnel appointments and promotions should be made on the basis of competence, without interference from "politicians" seeking to reward partisans.

7. Executives should control the expenditures of administrative units.

8. There should be sufficient staff services to provide the executive with the information necessary to understand and control the activities of subordinates.

50. Banfield and Wilson argue that, in American communities, an "Anglo-Saxon Protestant middle class political ethos is often found." Central to this ethos is "the obligation of the individual . . . to seek the good of the [whole] community" rather than foster narrow parochial interests. *City Politics*, 40–41.

51. In his comprehensive study of Canadian local politics, Donald Higgins writes, "The degree of competition in civic elections . . . helps account for considerable differences over time and place in participation by the civic electorate. It also helps account for the low rate of voter turnout in civic as opposed to federal and provincial elections." Higgins, *Local and Urban Politics in Canada*, 314. Also see Alford and Lee, "Voting Turnout in American Cities," 1192–1206; and Hansen, "Participation, Political Structure, and Concurrence," 1181–1199.

52. Salisbury and Black, "Class and Party in Partisan and Non-Partisan Elections: The Case of Des Moines," 584–592. It should be noted that the relationship found between party and partisanship is qualified. The authors write: "We may conclude that non-partisanship gives some additional weight to class by means of differential turnout, and this in turn gives upper income groups relatively greater power in the local community. Again, however, the effect is accounted for in terms of class rather than traditional party identification." *Ibid.*, 590. Also see Williams and Adrian, "The Insulation of Local Politics under the Nonpartisan Ballot," 1052–1063.

53. In a discussion of this issue, Higgins writes, ". . . one of the most obviously strong class biases built into almost all Canadian civic elections, is the election of candidates by the electorate at large rather than on a ward or electoral district basis." *Local and Urban Politics in Canada*, 324.

54. The term "grass-roots democracy" was coined more than 50 years ago. In 1935 the Governor of Kansas justified his opposition to the abolishment of county government by arguing that it would destroy "democracy at the grass roots." Then "ten years later . . . [the] Director of the United States Budget, observed that 'there are dynamics at the grass roots. These dynamics should be harnessed and used for the preservation and extension of democracy.'" Martin, *Grass Roots*, 1. For discussions of grass-roots democracy in the Tennessee Valley during the Great Depression, see Lilienthal, *TVA: Democracy on the March*, and Selznick, *TVA and the Grass Roots*.

55. Kotler, *Neighborhood Government*.

56. Pateman, *Participation and Democratic Theory*. See also Benello and Roussopoulos, eds., *The Case for Participatory Democracy*.

57. Hunnius, ed., *Participatory Democracy for Canada*. See also Roussopoulos, ed., *The City and Radical Social Change*.

58. See Axworthy, "The Best Laid Plans Oft Go Astray: The Case of Winnipeg." See also Wichern, "Winnipeg's Unicity after Two Years."

59. Fesler, "Approaches to the Understanding of Decentralization," 565.

60. *Ibid.*, 540.

61. Rayside, "Small Town Fragmentation and the Politics of Community," 103–120. There is also a somewhat dated Canadian study of the conservative nature of small town politics in Horace Miner's *St. Denis, A French Canadian Parish.*

62. See Magnusson's discussion of community activists and administrative decentralization in "Community Organization and Local Self-Government," 82–86.

63. ACIR, *Metropolitan Organization: The St. Louis Case*, 158. ACIR, *Metropolitan Organization: The Allegheny County Case*, 13–15. Also see Robert Dahl, who advanced a series of propositions on size and democracy after a careful examination convinced him that "for most citizens, participation in very large units becomes minimal and in very small units it becomes trivial." Dahl, "The City in the Future of Democracy," 960.

64. A resolution which was adopted at the 1978 annual AUMA convention indicates that the municipalities were not entirely convinced of the government's good intentions. The resolution reads: "WHEREAS the Government of Alberta has frequently stated its support of local autonomy, and WHEREAS over the years there has been a continuous erosion of the powers of local government bodies to exercise autonomous decision-making . . . BE IT RESOLVED that the Alberta Urban Municipalities Association urges the Government of Alberta to pass over-riding legislation which would require approval of the relevant local government association(s) prior to the passage of any legislation which would erode the local autonomy of municipalities, school boards or hospital Boards and health unit Boards." 1978 AUMA annual convention resolution no. 6 with the response by the Government of Alberta.

65. Alberta Legislative Assembly Debates, 18th Legislature, 4th Session, 100–101.

66. Alberta Legislative Assembly Debates, 19th Legislature, 3d Session, 303–304. In 1973 Lougheed reiterated the policy by saying that "our plan with regard to decentralization is one that extends throughout the entire province." Alberta Legislative Assembly Debates, 17th Legislature, 2d Session, 73–3956.

67. 1973 AUMA annual convention resolution no. 64 with the response by the Government of Alberta.

68. Alberta Legislative Assembly Debates, 18th Legislature, 2d Session, 782.

69. *Leader Post* (Regina), September, 1974.

70. *Edmonton Journal*, November 10, 1974.

71. Lougheed, "Think West" Conference.

72. Alberta Legislative Assembly Debates, 19th Legislature, 2d Session, 1140.

73. Alberta Legislative Assembly Debates, 17th Legislature, 2d Session,

58–3154. It rankled Calgary and its MLAs that some of the provincial government's departments in Edmonton were not being decentralized and relocated in Calgary. In a 1979 exchange between Calgary's Dennis Anderson (Currie) and Peter Lougheed over locating "government offices in places other than the city of Edmonton," Lougheed responded: ". . . the stated policy of the government in terms of decentralization of government operations has to do with the balanced economic growth of the province. Although there may be appropriate cases for recognizing that in terms of the city of Calgary, when I last checked the statistics I saw that Calgary was doing relatively well in terms of economic growth." Alberta Legislative Assembly Debates, 19th Legislature, 1st Session, 652.

74. 1974 AUMA annual convention resolution no. 76 with the response by the Government of Alberta.

75. 1975 AUMA annual convention resolution no. 122 with the response by the Government of Alberta.

76. See Feldman and Graham, "Intergovernmental Relations and Urban Growth," 204–210.

77. Alberta Legislative Assembly Debates, 20th Legislature, 3d Session, 1246.

78. Alberta Legislative Assembly Debates, 21st Legislature, 3d Session, 429.

79. Alberta Legislative Assembly Debates, 22d Legislature, 3d Session, 1460.

80. Day, "Edmonton Civic Politics 1891-1914," 48.

2 Intergovernmental Relations

1. The federal government is given municipal responsibilities in the territories. On this point it is worth examining *Dinner* v. *Humberstone* (1896), 26 S.C.R. 252 (S.C.C.).

2. Pawluk, "A 'Marble Cake' View of Canadian Federalism," 9.

3. Alberta Legislative Assembly Debates, 18th Legislature, 2d Session, 1443. Grant Notley (NDP) put Premier Lougheed in the awkward position of defending his colleague. Lougheed explained: "Constitutionally, municipal governments are not in the same relationship to the provincial government as the provincial government is to the federal government." *Ibid.*

4. Tindal and Tindal, *Local Government in Canada*, 161.

5. Canadian Federation of Mayors and Municipalities, *Puppets on a Shoestring*, 1.

6. Tindal and Tindal, 253.

7. Grodzins, "The Federal System," 265. See also Grodzins, *The American System: A New View of Government in the United States.*

8. Elazar, *American Federalism: A View from the State*, 76.

9. Pawluk, 91.

10. *Ibid.*, 29.

11. Federation of Canadian Municipalities Task Force on Constitutional Reform, *Municipal Government in a New Canadian Federal System*, 5–7.

12. Pawluk, 19–21.

13. Pawluk discusses this idea throughout her study.

14. Typifying this interest was the Federation of Canadian Municipalities Task Force on Constitutional Reform. See *Municipal Government in a New Canadian Federal System.*

15. Alberta Legislative Assembly Debates, 21st Legislature, 3d Session, 814.

16. Betke, "The Development of Urban Community in Prairie Canada: Edmonton, 1898–1921," 307–318.

17. Betke, 319. By 1921 Edmonton's per capita debt of $439, the highest in Canada, was more than twice that of Montreal and Winnipeg and half again that of Vancouver and Toronto.

18. *Edmonton Journal*, October 21, 27, 1913. *Edmonton Bulletin*, transcript of 3d Legislature, 1st Session, September 16 - October 25, 1913. Another lucrative right, to impose hotel licensing fees, was taken from municipalities in 1913 and the fees subsequently doubled by the provincial government. Municipalities argued that the regulation of hotels was solely their responsibility. The province's counter-argument was that since hotels sold liquor the province had the right to regulate and tax them. See *Edmonton Journal*, March 20, 1915.

19. Betke, 327.

20. *Edmonton Bulletin*, March 6, 1915; transcript of 3d Legislature, 3d Session, February 25 - March 6, 1915. Ironically, the legislature believed that an independent public utilities commission with strong powers would be objective and above politics.

21. *Edmonton Bulletin*, March 13, 1918.

22. *Edmonton Bulletin*, March 15, 1918.

23. Edmonton's income tax exempted the taxable income of single individuals up to $600 and "every other person" up to $1,200. A tax credit of $42.50 against their land tax was given to individuals with an income of more than $5,000. The tax rate was .5 percent on the first $500 of taxable income, 1 percent on the next $500, 1.5 percent on the next $1,000, 2 percent on the next $1,000, 5 percent on the next $5,000, and 8 percent on all income over $10,000. Bank income was 1 percent on the amount of the one-year average of the deposit at a local branch.

24. Calgary's tax structure was much like Edmonton's except that the basic exemption was $1,000 for single individuals and $1,500 for married ones.

25. In order to make the loss of the service tax more palatable, the premier promised it would be offset by a rebate of income tax revenue to the cities for two years. In its first year the provincial income tax revenue by city was as follows: Calgary, $188,915; Edmonton, $188,915; Lethbridge, $19,894; Medicine Hat, $11,996; Drumheller, $6,550. The amount the province rebated to the cities was: Calgary, $60,000; Edmonton, $60,000; Lethbridge, $3,000. No rebate was made to Medicine Hat or Drumheller. *Edmonton Journal*, February 17, 1933.

26. Liberals in the provincial assembly made a strenuous but unsuccessful attempt to amend the Income Tax Act to allow a deduction equal to the amount of the Supplementary Revenue Tax paid.

27. *Edmonton Bulletin*, March 3, 1931; transcript of 7th Legislature, 1st Session, January 29 - March 28, 1931.

28. Walchuk, *Alberta's Local Governments*, 53.

29. Bettison, Kenward, and Taylor, *Urban Affairs in Alberta*, 75.

30. *Ibid.*, 78–82.

31. Hanson, "Provincial Grants in Alberta," 469.

32. Bettison, Kenward, and Taylor, 150.

33. *Ibid.*, 151.

34. Alberta Legislative Assembly Debates, 17th Legislature, 1st Session, 19–14.

35. In the legislative assembly in 1974 Lougheed emphasized that his policy on revenue sharing had not changed; in 1977 before the Alberta Urban Municipalities Association he re-emphasized that municipalities should not expect any modification of this policy. Alberta Legislative Assembly Debates, 17th Legislature, 3d Session, 2412; *Edmonton Journal*, September 15, 1977.

36. Alberta Legislative Assembly Debates, 17th Legislature, 3d Session, 605.

37. Farran was well qualified, since he had been a Calgary alderman for a number of years and in 1972 chaired the Citizens' Budget Advisory Committee for the capital budget.

38. 1977 AUMA annual convention resolution no. 6 with the response by the Government of Alberta.

39. McMillan and Plain, *The Reform of Municipal-Provincial Fiscal Relationships in the Province of Alberta*, VI–8, 9.

40. Alberta Provincial-Municipal Finance Council, *Report of the Provincial-Municipal Finance Council on the Responsibilities and Financing of Local Government in Alberta*, 190–217.

41. A year later the minister reiterated Lougheed's policy. Alberta Legislative Assembly Debates, 19th Legislature, 3d Session, 702, 1077; Alberta Legislative Assembly Debates, 19th Legislature, 4th Session, 814. Moore lost his credibility when he maintained that conditional grants were really unconditional, and that the government provided conditional grants to municipalities simply because that is what the municipalities demanded. On the former point he said, "There have been grants to every single municipality in this province, to improvement districts in the rural areas, to the special areas, the MDs, and the counties for the work they necessarily have to carry out today in maintaining their local road system." Alberta Legislative Debates, 19th Legislature, 1st Session, 296. On the latter point he said, " . . . the conditional grants that are offered to municipalities in a variety of ways are there, to a large extent, because of requests by municipal governments and their citizens. . . . They [the municipalities and the citizens] don't want that replaced with a straight dollar transfer." Alberta Legislative Assembly Debates, 19th Legislature, 3d Session, 1129.

42. The ostensible reason for opposing the gas tax was that it was regressive and would be much more of a burden for low-income people in the province.

43. *Municipal Counsellor* 29 (November/December 1984): 13. Under the new formula "the equitable grant entitlement for each municipality is calculated under the revised formula on the basis of 'relative fiscal capacity'—a means of relating the assessment base and demands for services in one community (taking into account such factors as population size and kilometres of roads to be maintained) to the average for all municipalities in its broad class (urban, rural, or summer village)." *Municipal Counsellor* 33 (May/June 1988): 13.

44. Alberta Legislative Assembly Debates, 21st Legislature, 3d Session, 814.

45. However, as a result of the 1984 change in the grant formula, the grants for 20 municipalities were reduced from the previous year's level, the grants for 102 municipalities were frozen, and grant increases for 48 municipalities were less than the consumer price index.

46. Explaining how a job creation grant could be unconditional, Dennis Anderson, Minister of Municipal Affairs, said: "While we have asked that the municipalities look at their employment needs when they utilize these funds . . . it is open to the municipality to use that in the best interests of their public, and there are municipalities in the province where employment itself isn't the primary consideration." Alberta Legislative Assembly Debates, 21st Legislature, 3d Session, 673.

47. A financial sleight of hand enabled the provincial government to develop its AMPLE program. In 1981 and 1982 the Alberta Municipal Financing Corporation (AMFC) borrowed funds at extremely high rates which it loaned to municipalities at 9 percent. Much of this municipal borrowing was amortized over 20 to 25 years. In September 1986 the AMFC began over a two-year period to refinance $1.15 billion of debt at lower rates and for five- to seven-year periods. As the Minister of Municipal Affairs, Dennis Anderson, explained, "This series of AMFC transactions . . . has resulted in savings to the Municipal Debenture Interest Rebate Program, because it is now providing subsidy dollars up to the 12.5 percent rate instead of the rates upward of 17 percent which reigned in earlier years. These are the savings which the government is passing on to municipalities through the AMPLE program." *Municipal Counsellor* 34 (January/February 1989): i.

48. The Municipal Police Assistance Grant was paid to all municipalities which provided for their own policing either with their own police force or under contract with the RCMP. The grant formula was based on the number of police officers either on the force or under contract. The Public Transit Operating Grant was made to municipalities operating a transit service, using a per capita formula.

49. The APT program had its genesis under Premier Lougheed. Minister of Municipal Affairs Julian Koziak struck a committee made up of members of the various municipal associations to review the provincial grant system in 1984. The report submitted to the government in November 1985 called for the province to move away from conditional grants "to a comprehensive unconditional grant system." *Edmonton Journal*, December 5, 1985.

50. Alberta Legislative Assembly Debates, 21st Legislature, 3d Session, 661.

51. Higgins, *Local and Urban Politics in Canada,* 79.

52. Feldman and Graham, *Bargaining for Cities,* 21–27. They add that using municipal associations "for the conduct of important intergovernmental affairs . . . may well have stifled the emergence of much public concern about important [municipal] intergovernmental concerns." They also maintain that associations are not accountable to the public.

53. Siegel, "Provincial-Municipal Relations in Canada: An Overview," 314.

54. Feldman and Graham, 24.

55. In 1991 it represented 100 percent of the province's cities and towns, 99 percent of the villages, and 92 percent of the summer villages.

56. Alberta Urban Municipalities Association. *Commemorative Brochure of the Alberta Urban Municipalities Association,* 5.

57. Dates of incorporation of cities with individual charters: Calgary, 1893; Edmonton, 1904; Lethbridge, 1906; Medicine Hat, 1906; Wetaskiwin, 1906; Red Deer, 1913; Drumheller, 1930.

58. In 1983 and 1984 there were discussions in Edmonton about whether or not the city should drop out of the AUMA and lobby the government directly. It was said that the organization was primarily representing the interests of smaller communities and not those of the cities. The city did not drop its membership, but its AUMA support was tepid at best. In 1986 over 1,400 delegates and spouses from across the province attended the AUMA's annual convention in Edmonton. Two Edmonton aldermen regularly attended the sessions, while a few other Edmonton aldermen and the mayor attended sporadically.

59. *Municipal Counsellor* 29 (November/December 1984): 12.

60. In 1985 the Mayor of St. Albert said the AUMA had "difficulty believing that the province sees us as a legitimate form of government that should be consulted . . . it sees us as being the same as the local 4-H club." *St. Albert Gazette,* March 20, 1985. Ray Martin, the NDP leader, also alludes to this disillusionment in a wide-ranging discussion of municipal issues. See Alberta Legislative Assembly Debates, 20th Legislature, 2d Session, 967–969.

61. After the delegates to the 1984 AUMA convention passed a resolution urging the government to consult with municipalities "in advance of any legislative and program announcements" that affected them, the government responded favourably. See 1984 AUMA annual convention resolution no. B1 with the response by the Government of Alberta.

62. However, shortly after Don Getty became premier he called for a meeting with the AUMA board to discuss provincial-municipal issues. He told the board there would be other such meetings in the future. *Edmonton Journal,* January 4, 1986.

63. *Edmonton Journal,* November 21, 1991.

64. Alberta Association of Municipal Districts and Counties, *Story of Rural Municipal Government in Alberta,* 9.

65. On December 31, 1932, the cities had a debt of $76,137,376; towns, $2,456,752; and villages, $66,124. Municipal districts had a debt of only $17,974. *Edmonton Journal*, February 15, 1933.

66. Within the AAMD&C are four regional municipal organizations designated as directorate zones. The Central Alberta Association of Municipal Districts and Counties, with a membership in central Alberta, was organized in 1934 and the Foothills Little Bow Municipal Association, with a membership of southern Alberta municipalities, was organized in late 1934 or early 1935. The Edmonton Union of Municipal Districts and Counties, with a membership of municipalities surrounding the city, was organized in the late 1930s and the Northern Alberta Association of Municipal Districts and Counties was organized in the early 1960s. All of the organizations hold meetings to discuss concerns and present a common front to the government on pertinent policy issues.

67. In 1955 a number of rural municipalities experienced difficulty in obtaining liability insurance. The AAMD&C's legal advisor was also the president and general manager of U.G.G. Ltd. and U.G.G. Insurance Agencies, which represented six major insurance companies in Alberta. Jubilee Insurance was incorporated and licensed as an agent in Alberta, and the policies were prepared by U.G.G. insurance agencies. A 1973 agreement between the AAMD&C and the Alberta School Trustees' Association gives these two associations equal representation on Jubilee's board.

68. Weidenhamer, *A History of the Alberta School Trustees' Association*, 26.

69. *Ibid.*, 33.

70. Roberts, "The Alberta School Trustees' Association—A Study of the Activity of a Social Organization in the Alberta Educational System," 120.

71. Feldman and Graham question whether it is possible for a municipal association helped in the way the government has helped the ATA to remain objective and independent of the government's influence. See *Bargaining for Cities*, 21–27.

72. *Ibid.*, 43.

73. Walchuk, 91–93.

74. *Pincher Creek Echo*, March 1, 1988. This approach can be contrasted with that of MLA Jack Campbell, who, it was reported in 1987, was to meet with Sylvan Lake's town council for the first time in three years. See *Sylvan Lake News*, May 26, 1987.

75. *Grand Centre-Cold Lake Sun*, July 19, 1988.

76. In Edmonton in 1986, controversy developed over whether a section of a proposed LRT (Light Rail Transit) line was to run above or below ground. Weighed in the balance were an additional $22 million cost for an underground line against the destruction of a close-knit neighbourhood by a surface route. The area's MLA and Attorney General, Neil Crawford, told his constituents that he would "find the funds to cover the additional costs for the underground line." The Minister of Transportation responded, "that's a budget matter . . . he can't guarantee funds are coming in the future," and

then indicated that funding might not be available for the city's southside line. When Getty was queried about his ministers' differences of opinion, he replied that "it's our new style." *Edmonton Journal,* March 6, 1986.

77. *Edmonton Journal,* October 19, 1983.

78. *Edmonton Sun,* March, 22, 24, 1987.

79. *Edmonton Sun,* March 27, 1988; After Getty apologized Decore staked out the political high ground and said: I invite him [Getty] to continue his barbs against me . . . but leave the council alone." *Edmonton Journal,* March 29, 1988. It is worth noting that Decore did not limit his political attacks to provincial Tories. In September he accused Edmonton Tory MP Murray Dorin of ignoring his constituents when he would not support Decore's effort to obtain federal funds to upgrade the city's deteriorating infrastructure. *Edmonton Journal,* September 11, 1987.

80. *Edmonton Journal,* March 30, 1988. Getty was in such a hurry to attack Decore that it seems the projects and their cost estimates were thrown together at the last minute. As an example, he included $5.7 million to renovate the University of Alberta's Hub Mall. The project was almost completed, needing only $40,000 from the 1988/89 budget for the finishing touches. Getty also included $74 million for work on Edmonton's Royal Alexandra Hospital when it was only budgeted for $800,000.

81. *Edmonton Sun,* April 3, 1988.

82. *Edmonton Sun,* September 23, 1988.

83. *Edmonton Sun,* October 19, 1988; *Edmonton Journal,* November 1, 1988.

84. After he resigned, Decore, always the masterful politician, said that he did not believe Getty would be so petty as to punish the city just because he happened to be a Liberal. *Ibid.*

85. *Edmonton Journal,* March 30, 1989. MLA Nancy Betkowski, Chairperson for the Edmonton Area Government Caucus, explained the government's position: ". . . it was determined that the most effective ongoing consultative and decision-making mechanism would be on a government to government basis . . . it is the intention of the Edmonton Area Government Caucus to meet on a regular basis with Edmonton City Council to review particular issues between our two governments." Betkowski, Letter to Jack Masson, November 6, 1989.

86. *Edmonton Journal,* May 27, 1989.

87. The news media had suggested that the premier orchestrated the exclusion of the opposition members from the celebration. Hartman addressed this allegation in his letter of apology when he wrote: "contrary to certain public reports, at no time was there ever a suggestion by the premier's office or by members of the Calgary caucus to exclude opposition party representatives from participating in the event." *Calgary Herald,* June 3, 1989.

88. Holden, "The Governance of the Metropolis as a Problem in Diplomacy," 627–647.

89. When the Alberta Association of Improvement Districts held its annual meeting in Edmonton in 1985, the city was asked to send a representative

to the meeting. After the request was ignored, the organization's president, Arnold Jorgensen, said the association had been holding its annual meeting in the city since 1982 and "we haven't yet received any recognition from the city." *Edmonton Journal*, February 20, 1985.

90. For more than 35 years the city's interconnected storm and sanitary sewers have periodically dumped raw sewage into the North Saskatchewan River.

91. *Fort Saskatchewan Record*, July 17, 1985.

92. Some Edmonton city council members wanted to penalize the outlying municipalities, but Mayor Laurence Decore said that it was time for the city to cooperate with its neighbours. *Edmonton Journal*, May 14, 1988.

93. *Edmonton Journal*, October 18, 1990.

94. *Westlock Hub*, October 31, 1988.

95. In a similar situation the town of Sundre was determined to prevent the County of Mountain View from rezoning property very close to the town's boundaries for a mobile home park. In a discussion of the negotiations on the issue, a Sundre councillor said, "To say we don't agree with something and then have them go ahead and make steps to do it anyway doesn't make us feel like we have much say in the matter." *Didsbury Review*, September 22, 1988.

96. *Grand Centre-Cold Lake Sun*, February 14, 1989. At about the same time, Improvement District No. 18 was involved in a bitter controversy with the Town of Lac La Biche over a water and sewer sharing agreement which the two had negotiated in 1986.

97. *Sunny South News*, May 18, 1988.

98. *Edmonton Bulletin*, transcript of 7th Legislature, 1st Session, January 29 - March 28, 1931. See also March 3, 1931.

99. *Edmonton Sun*, January 7, 1987. Klein said, "Remember when Pierre Trudeau said Edmonton isn't the end of the world, you can just see it from there. Well, when Louis Riel was fighting for the West he couldn't have had Edmonton in mind."

100. *High River Times*, December 17, 1986.

101. *Municipal Counsellor* 35 (March/April 1990): 3–4.

102. Baldwin, "Recreational Planning in Small Towns and Rural Areas: The Need for Inter-Municipal Cooperation," 95.

103. *High River Times*, May 16, 1989.

104. *Sunny South News*, October 19, 1988. This agreement replaced one signed in 1972. However, the previous agreement did not include Coalhurst and it had different funding guidelines.

105. *Representative*, August 23, 1988. The province offered to assume financial responsibility for 40 percent of the cost of the study. Of particular interest is that the other municipalities were apparently unconcerned that as both a member of the task force and a party to the agreement, Edmonton would, in fact, be negotiating with itself.

106. *Edmonton Journal*, December 28, 1990.

107. Higgins, 104. Higgins cites the Bureau of Municipal Research's 1976 publi-

cation, "The Federation of Canadian Municipalities: In Search of Credibility," for much of his material.

108. Feldman and Graham, 20–21.

109. The rationale the government used to provide funds for housing was that since the disaster was directly linked to the war, the commission could be funded under the War Measures Act.

110. Anderson, "Programs in Search of a Corporation: The Origins of Canadian Housing Policy 1917–1946," 5.

111. Carver, *Compassionate Landscape*, 54. The Dominion Housing Act provided small loans for individual and corporate builders. The federal government would loan 20 percent of the cost, private lending institutions would supply 60 percent, and the builder was expected to pay 20 percent. Particularly important is that the act authorized lenders to exceed statutory loan ratios and make loans for as much as 80 percent of the value on new home construction. Prior to the legislation trust companies and life insurance companies were the major mortgage lenders but were restricted by statute to a loan of no more than 60 percent of a new home's value. This change in the loan ratio enabled many more people to purchase a home.

112. For a full discussion see Mallory, *Social Credit and the Federal Power in Canada*, 39–152. The Credit of Alberta Regulation Act gave the province power to regulate the credit policy of chartered banks in the province and the Judicature Act Amendment Act prevented anyone from using the courts to challenge the validity of provincial statutes. In short, the latter act prevented the banks from challenging the former act.

113. Finkel, *The Social Credit Phenomenon in Alberta*, 68. There was not a total boycott, for a number of insurance companies loaned money in the province under the federal government's Home Improvement Plan of 1937, which guaranteed insurance company loans. Between 1937 and 1939, $2,154,000 was loaned to 5,018 households in the province. See Bettison, Kenward, and Taylor, 77.

114. The 1938 National Housing Act was particularly significant for municipal-federal relations. If a municipality provided a building lot for $50 or less, under a provision in the act the Crown paid property taxes for three years on houses whose purchase price was less than $4,000—100 percent of the tax in the first year, 50 percent in the second year, and 25 percent in the third year.

115. Under all of the housing acts, the federal government made mortgage loans jointly with the private lending institutions in a 25–75 ratio, with the federal government also guaranteeing the private lenders' loans.

116. In 1941 the government established a crown corporation to build residential housing in cities where war industries were located and where housing was scarce. "Wartime Housing Limited" was the federal government's first program for directly supplying housing to the citizenry. When the CMHC came into existence all of the assets of Wartime Housing Limited were transferred to it.

117. When the Minister of Finance introduced the bill, he said that it did not "adopt the views of those who believe that our municipalities should engage directly or through local housing authorities in a vast programme of state housing furnished largely by dominion government funds. . . ." Bettison, *The Politics of Canadian Urban Development*, 87.

118. *Ibid.*, 96.

119. Dennis and Fish, *Low Income Housing*, 131.

120. *Ibid.*, 131–132. Humphry Carver, who had been brought into the CMHC in 1948 to take charge of NHA's directions on research and education, wrote about this new policy: "From a constitutional point of view it was, no doubt, strictly correct to unload upon the provinces some of the responsibilities for public action in housing. But for those of us who were more concerned about human needs than about the niceties of the constitution, it seemed like a shabby trick . . . the provinces had not shown the slightest interest in social responsibilities for housing; provincial legislatures were still dominated by rural voters and were most unlikely to show any leadership in solving the very difficult problems of low-income people in the centers of the big cities. . . ." Carver, 110.

121. *Ibid.*, 132.

122. Bettison, 110. He also writes that a planner in Edmonton claimed that "CMHC officials treated the provincial officials 'like kids, as if we knew nothing.'" *Ibid.*

123. Dennis and Fish, 145.

124. Another barrier to urban renewal participation in Alberta was that there was no enabling legislation in place which allowed municipalities to embark on public housing programs.

125. O'Brien, "The Ministry of State for Urban Affairs: A Municipal Perspective," 84.

126. *Ibid.*, 86.

127. Bettison, 20.

128. On this point see Feldman and Graham, 32–33.

129. Bettison, 23.

130. *Ibid.*, 28.

131. Alberta Legislative Assembly Debates, 17th Legislature, 1st Session, 19–15.

132. Canadian Federation of Mayors and Municipalities, Municipal Submissions to the Second Tri-Level Conference, "Housing and Land Use Strategy," Doc. no. TCT54, pp. 3–5; Municipal Submissions to the National Tri-Level Conference, "Transportation," Doc. no. TCT53, pp. 3–8.

133. Tri-Level Task Force on Municipal Finance, *Report*, 273–431.

134. Higgins, 111.

135. 1976 AUMA annual convention resolution no. 62 with the response by the Government of Alberta.

136. 1979 AUMA annual convention resolution no. L–9 with the response by the Government of Alberta.

137. Federation of Canadian Municipalities, *The Constitutional Role of the Municipalities in a New or "Renewed" Canadian Confederation.*

138. Federation of Canadian Municipalities, *Municipal Government in a New Canadian Federation System, Report of the Task Force on Constitutional Reform*, 126.

139. *Ibid.*, 50.

140. 1983 AUMA annual convention resolution no. F–7 with the response by the Government of Alberta.

141. *Edmonton Journal*, November 17, 1991.

142. The $15 billion figure was reached by estimating it would take $680 per capita for cities with a population of over 100,000 to repair the infrastructure damage.

143. *Globe and Mail*, February 6, 1987.

144. *Edmonton Journal*, February 7, 1987.

145. *Edmonton Sun*, February 14, 1989.

146. Doug Fee, the MP for the area, was unsympathetic. He explained that "the country is in a severe financial crisis and the main criticism I am getting from people who are calling me from home is that if anything the budget is not tough enough and there should have been more cuts in government spending." *Red Deer Advocate*, May 5, 1989.

147. Federation of Canadian Municipalities, "Emerging Issues for Canadian Municipalities," 5.

3 Urban Governmental Structures

1. The Municipal Statutes Review Committee recommended that a new Municipal Government Act add another dimension to municipal incorporations by making the number and the size of land parcels an integral factor for incorporation. A municipal district has to have a majority of its buildings on parcels of 1,850 square metres or larger. Conversely, for a village, town, or city to be incorporated, a majority of the buildings have to be located on parcels smaller than 1,850 square metres. Alberta Department of Municipal Affairs, Municipal Statutes Review Committee, *"The Municipal Government Act": Local Autonomy, You Want It, You Got It*, Part 4, 19–21. The benchmark 1,850 square metre figure is found in the Municipal Government Act definition of a hamlet. Section 1(f) reads in part: "A 'Hamlet' means an unincorporated community consisting of a group of 5 or more occupied dwellings, a majority of which are on parcels of less than 1850 metres."

2. After Fort Saskatchewan won an annexation bid in 1991, giving it a block of industrial land in the County of Strathcona, the Sherwood Park Chamber of Commerce discussed the possibility of Sherwood Park becoming a city to protect itself from annexation. The president of the chamber explained: "We're large and we have to look at this because if we were a city we wouldn't get annexed." *Edmonton Journal*, February 22, 1991.

3. Alberta Legislative Assembly Debates, 18th Legislature, 4th Session, 40. A number of major Canadian cities are governed under acts specifically tailored for them.

4. Under section 90(1) of the Municipal Government Act, the mayor "may suspend any official or employee, other than a municipal commissioner or municipal manager, and he shall forthwith report the suspension and the reasons . . . to the council not later than the next meeting." However, council has the last word on the suspension, for 90(2) states, "council may reinstate the official or employee suspended or may dismiss the official or employee."

5. Section 108 also serves another purpose. It prevents people who "lose" in the policy struggle from clogging the courts with continuing objections.

6. Crawford, *Canadian Municipal Government*, 110.

7. There is no need to designate the mayor a committee member since the mayor already sits *ex officio* on all council committees.

8. In the United States only mid-sized cities (population range 10,000 to 249,999) have more council-manager governments than mayor-council ones (2,702 to 1,315). In municipalities with a population under 10,000 the ratio is reversed, with 2,702 led by mayor-council governments and 1,315 by council-managers. A similar ratio is found in cities with populations over 250,000; 35 have mayor-council governments and 20 have council-managers.

9. Letter from Patricia Williams to Greg Poelzer, January 29, 1991.

10. *Lacombe Globe*, November 16, 1988.

11. Managers in the United States occasionally build an independent power base in the community or act as policy formulators in smaller communities with part-time mayors and councillors with little political and administrative expertise. A study of manager government in 45 communities found that the manager assumed the role of chief policy maker as well as that of administrator in the community. The study found that the manager's political role "includes efforts as a community leader and as a representative of community needs and interests before the local council. . . ." Perhaps of even greater political significance, the manager not only established council's policy agenda but also created the "menu" of policy alternatives. Wright, "The City Manager as a Development Administrator," 203–248.

12. Plunkett, *The Role of the Chief Administrative Officer*, 47.

13. *Ibid.*, 42–43.

14. Plunkett presents an excellent discussion of the relations between the chief administrative officer and his or her staff. See Plunkett, 41–42, 50–52.

15. Hickey, *Decision-Making Process in Ontario's Local Governments*, 275.

16. The powers delegated to the board are so broad they can be interpreted, in some instances, as being executive powers.

17. Lightbody, "Edmonton," 274.

18. On the other hand, Paul Hickey, a student of Canadian local government, maintains it is impossible for the mayor of a large city to fulfil both politi-

cal responsibilities and the duties of a chief administrative officer. Moreover, "since the mayor is the chief elected officer, he will dominate the discussions and the decisions of the board—even if he is not the chairman of the board. . . ." Hickey, 218–219.

19. Wood Gordon, "City of Medicine Hat Organizational Review," 24.

20. George B. Cuff and Associates Ltd., "City of Medicine Hat Legislative and Administrative Review," 27, 30.

21. *Medicine Hat News*, January 8, 1985.

22. This could be remediated by placing final authority for administration with the mayor, who would be responsible for all of the commission board's decisions. This change would give the mayor power to hire and fire commissioners. Thus, the mayor would become a powerful commission board chairperson.

23. Lightbody, "Edmonton," 274.

24. Lightbody, "The Political Traditions of a Prairie Canadian City," 16.

25. *Fort McMurray Today*, December 12, 1984.

26. An editorial in the January 21, 1987, *Fort McMurray Express* argued that by eliminating two commissioners the city would save $250,000. The editorial concluded that "the bottom line is our administrative staff have shown it can handle the job of our two departed commissioners."

27. On the other hand, Edd LeSage maintains that when council-commission government is examined closely, it is found that power is concentrated in the hands of a small number of senior administrators at the top of the governmental structure.

28. *Edmonton Bulletin*, November 16, 29, 1923.

29. Higgins, *Local and Urban Politics in Canada*, 161.

30. The term council-executive committee is used in a variety of contexts. Lightbody's "Pop Goes the Gopher: Municipal Innovation with Edmonton's New Executive Committee" discusses the evolution of the concept. He notes that the Tindals found something like an executive committee in Montreal during the 1850s and that Alan Artibise discusses a form of executive committee in Winnipeg at the turn of the century.

31. In 1988 the Westlock council considered establishing a liaison committee composed of the chairs of the council's other standing committees. Among its responsibilities the liaison committee would review all of the standing committees' bylaw and policy proposals. This provision galvanized opponents, who defeated what might have become an executive committee. One of them explained: "I see it growing into an inner cabinet power group." *Hub*, August 15, 1988.

32. Lightbody, "Pop Goes the Gopher," 8–9.

33. Even after the decision was made to restructure, one councillor continued to criticize the executive committee system. However, it is likely the tirade against the executive committee system was merely a means to attack Decore, whom the alderman openly criticized at every turn. The alderman lost his seat in the October 1986 election.

34. *Municipal Counsellor* 27 (November/December 1982): 16.

35. George B. Cuff and Associates Ltd., "City of Medicine Hat Legislative and Administrative Review," 11.

36. It was recommended that some of the committee's responsibilities should include: "[1] to review, monitor and recommend changes to the corporate organization structure; [2] to recommend and oversee management audits of parts of the organization or the organization as a whole; [3] to review recommended policy alternatives; provide Council input; and check for consistency; [4] to recommend policy to Council and to ensure that a comprehensive policy manual is developed and made available to all members of Council and senior staff (i.e. Commissioners, Department Heads, others); [5] to review the performance of the four Commissioners and other senior staff (e.g. City Clerk, City Solicitor); to provide Council with an opportunity to participate effectively in the review; and to provide feedback as a Committee to those being reviewed." *Ibid.*, 21.

37. Lightbody writes that this was done "to avoid the various problems that would be associated with either the Mayor's personal nomination or an election/recall by the Council as a whole." See "Pop Goes the Gopher," fn. 44.

38. Adrian and Press, *Governing Urban America*, 353.

39. *Bonnyville Nouvelle*, March 14, 21, April 25, 1989. In Fort McMurray in 1987, an ex-mayor and city alderman charged council with increasing membership on outside boards and committees in order to exercise greater control over them. However, one of the aldermen said the decision to increase aldermen was made to keep a closer watch on the mayor. The mayor maintained that there was no ulterior motive in increasing the number of aldermen on boards and committees, since it was done on the basis of a consultant's recommendation. *Fort McMurray Today*, January 13, 1987.

40. *Medicine Hat News*, October 29, 1986.

41. George B. Cuff and Associates Ltd., "City of Lloydminster Legislative and Administrative Review," 33.

42. The member who lost her position charged the mayor with "influence peddling" and then said, "I just cannot believe the system. This is supposed to be a democracy; obviously it isn't." *Calgary Herald*, November 10, 1986.

43. *Edmonton Journal*, March 18, 1987.

44. *Calgary Herald*, October 27, 1987.

45. When a village is incorporated, there is a division of assets with the rural municipality based primarily on the rural municipality's financial statement for the previous year. Any arrears on taxes for property located in the new municipality accrue to it. If the new village municipality and the rural municipality cannot reach an agreement, the Department of Municipal Affairs will negotiate a settlement as a last resort.

46. Section 27(1)(b)(ii) of the act states that "if the council of a village having a population of at least 250 persons so authorizes, [it] by by-law, shall consist of 5 councillors." However, the Municipal Statutes Review Committee rec-

ommends that a village council be allowed to increase its membership to five regardless of the village population. See Alberta Department of Municipal Affairs, Municipal Statutes Review Committee, "*The Municipal Government Act*": *Local Autonomy, You Want It, You Got It*, Part 5, 50.

47. The Municipal Statutes Review Committee does not even acknowledge the advantage of having the chief executive selected from the council. Rather, in order to give councils even greater choices the committee recommends that "a village, summer village . . . council may pass a bylaw saying that the chief elected official is to be elected by a vote of the electors of the entire municipality." *Ibid.*, Part 5, 54.

48. The only restriction on the date of the election is that it has to be four weeks after the nomination day for candidates.

49. Whether the office is physically located in the village or outside, it must have pertinent equipment such as a typewriter, calculator, photocopier, and fire-proof file cabinet. It also must contain assessment and tax rolls, legislative statutes, a bylaw register, and a minutes book.

50. Hanson, *Local Government in Alberta*, 87–88.

51. Preceding the New Town Act were the attempts of the Provincial Planning Advisory Board in 1953 and 1954 to direct planning and development in the fast-growing Drayton Valley area.

52. "Slave Lake—A Rapid Growth Town Seeking New Town Status," *Municipal Counsellor* 20 (First Quarter, 1976): 2–3.

53. A geographer examining the rivalry between the village and the town writes: "The competition between the two fire brigades was so great that the one was not allowed to cross the border into the other's territory. Finally the town fire brigade petitioned town council to allow the village fire brigade free access into the town, without renunciation, in case of an emergency, on the condition that the same privilege would be granted to them within the village boundaries." Dykstra, "The Political Geography of a Border Settlement: Lloydminster, Alberta-Saskatchewan," 45.

54. For example, Alberta's Agricultural Pest Act (Chapter 2) and Saskatchewan's Gas Inspection and Licensing Act (Chapter 368) and Special-Care Home Act (Chapter 275) apply to the whole city. On the other hand, Alberta acts which only apply to the Alberta portion of the city include the Municipalities Assessment and Equalization Act (Chapter 252), the Electric Power and Pipeline Assessment Act (Chapter 119), the Crown Property Municipal Grants Act (Chapter 82), the Municipal and Provincial Properties Valuation Act (Chapter 248), Section 41 of the Alberta Government Telephone Act (Chapter 12), and Section 129 of the School Act (Chapter 329).

55. Saskatchewan businesspeople made token sales tax payments on purchases of office and business equipment for their own use.

56. Reported by Dykstra and Ironside, "The Effects of the Division of the City of Lloydminster by the Alberta-Saskatchewan Inter-Provincial Boundary," 271.

57. Dykstra, 47.

58. Alberta Department of Municipal Affairs, *The Park Town of Banff*, 5.

59. *Ibid.*, 37.

60. Crawford, *Report of the Institute of Local Government*, 24–28; Canada, *Report of the Royal Commission on Government Organization*, vol. 2, 38–40; Plunkett et al., *A Form of Municipal Government and Administration for Banff Townsite*, 36–44; Canada, *Sixth Report of the Standing Committee on Northern Affairs and Natural Resources*, 131–182; Parks Canada, *Resident Involvement in Park Townsite Administration*; Alberta Department of Municipal Affairs, *The Banff-Jasper Autonomy Report*; Alberta Department of Municipal Affairs, *The Park Town of Banff*.

61. Alberta Department of Municipal Affairs, *The Banff-Jasper Autonomy Report*, 12.

62. Environmental Minister McMillan assured Banff residents that the federal government would never allow uncontrolled Banff growth which would adversely affect the park. "We would urge and insist on a regime that would make the National Parks Act the ultimate authority, so that when there are conflicts between any decisions made at the local level and decisions that have to be made to protect the national park system as a whole, the National Parks Act would click in and the decisions would favour the national park." *Banff Crag and Canyon*, June 8, 1987.

63. *Calgary Herald*, October 22, 1986.

64. *Calgary Herald*, June 15, 1988.

65. *Banff Crag and Canyon*, June 15, 1988.

4   Rural and Evolving Forms of Local Government

1. A herd district was formed when two-thirds of the voters in at least four townships applied to the Lieutenant-Governor. A fire district was formed when a majority of persons who had lived at least three months in the proposed district (minimum area 36 square miles, maximum area 144 square miles) applied to the Lieutenant-Governor. Each resident was taxed four dollars a year, payable either in cash or by labour at the rate of one dollar a day per person, or two dollars a day if the worker used his own team of horses.

2. MacIntosh, "Opening Speech."

3. Hanson, *Local Government in Alberta*, 24–25.

4. Rural municipalities were also empowered to cooperate in the formation of hospital districts and hail insurance districts. In addition, the collection of tax arrears was transferred from the Department of Municipal Affairs to the rural municipalities.

5. Gibson, "History of Improvement Districts," 4.

6. *Ibid.*, 5.

7. *Story of Rural Municipal Government in Alberta*, prepared by the Alberta Association of Municipal Districts and Counties, contains numerous accounts of early Alberta municipal district councils paying children a bounty ranging from half a cent to one cent for each gopher tail.

8. Although the Department of Municipal Affairs designates the population figures as being for 1989, except for Bighorn and Brazeau, with 1988 municipal censuses, the figures are based on the 1986 federal census.

9. Alberta Association of Municipal Districts and Counties, *Story of Rural Municipal Government in Alberta*, 468.

10. *Ibid.*, 515.

11. Section 128 of the School Act, R.S.A. 1980, governs the requisitions.

12. It should be noted that the reeve favoured increasing the size of council. See *Calgary Herald*, July 31, 1983.

13. Alberta Association of Municipal Districts and Counties, 403–404.

14. This is not to say that conflicts over differing values do not occasionally erupt in smaller towns and rural areas. In 1988 councillors in the Municipal District of Bonnyville approved a piggery with a manure pond which would have an extremely unpleasant odour when it was emptied twice a year. The piggery was to be located two miles from town. Citizens and the business community complained that such agricultural operations should not be located near residential areas.

15. Municipal Affairs cannot be faulted for its actions in the creation of a new self-governing municipal district, for citizens are certainly better represented in the new municipal district than they were when they were taken for granted or ignored by one of the five municipalities which had previously administered the area. However, the department seemed much more concerned about the assessment and financial ability of the new government unit than its ability to function democratically.

16. Hanson, 62.

17. Alberta Department of Municipal Affairs, "Reorganization of Rural Local Administration in Alberta," 3.

18. Initially, if a school requisition was more than 20 percent over the previous year's requisition the municipal district could refer it to the Public Utilities Board for a ruling. In 1952 the 20 percent limitation was removed. Somewhat later municipal councils also were given power to control school board requisitions. Under the School Act a municipal council could apply to the Local Authorities Board within 60 days after it had received a school authority requisition if it considered a school board's requisition to be excessive. The Local Authorities Board had the power to amend the requisition.

19. It is worth noting that the Alberta Association of Municipal Districts passed a resolution at its 1931 annual convention calling for the provincial government to implement a county system of government as soon as possible. See Alberta Department of Municipal Affairs, *Local Rural Self-Government in the Province of Alberta*, 3. But perhaps more important was a 1961 radio address by Minister of Municipal Affairs A.J. Hooke, who explained, "I believe that those who levy taxes should be the same people as those who decide how local revenues should be spent. I believe it is easier to place responsibility for the level of the mill rate when the same authority is in

charge of all local spending." *Grande Prairie Daily Herald Tribune*, December 18, 1987.

20. Alberta Department of Municipal Affairs, "After Twenty Years," 4.

21. Alberta Association of Municipal Districts and Counties, 88.

22. When Minister of Municipal Affairs C.E. Gerhart addressed Grande Prairie's municipal council on the merits of the county system, he said that if the hospital district wanted to join a new county it could easily be arranged. Alberta Association of Municipal Districts and Counties, 74.

23. Although the Department of Municipal Affairs designates the population figures as being for 1989, with the exception of Lamont, Strathcona, and Wheatland, the figures are based on the 1986 federal census.

24. For example, Eric Hanson writes, "It is to be hoped that the number of counties will increase in the future, and that, somehow, hospital districts can be tucked in under the county quilt." *Local Government in Alberta*, 69.

25. In 1991 the Minister of Municipal Affairs was considering a change to the County Act which would have permitted reeves to be elected at-large from the entire county. At the annual meeting of the Alberta Association of Municipal Districts and Counties (AAMD&C) a straw vote indicated that 80 percent of the delegates were opposed to such a change. See *Municipal Counsellor* 36 (May/June 1991): 18.

26. In practice, all county councillors become members of the education committee.

27. If the reeve is a separate school supporter, he or she is placed in an impossible position, since the reeve sits *ex officio* on all county boards, commissions, and committees and therefore is automatically a member of the education committee; however, as a separate school supporter the reeve is ineligible to serve on the committee.

28. When the Town of Leduc wanted to expand its high school facilities in 1983, the county turned down its request for $11 million to match funds previously approved by the province. Leduc had been considering applying for city status for some time and when a study found that an independent school system was feasible, the administration decided to apply for city status to enable it to establish and run its own school district.

29. The committee prepared reports in 1983 and 1985. On the basis of the 1985 report, Bill 53 to amend the County Act was proposed by Neil Crawford to implement some of the recommendations of the committee. The bill received only first reading and died on the order paper.

30. According to the report: ". . . the Act should provide for a modified system of representation upon the request of the local authorities affected (the county council and the board of education or the county council and a two-thirds majority of the councils of the educational units). This option provision would enable a modified representation system, deemed suitable by the local authorities, to be approved for any county." See Alberta Department of Municipal Affairs, "County Act Review Report," 4.

31. *Ibid.*, 5.

32. *Ibid.*
33. Alberta Teachers' Association, "Submission to Minister of Municipal Affairs Regarding the County Act," 1. The same year, irritated by the ATA's opposition to county government, the delegates to the Alberta Association of Municipal Districts and Counties passed resolution no. 15 (ER7), which would give counties a major voice in changes made to the County Act.
34. *ATA News*, February 27, 1987.
35. If a council receives a petition requesting either a continuation of county status or reversion to municipal district status and the petition has been signed by not less than 5 percent of the county's population, a vote shall be held. However, it is unclear whether a vote can be taken only at the end of the four-year period after a county is formed or whether it can be held at any time. It is also unclear whether or not having held an election on the county form of government precludes another election.
36. Three of the four rural councillors foresaw that reapportionment would eventually occur and urban councillors would predominate on council. For this reason, the councillors favoured splitting the county, with Sherwood Park becoming a city. In order to make this option politically palatable they suggested that a portion of the Refinery Row industrial area be included in the new city to provide it with a strong financial base.
37. A spokesman for Parents for Change said the issue was "the dilemma we face as county residents at election time . . . to choose between someone knowledgeable concerning heavy equipment, road load tolerances and weed control and someone aware of school curriculum, transportational and instructional needs." *Grande Prairie Daily Herald Tribune*, February 9, 1989.
38. *Rocky View/Five Village Weekly*, May 23, 1989. It is particularly relevant that the newspaper account of the meeting indicates that little was said about political accountability and responsibility, which were the basis for the implementation of the county system, but rather the Municipal Affairs spokesperson said, "the county system really means the merger of the municipality and the school district into one corporation with one tax bill and one local government, sort of a one-stop shopping concept."
39. At the 1990 annual meeting of the Alberta Teachers' Association a resolution was passed to "urge the Government of Alberta to amend the County Act in such a way as to ensure that the county council and the board of education are two completely separate entities, each with complete fiscal and managerial independence."
40. Brown, "The Evolution of Hospital Funding in Alberta," 33.
41. If an amalgamation involves a municipal hospital district, the newly amalgamated unit is called a general hospital district.
42. An Alberta Hospital Association (AHA) study published in 1984 reports that while 65.7 percent of district boards have either five or six members, only 14.3 percent of the provincial boards and 15.6 percent of the voluntary boards are that small. On the other hand, only 14.6 percent of all of

the hospital boards in the province have more than ten members. See Radcliffe, "Alberta Trusteeship: Strength in Caring," 33.

43. *Ibid.,* 13–14.

44. 1983 AUMA annual convention resolution no. F–2.

45. Alberta Legislative Assembly Debates, 20th Legislature, 2d Session, 1040–1041.

46. Radcliffe, 25.

47. A major empirical study on hospital board representation is needed to examine whether there are differences in how directly and indirectly elected hospital trustees perceive and represent their constituents and relate to other board members.

48. Alberta Legislative Assembly Debates, 21st Legislature, 2d Session, 1159–1161.

49. The Rev. William Roberts spoke of a letter sent by a hospital district board chairperson to the minister which mentioned this patronage. Alberta Legislative Assembly Debates, 21st Legislature, 2d Session, 1163–1164.

50. Alberta Legislative Assembly Debates, 21st Legislature, 3d Session, 1761–1762.

51. *Stettler Independent,* October 28, 1987.

52. *Stettler Independent,* February 17, October 12, 1988.

53. *Wetaskiwin Times-Advertiser,* January 31, March 21, 1989.

54. *Grande Prairie Daily Herald Tribune,* February 9, 1989.

55. *High River Times,* May 16, 1989.

56. Canada's first irrigation legislation was enacted in 1894. The North-West Irrigation Act had two basic principles: (1) since the ownership of surface water is vested in the Crown, this water and the right to its use cannot become private property; and (2) water use is regulated by the Crown through licensing and consequently the right to use water can be cancelled if there is abuse.

57. The district administrator asked to remain anonymous.

58. The remaining 10 percent came from the interest on a promissory note and the unspent portion of the 1989 grant.

59. In 1991 the Holden Drainage District had 157 electors and the Hay Lakes Drainage District had 40 electors. *Alberta's Local Governments,* by Walter Walchuk, published by the Department of Municipal Affairs in 1987, states that the average number of district "members/voters" is 66. However, it is unlikely that the number of people who participate in district elections is as large as the number of drainage district members.

60. Letter from Terry Pederson, Holden Drainage District Secretary-Treasurer, to Yi-chong Xu, October 9, 1991.

61. Alberta Department of the Environment, *Edmonton Regional Utilities Study,* i.

62. It is not coincidental that the functions and political structure recommended for regional service commissions closely resembled those of the regional service districts in British Columbia, for councillors and govern-

ment officials, primarily from Edmonton's outlying municipalities, spent three days in Vancouver examining the regional district concept employed in British Columbia. They learned that the Greater Vancouver Regional District had begun ten years earlier as a water and sewer board and had grown to include hospitals, pollution control, regional planning, regional parks, and even labour relations. Although Edmonton's chief corporate planner did not believe a regional district was appropriate for the Edmonton region, most representatives from the outlying areas were enthusiastic about the concept.

63. Edwards, "Economies of Scale," 13.
64. In early 1992 discussions were being held on the formation of the Mountainview Regional Water Commission in the Didsbury-Olds corridor.
65. Pocklington, *The Government and Politics of Alberta Metis Settlements*, 6–7.
66. Pocklington notes that the Catholic board of management informed the government that it wanted to terminate the leases it had negotiated. *Ibid.*, 8.
67. *Ibid.*, 12.
68. *Ibid.*, 24–26.
69. *Ibid.*, 34.
70. The Metis Settlement corporations are: Buffalo Lake, with 34,720 hectares (85,760 acres); East Prairie, with 32,647 hectares (80,640 acres); Elizabeth, with 25,601 hectares (63,236 acres); Fishing Lake, with 37,957 hectares (93,760 acres); Gift Lake, with 83,951 hectares (207,360 acres); Kikino, with 44,825 hectares (110,720 acres); Paddle Prairie, with 163,168 hectares (403,027 acres); and Peavine, with 82,233 hectares (203,113 acres).
71. Pertinent parts of Section 224 state that General Council Policies come into effect 90 days after they are received by the minister unless: "(a) the Minister by order approves the Policy in writing at an earlier date in which case the Policy comes into effect when it is approved, or on any later date specified in the Policy, or (b) the Minister vetoes the Policy or any portion of it by notice in writing to the President of the General Council. (2) A General Council Policy or any portion of it that is vetoed by the Minister has no effect. (3) A copy of an order or notice under subsection (1) must be sent to each settlement council."
72. In 1987 there were charges of fiscal mismanagement at the Buffalo Lake colony and charges of nepotism and corrupt election practices at the East Prairie colony. When Pocklington questioned residents in two settlements he discovered a pervasive belief that councillors favoured themselves and their relatives when the council allocated such things as housing and land to settlement residents. See Pocklington, 103–122.
73. Alberta Legislative Assembly Debates, 22d Legislature, 1st Session, 2178–2184, 2262–2264.
74. "Breaking New Ground: Metis Leaders Work Out Details for Self-Administration of Settlement Lands," *Municipal Counsellor* 30 (September/October 1985): 7–9.

75. Alberta Legislative Assembly Debates, 22d Legislature, 2d Session, 1665–1670.
76. Population figures for improvement districts 4, 6, 9, 12, 13, 14, 16, 19, 20, 21, 23, and 24 are based on the June 1986 federal census. The population figure for Improvement District No. 5 is based on a May 1990 municipal census; the figure for Improvement District No. 8 is based on a January 1988 municipal census; the figure for Improvement District No. 15 is based on a June 1991 municipal census; and the figure for Improvement District No. 18 is based on a January 1990 municipal census.
77. Gibson, 7.
78. Alberta Legislative Assembly Debates, 17th Legislature, 3d Session, 1975.
79. In the first session of the 1972 legislature, when the issue was whether "resident advisory committees" should have more power, both the government members and the opposition suggested that some improvement districts should be upgraded so that they might contribute a much larger share of funds for their operation. Alberta Legislative Assembly Debates, 17th Legislature, 1st Session, 76–77.
80. *Medicine Hat News*, March 22, 1984.
81. A portion of Improvement District No. 10 had been a municipal district until 1956, when the area's coal mining industry collapsed. The area was returned to improvement district status until the government felt it had the population and resources to be financially self-sufficient. When the area was restored to municipal district status in 1985 it had more land, 1.87 million hectares, than any other municipal district in the province. It also had a population of 9,200 and an ever-increasing tax base as oil and gas activity throughout the area continued to grow.
82. Improvement Districts Association of Alberta, "A Framework Proposal for Increased Local Government Autonomy for Improvement District Residents," 4.
83. Alberta Department of Municipal Affairs, "The Rural District: A Concept of Transitional Municipal Government." Surprisingly, although a "corporate strategy" is discussed in the Municipal Affairs report and the Rural District Act, such a strategy is never defined.
84. It should be noted that Municipal Affairs was merely following government policy. The government emphasized when it shepherded the act through the legislature that it reflected the interests of improvement district councils. See Alberta Legislative Assembly Debates, 22d Legislature, 3d Session, 1643–645.
85. Gorman, *A Land Reclaimed*, 15–16, 46–54. Gorman notes that shortly after they broke the prairie sod some farmers had a yield as high as 40 bushels to the acre. Since prices for quality hard wheat were as much as $1.35 a bushel, they began taking out large loans to purchase expensive new equipment. When yields and prices began to decline, the farmers were unable to repay their loans and lost everything.
86. *Ibid.*, 82.

87. In 1932 an employee of the Alberta Department of Agriculture, O.S. Longman, produced the "Berry Creek Report" on the exodus of settlers from the Hanna District, and three years later Donald Cameron presented a report on soil conservation. Gorman discusses both reports. *Ibid.,* 104–122.
88. Hanson, 87.
89. Gorman, 130–131.
90. Martin, "The Special Areas of Alberta," 18.
91. Gorman, 165.
92. Martin, 18–19.
93. Grover, "A Celebration of Success," 22.
94. *Ibid.*
95. Walchuk, 147–149.
96. A number of years ago the Peace River Planning Commission estimated that there were approximately 900 hamlets. In January 1992 the Department of Municipal Affairs placed the number of hamlets at 378.
97. The 1981 federal census contains a belated reference to hamlets in the following definition of an unincorporated place: "A cluster of 5 or more permanently occupied dwellings, known by a locally recognized name and located within a rural municipality or unorganized territory. Unincorporated places do not have a local government; most of them do not have legal boundaries." Canada. *1981 Census Dictionary*, 55.
98. In 1985 the County of Grande Prairie was anxious to have Bezanson and Teepee Creek designated hamlets so that each community would be eligible for a $15,000 base street grant plus $80 per capita. It should be noted the grant was cost-shared and the county would have to pay 25 percent of the cost for each community. *Grande Prairie Daily Herald Tribune,* May 31, 1985.
99. *Rocky View Times,* September 22, 1987.
100. *Rocky View/ Five Village Weekly,* September 22, 1987. A Rocky View counsellor attending the meeting questioned the proponent's figures and pointed out that since the municipal district did not budget on a divisional basis there was no reason to expect that all of the revenue raised in the municipality should stay in it.
101. The manager of the municipal district explained why a special election was called in September rather than waiting less than three weeks and placing the question on the municipal election ballot: "The decision . . . was made to avoid any possibility of the incorporation becoming an issue during the municipal elections." *Rocky View/Five Village Weekly,* May 2, 1989.
102. *Fort McMurray Today,* April 5, 1989; *Edson Leader,* April 25, 1989.

5 Governmental Reorganization

1. Maxey, "The Political Integration of Metropolitan Communities," 229.
2. Plunkett, *Urban Canada and Its Government,* 80.
3. Donald Rowat, one of Canada's leading academic authorities on governmental reorganization, has said that Victor Jones's *Metropolitan Govern-*

ment, written in 1942, shaped many of his ideas. Jones's theories are directly descended from those of Paul Studenski.

4. *Spillover effects* are defined as the effects on a municipality caused by the actions of an adjoining municipality. As an example, if one municipality permits heavy industry on its perimeter there may very well be unfavourable spillover effects of noise, smoke, dirt, and odour for the residents of the adjoining municipality. Conversely, if a municipality builds a park on its perimeter, residents of the adjoining community would enjoy the favourable spillover effects of increased recreational facilities and aesthetic enhancement.

5. Ostrum, Tiebout, and Warren, "The Organization of Government in Metropolitan Areas," 831–842.

6. U.S. Advisory Commission on Intergovernmental Relations, *The Organization of Local Public Economies*, 1. The report notes that the distinction between production and provision was first made in 1953 by Richard Musgrave in *The Theory of Public Finance: A Study in Public Economy*.

7. *Ibid.*

8. City of Edmonton, *Decision 1980: The Annexation Issue*, Section 7. A similar argument was made by Fort McMurray when it attempted in the 1970s to negotiate an industrial tax transfer agreement with Suncor Inc. and Syncrude Canada Limited, both of which were located outside the municipality's boundaries. It held that by providing expensive municipal services for workers who lived in Fort McMurray, the municipality was unfairly subsidizing the companies. After the tax transfer agreement expired in 1983 the Fort McMurray council discussed annexing the tar sand plants in order to capture their tax base.

9. On the other hand, it is argued that bedroom communities incur the expense of providing an educational system acceptable to their middle-class residents and costly services to enhance their low-density residential neighbourhoods. Therefore, the middle-class satellite community subsidizes the core city, which acquires a skilled labour force without having to pay for the expensive public services demanded by middle-class families.

10. *Grand Centre-Cold Lake Sun*, October 6, 1987.

11. *Newsmakers*, December 10, 1986; *Popular Press*, December 10, 1986. The reason the two municipalities did not amalgamate was that Entwistle's property taxes would have increased substantially. See *Western Review*, December 16, 1986.

12. City of Edmonton, *Decision 1980: The Annexation Issue*, Section 7.

13. U.S. Advisory Commission on Intergovernmental Relations, *Metropolitan Organization: The Allegheny County Case*, 3.

14. Hirsch, "The Supply of Urban Government Services," 509. Ian Wight, former manager of policy and research for Alberta Department of Municipal Affairs and an expert on reorganization, has said that "you really need 50,000 people before the economy of scale argument applies in Alberta." *Grand Centre-Cold Lake Sun*, May 26, 1987.

15. *Edmonton Journal*, February 27, 28, 1985.

16. *Calgary Herald*, April 16, 1988.

17. An example of this phenomenon occurred in the tiny hamlet of Rosedale, which Lacombe wanted to annex in the summer of 1989. The spokesperson for Rosedale's residents explained why almost 90 percent of them opposed annexation: ". . . the primary reason . . . is that we chose to live in a rural setting and would like to stay like that." *Red Deer Advocate*, May 11, 1989. However, it should be noted that Rosedale residents' property taxes would increase with annexation and they would receive significantly lower levels of service. Lacombe's mayor admitted that the people in the area proposed for annexation would be very aware of a drop in their services. *Red Deer Advocate*, June 20, 1989.

18. Many large-city office-holders and administrative personnel in both the public and private sectors favour expansion because increased prestige and higher salaries are characteristically found in larger governments.

19. *Medicine Hat News*, April 3, 1985.

20. Bettison, Kenward, and Taylor, *Urban Affairs in Alberta*, 69–117.

21. Alberta, *Report of the Royal Commission on the Metropolitan Development of Calgary and Edmonton*, iv–v.

22. *Ibid.*, Chapter 14.

23. *Ibid.* When Edmonton made its bid to the Alberta Local Authorities Board to bring all of the outlying communities in the region into its fold in 1980 it also relied on Maxey's assumption that a metropolitan area was a single undifferentiated social and economic entity. This can be seen in its submission: ". . . the major components within the Edmonton boundary proposal . . . [constitute] one urban or metropolitan unit, characterized often as one socio-economic unit, within which there exists a high degree of interdependence or community of interest." City of Edmonton, *Submission to the Local Authorities Board of Alberta on Behalf of the City of Edmonton*, iii.

24. Smith, "Community Aspirations, Territorial Justice and the Metropolitan Form of Edmonton and Calgary," 189.

25. In 1954/55 Edmonton received $6,430,000 in provincial assistance; in 1958/59, $16,190,000. Bettison, Kenward, and Taylor, 151.

26. A plebiscite was held in the area and 67.2 percent of the residents supported amalgamation. The provincial government provided "transitional capital assistance" during the amalgamation process.

27. Forerunners of the LAB were the Board of Public Utilities Commissioners (1915 through 1960) and the Public Utilities Board (1950 to 1961), the LAB's immediate predecessor.

28. Alberta, *Revised Statutes of Alberta*, 1980.

29. Hanson, *The Potential Unification of the Edmonton Metropolitan Area*, xii.

30. See Steil, "The Politicizing of Annexation in Alberta," 40–42. One of the more curious provisions in the cabinet's decision was that the city was awarded substantially more land on its northeastern boundary than it bid for in its annexation proposal. A possible explanation is that since the Min-

ister of Housing and Public Works, Thomas Chambers, had spent in excess of $35 million secretly assembling land for another housing complex, unbeknown to the Edmonton administration, the cabinet decided to facilitate the whole process by annexing the land for the city.

31. In March 1981 one of Edmonton's consultants stated that, estimating conservatively, the city has spent $3 million on consultants. As of March 1, St. Albert had spent $560,000 on attorneys and consultants; the Municipal District of Sturgeon and the County of Parkland, $450,000; the County of Strathcona, $2,982,549 (since 1977). *Edmonton Journal*, March 5, 12, 1981. A political scientist discussing metropolitan reorganization in Canadian cities concludes that, "Although Canadian suburbanites have generally tried to resist either annexation to the central city or metropolitan government, they have done so without the passion or commitment of their American counterparts." Sancton, "Conclusion: Canadian City Politics in Comparative Perspective," 301. Although the argument may apply to Canadian cities generally, it was not true in the Edmonton case. Residents of St. Albert and Sherwood Park held outdoor rallies and marches, displayed bumper stickers, gathered petitions with thousands of names, and wrote innumerable letters to their community newspapers as well as to the *Edmonton Journal*, all adamantly opposing amalgamation.

32. *Representative* (Leduc), May 7, 1985.

33. Edmonton had used a similar projection in its annexation proposal. See Steil, "Annexation Criteria in Alberta," 12–15.

34. *Representative*, October 28, November 11, 1986. Mayor Klak wanted the timing of the annexation proposal tied to the start-up of the Genesee power plant. He maintained that this would minimize annexation's financial effect on the county. *Representative*, May 19, 1987.

35. *Representative*, December 9, 1986.

36. *Representative*, January 20, 1987.

37. *Representative*, February 2, 1988.

38. Surprisingly, the LAB admitted that "the Airport and Nisku will continue to operate as constraints to the City and its aspirations for legitimate future growth." *Summary of the Leduc Annexation Decision*, 5.

39. *Edmonton Journal*, February 15, 1991. The Minister of Municipal Affairs, in particular, lauded the consultation process between the two municipalities which the government had set in motion. Alberta Legislative Assembly Debates, 22d Legislature, 3d Session, 1014.

40. Perhaps Calgary had examined what had occurred in Edmonton. Peter Smith explained that during the 1950s Jasper Place and Strathcona acted "as safety valves for Edmonton." Somewhat later Edmonton realized "that Jasper Place and Strathcona were erecting barriers against Edmonton's eventual expansion—barriers of a scale and kind that Calgary did not have to face on its boundaries." Smith, "Community Aspirations, Territorial Justice and the Metropolitan Form of Edmonton and Calgary," 186.

41. The 96-member local chapter of the Urban Development Institute (UDI) enthusiastically supported Calgary's bid for more land. The Institute's chair warned that if the city were not successful in its annexation bid land prices would increase. *Rocky View/Five Village Weekly*, April 11, 1989.

42. Calgary's task was far easier than the one Edmonton had in 1979 and 1980. Calgary was negotiating for low-density farm land rather than an area with high-density middle-class suburban housing.

43. For a detailed discussion of the 1989 annexation see Brown, Miller, and Simpkins, "The City of Calgary's Comprehensive Annexation," 39–78. The authors show the city made several tactical errors in its submission to the LAB. Perhaps the biggest surprise for the city was that the order emphasized that "intermunicipal agreements do not provide a substitute for justifying a need for land."

44. To buttress his argument he pointed out that the towns and their citizens were already linked in a number of areas: (1) teenagers from Redcliff went to high school in Medicine Hat; (2) Medicine Hat supplied Redcliff with electric power and natural gas; (3) Redcliff's sewer lines ran into Medicine Hat's sewage lagoon; (4) since Redcliff did not have a hospital, residents used the hospital in Medicine Hat; and (5) 75 to 80 cents of every Redcliff consumer dollar were spent in Medicine Hat. *Medicine Hat News*, April 3, 1985.

45. There were two precedents for such a grant. When municipalities in the Crowsnest Pass were amalgamated in 1979 the provincial government provided a grant so that all of the amalgamated communities, from the very beginning, would receive the same level of service. After Edmonton's large-scale annexation in the early 1980s, the rural municipalities which lost sizeable portions of their territory were given grants to ease the adverse impacts on them.

46. *Medicine Hat News*, April 10, 1986.

47. Plunkett and Lightbody, "Tribunals, Politics and the Public Interest," 207–221.

48. *Ibid.*, 211–218.

49. *Ibid.*, 219.

50. Criticism of the LAB process is not restricted to the academic community. In an exchange between Kurt Gesell, a government backbencher, and Ray Speaker, Minister of Municipal Affairs in the legislative assembly in 1990, Gesell asked for assurance that the LAB process would be revamped so that it would be less "confrontational." Alberta Legislative Assembly Debates, 22d Legislature, 2d Session, 2419.

51. Lightbody, "With Whom the Tolls Dwell," 55.

52. *Calgary Herald*, July 20, 1982; *Red Deer Advocate*, July 21, 1982.

53. The annexed lands in northeast Edmonton have class one soil and with a 124-day frost-free period the land is ideal for intensive truck gardening.

54. *Edmonton Journal*, March 29, 1982.

55. *Mainstream* (Edmonton), April 18, 1979.

56. *Edmonton Journal*, November 24, 1981.

57. The president of the firefighters' union pointed out that the fire department had added only 20 men to the city's 960-member force, although annexation had doubled the area the department had to serve. The Edmonton fire chief admitted that the department would be unable to provide the same level of service in the newly annexed areas as that provided in the rest of the city. *Edmonton Journal*, June 30, 1982.

58. Alderman Bettie Hewes advocated expanding the number of wards to eight, with each one served by two councillors. *Edmonton Journal*, April 14, 1982. However, her concerns about representation and her expanded ward plan had little council support.

59. The announcements were as follows: (1) the province would rebate 80 percent of the increase from 1981 to 1982; (2) for 1983 the province would rebate 80 percent of the 1982 rebate; (3) for 1984 the rebate would be 60 percent of the 1982 rebate; (4) for 1985 the rebate would be 40 percent of the 1982 rebate; (5) for 1986 the rebate would be 20 percent of the 1982 rebate. A rebate for any given year which worked out to less than $100 would not be paid.

60. *Edmonton Journal*, January 30, 1983.

61. *Edmonton Journal*, March 8, 1983. Ewasiuk pointed out that, "basically, most of the land we annexed was rural, which really doesn't give us much of a tax base." The County of Strathcona reeve, Warren Thomas, was less than enthusiastic about the proposal: "Sure, we want all of the land back, not just bits and pieces. We don't just want high cost areas to service." *Sherwood Park News*, March 16, 1983.

62. *Edmonton Journal*, October 17, 1985.

63. *Edmonton Journal*, July 13, 1986.

64. *Edmonton Journal*, July 16, 1986.

65. *Herald Sunday Magazine* (Calgary), 11–12.

66. *Rocky View/Five Village Weekly*, February 9, 1988.

67. *Edmonton Journal*, April 12, 1918.

68. The amalgamation resulted in savings as well as cost increases. The number of municipal administrative and general staff decreased from 69 before amalgamation in 1979 to 44 in 1983.

69. This annexation was not totally without controversy. Since over 400 people lived in the area to be annexed, the improvement district's chairperson was concerned about the loss of provincial grants awarded on a per capita basis: "We lose all that tax base and all that grant base and that's going to make a difference to the ID." *Medicine Hat News*, March 17, 1982.

70. The annexation area included $2.06 million of taxable property; however, while the area contributed $227,600 in revenue to the county in 1980, service to its residents cost $212,800.

71. Although it agreed to freeze farmers' taxes in the proposed annexation area

for five years, Lloydminster was not able to work out an agreement with the rural municipality of Britannia.

72. An exception was Mayor William Hawrelak who, in his last term of office (October 1974 through November 1975) and just before he died, was very close to putting the finishing touches on an expansion agreement with the County of Parkland and the Municipal District of Sturgeon.

73. Peter Smith, a noted geographer and authority on governmental reorganization in Edmonton and Calgary, maintains that this assertion needs to be explained if one is to understand the dynamics of governmental reorganization in the two cities. "Given that political relations in the Edmonton metropolitan area are peculiarly fractious, from what does the fractiousness derive and why has it not been characteristic of the Calgary area as well? The interpretation . . . is that the explanation is basically geographical. The differences in political behavior are themselves rooted in differences in spatial form between the two metropolitan areas. Those differences in form have been reinforced, in turn, as outcomes of the differences in political behavior, but they derived initially from different patterns in the circumstances of community origin and development." Smith, "Community Aspirations, Territorial Justice and the Metropolitan Form of Edmonton and Calgary," 182.

6 Policy Makers and Democracy

1. Braybrooke and Lindblom, *A Strategy of Decision*, 40.
2. Lindblom, "The Science of Muddling Through."
3. Dye, *Understanding Public Policy*, 31–32; Simon, *Administrative Behavior*, 38–41, 240–244.
4. See Aucoin, "Theory and Research in the Study of Policy Making," 14, for a criticism of incrementalism by a Canadian policy analyst.
5. Etzioni, *The Active Society*, 282–309. Two Canadian urban analysts take issue with the notion that rational policy making is so complex and difficult that decision makers resort to incremental policy making by default. In *Bargaining for Cities*, Lionel Feldman and Katherine Graham argue that there are two reasons why municipalities make policy incrementally. One reason is that a fragmented municipal political and administrative structure discourages "concerted action" in dealing with other governments. Another reason is that in intergovernmental affairs elected officials tend to become involved "on a functional basis, a pattern which compartmentalizes—rather than co-ordinates—the local approach." See pages xxii and xxiii. The differences in interpretation may be a function of their focus on policy making in an intergovernmental setting.
6. There is one exception to the requirement that a municipality must have a specific delegated power in order to enact a bylaw. A municipality has an implied power to carry out its delegated powers. For example, if a provincial act should give municipalities the power to regulate the type of materi-

als that can be used in building construction, there is an implied power that municipalities can hire construction inspectors.

7. Section 104(2) of the MGA reads: "In the event of the inability, neglect or failure of one or both of the parties named in subsection (1) to sign, the council by resolution in any particular case may authorize the persons it designates in the resolution to sign the by-law."

8. One exception is that it is necessary to have the assent of the electorate if the bylaw to be amended or repealed came about through the plebiscite process. Another exception is an amendment or repeal of a bylaw relating to council procedure. See Section 109(3)(a) of the MGA.

9. *Red Deer Advocate*, July 24, 1986; *Fort McMurray Today*, November 6, 1986.

10. Alberta Legislative Assembly Debates, 20th Legislature, 1st Session, 1303.

11. See Lightbody, "'Wild Bill Hawrelak,'" 47.

12. Lightbody, a participant-observer, describes Decore's electoral strategy in "The First Hurrah."

13. However, Klein faltered politically in 1988, when he hired for his own staff a $43,000 protocol officer at a time when his administration was grappling with an extremely large city debt.

14. Blake, "Role Perceptions of Local Decision-Makers," 95.

15. *Edmonton Sun*, December 23, 1985.

16. Higgins, *Urban Canada*, 96.

17. *Edmonton Journal*, January 19, 1989.

18. Bettison, Kenward, and Taylor, *Urban Affairs in Alberta*, 501.

19. In an interview with a *City Magazine* reporter Decore briefly discusses his working relationship with council. See Hicks, "A Better Deal for Cities."

20. *Alberta Report*, November 3, 1986.

21. *Sherwood Park News*, November 5, 1986. In the same interview Common said, ". . . it is a reasonable assumption that I was elected reeve in part because my division does bridge the gap between urban and rural." He added that his ties with the Tory Party also could influence his role as reeve.

22. *Calgary Herald*, June 26, 1986.

23. *Edmonton Journal*, February 16, 1984; *Alberta Report*, March 5, 1984.

24. Mayor Jan Reimer considered using one of her *ex officio* powers as mayor to attend a meeting of the utilities and public works standing committee and cast a vote for her candidate. However, on second thought she decided that "at this point in time, given that the committee has to work together over the next year, it was best they try to sort it out among themselves." *Edmonton Journal*, November 13, 1991.

25. *Representative*, May 14, 1985.

26. *South Peace News*, March 18, 1987.

27. *South Peace News*, September 16, 1987.

28. *St. Albert Gazette*, February 8, 1989.

29. *Lethbridge Herald*, March 18, 1989.

30. *Fort Saskatchewan Record*, May 3, 1989.

31. *Strathmore Standard*, March 12, 1986.

32. Alderman Ken Kozak explained why he supported unorthodox positions: "I like to consider myself somewhat innovative and creative." *Edmonton Journal*, February 16, 1992.

33. *Calgary Herald*, December 15, 1988.

34. *Edmonton Journal*, December 15, 1990. In 1986 Mackenzie and Reimer ran successfully together as Urban Reform Group Edmonton (URGE) candidates.

35. The case for immunity was made in 1975 by Ho Lem, a Social Credit MLA who had been a Calgary alderman. He also introduced bill no. 214 to amend the MGA to give municipal legislators immunity for council meeting discussions. The bill only received first reading. See Alberta Legislative Assembly Debates, 17th Legislature, 4th Session, 311.

36. On the basis of the sociological literature on friendship patterns, it can be postulated that social and work relationships among councillors are decidedly different on councils which are primarily middle-class and those which are working-class. See Athanasiou and Yoshioka, "The Spatial Character of Friendship Formation," 43–65; Schutte and Light, "The Relative Importance of Proximity and Status for Friendship Choices in Social Hierarchies," 260–264; Allan, "Class Variation in Friendship Patterns," 389–393; and Verbrugge, "The Structure of Adult Friendship Choices," 576–597.

37. McAlpine and Drabek, "Decision-Making Coalitions on Non-partisan Councils," 821.

38. Masson, "Decision-Making Patterns and Floating Coalitions in an Urban City Council."

39. *Alberta Report*, April 28, 1986.

40. *Post*, April 26, 1988.

41. Easton and Tennant, "Vancouver Civic Party Leadership," 19–29; Clarkson, "Barriers to Entry of Parties in Toronto's Civic Politics," 206–223; Alexander, "The Institutional and Role Perceptions of Local Aldermen," 124–140; Bourassa, "Les élites politiques de Montréal," 87–109.

42. Long and Slemko, "The Recruitment of Local Decision-Makers in Five Canadian Cities," 553.

43. Lightbody, "Edmonton: Gateway to the North," 271–272. Particularly intriguing was Lightbody's finding that few lawyers ran for council in the 1977, 1980, and 1983 elections.

44. Ed Ewasiuk, a labour leader and community activist, was elected to council in 1980. In October 1989 Brian Mason, a bus driver who captured a council seat with labour's support, was identified as working class since he trumpeted his occupation and class in his political campaign. However, Mason has a BA degree from the University of Alberta and had been an advisor to Ewasiuk.

45. Wilson, *Women, the Family and the Economy*, 120–125. A study that compared all of the female candidates who contested federal and provincial elections between 1945 and 1976 and women who contested municipal offices in 24 selected communities during the same period found that

"women are significantly more likely to achieve election at the municipal level." Of women who were elected in their first attempt, 58.9 percent did so in municipal elections, 18.26 percent in provincial elections, and 6.85 percent in federal elections. Vickers, "Where Are the Women in Canadian Politics?" 45–46.

46. *Edmonton Journal*, October 22, 1989.
47. *News*, June 29, 1988.
48. Under the Municipal Government Act a council member can be called either a councillor or an alderman. However, the term alderman has traditionally been used in larger communities and councillor in smaller ones.
49. *Red Deer Advocate*, November 29, 1983.
50. *Edmonton Journal*, January 21, 1986.
51. *Calgary Herald*, February 16, 1987.
52. Drackley, Willson, and Steil, "Profile of the Consulting Planning Industry in Canada," 7.
53. Duffy, "Hiring a Consultant: Not a Fairy Story," 4.
54. *Edmonton Journal*, May 26, 1985.
55. Kagi, "The Role of Private Consultants in Urban Governing," 54–55.
56. *Airdrie Echo*, January 18, 1989.
57. *Representative*, October 22, 1985.
58. *Grande Prairie Daily Herald Tribune*, January 18, 1985.
59. Most council decisions to employ outside consultants elicit little public controversy. An exception was the proposal made by Calgary's chief commissioner, George Cornish, in 1987. Cornish, who was 56, decided that his job was too stressful and that he wanted to work only part-time and as a consultant. Cornish worked out an arrangement whereby he would retire but be employed by the city as a part-time consultant for three years for an annual salary of $33,000. Both aldermen and the public expressed concern about Cornish's "golden parachute."
60. *Edmonton Journal*, July 3, 1985.
61. *Ibid.* More was at issue than whether the work should be done by Stanley and Associates or the public sector. After Stanley had been awarded the management consultant contract it purchased Cheriton Engineering, which subsequently obtained a $700,000 contract to work on design and provide mechanical and electrical engineering services for the LRT's southern leg. Questions were raised as to how objective Stanley, as the general consultant, could be in evaluating the work of one of its subsidiaries.
62. An exhaustive legalistic study of conflict of interest was made by the Conflict of Interest Committee of the Association of Municipalities of Ontario in the early 1980s. Although the study deals primarily with Ontario and is somewhat dated, several important conflict of interest cases in Alberta are examined. See Smither, *Municipal Conflict of Interest*.
63. *Calgary Herald*, February 26, 1983.
64. *Chronicle*, April 25, 1989; *Lethbridge Herald*, June 6, 1989.
65. *Grande Prairie Daily Herald Tribune*, May 23, 1989.

66. When a case of conflict of interest was brought before the court the judge ruled that the mayor's vote on the three-person council was an error in judgement and that he was not guilty.

67. For a description of the transaction, see Lightbody, "'Wild Bill Hawrelak,'" 37.

68. *Ibid.*, 41.

69. *Calgary Herald*, December 17, 1990.

70. In a discussion of conflict of interest, Grant MacEwan, respected long-time politician and Lieutenant-Governor of Alberta, wrote: "Under no circumstances should the public official be party to transactions between government in which he has a voice and any company or agency in which he holds an interest. . . . the man in public office, if acting wisely, will remove all possibility of serving himself through his position. In other words, there must be no grounds for suspicion that he could be serving two masters." MacEwan, *Poking into Politics*, 176.

71. *Calgary Herald*, December 3, 1913.

72. *Calgary Herald*, December 6, 1917.

73. Under the federal Income Tax Act, one-third of the remuneration of a councillor is nontaxable.

74. *Edmonton Journal*, June 27, 1986. In all fairness it should be noted he was not opposed to salary increases for council members.

75. When the Kosowan Committee was established, Alderman Percy Wickman said that council agreed to accept its recommendations and that "whether we're happy or not with them doesn't make any difference." *Edmonton Journal*, June 19, 1986. After the 1986 election Decore referred the salary issue to the secretary of his executive committee, John Woychuk, who reported to the committee that Edmonton's aldermen were badly underpaid. His report and his salary recommendations were used by council to justify their increases in salary. See *Edmonton Sun*, February 11, 1987. Woychuk's recommendation is particularly interesting since in a Canada-wide examination of municipal councils for 1984 Donald Higgins found that the salary of the Edmonton council was well above the average. Higgins, *Local and Urban Politics in Canada*, 386–388.

76. *Edmonton Journal*, February 12, 1987. A similar situation occurred in Claresholm in 1989 when the council went into an in camera session to discuss wages for the town's senior staff. The mayor explained that "after conducting our senior staff evaluations and wage increases, the council drifted naturally into discussion of its [own] remuneration." Although a council salary increase was not on the meeting's agenda the council came out of its in camera session into full council and a motion was introduced to increase council salaries. The salary motion had three readings and was unanimously passed, all in the same evening. *Claresholm Local Press*, January 25, February 1, 1989.

77. This move by Alderman Hayter was particularly surprising since he was one of the higher paid Edmonton aldermen because he sat on a number of

municipal boards and commissions. His rationale for a substantial salary increase was that Calgary aldermen had increased their salaries and he worked just as much as any MLA.

78. *Edmonton Sun*, September 26, 1989.

79. Remuneration data is based on a mail survey by the author of all Alberta urban and rural municipalities. Although the Alberta Urban Municipalities Association (AUMA) collects extensive data on the remuneration of municipal elected officials each year, its policy is not to release the data.

80. City of Calgary, "Report of the Committee on Council Remuneration," 10.

81. *Crowsnest Pass Promoter*, March 3, 1986.

82. Letter from Lutz Perschon to Jack Masson, March 5, 1991.

83. Council members actually are paid at a per-meeting rate which has been computed to ascertain annual salaries.

84. *Edmonton Journal*, February 12, 1987.

85. *Mercury*, November 1, 1988.

86. *Calgary Herald*, September 11, 1988.

87. *Edmonton Journal*, March 23, 1989.

88. *Calgary Herald*, June 7, 1989.

89. Particularly surprising is that the city had asked the Alberta Association of Architects to assist in a planning competition some six weeks before the Dub decision was announced and twelve architectural firms had planned to enter the competition. *Edmonton Journal*, March 9, 1988.

90. *Edmonton Journal*, November 18, 1989.

91. The *Edmonton Journal*'s city hall reporter, John Geiger, interviewed newly elected Brian Mason and then wrote: ". . . only 48 hours after the municipal election, city council huddled over its Grey Cup game plan. A short time later forms were circulated, to be filled out by those wanting to make the trip . . . Mason . . . said he wasn't used to such perks and found the free trip grab 'a bit much.'" *Edmonton Journal*, November 21, 1989.

92. A simple regression formula was used to compare aldermanic salaries with the size of city populations.

93. Sancton and Woolner, "Full Time Municipal Councillors: A Strategic Challenge for Canadian Urban Government," 504.

94. The AUMA 1979 convention resolution no. 61 was put forward by the Town of Claresholm.

7 Bureaucratic Behaviour and Democratic Institutions

1. On the other hand, Section 94 of the Municipal Government Act (MGA) clearly states that if a manager or commissioner has a direct or indirect business contract with the municipality, that person is in conflict of interest and is subject to immediate dismissal. In 1983 a question arose as to whether or not the town administrator in Rimbey violated the act, since he owned 25 percent of Eastview Development, which did business with the town. The mayor said that the pertinent section of the act mentions "town managers, mayor or commissioners—we won't know whether that includes

town administrator or not . . . whether town administrator is the same as town manager—things like that." *Red Deer Advocate*, December 2, 1983.

2. Under Section 94 of the MGA a commissioner or manager can be dismissed without notice and compensation if the person has a direct or indirect interest in a contract with the municipality. Moreover, if a senior administrator is involved in fiscal mismanagement, linked to theft, or has committed a misdemeanor, he or she can usually be dismissed with cause.

3. At this point the secretary-treasurer, who was attending the meeting, became annoyed and said, "I don't need any more power. I didn't request the change." *Tribune*, November 24, 1987.

4. This provision applies only to villages, summer villages, and municipal districts.

5. *Edmonton Journal*, September 8, 1990. However, several days later Picherack met with representatives of the Edmonton Caribbean Cultural Association and the St. Kitt and Nevis Edmonton Association and resolved his differences with them. See *Edmonton Journal*, September 14, 1990.

6. This is the official position of the Department of Municipal Affairs. Speaking before the 1986 annual convention of the Alberta Association of Municipal Districts and Counties (AAMD&C), the director of the department's municipal services branch, John McGowan, told the delegates: "Council's role is to establish policy, the administration's role is to carry it out." "Taking the Team Approach," 7–8.

7. Caraley, *City Governments and Urban Problems*, 268.

8. The public administration profession distinguishes between administrative generalists and specialists. Specialists have expertise in particular service areas such as firefighting or the administration of a fire department. Generalists have an overall knowledge of the administrative process that they are able to apply to any organization, no matter how specialized its goals.

9. Sayre and Kaufman, *Governing New York City*, 420–421.

10. Decore, "Politics."

11. *News*, June 8, 1988.

12. Lipsky, "Street-Level Bureaucrats and the Analysis of Urban Reform" and "Toward a Theory of Street-Level Bureaucracy"; Gardiner, "Police Enforcement of Traffic Laws"; Derthick, "Intercity Differences in Administration of the Public Assistance Program."

13. In addition, the manager was awarded a substantial number of employment benefits including a car, the payment of moving expenses, membership in the Centre Club, six weeks' vacation a year, a dental plan, group life insurance, an accidental disability and death plan, and Alberta Health Care.

14. Every municipality in the province was asked to provide salary information for its senior administrators. However, fewer than half of the municipalities in each of the four categories answered the survey.

15. Letter from S.A. Heather-Kalau, Municipal Administrator for the Village of Coutts, to Jack Masson, March 1, 1991.

16. In 1976 Edward LeSage and Charles Humphrey, using a proportional strat-

ified sample, selected 192 administrators (from larger municipalities, villages, counties, and municipal districts) who were sent questionnaires relating to the skill requirements and training needs of municipal administrators. They had a 70 percent return rate—158 questionnaires were returned, of which two were not usable. LeSage and Humphrey, "Alberta Municipal Administrators' Survey." In 1983 a follow-up study of municipal administrators was conducted by Edna Einsiedel. She too used a proportional stratified sample; 153 respondents returned the questionnaire, a response rate of 67 percent. Einsiedel, *Survey of Alberta Chief Municipal Administrators and Municipal Development Officers*.

17. Einsiedel, *Survey of Planning Needs and Training Preferences of Alberta Elected Officials*.

18. *Ibid*. It is important to note that even though these were the two most frequently mentioned problem areas, each was identified as a problem by only 7 percent of the elected officials who responded to the survey.

19. The mayor justified his actions on the basis of Section 51(1)(c) of the MGA, which states that "The mayor is the chief officer of the municipality and shall supervise and inspect the conduct of all officials of the municipality in the performance of their duties." George Cuff, long-time mayor of Spruce Grove and a municipal consultant, discusses elected officials who insist on closely monitoring the bureaucracy. He writes: ". . . I find in many municipalities councillors who, when referring to a particular function of the community, describe it as 'my department.' Instead, what the councillor is actually describing is the work of a committee on which he has been chosen to serve. Unfortunately, this group of councillors mistake their role as policy advisors on committees and policy decision-makers on council with that of the staff role of administrator. Councillors who fall into this trap do not fully comprehend their role as an elected official. Instead, they believe that the public 'hired' them to do a job rather than elected them to provide leadership. Thus, we have the spectre of elected officials becoming so buried in 'administrivia' that they are unable to see the larger picture." Cuff, "Fatal Flaws: Beware of Problems Which Can Plague a Council," 6.

20. *Dispatch*, March 23, November 2, 1988. Unfortunately, the town's elected officials did not understand the nature of the problem. They decided to convert the position of administrator into that of a manager and to hire a consultant to recruit a suitable candidate.

21. *Edmonton Report*, July 3, 1981.

22. The manager had been terminated without cause, which was allowed as long as he was paid one-quarter of his $38,000 annual salary. His attorney argued that his termination contravened Section 90 of the MGA, which stated that a manager had to be "furnished with a written statement of the reasons" and must be allowed "a reasonable opportunity to be heard before the council." Court of Queen's Bench Justice Ross McBain held the section did not apply for persons hired "at the pleasure" of city council.

23. *Medicine Hat News*, February 10, 1988; *Brooks Bulletin*, February 17, 1988.

24. At the 1987 AAMD&C convention attorney Leo Burgess advised the delegates on the applicable provisions of the common law as it related to a municipality dismissing employees and being subject to a charge of wrongful dismissal. He cited five common situations where the court has held the employer to be in the wrong. They are: (1) a unilateral reduction in salary or hours; (2) a substantial demotion in job responsibility; (3) a change in responsibility which results in a loss of authority, power, or status even though there may be no change in salary; (4) job reassignment as a consequence of a departmental reorganization and: (5) a job relocation. "Lawyer Outlines Dismissal Guidelines," 10–11.

25. Although a number of publicized negotiated settlements involving dismissals occurred during Decore's reign as mayor, the phenomenon was not unique to his administration. Early in Jan Reimer's administration a settlement was negotiated with the city's manager of environmental services. Although his duties ended on December 31, 1990, he was to receive $200,000 between his termination date and August 1992, when he would be eligible for early retirement. *Edmonton Journal*, December 13, 1990.

26. Although the city's position was that the community coordinator did not have a contract with the city, during the trial the defence counsel for the city admitted that Gordeyko's "contract is valid . . . and binding on the city." *Edmonton Journal*, March 20, 1986.

27. The total dollar value amount of the settlement was higher. The city solicitor, who was 52 years old, received $160,000 plus remuneration for legal fees up to $10,000 and "an amount equal to the benefits he would have received if he'd stayed with the city to age 55." *Edmonton Sun*, May 5, 1989. Alderman Jan Reimer in particular was critical of the city administration's lack of control over the city's law department. She argued that if the legal department had been responsible to the city manager allegations of sexual harassment could have been handled internally instead of being brought before council. *Edmonton Journal*, January 29, 1987.

28. *South Peace News*, October 19, 1988.

29. *South Peace News*, March 6, 1988.

30. Two very different versions of the incident were presented at Brodie's court hearing. Not at issue was that Miyauchi invited a town employee, Rita Gara, into the town hall coffee room to discuss some personal problems they had been having. Since relations between the two had been strained, the town manager entered the room and told Miyauchi to stop talking and to leave. At this point it is unclear whether Brodie began pushing her out of the room or whether there was just a shouting match. Gara said she did not see what had happened since her view had been blocked. *Brooks Bulletin*, October 19, 1988; January 18, 1990. Miyauchi, letter to Jack Masson, October 4, 1989.

31. *Edmonton Journal*, November 1, 1990.

32. *Edmonton Journal*, November 15, 1990.

33. *Alberta Report*, December 22, 1986.

34. When the retirement package was announced, a *Calgary Herald* writer contacted municipal officials in seven other large cities in Canada to determine whether they had negotiated similar settlements with their senior bureaucrats. None had and the director of personnel in Toronto said that "it's a practice we discourage, we think retirement is retirement." *Calgary Herald,* July 27, 1987.

35. *St. Albert Gazette,* July 27, 1988.

36. *Chronicle,* April 19, 1988.

37. Cuff, "Views from the Top," 13.

38. *Lethbridge Herald,* May 28, 1987.

39. Section 93 of the MGA, which states that "the mayor is, by virtue of his office, a commissioner in addition to those appointed by the council," gives the mayor the authority to hold power as both an elective and an administrative official.

40. *Vegreville Observer,* May 19, 1987.

41. See Millerson, *The Qualifying Associations,* for an often cited review of the literature. More recent discussions of the development of occupations and professions are found in the JAI Press series, *Current Research on Occupations and Professions.*

42. Goode, "Encroachment, Charlantism, and the Emerging Professions." Harold Wilenski defines an abstract body of knowledge as "a combination of intellectual and practical knowing, some of which is explicit (classifications and generalizations learned from books, lectures and demonstrations), and some implicit ('understanding' acquired from supervised practices and observation)." He argues that this body of knowledge should be neither too vague nor too precise, too broad nor too narrow, and that it should be definable yet not so definable that it can be easily mastered. He argues that an ideal of service is a norm prescribing that solutions should be based on a client's needs and not the needs of either the professional or society. See Wilenski, "The Professionalization of Everyone?"

43. For an academic discussion of public administration professionalism, see Price, *The Scientific Estate,* 120–269; Schott, "Public Administration as a Profession: Problems and Prospects"; and Rabin, "Professionalism in Public Administration: Definition, Character and Values." For a discussion of local government managerial professionalism, see Stillman II, *Rise of the City Manager: A Public Professional in Local Government;* and Reisman, "Dual Identities of City Managers and School Superintendents."

44. Adams, "Prolegomenon to a Teachable Theory of Public Administration," 97.

45. See Stillman II, *The Rise of the City Manager,* for a full discussion of the city management movement. For a wide-ranging collection of essays on the city management profession, see Harlow, *Servants of All: Professional Management in City Government.*

46. See Moyer, ed., *The ASBO Chronicles: 75 Years of Building the School Business Management Profession.*

47. The more important tests POARA uses to determine whether an organiza-
    tion is a professional association are whether:
    - the association serves to protect the public against incompetence and
      fraud that could affect the life, health, welfare, safety, and property of the
      public;
    - the association represents a group of persons practising an identifiable
      profession;
    - the association represents persons whose primary object is to advance
      the interests of a profession;
    - the association has a continuing education program for its members;
    - there are academic and experience requirements for registration as a
      member of the association;
    - a significant proportion of persons engaged in the profession are seeking
      registration, relative to the total number of persons in Alberta who are
      engaged in the profession;
    - other professional associations support the association's application for
      registration as a professional organization.
48. Agocs, "Affirmative Action, Canadian Style," 160.
49. Abella, *Equality in Employment*, 7–8.
50. Agocs presents an example. ". . . if 10 percent of the local university's grad-
    uating class of engineers are women, the organization might seek to achieve
    roughly 10 percent female representation across the ranks of its engineer-
    ing staff over a specified period of time; the proportion would be expected
    to increase as the representation of women in the relevant labour market
    increased." Agocs, 150.
51. *Ibid.*
52. A November 4, 1989, letter to Town Manager James Mulek requesting
    information on the recreation director's termination was not answered.
53. *Calgary Sun*, May 17, 1989.
54. *Calgary Herald*, May 15, 1989. It should be noted that the coordinator
    could say little more, since the city's administration was adamantly
    opposed to a program of preferential hiring. The "Commissioners' Report"
    of June 20, 1989 (C89-65/3) states: "Affirmative Action differs from
    employment equity in that an outside agency or court establishes inflexible
    quotas and timetables upon an employer, requiring a preferential selection
    basis which may be in conflict with the principle of equal opportunity."
55. In fact, Edmonton prided itself that a higher percentage of women were in
    the civic workforce than in Calgary. When library and telephone personnel
    are included, women comprise 29 percent of the Edmonton civic work-
    force. However, when these groups are excluded to make the data compara-
    ble to that of Calgary, the percentages are virtually the same.
56. *Edmonton Journal*, February 22, 1992.
57. *Ibid.*
58. *Edmonton Journal*, March 6, 1992.

8 Interest Groups and Democracy

1. Frederick Engelmann and Mildred Schwartz define interest groups as "organizations designed to put forward group demands, to infuse them into the political system and thereby take the first step toward obtaining political outputs in response to these demands." Engelmann and Schwartz, *Canadian Political Parties*, 142.

2. Social scientists have been attempting to define the concept of power for decades. One of the simplest definitions was formulated by Robert Dahl, who said, "My intuitive sense of power . . . is something like this: A has power over B to the extent that he can get B to do something that B would not otherwise do." Dahl, "The Concept of Power," 202.

3. Higgins, *Local and Urban Politics in Canada*, 291.

4. *Edmonton Journal*, October 17, 1984.

5. Long, "The Local Community as an Ecology of Games," p. 407.

6. *Representative*, June 2, 1987.

7. *St. Albert Gazette*, October 9, 1985.

8. *Didsbury Review*, February 25, 1987.

9. Full membership is restricted to land developers; associate members include architects, engineers, bankers, and municipal and provincial government bureaucrats.

10. A past UDI president, Peter Nesbitt, explains how private developers came to work closely with government. "Up until the early fifties, development in Alberta was conducted almost exclusively by the Public Sector itself. However, staff shortages and the ever escalating cost of installing the large diameter trunklines required to service growing communities made this an increasingly more difficult commitment to fulfill. To help alleviate the problem in Calgary, an agreement was reached between the City and the private developers whereby the City would install the trunklines and recover the cost from the developer. This arrangement gave rise to what we know as 'acreage assessment' and established the first 'Development Agreement' between the public and private sectors. It was signed on October 15th, 1955." Urban Development Institute, *Alberta UDI Report*, October 1989, 3–4.

11. *Ibid.*, 2.

12. Membership in a municipal chapter automatically confers membership in the Alberta and national organizations, which are funded by a portion of the municipal chapter members' annual dues.

13. At one point the whole gallery erupted in laughter after the mayor became so flustered in his attempt to silence Nader Ghermezian that he told "Alderman Ghermezian" to be quiet. *Edmonton Journal*, September 15, 1983.

14. Caragata, *Alberta Labour*, 48–49.

15. *Ibid.*, 51.

16. *Ibid.*, 82–83.

17. An advertisement run in the *Edmonton Journal* by the Edmonton Firefighters Union warned that "a child's life may be lost" if firefighters were laid off.

18. *Edmonton Journal*, September 21, 1989.
19. Alberta Association of Municipal Districts and Counties, *Story of Rural Municipal Government in Alberta*, 57.
20. *Ibid.*, 62.
21. Every teacher in the province is a member of the association. In 1991 there were 26,301 full-time, 3,308 part-time, and 3,743 substitute teachers. There were 82 regular locals and eight student locals composed of university undergraduates.
22. Higgins, *Urban Canada*, 206.
23. Pilkington, Letter to Jim Rochlin, August 19, 1983.
24. Price, Letter to Jim Rochlin, undated, 1983.
25. As enthusiasm for the tax revolt waned, more than half of the residents who appealed their assessment did not even show up for their court date.
26. *Western Review*, April 30, 1991.
27. *Wetaskiwin Times-Advertiser*, April 21, 1987.
28. Pilkington, Letter to Jim Rochlin, August 19, 1983.
29. *Wetaskiwin Times-Advertiser*, November 8, 1988.
30. *Athabasca Advocate*, October 31, 1988.
31. The Neighborhood Club Movement began in Rochester, New York, in 1907 and quickly spread both east and west.
32. *Edmonton Journal*, December 6, 1926.
33. Lightbody, "Edmonton," 268.
34. *Edmonton Journal*, February 25, 1986; *Edmonton Examiner*, March 3, 1986.
35. In 1987 a similar attempt was made by members of an Italian group in Calgary to rename a street "Corso Italia," but they had not done their political homework and the proposal was criticized by other ethnic groups living in the area.
36. Lightbody, "Edmonton," 269.
37. *Poundmaker*, May, 1973; *Edmonton Journal*, December 19, 1973.
38. Dickerson, Drabek, and Woods, "A Performance Approach to Urban Political Analysis," 68.
39. Gilsdorf, "Cognitive and Motivational Sources of Voter Susceptibility to Influence," 624.
40. Wright and Boynton, "The Media, the Masses, and Urban Management," 15.
41. Gilsdorf, 633.
42. Black, *Politics and the News*, 202.
43. Greenberg and Dervin, "Mass Communication among the Urban Poor," 236. While 41 percent of the general American population relied on newspapers for local news, only 22 percent of the study's low-income respondents did so. This may explain why a study in the American Midwest which examined the relationship between split-ticket voting and different sources of information found that more than twice as many people believed television reports as believed newspapers (52.6 percent to 25.3 percent). However, the study found that the "print media" sources of information had a stronger relationship with split-ticket voting.

44. Gilsdorf, 637.
45. As a hypothetical example, although letters to the editor may be running five-to-one opposing the imposition of charges for the use of community recreational facilities, an editor who favours charges may publish three letters favouring charges to every one which is opposed.
46. Black, 201.
47. *Didsbury Review*, March 11, 1987.
48. *Mercury*, August 25, 1987.
49. For a detailed account of the controversy see Hill, "Social Credit and the Press."
50. *Alberta Report*, November 2, 1979.
51. *Review*, April 21, 1987.
52. *Grove Examiner*, May 10, 1989.
53. *Rocky View/Five Village Weekly*, January 13, 1987.
54. *Sherwood Park News*, March 11, 1987.
55. *Lac La Biche Post*, June 9, 1987.
56. *Edmonton Journal*, March 20, 1981.
57. *Edmonton Journal*, October 2, 1982.
58. *Grand Centre-Cold Lake Sun*, December 16, 1986, and February 3, 1987. Also see *Bonnyville Nouvelle*, December 16, 1986.
59. *Edmonton Journal*, December 6, 1984.
60. *Edmonton Journal*, October 30, 1990.
61. *Stettler Independent*, August 19, 1987.
62. *Lethbridge Herald*, November 14, 1984.
63. *Whitecourt Star*, February 11, 1987.
64. *Edmonton Journal*, November 17, 1989.
65. Lowi, *The End of Liberalism*.

9 Parties, Representation, and Elections

1. Hawley, *Nonpartisan Elections and the Case for Party Politics*, 9.
2. At the turn of the century, "nonpartisan elections were almost unheard of, but by 1929 they could be found in 57 percent of the cities with more than 30,000 population." *Ibid.,* 14.
3. Anderson cites examples of greedy aldermen in Montreal, Toronto, Winnipeg, and Calgary who were found guilty of using their positions to further their own private economic interests. Anderson, "The Municipal Government Reform Movement in Western Canada, 1880–1920," 92–93.
4. *Ibid.,* 85.
5. Foran, "The Calgary Town Council, 1884–1895," 42.
6. *Ibid.,* 44.
7. Anderson, 85.
8. Gaetz, "Municipal Legislation," 26.
9. Macpherson, *Democracy in Alberta*, 20–27.
10. *Ibid.,* 24–25.
11. Some politicians still espouse the same concept of the role of politics in city

government. As an example, Lance White, an Edmonton council member in 1986, said that he opposed party politics because city council did not deal with philosophical issues. He justified his statement by saying that "A road or a pothole doesn't know if it's right or left of center." Of course he is right about the pothole, but whose pothole is repaired and in what part of town is a political issue with philosophical underpinnings. White sees himself as merely an administrator: "By and large, what the city government is in charge of is roads, sewers, water and safety protection. I can't see ideology entering into these decisions." *Edmonton Journal*, July 17, 1986.

12. Macpherson, 28–61.
13. Major Clifford Douglas, *Social Credit*, cited in Macpherson, 127.
14. Aberhart, "The Democratic Monetary Reform Organization of Canada," cited in Macpherson, 204.
15. The 1968 Edmonton data are found in Gilsdorf, "Cognitive and Motivational Sources of Voter Susceptibility to Influence," 626. The 1971 survey is reported in Masson, "The Ebb and Flow of Municipal Party Politics in Alberta," 360.
16. Gibbins et al., "Attitudinal and Socio-Demographic Determinants of Receptivity to Civic Partisanship," 11.
17. On the other hand, James Lightbody, a principal Decore campaign strategist and advisor, writes: "Issues in the election were addressed in a manner calculated to appeal to the city's strong non-partisan traditions." "The First Hurrah," 37.
18. A 1983 survey of senior municipal administrators in Alberta found that only three cities, three towns, and one village had any form of party politics. The survey, carried out by the author in the early spring of 1983, consisted of a mail-out questionnaire with follow-up letters, postcards, and telephone calls for those not responding. The response rate was 83 percent for cities, 73 percent for towns, and 64 percent for villages. The municipalities identified as having some form of party organization were Edmonton, Calgary, Lloydminster, High River, Vulcan, and, surprisingly, the small village of Ferintosh.
19. Walchuk, *Alberta's Local Governments*, 291–293.
20. Safire, *The New Language of Politics*, 289, cited in Hawley, 143.
21. A number of American studies examine the "partisan bias of nonpartisan elections." See Lee, *The Politics of Nonpartisanship*, 55–59; Adrian and Williams, "The Insulation of Local Politics under the Nonpartisan Ballot," 1063; Rogers and Arman, "Nonpartisanship and Election to City Office," 941–945; Salisbury and Black, "Class and Party in Partisan and Nonpartisan Elections," 584–592; and Hawley, 31–39.
22. Anderson, 94.
23. Lightbody, "Edmonton," 266.
24. *Globe and Mail*, January 13, 1984.
25. Lightbody, "Edmonton," 271–272.
26. Lightbody, "The Rise of Party Politics in Canadian Local Elections," 200.

27. *Ibid.*

28. Siegal, "City Hall Doesn't Need Parties," 26–27.

29. Anderson, 94.

30. Caragata, *Alberta Labour*, 95.

31. *Ibid.*, 95.

32. *Ibid.*, 116.

33. *Ibid.*, 118.

34. In more recent times federal-provincial parties in other provinces have occasionally attempted to run candidates in local elections. The exception is the Progressive Conservative Party, which has avoided direct involvement at the municipal level and relied on business-oriented municipal parties to further right-of-centre municipal goals. In the 1969 Toronto municipal election the Liberal Party fielded Stephen Clarkson, a high-profile candidate, for mayor and 16 aldermanic candidates for 22 council positions. Clarkson was badly defeated and only two of the Liberals won council seats. Candidates occasionally run as New Democrats, "but even that party does so only sporadically and selectively" and "it often appears to be half-hearted and it is therefore often taken only half seriously." Higgins, *Local and Urban Politics in Canada*, 336–337. The New Democratic Party ran municipal candidates in Toronto in 1969, and until recent years sporadically ran candidates in Vancouver and Winnipeg.

35. Lightbody discusses this aspect of his campaign strategy in "The First Hurrah," 35–41. In addition to the nonpartisan thesis are a number of other explanations why senior parties have tended to avoid contesting municipal elections, See Lightbody, "The Rise of Party Politics in Canadian Local Elections"; Clarkson, "Barriers to Entry of Parties in Toronto's Civic Politics"; and Masson, "The Ebb and Flow of Municipal Party Politics in Alberta," 356–368.

36. Masson, "The Ebb and Flow of Municipal Party Politics in Alberta," 357–358.

37. *Lethbridge Herald*, October 3, 1968.

38. Richwood, "Urban Reform Movements in Lethbridge," 4.

39. Rae, *The Political Consequences of Electoral Laws*, 86.

40. *Edmonton Bulletin*, December 11, 1922.

41. For a detailed discussion of proportional representation and the single transferable vote system see Mackenzie, *Free Elections*, 61–84.

42. *Edmonton Bulletin*, December 13, 1923.

43. *Edmonton Bulletin*, December 14, 1927.

44. In Edmonton the city clerk cautioned people not to mark their ballots with an "X" before each election, almost to no avail.

45. *Edmonton Journal*, December 8, 1922.

46. Letter from Calgary's city clerk to Regina's city clerk, September 14, 1921. Calgary Glenbow Museum, "Files of the City Clerk," Box 200 f.f. 1172. Copy of letter in correspondence of Max Foran to Jack Masson, October 4, 1983.

47. *Edmonton Bulletin*, December 13, 1927.

48. *Edmonton Bulletin*, December 9, 1927. However, five years earlier an *Edmonton Journal* editorial had argued: "It is said that when a voter is called upon to cast his ballot on the proportional representation system he will be so confused that he will prefer not to vote at all. The average elector is really not such a stupid fellow as those who make this argument assume. As between candidates he always has well defined preferences. . . ." *Edmonton Journal*, December 2, 1922.

49. *Calgary Herald*, December 11, 1917.

50. Proportional representation was introduced in council in 1916 and on December 11 of the same year the issue went to plebiscite, where it passed 2,901 to 1,394.

51. Foran, 264.

52. In the 1959 plebiscite on the ward system 12,497 were in favour and 6,975 opposed. In the 1960 plebiscite 20,263 were in favour and 9,262 opposed. Under the City Act of the time a plebiscite required a two-thirds vote to pass.

53. *Calgary Herald*, October 19, 1961. Just one year later, however, when only 17.8 percent of the eligible electorate voted and two veteran aldermen were defeated, the same paper ran an editorial claiming that with a ward system political unknowns can be elected and "it shows what can be accomplished by a determined minority bearing a grievance which may or may not be well founded." *Calgary Herald*, October 18, 1962.

54. *Calgary Herald*, October 14, 1971.

55. *Calgary Herald*, June 26, 1974.

56. 1975 AUMA annual convention resolution no. 130 with the response by the Government of Alberta.

57. *Edmonton Journal*, December 6, 1922.

58. *Edmonton Journal*, December 8, 1922.

59. *Edmonton Bulletin*, November 29, 1927.

60. *Edmonton Journal*, December 9, 1927.

61. *Edmonton Journal*, December 8, 1927.

62. The wording was: "Are you in favor of abolishing the system of electing the mayor and aldermen by the proportional representation system and returning to the system provided by the Edmonton charter in force before the adoption of election by the proportional representation system now used?"

63. *Lethbridge Herald*, December 12, 1923.

64. *Lethbridge Herald*, December 7, 1928. The editorial presented a convoluted argument opposing proportional representation.

65. Hansen, "Participation, Political Structure, and Concurrence."

66. *Calgary Herald*, October 19, 1962.

67. *Grande Prairie Daily Herald Tribune*, November 12, 1986.

68. *Calgary Herald*, September 7, 1988.

69. *Edmonton Journal*, April 13, 14, 1988.

70. *Edmonton Journal*, May 9, 1988.

71. Anderson, 89. James Lightbody describes how in 1920 Winnipeg's business community, aided by an anti-labour rural-based Manitoba legislature, managed to undermine the council representation afforded labour by the ward system. The number of wards was reduced from seven, with two members each, to three, with six members each. See Lightbody, "Electoral Reform in Local Government," 312–319.

72. At that time the size of an average ward in other Canadian cities varied between 2.4 and 4.4 square miles. In Edmonton the average size was 30.25 square miles.

73. *Edmonton Journal*, March 18, 1969.

74. Jerry Hough presents a hypothetical example contrasting electoral outcomes for a strip-ward system and one following homogeneous class boundaries. "Imagine an area populated in its northern half by 50,000 affluent persons and in its southern half by 50,000 poor persons, an area in which the northern half casts three times as many votes as the southern. If two electoral districts are created and the boundary is drawn along a north-south line, then each district will have 25,000 persons of each income level. It might well be predicted that the representative or representatives in each district would be much more sensitive to the demands of the northern area with its larger number of effective votes. If the boundary is drawn east-west along class lines, however, then the poor will obtain representation equal to that of the affluent, despite their lower turnout rate." Hough, "Voters' Turnout and the Responsiveness of Local Government." 295–296.

75. In 1989 the issue of ward residency was raised a number of times at election forums. In Ward 2, five of the eleven council candidates lived outside their ward. Surprisingly, one of the newly-elected councillors, Brian Mason, lived in Ward 4 but ran for a seat in Ward 3. He promised at an election forum that if elected he would take up residence in Ward 3, which he did. *Edmonton Sunday Sun*, October 1, 1989.

76. An extensive survey with 1,439 respondents was carried out in order to determine the citizenry's satisfaction with the city's political and governmental institutions. Only 2.1 percent of the sample were completely satisfied with the system of political representation, while 30 percent believed there should be "more or smaller wards." See Gilsdorf, "Political Satisfaction and Municipal Political Processes in Edmonton," 10–12.

77. *Edmonton Journal*, October 26, 1986. In 1983 council defeated a proposal which would have decreased the number of representatives to eight by establishing eight single-member wards.

78. *Edmonton Journal*, November 5, 1986.

79. *Edmonton Journal*, September 23, 1987. The vote on the ward proposal was six in favour and seven opposed. *Edmonton Sun* columnist Allan Bolstad may have influenced council's decision, since he was writing on the evils of a small-ward system: "Chopping the wards in half immediately raises the spectre of single issue candidates. . . . If you make the wards too small can-

didates won't have any incentive to balance their views with the needs of other city residents." *Edmonton Sun*, September 15, 1987.

80. *Edmonton Journal*, September 17, 1987.

81. The number of eligible voters in Ward 6 in southeast Edmonton was cut by 10,000 and the boundaries of wards 2, 3, and 4 were rearranged so that the number of eligible voters in Ward 2 was increased by 3,000, in Ward 3 by 6,300, and Ward 4 by 1,200.

82. *Edmonton Journal*, August 25, 1989.

83. *Edmonton Journal*, November 2, 1989.

84. Much of the information on Calgary's ward system was taken from Stan Drabek, "The Calgary Ward System."

85. The bylaw establishing the ward system specified that "the number of electors residing in each ward . . . be substantially equal." This provision eventually required that the ward boundaries be restructured as a result of Calgary's dramatic population increase in the 1960s.

86. In the winter of 1961 an amendment to the City Act eliminated the supermajority requirement so that a ward system could be implemented with a bare 51 percent majority.

87. *Calgary Herald*, October 13, 1960.

88. Drabek, 11.

89. The only time ward representation was even a topic was in the 1981 debate over Edmonton's massive annexation bid. Edmonton (Mill Woods) MLA Milt Pahl suggested, half in jest, that Mill Woods be given ward status. Alberta Legislative Assembly Debates, 19th Legislature, 3d Session, 896.

90. See Alberta Legislative Assembly Debates, 17th Legislature, 3d Session, 122; and 17th Legislature, 4th Session, 386.

91. The board argued that the adoption of a ward system should be determined by a plebiscite.

92. One of the nine trustees was to be elected from each of six wards whose boundaries were the same as the six municipal wards. The three other trustees were to be elected from the second-place finishers in three twinned wards, wards 1 and 4, 2 and 3, and 5 and 6. However, the second-place finisher would represent only the ward he or she ran in and not the composite ward.

93. The terms "plebiscite" and "referendum" often are used interchangeably; however, some scholars have made a distinction between the two, noting that plebiscite is a much older term dating to the fourth century B.C., while referendum did not appear until the seventeenth century.

94. Although municipal plebiscites have been little studied in Alberta, in British Columbia an examination of 109 municipal plebiscites held between 1964 and 1968 found that the greater the size of the municipality, the lower the referendum turnout. Of particular importance, there was no relationship between municipality size and whether or not the referendum was approved. Sproule-Jones and Van Klaveren, "Local Referenda and Size

of Municipality in British Columbia: A Note on Two of Their Interrelationships," 48–49.

95. Section 113(1) of the School Act states that the petition must be signed by at least:

   a. 2% of the electors in a district or division having 10,000 electors or more,

   b. 5% of the electors in a district or division having less than 10,000 but 5,000 electors or more,

   c. 10% of the electors in a district or division having less than 5,000 but 500 electors or more, or

   d. 15% of the electorate in a district or division having less than 500 electors.

96. *Tribune*, July 26, 1988.

97. An escape clause in Section 328 of the Municipal Government Act states that if the capital debt to be incurred is to be repaid in three years and "yearly payments of principal and interest . . . do not exceed . . . 5 mills" the proprietary electors' approval is not required.

98. Cronin examines the finance issue in his study of the initiative, referendum, and recall and concludes, "Although the expenditure of large sums does not automatically guarantee the outcome of a ballot issue campaign, money well spent or one-sided spending on ballot propositions has about the same effect as in candidate elections. Just as in candidate races, money buys crucial resources. . . . However, money well spent in the last ten days probably makes more of a difference in an issues campaign." Cronin, *Direct Democracy*, 109. A study of referendums found that the side spending the most money won 78 percent of the time. See Zisk, *Money, Media, and the Grass Roots*, 245.

99. *Alberta Report*, December 7, 1979.

100. Masson, "Some Preliminary Findings on the Plebiscite Petition."

101. The attitude of municipal representatives is summed up by Bettie Hewes, who was an Edmonton councillor at the time. She said that citizens had a right to petition against capital spending projects but questioned "the wisdom of the provincial government act that allows them to do so." *Alberta Report*, June 5, 1981. This was said after the cost of the Edmonton Convention Centre had skyrocketed from $32 million to $90 million. It was the soaring costs, from $22 million to $32 million, that had sparked the plebiscite campaign in the first place.

102. Alberta Legislative Assembly Debates, 20th Legislature, 3d Session, 273. The amendment's key section was "No plebiscite pursuant to this section would be valid unless the number of votes cast in the plebiscite were greater than 66 and two-thirds [per cent] of the total votes cast in the preceding election."

103. Resolution no. A16 read in part: ". . . be it resolved that the Alberta Urban Municipalities Association request the Government of Alberta to amend the Municipal Government Act to require petitions to be obtained within 6

months prior to the date of the petition being filed with the Municipal Secretary and that all signators date their signature on the petition."

104. *O'Callaghan* v. *Edmonton.*

105. *Ewasiuk* v. *Edmonton.*

106. *Lethbridge Herald*, December 20, 1984. A somewhat dated study of the
plebiscite in British Columbia municipalities found an inverse relationship
between municipal population size and voter turnout for plebiscite elections. In other words, the larger the municipality, the lower the turnout,
and the smaller the municipality, the higher the turnout. See Sproule-Jones
and Van Klaveren, "Local Referenda and Size of Municipality in British
Columbia," 48–49.

107. *Lethbridge Herald*, August 25, 1987.

108. Cronin, 211–212.

109. The 1907 federal Lord's Day Act prohibits virtually all activities except worship between midnight Saturday and midnight Sunday. There is, however, a
provincial provision which Alberta adopted by enacting the Alberta Lord's
Day Act. The provincial act allows municipalities to "opt out" of the federal
act and, among other things, permits Sunday movie attendance.

110. Cronin found that, in general, the electorate was not any more misinformed than elected officials. See *Direct Democracy*, 60–89.

111. *Leader*, May 17, 1988.

112. *Edmonton Journal*, September 23, 1986.

113. Section 30(2) of the Local Authorities Election Act reads: "The candidate's
deposit shall be returned to him (a) if he is declared elected, (b) if he
obtains a number of votes at least equal to 1/2 of the total number of votes
cast for the candidate elected with the least number of votes, or (c) if he
withdraws his name as a candidate. . . ."

114. In 1987 Edmonton Council's public affairs committee supported a proposal by Alderman Ron Hayter that the number of nomination signatures
be increased to 100 for mayoral candidates and to 25 for aldermanic candidates.

115. Saskatchewan. *Final Report of the Advisory Committee on Local Election
Financing*, 25.

116. More than 15 months after Laurence Decore won the 1983 mayoralty race
in Edmonton he still had substantial campaign debts despite having held a
series of fund-raisers.

117. Alderman Ron Hayter made a full disclosure of his campaign contributions
but stopped in 1980 when no other candidates would do so.

118. Although federal legislation requires candidates to disclose campaign contributions in excess of $100, the provincial disclosure limit is $375. In order
to make disclosure more palatable to the other candidates Reimer used the
higher provincial figure rather than the much lower federal one.

119. The incumbent mayor, Terry Cavanagh, told the *Edmonton Journal* that he
believed in making a full disclosure of campaign donations, but shortly
after he consulted with his campaign committee and finance chairperson

he explained that he had made a mistake and that neither the names of contributors nor the amounts of their donations would be made public. *Edmonton Journal*, September 20, 1989.

120. Alberta Urban Municipalities Association 1989 Resolution no. A12.

121. Her nonpayment of taxes probably was an oversight, since if she had made a conscious attempt to avoid paying taxes she would have registered her business as a limited company which would have been responsible for the taxes rather than Chichak.

122. However, Chichak was fined $200 in provincial court for signing a false statement about her taxes.

123. Since the election data are based on a 1991 mail survey with a 52 percent response rate from towns, there are undoubtedly a number of others in which council members and mayors were elected by acclamation in 1986 and 1989.

124. Letter from Padey Lapointe to Greg Poelzer, February 15, 1991.

125. The survey response rate was 63 percent from municipal districts and 60 percent from counties.

126. Letter from Jim Kincaid to Jack Masson, March 8, 1991.

127. Letter from Roger Laflamme to Jack Masson, March 19, 1991.

128. Letter from Joyce Sydnes to Jack Masson, March 5, 1991.

129. Letter from Veronica Andruchiw to Jack Masson, March 21, 1991.

130. *Calgary Herald*, October 15, 1964.

131. An example of this phenomenon occurred in Calgary in 1962, when the turnout rate was only 17 percent in a year the mayor was not up for election.

132. Over a period of years the author has presented seminars to municipal managers, administrators, clerk-treasurers, and council members. Time after time they have argued that there is a much greater sense of civic pride and responsibility in smaller communities than in larger ones.

133. *Edmonton Journal*, May 28, 1986.

134. This argument was made some time ago by John Sewell in his discussion of Toronto municipal politics, *Up against City Hall.*

135. *Edmonton Journal*, October 7, 1989.

136. *Edmonton Journal*, September 14, 1989.

137. *Edmonton Journal*, October 11, 1989.

138. However, there are exceptions. In the 1989 election in Crowsnest Pass, mayoralty candidate Wayne Terriff, in discussing his opponent, candidly said that "we don't differ much on the issues." *Calgary Herald*, October 14, 1989.

139. *Edmonton Journal*, October 11, 1989.

140. To prevent electors from making frivolous recount requests the judge assesses the costs, among other things, on the basis of whether there have been "vexatious conduct, unfounded allegations or unfounded objections on the part of the applicant or any person served with a notice." Section 113 of the Local Authorities Election Act also states that "the costs may . . .

be taxed in the same manner and according to the same principles as costs are taxed between solicitor and client."

141. Section 127 of the Local Authorities Act also states that an elector can contest the validity of a vote on a bylaw or question.

142. *Edmonton Journal*, October 21, 1989.

10 Finance, Democracy, and Policy Making

1. Wight, "The Public Sector Context," 6. Despite his reservations, Wight does not say that strategic planning is inappropriate for the public sector.

2. Some municipal councils employ these basic budgeting rules in reverse order. Rather than using revenue factors to determine expenditure levels, they focus on the services they want to provide and then calculate the necessary revenue.

3. Although out of date, Ridler shows that the percentage of municipal revenue derived from the property tax in Canadian municipalities decreased from 78.3 percent in 1953 to 41.8 percent in 1973, with the difference taken up by other revenue sources. Ridler, "Fiscal Constraints and the Growth of User Fees among Canadian Municipalities," 432.

4. Although many municipalities employ their own assessors, Municipal Affairs assessors do the assessing on an hourly fee basis for over 300 rural and urban municipalities. Municipalities other than cities which do their own assessing receive a grant from Municipal Affairs for 25 percent of the assessment cost of a general assessment.

5. After a base value is calculated, other factors are taken into consideration, such as traffic flows, zoning, and the location of the property in relation to educational and recreational facilities, shopping centres, and churches. Assessors use a regulated formula to estimate improvements to land in the form of houses and other buildings. A building's new replacement cost is carefully depreciated on the basis of its condition and age.

6. A land developer speaking before the Urban Development Institute denied that the conversion of land was a tax loophole. He argued that with the economic downturn the land had to be put to its best use, which in some cases was farming. He said, "But surely the municipal government must realize there are no speculators left." *Edmonton Journal*, March 22, 1985.

7. The Municipal Taxation Act defines farmland in Section 1(j) as follows: "farm land means land used for farming operations and consisting of one parcel or more than one parcel operated as a unit (i) by a person who derives from the farming operation on that parcel or unit an income sufficient to provide a livelihood, if the parcel or unit contains 20 acres or more or has been reduced to less than 20 acres by expropriation, or (ii) by a person who derives his principal income from the farming operations . . . if the parcel or unit contains less than 20 acres."

8. "Equity in Taxation," *Municipal Counsellor* 33 (July/August 1988): 10.

9. *Edmonton Journal*, February 22, 1991.

10. Tax specialist Roger Smith is not convinced by such arguments. In a discus-

sion of the split mill rate he writes, "I can find no economic justification for taxing business properties more heavily than non-business properties in order to finance schools." Smith, "A Critique of Property Taxation," 27.

11. In 1983 a political columnist wrote: "Probably, nobody knows exactly how much the city [Edmonton] foregoes in property taxes each year, but in only one category—senior citizen and handicapped housing—the estimate is $3.7 million in 1983. Calgary, which has fewer projects than Edmonton, estimates that it will be losing $1.57 million in taxes on housing for the elderly and handicapped this year." *Edmonton Journal*, May 11, 1983.

12. The groups and the exemptions they were seeking were the German Canadian Club of Calgary ($35,000), the Austrian Canadian Cultural Center ($35,000), the Croatian Canadian Centre ($30,000), the Polish Canadian Cultural Centre ($35,000), and St. Vladimir's Ukrainian Orthodox Centre ($6,500).

13. In Hinton the Moose Hall changed its name to the Cultural Centre in 1987 in order to be eligible for $418,000 in federal grant money. After the federal government turned down the request the Moose Hall/Cultural Centre requested funding from the town council.

14. *Fort McMurray Today*, June 23, 1988.

15. Alberta Department of Municipal Affairs, "Annual General Assessments: The Spruce Grove Experience," 11.

16. "Unravelling a Mystery," *Municipal Counsellor* 36 (July/August 1991): 6. One of the reasons people were enthusiastic about 100 percent market assessment was that the town's council and administration made a concerted effort to explain to ratepayers what was being done and how it would be beneficial to them.

17. Using the same three-bedroom example, property taxes for cities outside of the province are: Vancouver, $1,355; Regina, $1,675; Winnipeg, $1,711; Toronto, $1,591; Ottawa, $2,074; Halifax, $1,428; North York, $2,107.

18. As an example, Alderman Bruce Campbell's taxes increased from $3,042 to $6,232 after the reassessment. After taking into account the 13 percent limit, he was eligible for a $2,794 tax rebate. Mayor Laurence Decore was eligible for a $350 rebate, Alderman Mel Binder a $827 rebate, and Pat Mackenzie a $505 rebate. *Edmonton Sun*, September 6, 1987. In fairness, it should be noted that Bruce Campbell donated his property tax rebate to the YMCA.

19. The appeal processes in Alberta and British Columbia are similar; in other provinces the appeal process is more difficult. See Makuch, *Canadian Municipal and Planning Law*, 103–105.

20. The four citizens were a business person, a farmer, a country residence member, and a member at large.

21. *Canmore Leader*, September 23, 1987.

22. *Edmonton Journal*, November 15, 1988.

23. *Calgary Herald*, March 25, 1988.

24. *Edmonton Journal*, March 29, 1989.

25. *Edmonton Journal*, August 8, 1987.

26. In 1990 the city's Auditor General, Ed Powell, re-examined the agreement the city had made with Triple Five. Powell found that over a 40-year period the tax concession deal would produce $74 million in benefits from property and business taxes and parkade revenue. However, when inflation and the rate of interest are taken into consideration, the city will have a net loss of $11.6 million over 40 years. *Edmonton Journal*, November 15, 1990.

27. Mayor Terry Cavanagh, in explaining why Triple Five had been given preferential treatment, said the company was in the midst of seeking additional financing and if it was revealed that it could not pay its taxes, investors would be frightened away. *Edmonton Journal*, June 15, 1989.

28. Reimer cited 908 parking stalls being built when a city lease agreement with a developer called for 1,000 spaces and plans for a major development which included a hotel that was later eliminated from the project. *Edmonton Journal*, November 11, 1989.

29. When Edmonton confronted the provincial government's Alberta Telephones over the right of Edmonton Telephones to the revenue for long-distance calls, Mayor Decore at one point said, "I think they're frightened to death of the CRTC, the way we're frightened to death by the Public Utilities Board [PUB] . . . which has been negative in its dealings with Edmonton Telephones in the past." *Edmonton Journal*, March 7, 1984, quoted in Lightbody, "With Whom the Tolls Dwell," 51. The city also has had a dispute with the PUB over the construction of its Genesee power plant. In May 1977 the province approved in principle the Genesee project and in November 1980 the Energy Resources Conservation Board gave its approval, which it reaffirmed in 1986. On February 15, 1989, the PUB ruled that the Genesee plant was not needed and it prohibited Edmonton Power from increasing its 1989 base rate to help pay for the plant.

30. *Edmonton Journal*, October 25, 1991.

31. Medicine Hat was so successful in operating and marketing its utilities that in 1982 it purchased an adjoining gas field to boost its reserve and make it self-sufficient in gas well into the 21st century.

32. A 1988 Department of Municipal Affairs publication discusses how local improvement costs are determined: "The cost . . . is charged against the abutting properties as a 'special frontage assessment'. The cost of the project is divided by the number of lineal feet of property affected to produce a rate per front foot. This rate multiplied by the frontage of an individual property indicates that property's share of the cost. Corner lots or irregular parcels . . . are treated specially so that they bear a fair and equitable share of the cost. A council may also establish a 'unit rate bylaw' which provides a standard rate to be used for any type of local improvement project during the year. For example, if a number of sidewalk replacement programs were proposed, the average cost per foot could be calculated and that rate would

be used for all sidewalk replacement projects." Alberta Department of Municipal Affairs, Municipal Statutes Review Committee, "How Should Municipalities Be Financed?" 6.

33. Ridler, 429–436.

34. Nevertheless, the installation of parking meters has sparked political protests in a number of communities where residents feel they have a right to free parking. Merchants oppose metered parking because they fear the public will change its buying habits and shop in centres and communities which provide free parking.

35. *Red Deer Advocate*, July 31, 1982.

36. *Medicine Hat News*, March 13, 1981.

37. *Grande Prairie Daily Herald Tribune*, September 9, 1981.

38. Osborne and Gaebler, *Reinventing Government*, 47.

39. See Savas, "Municipal Monopolies Versus Competition in Delivering Urban Services," 473–500; Bish, "Improving Productivity in the Government Sector," 203–237; and Rehfuss, *Contracting Out in Government*.

40. *Edmonton Journal*, January 23, 1986.

41. Mayor Decore called on council's business-oriented members to support him. *Edmonton Journal*, January 18, 1986.

42. *Calgary Sun*, May 25, 1989.

43. *Edmonton Journal*, May 13, 1989. "Beyond the Bottom Line" cited one case of a contractor hired to paint several thousand fire hydrants who colour-coded two-thirds of them incorrectly and did such a poor job that the undercoat was visible on many. In another case, a contractor who defaulted on a major sewer upgrading project which had to be completed by the city was awarded another contract in excess of $5 million the following year. The report also noted that improperly compacted roadwork done by private contractors cost the city $1.5 million a year to repair and that poorly constructed roads and sidewalks were to be found in half of the subdivisions developed since the economic downturn.

44. *Edmonton Journal*, February 16, 1991.

45. *Edmonton Sun*, May 23, 1989.

46. Another excellent study is McDavid and Schick, "Privatization versus Union-Management Cooperation," 472–488.

47. Alberta Legislative Assembly Debates, 17th Legislature, 3d Session, 2412–2413.

48. 1974 AUMA annual convention resolution no. 85 with the response by the Government of Alberta.

49. Alberta Legislative Assembly Debates, 19th Legislature, 2d Session, 843; 19th Legislature, 3d Session, 702; 19th Legislature, 4th Session, 814.

50. Larger municipalities supported the resolution and smaller ones opposed it.

51. The provincial government had widespread public support when it abolished the provincial gasoline tax in March of 1978. Evidently Premier Lougheed felt this support was worth the loss of $95 million in annual rev-

enue. Many AUMA delegates were afraid that if a new gas tax were adopted for their benefit, the province would disclaim any responsibility for it.

52. In 1983 New Democrat MLA Ray Martin introduced the Provincial-Municipal Resource Revenue Sharing Act which allocated to the municipalities 8 percent of the revenue from nonrenewable resources. The bill received only a first reading. Alberta Legislative Assembly Debates, 20th Legislature, 1st Session, 1243.

53. Ed Oman, a Tory MLA from Calgary, tried to explain: "I was really dumbfounded . . . when the Alberta Urban Municipalities Association was persuaded, without a proper look, by a few people who I think wanted to embarrass the government . . . persuaded that assembly [AUMA convention delegates] in the last week to turn down the suggestion of its own committee. . . ." Alberta Legislative Assembly Debates, 19th Legislature, 3d Session, 1138.

54. *Grande Prairie Daily Herald Tribune*, October 2, 1981. It is worth noting that the minister said that if the AUMA should reverse its position, the government again might consider a gas tax revenue policy to help municipalities.

55. Walchuk, *Alberta's Local Governments*, 94–95. It is interesting that the government specifically directed the advisory committee not to consider sharing income tax revenue with municipalities, for this method of revenue sharing is employed in both Manitoba and British Columbia. In *Local and Urban Politics in Canada*, p. 101, Higgins notes that since 1976 Manitoba has designated 1 percent of its corporate income tax revenue and 2.2 percent of personal income tax revenue for municipalities. Similar policies are in place in British Columbia. AUMA members have discussed the sharing of income tax revenue, but have never been given the slightest encouragement by the provincial government.

56. 1982 AUMA annual convention resolution no. B4 with the response by the Government of Alberta.

57. 1984 AUMA annual convention resolution no. A2 with the response by the Government of Alberta.

58. Alberta Legislative Assembly Debates, 19th Legislature, 1st Session, 296.

59. "Grants Will Come with Fewer Strings," *Municipal Counsellor* 31 (January/February 1986): 12.

60. AMPLE funding was to come from savings incurred as a result of changes made in the Municipal Debenture Interest Rebate Program. In 1981 and 1982, when interest rates were extremely high, the Alberta Municipal Financing Corporation (AMFC) borrowed funds for the financing of municipal debt at the prevailing rate for a five to seven year period rather than the normal 20 to 25 years. It was calculated that when $1.16 billion of this debt came due for refinancing between 1986 and 1989 it would be refinanced substantially below the initial rate. Moreover, the AMFC capped its interest subsidy at 12.5 percent. It was these savings which were to fund the AMPLE program.

61. Although the funds were to be awarded on a per capita basis for municipalities with very small populations, the minimum base grant was $3,000.

62. Other than the stimulation of employment, the only activity municipalities were encouraged to spend their AMPLE funding on was an examination of their futures. Six months before the futures program was formally announced, Minister of Municipal Affairs Dennis Anderson suggested municipalities hold back some of their AMPLE funds so they would be able to participate.

63. In a 1988 legislative debate Progressive Conservative Harry Alger explained how municipalities' use of funds furthered provincial goals. "While we have asked that the municipalities look at their employment needs when they utilize these [AMPLE] funds, in fact it is open to the municipality to use that in the best interests of their public, and there are municipalities in the province where employment itself isn't the primary consideration. There aren't many—most of us have employment concerns—but there are some of the smaller communities where there is not a direct concern, though ultimately all of the money expended will be likely to improve the employment situation for individuals." Alberta Legislative Assembly Debates, 21st Legislature, 3d Session, 672.

64. Although the grant was labelled as unconditional, Minister of Municipal Affairs Dennis Anderson said that "we will continue to identify on the cheque and on the cheque stub the various components which will make up that one grant—in doing so, underlining the priorities of this government. . . ." Alberta Legislative Assembly Debates, 21st Legislature, 3d Session, 661.

65. With the exceptions of Edmonton and Calgary, the following formula was used to allocate unconditional grants from 1979 to 1982: (1) each municipality was given a base amount of funds that could not be less than the previous year's assistance; (2) a municipality's fiscal capacity was used in equalizing grants on a per capita basis; and (3) if a municipality's population had increased 5 percent or more in the previous year an additional sum was allocated to it on a per capita basis. Unconditional grants made to Edmonton and Calgary were based on the grants given in 1979 plus the level of inflation each year. In 1983 the province simply used a municipality's 1982 funding as a base and increased the amount by 5 percent.

66. Two economists examined municipal equalization programs in three provinces and concluded that although Alberta's was the simplest, it did "little equalizing." See Auld and Eden, "A Comparative Evaluation of Provincial-Local Equalization," 515–528.

67. "Municipal Assistance Grants," *Municipal Councillor* 34 (July/August 1989): 13.

68. McMillan and Plain, *The Reform of Municipal-Provincial Fiscal Relationships in the Province of Alberta*, I–19.

69. McMillan and Plain argue that ". . . provincial bureaucrats also favour conditional programs which, because they require considerably more bureaucratic involvement, afford a fertile area for bureaucratic empire

building.... Between 1969 and 1977, transfers to Alberta municipalities grew ... 26%. Provincial departmental employment over this same period [had] a growth of 27%. This suggests that as the provincial grant system became more complex, the provincial government bureaucracy grew relative to the provincial population thereby imposing a heavier burden on the Alberta taxpayer. Clearly other factors must be taken into account in considering these trends, however, one suspects that there is a grain of truth in the high correlation between the growth of the bureaucracy, the increase in the conditional grant system and the loss of municipal autonomy." *Ibid.,* III–16.

70. McMillan and Plain cite a report by Edmonton, "whose conditional funding rose from 44% to 84% of transfers between 1966 and 1976," the consequence being a "loss of control over policy, the reduction of local autonomy, the distorted decisions, and the reduced flexibility of their operations." *Ibid.,* I–29.

71. Western Canada Lottery Corporation's revenue is derived from the Express, Provincial, Super Lotto, Lotto 6/49, and Lotto 6/36 lotteries and various instant lottery schemes. Alberta's share of the lotto revenue was $88 million in the 1988 fiscal year.

72. When the amounts of lottery fund grants were listed by riding, the six ridings receiving the most money were held by Tories, including Lotteries Minister Ken Kowalski and Premier Don Getty. Nevertheless, Kowalski said charges that the government was doling out lottery funds on the basis of political considerations were unfounded. As proof, he claimed that the average grant to opposition ridings was about $17,000 more than that to ridings held by government members.

73. *Edmonton Journal,* November 10, 1989.

74. *Edmonton Examiner,* December 8, 1986. However, since the census would have cost $300,000 for each of those years the loss in revenue would have been about $600,000.

75. *Red Deer Advocate,* June 10, August 14, 1987. When it was found the town's population was substantially less than what was initially claimed, another problem arose. With a population of over 2,000, the town had been eligible to place a second representative on the county school board, and two were elected in the 1986 municipal election. When the population was found to be less than 2,000, the town was entitled to only one representative.

76. In a discussion of the federal government's grant in lieu of taxes for the city, Calgary's director of assessment said, "there is no difference between the tax assessment the city would charge for the land and buildings, if they were owned by private citizens or businesses, and the amount granted to the city by the federal government. It is substantially identical to what one would collect from the same property if you or I owned it." *Calgary Herald,* September 30, 1982.

77. It should be noted that until 1984 there was no appeal process for a municipality questioning the amount of a federal grant in lieu of taxes.

78. The AUMA pointed out to its members that "the reduction is actually more

than the stated 6% as school and other requisitions are based on the full assessed value of the Grants in Lieu properties. If requisitions make up one-half of [a] municipality's property tax, the 6% reduction becomes approximately 9%." Alberta Urban Municipalities Association, *Urban Perspectives* 10 (June 1990), 2.

79. Ken Kowalski merely said: "... in order to determine what level of funding the province would provide by this grant in lieu of tax to any particular municipality, we have to have a standard that we would have to follow. So basically we ask the municipality to determine what their assessment level is, and in this year we'll provide them 94 percent of that level." Alberta Legislative Assembly Debates, 22d Legislature, 2d Session, 2353.

80. Properties of the Alberta Liquor Control Board and the Alberta Telephone Commission are also exempt under the act, but Section 18 of the Liquor Control Act and Section 44 of the Alberta Government Telephone Act provide for grants to be paid in lieu of property and business taxes for these installations.

81. At the 1978 AUMA annual meeting a general resolution on the payment of grants in lieu of taxes was passed. It read in part: "BE IT RESOLVED that the AUMA request that the Government of Alberta recognize property taxes on all provincially owned properties as a legitimate charge on the provincial revenues." 1978 AUMA annual convention resolution no. 12 with the response by the Government of Alberta.

82. Report by the City of Edmonton's Real Estate and Housing Department, 2.

83. Bird and Slack, *Urban Public Finance in Canada,* 11.

84. Although the corporation initially derived its funds from the Treasury, between 1959 and 1970 it increased its capital base by selling bonds and "in 1966 the province began assigning much of its share of Canada Pension Plan funds to the AMFC, and in 1977 the Alberta Heritage Savings Trust Fund became a source of funds." Walchuk, 72. It is also worth noting that in its early years the AMFC established a $40 per capita borrowing limit for municipalities. The limit was increased in 1967 and 1974 and entirely removed in 1974.

85. There are two credit rating agencies in Canada, the Dominion Bond Rating Service and the Canadian Bond Rating Service, and two in the United States, Moody's Investors Service and Standard and Poor's Corporation.

86. Federal legislation allowing tax-free municipal bonds is unlikely for two reasons. First, the federal government would be deprived of revenue. Second, even if the federal government were sympathetic to the plight of Canadian municipalities and willing to make a financial commitment to them, it is improbable that it would favour tax-free bonds, for, based on the American experience, they are seen by the public as a tax loophole for the wealthy. A person normally must be in an upper tax bracket before it is advantageous to buy tax-free bonds. Furthermore, if all of a wealthy person's capital is invested in tax-free bonds the person's interest income, no matter how large, is exempt from taxation. At a time when federal and

provincial taxes are rising, a tax scheme enabling the wealthy to escape taxation completely would be politically unwise and would probably lead to greater tax cheating and use of the underground economy by the working and middle classes, who already feel that the tax system is weighted to the advantage of business people and the wealthy.

87. It was not just a series of external events which made it difficult for Calgary to balance its budget. In May 1988 the city's Director of Finance notified council's finance and budget committee that although a balanced budget had been prepared for 1987, a number of miscalculations would leave the city $4.4 million short. The biggest error was in the estimation of grants in lieu of tax payments from the provincial and federal governments. Receipts from utilities and from the business tax also were overestimated. *Calgary Herald*, July 21, 1987.

88. The provincial government was not very sympathetic to the municipality's plight. The Minister of Municipal Affairs described his meeting with the Stony Plain council as follows: "They [the council] recognized the foolishness of those decisions [of previous councils] and wondered if there were ways in which they might unload some of the lands that were purchased and developed, and looked at other ways in which the burden on their taxpayers might in some way be alleviated. There were two ways in which I . . . suggested I might be able to look at some small relief. One was in terms of the acceleration of the support under the municipal debenture interest rebate program, so that money came sooner rather than later. But there was recognition by the council that the major responsibility for the decision-making that would take that municipality out of the present set of circumstances rested on their shoulders." Alberta Legislative Assembly Debates, 20th Legislature, 1st Session, 1714.

89. It is surprising the village council did not enter into an agreement with the developer, since in 1981 the Plamondon General Municipal Plan had as one of its major objectives that "developers contribute to servicing costs." In order to do this "developers will be expected to provide or pay for the installation of utilities. . . . This will require the developers to enter into development agreements with the village." Alberta Department of Municipal Affairs, *Plamondon General Municipal Plan 1981*, 31.

90. The town appealed to the Alberta Court of Queen's Bench, which upheld the Land Compensation Board's decision.

91. *Edmonton Journal*, November 17, 1983.

92. *St. Albert Gazette*, May 28, 1986.

93. *Edmonton Journal*, December 2, 1989.

94. *Edmonton Journal*, December 13, 1990.

95. *Calgary Herald*, November 4, 1988.

96. *Edmonton Journal*, November 15, 1988.

97. Ironically, it is the provincial government which has been negligent in its budgeting and creative in its accounting. As an example, when the Municipal District of Cypress was created from Improvement District No. 1, it was

found that the Village of Alderson, dissolved in 1936, abandoned in 1950, and without buildings, owed $325,000 in uncollected property taxes dating back to the 1920s which the province had been carrying on its books as receivables for years. Three years later the District Manager of Cypress wrote off the whole amount explaining, "If taxes are listed as receivable on the books, there's some hope of collecting them in the future, they are not . . . so they were written off." *Medicine Hat News*, March 16, 1989.

11   Municipal Activities

1. The classification system is a derivation of one developed by Vincent and Elinor Ostrom. See "Public Goods and Public Choices," in Savas, ed., *Alternatives for Delivering Public Services: Toward Improved Performance*, 7–49.
2. Osborne and Gaebler, *Reinventing Government*, 34–48.
3. Thompson, "The City as a Distorted Price System," 31.
4. *Edmonton Journal*, June 17, 1989. In most Alberta municipalities recreational facility user fees have not been controversial, although many Calgarians were angry in 1988 when a council financial task force recommended a 10 percent tax on sporting and entertainment events. One golfer summed up the feelings of the golfing community when he said, "they are really quick to increase user fees for golf courses but they are slow on improvements." *Calgary Herald*, October 19, 1988.
5. Critics have argued that since fire departments are a public monopoly they have no incentive to become more innovative. The example almost always used to make their argument is the privately run Rural/Metro Fire Department Incorporated in Arizona. It contracts with Scottsdale and other communities in the area for fire protection, with the communities being responsible for providing the fire halls. In order to cut costs the company has been innovative in several areas. It developed "The Snail," a remote-controlled track vehicle for fighting fires too hot for firefighters to approach. The company also developed its own fire trucks for less than it would have had to pay on the market. As a result of these innovations and because neither the company nor the city pays fringe or retirement benefits, firefighting costs in Scottsdale have been approximately 25 percent of the national average for cities of its size.
6. If a department does not have an investigative capability the investigations are carried out by either the RCMP or the Provincial Fire Commissioner.
7. See Coulter, MacGillivray, and Vickery, "Municipal Fire Protection Performance in Urban Areas," 256.
8. *Record-Gazette* (Grimshaw), May 18, 1988.
9. McDavid, "Part-Time Fire Fighters in Canadian Municipalities," 386–387.
10. As late as 1984 there were functioning outhouses in Edmonton's core. See *Edmonton Journal*, August 15, 1984.
11. *Edmonton Journal*, February 1, 1991.
12. Bird and Slack, *Urban Public Finance in Canada*, 90.
13. In Calgary there is a small differential built into the unmetered fee; proper-

ties with higher assessments have slightly higher water fees than those with lower assessments. In Medicine Hat unmetered homes are levied a basic flat fee plus an additional charge per foot of frontage.

14. Ironically, one of the arguments made for opposing metering all Calgary residences was that it would reduce water consumption and delay the construction of a new $100 million water treatment plant.

15. A consultant hired by Calgary in 1983 admonished the city for dumping partially treated sewage into the Bow River, thereby subjecting downstream farm families and recreational users to cholera and typhoid fever. Calgary's response was that it could not afford a higher level of treatment. See *Alberta Report*, February 21, 1983.

16. *Calgary Herald*, November 15, 1988.

17. It is important that the act's procedures are carefully followed, otherwise the citizenry may be thwarted. In 1983 the fluoridation issue was placed before the electorate in the Town of Brooks, of whom 56 percent favoured fluoridation. Its proponents assumed there would be a delay because of tight budgeting, but when council was queried about the matter in 1988 the mayor explained that the 1983 vote was just an advisory opinion poll since a bylaw on fluoridation had never been introduced. See *Brooks Bulletin*, February 3, 1988.

18. Hahn, "Voting in Canadian Communities," 467.

19. The basis for making this assertion was that "the Russians use it on their slave laborers to rob them of their will to resist." *New York Times*, April 11, 1955. At a New York State Legislative Committee hearing, a representative of an antifluoridation committee testified, "You can call this forced mass medication, but it might turn out to be mass liquidation." *New York Times*, March 5, 1953.

20. Six municipalities had fluoridation by default since they contracted for water from a community that had adopted fluoridation. Beaumont, the Canadian Forces Base at Namao, Leduc, Sherwood Park, and St. Albert had to accept fluoridation or seek alternative water sources when Edmonton fluoridated its water in 1967. A similar situation occurred in 1969 in Grand Centre.

21. As in the 1960s, five of the communities had fluoridation by default.

22. Ross Brown continues to use the Calgary Safe Water Association to oppose fluoridation whenever he has the opportunity.

23. Even before the city implemented programs to reduce its garbage production the amount decreased with the onset of Alberta's 1980s recession.

24. In 1982 Edmonton's Utilities and Protection Service Commissioner made a distinction between garbage dumps and landfill sites, declaring that the city has had dumps in the past but today it has landfill sites that are packed with landfill material and ground garbage and then graded, making them much more aesthetically acceptable than the old dumps. *Edmonton Journal*, June 10, 1982. Neither the citizenry nor the media seem to make the fine distinction made by the commissioner.

25. *Edmonton Journal*, December 27, 1990.

26. At about the same time city engineers stated that it was necessary to commence work on a landfill site immediately. Council approved in principle the use of sludge lagoons on Clover Bar for a landfill site.

27. In October 1990 Klein said that Edmonton was warned as early as 1980 that the river valley was not the place for a garbage dump. Moreover, "there can be no doubt that he [Mayor Decore] was advised very strongly in 1985 . . . that the river valley should be avoided whenever possible." *Edmonton Journal*, October 12, 1990.

28. *Edmonton Journal*, October 13, 1990.

29. McDavid, "Residential Solid Waste Collection Services in Canadian Municipalities," 24. McDavid cautions: "Although costs per household vary with collection method, it is important to remember that the comparison does not control for the influence of other variables. In other words, when we examined the difference between public and private collection costs, we assumed . . . that everything else was held constant. That is, technologies and service levels were equalized for public and private producers. Clearly that assumption needs to be relaxed. Private companies, for example, use a larger percentage of larger hauling vehicles, which could itself influence costs per household." *Ibid.*, 27.

30. McDavid and Schick, "Privatization versus Union-Management Cooperation," 487.

31. Bettison, Kenward, and Taylor, *Urban Affairs in Alberta*, 104.

32. In order not to erode the powers of the provincial government, "urban renewal was to be handled by the provincial government entering into an agreement with its municipalities and with federal authorities, or by a municipality entering an agreement, after obtaining provincial approval direct with federal authorities." *Ibid.*, 171.

33. In 1973 the development firms in Edmonton and the number of acres they controlled were: Nu-West, 158; Bramalea, 44; Western, 3,923; Dawson, 58; MacLab, 911; BACM Ltd., 1,500; Great Northern, 2,807; Allarco, 8,803; and Melton, 1,815. In Calgary the firms and numbers were: Campeau, 37; Nu-West, 1,759; Bramalea, 211; Western, 2,063; Dawson, 1,400; Paragon, 30; Carma, 4,500; and Melton, 920. Spurr, *Land and Urban Development*, 204–205. Spurr explains how the land monopoly occurred in Edmonton. "As most of Edmonton's private land banks were assembled in the 1960s at prices below $4,000 per acre, and held at relatively low interest rates, their production costs are greatly exceeded by current prices. This relationship between costs and prices translates, in the view of other actors in land (such as financial institutions, governments and sub-contractors) as relatively low risk, so the land bank owners obtain a self-perpetuating competitive advantage over other developers. In other words, concentration in land markets leads to further concentration at the expense of competition and particularly, the entry of new, smaller developers." *Ibid.*, 155.

34. Alberta Department of Housing, *Provincial Housing Programs in Alberta*, 30.

35. *Grande Prairie Daily Herald Tribune*, September 9, 1981.

36. There were three different types of land purchase agreements: (1) a trunk servicing program which usually had a ten-year life-span; (2) a residential and industrial land program which usually had a five-year life-span; and (3) a residential and industrial land bank program which usually had a 15-year life-span.

37. The effect of this was that the province's Residential Land Program, Industrial Land Program, and Revolving Trunk Servicing Program were, for all intents and purposes, eliminated.

38. Lightbody discusses the province's role in sparking opposition to roadways in Edmonton. He writes: ". . . a provincial statute . . . became the unintended catalyst for citizen opposition. The province now required that municipal applicants for conditional grants in support of transportation designs hold public hearings prior to approving a general transportation by-law. Hearings on the METS proposals served to spark a citizen revolt. In contrast to the three individuals opposed to the MacKinnon freeway in 1964, twenty-two groups or individuals demonstrated before the meeting in 1971. . . ." Lightbody, "Edmonton," 269.

39. A University of Alberta engineering professor, J.J. Bakker, prepared a report reviewing transportation needs and options for Edmonton in 1968. He argued that freeways converging on the downtown would be clogged with cars and recommended that two freeways be eliminated and replaced by a rapid transit line. Although he was critical of parts of the METS plan he did not argue that it should be totally replaced. It should also be noted that the city administration and citizen groups committed to the development of an LRT system frequently justified it on the basis of a booklet entitled *The Immorality of the Motorcar*, produced in 1971 by Professor Gerry Wright and his students in the Faculty of Extension at the University of Alberta. The booklet presented a series of arguments proclaiming the efficiency of an LRT system in areas such as capacity and cost. The booklet argued that once an LRT system was in place people would use it rather than their own automobiles. In 1991 two economists evaluating the Edmonton system wrote that no cost benefit analysis was ever done. "Indeed, the 1983 study produced by the City of Edmonton's Transportation Management to recommend a particular alignment for the south extension . . . is stunningly incomplete in its analysis . . . there is no indication that the authors of the report are familiar with the economic literature on the costs and benefits of rail rapid transit relative to bus transit or the expansion of the road network." Kim and West, "The Edmonton LRT: An Appropriate Choice?" 175.

40. The first leg of the LRT was extended into the northeast area because Mayor Ivor Dent wanted to have a showcase system in place to transport people between the stadium, where the 1978 Commonwealth Games were to be held, and the city's downtown.

41. City of Edmonton Planning Department, *North-East LRT Evaluation Study*, 3.

42. Kim and West, 173–182.

43. *Edmonton Journal*, December 2, 1991.

44. Kim and West, 175.

45. *Edmonton Journal*, March 7, 1992. Even though the LRT has had dismal ridership figures, Edmonton transportation planners are so determined to "make the LRT system work" that all of the funding for capital development is spent on the LRT system and virtually none is reserved to repair and upgrade the bus system. The city transportation manager, John Schnablegger, explained that LRT is so efficient that by the time it is extended south from the university to the Southgate Shopping Centre 40 fewer buses will be needed. Implicitly, he argued it is not necessary to upgrade the bus system. *Edmonton Journal*, November 12, December 8–9, 1990.

46. The per capita grant was set at $11.00 until 1985, when the amount was reduced to $10.78 per capita. Several years later it was increased to $10.98 per capita, and effective April 1990 increased 3 percent to $11.10.

47. *Red Deer Advocate*, September 30, 1986.

48. "Report of the Alberta High Speed Rail Review Committee," June, 1986. For a report which concludes that the service would have high use and be economically feasible, see Alberta Department of Economic Development, "Rail Passenger Service in the Calgary-Edmonton Corridor," July, 1985.

49. *Edmonton Journal*, November 15, 1991.

50. The neighbourhood leader, a 55-year-old University of Alberta biochemist, explained, "It's not a good feeling you've angered so many people. But I'm not trying to anger them. I'm trying to get a point across." *Edmonton Journal*, October 31, 1989.

51. It could be argued that if the area is rezoned for higher density, some of the residents will be financial winners.

52. The Community Recreation/Cultural Grant Program is the predecessor of the Major Cultural/Recreation Facility Development Program, the Project Cooperation Program, and the Operation Assistance Program.

53. In 1987 the government announced that the program would be extended but no additional monies would be committed. Therefore, the annual grant was halved.

54. Under the Libraries Act a charge cannot be assessed for use of materials within the library building.

55. *Edmonton Journal*, February 8, 1991.

56. *Bonnyville Nouvelle*, April 4, 1989.

57. Municipalities are represented on the district board under the provision of Section 6 of the Health Unit Act.

58. MacGregor, *Edmonton*, 246–247.

59. Those making this argument maintained that property taxes should pay only for services used either directly or indirectly by the property owner. Since the recipients of welfare rarely owned property, it was argued that

property owners were paying for a service for which they received little or no benefit.

60. Bella, "The Goal Effectiveness of Alberta's Preventive Social Service Program," 144.

61. *Calgary Herald,* April 25, 1988.

62. *Edmonton Journal,* March 14, 1985.

63. Although BRZs have been successful in some communities, the basic premise that the downtown core can again become an area's main shopping centre is controversial. In Edmonton, the decline of downtown retail shopping began in the late 1960s after the opening of Southgate Shopping Centre in a suburban area. After the 1980s development of the West Edmonton mega-mall with over 800 shops, a 50,000 square foot amusement centre, and free parking, the shopping patterns of tens of thousands of people changed and they seldom ventured downtown. Retail activity in Calgary follows a similar pattern as shopping centres follow new housing being built in outlying areas.

64. Edmonton became over-enthusiastic in its business development. A 1988 study found that although seven entities with a total budget of $7 million were promoting the city's economic development, they had no overall strategy and often worked at cross purposes. The seven are the Downtown Business Association, Edmonton Downtown Development Corporation, Downtown Parking Advisory Board, Edmonton Economic Development Authority, Edmonton Research Park Authority, Edmonton Convention and Tourism Authority, and Edmonton Convention Centre Authority. *Edmonton Journal,* November 30, 1988.

65. *Alberta Report,* April 7, 1986.

66. Osborne and Gaebler, *Reinventing Government,* 23–24.

67. Another factor was involved. "In the early years of Edmonton's development, it was natural for the city's dominant anglo elite to affect British pretensions. In 1911, the map-makers Driscoll and Knight surveyed and identified new subdivisions with fashionable monikers like Belgravia, Mayfair, and Lansdowne (after the prestigious London districts). As a clear indication of the evolving distribution of influence in the city's social and political mix, Mayfair Park, which surrounds the prestigious private golf and country club [was given] the same name." Lightbody, "Edmonton's Official Flower," 1–9. Over time the city's ethnic mix changed and the fight over the name change was a manifestation of this.

68. The chain is made primarily of beaver pelt to symbolize the city's location on the North Saskatchewan River. Woven into the chain are a variety of badges and symbols which represent some aspect of the city's past: the city's crest, a Hudson's Bay Company seal, and badges representing pertinent army regiments, police forces, and naval and air force squadrons.

69. Councils have designated an assortment of objects as officially representing their municipalities. In his light-hearted description of the choice of the marigold as Edmonton's official flower and the selection of the city's offi-

cial tartan, Lightbody notes that "A furious debate ensued over the extent of blues and purples in the design." "Edmonton's Official Flower," 1–9.

70. *Edmonton Journal*, April 28, 1987.

71. *Camrose Canadian*, February 25, 1987.

72. *Edson Leader*, November 22, 1988.

73. *Fort McMurray Today*, October 3, 1985.

74. Lightbody, "Edmonton's Official Flower," 8.

75. Makuch, *Canadian Municipal and Planning Law*, 122. The chapter entitled "Municipal Authority and Judicial Review," 107–139, should be read in its entirety.

76. Just as the campaign to place the disarmament question on municipal ballets was gaining public support, the Soviet Union downed a Korean airliner and disarmament ardour cooled across the province. As just one example, Medicine Hat's council had voted in 1982 to place the issue on the ballet, but on September 6 the council voted by a five to three margin not to hold the referendum. Grande Prairie's Peace Association of Nuclear Awareness acknowledged that the Korean airline tragedy was likely a factor when council defeated a motion to place the measure on the ballet.

77. In particular, the council wanted to disassociate itself from the World Federalists of Canada. Councillor Don Moore explained, "It's almost embarrassing to be associated with that." *Crossfield Chronicle*, December 30, 1986.

78. *Reporter*, August 24, 1988.

79. *Edmonton Journal*, October 9, 1991.

80. *Journal* (St. Paul), April 13, 1988.

81. All of the candidates were sent a questionnaire asking whether they favoured free-standing abortion clinics and whether they favoured civic funding for planned parenthood. Many of the candidates refused to answer the questions on the grounds that abortion policy was not a municipal issue.

82. Until 1988 only communities with populations of 1,500 or less were entitled to law enforcement provided by the province. Penhold's chief executive attributed the change to 2,500 to lobbying by delegations of small town residents and their MLAs. *Red Deer Advocate*, May 17, 1988. Ironically, while the province was planning to shift the population figure from 1,500 to 2,500 and thus police more communities and larger numbers of people, it also was cutting personnel. At the 1988 annual convention of the Alberta Association of Municipal Districts and Counties, Marvin Moore told the delegates that in the previous two years he had cut back the provincial force by 140 officers. However, he said that he intended to hire 80 new officers who would be deployed across the province wherever they were needed. *Wetaskiwin Times-Advertiser*, November 29, 1988. After the federal government announced that by 1991 municipalities with a population of less than 15,000 would have to pay 70 percent of the cost of their policing by the RCMP, delegates at the 1989 annual meeting of the Alberta Urban Munici-

palities Association passed a resolution "that all municipalities in the Province of Alberta with a population of 5000 or less receive policing services at no direct cost."

83. In a controversial case in which an RCMP officer strip-searched a man in the front of two female companions, a complaint was laid with the province's Law Enforcement Appeal Board. The RCMP refused to appear before the board, claiming that it was allowed to handle its own internal affairs under federal legislation. The case was finally resolved in the summer of 1981 when the Supreme Court of Canada ruled that the RCMP is not subject to provincial police conduct boards.

84. An Edmonton political columnist writes that the city's police board has been the "volunteer board of choice for the more fortunate in our community. . . . Current police commission members include two lawyers, a medical doctor, a professional engineer and an educator. It might not be an exaggeration to say that the closest some have come to violent crime is having the antenna of their BMW bent." *Edmonton Journal*, February 9, 1991.

85. *Medicine Hat News*, October 19, 1984.

12   Planning and Democratic Institutions

1. The Canadian Institute of Planners defines planning as "the scientific, aesthetic and orderly disposition of land, with a view to securing physical, economic and social efficiency, health and well-being in urban and rural communities." For a discussion of the reaction of Canadian planners to this definition, see Sells, "Selected Material from the Report on the Questionnaire on the Future of the Planning Profession."

2. A good discussion of the tensions generated between planners and elected decision makers is found in Catanese, *Planners and Local Politics.*

3. *Calgary Herald*, December 5, 1985.

4. Burton, "The Seven Deadly Sins of Planning," 14.

5. Van Nus, "The Fate of City Beautiful Thought in Canada, 1893–1930," 163. For a general discussion of the evolution of city planning see Brunt, *The History of City Planning*, and Kaplan, *Reform, Planning and City Politics.*

6. Van Nus cites an article in the 1911 *Canadian Municipal Journal*, an organ of the planning profession: "Magnificent avenues, leading to grand buildings, are desirable. Lovely and artistic parks should be in every city. But the dwellings in which those live who cannot get away from their homes the whole year long, really decide whether any city is to be healthy, moral and progressive. The common people are in the great majority; their proper accommodation is the greatest problem." In Van Nus, 171.

7. For graphic examples of these conditions see Artibise, *Winnipeg: A Social History of Urban Growth.*

8. According to Michael Simpson, "Adams was almost in the position of being unable to join his own foundation for he qualified as a surveyor only in 1913. He may have taken up professional studies simply to meet the T.P.I.'s

membership requirements or to reinforce his authority as the Local Government Board's Town Planning Advisor." See Simpson, *Thomas Adams and the Modern Planning Movement*, 67.

9. The commission comprised federal ministers for agriculture, the interior, and mines who sat *ex officio,* as well as representatives from the provincial government who were responsible for natural resources. There was also an unusual membership provision which allowed the Governor in Council to appoint a professor to the council from a university from each province. Armstrong, "Thomas Adams and the Commission of Conservation," 18.

10. Simpson, *Thomas Adams and the Modern Planning Movement,* 79.

11. The Prime Minister's explanation for the abolishment of the commission was that its organizational structure had "no relationship to any minister" and it had always been seen as a temporary organization. Armstrong, 32–33.

12. Simpson, *Thomas Adams and the Modern Planning Movement,* 102.

13. It is important to note that by 1930 Adams's philosophy on planning was almost wholly rejected by the Canadian planning profession. Only later was there a rebirth of his ideas.

14. Simpson, "Thomas Adams in Canada, 1914–1930," 5.

15. Rutherford, "Tomorrow's Metropolis," 379. Also see Kaplan, 113–209.

16. Gerecke, "The History of Canadian City Planning," 13. Matthew Kiernan, in discussing the period between the wars, writes: "Only one Canadian city (Toronto) even had a planning department and those few cities and towns which did have plans and zoning bylaws at all (Vancouver, Edmonton and Windsor, for example) had grossly outdated ones." Kiernan, "Urban Planning in Canada," 12.

17. Gerecke identifies the solutions to urban problems proposed by the LSR: (1) public housing estates for low-income families; (2) government housing corporations; (3) socialist housing plans based on the "neighbourhood unit"; (4) comprehensive plans based on surveys; and (5) housing designs "to liberate the housewife from the monotonous servitude of domestic chores." In addition, the league wanted to eliminate "rake-offs" by promoters, monopolies in building supplies, and the compulsory purchase of inner-city lands for less than their "fictitious" value. Gerecke, 22.

18. Gunton, "Origins of Canadian Urban Planning," 97–98.

19. Kiernan, "Urban Planning in Canada," 13–14.

20. Clark, "Planners as Professionals," 51.

21. Page and Lang, "Canadian Planners in Profile," 8.

22. Kiernan, "Ideology and the Precarious Future of the Canadian Planning Profession," 18.

23. Sixty-six percent of the respondents in the survey believed that the comprehensive plan ought to provide a general guide to community planning. However, the survey showed that only 16 percent of Canadian planners felt that planners should be a part of a larger process governed by political considerations. A manifestation of the apolitical stance of American planners is

found in a 1974 comprehensive survey of members of the American Institute of Planners; 48 percent indicated that planners should not be involved
in the political process, 32 percent took a moderate position, and only 20
percent believed planners should take positions on political issues. Vasu,
Politics and Planning, 34. Other studies of American planners have found
that many are not just apolitical but anti-political. A 1963 survey of student
planners at the Massachusetts Institute of Technology found that "76 per
cent saw politicians as selfish. Not one respondent believed politicians
could be more than 'slightly' altruistic." Rabinovitz, *City Politics and City
Planning*, 135.

24. Kiernan, "Urban Planning in Canada," 14.

25. Page and Lang, 3.

26. Smith, "The Principle of Utility and the Origin of Planning Legislation in
Alberta, 1912–1975," 202–203.

27. P.J. Smith explains how this omission of planning for the community's core
area came about: ". . . earlier versions of the housing act had already given
substantial powers of intervention to local governments, including the
right to carry out slum clearance and redevelopment schemes. The special
contribution of the 1909 Act was to extend that right of intervention
beyond the existing built-up areas. Whether out of ignorance, or because
they were not thought to be relevant in Canada, the planning powers of the
housing section of the 1909 Act were ignored in both New Brunswick and
Alberta." *Ibid.*, 209.

28. *Ibid.*, 210–211.

29. *Ibid.*, 208.

30. Bettison, Kenward, and Taylor, *Urban Affairs in Alberta*, 44.

31. Smith, "The Principle of Utility and the Origin of Planning Legislation in
Alberta, 1912–1975," 213.

32. Smith, "American Influences and Local Needs," 7.

33. *Ibid.*, 11.

34. *Ibid.*, 16.

35. At this time the province was making substantial changes in its local governments. In the same year the County Act was enacted to streamline rural
government and in the following year the City Act was passed to provide
cities with uniform charters.

36. Gordon and Hulchanski, *The Evolution of the Land Use Planning Process in
Alberta, 1945–1984*, 6. A Department of Municipal Affairs publication
describes the limited powers of the district planning commissions. "A
Commission was responsible upon the request of a municipality for the
preparation of general plans and zoning bylaws for municipalities situated
within the boundaries of the District, and for advising on planning matters
of a general nature or involving two or more municipalities." Alberta
Department of Municipal Affairs, *Planning in Alberta*, 2.

37. Shannon, "Rural Planning Re-Evaluated," 101.

38. The funding formula and mechanism seemed to work reasonably well until

1983, when the municipal requisition to the Planning Fund was reduced by 25 percent. As a consequence the board reduced its funding to the commissions, which were forced to reduce their staffs. In 1985 at the annual meeting of the Alberta Urban Municipalities Association a resolution was carried that the provincial government ". . . suspend any further budget and staff cuts related to regional planning commissions and, where necessary, increase financial support by way of the Alberta Planning Fund, thus enabling regional planning commissions to again provide a satisfactory level of services to meet the required needs of their municipalities." In 1986 the funds the Red Deer Regional Planning Commission received from the Planning Fund were cut by 29 percent. The director of the commission was incensed, since the commission had already cut 10 of its 36 positions over a three-year period. *Red Deer Advocate*, October 18, 1986.

39. Gordon and Hulchanski, 11.

40. Alberta Department of Municipal Affairs, Inter-Agency Planning Branch, "Summary of Preliminary Findings of the Regional Planning System Study," 12.

41. Smith, "The Principle of Utility," 215–216.

42. Smith, "The New Planning Act in Alberta," 120–123.

43. The Director of Administration explained why regional plans were unacceptable to the Alberta Planning Board: "Generally speaking the proposed regional plans were too lengthy, too repetitive, too prescriptive and were seen by the Board as infringing upon the autonomy of their member municipalities and over-lapping into the exclusive jurisdictions of the Provincial and Federal governments in some respects and some instances. Most of the proposed plans were management and control documents as opposed to providing guidance and direction to their municipalities and some contained policies which would control economic and social development which are seen by the Board as going beyond the mandate and jurisdiction of regional planning commissions." Suelzle, letter to Jack Masson, July 12, 1983.

44. *Ibid.*

45. *Calgary Herald*, January 26, 1986.

46. A few larger municipalities have been given the authority to act as their own subdivision approving authorities. For areas of the province not served by regional planning commissions, the Planning Service Division of Alberta Municipal Affairs is the approving authority.

47. *Wetaskiwin Times-Advertiser*, December 16, 1985.

48. Horace Seymour, appointed in 1928 as the province's first Director of Town and Rural Planning, "believed that all members of a community should be given an opportunity to express their views about the community needs and future before any bylaw was adopted. His concern, however, was more for the technical qualities of the planning policies, and their acceptability, than for the principles of participation and popular control." Smith, "American Influences and Local Needs," 22. Seymour's ideas were incorpo-

rated into the 1929 Act that required public hearings as one of the precon-
ditions for the adoption of a comprehensive plan. But, as Smith notes, "In
general, the public hearing was thought to be most applicable to zoning bylaws or ordinances, and . . . it was designed to protect individual interests
in real property." *Ibid.*, 23.

49. "Advocate planners . . . reject both the notion of a single 'best' solution,
and the notion of a general welfare which such a solution might serve.
They take the view that any plan is the embodiment of particular group
interests, and they therefore see it as important that any group which has
interests at stake in the planning process should have those interests articu-
lated in the form of a plan. Planning in this view becomes pluralistic, and
partisan. . . ." Peattie, "Reflections of an Advocate Planner," 81.

50. It is not in the government's interest to activate citizen groups or to provide
them with resources so that they will impede and frustrate "the workings of
government." Undoubtedly, it is for this reason that Alberta and other
provinces have been very cool to suggestions that advocate planners be
hired and funded by the province or municipality to provide assistance to
community groups. The few American communities that have employed
advocate planners have had an extremely strong commitment to grass-
roots democracy.

51. Gordon and Hulchanski, 17.

52. Alberta Legislative Assembly Debates, 20th Legislature, 2d Session, 1.

53. "Fine-tuning the System," *Municipal Counsellor* 33 (July/August, 1988): 5.

54. Until 1988 a local subdivision approving authority (SAA) did not have the
discretion to turn down a planning proposal which was just short of the
standards imposed by a local land-use bylaw. Dennis Anderson explained,
"The SAA had little choice but to refuse the application and suggest that
the landowner appeal it to the Alberta Planning Board, whose decisions
aren't bound by the details of the local bylaw. The SAAs would often even
forward recommendations to the board in support of the owner." *Ibid.*, 7.

55. In order to have its environmental reserve actions approved by the Alberta
Planning Board, a municipality had to post a public notice on the site and
in the newspaper. If anyone objected, a public hearing had to be held.

56. Under Section 22 of the Planning Act the Minister of Municipal Affairs
designates which governmental units will be given representation and how
many representatives each will have on the commission. The minister is
given the responsibility to designate councils which will have commission
representation.

57. Alberta Association of Municipal Districts and Counties and Alberta Urban
Municipalities Association, "Municipal Attitudes towards Regional Planning in Alberta," 22.

58. Alberta Planning Board Annual Spring Seminar, 1983.

59. Alberta Association of Municipal Districts and Counties and Alberta Urban
Municipalities Association, 19.

60. In 1980 and 1981, Thomas Burton examined the perceptions of regional

planning commissions held by developers, citizen groups, planning-related professions (surveyors, architects, and engineers), regional planning commission planners, and planners in the private sector. Altogether, 60 people were extensively interviewed. Burton concludes: "The most contentious issue . . . had to do with the Commissions' subdivision approval authority. The developers were about equally divided on whether or not this authority should be transferred from the Commissions to the municipalities, as were the citizens. The other three groups favoured its retention by the Commissions, although the planning-related professionals did suggest that the municipalities should be given greater autonomy (but not subdivision approval authority)." Burton, *The Roles and Relevance of Alberta's Regional Planning Commissions,* 87–88.

61. Alberta Department of Municipal Affairs, "Era of the Regional Plan."
62. Bettison, Kenward, and Taylor, 502–509.
63. Alberta Department of Municipal Affairs, Inter-Agency Planning Board, "Summary of Preliminary Findings of the Regional Planning System Study," 53.
64. Grover, "Future Directions for Community Planning," 15–16. Grover may have been influenced by William Perks and Lydia Ind Kawun, who presented a strategic planning model for Alberta's smaller communities in 1986. "The process itself and the ends we propose be pursued call into play a developmental perspective shaped by concerns for municipal and community organization, community-based partnerships for plan implementation, role-casting and a networking of resources." Perks and Kawun, "Strategic Planning for Small-Town Community Development," 28.
65. *City Magazine* 11 (summer/fall 1989), 1.
66. Young, *Post Environmentalism,* 159.
67. Richardson, "Four Constituencies Revisited: Some Thoughts on Planners, Politicians and Principles," 16.

13 Education Politics and Government

1. Tucker and Zeigler, *The Politics of Educational Governance,* 43–44.
2. Kratzmann, Byrne, and Worth, *A System in Conflict,* 6–7.
3. The Kratzmann Report states: ". . . the school bears the brunt of family and social dislocation. Because of such disrupting forces, an increasing number of pupils are depressed, angry, and rebellious, and they express these feelings often through aggressive behavior or withdrawal. . . . One professional [education] fraternity . . . in discussing this role and responsibility for teachers, has concluded that more than ever before 'teachers are expected to be the shock absorbers of society.'" *Ibid.,* 15.
4. See Child, "The Ryerson Tradition in Western Canada, 1881–1906."
5. Goresky, "The Beginning and Growth of the Alberta School System," 37–39.
6. Hanson, *Local Government in Alberta,* 11. Almost immediately after the passage of the 1884 School Act complete changes were being planned.

Under the School Ordinance of 1885 grants were given to schools on the following basis:

I. Teacher qualification

   A. A $250 annual grant to a school employing a teacher with a third class or provisional certificate

   B. A $300 annual grant to a school employing a teacher with a second class certificate

   C. A $350 annual grant to each school employing a teacher with a first class teacher's certificate

II. Attendance

   A. A $2.00 per student annual grant to a school open for at least one term, with a minimum average of eight students, each of whom attends school at least 100 days

   B. A $2.50 per student annual grant to a school open during winter and summer terms, with a minimum average of eight students, each of whom attends school at least 160 days

   Goresky, 57–58.

7. Cited in Stamp, *School Days*, 27.

8. Consolidated school districts were simply composed of two or more districts that had agreed to amalgamate. It is worth noting that the original school districts "are not dissolved, they are consolidated into one jurisdictional unit with one board elected from the entire area." Alberta Municipal Affairs, Municipal Administrative Services Division, *Municipal and Local Administrative Bodies in Alberta 1941–1981*, 29.

9. Alberta Department of Education, *Annual Report, 1933*, 33.

10. Alberta Department of Education, *Annual Report, 1935*, 47.

11. *Ibid.*, 134.

12. The ATA's first secretary-treasurer was J.W. Barnett, who had been the president of a local of the British National Union of Teachers. Barnett centralized the functions of the ATA and substantially increased his own powers. See Ramsay, "The Alberta Teachers' Alliance as a Social Movement," 1–45.

13. In a discussion of the 1921 election, Ramsay writes, "Because the Liberal Government and the Minister of Education, Dr. G.P. Smith, had developed policies opposite to those of the Alliance, the teachers' movement became involved in the 1921 provincial election. Their involvement was basically limited to a few days of campaigning for John Barnett." *Ibid.*, 33.

14. In the 1930s Turner Valley's small school districts could not cope with a mushrooming population caused by the oil boom and the Minister of Education consolidated a number of them with virtually no opposition. So many people had moved from the Berry Creek region in the southeastern part of the province that the school districts were not economically viable. As a consequence, 67 districts were combined into a single unit and a substantial amount of the small districts' liabilities was written off. See Goresky, 148–150.

15. In 1929 Aberhart was admonished by the chair of the Calgary School Board

for spending so much time with his radio broadcasts and religious work in his own church. He "claimed that Aberhart was ordered to resign as leader of Westbourne Church if he wished to keep his position at Crescent Heights High." Aberhart must have resented having to resign. One can speculate that his unpleasant experience with the Calgary board may have affected his attitude towards the ASTA. See Elliott and Miller, *Bible Bill,* 85–90.

16. Aberhart's cohort and successor, Ernest Manning, said in a 1970 interview that "education wasn't much of an election issue in 1935, as people had more immediate concerns." See Oviatt, "The Papers of William Aberhart as Minister of Education, 1935–1943," 38. Nevertheless, since 13 of the 57 newly elected Social Credit MLAs were teachers, educational issues must have been of concern in party caucus and the cabinet.

17. Despite Aberhart's commitment to bettering the conditions of teachers, it was 1948 before the government began paying into the Alberta Teachers' Association pension fund.

18. Oviatt, 48.

19. The districts amalgamated into divisions did not cease to exist but their functions as local school authorities were terminated. A Municipal Affairs publication notes that by "1981 there were 4362 school districts in existence, of which 4237 had been amalgamated into school divisions or counties." Alberta Municipal Affairs, Municipal Administrative Services Division, *Municipal and Local Administrative Bodies in Alberta 1941–1981,* 28.

20. For a discussion of the changing philosophy of education during this period see Patterson, "The Establishment of Progressive Education in Alberta."

21. Aberhart joined the ATA in 1919 and remained a member until he let his membership lapse in 1923. Although he was offered the opportunity to become the president of the ATA in 1927, he never rejoined. See Elliott and Miller, 48.

22. Roberts, "The Alberta School Trustees' Association—A Study of the Activity of a Social Organization in the Alberta Educational System," 143–144.

23. Ironically, the Department of Education's *Annual Report, 1915* (pp. 13–14) noted: "An examination of the statistical returns . . . show[s] that whereas fairly substantial increases in school enrollment are recorded with respect to the two largest centres—Edmonton and Calgary—the enrollment for the smaller cities and the towns has undergone comparatively slight changes, so that the net increase during the year is accounted for chiefly by the development of the rural communities. It would thus appear . . . that the rural communities have received an impetus which will enable them to hold the majority for years to come."

24. It should be noted that subsequently enrollments increased somewhat and in 1990 the school was being utilized at 35 percent of its capacity.

25. A twelfth Edmonton school, King Edward, closed its junior high component but continued to operate its primary school component.

26. The public system also closed down half of the school operations in nine schools.
27. Goresky, 116.
28. *Ibid.*, 128.
29. Dent, "The Evolution of School Grants in Alberta," 29–30.
30. *Ibid.*, 54.
31. Hanson explains: "With a uniform levy on all taxed property, the level of taxes paid serves the same purpose as the level of assessments for indicating ability to pay. Thus the SFPF levy in any given year is a proxy for the level of assessment, being a uniform percentage or mill rate. One can say that the higher the SFPF levy of a district, the higher its assessment and ability to pay, and vice versa. The SFPF levy is also a valid measure of the tax burden of a district, and can be used to gauge the equity of school taxation among districts." Hanson, "The School Foundation Program in the 1970s," 83.
32. A major part of the grant was $105 for each student enrolled in grades one through twelve. Another part of the grant was based on the academic qualifications of teachers employed by a district. It varied from $2,100 for teachers with less than two years of teacher education to $3,700 for teachers with six or more years of formal teacher training.
33. Alberta, *Task Force on Provincial-Municipal Fiscal Arrangements in Alberta*, 1.
34. The recommendation was not that each school would receive 85 percent of its funds from the province but rather "some school jurisdictions might receive more or less than 85% support, depending on local decision-making, local wealth, and other relevant circumstances provided for in the grants system." Alberta Department of Education, "Financing Schooling in Alberta," 15.
35. One example is a 1986 ASTA resolution (26Z/86) which read: "Be it resolved that the Alberta School Trustees' Association urge the Government of Alberta to increase the level of funding to Alberta school boards to reflect 85 percent of the total cost of educating children in this province." Another example is the AUMA Board of Directors 1987 resolution which read: ". . . be it resolved that the Alberta Urban Municipalities Association request the Government of Alberta to meet its responsibility by funding 85% of kindergarten to grade 12 education costs with local property taxation used to collect the other 15%." In 1989 the AUMA convention urged the government "to remove the funding of education from the property tax and have this service funded through the general revenues of the Province of Alberta." 1989 AUMA annual convention resolution no. A13.
36. 1981 AUMA annual convention resolution no. 3 with the response by the Government of Alberta.
37. 1984 AUMA annual convention resolution no. B5 with the response by the Government of Alberta.
38. Fiscal capacity is a school jurisdiction's ability to raise revenue; the less revenue it is able to raise, the greater its grant. The greater the sparsity, the

more likely it is a jurisdiction with small schools, low pupil/teacher ratios, and higher bussing costs. The greater the distance a school jurisdiction is from a major urban supply centre, the greater the shipping costs, and the greater the likelihood that teachers will have to be paid isolation pay and provided with special housing. The Equity Grant replaced the Supplementary Requisition Equalization Grant, Small Jurisdiction Grant, Small School Assistance Grant, and the Location Allowance and Teacher Housing Unit Grant. The Declining Enrollment and Private School Opening grants were eliminated.

39. *Edmonton Journal,* January 15, 1991. Left unsaid was that the two public boards in Edmonton and Calgary, which opposed corporate pooling, skewed his figures.

40. Alberta Urban Municipalities Association, "Education Financing Position," 2–3.

41. Alberta Legislative Assembly Debates, 21st Legislature, 4th Session, 5.

42. Alberta Department of Education, "Education Trust Fund: A Proposal to Bring Equity to Educational Financing," 2–4.

43. Delegates voted to change the meaning of the acronym ETEC to the Education Trust Equity Council.

44. Tucker and Zeigler, 44.

45. Boyd, "School Board–Administrative Staff Relationships," 104.

46. Zeigler and Jennings, *Governing American Schools,* 163–164.

47. Gour, "The Role of Schooling—A Trustee Perspective," 90, 92.

48. Langlois, "Who Will Lead?" 346.

49. Section 232 of the School Act states that the board shall call a public meeting when it receives a petition for one signed "by 25% of the parents, who are also electors, of the students in a school, or by the lesser of 2,000 electors, and 25% of the electors." If a board or district is not wholly or partly situated within a city, then a public meeting has to be called when the board receives a petition "by 100 electors, or by a majority of the electors."

50. An exception is that a resolution can be made for the council to revert back to an open meeting. See the School Act, Section 54(4).

51. Section 59(1) of the School Act reads: "At any reasonable time, an elector of a district or division may with respect to the board of that district or division inspect any 1 or more of the following items: (a) the agenda of any public meeting or board meeting; (b) the minutes of any public meeting or board meeting; (c) a budget adopted by the board; (d) a by-law of the board; (e) an agreement entered into by the board; (f) an account of the board; (g) a financial statement prepared to a requirement of this Act."

52. Tucker and Zeigler, 44.

53. *Edmonton Journal,* October 30, November 1, 1990.

54. *Edmonton Journal,* December 16, 1990. The board chair, a supporter of a substantial salary increase, maintained that it was an error to estimate that board members would attend between 30 and 60 special meetings a year.

55. Beaudry, "An Investigation into the Backgrounds, Roles, and Educational Attitudes of Alberta Public School Trustees," 50–52.
56. *Ibid.*, 48–50.
57. Section 55(3) provides an escape clause, although it is not one the minister prefers to use. The clause reads, "The Minister may order that when the number of trustees has fallen below the quorum the remaining trustees shall be deemed to be a quorum until elections are held to fill the number of vacancies required to achieve a normal quorum."
58. Alberta School Trustees' Association, *1990 Handbook,* 27.
59. *Ibid.*, 26. Motion 10M/90.
60. *Ibid.*, 24. Motion 9M/90.

14 Concluding One Era of Governance and Beginning Another

1. Osborne and Gaebler, *Reinventing Government,* 110.
2. *Ibid.*, 74.
3. Alberta Department of Municipal Affairs, *A New Municipal Government Act for Albertans,* 3.
4. The Department of Education maintained that a reduction in the number of school boards would increase the amount of control certain groups would have over education. This was to be done by establishing school-based management committees. Unfortunately, the membership of the committees and their responsibilities were left undefined. A fact sheet distributed on February 24, 1994, states: "The restructuring is based on increased responsibility and involvement of parents, business and the community, with more authority at the school level." Alberta Department of Education, "Facts about Changes to Education," 8.

Appendix: Local Political Parties

1. Day, "Edmonton Civic Politics, 1891–1914," 60–61.
2. *Minutes of the Edmonton Trades and Labour Council,* November 4, 1907, cited in Anderson, "The Municipal Government Reform Movement in Western Canada, 1880–1920," 99.
3. Day, 65.
4. Lightbody, "Edmonton," 260.
5. *Ibid.*
6. The seven-point platform called for (1) public ownership of public utilities; (2) collective bargaining; (3) a conference with the Dominion and provincial governments to bring about a more equitable system of taxation and the distribution of taxes; (4) abolition of property qualifications for candidates for all municipal offices; (5) strict enforcement of traffic, fire, and health regulations; (6) a municipal effort to convince the Dominion and provincial governments to provide work or full support for the unemployed, in short, making unemployment a responsibility of the state; and (7) no reduction in corporate taxation if it adversely affected the liv-

ing standard of the average citizen. See *Edmonton Bulletin*, November 14, 1923.

7. The school board losses were particularly ironic, since the party's platform included a strong and well defined education plank which both aldermanic and school trustee candidates referred to throughout the campaign. Among other things, the platform called for constructing permanent school buildings and phasing out temporary buildings as soon as possible, "an adequate health policy for the schools," and free school books and supplies. The party was cognizant of the importance of the teaching function and called for a "normal school" (school for the teaching of educational methods and philosophy) for Edmonton.

8. Ogilvie, CC council candidate in 1936, cited in Betts, "The Edmonton Aldermanic Election of 1962," 31.

9. *Ibid.*, 40.

10. Finkel, *The Social Credit Phenomenon in Alberta*, 50.

11. *Edmonton Journal*, September 21, 1954.

12. Ivor Dent, who successfully ran for mayor in 1968 strictly as an independent, decrying party politics in general and the Civic Party affiliation of his opponents in particular, was an EVA candidate in 1957. At that time, he was a strong proponent of parties at the local level. *Edmonton Journal*, October 2, 1957.

13. The original EPOA was born and died in 1936. The defunct organization's name was adopted in 1957 by the CC dissidents.

14. Both the CRA and the CC endorsed Elmer Roper for mayor.

15. Yet another organization was founded in 1960 to contest the public school board elections. The Better Education Association (BEA) defeated both CRA and CC candidates and won all the positions on the school board.

16. For the first time in Edmonton's history an alphabet party contested the city's separate school board elections when, in 1961, the Separate School Voters Association (SSVA) ran a full slate of candidates.

17. In 1963 another new party was formed to contest the public school board elections; the Quality Education Committee (QEC) nominated four candidates, of whom one was elected.

18. A UVO candidate caustically remarked of this name change, "Last year we had the CGA. This year it's the Better Civic Government Committee; maybe someday we'll have the Even Better Civic Government Committee." *Edmonton Journal*, October 9, 1964.

19. In 1964 the BEA, QEC, and BCGC were seeking seats on the public school board.

20. *Edmonton Journal*, October 11, 1966. Another candidate said, "I'm not sure what it [BCGC] stands for . . . Bandits and Crooks, Gangsters and Criminals?" *Ibid.*

21. Even some of the candidates were confused. As an example, the *Edmonton Journal* reported: "Alderman Morris Weinlos . . . qualified for the Most Embarrassing Moment of the Civic Election award—he forgot which slate

he is running on. . . . Dr. Weinlos was in the process of telling voters of his pride to be associated with . . . stumbled, then came out with: 'Better Civic Action Committee.' Dr. Weinlos, in the past, ran on the Better Civic Government Committee slate. The group has disbanded and he is now a member of Les Bodie's United Civic Action Party." *Edmonton Journal*, October 3, 1968.

22. A by-election was held in 1970 to replace a councillor who had died in 1969. Normally the vacancy would have remained open until the 1971 election. However, council wished to place an important plebiscite before the electorate and so it decided to combine the plebiscite with the by-election. For this single position, all the candidates ran as independents.

23. BEA did run candidates for the school board; however, most of them lost.

24. Lightbody, "Edmonton," 260–266.

25. *Ibid.*, 287, note 74.

26. Lightbody and Gerry Wright, a founder of URGE who ran successfully for council as one of the party's candidates, discuss in a conference paper the organization's founding, the makeup of its membership, and the focus of its policy goals. On its social composition they say: "A political neophyte in the practical sense, URGE was middle class and drawn from the ranks of government and private social agencies, the neighborhood protectionist groups and a handful of academics." The first URGE platform, written in September 1973, had four basic tenets: "1. the preservation of the river valley and its communities; 2. citizen participation and improvement of the ward system; 3. better public transit in a balanced transportation system; 4. preservation of older neighborhoods. . . . From this time onwards, all else became either derivatives or extensions of these four tenets." Lightbody and Wright, "Urban Innovation?" 29, 32–33.

27. Foran, "The Civic Corporation and Urban Growth," 175.

28. The Citizens' Slate comprised five business and professional men and two returning war veterans who had been commissioned officers.

29. Foran, "The Civic Corporation and Urban Growth," 261.

30. Foran notes that "Labour's share of the popular vote hovered around twenty five percent" throughout the 1920s. *Ibid.*, 262.

31. *Ibid.*, 264–265. The argument that proportional representation did not help labour is a controversial one, especially as proportional representation normally gives a minority an advantage. The only way it could be determined whether Calgary's proportional representation operated to the benefit of labour would be to examine voting data of the period. Foran has not done that.

32. Finkel, 50.

33. The UCLG became the Civic Labour Association (CLA) in 1951.

34. *Calgary Herald*, October 9, 1959.

35. In the 1962 election one of the NHBA candidates received an endorsement from the CLC, although the person was not included on the CLC slate.

36. *Calgary Herald*, September 27, 1961. In 1964 a UCA spokesman, in a candid statement, said that the organization collected between $5,000 and $8,000 annually from private donors, using the money to provide partial financial support for UCA candidates. *Calgary Herald*, September 15, 1964.
37. *Calgary Herald*, September 18, 1967.
38. Perhaps one of the reasons for the defeat of party candidates is found in a Ward Seven Hillhurst-Sunnyside community survey in which 67 percent of respondents indicated that they "preferred that their ward alderman stand alone and not be bound to any city-wide electoral organization." Drabek and Woods, "Calgary: The Boom Ends," 14.
39. The key feature of commission government is a small number of representatives elected on a nonpartisan ballot. In the case of Lethbridge, the number of representatives was seven. Each elected representative, known as a commissioner, is responsible for one or more municipal departments. This system is adopted to fuse the policy-making and administrative arms of city government. The commissioners elect one of their own members to be mayor. Normally the mayor is also the city's finance commissioner.
40. Lovering was first involved in Lethbridge politics when he made an unsuccessful bid for the school board in 1917. Thereafter, politics became his advocation, as he was involved in virtually every municipal campaign and came to be known as a man "who stirs up things." *Lethbridge Herald*, December 6, 1924.
41. The commissioners became councillors, with the manager being held responsible to the council. The mayor continued to be elected internally by council members. It was not until 1961 that the citizenry, in another plebiscite, decided that the mayor should be directly elected.
42. *Lethbridge Herald*, October 3, 1927.
43. In a field of six, three DLP candidates ran for three school trustee positions and all lost.
44. Soon after the election the ICWA was disbanded.
45. Only seven people attended the CLO's nomination and organization meeting. In order to broaden the party's support base before election day, the organization's name was changed. *Lethbridge Herald*, September 30, 1955.
46. *Lethbridge Herald*, October 19, 1977.
47. In a October 5, 1990, letter the Assistant City Clerk, Dianne Nemeth, wrote Greg Poelzer, "I spoke to one of the members backing this Association and they felt that such backing proved to be a failure due to the political differences each of the five candidates had. Further, many people refused to back the CGA candidates as they felt they were being told how to vote."

Bibliography

Books

Adrian, Charles R., and Charles Press. *Governing Urban America.* 4th ed. New York: McGraw-Hill, 1972.

Artibise, Alan F.J. *Winnipeg: A Social History of Urban Growth, 1874–1914.* Montreal: McGill-Queen's University Press, 1975.

Banfield, Edward C., and James Q. Wilson. *City Politics.* Cambridge, Mass.: Harvard University Press, 1965.

Benello, C. George, and Dimitrios Roussopoulos, eds. *The Case for Participatory Democracy.* New York: Viking Press, 1971.

Bettison, David G. *The Politics of Canadian Urban Development.* Edmonton: University of Alberta Press, 1975.

Bettison, David G., John K. Kenward, and Larrie Taylor. *Urban Affairs in Alberta.* Edmonton: University of Alberta Press, 1975.

Bird, Richard M., and N. Enid Slack. *Urban Public Finance in Canada.* Toronto: Butterworths, 1983.

Bish, Robert, and Vincent Ostrom. *Understanding Urban Government: Metropolitan Reform Reconsidered.* Washington, D.C.: American Enterprise Institute, 1973.

Black, Edwin. *Politics and the News.* Toronto: Butterworths, 1982.

Boyer, J. Patrick. *Lawmaking by the People.* Toronto: Butterworths, 1982.

Braybrooke, David, and Charles Lindblom. *A Strategy of Decision: Policy Evaluation as a Social Process.* New York: Free Press, 1963.

Brunt, Michael Hugo. *The History of City Planning.* Montreal: Harvest House, 1972.

Burton, Thomas L. *The Roles and Relevance of Alberta's Regional Planning Commissions.* Edmonton: Department of Recreation Administration, University of Alberta, 1981.

Butler, David, and Austin Ranney, eds. *Referendums: A Comparative Study of Practice and Theory.* Washington: American Enterprise Institute, 1978.

Caragata, Warren. *Alberta Labour: A Heritage Untold.* Toronto: James Lorimer, 1979.

Caraley, Demetrios. *City Governments and Urban Problems: A New Introduction to Urban Politics.* Englewood Cliffs, N.J.: Prentice-Hall, 1977.

Carver, Humphrey. *Compassionate Landscape.* Toronto: University of Toronto Press, 1975.

Catanese, Anthony James. *Planners and Local Politics: Impossible Dreams.* Beverly Hills, Calif.: Sage, 1974.

Crawford, Kenneth G. *Canadian Municipal Government.* Toronto: University of Toronto Press, 1954.

Cronin, Thomas E. *Direct Democracy: The Politics of Initiative, Referendum, and Recall.* Cambridge, Mass.: Harvard University Press, 1989.

Dahl, Robert. *Who Governs? Democracy and Power in an American City.* New Haven: Yale University Press, 1961.

Dahl, Robert, and Charles Lindblom. *Politics, Economics, and Welfare: Planning and Political-Economic Systems Resolved into Basic Social Processes.* New York: Harper & Brothers, 1953.

Dennis, Michael, and Susan Fish. *Low Income Housing: Programs in Search of a Policy, Summary and Recommendations.* Toronto: Hakkert, 1972.

Dye, Thomas R. *Understanding Public Policy.* Englewood Cliffs, N.J.: Prentice-Hall, 1972.

Einsiedel, Edna F. *Survey of Alberta Chief Municipal Administrators and Municipal Development Officers.* Edmonton: Local Government Studies, Faculty of Extension, University of Alberta, 1983.

_____. *Survey of Planning Needs and Training Preferences of Alberta Elected Officials.* Edmonton: Local Government Studies, Faculty of Extension, University of Alberta, 1983.

Elazar, Daniel J. *American Federalism: A View from the States.* New York: Crowell, 1966.

Elliott, David R., and Iris Miller. *Bible Bill: A Biography of William Aberhart.* Edmonton: Reidmore Books, 1987.

Engelmann, Frederick C., and Mildred A Schwartz. *Canadian Political Parties: Origin, Character, Impact.* Scarborough: Prentice-Hall, 1975.

Etzioni, Amitai. *The Active Society: A Theory of Societal and Political Processes.* New York: Free Press, 1968.

Feldman, Lionel D., and Katherine A. Graham. *Bargaining for Cities: Municipalities and Intergovernmental Relations: An Assessment.* Toronto: Institute for Research on Public Policy, 1979.

Finkel, Alvin. *The Social Credit Phenomenon in Alberta.* Toronto: University of Toronto Press, 1989.

Gordon, Michael, and J. David Hulchanski. *The Evolution of the Land Use Planning Process in Alberta, 1945–1984.* Toronto: University of Toronto Centre for Urban and Community Studies, 1985.

Gorman, Jack. *A Land Reclaimed: A Story of the Special Areas in Alberta.* Hanna, Alberta: Gorman & Gorman, 1988.

Grodzins, Morton. *The American System: A New View of Government in the United States.* New Brunswick, N.J.: Transaction Publications, 1983.

Hanson, Eric. *Local Government in Alberta.* Toronto: McClelland and Stewart, 1956.

Harlow, LeRoy F., ed. *Servants of All: Professional Management in City Government.* Provo, Utah: Brigham Young University Press, 1981.

Hawley, Willis D. *Nonpartisan Elections and the Case for Party Politics.* New York: John Wiley, 1973.

Higgins, Donald. *Local and Urban Politics in Canada.* Toronto: Gage, 1986.

_____. *Urban Canada: Its Government and Politics.* Toronto: Macmillan, 1977.

Hunnius, Gerry, ed. *Participatory Democracy for Canada: Workers' Control and Community Control.* Montreal: Black Rose Books and Our Generation Press, 1971.

Jones, Victor. *Metropolitan Government.* Chicago: University of Chicago Press, 1942.

Kaplan, Harold. *Reform, Planning and City Politics: Montreal, Winnipeg, Toronto.* Toronto: University of Toronto Press, 1982.

Kotler, Milton. *Neighborhood Government: The Local Foundations of Political Life.* New York: Bobbs-Merrill, 1969.

Lee, Eugene C. *The Politics of Nonpartisanship.* Berkeley: University of California Press, 1960.

Lilienthal, David. *TVA: Democracy on the March.* New York: Harper & Brothers, 1944.

Lowi, Theodore J. *The End of Liberalism.* New York: W.W. Norton, 1969.

MacEwan, Grant. *Poking into Politics.* Edmonton: Institute of Applied Art, 1966.

MacGregor, J.G. *Edmonton: A History.* Edmonton: Hurtig, 1975.

Mackenzie, W.J.M. *Free Elections.* London: George Allen and Unwin, 1958.

Macpherson, C.B. *Democracy in Alberta: Social Credit and the Party System.* 2d ed. Toronto: University of Toronto Press, 1962.

Makuch, Stanley. *Canadian Municipal and Planning Law.* Toronto: Carswell, 1983.

Mallory, J.R. *Social Credit and the Federal Power in Canada.* Toronto: University of Toronto Press, 1954.

Martin, Roscoe. *Grass Roots.* Alabama: University of Alabama Press, 1957.

Millerson, G. *The Qualifying Associations.* London: Routledge & Kegan Paul, 1964.

Miner, Horace. *St. Denis, A French Canadian Parish.* Chicago: University of Chicago Press, 1966.

Moyer, Linford F., ed. *The ASBO Chronicles: 75 Years of Building the School Business Management Profession.* Reston, Va.: Association of School Business Officials, 1985.

Osborne, David, and Ted Gaebler. *Reinventing Government.* Reading, Mass.: Addison-Wesley, 1992.

Pateman, Carole. *Participation and Democratic Theory.* Cambridge, England: Cambridge University Press, 1970.

Pitkin, Hanna. *The Concept of Representation.* Berkeley: University of California Press, 1967.

Plunkett, Thomas J. *The Role of the Chief Administrative Officer.* Toronto: Institute of Public Administration of Canada, 1992.

———. *Urban Canada and Its Government: A Study of Municipal Organization.* Toronto: Macmillan, 1968.

Pocklington, T.C. *The Government and Politics of the Alberta Metis Settlements.* Regina: Canadian Plains Research Center, 1991.

Price, Don K. *The Scientific Estate.* Cambridge, Mass.: Harvard University Press, 1965.

Rabinovitz, Francine F. *City Politics and City Planning.* New York: Atherton Press, 1969.

Rae, Douglas W. *The Political Consequences of Electoral Laws.* New Haven, Conn.: Yale University Press, 1967.

Rehfuss, John A. *Contracting Out in Government.* San Francisco: Jossey-Bass, 1989.

Roussopoulos, Dimitrios, ed. *The City and Radical Social Change.* Montreal: Black Rose Books, 1982.

Sayre, Wallace S., and Herbert Kaufman. *Governing New York City: Politics in the Metropolis.* New York: W.W. Norton, 1965.

Selznick, Philip. *TVA and the Grass Roots.* New York: Harper and Row, 1966.

Sewell, John. *Up against City Hall.* Toronto: James Lewis & Samuel, 1972.

Simon, Herbert A. *Administrative Behavior.* 3d ed. New York: Free Press, 1976.

Simpson, Michael. *Thomas Adams and the Modern Planning Movement: Britain, Canada, and the United States, 1900–1940.* London: Mansell, 1985.

Smither, Michael J. *Municipal Conflict of Interest.* St. Thomas, Ont.: Municipal World, 1983.

Spurr, Peter. *Land and Urban Development: A Preliminary Study.* Toronto: James Lorimer, 1976.

Stamp, Robert M. *School Days: A Century of Memories.* Calgary: Calgary Board of Education, 1975.

Stillman II, Richard J. *Rise of the City Manager: A Public Professional in Local Government.* Albuquerque: University of New Mexico Press, 1974.

Studenski, Paul. *The Government of Metropolitan Areas in the United States.* New York: National Municipal League, 1930.

Tindal, Charles R., and S. Nobes Tindal. *Local Government in Canada.* 3d ed. Toronto: McGraw-Hill Ryerson, 1990.

Tucker, Harvey J., and Harmon Zeigler. *The Politics of Educational Governance: An Overview.* Eugene, Oregon: ERIC Clearinghouse on Educational Management, University of Oregon, 1980.

Vasu, Michael Lee. *Politics and Planning: A National Study of American Planners.* Chapel Hill: University of North Carolina Press, 1979.

Walchuk, Walter. *Alberta's Local Governments: People in Community Seeking Goodness.* Edmonton: Alberta Department of Municipal Affairs, 1987.

Weidenhamer, T.C. *A History of the Alberta School Trustees' Association.* Edmonton: Alberta School Trustees' Association, 1971.

Wilson, S.J. *Women, the Family and the Economy.* Toronto: McGraw-Hill Ryerson, 1982.

Wright, Gerald. *The Immorality of the Motorcar.* Edmonton: Community Resources Development Division, Faculty of Extension, University of Alberta, 1971.

Young, John. *Post Environmentalism.* London: Belhaven, 1990.

Zeigler, L.H., and M.K. Jennings. *Governing American Schools: Political Interaction in Local School Districts.* North Scituate, Mass.: Duxbury, 1974.

Zisk, Betty. *Money, Media, and the Grass Roots: State Ballot Issues and the Electoral Process.* Beverly Hills, Calif.: Sage, 1987.

Chapters and Articles

"Access to Information." *Municipal Councillor* 33 (January/February 1988): 7–8.

Adams, Guy B. "Prolegomenon to a Teachable Theory of Public Administration." In *Public Administration Education in Transition,* edited by Thomas Vocino and Richard Heimovics, 93–114. New York: Marcel Dekker, 1982.

Adrian, Charles, and Oliver Williams. "The Insulation of Local Politics under the Nonpartisan Ballot." *American Political Science Review* 53 (December 1959): 1052–1063.

Agocs, Carol. "Affirmative Action, Canadian Style: A Reconnaissance." *Canadian Public Policy* 12 (1986): 148–162.

Alexander, Alan. "The Institutional and Role Perceptions of Local Aldermen." In *Emerging Party Politics in Urban Canada,* edited by Jack K. Masson and James D. Anderson, 124–140. Toronto: McClelland and Stewart, 1972.

Alford, Robert R., and Eugene C. Lee. "Voting Turnout in American Cities." *American Political Science Review* 62 (September 1968): 1192–1206.

Allan, Graham. "Class Variation in Friendship Patterns." *British Journal of Sociology* 28 (September 1977): 389–393.

Anderson, James D. "The Municipal Government Reform Movement in Western Canada, 1880–1920." In *The Usable Urban Past: Planning and Politics in the Modern Canadian City,* edited by Alan F.J. Artibise and Gilbert A. Stelter, 73–111. Toronto: Macmillan, 1979.

Armstrong, Alan H. "Thomas Adams and the Commission of Conservation." In *Planning the Canadian Environment,* edited by L.O. Gertler, 17–35. Montreal: Harvest House, 1968.

Athanasiou, Robert, and Gary A. Yoshioka. "The Spatial Character of Friendship Formation." *Journal of Environment and Behavior* 5 (March 1973): 43–65.

Aucoin, Peter. "Theory and Research in the Study of Policy Making." In *The Structure of Policy Making in Canada,* edited by G. Bruce Doern and Peter Aucoin, 10–38. Toronto: Macmillan, 1971.

Auld, D.A.L., and Lorraine Eden. "A Comparative Evaluation of Provincial-Local Equalization." *Canadian Public Policy* 13 (1987): 515–528.

Axworthy, Lloyd. "The Best Laid Plans Oft Go Astray: The Case of Winnipeg." In *Problems of Change in Urban Government*, edited by M.O. Dickerson, S. Drabek, and J.T. Woods, 105–123. Waterloo: Wilfred Laurier University Press, 1980.

Baldwin, Thomas W. "Recreational Planning in Small Towns and Rural Areas: The Need for Inter-Municipal Cooperation." *Alberta Journal of Planning Practice* 5 (Fall 1987): 84–98.

Bella, Leslie. "The Goal Effectiveness of Alberta's Preventive Social Service Program." *Canadian Public Policy* 8 (Spring 1982): 143–155.

Bish, Robert L. "Improving Productivity in the Government Sector: The Role of Contracting Out." In *Responses to Economic Change*, edited by David Laidler, 203–237. Toronto: University of Toronto Press, 1986.

Bourassa, G. "Les élites politiques de Montréal." In *Emerging Party Politics in Urban Canada*, edited by Jack K. Masson and James D. Anderson, 87–109. Toronto: McClelland and Stewart, 1972.

Boyd, William L. "School Board–Administrative Staff Relationships." In *Understanding School Boards*, edited by Peter J. Cistone, 103–129. Toronto: Lexington Books, 1975.

"Breaking New Ground." *Municipal Counsellor* 30 (September/October 1985): 7–9.

Brown, E.C., R.M. Miller, and B.D. Simpkins. "The City of Calgary's Comprehensive Annexation." *Alberta and Northwest Territories Journal of Planning Practices* 8 (Winter 1989): 39–78.

Burton, Thomas L. "The Seven Deadly Sins of Planning." *Alberta Journal of Planning Practice* 2 (Summer 1983): 7–18.

Child, Alan H. "The Ryerson Tradition in Western Canada, 1881–1906." In *Egerton Ryerson and His Times*, edited by Neil McDonald and Alf Chaiton, 279–301. Toronto: Macmillan, 1978.

Clark, Ron. "Planners as Professionals." In *The City Book*, edited by James Lorimer and Evelyn Ross, 46–53. Toronto: James Lorimer, 1976.

Clarkson, Stephen. "Barriers to Entry of Parties in Toronto's Civic Politics: Towards a Theory of Party Penetration." *Canadian Journal of Political Science* 4 (June 1971): 206–223.

Coulter, Philip B., Lois MacGillivray, and William Vickery. "Municipal Fire Protection Performance in Urban Areas: Environmental and Organizational Influences on Effectiveness and Productivity Measures." In *The Delivery of Urban Services*, edited by Elinor Ostrom, 231–260. Beverly Hills, Calif.: Sage, 1976.

Cuff, George B. "Fatal Flaws: Beware of Problems Which Can Plague a Council." *Municipal Counsellor* 33 (March/April 1988): 5–7.

_____. "Views from the Top." *Municipal Counsellor* 34 (January/February 1989): 12–13.

Dahl, Robert. "The City in the Future of Democracy." *American Political Science Review* 61 (December 1967): 953–970.

_____. "The Concept of Power." *Behavioral Science* 2 (July 1957): 201–215.

Day, John P. "Edmonton Civic Politics, 1891–1914." *Urban History Review* 3 (1977): 42–68.

Derthick, Martha. "Intercity Differences in Administration of the Public Assistance Program: The Case of Massachusetts." In *City Politics and Public Policy*, edited by James Q. Wilson, 243–266. New York: Wiley, 1968.

Dickerson, M.O., S. Drabek, and J.T. Woods. "A Performance Approach to Urban Political Analysis: The Calgary Case." In *Problems of Change in Urban Government*, edited by M.O. Dickerson, S. Drabek, and J.T. Woods, 61–81. Waterloo: Wilfred Laurier University Press, 1980.

Drackley, Don, Gary Willson, and John Steil, "Profile of the Consulting Planning Industry in Canada." *Plan Canada* 30 (May 1990): 5–17.

Duffy, Ron. "Hiring a Consultant: Not a Fairy Story." *Municipal Counsellor* 29 (May/June 1984): 4–5.

Dykstra, Theodore L., and R.G. Ironside. "The Effects of the Division of the City of Lloydminster by the Alberta-Saskatchewan Inter-Provincial Boundary." *Cahiers de Geographie de Quebec* 16 (September 1972): 263–283.

Easton, Robert, and Paul Tennant. "Vancouver Civic Party Leadership, Backgrounds, Attitudes and Non-Civic Party Affiliations." *B.C. Studies* (Summer 1969): 19–29.

Edwards, Cheryl. "Economies of Scale." *Municipal Counsellor* 36 (May/June 1991): 12–13.

"Equity in Taxation." *Municipal Counsellor* 33 (July/August 1988): 10.

Feldman, Lionel D., and Katherine A. Graham. "Intergovernmental Relations and Urban Growth: A Canadian View." In *Politics and Government of Urban Canada*, 4th ed., edited by Lionel D. Feldman, 202–245. Toronto: Methuen, 1981.

Fesler, James W. "Approaches to the Understanding of Decentralization." *Journal of Politics* 27 (1965): 537–567.

"Fine-tuning the System." *Municipal Counsellor* 33 (July/August 1988): 5–10.

Gaetz, H.H. Paper presented to the Union of Alberta Municipalities Convention, 1909. Published as "Municipal Legislation" in *Emerging Party Politics in Urban Canada*, edited by Jack K. Masson and James D. Anderson, 26–29. Toronto: McClelland and Stewart, 1972.

Gardiner, John A. "Police Enforcement of Traffic Laws: A Comparative Analysis." In *City Politics and Public Policy*, edited by James Q. Wilson, 151–172. New York: Wiley, 1968

Gerecke, Kent. "The History of Canadian City Planning." *City Magazine* 2 (Summer 1976): 12–23.

Gilsdorf, Robert. "Cognitive and Motivational Sources of Voter Susceptibility to Influence." *Canadian Journal of Political Science* 6 (December 1973): 624–638.

Goode, William. "Encroachment, Charlantism, and the Emerging Professions." *American Sociological Review* 25 (December 1960): 902–914.

"Grants Will Come with Fewer Strings." *Municipal Councillor* 31 (January/February 1986): 12.

Greenberg, Bradley, and Brenda Dervin. "Mass Communication among the Urban Poor." *Public Opinion Quarterly* 34 (Summer 1970): 224–235.

Grodzins, Morton. "The Federal System." In *Goals for Americans, Programs for Action in the Sixties, Comprising the Report of the President's Commission on National Goals*, 265–375. Englewood Cliffs: Prentice-Hall, 1960.

Grover, Archie R. "A Celebration of Success." *Municipal Counsellor* 33 (September/October 1988): 22.

_____. "Future Directions for Community Planning." *Alberta and Northwest Territories Journal of Planning Practices* 8 (Winter 1989): 7–22.

Gunton, Tom. "Origins of Canadian Urban Planning." In *The Canadian City*, edited by Kent Gerecke, 93–114. Montreal: Black Rose Books, 1991.

Hahn, Harlan. "Voting in Canadian Communities: A Taxonomy of Referendum Issues." *Canadian Journal of Political Science* 1 (December 1968): 462–469.

Hambleton, Robin. "Consumerism, Decentralization and Local Democracy." *Public Administration* 66 (Summer 1988): 125–147.

Hansen, Susan B. "Participation, Political Structure, and Concurrence." *American Political Science Review* 69 (December 1975): 1181–1199.

Hanson, Eric J. "Provincial Grants in Alberta." *Canadian Tax Journal* 1 (September/October 1953): 468–480.

Hewes, Bettie. "Listen, Consult and Be Accountable." *Municipal Councillor* 31 (November/December 1986): 4–5.

Hicks, Graham. "A Better Deal for Cities." *City Magazine* 8 (Fall 1986): 31–34.

Hirsch, Werner. "The Supply of Urban Government Services." In *Issues in Urban Economics*, edited by Harvey S. Perloff and Lowden Wingo, Jr., 477–524. Baltimore: Johns Hopkins Press, 1968.

Holden, Matthew, Jr. "The Governance of the Metropolis as a Problem in Diplomacy." *Journal of Politics* 3 (August 1964): 627–647.

Hough, Jerry F. "Voters' Turnout and the Responsiveness of Local Government: The Case of Toronto." In *Politics Canada*, 3d ed., edited by Paul W. Fox, 284–299. Toronto: McGraw-Hill, 1970.

Kagi, Herbert. "The Role of Private Consultants in Urban Governing." *Urban Affairs Quarterly* 5 (September 1969): 45–58.

Kiernan, Matthew. "Ideology and the Precarious Future of the Canadian Planning Profession." *Plan Canada* 22 (March 1982): 14–24.

_____. "Urban Planning in Canada: A Synopsis and Some Future Directions." *Plan Canada* 30 (January 1990): 11–22.

Kim, John, and Douglas S. West. "The Edmonton LRT: An Appropriate Choice?" *Canadian Public Policy* 17 (June 1991): 173–182.

Langlois, H.O. "Who Will Lead?" In *The Organization and Administration of Education in Canada*, edited by E.D. Hodgson, J.J. Bergen, and R.C. Bryce,

345–347. Edmonton: Department of Educational Administration, University of Alberta, 1980.

"Lawyer Outlines Dismissal Guidelines." *Municipal Councillor* 32 (May/June 1987): 11–12.

Lightbody, James. "Edmonton: Gateway to the North." In *City Politics in Canada*, edited by Warren Magnusson and Andrew Sancton, 225–290. Toronto: University of Toronto Press, 1983.

_____. "Edmonton's Official Flower." *Alberta* 2 (Fall 1989): 1–9.

_____. "Electoral Reform in Local Government: The Case of Winnipeg." *Canadian Journal of Political Science* 11 (June 1978): 312–319.

_____. "The First Hurrah: Edmonton Elects a Mayor, 1983." *Urban History Review* 13 (June 1984): 35–41.

_____. "The Political Traditions of a Prairie Canadian City." *Local Government Studies* 10 (June 1984): 11–24.

_____. "The Rise of Party Politics in Canadian Local Elections." In *Emerging Party Politics in Urban Canada*, edited by Jack K. Masson and James D. Anderson, 192–202. Toronto: McClelland and Stewart, 1972.

_____. "'Wild Bill Hawrelak.'" In *Your Worship*, edited by Allan Levine, 32–48. Toronto: James Lorimer, 1989.

_____. "With Whom the Tolls Dwell: The Great Edmonton Telephone Dispute, 1984–1987." *Canadian Public Administration* 32 (Spring 1989): 41–62.

Lindblom, Charles. "The Science of Muddling Through." *Public Administration Review* 19 (Spring 1959): 79–88.

Lipsky, Michael. "Street-Level Bureaucrats and the Analysis of Urban Reform." *Urban Affairs Quarterly* 6 (June 1971): 391–409.

_____. "Toward a Theory of Street-Level Bureaucracy." In *Theoretical Perspectives on Urban Politics*, edited by Willis D. Hawley et al., 196–213. Englewood Cliffs, N.J.: Prentice-Hall, 1976.

Long, J. Anthony, and Brian Slemko. "The Recruitment of Local Decision-Makers in Five Canadian Cities." *Canadian Journal of Political Science* 7 (September 1974): 550–559.

Long, Norton E. "The Local Community as an Ecology of Games." In *Urban Government*, edited by Edward C. Banfield, 400–413. New York: Free Press, 1961. First published in *American Journal of Sociology* 64 (November 1958): 251–261.

MacIntosh, G.H. "Opening Speech to the Fifth Session of the Second Legislature of the Northwest Territories." In *Northwest Gazette* 2 (August 1894).

Magnusson, Warren. "Community Organization and Local Self-Government." In *Politics and Government of Urban Canada*, 4th ed., edited by Lionel D. Feldman, 51–86. Toronto: Methuen, 1981.

_____. "The Local State in Canada: Theoretical Perspectives." *Canadian Public Administration* 28 (Winter 1985): 575–599.

Masson, Jack K. "Decision-Making Patterns and Floating Coalitions in an Urban City Council." *Canadian Journal of Political Science* 8 (March 1975): 128–137.

_____. "The Ebb and Flow of Municipal Party Politics in Alberta." In *Society and Politics in Alberta: Research Papers,* edited by Carlo Caldarola, 356–368. Toronto: Methuen, 1979.

_____. "Edmonton: The Unsettled Issues of Expansion, Governmental Reform and Provincial Economic Diversification." In *Politics and Government of Urban Canada,* 4th ed., edited by Lionel D. Feldman, 431–447. Toronto: Methuen, 1981.

Maxey, Chester C. "The Political Integration of Metropolitan Communities." *National Municipal Review* 11 (August 1922): 229–253.

McAlpine, Scott, and Stan Drabek. "Decision-Making Coalitions on Non-partisan Councils: A Small City/Large City Comparison." *Canadian Journal of Political Science* 24 (December 1991): 803–829.

McDavid, James C. "Part-Time Fire Fighters in Canadian Municipalities: Cost and Effectiveness Comparisons." *Canadian Public Administration* 29 (Fall 1986): 377–387.

_____. "Residential Solid Waste Collection Services in Canadian Municipalities." Victoria, B.C.: School of Public Administration, University of Victoria, 1983. Monograph.

McDavid, James C., and Gregory K. Schick. "Privatization versus Union-Management Cooperation: The Effects of Competition on Service Efficiency in Municipalities." *Canadian Public Administration* 30 (Fall 1987): 472–488.

"Municipal Assistance Grants." *Municipal Councillor* 34 (July/August 1989): 13–18.

O'Brien, Allan. "The Ministry of State for Urban Affairs: A Municipal Perspective." *Canadian Journal of Regional Science* 5 (1982): 83–94.

Ostrom, Vincent, and Elinor Ostrom. "Public Goods and Public Choices." In *Alternatives for Delivering Public Services: Toward Improved Performance,* edited by Emanuel S. Savas, 7–49. Boulder, Colo.: Westview Press, 1979.

Ostrom, Vincent, Charles Tiebout, and R. Warren. "The Organization of Government in Metropolitan Areas: A Theoretical Inquiry." *American Political Science Review* 55 (December 1961): 831–842.

Peattie, Lisa. "Reflections of an Advocate Planner." *Journal of the American Institute of Planners* 34 (March 1968): 80–87.

Perks, William T., and Lydia Ind Kawun. "Strategic Planning for Small-Town Community Development." *Alberta Journal of Planning Practice* 5 (Fall 1986): 28–45.

Plunkett, Thomas J., and James Lightbody. "Tribunals, Politics and the Public Interest: The Edmonton Annexation Case." *Canadian Public Policy* 8 (Spring 1982): 207–221.

Pocklington, T.C. "Democracy." In *Liberal Democracy: An Introduction to Politics and Government in Canada and the United States,* edited by T.C. Pocklington, 2–29. Toronto: Holt, Rinehart and Winston, 1985.

Protasel, Greg. "Abandonments of the Council-Manager Plan: A New Institutionalist Perspective." *Public Administration Review* 48 (July/August 1988): 807–812.

Rabin, Jack, ed. "Professionalism in Public Administration: Definition, Character and Values." *American Review of Public Administration* 16 (Winter 1982): 303–412.

Rayside, David M. "Small Town Fragmentation and the Politics of Community." *Journal of Canadian Studies* 24 (Spring 1989): 103–120.

Reisman, Jane. "Dual Identities of City Managers and School Superintendents." In *Current Research on Occupations and Professions,* edited by Helena Z. Lopata, 199–216. Greenwich, Conn.: JAI Press, 1987.

Richardson, Nigel H. "Four Constituencies Revisited: Some Thoughts on Planners, Politicians and Principles." *Plan Canada* 30 (March 1990): 14–17.

Ridler, Neil B. "Fiscal Constraints and the Growth of User Fees among Canadian Municipalities." *Canadian Public Administration* 27 (Fall 1984): 429–436.

Rogers, Chester B., and Harold D. Arman. "Nonpartisanship and Election to City Office." *Social Science Quarterly* 51 (March 1971): 941–945.

Rutherford, Paul. "Tomorrow's Metropolis: The Urban Reform Movement in Canada, 1880–1920." In *The Canadian City: Essays in Urban and Social History,* edited by Gilbert A. Stelter and Alan F.J. Artibise, 368–392. Toronto: McClelland and Stewart, 1977.

Salisbury, Robert H., and Gordon Black. "Class and Party in Partisan and Nonpartisan Elections: The Case of Des Moines." *American Political Science Review* 57 (September 1963): 584–592.

Sancton, Andrew. "Conclusion: Canadian City Politics in Comparative Perspective." In *City Politics in Canada,* edited by Warren Magnusson and Andrew Sancton, 291–317. Toronto: University of Toronto Press, 1983.

Sancton, Andrew, and Paul Woolner. "Full Time Municipal Councillors: A Strategic Challenge for Canadian Urban Government." *Canadian Public Administration* 33 (Winter 1990): 482–505.

Savas, E.S. "Municipal Monopolies Versus Competition in Delivering Urban Services." In *Improving the Quality of Urban Management,* edited by Willis D. Hawley and David Rogers, 473–500. Beverly Hills, Calif.: Sage, 1974.

Schott, Richard L. "Public Administration as a Profession: Problems and Prospects." *Public Administration Review* 36 (May-June 1976): 253–259.

Schutte, Jerald G., and John M. Light. "The Relative Importance of Proximity and Status for Friendship Choices in Social Hierarchies." *Social Psychology* 41 (September 1978): 260–264.

Sells, James. "Selected Material from the Report on the Questionnaire on the Future of the Planning Profession." *Plan Canada* Special Issue (June 1982): 26–30.

Shannon, Wes. "Rural Planning Re-Evaluated." *Alberta and Northwest Territories Journal of Planning Practices* 8 (Winter 1989): 99–120.

Siegal, David. "City Hall Doesn't Need Parties." *Policy Options* 8 (June 1987): 26–27.

_____. "Provincial-Municipal Relations in Canada: An Overview." *Canadian Public Administration* 23 (Summer 1980): 281–317.

Simpson, Michael. "Thomas Adams in Canada, 1914–1930." *Urban History Review* 11 (October 1982): 1–15.

Smith, P.J. "American Influences and Local Needs: Adaptations to the Alberta Planning System in 1928–1929." In *Power and Place: Canadian Urban Development in the North American Context,* edited by Gilbert A. Stelter and Alan F.J. Artibise, 109–132. Vancouver: University of British Columbia Press, 1986.

_____. "Community Aspirations, Territorial Justice and the Metropolitan Form of Edmonton and Calgary." In *A Social Geography of Canada: Essays in Honour of J. Wreford Watson,* edited by Guy M. Robinson, 179–196. Edinburgh: North Publishing Company, 1988.

_____. "The Principle of Utility and the Origin of Planning Legislation in Alberta, 1912–1975." In *The Usable Urban Past: Planning and Politics in the Modern Canadian City,* edited by Alan F.J. Artibise and Gilbert A. Stelter, 196–225. Toronto: Macmillan, 1979.

Smith, Phyllis. "The New Planning Act in Alberta." *Plan Canada* 20 (June 1980): 120–123.

Sproule-Jones, Mark, and Adrie Van Klaveren. "Local Referenda and Size of Municipality in British Columbia: A Note on Two of Their Interrelationships." *B.C. Studies* 8 (Winter 1970-71): 47–50.

Steil, John. "Annexation Criteria in Alberta." *Alberta and Northwest Territories Journal of Planning Practices* 7 (Winter 1988): 9–29.

_____. "The Politicizing of Annexation in Alberta." *Alberta Journal of Planning Practice* 2 (Summer 1983): 26–45.

"Taking the Team Approach." *Municipal Counsellor* 31 (November/December 1986): 6–10.

Thompson, Wilbur. "The City as a Distorted Price System." *Psychology Today* 2 (August 1968): 28–33.

Tiebout, Charles M. "A Pure Theory of Local Expenditure." *Journal of Political Economy* 64 (October 1956): 416–424.

"Unravelling a Mystery." *Municipal Counsellor* 36 (July/August 1991): 5–6.

Van Nus, Walter. "The Fate of City Beautiful Thought in Canada, 1893–1930." In *The Canadian City: Essays in Urban and Social History,* edited by Alan F.J. Artibise and Gilbert A. Stelter, 162–185. Toronto: McClelland and Stewart, 1977.

Verbrugge, Lois. "The Structure of Adult Friendship Choices." *Social Forces* 56 (December 1977): 576–597.

Vickers, Jill McCalla. "Where Are the Women in Canadian Politics?" *Atlantis* 3 (Spring 1978): 40–51.

Wilenski, Harold. "The Professionalization of Everyone?" *American Journal of Sociology* 71 (September 1964): 148–149.

Williams, Oliver P., and Charles R. Adrian. "The Insulation of Local Politics under the Nonpartisan Ballot." *American Political Science Review* 53 (December 1959): 1052–1063.

Wright, Deil S. "The City Manager as a Development Administrator." In *Comparative Urban Research*, edited by Robert T. Daland, 203–248. Beverly Hills, Calif.: Sage, 1969.

Wright, Deil S., and Robert Paul Boynton. "The Media, the Masses, and Urban Management." *Journalism Quarterly* 47 (Spring 1970): 12–19.

Wright, Ian. "The Public Sector Context." *Municipal Counsellor* 35 (September/October 1990): 6–7.

Government Publications

Abella, Rosalie S. *Equality in Employment: A Royal Commission Report.* Ottawa: Minister of Supply and Services, 1985.

Alberta. *Report of the Royal Commission on the Metropolitan Development of Calgary and Edmonton.* Edmonton: Queen's Printer, 1956.

_____. *Revised Statutes of Alberta.* Edmonton: Queen's Printer, 1980.

_____. *Task Force on Provincial-Municipal Fiscal Arrangements in Alberta.* Edmonton: Queen's Printer, 1972.

Alberta. Department of Economic Development. "Rail Passenger Service in the Calgary-Edmonton Corridor: The Government of Alberta Position." Edmonton: Department of Economic Development, July 1985.

_____. "Report of the Alberta High Speed Rail Review Committee." Edmonton: Department of Economic Development, June 1986.

Alberta. Department of Education. *Annual Report,* various years. Edmonton: Department of Education.

_____. "Education Trust Fund: A Proposal to Bring Equity to Educational Financing." Edmonton: Department of Education, January 21, 1991.

_____. "Facts about Changes to Education." Edmonton: Department of Education, February 24, 1994.

_____. "Financing Schooling in Alberta." Edmonton: Department of Education, 1982.

Alberta. Department of the Environment. *Edmonton Regional Utilities Study.* Edmonton: Department of the Environment, 1978.

Alberta. Department of Housing. *Provincial Housing Programs in Alberta.* Edmonton: Department of Housing, 1983.

Alberta. Department of Municipal Affairs. "After Twenty Years." Edmonton: Department of Municipal Affairs, 1971.

_____. "Annual General Assessments: The Spruce Grove Experience." Edmonton: Department of Municipal Affairs, undated.

_____. *The Banff-Jasper Autonomy Report.* Edmonton: Department of Municipal Affairs, 1972.

_____. "County Act Review Report." Edmonton: Department of Municipal Affairs, 1987.

_____. "Era of the Regional Plan: A Discussion Paper for the Annual Spring

Seminar." Presented by the Alberta Planning Board at the Annual Spring Seminar, Jasper, April 26–29, 1983.

_____. *Local Rural Self-Government in the Province of Alberta.* Edmonton: Queen's Printer, 1941.

_____. "Municipal Government in Alberta." Edmonton: Department of Municipal Affairs, 1989.

_____. *A New Municipal Government Act for Albertans.* Edmonton: Department of Municipal Affairs, 1992.

_____. *The Park Town of Banff: An Option for Local Government.* Edmonton: Department of Municipal Affairs, 1980.

_____. *Plamondon General Municipal Plan, 1981.* Edmonton: Department of Municipal Affairs, 1981.

_____. *Planning in Alberta.* Edmonton: Department of Municipal Affairs, 1980.

_____. "Reading the Environment: Public Sector Takes its Cues from Corporate Executives." *Municipal Counsellor* 35 (September/October 1990): 2–7.

_____. "Reorganization of Rural Local Administration in Alberta." Edmonton: Department of Municipal Affairs, 1941.

_____. "The Rural District: A Concept of Transitional Municipal Government." Edmonton: Department of Municipal Affairs, 1990.

Alberta. Department of Municipal Affairs. County Act Review Committee. "County Act Review Report." Edmonton: Department of Municipal Affairs, April 1987.

Alberta. Department of Municipal Affairs. Inter-Agency Planning Branch. "Summary of Preliminary Findings of the Regional Planning System Study." Discussion paper. Edmonton: Department of Municipal Affairs, September 15, 1981.

Alberta. Department of Municipal Affairs. Municipal Administrative Services Division. *Municipal and Local Administrative Bodies in Alberta 1941–1981.* Edmonton: Department of Municipal Affairs, 1982.

Alberta. Department of Municipal Affairs. Municipal Statutes Review Committee. "How Should Municipalities Be Financed?" [Preliminary Draft, Discussion Paper no. 4.] Edmonton: Department of Municipal Affairs, 1988.

_____. *"The Municipal Government Act": Local Autonomy, You Want It, You Got It.* Edmonton: Department of Municipal Affairs, [fall 1990].

Alberta. Department of Municipal Affairs. Provincial-Municipal Finance Council. *Report of the Provincial-Municipal Finance Council on the Responsibilities and Financing of Local Government in Alberta.* Edmonton: Department of Municipal Affairs, 1979.

Alberta. Local Authorities Board. *Summary of the Leduc Annexation Decision.* Edmonton: Local Authorities Board, April 6, 1988.

Alberta Hansard. *Alberta Legislative Assembly Debates.* Edmonton: Queen's Printer, 1971 through 1989.

Canada. *1981 Census Dictionary.* Ottawa: Supply and Services Canada, 1982.

_____. *Report of the Royal Commission on Government Organization* (The

Glassco Commission). Vol. 2, *Supporting Services for Government.* Ottawa: Queen's Printer, 1962.

_____. *Sixth Report of the Standing Committee on Northern Affairs and Natural Resources, 1966.* Ottawa: Queen's Printer, 1966.

Canada. Parks Canada. *Resident Involvement in Park Townsite Administration, Western Region.* Ottawa: Queen's Printer, 1970.

Canada. Tri-Level Task Force on Municipal Finance. *Report.* Ottawa: Supplies and Services, February 1976.

City of Calgary. "Report of the Committee on Council Remuneration." [Commonly referred to as The Kirby Report.] Unpublished, June 14, 1985.

City of Edmonton. *Decision 1980: The Annexation Issue.* Edmonton: City of Edmonton, 1981.

_____. *Submission to the Local Authorities Board of Alberta on Behalf of the City of Edmonton.* Edmonton: City of Edmonton, 1980.

City of Edmonton. Planning Department. *North-East LRT Evaluation Study.* Edmonton: City of Edmonton, 1979.

City of Edmonton. Real Estate and Housing Department. "Report." May 4, 1982.

Gibson, J. Neil. "History of Improvement Districts." Edmonton: Department of Municipal Affairs, 1986.

Hanson, Eric. *The Potential Unification of the Edmonton Metropolitan Area.* Edmonton: City of Edmonton, 1968.

Hickey, Paul. *Decision-Making Process in Ontario's Local Governments.* Toronto: Ministry of Treasury, Economics and Intergovernmental Affairs, undated.

Kratzmann, Arthur, Timothy C. Byrne, and Walter H. Worth. *A System in Conflict: A Report to the Minister of Labour by the Fact Finding Commission.* Edmonton: Alberta Department of Labour, 1980.

Municipal Counsellor, various issues.

Plunkett, Thomas J., et al. *A Form of Municipal Government and Administration for Banff Townsite.* Ottawa: Queen's Printer, 1964.

Saskatchewan. *Final Report of the Advisory Committee on Local Election Financing.* Regina, Saskatchewan: Advisory Committee on Local Election Financing, 1990.

U.S. Advisory Commission on Intergovernmental Relations. *Metropolitan Organization: The Allegheny County Case.* Washington, D.C.: 1992.

_____. *Metropolitan Organization: The St. Louis Case.* Washington, D.C.: 1988.

_____. *The Organization of Local Public Economies.* Washington, D.C.: 1987.

Cases

Dinner v. *Humberstone* (1896), 26 S.C.R. 252 (S.C.C.).

Ewasiuk v. *Edmonton* (1979), 23 A.R. (C.A.).

Journal Printing Co. v. *McVeity* (1915), 33 O.R. 166.

O'Callaghan v. *Edmonton* (1978), 6 Alta. L.R. (2d) 307, 12 A.R. 563, 7 M.P.L.R 140 (Dist. Ct.).

Newspapers

Advance (Vauxhall).
Advocate (Red Deer).
Airdrie Echo.
Athabasca Advocate.
Banff Crag and Canyon.
Bonnyville Nouvelle.
Brooks Bulletin.
Calgary Herald.
Calgary Sun.
Camrose Canadian.
Canmore Leader.
Chronicle (Cardston).
Claresholm Local Press.
Crossfield Chronicle.
Crowsnest Pass Promoter.
Didsbury Review.
Dispatch.
Edmonton Bulletin.
Edmonton Examiner.
Edmonton Journal.
Edmonton Report.
Edmonton Sun.
Edmonton Sunday Sun.
Edson Leader.
Fort McMurray Express.
Fort McMurray Today.
Fort Saskatchewan Record.
Freelancer (Mayerthorpe).
Globe and Mail.
Grand Centre-Cold Lake Sun.
Grande Prairie Daily Herald Tribune.
Grove Examiner.
Herald Sunday Magazine (Calgary).
High River Times.
Hinton Parklander.
Hub.
Journal (St. Paul).
Lac La Biche Post.
Lacombe Globe.

Leader.
Leader Post (Regina).
Lethbridge Herald.
Mainstream (Edmonton).
Medicine Hat News.
Mercury.
News (Nanton).
Newsmakers (Stony Plain/Spruce
    Grove).
Nouvelle.
Okotoks Western Wheel (Okotoks).
Pincher Creek Echo.
Popular Press (Evansburg).
Post (Fairview).
Poundmaker.
Record-Gazette (Grimshaw).
Red Deer Advocate.
Reporter (Stony Plain).
Representative (Leduc).
Review (Milk River).
Rocky View/Five Village Weekly.
Rocky View Times.
St. Albert Gazette.
Sherwood Park News.
Slave Lake Scope.
South Peace News.
Stettler Independent.
Strathmore Standard.
Sunny South News.
Sylvan Lake News.
Triangle (Lamont).
Tribune (Redwater).
Vegreville Observer.
Wainwright Star Chronicle.
Western Review (Drayton Valley).
Westlock Hub.
Wetaskiwin Times-Advertiser.
Whitecourt Star.

Reports, Theses, and Miscellaneous Materials

Alberta Association of Municipal Districts and Counties. *Story of Rural Municipal Government in Alberta.* Edmonton: Alberta Association of Municipal Districts and Counties, 1983.

Alberta Association of Municipal Districts and Counties and Alberta Urban Municipalities Association. "Municipal Attitudes towards Regional Planning in Alberta." Edmonton: Alberta Association of Municipal Districts and Counties and Alberta Urban Municipalities Association, 1980.

Alberta Report, various issues.

Alberta School Trustees' Association. *1990 Handbook.* Edmonton: Alberta School Trustees' Association, 1990.

Alberta Teachers' Association. *ATA News,* various issues.

_____. "Submission to Minister of Municipal Affairs Regarding the County Act." Edmonton: Alberta Teachers' Association, 1987.

Alberta Urban Municipalities Association. *Commemorative Brochure of the Alberta Urban Municipalities Association.* Edmonton: Alberta Urban Municipalities Association, 1980.

_____. "Education Financing Position." Edmonton: Alberta Urban Municipalities Association, 1988. Mimeo.

_____. *Urban Municipal Survey.* Edmonton: Alberta Urban Municipalities Association, Fall 1990.

_____. *Urban Perspectives* 10 (June 1990).

Anderson, George. "Programs in Search of a Corporation: The Origins of Canadian Housing Policy 1917–1946." Housing Policy in Canada Lecture Series No. 1. Ottawa: Canada Mortgage and Housing Corporation, 1987.

Beaudry, Lawrence A. "An Investigation into the Backgrounds, Roles, and Educational Attitudes of Alberta Public School Trustees." M.Ed. thesis, University of Alberta, 1978.

Betke, Carl F. "The Development of Urban Community in Prairie Canada: Edmonton, 1898–1921." Ph.D. dissertation, University of Alberta, 1981.

Betts, George. "The Edmonton Aldermanic Election of 1962." Master's thesis, University of Alberta, 1962.

Blake, Donald. "Role Perceptions of Local Decision-Makers." Master's thesis, University of Alberta, 1967.

Brown, Kenneth E. "The Evolution of Hospital Funding in Alberta." Major Paper for Master of Health Service Administration, University of Alberta, 1983.

Canadian Federation of Mayors and Municipalities. "Emerging Issues for Canadian Municipalities." Draft Report. Markham, Ont: December 1990.

_____. Municipal Submissions to the National Tri-Level Conference, "Transportation," Doc. no. TCT53.

_____. Municipal Submissions to the Second Tri-Level Conference, "Housing and Land Use Strategy," Doc. no. TCT54.

_____. *Puppets on a Shoestring: The Effects of Municipal Government on Canada's System of Public Finance.* Ottawa: Canadian Federation of Mayors and Municipalities, 1976.

City Magazine, various issues.

Crawford, Kenneth. *Report of the Institute of Local Government.* Kingston, Ont.: Institute of Local Government, Queen's University, 1959.

Decore, Laurence. "Politics." Speech before the Orientation for Candidates for Municipal Office Symposium, University of Alberta, September 6, 1989.

Dent, Ivor. "The Evolution of School Grants in Alberta." M.Ed. thesis, University of Alberta, 1956.

Drabek, Stan. "The Calgary Ward System." Unpublished paper, prepared for the City of Vancouver Electoral Reform Commission. University of Calgary, undated.

Drabek, Stan, and John Woods. "Calgary: The Boom Ends." Paper presented at the annual meeting of the Canadian Political Science Association, University of Guelph, June 1984.

Dykstra, Theodore L. "The Political Geography of a Border Settlement: Lloydminster, Alberta-Saskatchewan." Master's thesis, University of Alberta, 1970.

Federation of Canadian Municipalities. "Emerging Issues for Canadian Municipalities." Draft report. Markham, Ontario, December 1990.

_____. *The Constitutional Role of the Municipalities in a New or "Renewed" Canadian Federation.* Ottawa: Federation of Canadian Municipalities, 1979.

_____. Task Force on Constitutional Reform. *Municipal Government in a New Canadian Federation System: Report of the Task Force on Constitutional Reform.* Ottawa: Federation of Canadian Municipalities, 1980.

Foran, Maxwell. "The Calgary Town Council, 1884–1895: A Study of Local Government in a Frontier Environment." Master's thesis, University of Calgary, 1970.

_____. "The Civic Corporation and Urban Growth: Calgary, 1884–1930." Ph.D. dissertation, University of Calgary, 1981.

George B. Cuff and Associates, Ltd. "City of Lloydminster Legislative and Administrative Review." Report submitted to City Council, 1986.

_____. "City of Medicine Hat Legislative and Administrative Review." Report submitted to City Council, November 4, 1985.

Gibbins, R., S. Drabek, M.O. Dickerson, and J.T. Woods. "Attitudinal and Socio-Democratic Determinants of Receptivity to Civic Partisanship." Paper presented at the annual meeting of the Canadian Political Science Association, University of Western Ontario, London, June 1978.

Gilsdorf, Robert R. "Political Satisfaction and Municipal Political Processes in Edmonton: An Analysis of Data from the Citizens' Concerns Survey." Unpublished paper, an addendum to the City of Edmonton's Task Force on City Government Committee, July 1980.

Goresky, Isidore. "The Beginning and Growth of the Alberta School System." M.Ed. thesis, University of Alberta, 1945.

Gour, Noel R. "The Role of Schooling—A Trustee Perspective." M.Ed. thesis, University of Alberta, 1983.

Hanson, Eric J. "The School Foundation Program in the 1970s." Edmonton: Alberta Teachers' Association, undated. Mimeo.

Hill, Robert C. "Social Credit and the Press: The Early Years." Master's thesis, University of Alberta, 1977.

Improvement Districts Association of Alberta. "A Framework Proposal for Increased Local Government Autonomy for Improvement District Residents." Edmonton: Improvement Districts Association of Alberta, 1989. Mimeo.

LeSage, Edward, and Charles Humphrey. "Alberta Municipal Administrators' Survey." Edmonton: 1977. Mimeo.

Lightbody, James. "Pop Goes the Gopher: Municipal Innovation with Edmonton's New Executive Committee." Edmonton: 1988. Mimeo.

Lightbody, James, and Gerry Wright. "Urban Innovation? Conditions Underpinning the Transformation of Movement into Party: The Case of the Urban Reform Group of Edmonton, Canada." Edmonton: 1989. Mimeographed paper prepared for FAUI Workshop, Paris.

Lougheed, Peter. Speech to the "Think West" Conference, September 28, 1977.

Martin, L.S. "The Special Areas of Alberta: Origin and Development." Report prepared for the Honourable G.E. Taylor, Member of the Legislative Assembly of Alberta, July 20, 1977.

Masson, Jack K. "Some Preliminary Findings on the Plebiscite Petition: The Reasons People Signed the Convention Centre and Downtown Redevelopment Plebiscite Petitions." Paper presented at the Conference on Referenda and Plebiscites, University of Calgary, March 20–21, 1980.

McMillan, Melville L., and Richard H.M. Plain. *The Reform of Municipal-Provincial Fiscal Relationships in the Province of Alberta.* Edmonton: Alberta Urban Municipalities Association, 1979.

Oviatt, Barrie Connolly. "The Papers of William Aberhart as Minister of Education, 1935–1943." M.Ed. thesis, University of Alberta, 1971.

Page, John, and Reg Lang. "Canadian Planners in Profile." Paper presented at the annual meeting of the Canadian Institute of Planners, Toronto, June 27, 1977.

Patterson, Robert Steven. "The Establishment of Progressive Education in Alberta." Ph.D. dissertation, Michigan State University, 1968.

Pawluk, Lorna. "A 'Marble Cake' View of Canadian Federalism." Master's thesis, University of Alberta, 1979.

Radcliffe, Lois. "Alberta Trusteeship: Strength in Caring." Presidential Paper of the Alberta Hospital Association. Edmonton: 1984.

Ramsay, Ralph Douglas. "The Alberta Teachers' Alliance as a Social Movement." Master's thesis, University of Calgary, 1978.

Richwood, Roger R. "Urban Reform Movements in Lethbridge." Paper presented at the annual meeting of the Canadian Political Science Association, University of Alberta, Edmonton, June 1975.

Roberts, William Glyndwr. "The Alberta School Trustees' Association—A Study of the Activity of a Social Organization in the Alberta Educational System." Ph.D. dissertation, University of Alberta, 1966.

Smith, Roger. "A Critique of Property Taxation." Edmonton, June 1976. Mimeo.

Urban Development Institute. *Alberta UDI Report.* Edmonton: Urban Development Institute, October 1989.

Wichern, P.H., Jr. "Winnipeg's Unicity after Two Years; Evaluation of an Experiment in Urban Government." Paper presented at the 46th Annual Meeting of the Canadian Political Science Association, Toronto, June 3–6, 1975.

Wood Gordon. "City of Medicine Hat Organizational Review." Report submitted to City Council, June 7, 1982.

Index of Places

Index of Persons, Subjects and Acts